CHOICES, CHANGES & FRIENDS

1970s After Divorce

A Memoir

Alice Parker

ISBN 978-1-955156-03-5 (paperback)
ISBN 978-1-955156-04-2 (hardcover)
ISBN 978-1-955156-05-9 (digital)

Copyright © 2021 by Alice Parker

All rights reserved. No part of this publication may be reproduced, distributed, or transmitted in any form or by any means, including photocopying, recording, or other electronic or mechanical methods without the prior written permission of the publisher. For permission requests, solicit the publisher via the address below.

Credits for the Front cover:

The overall design is by Cheryl McDonald - www.CherylMcDonaldCreative.com

Front Photo credit: The Chicago Theatre - Raymon Sutedjo - The CC by SA 3.0.

Prudential Place by Diego Delso - Sears Tower by Kelly Martin.

Back Cover headshot by Obediah Harrison, Icarus Independent Productions.

Rushmore Press LLC
1 800 460 9188
www.rushmorepress.com

Printed in the United States of America

DEDICATION

To Karen, Maureen and Gail

We did the best we could with what we knew.   No regrets.

Additional information - Jim and Sharon - thank you.

A true Memoir -
Only names of some people and places are changed.

All poems by the Author - Alice Parker

CONTENTS

Introduction	**Page 8**
The Past	11
Prologue	12
SECTION 1: BACKGROUNDS OF THE FOUR	19
When Do the Losers Win & Other Fairy Tales	20
Chapter 1: April	21
Warranty Unguaranteed	56
Chapter 2: Connie	57
Letting Go	74
Chapter 3: Michael	75
Lessons	99
Chapter 4: Beth	100
SECTION 2: LIFE AFTER THE DIVORCES	137
Infinity	138
Chapter 5: September, 1971	139
Touch Me	152
Chapter 6: Making a Sandwich	153
Time & Love	165
Chapter 7: Not Who I Dreamed	166
Circles & Squares	174
The Real You	174
Chapter 8: Lost or Sober	175
Glimmering Presence	184
Chapter 9: Comings and Goings	185
Not Enough	192
Chapter 10: Breaking Up	193
Dawn Rising	205

Chapter 11: A Glimmering Presence	206
Tomorrow	216
Chapter 12: If I Only Knew	217
Unrequited Thoughts	228
Chapter 13: Learning Lessons	229
Dream People	242
Chapter 14: Where is the Love	243
A Woman on Women	254
Chapter 15: To Party Hearty	255
Sorrow and Joy	268
Chapter 16: More Lessons Learned	269
The Magic Land	280
Chapter 17: Is this Love?	281
Fly Away	289
Chapter 18: Brief Chance of Love	290
Reflections	298
Sure Sign of Hope	298
Chapter 19: Not the Usual Status Quo	299
A Friendship	307
Chapter 20: You Got A Friend	308
Retake	315
Chapter 21: Surprise! Surprise!	316
Independence	325
What Price Freedom?	325
Chapter 22: On the Move	326
The Support Searches	335
Chapter 23: Moving On Out	336
Crossing & Burning Bridges	351
Chapter 24: Choices for Change	352
About # 30	370
Chapter 25: Crossing Borders	371
If the Shoe Fits	378
Chapter 26: Little Lies Become Bigger	379
Far and Away	388
Chapter 27: Family Matters Hurt	389
A View From the Past	400

Sunrise	400
Chapter 28: Education Versus Learning	401
Almost Always Counts	413
Chapter 29: Your Basic Farmer's Daughter	414
My Son	422
Chapter 30: The Judgment & the Judge	423
To Find Me	439
Chapter 31: New Opportunities in OKC	440
Female Knowledge	453
Chapter 32: It's Not Over, Till It's Over	454
Déjà Vu	465
Chapter 33: Picking Up Life's Pieces	466
The Conversation	478
Chapter 34: Cold Turkey and Lies	479
The Spacial Experience	487
Chapter 35: Escape the Mundane	488
Underestimating Women	499
Chapter 36: Why Does Starting Over Hurt So Bad	500
Ode to a Man Unknown	510
Chapter 37: New Men - New Lives	511
Blossoming	521
Chapter 38: Escape and Return	522
SECTION 3: THE FOLLOWING DECADES	530
Mystery of Secrets	531
Chapter 39: Rushing Into the 80s	532
Changing Lifetimes	553
Chapter 40: Chasing the 90s	554
Little Barometers	575
Chapter 41: Acknowledging the Millennium	576
My Friend	588
Chapter 42: Last Reunions and Goodbyes	589
Epilogue	622
An Old Soul	625

INTRODUCTION

During the early 1970s, the United States was in quite an upheaval It seemed that there were protest marches of all types going on everywhere, against everything, but especially the war, the government and the inequality of the sexes. But our four main characters: Beth, Connie, Michael and April were never vocal concerning the Viet Nam war, nor the inequality of the sexes, and no bra-burning was considered. In their Chicago western suburbs, a much smaller revolution was going on, but its momentum was building.

Not related in any way to these other marches, as these participants had a much lesser-known problem: overdosing on Tupperware and other Home parties, as well, too many visits from their Avon ladies It was truly a case of suburban-blight brought on by television-burnout and sexually-inept/non-attentive husbands The wine, women and dance of their youth had turned into beer, the 'ole-lady' and TV This might have been acceptable to their mothers, but not these ladies They wanted more

The heartland of America is truly different from the East or West Coast. Chicago, in all of its vastness, never had the sophistication of New York, nor the experimental-taste of Los Angeles and it cannot begin to comprehend the slow-motion attitude of the South. Chicago had always been the melting pot of the great middle-class, whose main drive is the work ethic of 'nose to the grindstone, shoulder to the wheel,' meaning one must always work for a living and fun is almost a sin. Even the most-modern Chicagoan, in the 1970s was only one or two generations re-moved from the farm or Eastern Europe, where life was defined as an honest day's work. This background also carried over to the separation of the sexes - man's work and woman's work, clearly defined and expected to be followed.

The 1960s were the catalyst to changes that made the 1970s explode, with no map or direction, much less a guru to answer the questions of what to do with one's life after divorce. Thus, amazing mistakes, with irony sometimes realized from their naiveté. This path to discovery of learning lessons to grow up, has no yellow bricks, and never a castle of green or any other color in site. There's not even a flagrant, hand-painted sign or writing on any wall that could guide or direct these ladies. When not a church-goer, where does one find a man to converse with, if not a bar. Yes, there were few choices, and fewer good-finds.

Perhaps the generation more than any other, which perpetuated the changes of all this, was the Baby-Boomers growing up in the 1950s and 1960s. It was in this era, that our four characters spent their formative, school years and got married, *way too soon*. The numerous rules, morals, regulations, etcetera, inundated by family-culture, society/religion and school, created either the adaptive or rebellious child. And usually, even the adaptive-child went through some period of rebellion, either in their late teen-years, or more effectively, in their twenties - after divorce.

The cure for a change, for these young housewives and mothers, was thought to be getting a job to get out of the house, and to regain some knowledge of self. Listening to 'Ernie and Bert' recite repetitive numbers and letters does become monotonous five days a week. But a job was not the solution, it was the beginning of awareness that PTA meetings, and exciting trips to the emergency room for their children was no longer satisfying for a twenty-five-year old woman. There was a whole other life to live that their mother's had never told them about, and they believed it wasn't too late to try for it. There was only one way for them to break-out of the mold, that their heritage had set-up for them. It was not acceptable, for they, the parents had never done it. "Being unhappily married is just part of living, and you have to learn to make the best of it." They had all been told, or it had been demonstrated constantly in front of them.

Working in the real world, they began to see that they certainly weren't living their own lives. So, when this little growing-revolution wanted more out of life, they then chose the alternative - divorce.

They knew it would not be easy, as it held no guarantee of happiness, *but winners risk* - they'd also heard - and that they decided to do. They also acknowledged that the dilemma did not solely lie with their husbands, children or family life. But it was easier to work on one problem at a time, and working on themselves not only seemed like a good idea, but they were certainly more cooperative about it.

Deciding what they wanted for themselves was not going to be quick or simple. Divorce was not the total answer, it was the opportunity to start a new life where choice was yours, no longer controlled by parents or husband. Yet, at this time, how could they have the right answers when they were still trying to formulate the questions about what they did want . . . from life, for themselves and in a good relationship. Whatever that was, and if they would know it when they found it, or if they ever would. And, if that choice was a mistake, then you learned from it and to not repeat it. Then you shared that wisdom with another divorcee, or woman looking to gain her freedom, and be ready to learn from your lesson. But, most importantly, you still supported each other in the Freedom quest. There was an irony to all of this, that they would frequently and painfully learn.

THE PAST

Many women think
      once they catch that golden ring,
they can ride-free on the carousel of marriage -
      happily ever after.

Unfortunately, it usually turns out
      to be a shabby merry-go-round,
          that ends up playing
      the same old tune.

PROLOGUE

NOVEMBER, 1974

In the small kitchen, Beth popped the cork on the third bottle of Cold Duck. She more than realized she did not need anything else to drink - already at least half-drunk. But, it was her party, her special night, her twenty-ninth birthday - la-de-da. Astrologically, her Saturn Return, and that was supposed to be pivotal - April reported. And hopefully, the end of her turbulent-twenties almost upon her, what would be next - now, almost three-years after her divorce? As Beth raised the glass of cool, pink liquid to her mouth, she began to think of the future-racing toward her. By the time she reached thirty, she really wanted to have her life together. The joke being: "If you get all your shit-together, can you still carry it?"

This meant she'd have to have her life-goals set - no more of this wild-living, crazies in the fast-lane. Her decision to experience 'everything,' had been denied her growing up in an almost-cloistered middle-class, midwest-youth must be finished, as she settled down to getting her life in control. The approaching maturity loomed with shades of remarriage, a good step-father for Jeremy, like a nightmare, and definitely not something she wanted to deal with at this time, or supposedly, happy occasion. In her Southern-falsetto, with definite shades of Scarlett O'Hara, she mumbled to herself, "I'll worry about that tomorrow …"

Almost be expected of her to get bombed, she rationalized. Once again, she took another sip, rather more a gulp of the soothing-alcohol, it wasn't bad for the price. At least she never bought the cheapest, but the best her limited-budget could afford. Money was not that much of a problem, except for the fact no matter how much she had, she usually seemed to spend more. Her house-cleaning business was doing well, yet she expected more. She knew she was, or at least could be, well-accomplished if . . . allowing herself, yet not satisfied with herself. This discontent in her life popped its ugly head up, at the most inopportune times. Once again, she would try to drown it.

Another swallow, as she thought how philosophical - even prophetic she became when soused. Only pearls-of-wisdom rolled off her tongue - how trite, really? She snickered to herself, how she had all the confidence in the world about her success, when a drink in her hand. Yet, she knew she wasn't real. She wondered how often the others had seen through her, and her true insecurities. They did say something once in a while that burst her bubble, but most of the time they went along with her hopes and dreams. They were her friends, and that was what they're for, right? Only lie when the truth hurts, too much. Beth took a last sip before re-entering the living room - as if magically, through her colorful, 'hippy-dippy' plastic-beaded-strands across the doorway separating the rooms -and back into the laughing-group of female friends.

She felt as if preparing to meet a new, waiting lover. She ruffled-up her long, curly-blonde hair, and fixed her well-known smile on her face. She started jabbering loudly, "Well is everybody ready for another drink?" as if she had never left the room, nor the conversations mentally or physically. Refilling the glasses of each, she began thinking how truly-different they were from each other, her being the connector of them all. Her closest friends - the four of them - had been through so much together. Beth felt that she was the best friend to each of them, yet they weren't best friends to each other. She brought them all together, and usually kept them so.

Michael, seated nearest the kitchen doorway, was somewhat nervous, regularly running her hand through her shoulder-length, curly-red hair when she laughed. She'd be more relaxed once Mike got there, Beth's older, married-brother. He'd become such a large part of Michael's life, now they were lovers. Only with him, did she feel complete, and almost calm. Still, she was laughing - maybe pushing it - so her pretty 'chipmunk' cheeks buried her soft, olive-green eyes. She looked so much younger than her twenty-eight years. Maybe it was her free-lifestyle, since still rebelling against 'the establishment' in her own ways. Yet, with Mike's teenage boys, she was totally comfortable - being so much that kid herself. Since Mike though, she had adjusted to the point, that she no longer said, or did *too* many things just for shock-value.

Seated next to Michael was Connie, so they could hold their own 'stinging' discussion of the others. Connie's forte was mouthing-off zingers, mainly learned from Cam, her married-lover. Collusion was not the usual-thing between them, but they'd recently became closer with the sharing of their clandestine-affairs. Connie was different in more ways that just looks. She was taller, and her serious-looking, olive-colored face was thinner. Her beautiful, usually long, dark-auburn hair was now just to the nape of her neck, and frosted all over in a long shag. It was a more fun-look for her, as she needed fun, excitement and male-attention.

Connie had a self-confident and hard-working view in her velvet-brown eyes, of a woman determined to make money -which she did at every opportunity. She was two years younger than Beth, but years older than any of them with her life/sex experience. Most people who met her, only saw the quiet-coldness that protected her on the outside, and seldom the soft-warmness, hidden inside. Connie and Michael did share the freedom of not having their children living with them, and accepted this as the best decision for the time being. Beth asked Connie not to pick on April - for whom she had little love. Except for a few zingers, she was keeping quiet enough, so only Michael heard her remarks in the small living room.

Part of the problem, April considered herself to be the intellectual-one, and maybe in aspects like exploring metaphysics, she was. Perhaps too, in being the only one at this time, who had found her creative interest and current career - astrology. Being very good at it, one had to give her that, though she put drama into everything.

She was pouring over the figures, working-up Beth's Saturn Return as her birthday present. April particularly loved figuring-out Beth's future, as she purported her chart the most fascinating to work on. She even used it in her astrology classes taught at the County College. Just finishing, as Beth topped off her glass with the Cold Duck, April in reality, was the only one among the four who did not drink to any extent. And, she reminded them of it on a regular basis.

Taking off her glasses, she ran her long, thin hand through her now short, black hair. Leaning back, she stretched her small body like a cat, ready to make a significant purring-announcement for attention. Beth silenced them, and April read in her best contrastingly-high sing-song-voice. Her dramatics at work, with the center of attention - except for a few sighs, and a giggle out of Michael from one of Connie's remarks - they were all raptly listening.

"Well," April began slowly, "it looks like another interesting year for Beth - both in business and pleasure . . . " Giggles went around, those all knowing Beth's amorous-sexual side.

The three other guests, very involved in some way with Beth, were entranced. The only real newcomer to the group was Lori. She was a cleaning-customer of Beth's, who had become a friend over the past six months. Lori was an artist, newly-divorced and though older, used Beth's knowledgeable-shoulder to frequently cry on, and would regularly seek advice from her. Beth talked to her many times before and after Lori's divorce. In the early-70s, no women's networking, or support groups existed to guide or inform those seeking a divorce. Or even those who considered the option of a more independent - less male-controlled life.

Beth had invited Lori, to meet the friends she'd told her so many stories about. Lori, in her late-thirties, had never experienced some of the wild-times the four of them had gotten involved in, since their divorces just two or three years before. Especially Beth, who had been the 'kid-in-a-candy-store,' trying to sample as many men as she could, after such an arid-marriage. Lori sat quietly, absorbed in this interestingly-mixed group of divorced women. Considering some of the stories she'd heard, perhaps she expected a more spectacular, or vampy-looking group. But then, it hadn't been that long before, they had all been middle-class, mid-American suburbanite-housewives. Perhaps they'd all taken the term - "do your own thing" too, literally.

Another one, in attendance of the reading was Sybil - Michael and April's long-time acquaintance, and very-trying friend. Barely-thirty herself, rather pretty, but her unstable-personality could be very off-putting. She sat and drank, and bitched about one thing after another. Granted, her life had been more colorful and 'certifiable' than any of theirs, but also completely erratic, and totally unbelievable. Any new fad, craze or language-phrasing-slang, she was the first to try and experience it, never considering any consequences. Beth had difficulty having empathy for Sybil, as she truly was her own worst enemy - quite self-destructive.

On the opposite end of the spectrum was Marie, Beth's thirteen-year older sister. She still tried to catch her breath, having just arrived. As with everything else in Marie's life - alway done at the last minute - her decision to escape her pathetic-husband and three, cloyingly-dependent daughters, to join in celebration. Although Marie looked much younger than her forty-two years, her beliefs were not.

She could not let go of the supposed-security of her desperately-bad marriage, just 'on-the-chance-of-happiness' in the single-divorced life. But Marie did love associating, on-the-fringe of her sister's divorced-friends' lives. Perhaps, she believed she could absorb something by osmosis from a close proximity. It made her existence somehow more bearable, and sometimes even palatable. The Aquarius-Marie always lived in a dream-world, wishing she had tried a few of the things Beth and the others had done. Of course, Marie wanted only the good times. In her fantasy world, no hardships, broken-hearts or pain could exist.

April would be the first to hit thirty in just five-short months. She looked older, but then she had that kind of face, and looked twenty-five at eighteen. She smiled even less than Connie, and took absolutely everything seriously. Her small, dark eyes were quite penetrating, but it was her tongue that could cut-deep, saying whatever she thought was right, or needed to be said in her self-righteous way. Somehow, that ugly habit took something away from her looks.

April crossed her short, thin legs and began her nervous leg-swing. This practice almost kept beat to the tone of her voice, stopping precisely when emphasizing some point in her dialogue. Of course, for more affect at a critical point, she stopped to light a cigarette and take a small sip of the wine. Connie groaned at the staging, but also had become part of the captured-audience. Her hazel eyes rolled-up and sideways, until she got a snicker out of Michael.

When April had finished reading the astrology chart, Beth took over the floor thanking April for her insightful proclamations. Once again, she'd said that Beth would do great things with her life. She would become a famous writer of books and poetry - she would be rich and famous . . . etcetera, la de da. Beth went back to college shortly after her divorce, concentrating on those skills, and even considering going back into her advertising career, which had been creatively-challenging. The cleaning - party-servicing business she, Connie and Michael started together was doing well, with over fifteen women working for them. But Beth still wanted something else - more. That damned discontent again!

Beth tried to believe in herself and what April said. With another large gulp of the wine, and a drag on her cigarette, she continued to talk for a minute - whether they were listening or not. In her mind's eye, her five-foot-seven frame carried maybe one hundred and forty-five, curvy pounds, accented by those bedroom, blue-green eyes, many men and women complimented her on.

A sometimes-beautiful, brilliant person, who laughed and smiled all the time on the outside - the inside, well, another story. She had a statement she wanted to make to the world about life after divorce, and get the world to listen. The four of them had come a long way since those first, new days of freedom. Yes, they made a lot of mistakes, struggling to achieve small steps up from what they learned. Her drive was to share those accomplishments/ mistakes with other women, for them to be able to do better in achieving their freedom.

Beth finished talking, and slipped into the recesses of her inebriated-mind, to think once again about all those steps, that had helped them change-grow in the past few years. How to grow up in one easy lesson - get a divorce! Of course, no one told them the lessons actually take years to learn, with no guarantee that they would ever *graduate* to real happiness. Shit, it was a bitch to grow up, when you were already supposed to be an adult! She finished her part in the evening's festivities, and willing to give the stage to whomever wanted it to babble on about whatever. Content in her mind to drink and smoke, she felt herself rise above the din-filled room. She mind-traveled back into the past, since in all truth - she was afraid to go into the future alone.

SECTION 1
BACKGROUNDS OF THE FOUR

When Do The Losers Win & Other Fairy Tales

Life in Fantasy Land is so grand
-until someone pops the bubble.

Did Cinderella live happily ever after,
or did she end-up with dish-pan hands?

If I kissed a spell-bound frog, would he
turn into a Prince, or would I turn into a frog?

If Sleeping Beauty was kissed awake,
would she have insomnia the rest of her life?

I've been patiently waiting on my front porch, for
my knight-in-shining-armor to take me away from all this!

Was Snow White pure and virginal,
or was she just neat and clean?

Crusader Rabbit will save us all from ourselves - I hope!

You've never been to Wonderland,
until you've been there with Alice!

When you wish upon a star,
It does make a difference who you are!

Fairy Tales won't come true, they don't happen to you,
no matter what age you are.
Plunk Your Magic Twanger - Froggie! Tinkerbell is a Fairy!

CHAPTER 1

April

Besides being a change-of-life baby to her forty-one year old mother, April Ramson, born in April of 1945, was an only child Her overweight mother, had a serious heart condition, while her obsessive-paranoid father made life difficult in weird ways   Beth didn't remember April sitting in the next row, and two seats up from her in first grade, but as April told the story so often, Beth had shared her milk-money with her. April was plump back then, and very quiet Sadness filled April's mind, and gave her dark eyes that unspoken lost-look on life. The culmination of which was her mother's death, that same year school started.

April could sit for hours in their small, house-trailer staring off into space, aching from the loneliness   Not being allowed playmates or friends, because her father didn't trust anyone, she was basically by herself everyday that he worked   Her mother's sister - Aunt Sissy and her Uncle Art lived next door, but she didn't spend time inside with them, unless it was foul weather. April learned the last few years of her mother's life to be quiet, and not disturb anyone. Even when older, and not in school, she stayed inside the trailer to sketch models from the newspaper for hours.

Though, this only made her feel fatter and ugly. April fantasized about being grown-up - as a slim, beautiful model wearing all those gorgeous clothes in bright, rainbow-colors The drab-grays and browns or blacks that her father bought for her, had no excitement at all They looked like miniature-versions of old ladies' clothes   He would buy dresses big enough to last two years - first they'd bag-all-over, and second year, they were too tight. Aunt Sissy gave up trying to talk to him about April's clothes, or anything else regarding her life, as her father wanted no advice. April's fantasies and dreams kept her going from day to day. Yes, Cinderella was alive and well, living in the trailer-court waiting for her Prince Charming to come and put the glass slipper on her foot, as *it* would transform her into a beautiful Princess.

In the real world - from prior rejection - April was afraid other kids wouldn't like her, so she didn't try to associate with most them. Sometimes she'd go to her Aunt Sissy's for consoling, but she was ineptly-cool, having no children of her own. Truth be known, she didn't even like them, and always held April at arm's-length for any affection. With no real mother substitute, she appreciated the occasional attention from Beth, but there was little beyond their school contact.

Her father had difficulty being a single parent since he wanted a partner, not a little girl to take care of, in the limited time off from his structural, iron-worker's job. He resented the fact that she was alive and his wife was dead - which he blamed the stress of April's birth, and natal-care as the major cause of it. He often became morse, placing the burdens of his life on April -constantly telling her how lonely he was without her mother, and being *stuck* raising her. Besides being tight and stingy, with his money only for the necessities, he took his general frustrations out on April with physical abuse. She really never had anyone to teach her how to have fun. She sometimes talked to herself for hours, then the silence reminded her of the vacuum she lived in. This closed-mouth life was not typical of the opinionated Aries, she'd release in later years.

About a year after her mother died, her father decided to pack-up their trailer and pulled it to California. Perhaps he thought he'd get more work there, with all of the high-rise buildings his union said were being built. Now, April didn't even have her Aunt Sissy around, for the little comforting that she did get from her. Shortly after they moved into the new trailer court, some of the children there wanted to play with April. Her father was rarely around to yell and scare them off, so she was anxious to have some friends that wanted to play 'dress-up.'

Without having had much adult supervision when around friends, she didn't have any other clothes to play with, so April took out her own clothes to use. Not too long after they had started playing, her father came home early from work. When he saw what they were doing, he slapped the unknowing, rare-smile off her face.

The other children fled for their homes in terror, not knowing what was happening, or why. Her father dragged her into the trailer, beating and kicking her with every step. She never tried to fight back, accepting what she believed was just her fate. Hearing the screams over and over, the neighbors finally called the police. This was not the first, nor the last time she was so badly beaten, that she couldn't go to school. Then, for the same lack of real reasoning which had brought them to California, he returned them to the same Chicago suburban-area trailer park the next year.

April continued to gain weight - food her sole-consolation in her meager life. Her thick, straight black hair was kept short, which only made her little, round face look like a malleable, pale-colored ball. Still, she was attracted to boys, even if they didn't respond to her, as she wanted the same attention all the other grade-school girls craved. Ellis Cooney was April's first crush, and with her size, she probably could have made two of him. He obviously didn't feel the same about her. How flattered could a fourth-grade boy be, when the fattest girl in school was after him? Most boys his age, usually didn't even like a pretty girl attracted to them.

At least with her return to the suburbs, April and Beth were able to become better friends, with Beth frequently inviting her over during lunch break. Otherwise, April walked to the corner store to get something to eat, that often was not very healthy. The grade school in those days had no lunch program. Through Beth, April met several of her friends, and at least began to have more involvement with other girls, if not the boys. Most importantly, it gave her an idea of what a more 'normal' family life was all about.

Mothers baked cookies and cakes, or those who worked full or part-time, bought them. They were there helping with clothes choices - whether home-made or store bought, and buying toys or board games to play with. Learning how to interact, April began to stop by either Beth's house, or the other girls, who were on her walk home from school. Real friendships were being built, and she felt an acceptance she'd never known before.

By the fifth grade, April's father moved them further west, out into a more rural suburban area He'd bought a small house, and soon her Aunt Sissy and Uncle Artie moved out there, too At her father's insistence, April started taking care of the house and the cooking, which consisted mainly of hamburgers - all she was ever taught.

For this, she was allowed to visit occasionally with her old friends back in Elmwood at Christmas and birthday parties Her father drove her there, usually waiting in the car, and only rarely coming in to visit with the other parents.

As April got older and more independent, she continued to not get along with her father. More from his moodiness - or probably depression - rather than lack of work, he went for long periods of time not working. The money they did have, she began to realize, he hid in the house because he didn't trust the banks. But the furious and frustrated April never found it, no matter how well she looked. What good was her father, if he couldn't provide the money she needed and wanted for a better life?

Sometimes there was no food at all, so she'd have to go over to eat at Sissy's, or the minister's house, she recently met. She still returned to her father out of guilt or feeling sorry for him, though she didn't understand his strange behavior, and the occasional physical abuse of her

Now beginning high school, not having been exposed to, or at least a casual knowledge of any 'good' men, the first seeds were unknowingly planted to hate men, and their control over her. This was subconscious at first, as the real, ugly-truth was soon to come out. No one knew about the strange relationship April had with her father, though she tried several times to tell Aunt Sissy.

When she was eight, he started to sleep with her - he in clothes, her without He told her whatever he did was not to be told to anyone. He also told her, that these were things the *'naughty'* boys would do to her, if she wasn't careful. (Almost directly out of the case reports of what most incestuous-relatives say.) At first, because she was so young, he only fondle her body and kissed her. Somehow, she knew it wasn't quite right, but he was her father so she believed he was doing what was *right* for her - teaching her, protecting her -she trusted him.

Of course, it felt good to be touched, and it *was* the only affection he showed her. Before long, her father was having oral sex with her. He played with April's genitals, almost making a game out it, as he showed her how to masturbate, even while too young to have a climax of any kind. As she matured, he played with her budding breasts, kissing and sucking them. He did not do any outward masturbation himself in front of her, as if fulfilling this was all for *her* to be aware of.

With age, not really wanting him to continue, as she didn't want him near her. April again tried to tell Aunt Sissy. But as she was about say something more specific, about the way her father was kissing and touching her, Sissy'd remind her that he loved her the *best he knew how*. Years later, she realized Sissy must have known, but didn't want to acknowledge it, as that meant she'd have to *do something* about it.

By the time she was a high school teenager, her father was coming to her bed nude. She learned to manipulate him into working more, so she felt at least she got money to spend for herself out of the whole ugly process. But even that was no longer enough, as he began by pulling at her nightgown, and trying to place himself on top of her. When he tried to actually penetrate her with his penis, she pushed him off.

Finally, she decided she had to tell someone who might listen, and give her advice. The next day, she told an older girl at the bus stop who had befriended her. The girl was aghast a father could do such things. She convinced April to go to the authorities, or at least to ask her Aunt Sissy for help in reporting it. Her Aunt didn't want to believe her at first, but then April reminded her of all the times Sissy had been at the door, and it took so long for her father to answer.

She contacted the authorities, and they put him in jail, but April never prosecuted him in court, as Aunt Sissy talked her out of it. In her own mind, and to his face, April *never* let her father forget how much she hated him. Still, he was her father, and only direct blood relative. Even after he died, she had not relented in forgiving him for molesting her. The ugly-evil poisoned her, and unfortunately affected all her future relationships with men.

April began living at the local minister's house after the abated court trial. A better alternative to the orphanage, where the court wanted to send her, when her inconsiderate and insensitive Aunt refused to take her. On the more positive side, also at this time she met Wally on a *blind*-date. It was courtesy of his cousin Ron, who was in her class at school. April, now sixteen to Wally's nineteen, he considered it more of a *pseudo*-date. For Wally, known as a big swinger with a lot of girls, normally wouldn't want to be seen with someone fat like April. What reason Wally did consider taking her out, April never understood.

From beginning to end, a strange date - if even called that since Ron came with him to pick her up, and sat in between them riding in the car to the movies. At the show, Wally bought himself and Ron popcorn, but they both offered her some, as she sat between them. Afterwards, they all talked about generalities and Wally took her right home without any acknowledgement of the whole evening. She figured scratch that one, until a few days later when he called.

April thought at first he must have her mixed up with some other girl, since he knew so many. He then told her he felt comfortable with her, and asked if she'd like to go for a ride. She knew he didn't want to drive her through town, to be seen with her, but she didn't mind. Being out with a good looking guy, who wanted to be with her was enough.

His thick, brown hair was set off by his soft, brown eyes, with a quick smile that made her feel almost happy. Wally's shoulders seemed so broad on his five-foot eight-inch frame. The sort-of-real 'dates' continued on for several more occasions, with him never making a move. Perhaps Aunt Sissy knew best about her not testifying, as her name would have gotten out regarding the situation. Considering April's age, Wally must have believed she was a truly, innocent virgin, living with the minister and all. If that presumption worked for him, she had no intention of telling him anything different.

They talked about all sorts of things, with April being the talkative one, and for the first time the center of someone's total attention. The usually quiet Wally began to open up to her about his life, more like to a confidential sister/friend. When he didn't see her, he'd call her to talk about his problems with other girls or things. One night, wanting more than just his friendship, she casually asked if she could wear his class ring - just for the night. He had no idea she was already falling for him.

Interestingly, after Wally gave her the ring, there were no calls for a week, and no information from Ron regarding him. April kept wearing his ring, while blatantly informing anyone who asked about it, whose ring it was. The grapevine responded, and Wally told Ron to *tell* her to give his ring back. This hurt, he could of at least called himself to ask her. That night, coming out of a movie theater with a girlfriend, she saw him driving around with a bunch of his friends.

As before, he ignored her when with them, but her confidence built up from being with him, she was ready to show him how she's changed. When she saw his car coming around the block a second time, she went out in the street to stop him. Hands held high, with all the dramatics she could possibly create, she removed the ring without a word. She then slowly reached into the car, and dropped it into his lap. As graceful as a pregnant-gazelle, she walked back to the sidewalk without looking back, only glancing at her pop-eyed girlfriend, now freaking-out. Thank God, Wally quickly sped away, because upon reaching the sidewalk April fainted.

Not quite two weeks later, Wally called her out of loneliness, This time when he took her out they would kiss, *'neck'* and sometimes even *'pet.'* To get more leveraged-freedom from under the minister's watchful eye, April moved back in with her father, after his insistent requests. He agreed to never touch her again, or have any control whatsoever over her life. Wally was working for the county, and painted ballot-boxes green before the election. One night, she came home with 'green-fingerprints' on her white blouse, across her full breasts. She proudly taunted her father, but he knew better than to make any comment.

When Wally was laid off, without a lot of forethought, he joined the Navy. As several friends had already gotten their Draft-notices, he wanted to have a choice other than the Army. April started writing to him, again as a friend. But as time went by, the loneliness crept in and Wally's letters started to be filled with love for the only girl who had listened, and seemed to care for him alone - faithfully.

When he came home on his first leave, April tried to get him to have sex with her, but he wouldn't. He'd known so few virgins, he felt she was special, so he wanted to save her. Though she had done little to reduce her weight, that was no longer a real concern for him - he'd fallen in love with the sweet-persona that she presented so well to him.

After Wally returned to the West Coast, out of a combination of curiosity and sexual frustration, April began running around with a guy named Billy. Though she knew his unsavory background, she kept seeing him because he did not have Wally's scruples regarding her virginity - he definitely *would* have sex with her.

So, sixteen-year old April lost her virginity to this twenty-three year old married man, who was also an ex-convict, bisexual and a drug addict. Definitely *not* the Cinderella and Prince Charming story, she had dreamed of as a little girl, for it also happened in the care-taker's house of the local mental institution. Still, being anxious to learn about sex, and he being more than happy to teach her. They devoured each other, like the world was going to end any moment.

Michael, April's only close girlfriend, along with her boyfriend Tim, were the only ones who knew about the unlikely duo, and their wild, sex-escapades. Of course, as they continued to not be able to keep their hands off each other in public places, shortly everyone knew about Billy and April's involvement, too. The woman who owned the coffee shop, where they hung out, told April's father - basically because she was afraid Billy's wife was going to kill April. She had threatened a previous woman, and she was crazy enough to do it.

When April got home at 5:30 the next morning, her father sweep her up into his car, and drove her to Texas to stay with a friend. He'd heard the rumor she was also pregnant. She didn't know if she was or not, but bleeding on the bumpy-ride down ended any problem she might have had. She stayed about three weeks in Texas, before taking a bus back. The whole incident scared April enough, so she stopped seeing Billy.

Yet, through all this, she *still* faithfully-wrote love letters to Wally, with insinuations that her virginity was *absolutely* intact for him only. Next, April went into Chicago to pick up sailors coming in from the Great Lakes Naval Training Station. Her dual-life was not acceptable to her father, but if he said anything, she'd increase her activity. As she continued writing to Wally of her love and virtue, it at last paid off when he sent her the *specific* wedding rings she'd requested. They were to be married when he came home on leave.

She lost fifty pounds, but more to look good for her wedding photos, than actually for him. She looked terrific, and let everyone know who had *ever* made fun of her when fat. It took her two and a half years to capture him - as she considered him a conquest. Not yet eighteen, nothing had ever before made April feel more highly respected, than to tote-around an engagement ring, backed up with love letters from an older guy in military service.

She greatly enjoyed all the new attention from her friends, as well the peer-group who had judged her so harshly. April admitted to Michael that she didn't know if she loved him, as much as she worshipped him, regarding that he wanted to marry her. Wally on the other hand, would have admitted that marrying April meant regular sex, someone to cook, clean and care for him. Since she lost so much weight, he was sure she'd be someone that would be *eager to please* him. This fulfilled Wally's insecurity regarding keeping a good woman. Neither one had a clue, or knew what the other was expecting in, or from their marriage. Besides April, couldn't wait to get away from her father.

Now it was all about the wedding, the dress and how April could make her father pay for it all. She decided in choosing her wedding party, from a mix of the old neighborhood friends she'd kept in touch with, and new high school friends who had been loyal to her. Pollyanna, who her father had always made a point to compliment - the pretty-blonde, younger sister she'd met through Beth - was first choice as Maid of Honor.

She wanted to prove to all them, she - April - could get married before any of them did. It also guaranteed *everyone* in the old neighborhood would know of the wedding. Michael didn't want to be Maid of Honor - being Bride's Maid was more than enough to deal with. In her opinion, it was all getting very boring, with the date still being a long way off yet. April kept telling Michael, and anyone else who would listen, that Wally had changed her feelings about men. "He's different, not like my father." Naturally, she never spoke of Billy, or the other men she'd picked-up-with over the past year. Later, April would muse: "When you *think* you're in love, they always *seem different*."

Beth would only be getting an invitation, because April was still pissed at her from the scene she created in accusing Beth of trying to steal Wally from her. The first time Beth met Wally, he and April had only gone out a few times, but she wanted to bring him in to meet her old neighborhood friends. So, Beth got six couples - friends who knew April - set to go for a Saturday at Brookfield Zoo. Though called *dates*, it wasn't really that formal, with only a few of the girls going-steady with the guys they brought. Beth, always the flirt, teased around with all the guys, as her date was just a good *buddy*. But when she started in on Wally, April really blew her cool in a big way, revealing how insecure and jealous she was.

Wally, another guy and Beth supposedly *got lost*, for over an hour. Beth hid behind her own real virginity, as she'd seductively-tease with absolute fake-innocence. She knew nothing of what April had done with her sex life, since they were living so many miles apart. Beth laughed a lot, trying to have a good time, while-covering up her own sexual frustration, since it was 1962. By the time the three rejoined the others for the picnic lunch, Beth was getting looks like someone would put her in the lions' cage. April, years later, brought up that Beth had tried to take Wally away from her, but *she* managed to hold on to him. Beth only shook her head and laughed. Wally was a nice guy, but to her, even back then, rather boring, not very clever.

April really didn't know what kind of bed she had made for herself, until she was supposed to get laid in it. She counted up the actual days she'd spent with Wally, and it was about two months out of the two years they knew - dated each other. She began to realize, she didn't know very much about him at all, and especially not about his family - most of whom were *not* planning to come down from Wisconsin for the wedding.

Wally honestly told her about the women he'd been with, while on leave in the Orient and the West Coast. But April clung to her *virgin story*, as far as he knew. Her actions, on their wedding night, were an equal combination of scared of being found out and anxious-horniness. That feeling of wanting something you know about, but can't show your knowledge of. In all her nervousness, she forgot to change clothes as they left for the expensive, resort hotel she had insisted on having. She then insisted they drag-along Pollyanna, and Wally's younger brother Doug, who had been Best Man.

The scene at the reservation desk qualified as a good imitation of a comedy routine, with the desk manager staring at April in her wedding dress, while Wally proudly announced for everyone within earshot to hear, "The Bridal Suite." Pollyanna and Doug stayed almost an hour drinking champagne, since April wouldn't let them leave. Finally when they left, she locked herself in the bathroom. Later that night, after the marriage was consummated, Wally was still surprised that the girl who had chased him so, would have hid in a bathroom. Maybe she'd been a bit over-convincing about her virginity.

The following day they left for Wisconsin, and April's first meeting of Wally's family. He had never talked about them, and in all reality she'd never asked, so she didn't know what she was getting into at all. They lived on a small farm, which was rather run-down. Though they had lived there for fifteen years, his father had never put in plumbing, and there was only one electric line to the house. Wally's five, younger siblings slept in the unheated, upstairs loft. He was not surprised, nor did he speak against it, when the newlyweds got to sleep there, too. The middle of January, but not concerned, for they had their love to keep them warm -even if in an audience.

During the night, April had to pee, but refused to go outside, so she suffered through, until Wally found a cup for her to use They both wanted sex, but patiently waited until everyone sounded like they were asleep When in the throws of hot passion, she never noticed if anyone woke up or not It was ignorant bliss, but still she insisted they move-up their plans to leave for Long Beach -privacy and indoor plumbing And thus, the honeymoon was over, so it was time for her to become the *hausfrau*

April attacked her long-sought after job of a housewife, like a true bull-in-a-china-shop. To say she was inept, was in error for Wally would eat anything, and cleanliness was not at the top of his list She shouldn't be criticized, because everyone is usually not a great, gourmet-cook when first starting out. The one thing they did perfect was sex, which would keep him happy They practiced sex five, sometimes ten times a day April hoped that with the volume, Wally would become a more versatile lover But then, she couldn't make any suggestions of her own, or share comparisons, as she had no married friends. He, of course, thought he had satisfactorily gotten *the job* done

The first disappointing incident was when April realized Wally's problem with making decisions. He was sent to buy polish for the Admiral's boat. Even with the product name on a piece of paper in front of him, he could not decide which one to choose. April may not have done well in school, but she wasn't stupid. She stood there completely stunned at first, then she grabbed the right can of wax and walked to the counter. After a while, it continued to bother her that they were broke all the time. He didn't want her to work, because he wanted them to be together whenever he had time off the ship, which was not regularly scheduled.

They lived on one hundred and eighty dollars a month Seventy-five of that went for rent, which didn't leave much for everyday expenses, much less splurges Still, one day he insisted on going into town for a haircut, because the ones on the ship -although free - were not very good, he thought. When he returned *three* hours later, she could see him through the apartment window counting his change coming up to the door. Also obvious, he was drunk. She did not fully realize until then, he'd come from a family where drinking was more than a social habit. With only bottle-return-money, she scrounged for her cigarettes, she'd been smoking cigarette-butts, and he went out drinking! Though these things hurt, she told herself that she loved him. Yet, she wasn't sure about his continued feelings for her, if his drinking was more important than her.

Wally was soon to leave for his first, long tour-of-sea-duty since their marriage. He'd be gone six months, and asked April to promise she wouldn't cry at the ship, as it embarrassed him. When the day came, she stood on the ship surrounded by hundreds of crying-wives with their children, but her eyes stayed dry.

She'd not break her promise, she would be strong. As their last moments slipped away, all that was left were their eyes staring at each other, telling all the deep feelings that neither one of them dared to speak. Their bodies had been absorbed into the masses of people with everyone - everything becoming a blur. It was the first time April felt Wally truly loved her. Even if he never spoke it aloud, his eyes had whispered every romantic word his inarticulateness could not say.

When the whistle blew, April slowly brushed her cheek against his. She knew she was not strong enough for a last kiss. She wanted only the memory of how they had been one hour before in bed. With all the strength she had left, she turned to walk off the ship, not looking back once. As she reached the dock, she turned facing him, then reached her arm up, as if to touch him instead of waving goodbye. He then leaned over the railing, to reach his arm down to her. She knew she had gotten to him, and he would be in her grasp, as long as *she* wanted to hold onto him. She realized the power in the drama of her performance - and how easy it had been to do.

Her father - at Wally's request - had come out to California to return April to Illinois, and he took her back to the apartment to finish packing. But she would not return to her old men-chasing days - when April was loyal, she was one-hundred-per-cent. The only time in the six months she went out, was to suburbia's 'every housewife's favorite thrill' - a Tupperware party.

But loyalty could not be said of her husband, as the letters and pictures Wally sent were obliviously to his wife's feelings, as more than descriptive. With his braggart, insensitive ego, he wrote of the lovely, *friendly* Japanese and Filipino girls. Probably, as if to prove his prowess, the photos showed him with his buddies in bars surrounded by these *lovelies*. To him, this is what they did, as in the usual to be expected, with no apologies or excuses. Yet, no matter what he said or did, her stoic-faithfulness remained dauntless, for now. She may have accepted these military circumstances, but she would never forget them.

Beth went out to visit April and Wally in Long Beach, the summer after she had started working in Chicago. It was 1964, after a year at the university, she'd started dating Bruce, and also commuting to Chicago with her childhood friends, sisters Priscilla and Pollyanna - April's former maid of honor. They decided to take a vacation together out west by bus, and while in California, stayed with April and Wally a few days She had only recently rejoined him

Beth hadn't seen her in years, since away in college when they wed - taking her finals the excuse for not attending. The trip was both detrimental and beneficial to the friendships. The sisters picked at April, and tried to get her to side with them against Beth regarding Bruce. April refused to condemn a man she'd never met. Besides, Beth made him sound more like the man she wanted him to be, than the man he was. When April stuck by her, Beth knew they would someday again be close friends.

As for April, the marriage-bliss had worn-off. They weren't "in love," she *maturely* said, but they did have a 'bond of love.' She'd learned to live with him, and he with her, so married a year and a half, it had all the common-earmarks of lasting. Then, of course, she didn't know how much she could change and grow, especially when she had gotten married at eighteen. Trauma of her miscarriage already tested their married life, a few months before. In her fifth month, April'd been exposed to German measles, so she knew the miscarriage was for the best. Also, she realized Wally could not handle any kind of serious, or emotional problems.

While she was in the hospital, he escaped from it all by drinking with his buddies. Not being able to face the pain of loss, he evaded it. She chose to take the reaction as, him not caring what happened to her. He didn't talk of his feelings at all, nor come to visit her in the hospital. Again, this neglect in her eyes, added to the soon growing list of love-infractions.

Almost a year later, Wally received his discharge from the Navy, and they moved back to the Chicago suburban area. April, again pregnant, so Wally's factory job made them still pinch-pennies, and she didn't work for fear of another miscarriage. Then, when she was almost in her ninth month, her Aunt Sissy died. Her Uncle and Aunt had been living in Tucson for some time, but she couldn't take a plane in her condition, so her father went alone.

Though, she hadn't been really close to Sissy, she was the closest thing to a mother that she'd ever known. But April was very concerned about staying calm for the baby's sake. By that evening, she was pretty much under control until Wally decided to go out drinking with his brother. He couldn't stand being around her so upset, with continuous crying, though she begged him to stay and comfort her.

He coolly replied, "Why should I mourn for your Aunt, when she never liked me anyway?" He took his stance, and the whole emotional situation made him easily agitated.

Shocked, but she tried to explain. "Wally," she pleaded, "I'm not asking you to mourn for Sissy. I'm asking you to stay, comfort me and hold me . . . I just don't want to be alone. It makes me feel better . . . to have you here with me." She sat curled on the couch, hoping he would see how small and vulnerable she was.

His whole family-instilled-ancestry of showing emotions to *not* be masculine could *not* be changed, even if he did love her. He began to feel cornered, and thinking that a man sitting around comforting his wife was rather weak and sappy. Still, he did not have the communication skills to explain it all, or reveal his inadequacies and fears to her. Instead he said, "I gotta go, Doug is waiting." With that, he quickly gave her a kiss on the forehead, heading out the door.

April's voice trailed off, as it echoed against the closing door, "Wally, please . . . " This new hurt opened her eyes even more about him. Soon, she was not only crying for her Aunt, who had never been capable of loving her the way she wanted, but also for herself not being loved the way she wanted. She'd been alone too many times already in her life, facing one crisis after another. She'd thought if she married, she'd never be alone, but she was wrong. Marriage was not the answer to her loneliness. Perhaps her child would help her be happy.

Sometimes April wished she had not begged her father to get Wally into the structural-iron workers' union. But as he worked harder, and moved up in the ranks, she became aware of the money - specifically what it could do for *her*. If she had money, she felt no one could look down on her. It soon became Wally's goal, too, having come from poverty. He never had any *real* money before, and it could make *him* a big-man, especially when he bought most of the rounds of beer for his new-found friends at the bar.

Soon after their daughter, Deidra was born, they bought a track-house in one of the new developments sprouting-up all over the western suburbs in the mid-1960s. The little houses looked like differently-painted boxes, and sat on the curved, winding streets, with little sapling trees outlining the middle-class-maze. Perhaps there was safety in this anonymity, and at least April would never be alone, surrounded by so many other housewives. In time, just as a house is not a home, she became very lonely in this crowded neighborhood, where she knew few of the women.

The first time Beth came to visit, she absentmindedly left the address at home, and with only the description of the house color. She ended up driving around the lanes, and avenues, and parkways for forty-five minutes passing April's house three times. She felt like *Alice in Wonderland* without the excitement of meeting the White Rabbit. Beth wondered if Wally ever went into the wrong house, after one of his drinking-episodes. She went back to the gas station to call April on the payphone. The second time Beth was there, she drove in the wrong driveway, and rang the wrong bell. That neighbor had painted their box-house the same color as April's!

On that first visit, April led Beth from room to room pointing out custom drapes, their color television, professional photos of their wedding and Deidra's baby photos. Everyone of her possessions were regarded as if the price-tags should've been attached - to be more impressive. She droned on ad nauseam, expecting some gush or something of admiration from Beth.

Yes, they were more than what Beth had, but also what she didn't like or want. Yes, of course, proud of her house - better than the trailer she was raised in. And, she was glad to have *someone* over to show it off to, but that was not the sort of thing that impressed Beth. April wore *her* new money status like a fur coat. At the same time, she never ceased to mention to people that *she* was the one who got Wally his job in the union.

April tried to act so happy those first few years, in her pretend-picture-perfect house in the make-believe suburb. Yet, her acting barely concealed how deeply, empty-inside she actually felt. The only pleasures she got were from playing with Deidra, and them continuously shopping for more possessions for them both. Unconsciously, she believed they'd take the place of a husband who was never home, or spending any of his free time with her. Wally worked a new construction job that ran twelve to sixteen hours a day, six or seven days a week. Even when he did get off work early, he usually joined his buddies drinking, rather than coming home to her and Deidra.

At first, April tried to understand he needed time to unwind, but his drinking problem had never been every night before. Each evening by nine o'clock or so, she threw away the ruined dinners she'd kept warm for him. Many of those times, after he did get home, she also cleaned-up his vomit, when he got sick from drinking too much.

The pile of money lying on the kitchen table, at the end of every week with the check-stub, showed her how much this man was making for himself and her. Somehow it was not big enough to fill the void that had come into both their lives. While the alcohol also ruined his sexual desire, hers was gone mainly from his inattention to her. Ironically then, they had been happier when pinching-pennies.

As if for spite, April tried to see how much of the money she could spend. Beth shopped with her many times during those years, and could not believe how much she wasted on trinkets, toys and knick-knacks. She didn't think about a hobby or interest to keep her occupied. Her obvious loneliness was quite pathetic, as she toted Deidra from visiting over at Michael's house to Beth's house, and then back to Michael's again - trying to kill time. Each house was at least ten miles from the other, so getting gas with constant stops at McDonalds was her routine, along with whatever retail store they may wandered into.

The bitterness started building-up in her, until she had very little to say about or to Wally. What hurt her more than anything, when he was home, he still really didn't spend time with her. If he went out, he wouldn't take her with, and when at home he usually slept the time away. As with many wives, April felt he was ashamed of her, and her fault he drank. The only times they had sex were when he came home not too drunk to get an erection, but drunk enough he didn't know who was in bed with him.

April decided to go on a diet, realizing she'd let herself go long enough, using food once again for consolation. At only five-feet four-inches, she weighed over two-hundred pounds. The only way she knew to diet was to stop eating, and take those wonderful, little pills the doctor prescribed for her - in the language of their time - *speed*. Consequently, with this method, she was constantly fainting.

Many times while shopping, she stopped in at Michael's or Beth's for something to eat before she passed out again. The weight dropped off quickly, and within nine months she lost almost a hundred pounds. She looked terrific, and of course, it changed her personality drastically. She became that teenager again, resentful of all those who had previously looked down on her for being fat, or didn't feel her worthy of their friendship. And, Wally was at the top of that list this time.

Suddenly, April hooked herself-up with a company to start selling clothes at home-parties to build-up her wardrobe, as well get her out of the house several nights a week. She created a warm, lively-person from deep-down inside herself, who enjoyed being out on her own among lots of women. She soon realized that men began to notice her, nice men - the kind she'd never personally known in her life. Men who seemed to appear out of nowhere, and want to help her with this and that, as if she were fragile, or they simply wanted to be around her - to talk to her politely. To this she only observed, and politely responded back, without any encouragement for anything more. But it all was being filed-way for future reference.

Now, for two or three nights a week, there were no longer dinners warming in the oven. It was no longer unusual, for Wally to come home drunk to find his father-in-law there babysitting for Deidra. With no real reason to rush home, April sat to talk with her 'new friends' after the clothes demonstrations. She particularly liked these people, because they never knew the old, fat April, married to the drunkard-husband. To top it off, to her surprise, she had no problem talking, laughing and having a good time with these *strangers* either.

April enjoyed her slimness about a year, with her new vanity regarding it, as she worked hard to accomplish it. Soon with this pattern, Wally began accusing her of seeing other men. He could not understand why she needed to be out in the world, though communication with people was really all she wanted at this time. It was after eleven, when she came in to find Wally waiting up for her. At first she was happy by the surprise. "Well, hello dear." She walked straight over to kiss him, but he got up instantly from the couch to cross to the end of the room.

"Where the hell have you been?" April quickly realized he'd had enough to drink to make him suspicious of the late hour. Usually, he was sound asleep when she got home.

Since nothing to hide, she calmly said, "I was at Margaret Cummings in Downers Grove giving a clothes party, just as I am usually doing when I'm out." She went ahead to sit on the couch, as she was tired. When he didn't have a response, she continued. "After everyone left, I totaled up her order, which by the way, I made over $100 in commission."

When his eyes barely blinked at her accomplishment, she went on. "She then had to decide what free-clothes she wanted, as her hostess gift. She probably tried on everything I had on the rack in her size." She watched him, as he stood like a statue not moving or reacting.

"Afterwards, we had coffee and talked about our kids." She paused, then asked, "Where the hell do you think I was, standing on the corner selling these clothes?" She threw the one clothes bag still in her hand, onto the next couch cushion.

As he came alive, he became defensive, mumbling incomprehensibly. "How do I know that? . . . You could have been out screwing with some guy . . . or something?" He stepped forward as if gathering steam, "Since you lost all that weight . . . you're always gone . . . and you don't even fix dinner for me."

April now responded with a raised voice, as he hit a real cord of discontent. "Why should I cook, when you're never home in time to eat dinner anyway? I threw out more dinners than you ever ate! What difference does it make when you're drunk, if it's home-cooked or frozen, you can't taste it anyway?" She got up from the couch to head to the bedroom, then turned. "Besides, if you did eat, you only threw-up . . . *And I* was the one to always clean it up - you weren't!"

Wally could not handle the accusations, as he was supposed to be the one making them. Desperate, he yelled back, "That's not true!" She burst out laughing at the ridiculous denial. "Besides, you didn't lose the weight for me, you were only looking to get attention from other men." He was the pathetic one, so April sat back down on the couch, and lit a cigarette to attempt to calm them both down.

"If you really want to know, I lost the weight for myself, and hoping you, *My Dear* husband, might notice me *enough* to stay home, *and be sober*. Maybe even - hope beyond hope - want to make love to me in a *sober-condition*, so that you would know that the skinny-person lying under you was *actually your wife*. But, it didn't work." April slowly began to cry.

Wally walked over to the easy chair and sat down. She looked over at him, and that possibly he might be listening to her, she wiped her eyes and nose to continue. "So, I thought I would at least get out among people before I went totally berserk, since you obviously didn't care. It helped too, Wally," she began to control herself, "because I've found out that very few of the women out there are any happier than I am. Even if their husbands don't go out drinking with the guys, most of them still ignore their wives."

She looked at him, staring at her with a very lost-look in his eyes. After a moment of contemplation, April decided it was his ignorance of their whole relationship, and not the booze. "What I'm trying to say is, that if I don't see any *really* better marriages out there than mine, why would I be looking for another man to get involved with?" She decided not to add her true feeling, that most men were still just all alike - a bunch of self-centered, non-caring bastards.

Totally lost and confused, especially with the booze-affect wearing off, his spine was weakening in knowing what to say. It certainly seemed that April was telling the truth. All he knew was that he didn't want to lose her, or his darling, daughter Deidra. His defenses were still up, but he took a different mode. "OK, OK. I'll be home more often, and spend more time with you and Deidra, if you will stop being-gone to all these clothes-show-things, or whatever they are. You know I love you, and I want us to stay together." He seemed to have heard her.

Once again, April believed him because, he was the only happiness she'd known in her life, for even these few years. She still had a piece of her heart left for Wally - she wouldn't for long though, if he kept breaking his promises, which would chip that last piece away also. And so, the pattern was started with him changing - to quit drinking, while she believed he was doing it, and be so proud of him for it. Then, the trust being broken, as the promises were made over and over again, around they went. She could not get him to acknowledge at all, that he truly had a drinking problem, which even she knew was key to his success in stopping.

Then, they both made the most-fatal-mistake, so many couples looking for the magic band-aid make. They committed to have another child, to give him more responsibility and reason for not drinking. It sounded like the easiest solution with both agreeing, yet no consideration of what kind of a marriage, they were bringing that unknowing child into.

Question April should have thought of was: "Why wasn't the first child - Deidra - enough to make him responsible and quit drinking?" Yet, Wally did do very well through most of her new pregnancy, then his ten-year High School Reunion came up. When she looked at the invitation, she saw it was close to her due date, yet relented for him to go ahead to Wisconsin. He had been doing so good, and they had been getting along so well together. He was such a good father to Deidra, as well being so helpful to her during the pregnancy. She really didn't want to test him, to see if he would go, if she did ask him not to go.

As fate would have it, Wally had just gotten to Wisconsin - he took a week's vacation to be able to visit with everyone and really celebrate with all of his friends - and April went into early labor. When she called to his home, his mother was the one who answered. After all the kids she had on her own, she saw no need to bother Wally, as he was bar-hopping with his brothers and friends. "He works hard to give you a good life, so he deserves to have some fun, but do call back once the baby comes. We'd like to know what you had," she said.

April turned to Michael to see her through the whole drawn-out delivery, as she'd been down that path of a negligent husband, also. For April though, this destroyed the last love she'd been able to hold onto for Wally. He just could not be there when she needed him - not physically or especially emotionally. Yes, she knew he still loved her in his own way, but he was not capable of showing it. Then the crowning straw came - though he had a new, baby daughter at home - Wally decided to stay an extra day in Wisconsin, rather than returning immediately. Once back, April was cold to him, and remained controlled of her feelings the rest of their marriage.

April quickly lost the pregnancy weight, and made real plans to change her life. Wanting to get more in touch with herself, she read a lot of metaphysical books, took hypnosis lessons the summer of 1971. She dragged along Michael to join in expanding their self-images. April soon had a crush on the instructor and another student, too. These classes were for learning to be a hypnotist, so the beginning of her interest in the occult, then astrology. The crushes went no place - just the necking and petting attention again - yet, also affirmed she was attractive to some interesting men.

At the same time, Wally's faults - short-comings became blaring issues. She'd begun rejecting him in bed when he was drunk, and when he wasn't, she'd just lay there waiting for him to finish.

April spent her days reading her metaphysics or astrology, and evenings with Michael practicing her hypnosis. Wally continued to drink, not even bothering to apologize for his actions. Since he rarely read anything but a newspaper, he had no interest in her new activities, so more limited their conversations. As April's life expanded daily, the nothingness between them had to be acknowledged. They barely talked about the girls, and he still didn't want to take her out, though now slim. When at home, he fell asleep on the couch by ten. The money factor no longer had much influence over keeping her in the marriage.

Arguing or criticizing each other more, April simply went out more often, even if by herself. Several times she went to a small bar-discotheque, quite a distance from the house because she loved to dance so much, and felt better about it now being thin. Tim Brennan, Michael's husband, frequented such bars to drink and pick-up women. That particular night, he had Wally and a few other guys with him.

April was dancing with a guy, when they both noticed her, and pointed her out to the others. Before Wally got-up to say something to her, she left with the guy. Though they went out the door together, they left in separate cars, but Wally didn't bother to check that part out. Just a guy who had talked and danced with April - something Wally never did either - and they were going for coffee.

An innocent incident, but Wally being a jealous, insecure husband with a wife he could now be jealous of, didn't want to know the facts, of his own negligence being the cause. With prodding insinuations from his supposed-good buddies - especially Tim from his own usual cheating experience - everything conceivable was going on in Wally's mind. April got home long before he did, as they had kept drinking. She knew when he came stomping into the bedroom and flicked on the lights, he had somehow known where she'd been. She also figured he was so drunk, nothing she said would convince him it was innocent.

April stared at Wally as he began his tirade. "Well, you think because you're all snuggled in bed, I don't know you've been screwing that guy you were dancing with at the bar?" He stepped closer, so April couldn't get a word in as he continued. "You think if you go to some-out-of-the-way-place you won't get caught, huh? Well, Tim and all of the rest of the guys saw you hanging onto him, and then leaving together. Go ahead, just try to deny it . . . I've got witnesses this time!" He started to sway in his inebriated state, then put his hand against the wall.

Though April felt it futile, she decided to make her statement anyway, and calmly began, "Yes, we left together, drove to a coffee shop in separate cars. I had an interesting conversation with a sober, intelligent man who was interested in what *I* also had to say. To my knowledge, restaurants don't allow people to screw in them, even if you're quiet and under the table. He kissed me lightly good night, and I drove home by myself." She pulled herself up from under the covers, and sat with her arms crossed in front.

Wally, teetered back and forth totally wasted, as leaning wasn't helping, he was too far gone. April knew he'd pass-out any moment, and not remember a word either of them said. "You, *asshole,* can believe me or not. I don't give a shit, and . . . I really don't think you would have either, if you hadn't been egged-on by your so-called drunken friends. I'm sure Michael will be interested where Tim was this evening. Good Night!"

She rolled over, scooted back down and pulled the covers over her head. Moments later, she heard him crash to the floor, somewhere between the bedroom and bathroom. She thought of getting up to check on him, then decided not to bother.

The first night April did pick-up a guy, was right after her hypnosis classes finished, and her crush ended. She and Michael were to meet Beth, and her single-girlfriend Carrie, at their favorite nightclub. They were running a little late from work at the restaurant, but still didn't expect to find Micheal and April sitting with two guys when they arrived. Whenever Beth went out with the girls, she'd always let any men they met know she was married.

Now, when she started to say something, April actually gave her a swift-kick under the table, with a look not to say it. This was hysterically funny to Beth, as the most exciting things April and Michael usually did was hold hands, or share a few naive kisses.

They had created their made-up scenarios about them-selves throughout the conversation. They looked forward to the big excitement of the men, usually asking them to join them in their rooms at the adjacent hotel. They both declined, as did Beth and Carrie when the same men, posed the same request to them later.

April had decided most of the men she met were only interested in available sex, and not enough conversation first for the compatibility she was looking for. Since she wasn't ready to take that big-step against her marriage, she soon decided to just stay home and loose herself in her reading. If it hadn't been for her interest in her growing collection of books, she really would have gone off the deep end. Beth and Michael began to worry, as she began to lose touch with daily life.

April was only existing through her books, and gotten heavy into the occult, with some weird phenomena. Objects were flying around the room, her bed moved at night, and visions - talking to her dead Aunt and Mother. After several months of strange happenings, Beth knew something had to be done to get April back into the living world. She wasn't even functioning as a mother to her children, once such an important part of her life. As well, she let the house go, only prepared the basics of sandwiches and TV dinners, too.

With Beth's excitement of building a new house closer to where April lived, competitiveness turned her on to also buying a new house. Her husband made the most money, so she needed the biggest house. But for April, this was not the best move - in the new house she had twelve rooms to wander around in, where the old one only had six. Beth called on a regular basis to talk her into going bar-hopping and dancing with her and Connie.

"Honest to God, April, you act as if we're jumping every man we dance with. We have a good time, and the music will put some life back into you!" She paused a second, and then continued, "Don't you remember how you love to dance? Bruce won't take me, and Wally doesn't take you, so we go out and dance without them. There are always good, fun men available where we go. It's just dancing with people of the opposite sex. You remember them don't you?"

Sitting in that big, reclining-chair with her short legs tucked under her, and her arms crossed in front, she almost yelled "I'm not going to screw some stranger!"

"Who said anything about sex?" We all go together and come home together. If Connie wants to pick someone up, she's on her own. I'm not really having sex except with Rob, and he's with his wife on weekends." Finally, Beth pried her out, as she agreed to show up at the Cafe' la France, where her and Connie worked.

At about ten o'clock that Friday night - and almost a smile on her face, she was ready. As they headed to downtown Chicago, Connie made it clear they were heading for the best places to dance and meet new, interesting people from all over. The music and crowds slowly got to April, as once again she found some reason for living. There was a world out there that she could be a part of, and dance her little butt-off, at the same time. It was one of the better nights for them all to let go, and enjoy some fun for themselves. Beth hadn't known at the time, how close April came to losing her marbles. She also didn't know, that April's marriage was in a state as bad as her own.

Several times April then met Connie and Beth at The Place, a discotheque next door to the Cafe'. She picked up several guys there, and either made out in the car, or went for coffee at their place. She still only wanted someone to talk to, or pay some attention toward her. The fact that she never got a weirdo who tried to rape her, or continued when she said stop, was an absolute miracle. Connie's favorite expression about April's stupid habit was, "She is unfucking believable." She never saw the danger in her being alone with some strange man, feeling she had good instincts about them, but it was quite a chance she was taking. In reality, they were the precursors regarding the 1977 movie, *Looking for Mr. Goodbar*, but luckier. Then, the end of November, April moved kids, clothes and furniture over to her father's house. She'd asked Wally for a divorce, to no avail. They'd been battling constantly, but she lasted only a week.

Her first real fling didn't come until months after Beth's divorce. Having lunch to celebrate, April told her about meeting Dean at the large, singles apartment complex community center, they'd been out to a couple of times before. They'd met some guys, but hadn't had sex with any of them. Easy to get into the 'private' residents' party - just give a name or apartment number. Beth noticed the Mail Center, so got some last names and numbers. She had tired of the married men at the Cafe' always hitting on her, and wanted some bona-fide single guys to dance and talk with sometimes.

April was doing ground-work, she said for when she found someone she wanted, she'd have the experience then of knowing how to act, and what to say. She knew her marriage was a lost cause, and only putting in her time, as she had nowhere else she could go with her two daughters. She agreed on having sex when Wally insisted on it to keep peace, to be able to go out when she wanted. She felt it had been years since they'd actually, passionately made love. She so wanted the romance in her life.

April met Dean the first week of February, when Beth was supposed to meet her there, but she got stuck working late. If April didn't want it to appear that she was alone, she'd keep walking around like she was looking for someone she was supposed to meet. The ploy worked many times, even when true. The guys would notice and ask who she was looking for, or if they could help. On her fourth time past the fireplace in an hour, Dean stopped to ask, so in her sweetest, little-girl-lost voice, she said, "My friend Beth, she must have gotten lost or something. She was to meet me an hour ago. I really don't know anyone, and I don't know what to do - wait or leave." She had continued to smile at him, as she glanced around and then back to him.

Needless to say, Dean was quite taken by her innocence, so being the White Knight, he offered: "My apartment is close by, would like to come over to call Beth?"

April noted immediately that he remembered her friend's name, which she took as a sign that he *was* paying attention. "How kind of you to offer," she replied so sweetly. "And, not that I don't trust such a nice guy as you, but you'll have to promise not to take advantage of my predicament." Up in Dean's apartment, she pretended to call Beth. She and Dean then talked, as she very carefully asked about his work and hobbies. She glanced around, not to seem that she was scrutinizing his living quarters, yet avoiding to give much information about herself.

Money, in and of itself, was *still* very important to her - she could *not* get involved with a man without money. Also, she wanted to make sure he wasn't married. She didn't want to be in the same boat as Connie and Beth - in love with married men. Beth said if a guy could afford Round-Tree Lake apartments, he had money, and one reason why they kept going there to party.

Dean turned on some music while April pretended to call Beth, then automatically took two wine glasses from the cabinet and filled them from a bottle - open, but corked on the counter. The convenience of it all did not attract her attention, as it should have. Dean then lifted a glass to April, which she took without commenting about not usually drinking, as he toasted her casually, "To finding each other." She smiled, nodded and sipped some of the wine.

Dean took that as his signal, leaned in close to her to slowly seduce her. She, at first, mumbled about thoroughly enjoying the attention. His hands had moved carefully over and under her blouse, with the kisses coming down her neck into her cleavage. April became caught up in her own film scenario, playing it to the hilt with little moans of enjoyment.

Then she whispered sweetly, "Need I remind you of your promise not to take advantage of me?" At no time had she pushed him, or his hands away.

He pulled his head back, as he couldn't believe she was for real, and had to look at her face. "How can you say 'no' when your clothes are half-off?" Her face was almost blank, as she'd learned to separate sex and emotional involvement during the last few years with Wally.

April slowly and quietly replied, "I wanted to make sure you want me for myself, and not just my body." The remark was probably one she heard in some movie to prove sincerity. Dean might have seen the same movie, for he resumed seducing her. Very dramatically she added, "If you really want me, you can wait until tomorrow!" This compromise put her in control of the final decision, and he was gullible enough to agree to her terms.

She then speeded home to Wally, getting the first of her many tickets. She had no regrets on her choice to meet Dean the following evening. They made love the way she'd known it, long before. When she retold the experience to Beth, only the soft music and candlelight were missing. She thought he was quite good, *but* it was her first comparison in years.

April had *a thing* about social/sexual diseases, in fact deep-down quite a hypochondriac about them. She was positive if she fooled around with more than one man at a time, 'her clitoris would turn green and fall off, or something more absurd.' Quite serious about it, she later warned the girls, they'd be committed to a mental hospital, because syphilis had eaten up their brains. Often her self-righteousness was mixed in, since she'd not always practice what she preached.

Because of this phobia, part of her first affair was the pact that she and Dean made with each other. No matter how kooky it sounded, April proudly stated how she put one hand on her heart, and the other on her crotch, and Dean did the same thing to his heart and penis. They then swore not have sex with anyone else without telling the other one, or thus released them from their promise, and their affair. Dean more than agreed, or perhaps he believed: *His penis in her bush, was better than two birds still in a tree. Or, as close to a 'sure thing,' as he'd get.*

Connie couldn't quit laughing, or retelling everyone she knew of April's ridiculous game of being faithful, when *she* was the one married. April told Dean that they could only see each other once a week until she separated from Wally, because a lot of money for her was involved. She believed Dean accepted every word she said. It would have been hard to decipher who was doing the better acting. They kissed, caressed and passionately made love again to double-seal the vows just taken. Afterwards, April got her second ticket speeding home.

After a few times with Dean, while much deliberation and thought, April decided he was not *all* she wanted in a lover. Back out looking, not really knowing what she was looking for, but now knowing a little better what she didn't want. She also believed, it would only be a matter of time before Wally accepted the facts and signed the divorce papers. Since she hardly cared, she went out as much as possible

On Friday night, once again at The Place dancing and waiting for Beth to get off work, April wandered around. Al spotted her. Her eyes so wide open, she didn't miss a single guy in the place, yet he'd been watching her before she noticed him. She did look spectacular that night, as she'd been working on her make-up, hair and clothes. During one of the breaks in the live music, she sat down on the stage with her soft drink. Al came strolling up to ask, "Could I share part of your stage?"

This, of course, made her light-up like a Christmas tree. Any reference to acting at all, and she had a script in her hand. Even with her playing the struggling-starlet, she was more sure of herself than he seemed.

An instant, purely physical attraction to one another was made. He actually primped more for the evening out than she had. Al wasn't much taller than Wally, but his coal-black hair glistened, almost manicured in a mod-cut. While his close-cut beard and mustache were perfectly trimmed, without a hair out-of-place. The charcoal eyes had just enough blue in them, so they were still believable. From head to toe, he looked like any moment he'd be cued to pose for some elegant men's magazine. Yet, all the time he was trying to look like the total-package had merely fallen-together, without any effort of his own.

They immediately shared stories, with him as lost and mixed up as she was - or so it appeared. He began slowly, as if painfully, pulling every word out hurt. Yet, the words fit together quite well, a more objective person would have noticed how well-rehearsed. He was separated from his wife and two kids. "For now, I'm staying at a friend's house, to take care of their horses, while they're on vacation." They talked continuously, squeezing in as much as possible until the band returned. After several dances, April definitely wanted to know this man better.

But, trying to talk above the band noise and usual crowd chatter, became impossible, so April suggested, "Why don't we go somewhere else . . . more quiet and intimate, but maybe still dance?"

Al's shy routine was more elusive when he hesitated to the proposition.

"Are you sure you want to leave here . . . with me? I mean didn't you have some friends you were meeting?" She looked at him wondering why such a good looking, well-built man would be so insecure about himself. Yes, he mentioned his wife made him feel so inadequate, because he didn't *earn very much money*, as a city, gas-line repairman, but still.

April stared a moment more, then in her most-mothering, reassuring smiling-voice she said, "I'll catch up with them later, I really want to spend time with you." They drove to a small lounge with more sedate music. The trio began to play the theme from *"Romeo and Juliet,"* as if on cue. Touching for the first time in the slow dance, after admiring each other's bodies, brought the intimacy up-close and very personal. That moment on, they were glued together like one single, fluid-body moving across the floor.
Though it was crowded, they never noticed another couple around them, or other movement, as catapulted into a dream-waltz, above everyone.

Moments after the music stopped, their bodies regained contact to the floor again. Suddenly, April felt embarrassed, as if she bared her most inner, personal feelings to this man, without saying a word. She couldn't even look at him, so when they sat down, she began to apologize for flinging herself upon him. "I really don't . . . usually throw myself upon men I've just met."

Al put his arm around her, to soothe the flustered, little girl replying, "I felt the electricity pull us close on the dance floor, too." She relaxed knowing she was not alone in her falling, and the conversation moved to even more personal. She then suggested they go for coffee at the place where he was staying, since he'd mentioned it was so close. This was not a coy game this time, she wanted him to make love to her, yet he had not made any direct passes, or even insinuated any intensions of doing so. Perhaps if she got them alone, he would get the idea to seduce her.

Minutes after they arrived at the stately, old country house, they were reclining in the living room listening to music and drinking coffee. The conversation reached the point where Al should have made some move toward her. Impatient, April turned herself to face him in anticipation. He finally leaned over and kissed her lightly. Just about to break away, the electricity took over once more, with the growing passion moving them into a prone position. She whispered, "Not here, take me to the bedroom." In her script, but *not* her expectations, in one fell-swoop, Al carried her off to his bedroom. One could only think there had been some magic potion in his coffee, to make such a change from his prior, shy-acting character into a daring-dude.

But no, it was only the beginning of *his* theatrics. April became so enthralled by this new role, she assumed *she* had solely inspired this transformation from reluctant lover he first portrayed. He didn't even want her to undress herself, he wanted that full pleasure of the scene to unfold his way. He slipped off her blouse with one hand, and with precision unsnapped her bra with the other. April became excited thinking of herself as a real character out of *Peyton Place*, or a Jacqueline Susann novel.

Al kissed her almost methodically all over her body, moving from one area to another as she reached a fever pitch. Wally now seemed totally inept in his love making. This man had found erogenous-zones, that April didn't even know she had. He took her leg and wrapped it around him, as he kissed up and down the back of her legs, moving slowly from her heel to the inside of her thigh. He lingered in the shallow-dip of her knee, while she began to squirm. With his free hand, he started to gently manipulate her clitoris. He moved up on her, never relenting with the action of his hands or mouth. By the time he penetrated her, she was already dissolving with another climax. She hadn't even realized he'd finished undressing her.

In between the rolling movements, he would whisper lines to her that she had always dreamed of hearing. It never occurred to her, they might not be original with him, or that she might not be the first he had whispered them to. So caught up with the fantasy and complete surrealism of it all, she could not actually believe it happening *to her with him.* She was lost, in a time and space-energy created by Al, in fulfilling her search for love. When it came her turn to seduce him, she seemed to be only seconds ahead of him, as he'd position her or move, in just the right direction. To her, their bodies overflowed together, knowing what the other one wanted before words were spoken.

Hours later, as she watched the morning light come slowly through the windows, her eyes turned to linger on the beautiful sleeping form of her lover. April knew she had found what she had *not known* she was looking for. She smiled devilishly, recapturing in her mind every fine moment of the glorious hours before, and how he had satisfied needs she never knew she had.

This hesitant lover - that she thought she had to seduce - was more than capable and passionate in every way. *"How was it that his wife could have overlooked this, or maybe even destroyed it?"* What a silly question of her, of all people to ask, April rationalized, when she felt Wally had done the same thing to her. April didn't bother to go home after her ethereal experience with Al. Instead, she called Beth, and asked if she would cover for her. This time Beth couldn't see how it would work.

She actually felt sorry for Wally that first morning, when he apologetically called her at six o'clock. He had already called Michael and several other friends, to no avail. He was waiting for the worst, or maybe perhaps the truth. He didn't hate Beth for her divorce, but he feared April would do the same thing, if she continued to associate with Beth and her *divorced* friends. Again, guilt by associations - divorce was a social disease, being caught by discontented housewives.

Beth coolly told Wally, "April's been here at my house all night talking. She's just left to go for a drive and think things over before she goes home." He wouldn't have believed it, except it had actually happened many times before, when they had been fighting. Waking-up from the alarm going-off, and turning-over to see that April hadn't been home, must have been a shock, since they *hadn't* been fighting recently. He never thought she would leave the big, new house and security of his money

April waited till her father arrived to babysit the girls, and Wally left the house. She went in, ignoring all her father's questions, changed clothes and took some money from the kitchen drawer. It was interesting that when it came to Al, it did not matter that he didn't have any money or a prestigious job. All that mattered was the love she could give, and receive from this man - more than she had ever dreamed was possible. She thanked her father for coming over, still ignoring his questions, gathered the girls and went to Michael's. She decided to start pressuring Wally again about the divorce. Maybe if she kept at him, he would give in and agree to it.

April saw Al every night, going home when she absolutely had to. Her father babysat, and tried to understand what was happening, with Wally not budging on the divorce. The following Saturday, April was at Beth's house with Al - Jeremy was with his father that weekend. They stayed after Beth left for work, to have a quiet place to talk. April then made her decision to leave both Wally and her kids. She could not leave Al, he'd become her *"life's blood,"* she cried, without any hesitation. With him, she justified she was happy, and it had only been unhappiness with her family. For someone who had been so overprotective - to the point of doting on her girls - this was a landmark decision.

Things began to move rapidly, and rather desperately from that point on. April and Wally had several big fights which were more screaming, yelling-fits filled with accusations, nasty remarks and name calling. This escalated with her pushing him, and him finally hitting back at her. It was all she wanted, so in a fit of anger she picked up the wall-phone, and hit him across the face with it. She'd only been coming back to see the kids, and get him to agree to the divorce. But it accomplished nothing, as they only fought and he called her vile names in front of the girls. April and Al actually got into the house, even after Wally had all the locks changed. She took the color television, the new living room set and the bedroom set, besides her clothes.

April now felt with Wally striking her she had enough to go to Beth's attorney. If someone had said the year before that April would give up her big house, as well her two, spoiled daughters and the money, friends would never have believed them. She had everything most women wanted *at that time*, but Beth understood what was missing. April was lonely, since she didn't have a caring husband, yet

Beth also knew from her own experience, April's new found sexual-escapade would not *completely* fill that void she had. She and Wally had a good sex life when they were first married, but a relationship built on sex alone never lasts. Though she tried to warn April, there was not much Beth could say, for in the throes of sexual-ecstasy, April definitely did not listen to anyone.

Those first few weeks, April and Al spent every spare moment together. Her fairy tale had come true, with the total elation of her Prince on the white horse carrying her away to his castle. It didn't matter to April, they *actually* stayed that first week and a half at his sister's house, with four kids running around. More like a fractured-fairy tale, but she ignored tacky-details over love. Finally, they got a small apartment in a building Al's mother owned. Happiness was theirs for the taking, except when his irate wife - she had NOT filed for divorce - or hostile Wally brought them back down to earth.

When April's divorce was over, everyone was still in a mild state of shock. Connie and Beth had been her witnesses, which was funny considering Connie had never even met Wally. For the nine years of marriage, April didn't have very much to show for it. She got to keep all the furniture she took, and an immediate compensation of five hundred dollars. There was also to be a small property settlement, once the house was sold. Some people felt that she didn't even deserve that, because she had been the one to walk-out on him, and their two kids for another man. The price she paid for her freedom was higher than most, so she better enjoy it as long as she could. Reality could be a bitch, as well heart-breaking.

Warranty Unguaranteed

Do I love you . . .
because I want to love someone?

Or do I question the love,
because it is not a permanent thing?

Is there a built-in obsolescence
in our love?

Will one of us have to be replaced
after a certain number of years?

Or is it the wear and tear we put on the love
that brings it to an end?

Few relationships of men or women,
can endure through time,
without a change of some kind.

CHAPTER 2

Connie

January, 1948, Constance Hope Stanswauski was born. Connie would always be a hard-working Capricorn, who loved money and a good time. Beth teased she married the first guy with a name easy to pronounce and spell. Connie was two years younger, but three grades behind Beth in school, because of her January birthday.

Her family didn't move into Elmwood until she was in the third grade, when the catholic school opened. She referred to her parents as the typical, arduous first-generation born in America. Being so close to poverty, money became her first, and most important security blanket. Both her parents worked, so they would never owe anyone, or be in debt to anyone. Credit or plastic money was not believed in by these people.

Not being at home, or having time to spend with their two daughters, was one reason why Connie did some things merely for attention's sake. Two years younger, Connie never did get along well with her sister Cheryl, and as they grew older, it got worse when jealousy crept in. Her father began comparing them, while still in grade school, as he felt Connie a lost-cause.

He'd always be very hard on her, and punish her regularly for pulling the usual, childhood pranks. Not just spank or hit her, but sometimes abuse where she couldn't go to school for the marks and bruises. She never saw her parents fight at all, so it seemed he took his 'life's frustrations' out on her. He never verbalized about wishing he'd had a son instead, so she truly did not know why he beat her so much. Since she didn't feel she deserved many of these punishments, they were never forgotten, and she'd later become revengeful regarding him. Yet, as she matured, Connie still tried to prove to them - and her father particularly as he died - that she was worthy of their love.

One time, out of the usual child-curiosity, Connie was playing 'doctor' with a little boy of the same age of five, right on the front steps of her home. If they had known what they were doing was wrong, they wouldn't have been on the front steps. Her mother didn't intervene when her father caught them, but punished only her. Connie's mother never stopped to explain to her what was wrong, if anything, about what she'd done. Since her mother believed old school - 'if she didn't talk about sex, they won't be curious about it, and maybe forget about it.' She felt she'd wait, at least until Connie got married to talk to her about *those* things.

To make up for some of the misunderstandings of Connie's childhood, there were the summer vacations in her younger years. The whole family traveled all over the country, camping for two or three weeks. It was a fun time, although rather young to remember most of them very well. What she did remember best was that they were happy together. Her father was very generous and good to her, when on vacation, or visiting relatives. It was this attention and togetherness, that she so missed the rest of the time.

So, she learned early to develop close friendships with the boys and girls in her neighborhood. Her closest friend was a girl named Pam. They were together constantly having fun, getting into trouble and trying not to get caught. They took turns riding-double on their bikes, until one of them would fall or get hurt, and then get punished for riding-double. They also loved to play with matches, but never did get caught when they accidentally set-fire to the abandoned building in the empty lot.

Connie got her first menstrual period when she was ten. All she knew about it was the sketchy information she'd gotten from school. She was a big girl, developed early, but also ran with an older, unsupervised crowd, because their parents worked also. Learning from the older girls, Connie started masturbating at eleven, enjoying the sense of secretiveness and pleasure not caught or punished. The whole catholic school education was about guilt, sin and confession, which became quite rote in practice for her, as to what she could get away with.

    Connie's first encounter with sex came at the age of thirteen, with a boy named Buddy. They were in his basement, with his mother upstairs making dinner. He took her on an old couch, and it was a mutual agreement, of plain curiosity. They'd been necking and petting for some time, yet it didn't happen in the heat of passion. He'd gotten an erection, so thought they'd see what they could do with it. They both knew other people who had tried it, and decided to see what it was like. Between the two of them, they knew barely enough to get the act accomplished.

    There were no sky rockets, bells ringing, or being carried away on a magic carpet. There wasn't much pain, and no blood. It was not at all what either heard from others. Needless to say, Connie did not have a climax, and Buddy didn't get too much out of it. But, they both decided not to give up, they would try again sometime. From this point on, Connie started on her long journey looking for satisfaction from sex. Other people seemed to enjoy it much more, that she figured if she continued trying maybe with age, and experience she'd make it. If she couldn't see sky rockets, at least a few twinkling stars would be nice.

    Connie didn't turn all her attention to sex immediately. She always loved animals, especially dogs. She'd bring home any strays she'd find, but her father would never let her keep them. Finally, on her fourteenth birthday he brought home a puppy so small, that he carried it in his pocket to surprise her. Soon, she got all the neighborhood kids together to have pet shows. They all had some trick they'd taught whatever pets they had. She was terrific with animals, and *they always* returned the love she had to give unconditionally. She never went in much for playing with dolls or dress-ups, as being domestic was not for her, when she could be playing outside with friends or her pets.

    Connie's parents dragged her to weddings and funerals for as long as she could remember, but she still wasn't prepared for her grandfather's funeral. They had been very close, as he lived next door since they'd moved there. She went to visit with him many times because she wanted to, he accepted her as she was, and gave her the attention she sorely needed.

She enjoyed talking and listening to him tell stories from his Croatian homeland. On the day of the funeral, she was very sick with the measles, so was left home alone in the dark room, and not to leave her bed. She was sixteen, and had never felt more alone in her whole life, especially knowing someone who truly loved her was now gone.

After that traumatic time, Connie felt the need to party and laugh as much as possible. She and her sister Cheryl joined together to have parties almost every day during school vacations, while her parents were at work. The group waited down at the corner grocery, until her mother got out-of-sight, so at eight-fifteen in the morning the parties began. The empty beer cases were piled to the ceiling.

Mass confusion - what any good booze-party had going for it was great - except there wasn't anyone over eighteen in the group. Unfortunately, they probably had as much experience in sex, as they did in drinking. There were kids throwing up in every conceivable place: the drain-tubs, trash cans and in the sink. The guys were pissing in the sink, down the floor-drain and in paper cups as well - which some dumb-jerk would drink occasionally.

Connie, through it all, was organized with a system to get rid of the leftover garbage. The guys took it over to the dumpster at the grocery store, where one of them worked. But, at one of the parties, the system almost broke down. Connie counted all the beer cans before the party started, then Cheryl on the clean-up end, counted them when throwing them into the bags to be taken away.

One can was missing, and panic struck. Everyone had to be out by three-thirty, because her mother came home at four-thirty. Even the falling-down-drunk kids were searching for *the* lone beer can. They moved the refrigerator, and practically tore the whole basement apart. At last, in desperation they gave up fifteen minutes before her mother walked in.

Connie was sure that her mother knew about the parties, simply because of the smell of beer and smoke - even with the fans going, the doors and windows wide open. But she never said a word to Cheryl or Connie. When her mother got home that night, she started dinner as usual. When she stepped on the kitchen trash-can lever, the lid opened to reveal the beer can to her.

She confronted Connie with it, as she calmly explained, "Oh that, I found it in front of the house, when I was coming home. I know Dad doesn't like trash left on the lawn." The plausibility was there, and Connie stood her ground. If her father had known about even one beer can, she wouldn't have lived to tell about it. With time, Connie's mother began to save her from her father's wrath. She realized this was connected to how he felt people would judge *him*, on his daughter's behavior. Another incident was closer, than Connie cared to remember.

At the school social club for a dance with her friends, Connie's father had taken her there, with very set rules to pick her up. She was not supposed to get into a car with anyone, and had been grounded for that previous action. After a while, the group she hung with decided to go get some beer and wine, figuring they had plenty of time to party. As usual, they never knew when to stop. When her father came early to pick her up, she had not gotten back. He looked everywhere for her in the center, then drove over to the school parking lot, looking for any of the cars he knew of her friends.

When he got back to the center, the cars they'd gone in were back. He marched inside, then dragged Connie out screaming and kicking. Without asking any questions, he started hitting her right in the middle of the parking lot. Not knowing he knew she'd been gone, she kept denying his screams about her being out drinking. From the noise of them yelling at each other,. a crowd began to gather, so he took her home. She, of course, had been drinking, and did smell of wine. He pushed her down in the kitchen chair, telling her mother she'd been drinking and, "God knows what else!"

Her mother looked her in the eyes, and said clearly, "No, she hasn't been drinking!"

"Yes, she has!" yelled her father, fiercely angry that she was not agreeing with him.

Her mother very, calmly bent-over, and put her nose to Connie's mouth and answered, "No, she hasn't! I can't smell a thing."

Her father was shaking now, and could only say, "If I ever catch her, I'll kill her!" Connie was saved by little more than the skin on her teeth.

She then decided to cut back on the drinking, and go back to getting some more sex experience instead. At least sex, she thought, didn't have any telltale-after-effects that could get her into trouble. She joined her girlfriend Pat with their boyfriends at Pat's house, while her mother worked - either they ditched school or waited for a day off, since the catholic schools had more holidays than the public. They never thought there was anything kinky, while having their group sex, as they didn't change partners, it was just fun to be together in one big bed. To the girls, it was like a 'sleep-over,' except guys were included - not a lot of emotion attached to the sex.

Pat and Connie *did* share this guy, Chuck, by one of them waiting her turn. Chuck was twenty-three years old, a little crazy and taking full advantage of the perfect set-up of two girls wanting to get some *sexual experience*. One would think, that he would have taught the girls some variations in sexual positions, but apparently Chuck wasn't too experienced beyond missionary-style himself. Connie hadn't gotten involved with any kind of oral sex, or physical variety at this time, and *still* hadn't had a climax. Chuck was always doing the positioning, with his satisfaction being the more important thing - very 1963.

Connie spent endless days with Chuck, though his fascination with guns scared the hell out of her. He had quite a gun collection, and kept most of them loaded with blanks. He'd have her hold up small targets, and shoot into the pillow. Common also, he would shoot into a hole in the ceiling. One day, she was coming around the corner with cookies and milk, when he started shooting blanks at her. The cookies and milk went flying, as well did Connie.

When they got back together, Chuck let Connie drive his car to make it up to her. Being an inexperienced driver, she clipped his car while avoiding another car. Chuck just laughed it off for the time being, and they kept cruising around town. Then one night a few days later, when he was drunk, he called to say he was going to shoot her for smashing up his car. Chuck said, "I know when you go to work and school . . . and I have someone watching you all the time." Connie, of course, believed him.

She was petrified, as she realized she was dealing with someone not playing with a full deck. Connie called her friend Peggy, to ask if her boyfriend, George, could come and stay with her at the drive-in where she worked. Eventually, from taking her to and from work, as well spending the evenings with her, looking out for Chuck, George soon broke up with Peggy to started dating Connie. It was now Thanksgiving of her sixteenth year.

Connie never thought to use a birth control - nor did the guys, they naively figured you only got pregnant when the sex was legalized. Where the idea came from, she had no idea. Then, on her seventeenth birthday, she discovered she was pregnant, and indefinitely not legalized. If she had said something to her mother, at the time she didn't get her period, she would have gotten her an abortion. So, the summer of 1965, Connie spent it in a home for unwed mothers in Milwaukee.

Not to be thwarted in having fun, she and George set up a system so they could continue with sex, even under the watchful eyes of the Catholic nuns. She asked her parents to come up one Sunday, and George came the following Sunday. This way visiting her parents one weekend, and have sex with George the next, while pretending to go to a movie with one of the girls at the home, Connie paid the girl from money her parents gave her. So, neither the nuns or her parents got suspicious or knew what she did.

Connie was one person who could have fun, no matter what the situation, so they went on picnics, or tramped around Milwaukee, as if never a care in the world. There was never any discussion as to what would happen, *when* it was time for her to have the baby. One advantage of her pregnancy, they never had trouble getting a motel room. Some of the girls at the home came from the local area, so they didn't want to go out. The nuns were not always understanding, even of the girls who had been raped.

A few of the girls had been there once or twice before, and these girls were treated badly. There were thirty-six girls in all, their ages ranged from thirteen to thirty-two. A couple of the girls had been married, and two raped. Besides the craft classes in the building, the movie theater near by, the county fair was only a short distance away. Connie learned to play solitaire eight-different-ways, and she soon became the Gin-Rummy "500" champion. She developed a close friendship with a Jewish girl, who taught her how to *play-to-win* at Scrabble.

Many of the girls were not Catholic, and some of them decided ahead of time they were going to keep their babies, but Connie hadn't thought about it either way. She, herself, for once in her life, was in a situation where no one around her, was better than the other. No matter what their background, they were all in the same boat, and she wasn't competing with her sister this time.

Not until the end of Connie's pregnancy, the realization of her situation struck her. She'd recently been the godmother to one of the girls, who had decided to keep her baby. Standing before the alter for the christening, she wondered what *she* would do about her own child. When her time came, with almost forty-two hours labor to go through, and no compassion or even the same doctor she'd seen previously. At the end, all by herself changed her, snd she decided to keep her son. She never developed a maternal instinct, a *possessiveness,* in the sense he was hers - by creation, and no one could take him away from her.

No plans of marrying George, but she knew she could not give up this baby she had given life to. Her parents were quite distressed with her, but nothing they said could get her to change her mind. He was *hers,* whatever happened next. Six weeks after Matthew was born, Connie married George, no one forced them, they just wanted to, and obviously without a lot thought put into it. If April's honeymoon was strange, Connie's was stranger, Connie, George and baby Matthew on the honeymoon. Connie was still bleeding, and no idea how to take care of her *live* doll.

The marriage progressed fairly well considering, and when she turned eighteen, a small inheritance from her grandfather was enough for a down payment on their own house. George got a job as a lineman for the telephone company, so only a few years married, they were going good. Once they moved into the house, the old parties started once again. This time with no time limit, and everyone could make as much noise as they wanted.

A new problem appeared, as George kept having little parties on his own when Connie had to stay home with Matthew. At first she understood, because these were high school buddies, coming home from Viet Nam. The under-standing only lasted so long, and then her patience were worn out.

Since the bedroom, didn't require much conversation, no big problem, but in the living room or dining table, the marriage became an uphill struggle. Not that their sex life developed beyond the high school status, but then Connie never got great kicks out of sex from any man. George didn't put a lot of effort into it, so he'd turned into a minute man, which never gave her a chance to find out what *could* happen.

And, he saw no need for improvement, or her not knowing how to talk about it all. But then, George moved from the booze to grass, without letting her know what he was doing. Completely ignorant about drugs, she thought his indulging more in the alcohol curbed his enthusiasm for sex. The time passed with neither communicating more than two people sharing the same residence. Likewise, having similar parents, neither was raised in an atmosphere of intimacy. You never miss what rapture might have been, lacking experience of it.

Into this situation, Connie let an old, friend named Ginger, temporarily move in with them. Unknown to her, Ginger was a pill-popper and marijuana-smoker too, so with her presence, George opened up with his pot-smoking. Connie decided she may as well join them, in having a good time. But she soon preferred the pills, since they were much faster and easier. Besides, she wanted to do her own thing. Although, if she had stuck to smoking pot, they probably would have stayed together, and had at least one other thing in common besides Matthew.

Since Connie thought she was having fun experimenting with the pills, she tried all of them that Ginger had - picking different colors, sizes and shapes for kicks. As typical, no forethought was in her mind. So, even as dopers, Connie and George went their separate ways with their habits. The girls were out one night, drinking at their favorite establishment, The Basement, or better known as the *'sewer,'* because of its unsavory clientele.

Then Ginger took off with a couple of guys to Chicago for some mescaline. Though Connie never had it before, she was more than willing to try it, taking a full-tab, without asking anyone how much was enough. *Way too much* for a beginner, as the night grew young, she flew like never before.

Connie dropped Ginger off at the house, to stay with Matt before he left for school. She then drove around the block till George went to work, not wanting him to know how high she was. When Connie finally fell into the house, she saw the walls coming in on her. The furniture was moving up the walls, which were now covered with pink and blue elephants. The yellow, rubber-duckies were bobbing in a row across the ceiling. She was riding the waves, numbly holding on for dear life, as she sat on the couch grabbing the cushions up to her sides. Suddenly, she pulled herself up, and went to the kitchen to see if Matt was eating his breakfast.

"Hi Mom, how ya doing?"

She couldn't believe her eyes, sitting at the table eating Cheerios was a skeleton shaped just like Matt, talking and sounding like Matt. There was no flesh, only bones. She said nothing, afraid her eyes would pop-out of her head. It was the most frightening thing she'd ever seen in her life. She returned to the couch trying to close her eyes, yet they kept popping back open, as if on a spring. Matt said nothing more to her, and went off to kindergarten.

Connie remained on the couch, as a party was still going on in head, but now people - presumably friends of Ginger's - had moved into her house. When George came home that afternoon, the house was a complete shambles. Someone tried to cook something, leaving the kitchen a disaster, and there were empty booze-bottles all over the house. George was not phased, and just sat down to roll a joint for himself to join the party. Matt was at the neighbors watching cartoons

There wasn't a lot of decision or discussion as to a second child, though Connie was not upset when she became pregnant. She enjoyed it somewhat before, and felt the natural progress of how things should be. No real knowledge of the effects of drugs or alcohol were known at the time, as she continued to do both. When Connie delivered her second son, a reality hit her - *'house-wifing'* was neither fun, nor profitable.

George didn't make enough money, if they wanted to party the way they liked. So, Connie started waitress-work when she was twenty, and moved up quickly to a rather classy restaurant, which introduced her to a whole, other kind of people. those throwing lots of money around.

These people, very temptingly, passed their money around generously. And, especially the men, were always on the look-out for young, impressionable women. Best in this category was Jerry Asher. Connie, of course, finally succumbed after only three attempts by his charm, wit, good looks and MONEY. No matter what her experiences before married, she had not played around after. Immediately, after starting to waitress, George accused her of screwing around, when just going out with the girls for drinks after their shift. She was shapely and attractive.

Now a different story, Jerry took her out three or four times to very expensive bars and nightclubs, the kind she'd never seen before. They petted a little, but he did not push her about sex. He knew what persuaded her, and when she was ready, he took her to one of the most expensive hotels in the area. As expected, she quickly fell for Jerry.

She thought he was the best-looking man she'd ever seen, and a superman in bed was also an attribute. But, what Connie liked the most, was the way he spread his money around, especially on her. The only problem, once he conquered her, Jerry didn't have enough room, or time for anyone else to love, but himself. He basically was a plastic-man with artificial feelings, he put on and took off as required to conquer the next ripe cherry.

To rub salt into the deep wound, once he knew Connie was hooked on him, he dropped her. And, to make sure she knew it, he brought another woman to the restaurant where she worked, asking for her to be their waitress. The whole experience took several months, but the bitter, hurt feelings lasted much longer. In retaliation, Connie merely chose another man from the line-up at the bar. Soon she learned, cheating was like potato chips, it didn't stop at one, and feelings could be turned off or on as needed. The current lover always paid the dues, for the debts of the men before. When she tried to change, someone brought up her colorful past, so she figured what was the use.

Connie had yet to achieve an orgasm, and still searching for the fireworks. No one would have ever believed, that it would be Cameron O'Brien who would have the magic touch. Twenty years older than Connie, he didn't have much of his blonde hair left, and a slim, trim waist was long gone. But, what Cam had was time, patience and a lot of good experience.

Cam also had a bag of well-rehearsed one-liners, that would have made *Henney Youngman* jealous. He was one of the funniest men she'd ever met, and laughter had often been missing from Connie's life. The night they met, he sat near the service-end of the bar, to talk to her when she came for her customers' drinks. He'd been recanting to her, "I'm madly in love with you . . . can't live another day, hour or minute without you . . ." Of course drunk, but he made her laugh. The fact someday he would mean it, was totally incomprehensible.

Connie did look good, with her long, dark-auburn hair, believing eyes and slow, insecure-smile making her a prime target for Cam. Then, the shapely breasts, small waist and long legs, didn't hurt either. He knew nothing about her reputation, but the 'good' bar friends, forthwith told him. By this time, he felt not only that he could change her, but that she *needed him* to change her. Connie didn't stop seeing other men, or stop taking a variety of pills.

It would be six months - July of 1969 - before she would begin idolizing Cam as a miracle-worker. He introduced oral sex on Connie, and at first Cam scared her, because she did not know what kind of freaky-thing this was. She stopped protesting, when it started feeling so good, but still no climax.

Very disappointed, Connie became a challenge to him, if the last thing he did, it'd be to give her real satisfaction. Cam wasn't faithful to her either, so he couldn't bitch when she ran around with other men. Besides his wife, he had *another* married girlfriend, much older than Connie. On his birthday in July, she finally had an orgasm.

Not quite tears in his eyes, but he was more satisfied than she was. Eight years since Connie started having sex, finally she found the fireworks and heard the bells. It was one reason why she first fell in love with him. Not the only man after, but few other men gave her orgasms. With time, they knew each other's bodies like their own.

Once Connie got started on oral sex, she felt an authority on it, with shameless-bragging-rights, especially after imbibing. Her new-found toy was giving her great joy. She teased Cam that he might be small one place, but he had a 'golden tongue.' It became her new motto: "When Cam dies, I'm going to have his tongue-bronzed, and wear it around my neck." From then on, everyone heard about Cam, and his battery-operated tongue. It certainly was nothing her mother would have ever told her about.

Things were not all peachy-keen for Cam and Connie, because he always tried to manipulate her in many degrading ways Whatever they had sex-wise, which he acknowledged was great, he still considered her *'just a waitress'* he picked up in a bar, not equal to him One time, he came to pick her up at the restaurant, acting real happy and told her, "I've got a motel room key from a friend, whose date passed out!" Believing him, wanting to share his luck, as well the room, she went to the motel with him There were empty bottles of gin and tonic, with the bed rumpled, but not used. Afterwards, he looked like the cat who just ate the canary. He'd used one room for both his women. He had been there earlier, with his older girlfriend Nancy.

Connie might have been naive sometimes, but not totally stupid. Something seemed slightly-fishy about the whole thing, with Cam giving *too much* of an explanation about the situation He did not know, Connie had found out about Nancy from some of her friends Key thing, she knew Nancy drank gin and tonic, and usually saw him at that motel When he tried to pull the same game the following week, she simply said, "No "

Connie did have a sharp memory, so not many people pulled the wool-over her eyes twice, but she could be a champion at doing the act to someone else. Cam waited for her to get off work every Friday night to get a room. Every Saturday, she came home around ten in the morning, using the story to George her car or a friend's broke-down.

She'd change clothes, then go back to the motel to meet Cam for another session. She was suppose to be getting somebody's car fixed, or giving somebody a ride. Connie pulled this off constantly, one week-end after another. She got a good laugh out of it, without thinking that George may have been totally wasted on weed with little care as to what she did.

As with many women, Connie cheated because of lack of affection. She could not have been flaunting it more obviously, so it merely became a game between them. By the time she and Cam were heavily involved, she had stopped having sex with George, what little there had been. He rarely had a comment to her coming and going, as it didn't seem to matter. He was so deep into his marijuana, nothing much did. She was totally unaware of what he was doing, while she was working, or gone out with whomever.

Cam did have some positive influence over Connie in more ways than sex. He was determined to get her out of the vicious-circle of pills and booze - though a heavy drinker himself. The solution was simple he thought, if he spent more time with her, then she wouldn't be with her friends at The Basement. It did work for a while, until he forgot her twenty-third birthday. The crux came, her expecting the attention and him giving a lame excuse why he couldn't go out with her. So, being her birthday, Connie went to the Fire-Lite restaurant - which was Cam's hangout with Nancy - for drinks with a girlfriend from work.

He came in with Nancy and another couple, walking right past Connie sitting at the corner table, since he was in his usual, jovial-half-bombed state. She called over the cocktail waitress, and ordered drinks for his group.

When Cam asked to whom he should thank for the drinks, she pointed to the two girls in the dark corner. Smiling, he swung around with glass in hand. He did not drop his glass, but he did drop his mouth open. In expectation, she raised her glass high to salute them.Cam marched over to her with a, "What are you doing HERE?" no longer jovial.

Connie calmly replied, "I didn't know it was a private club!"

That was the beginning of one of the worst nights she ever had. The girls left shortly, Connie having accomplished what she came to do. They went to The Basement, and proceeded to get stoned with all the usual dopers who were there. When Cam walked in a few hours later in his snazzy suit, it really opened some patrons' eyeballs. In his feeble way, he tried to make excuses for the evening.

"Listen, there's not much I can say . . . "

"You got that one right!" Too late, she was too far gone to care.

Still, he kept trying, "What I mean is, you know about Nancy, and I've really not been honest with you . . . " Trying to get her to leave, she refused in not too many polite words.

"That's two in a row for the clever man!" She looked around at the others she knew, who laughed when she rolled her eyes. Taking a deep breath, trying to rescue the situation, Cam continued, "Can't we get out of here . . . go some place private and talk . . . Connie, I really do care for you, and it upsets me to see you doing this . . ."

"Bingo Buster, that's three . . . You just struck out. If you cared, *you* would not *need* two girlfriends, plus a *wife*!" Now most of the group howled with laughter.

"You knew I was married from the start . . . "

She cut him off, at the perfect opening given her, turning to look straight at him. "Then why don't you take it home to her, maybe she'll listen to your story, because I don't care . . . Hit IT!"

Not five minutes after Cam left, Connie noticed her friend Rabbit, the head bouncer, had hurried from the bar for the pool room. It was obviously to break up a fight, which was not uncommon there. But loud gunfire, was not that common. When the noise was over, Rabbit was dead. He'd been a good friend to Connie and the others - he was married with several kids.

No one ever found out who killed him, or why. The shock was enough for Connie, she swore she'd never go down there again. Slowly she got away from the pills, as she got away from the dopers. She still bounced around with different men, but they were fewer, as she made-up with Cam, and he spent more time with her. It was time.

Connie asked George for a divorce, but he said no, saying he still loved her, and begged her not to leave him.

After six months of her never being home, he still didn't change his mind. Even when they went out with other couples, she'd flirt with other men. He looked all night for her one evening, finding her in a bar at the Holiday Inn. He dragged her out, the way her father had when she was a teenager. She broke away from him, and told him, "Don't you ever touch me again, you Bastard!" He finally left, as she went back into the bar.

Connie got fired from another waitress job, so stayed home playing housewife, mother and wino. One night, for no reason except horniness and booze, she had sex with George. Apparently, he had not been sitting at home just 'playing-with-himself.' He had improved tremendously. It was then, she decided to give it all another try - maybe she'd not been fair with him, and maybe he did love her after all.

Connie then got another restaurant job, where she recognized Beth from high school. But she barely remembered Connie, and what she did remember wasn't very good, so she wasn't overly friendly to her. Beth had been raised too strict and straight to associate with Connie's 'loose' group of friends.

Beth's best friend and neighbor had recently moved away. So, after a month of working close together, Beth began to think that Connie was not so bad, except for her *colorful* mouth. It was actually, shockingly funny to Beth. She kept asking Beth to go for a drink after work, and finally she accepted.

Before Beth knew it, they became best friends. Connie taught Beth to drink scotch, which at least got her off the vodka for a time. Getting to know her, Beth could see in her the freer person that she always wanted to be. When it came to their marriages, neither one had much good to say about their spouses.

One night Connie came home early from work to find Matt and Jeff, her sons, helping George roll joints. She then found out he had been taking the bill-money to buy grass and pills. That was the last straw, since she'd worked hard at cleaning-up her own act significantly. She figured that if she could get off drugs, there was no reason why he could not also.

When the F.B.I. came to the door one day, that was the definite end. They did not have a search warrant, which was lucky, since unknown to her, George had grass stashed all over the house. He also had marijuana growing behind the garage, she didn't know about. Truly, only because of Georgia, her Great Dane in the yard barking wildly, the F.B.I. didn't try to look.

The marriage was over, Connie wanted out with no further discussion. The fight they had was horrendous, with him kicking her in the kidney, which knocked her out. When she came to, she swore at him, "I will see you dead, if you ever hurt me again." Cam never pressured her about getting a divorce, but she felt that if she were free, she might win him in the long run. And, also tired of playing the motel game.

Connie's court date was on her seventh anniversary. George sent her flowers, and called begging her not to go through with it. She clearly told him, "Even if I break my leg going down the steps, it won't stop me!" Once they had the settlement though, he was one happy-camper. She sold the house to her parents, but stayed in it, with her child support paying her parents the rent. She paid off his new car, and he got several thousand dollars in cash, with a minimum child support for his salary. He was certainly going out of the marriage with more than he came into it.

Beth was babysitting for her court date, with the old going out and the new coming in. Connie ordered new furniture for the living room, and a new queen-sized bed for her and Cam. She gave all the old stuff to George for his apartment. Beth and Connie were now best friends, and her first divorced girlfriend. It had seemed so simple at the time for Connie, so Beth began to let the small, seed grow inside her own head. She didn't know if her marriage was any better or worse than Connie's, but sure a long shot from what she'd hoped.

Letting Go

Being involved alone
is the loneliest feeling.

When the love is gone,
holding on will not bring it back.

To cage a free bird is worse
than clipping its wings.

Smother love is
like dying a slow death.

Not even marriage gives one
the right to own another.

It's not till death do us part -
But, as long as we both shall love.

Please let me go,
for the love is already gone.

CHAPTER 3

Michael

The end of April, in 1946, Michael Shannon was born. Not so much, her parents wanted a boy first, but they named her Michael. Although when her brother, Webster-the-Third, came just thirteen months later, the family was complete. It wouldn't be until several years later, her parent's preference for him would be fully realized. She never tried to compete with Web, and be the tomboy-type. A small, frail child with bright, olive-green eyes, shone through a mass of short, curly-red hair.

Her size and lack of appetite, would cause many of her problems in the family. Her mother cooked special food for her, much to the outcries of her father, that she spoiled her. Since her father's hobby was cooking, and she refused to eat almost everything, she displeased him greatly. Sunday mornings were particularly a great turmoil for Michael. Everyone had to be up to fix breakfast together.

Web loved cooking with his father, and also had a natural talent for it. Michael dreaded it for multiple reasons, but mostly because her father said she never did anything right. She never followed her Taurus, Earth-Mother sign, but her freedom-dreaming Aquarius-moon sign pulled-on her. Because of this background, she was bored when her father made her stand-by to fry the bacon, and other menial chores.

Her mother understood somewhat, because she wasn't crazy either about the routine of cooking, she only liked the preparation of a special meal. Also, if her father was on one of his religious-spurts, they'd have to attend the six-thirty Mass, *before* the breakfast-cooking event. A back-sliding Catholic at times, but with several brothers who were Jesuits, it spurred him on.

Mr. Shannon was a perfectionist, and that did not help Michael to enjoy any chores. She dreaded the kitchen also, as he made her sit at the table until she ate everything on her plate. She sat staring at her plate, the food seeming to grow in front of her eyes, while he patiently worked the crossword puzzle. It was the only thing that she was more stubborn at.

Her procrastination was probably the biggest thorn in his side. A man who preached, "do it now," though he never practiced it. During the summer, she and Web had to dig dandelions out of the yard - five a day or twenty-five a week. Web went out Monday mornings, dug his twenty-five to be done with it. Michael, on the other hand, waited until five--thirty on Friday afternoon, then raced out to get hers dug before her father got home.

Psychologically, her father was a displaced -person, a genius who never found his niche. He couldn't find a job that fulfilled him, or one in which he could use his full potential. He changed jobs frequently, and was out of work much of the time. Her mother worked steadily to help them through the financial difficulties.

If Mr. Shannon was not a good provider in the monetary sense, he definitely was in an intellectual way. He read constantly to both Web and Michael, not just the usual story books, but novels and classics. Being a history buff, Mr. Shannon shared the true stories of many American heroes, revealing they were not all what they were cracked up to be.

This sometimes caused problems at school, when their history books told a different story. This questioning about America's finest, always made Michael look at everyone as an equal human being. No one, no matter who, ever got on a pedestal to her. Nothing ever really impressed her, not money, brains or talent, only *how* someone related or treated another human being.

She'd already begun to question much of the teachings of her public school. The free-spirit in her could not take the typical regimentation and authority being held over her. She soon transferred this same questioning to the indoctrinations of the Catholic church. This was frowned upon greatly, by both the church and her father.

At the age of nine, Michael wasn't all that different from the other neighborhood girls on basic things. To feel she belonged, she wanted the same toys and clothes they had. Since her mother worked in the local department store, she could ably fulfill those material wants and needs for her. But, when she wanted to join the local girls club, her parents hesitated.

She didn't realize it was a Protestant church-affiliated group. After great discussion and argument, her parents allowed her to join. Then, at the third meeting, she was promptly ostracized for being a Catholic, her first realization of prejudice and discrimination.

Several years later, she once again insisted on having her own way with her parents, for a two-week summer camp in Wisconsin. Again connected with another Protestant church. This one did accept Catholic children, guaranteeing they would be taken to Mass on Sundays. Michael didn't learn the 'catch-22' until stuck at the camp.

The kids weren't allowed to go swimming, until they learned certain passages from the Bible. Being Catholic, and totally unfamiliar with it, unlike the others who learned them in Sunday school and prior camps, she was lost. To top it all off, her camp-counselor took it upon herself to convert her from her Catholicism. Memorizing the passages were almost impossible, as she feared what her father would do if he found out.

On Sunday when her parents came to visit, she was afraid to tell them how miserable she was. Michael knew that it had cost a lot of money to send her to this religious-hell, she'd insisted on attending. Upon returning home, she never mentioned the camp again, except to say what a great time she had. She then requested to attend Catholic school that fall for seventh grade, and her father was thrilled that *he* finally reached her. She came to the conclusion that she *would* be better off staying with *her own kind*. Those junior high years would not become her worst two years, but then no schooling was fondly remembered by Michael.

At least her mother was not a moralist, and understood why at thirteen, Michael met her boyfriend on Friday nights at the indoor show - her father didn't allow her to go to the drive-in movies. When sitting down, they were the same height, but standing - he barely came to her shoulders. But his black hair, accentuated by velvet brown eyes, and being *'cute as the dickens'* was good enough for her.

The theater had a ruling about necking, and if caught, parents were called. Her mother came to pick them up, but never mentioned it to her father - to keep peace for all. She didn't lecture, but told Michael in the future to neck at home, if she wanted to do that. Likewise, she ruled Web on cigarettes and alcohol, as he started indulging in both when eleven. Michael didn't touch either while living at home.

She continued dating boys, but didn't experiment with sex, as terrified her father would find out. She enjoyed the attention that the affection of necking gave her. The first big love came the summer of her freshman year, taking a leather-crafts course to make up credits. Similar to many clever kids, she couldn't understand why so many classes she felt she'd never use were required.

The blonde, blue-eyed senior was her first older man - all of nineteen. He also didn't have much use for school, but had to graduate to get into the Marines. Amazingly, both her parents liked him, and even taught him to play bridge. This made her life more harmonious, boring, but acceptable.

At fifteen, Michael joined two girlfriends to go into Chicago to pick-up sailors. She created many excuses for the trips -shopping, museums or movie theaters. The sailor she got involved with was a guy named Sal, twenty-three, who thought she was eighteen. From New York, Sal was Catholic, tall, black hair and again the brown eyes. He never knew, neither did her parents, she had picked-up any other guys or sailors. She and Sal walked around Chicago, ate lunch, then went to the movies to neck - no restrictions at the Chicago Theatre. After several weeks dating, he decided to take a cab out to her suburb of Westfall to surprise her - he had no idea how expensive it would be. Michael, sitting at the breakfast table, saw him when he get out of the cab, and almost inhaled her food.

She ran outside to meet him, telling him that he was supposed to be the 'best friend of her girlfriend's cousin,' and that he was only nineteen. Even back then, she was good at inventing lies to cover her tracks. As she introduced him to her parents, they didn't quite believe the convoluted story she told. Trying to be more convincing, she added they met at the girlfriend's grandmother's house.

She squirmed a little, almost feeling her nose grow from so many lies. After that first fateful visit, her mother invited Sal back several times for Sunday dinner. Whether because he was a serviceman, or to see how many more lies she'd reveal, Michael never knew. But each time, she sweated-up-a-storm dancing around the truth. Sal also learned to take the commuter train when he came out -much cheaper.

Though her parents both liked him, they questioned his age and intention, until five months later when he talked about marriage. To him, Michael seemed the perfect-match, with her Catholic background, and having said 'no' to sex. Her complete attention to him, was an ego-booster, figuring that she'd probably *be grateful* to be married to him. Such a lovely day in Westfall Park, when his glorious, dreamed-future came to a screeching-halt.

Crystal, a 'trust-worthy' friend of Michael's told Sal her true age of fifteen. He yelled and screamed at her for almost an hour, "How could you have flaunted my love?" Almost in her face, he continued, "Could you not understand, I wanted to MARRY you! Did that not mean anything to you?" She mumbled a bunch of words about having such a good time together, but 'no.' She was not ready for marriage, so they never rode off into the sunset together.

Michael and a girlfriend occasionally took a cab into Westfall, and their usual driver was Tim. It only cost forty-five cents, so it was a cheap-thrill for Michael, with her crush on him. Twenty-one, five-ten, again blonde - blue-eyed, but this time he'd already been in the Marines. By Thanksgiving vacation, he asked her out for a date of a movie and hamburger.

But the opposite this time, for if there was ever a boyfriend both her parents disliked, it was Tim. It was that 'something' that her parent's radar just *knew* was wrong, or 'off' about him. She didn't care, and fit it into all the other things she'd given up, trying to please her father. A part of her that didn't care on the surface, and his displeasure gave her some rebellious joy.

They continued to go together despite the outcry from her parents, until a week before Christmas. They broke up because she refused to have sex with him. Tim couldn't understand, since she loved the necking and petting, why such a resistance for real sex. For the next week, she drove her family nuts playing *"Heart-Break Hotel,"* over and over, again and again. Any comment or complaint, she immediately broke into a deluge of tears. At the dinner table one night, her father finally said something about her moodiness. Web chanted, "She's in love!" She burst into tears, sobbing like he stabbed her, as she ran to her room.

Right after Christmas, they resumed, though Michael still wouldn't have sex. By Easter vacation, her fed-up parents sent her up to Minnesota to visit some friends. They had been their neighbors, with a daughter her age, she'd been close to. Their hope, that the separation would help break-up the relationship back-fired.

At the end of the week, Tim picked her up from the train station, and told her he'd marry her. If he couldn't get her one way, he was willing another. It wasn't as if he'd broadcast his dying-love for her, because he'd never said anything even close to that. Excitedly, she told her parents, and they could only ask "Why?" They were more numb, than shocked.

"Because I love him," the only answer she could give. There was no defending his flaws, and no extolling virtues, as he didn't have any - absolutely nothing outstanding about any of his characteristics. All he did was drive a cab, with no ambitions whatsoever for more. Even if he had money, he'd never been thoughtful or generous with any presents. None of this mattered to sixteen-year old Michael.

He wanted her *enough* to marry her, and *now* she was ready. She felt like he sacrificed his freedom, and for that she loved him - considering how much any teenager knew of love. Subconsciously, probably getting away from school requirements, and her father's control were factors, but ones she wouldn't realize till later.

Though understanding and loving, her mother wasn't one Michael could go to with her problems, or deep-rooted feelings. Not a cold woman, but also not a tremendous amount of patience. Mrs.

Shannon loved her two children very much, but would also be very happy when both were grown and on their own.

These points *allowed her* to encourage Michael to marry Tim, though she knew her to be irresponsible, as well as too young for such a decision. Maybe this was what Michael needed to grow up, and see life as it really was. Tim happened to know a Justice of the Peace in a nearby town, who didn't pay attention about Michael's birth certificate being changed. She looked older at sixteen, than she did later at twenty-six.

Michael's wedding night and honeymoon were the most bizarre of all Tim arranged to borrow the private house of the caretaker, on the grounds of a private mental hospital It was actually the same place April lost her virginity, though not the same person The night was memorable, not satisfying expectations of either of them.

Tim wanted a virgin, but one who at least knew what to do, even without having had the experience - a dichotomy of the impossible. Michael raised in the era of Walt Disney's romantic fairy tales, though not as brain-washed as April, had romantic aspirations simply adding to her enjoyment of necking and petting.

A quick-study learner from Tim's faulty directions, she was not. She might have adapted sooner, if he hadn't been so rough, or hurt her so much, in his anxiousness and actual ineptness. The bulk of his experience, acquired from 'professional' ladies, who knew how to handle energetic young men. Their 'honeymoon' was not improved upon by better sex or surroundings. Tim had another friend, who owned a funeral home. They thus spent their four-day honeymoon in the apartment above it In essence, 'house-sitting' while the owners were on vacation. That someone came in with a body one day, did not tend to lend romance to the already limited mood.

Michael never minded the mental hospital, because no one was around them, but the funeral home did creep her out. Though Tim was not a patient or understanding lover, she was glad to have the attention and affection she felt he gave her. Not knowing how bad the sex was, she knew she could get use to it.

She'd faced many other problems this way. Life in general, at least her life so far, was something that she accepted, and adapted as needed. It made it easier than arguing or fighting. As with her parents, she chose her battles, but rarely did the winning of them ever bring her the results she expected and wanted.

Her return home did not bring a warm reception, with her father ultimately so disgusted with her, that he erupted to disown her. He truly did not believe that she'd actually go through with it, though she never indicated any hesitation. Her mother also was quite upset that she did it, when she wasn't even pregnant. On the other hand, Tim's parents were thrilled - they were the witnesses for the wedding. The newlyweds' first house in the suburbs was rented for eighty-five dollars, and the beginning of a continuous string of moves and jobs for Tim.

The money for setting up the house was borrowed from both parents, since Tim currently had no job. There were four houses in a row, that rented for this miraculously low price. The first one had hookers in it, the second was theirs, the third another young couple and the fourth Tim's parents - who moved around a lot, too. About a month later, the other young couple decided they wanted to buy the house they were renting. When checking around about it, they found out the houses were repossessed, and suppose to be vacant. Everyone got evicted the next week.

They next moved to an apartment in Iowa. Tim got work there as a laborer in construction, and his step-father shared the apartment with them. Unfortunately, Tim's patience with Michael didn't improve in bed, and her lack of enthusiasm angered him greatly. Just as she could never please her father in whatever she did, now she didn't know how to please her husband.

Yet, they sometimes spent whole weekends in bed - when his step-father returned to Illinois - only getting out of bed to eat. Though older, Tim again was an example of a man who didn't have a lot of varied experience with sexual positions or techniques - especially not to satisfy his wife. The expectations were all on her, and she had no clue what she should do.

Then there was the fact of his phobia. Basically, he thought of sex as dirty, so jumped out of bed to wash *vigorously* after each coitus.

Still, it was the holding, touching and kissing that made Michael keep trying to improve, or do it better to make Tim happy.

She had someone to whom she could show affection and receive it in return, even if much less than what she gave. She knew she disappointed him where sex was concerned, but she had no one to talk to about it. Not that she was open or mature enough to discuss the subject, and he certainly wouldn't discuss the subject if asked, he just kept criticizing *her lack* in performing it.

But even bad sex has a result, and soon Michael was pregnant. Surprisingly, Tim was as happy as she was, but it didn't work out, as a miscarriage came in her sixth month. Here age and poor health condition the main cause, with being so thin and anemic. Luckily, her in-laws stopped in that day to see her, and found her passed-out across the bed hemorrhaging. They called the ambulance to rush her to the hospital, but the fetus had already aborted.

She wasn't conscious until the next day, with his mother signing for the D and C, because no one knew exactly where Tim was out drinking with his brother. He didn't show up at the hospital until late the next day. With no apology or real explanation for the delay, even his mother was upset with him, she rarely chastised him. So, Michael's first disappointment - when she needed him most -he hadn't been there. Only sixteen, and she almost died - all alone.

They came back to the Chicago area, out of a job and money. Something that became more than the normal situation. Not really learning from the prior experience, after only one menstrual period, Michael was pregnant again. They both again wanted it, like they were proving something to one another, and the people around them. Michael took this pregnancy well, trying to eat even when she didn't feel like it, and keeping herself positive about the happiness a child would bring to them. Then her father died. A completely-unexpected heart attack, as he'd never had problems before.

Michael couldn't believe how devastated she was, and the irony of the situation wasn't lost on her youth. He'd been one of the main reasons she wanted to get away from home, then he dies less than a year later. This realization took some of the credence out of her marriage, and perhaps how stupid the action had been.

They had never settled their differences, or cleared the air over so many disagreements. A part of her hoped that making him a grandfather would balance something between them. But now, she was the 'unforgiven-child,' who disappointed him on a regular basis - the last point being her marriage.

In many ways, she knew her father loved her, he just never took the time to tell her, and then his last words so filled with anger. In her grief, Michael realized she loved him more than she ever acknowledged. Their verbal jousting more a reflection of how much they were alike, than different. She couldn't believe how difficult the loss was for her, and Tim wouldn't accept her sadness at all, considering how she often referred to him so negatively.

She couldn't be at the wake with the coffin open, it overwhelmed her. Michael needed someone to lean on, but Tim was literally useless in his lack of feelings or understanding. The rest of her life, she'd be dealing with *the effects* of her father upon her, and *its affects* on how she related to other men she loved.

They moved twice more, before settling into the house that Michael'd been raised in. Her mother didn't feel she could live in it any more, so she rented it to them. Things didn't improve much after their son Travis was born. Michael so happy with the baby, but Tim couldn't or wouldn't hold a job. Her mother tried to talk to her about him, but Michael wouldn't listen. To admit now that she'd been wrong, was simply too late. She felt she must prove that she was not the failure that her father believed. "I love him, and that is all there is to it." She even refused to go to a family reunion in Seattle without him, when her mother offered to pay her way.

Yet, her mother didn't turn on her, she gave her money countless times to buy groceries. They both knew that Tim always found enough money to go out with the guys to drink, but he couldn't find *enough* to put food on the table. *His mother* accused Michael of not knowing how to manage the little bit of money they had. The fact she didn't have much to work with, didn't seem to matter. Tim did all of the spending of the big money, without ever asking for Michael's consent. Besides, she was under twenty-one, so couldn't sign most of the contracts for the things he bought, most were repossessed soon any way.

Though Tim was excited over Travis, it didn't improve his sense of responsibility. He could have bought her mother's house very cheaply, but he wouldn't have anything to do with it. He didn't want anything to tie him down permanently. So, when Mrs. Shannon needed to sell the house, they moved again. When Tim was fired from his last job, because he couldn't get up in the morning, Michael got a job as a waitress in a pizza joint. She never said anything to him about 'my' money, or I'm supporting you.

So, when he'd come to pick her up from work, she'd turn all the money over to Tim, never keeping a nickel for herself. With his continued spending habits, they didn't make ends meet and barely existed. Still, if he became restless babysitting at home with Travis, he'd take him over to his mother, to go out with his friends.

It became common for him to come home six-thirty in the morning, but Michael kept her stoicism, never saying a word, trusting him rather than suspecting he was running around with other women. If he said he was out drinking with his buddy Hal, then he was. When Hal's wife accused him of cheating, Michael did not do the same. She loved him, she kept telling herself that he wouldn't cheat on her.

Then, one night Tim came in early to pick up Michael at the pizza joint, with lipstick on the side of his mouth. She was horrified. She threw a napkin at him as she passed by, "Wipe off your face!" When they got to the car, she asked for an explanation, trying to remain calm. He decided to tell her the truth, and she fell apart, sobbing like a baby. She only wanted him to take her to her girlfriend's house. Barb knew for sometime, but never told her anything. Michael immediately blamed herself, "It's all my fault, because of my lack of enthusiasm for the sex."

The only way she could continue to exist was to say it did't matter, "I don't care . . . it doesn't change anything. It doesn't matter, I'm still his wife. It doesn't matter . . . " She kept repeating this, and eventually began to believe it. Michael mentally-built a very, neat shell around herself. She wouldn't let this affect her, though a very sacred thing had been broken - trust. Her motto became: "Expect nothing, and you will never be disappointed."

Not all down hill from there, as Michael went on as a family unit, if only in her own mind with no plans whatsoever of breaking-up. She was married, and that's what she planned to stay. She then made plans to get pregnant again. She wanted another baby, and maybe it would be girl - she was sure Tim would like to have girl, also. They tried for over a year, and by the time she got pregnant, he was elated. Still running around leading two lives, but working.

When Kristen arrived, so did euphoria, as Tim was truly excited to have a daughter. It thrilled Michael, and thinking how *her* being a girl never made her father happy. For the first time since their marriage, she felt like part of a family, and was never happier. Though Tim was being a loving father and husband, still unfortunately their perfection was short lived. Seven weeks after Kristen, Michael was pregnant again. Her doctor was shocked, how could *she* have done such a thing? Tim felt the same about it, how could *she*? Why did everyone blame her, just because *she* didn't want to *turn down affection* from her husband?

Everything was coming apart at the seams - a new baby, a toddler three and a half, her with morning sickness everyday. It *was* too much *for Tim*. He went back to running around, and started drinking more readily. Michael became a walking zombie. She had no time to recuperate after Kristen, to pull herself together. Seeing her little dream broken like cheap glass, didn't help either. Her marriage, what there was of it, became a vicious circle, and sometimes she didn't want Tim around to remind her of the reality.

One day after another was a daze. She sealed up her feelings in her air-tight Tupperware bowls, and put them on layaway. There were no real memories of Kristen growing that year, but fortunately her main attention did come from Tim - as he was around enough for that. Ankle-deep in soggy Cheerios, Michael functioned like a bad robot, frequently getting stuck and buffeting into a corner.

Jenny's was a very difficult delivery, with Michael almost bleeding to death. She didn't have a whole lot to live for, but struggled through hoping some day there would be more to life than what she'd experienced so far. The next four years became a dense fog, with Tim leaving Michael, then returning several months later. He set a pattern after a while, of leaving in September, returning before Christmas.

He'd never *actually* leave town, just continued to see his girlfriends right there, for everyone around them to know what he was doing. She also developed a pattern of going to April and Beth's lawyer to file for divorce, then always taking Tim back at the end. It became a sick-game of him buying her whatever she wanted to let him come back.

Once Tim had a good welding job, he had money to spread around. One year, he spent almost two hundred dollars on a Christmas tree, with lights and all the extra trimmings - as if these things made up for his absence. Another time, he bought Michael over six hundred dollars worth of crystal stemware, at twelve dollars a glass. She ended up selling it, to put food on the table when the job finished. He then bought a color television and stereo tape-deck, when he couldn't afford the down payment on a house, or so he said.

Around this time, Beth met Michael through April. Since Jeremy, Beth's son, was only weeks apart from Jenny, April thought Beth and Michael would have so much in common. Beth couldn't get over how *cool* she was - everything held inside. Michael didn't talk the 'housewife-language' of children, furnishings and shopping-sales. She'd simply sit in the group of women, never speaking unless someone singled her out.

If the subject turned to sex, she'd leave the room. She didn't enjoy cooking, so had no recipes to share, and rather mixed-up in her housekeeping. It was either knee-deep, or she'd go around polishing ashtrays, as soon as they were dirtied. But, a voracious reader she was, so did talk books, watched television - especially old movies for escapism. Beth was glad when she finally found a topic they could converse on.

Michael started eating when no one was around. Not only had she grown two inches since her marriage, but she finally gained about fifty pounds. She no longer looked like a waif, but a real woman with full breasts, a shapely buttock and thighs. Tim was not a large man, so they didn't have the appearance of a matched-couple any more. If some exciting thing did happen in her life, she rarely bothered to share it with anyone. Once she grew close to Beth, she trusted to share a special time, no one else knew about.

When Travis was still a baby, Michael met a guy who lived in the house in back of their yard. He was her age, and still lived with his parents. His name was Renie, he had a horse he let Travis pet and sit on, simply how they'd met. Renie was some one to talk to on those long nights, when Tim'd be out running around.

They sat on the grass in the backyard, after she put Travis to bed. He'd tell her about places he had been, and the people he met on his motorcycle road-trips. Soon they held hands, pretending it was only a friendly gesture, yet it meant much more to each of them. He was the first one to see her as a separate person, an individual, not just somebody's wife or mother.

Once in a while, they would kiss, but nothing more. Both were too afraid to let themselves go. A married woman with a child, you didn't do those things then. Renie listened to her reveal herself, and she'd listen to him. They could talk about anything under, and above the sun. He also said he saw her as - a Kewpie doll - her arms stretched-out with a big sign, *"Love ME. Please."* It amazed her, not knowing how much affection she needed, or was capable of giving.

Renie was leaving to go on a vacation up to Wisconsin on his motorcycle. Michael watched this free-spirit on his freedom-machine, as he rode off. He had asked if she'd go with him, but of course, she said 'no.' Before leaving, he gave her a copper bracelet, "A small token of what love should be, 'a never ending circle' where mutual love has no beginning and no end." There was nothing corny about the sincerity.

A few days later, she was in the backyard chatting with another neighbor. Before she realized it, the neighbor said, "Did you hear about Renie's accident? He was killed head-on, isn't that such a shame, a nice, young boy like that . . . " The neighbor continued to talk for another five minutes on other topics, but she never heard another word. Not fair or just, or even right or it could have possibly happened.

There could be no God who would do such a thing for no reason. Renie had so much to give, not only to her, but to the world in which he was so totally involved. Beth never forgot the story, and also never shared it with anyone. In the years to come, she'd often remember it when seeing the risky choices Michael made in her life, and the changes she took-on with them.

It would be a long time, before Michael let anyone into the private sanctum of her heart again. When she did, it'd be only a sliver of what she revealed before, and he was Tim's best friend, Derek He was so good looking and successful, that Tim never figured he'd have any interest in simple, basic Michael. Again, for her it started very slowly, actually years before they even kissed. Divorced when they first met, then remarried and divorced before they got physically involved. He had many women, no one ever thought he'd waste his time on the little housewife.

Michael was not ugly by any means, with her beautiful red hair and green eyes, yet she never developed her potential-appearance. She wore ill-fitting clothes, her hair in a domestic, short bubble, and not much make-up on her fair complexion. But, she was honest and sincere and his first two wives had not been, so Derek was very drawn to her. She was loyal to Tim, or so he thought, no matter what.

Michael was also very active with her children, being a den-mother for Travis' Cub Scouts, and she'd take Derek's children along with hers. Her house, and everything in it, were always open to him and others. Most of all, she listened, no matter what he had to say. He didn't have to put on a front for her, as he felt natural, at home.

But their relationship wasn't mutual, in that he only thought of her being Tim's wife, and the mother of his children. Derek didn't look at her on the level of an individual, a separate person away from them. Almost the mother-image of wholesomeness - as the President of the PTA should be. So sexually attracted to him, yet knew if she made any move, he'd run in fear of her humanness, rather than the Super-Mom, he thought of her

Michael saw a side of Derek, no-one else ever saw. With her, he was honest, vulnerable and open To everyone else, the boastful playboy, who had a bad case of narcissism. They sat up late nights, watching the old, old movies together, laughing at the cliches and crying at the lovers - sometimes having seen them so many times, they'd quote the dialogues to each other. Tim never thought anything of it. Sometimes, Derek's girlfriend Polly would be in another room sleeping, or waiting for him while he'd be sitting, holding hands, watching a movie for the tenth-time with Michael. She pretended it never bothered her, when Derek made love to other women while staying-over at her home.

Finally, if they wanted to be alone, they'd go to the drive-in. Michael'd use the excuse she had to get out of the house, away from the kids. They'd meet and neck, while watching the movie, never anything more. She felt if she had sex with him, it'd put her in the same class as his previous wives, since he'd caught them both cheating. This high-school-parody continued for more than a year before Michael told April. Not shocked, as it seemed logical because of the closeness to Derek for so many years. April, of course, encouraged her to sleep with him, but Michael refused. After her hypnosis classes with April, Michael did have more fortitude, but it never lasted long enough.

One hot summer night, Michael couldn't stand it any more. She didn't care what anyone said anymore. She and Derek had been getting further apart, and maybe this would bring them closer. They'd been out to their country-western hangout, and Derek was drunk, so she got in his car with him, and began to seduce him. Maybe it was the booze, or maybe he wanted it, too, but Derek didn't put up any resistance. When it was over, she wondered why she bothered. She didn't know if it was the cramped quarters, or the idea of it all, but it left a foul-taste in her mouth. She'd been wrong also, it did not bring them together, only further apart.

Not only the beginning of the end of her and Derek, but also the image that she'd held for so many years of herself to others. The 'mother' to everyone, taking care of their problems, always putting herself last, bending over backwards, compensating everyone, trying to make everybody happy. It was the old, inferiority-complex left-over from her father, who was never happy with her. She'd held her feelings in so often, so long that when she let go, and said something, people were totally shocked.

Michael always welcomed April, even when she came over almost everyday. When she finally told her how she felt about listening to her problems and complaints, April almost cried, yet the honesty eventually brought them closer. It wasn't true with other people, unfortunately, they couldn't accept the change she tried to make in herself. Michael had played at being 'Earth-Mother,' too long.

One night, sitting at a den mothers' meeting, listening to them argue over some trivial thing, she burst out with her opinion. She only got stares from the other women. A few minutes later, one of the fathers responded, "You're not really like the rest, are you?"

Not meant sarcastically, so she answered, "No. I guess I'm not, and I've been trying to fool myself that I fit in." She picked up her purse, and walked out while the others were still arguing. Sometimes, it is the very minute things, that releases the mind into seeing the truth. The finale came when Michael's crazy, mixed up friend Sybil, had sex with Tim, and *then* Michael fully opened her eyes.

Although, she said something to April about it, Michael didn't say anything to Sybil, since she couldn't be responsible for what she did in her *indisposed-condition.* She rescued Sybil a countless number of times from her feeble-attempts of suicide. Tim at last proved he'd screw anyone, when he took advantage of Sybil, in one of her 'booze and pills-state.' Michael finally figured he wasn't worth staying loyal to any more.

So, having sex with Derek changed not only her whole life, but her whole life-style. She couldn't think of him as someone to commit adultery with, yet that's what it's called, and the *'first time's always the hardest.'* She was done trying to making other people happy, now it was her turn. She'd stayed knee-deep in children and commitments for so long, that it would be a long, hard climb out of her self-dug rut.

It had been a hot-suburban summer of turmoil with Barb's marriage faltering, April's also and Sybil's usual problems just coping with life. So, at first, when Michael wanted to change, her friends didn't want to face it. As if *someone* had to stay behind, to be the rock for everyone else to cling to. They couldn't understand why she didn't want the job of consoling, since she'd never confided any of her own problems to them.

Michael had her first experience with alcohol shortly after the 'fling' with Derek. She was back out at Hillbilly Heaven, when she decided to have a drink to 'let it all go. ' Except for one time when she had a toothache at a wedding, she never drank before. She jumped right into the hard stuff - gin, and of all things, orange juice.

The next day was one she would long remember. She vomited all night, and had dry-heaves all morning. She had to attend a funeral on the hottest July afternoon - her good friend Crystal's twenty-nine year old husband had died. Derek and the icky memories of it, had not been worth the horrendous hangover.

Michael occasionally went out with April and Polly, Derek's girlfriend, but nothing more than socializing girl-talk Three weeks after the funeral, Crystal and Michael started going out with other interests on their minds Crystal'd been around a lot before, so she knew the places to go for guys.

Michael's inner-naivety felt Crystal really mourned her husband, so she must have been just lonely, she thought. Crystal introduced her to The Basement Rather ironic, because that past spring Connie had stopped going there. This was definitely not the place a former den-mother and President of the PTA would go.

After a month of going there, Michael met Donny. He came walking up to her and said, "You wanna ball?" Michael, in her acceptance of everyone, was neither offended or shocked. Donny was drunk, but he looked darling to her. They were in a large group of people, so she just ignored him. Later he came over to talk, and when she put money in the juke box, he asked her to dance. She'd find out later, it only happened when he was very, very drunk. When he asked her for her phone number, she simply answered, "I'm married "

"That doesn't bother me, if it doesn't bother you," Donny retorted The next night, she met him at the Longview, his usual hangout After a short conversation, they went to his trailer for sex Michael later explained, "It wasn't sex with a stranger, he really made love to me If Tim had acted that way on our wedding night, I never would have felt so negative about sex." Amazingly, Donny was gentle, kind and understanding about her nervousness.

His patience and tenderness made her melt, and he didn't jump out of bed to go wash up - he held her, caressing her softly. Donny treated her full breasts like goddesses, praising them with tender kisses. She never felt anything like this before. She could no longer stand to have Tim touch her breasts, as he was so rough, it made her flesh crawl. It had gotten to the point with Tim, that she'd just lie there, showing no emotion or feeling, waiting for him to finish.

Donny even wanted to make love when Michael had her menstrual period, which was mind-boggling to her. Tim walked a large circle around her, as if she were contaminated when she had her periods. There were so many differences in the way they had sex, but the most impressive one - Donny also gave her a climax. It happened on their fourth night together. She didn't know what was happening to her. She just kept saying, "Oh my God, my God. What are you doing to me?" He hadn't realized that she'd *never* had an orgasm. He thought she was just nervous. She wasn't looking for the climax, like Connie, she simply had no idea what it was supposed to be.

Afterwards, Michael did not just go nuts with the sex - like Connie, she became obsessed by it. Any time she was able to get away to be with Donny, she did. She worked her schedule out, so once Travis left for school, and Tim for work, she took the girls over to the neighbors. She returned in time to make dinner, and get everyone off to bed. Soon, she wasn't resisting Tim's attention in bed, she'd ask him. Afterwards, she lay quietly until hearing his breathing become even. She'd then slip away to be with her new-found love.

For a time, she felt that this was a symbol of real love, that she'd have sex with a man she loathed, in order to make love with the man she wanted. Michael returned home about four in the morning, when Tim might stir, and miss her. One night, she'd just walked in the door, when she heard Tim start to get up. She rushed in the bathroom to take her clothes off, and throw on a robe. She grabbed the dog, and stepped out the door before he came into view. She waited a minute before stepping back in with the dog.

Acting surprised to see him, she reported, "I couldn't sleep, so I was out walking the dog. Are you OK?" She developed a real secret pride in this new person, who controlled more of her life and feelings.

Donny worked evenings, so Michael spent her days with him. They were *very exciting* days, sitting in a bar watching him get drunk. At least her knowledge of television and movies began to pay off, as she played trivia with the other men in the bar, for free-beer for Donny. For someone who didn't drink, she learned how to hold-down a bar stool very well. Because his drinking rarely affected their sex life, she never let it bother her. She was one person who never let anything about a person change the way she felt about them - until it affected the way that person felt about her.

Once again, life played its little joke on her happiness. Of course, Michael didn't plan on getting pregnant, nor had she concerned herself about preventing it. Although, like April, she'd begun to think of the responsibility of a child, and how it might make Donny snap out of his drinking. How little Tim changed, never occurred to her was beyond comprehension they both had major flaws.

She was *still* living in a dream world, a new one albeit, but *still* not real-reality. The childish-thought that a child might keep Donny around longer, also occupied space, bouncing around in her brain. She didn't trust the fact that he might stay around *simply* because he loved and wanted her. Even when sure she was pregnant, it didn't seem to bother her one way or the other - she'd dealt with worse things. Positive it was Donny's, but she'd had sex with Tim throughout the month, too.

Then an odd feeling of relief came upon her, so she no longer had a real concern about the baby, as if she'd never have it - as in *have to* raise it. With no idea where this came from, Michael could not see herself raising another child. She almost snickered, visualizing the sight of sitting in a bar winning drinks with her trivia, and a baby propped-up with a bottle.

Through her changing mental-process, she quickly began shedding her housewife-skin, and growing a new one of a free person. She liked seeing herself as a *hippie-type*, letting her hair grow, and only wearing Levis. The masquerade didn't quite fit the person inside yet, but each day she became more comfortable doing things more for her rebellion choices, of what she wanted. This new person typified the 'teenager,' that she'd never got to be when she was young.

Michael still didn't drink or smoke, but she started using *speed* to keep going on her crazy - almost sleepless schedule. If her friends at the P.T.A could see her now - she really had changed. This year, instead of Tim leaving, she decided to leave him. April now divorced, suggested that she come stay with her, to see how she felt about a separation. This actually gave her easier access to her addiction to Donny. But, unfortunately, April wasn't as good covering Michael's tracks, as Beth'd been for April's. Tim clearly got a clue that Michael was running around on him, since she wasn't at April's apartment no matter when he came by to see her.

Tim came over another night, and April was in bed with a guy. She hoped Tim didn't notice his shoes, because of her planning to get back with Wally, again. Rattled, she told Tim that Michael was at Beth's mother's house - her father had a heart attack, so they were helping out. When Tim wanted to call there, she mumbled, talking him out of it, as it was too late. So obviously lying, he was getting angry. April quickly promised, she'd go over first thing in the morning, and bring Michael home to Tim herself.

After he left, April roused the guy out of her bed, to get Michael from Donny's. When she arrived, they were sitting in the living room, with Donny so drunk, he didn't understand why she left so quickly. April raced her back to the apartment, getting their stories aligned before she took her home. They were taking her dirty clothes out of the car, when Tim roared up in his car. He'd been waiting behind the building, to see where April went in such a hurry at three in the morning.

Without asking any questions, he punched Michael in the mouth. They yelled and screamed at each other for several minutes, before she broke away to jump in her car to drive home. He was in hot pursuit, with both doing ninety miles per hour all the way - where were the cops when she needed them? Michael's speeding was to no avail, as he continued to beat her when he got home. The following afternoon, she went back to Donny's. Not only surprised, but happy to see her, as he'd been so drunk, he'd thought *they* had a fight, and that's why she left in such a hurry.

Now rarely at April's, Tim checked-up anyway, so she said she'd go help him look for her. She did use enough sense to take him around to the bars further out in the suburbs. Because of this incident, Michael accused April of having sex with Tim. No reason why he wouldn't, since he'd slept with her other friends, Sybil and Barb, though both were drunk at the time. Whatever April's excuse, she said she never did. No accusing Tim, as he always denied having sex with anyone but Michael, even when several women told her they did have sex. It never ceased to amaze her, that women who knew him, still succumbed to his seduction line. Shocked, there were that many desperate women out there wanting attention.

The separation was short-lived, with Michael asking for a divorce, to no avail. Tim railed that he loved her, and when she told him she was pregnant, he wouldn't think of it. "This would be the baby that would hold their marriage together." Even Michael realized that was a pretty big job for such a little baby, and he was more delusional than she'd been to even consider that for Donny. The next few months proceeded in rounds - the knock-down and drag-out kind - with her ending up with a broken eardrum and three cracked ribs.

The culmination came with Tim's knee pressing her shoulder, while he beat on her face until she admitted to having sex with Donny. She'd made the obvious blunder of having Donny at her house for sex - perhaps subconsciously to retaliate, or show her independence. She'd been slow in them leaving, as getting in her car to take him home, Tim pulled into the driveway, home early from work. Cooly, she introduced him as Crystal's cousin, and while Tim didn't quite believe it at the time, he didn't forget it either.

The fight the next day, with all of the screaming, her neighbor did call the police. Michael had broken away from Tim, racing across the lawn when they drove up. From her physical condition and request, they took him away. She called her mother to come get her, as she couldn't drive. She packed all her clothes into a large, black, plastic garbage bag - virtually all she took out of ten and a half years of marriage.

About to turn twenty-seven, it took several months before the divorce hit the courts, as he was still resisting, not accepting her determination to leave him. Tim no longer had any idea who *this woman was,* that had once been his dutiful wife - not Christmas or any other holiday was going to bring her back. She also made the difficult decision to give him the three children, that would be the ultimate of responsibility for him to learn. Besides, she knew she'd never get child support out of him - on many occasions before, he'd clearly said that he'd leave the country first, and she knew he meant it.

Now time she lived her own life, which would be simpler and easier without her children. Michael knew being married so young, she never had time to spend on herself, or for herself. She'd been emotionally drained, for so many years running a marriage and family by herself. In truth, she didn't want to wait till she was forty to enjoy life. Her world truly had been limited by her own doing, but that she'd change. She also believed the kids would adjust, they always did somehow through the years of turmoil and moving constantly. She'd see them, as a better parent able to influence their lives. She figured Tim would remarry shortly, perhaps to someone willing to be adaptable, as she once was. Time would heal all wounds, in both her and the kids. There was always hope, she had learned it still existed.

Next on her list, Michael started to open her ears and eyes to the fact that Donny was an alcoholic. He'd been to the hospital twice to dry-out, but still went back to the bottle. They were quite a pair at the Longview, him drinking his beer and her drinking milk to keep her pregnant stomach together. As the sex started to wain, it soon became drudgery. Like many men, securely feeling he'd 'won' his woman, he took her for granted, as the 'little' brain between his legs, had a mind of its own. The point of no return came one night when having dinner. Donny casually, but smugly remarked, "It would take a hell-of-a-woman to get me off-the-bottle for good."

Michael threw down her fork to answer, "How about a hell-of-a-man?" It was then she knew it was over. She could compete with other women, she had, he'd cheated on her twice, and she'd forgiven him. But she knew no woman in the world could compete with a bottle or drugs.

Still, Donny could not let go gracefully, the same as Tim. Michael was back living with April, who was *back* with Wally. As if, she were the one to speak, she constantly told Michael what a waste of her life it'd be to stay with Donny. He called constantly, waking Wally up at three and four in the morning, until Michael came to the phone. She gave in, and agreed to meet him once more at the Longview the next day. They did nothing but fight. Proudly, Donny announced, "Fucking me, used to be more important than being with your kids!" It touched too close to the truth, which Michael could not face.

"That's it Buster!" she yelled, picking up a beer bottle, and hit him across the head. She would've lunged the broken end at him, if two customers hadn't stopped her. The bartender jumped over the bar, and with help dragged Donny out before he could retaliate.

A few nights later, Michael was sitting in The Basement with Frank, the biker. She'd watched him from afar many nights, in both awe and amazement of who he was - since he belonged to a rather, notorious motorcycle club. Quite a striking figure, with his long, dishwater blonde hair, captive-blue eyes and a strut of a walk, like he was ten feet tall. Talking quietly, when he casually asked if she wanted to go to his *'crib'* - apartment. She smiled, but declined, "I'd like to take a pass, I'm really tired." Then, in stumbled Donny looking for her and started yelling at her about Frank. She kept ignoring him, and asked Frank to do the same.

Finally, in his most suave manner, Donny asked, "Did you ever fuck him?" Frank's arm and leg muscles began to tighten so much, Michael could feel them against hers.

Michael turned and lied, "Yes, and he's very good!" Donny shrugged his shoulders and walked to the end of the bar. Perhaps he recognized Frank, and knew better not to get into it with him. She looked down once, he was gone and she never saw him again.

Frank then said, "Are you ready to go now?" Michael smiled as they left. After everything, her divorce was anti-climactic - over six months since she'd first left Tim. She only needed her mother as a witness, with the doctor and police reports. It took ten years to go over the hill to freedom, and then she went over pregnant - so much for a divorcee's carefree life.

Lessons

I've loved and lost,
and the losing was worthy of the love,
for the memories left behind.

I've loved and won,
and the winning wasn't worth
the struggle for the prize.

I've played the game so long now,
The winning and losing are much the same.

I've asked myself if it's been worth it all,
but I guess I've learned something,
so there's no need to question it.

CHAPTER 4

Beth

The middle of November, 1945, brought Elizabeth Carole Cordeau, the fourth child of Louise and Jacque - John. They'd not planned on her, as Louise almost forty, didn't even know she was pregnant until the doctor found a heartbeat. She carried a bunch of tumors, they were about to remove, so the doctor couldn't promise her a normal child. She didn't see the baby for almost a week, with the three operations following her delivery. Louise took every bit of her clothes off, as she counted fingers, toes and checked every inch carefully. Elizabeth only had a small birthmark on her upper left leg, and a slight heart murmur, the doctor said she would out-grow.

  Mike, her oldest brother, called her Bethie. They always got along fabulously, as she was a real tomboy. He was so much more fun than her next older brother, Chuckie, or the oldest, her sister-the-'princess,' Marie. But those tomboy activities got her into trouble, since her mother wanted her to stay quiet, which Marie did naturally. Not a ton of bricks could hold Beth down, as her mother restricted her constantly. At grade school, she fought Chuckie's fights, as Louise spoiled him terribly, he'd stand and cry. A big boy, he looked so silly, the other boys teased him, till she gave one a black eye, and another a bloody nose. Her mother was called to school, so embarrassed, "What will people say?" she kept repeating, as she coddled Chuckie.

  Beth, also accident prone, had numerous cuts and stitches from running the almost acre of land, in the south-east unincorporated section of Elmwood But her favorite was the five, silver maples she'd climb daily. Used as her pirate ships, with Mike's golf clubs in the branches for the canons - girls in one tree and sometimes the boys in another. One windy day, a few clubs had fallen, with Beth scrambling down to retrieve them. Her girlfriend called down, "Look Out!" as a 'woody' was flying towards her, Beth looked up as it hit her square in her mouth. Marie usually patched her up, but she'd left for art school in New York, a few weeks before. With so much blood, her girlfriend was afraid, so Chuckie went to get his mother.

Louise was furious, she had to stop cooking dinner, put a wet washcloth over Beth's mouth, and they walked up to the corner, to catch a bus to town for the doctor. She wouldn't dare think of asking a neighbor for a ride in their car - too, embarrassing. As fate would have it, waiting for a bus that only came every thirty minutes, one of the neighbors did come by going to the grocery store. When she saw all the blood on Beth, she insisted on taking them to the doctor. Her mother kept apologizing, "What a terrible tomboy Beth is, she won't stay quiet, and for sure now, she won't be as pretty as her sister."

Most of the boys in her younger years were more buddies, than boyfriends as they particularly liked Beth playing baseball with them - usually the only girl to do so. That summer after sixth grade, she had a bunch of neighborhood kids over to play ball in their large yard. Teenage Mike and a friend were watching, when he saw Beth running the bases on her long hit. Her young breasts had fully-popped and were bobbing as she ran, as his friend snickered. Mike hit him in the shoulder, and headed for the house. "Mother," he said coming in the back porch, "you better get Beth into town, and get her strapped down, she attracting the wrong attention."

Still, she had crushes on boys without any awareness on their part. A continuing heart-throb-buddy was Jack Dixon. He'd been more of a boyfriend to Pollyanna, as Beth was more a 'sister' type to him, since they attended the same Presbyterian church. He'd talk to Beth about all kinds of problems at home or school, or regarding other girls. When he moved into town, they stayed close because of their church activities. In high school, Beth's mother had gotten a small job in town, so her father got her a good, old car, a '52 Chevy - the first automatic. So excited, Beth soon learned how to drive at school and practiced with Mike.

Dix, as everyone called him, was the first guy to drive, and Beth the first girl. Actually April was, but it didn't count, since she was seldom back in the old neighborhood. When Beth got to drive her car to church, she let Dix drive it after. They loaded the car up with kids and took off. He had it up to almost ninety miles an hour, and the poor-thing almost popped its cork. Beth, still attracted to Dix, but he'd changed somewhat after moving into town, acting like he was better than she was. His social standing changed, though they didn't really have money, he tried to act like it and choose town-girls to date.

A lot of love in Beth's family, though it wasn't sometimes shown. Her hard-working father, John, loved his family, but left most of the discipline to Louise to handle and solve. Especially in the summer, he worked long hours in the road construction business, laying asphalt for the new interstate connecting from Chicago. Proud of his immigrant beginnings, of course, he wanted more for his children. He'd spent more time with Mike growing up, but he was younger then and not as tired. John never raised his voice or swore at any of them, and his only outside enjoyment was his bowling team and his lodge activities. Mike, who would go on to accomplish more than his father ever dreamed of, though always feel like he'd never filled his father's shoes.

Close to her father, as a child Beth climbed up in his lap to drink his coffee, when he came home. As the only child that took after his Belgium-French looks, the fair complexion, light hair and very, light blue eyes, he adored her.

Louise was quite different, she loved her children, but was easier and more affectionate to Marie and Chuckie. She liked that they depended on her more, and rarely went against anything she said. Marie had stood with her hands in the dishpan crying until her mother sent her to bed. She corrected her mistakes of lax-discipline of them onto Beth, and made sure that she redo any job until it was perfect. She also never allowed her to whine or cry, as Beth learned to stay more than an arm's-length away, as he mother's palm-slap left a mark and her back-hand could also. As three-quarters American Indian - Choctaw, Cherokee and Chickasaw, Louise was from a farm in Hattiesburg, Mississippi. The three other children had her more olive skin, dark hair and eyes.

But Mike was too independent for her, with Beth becoming more so. Louise did have have difficulties showing affection, feeling the more strict guideline turned out good children, that would do things 'right,' not causing scenes or make a lot of noise. She frequently used an apple tree-switch on Beth's back legs, until John saw the red marks, and told her he didn't want to ever see them again. She knew not to go against her husband's rare directives. With high school, Beth's relationship with her mother deteriorated, as she became more outspoken about how things everywhere were changing. Even with her early development, her mother could not accept her 'French' curves others mentioned at such a young age.

When she popped, no 'training-bra' or 'A-cup' was needed, as she went straight into a 'B' cup, then soon a 'C.' Louise checked to make sure Beth hadn't put toilet paper in her bra - it was all her. At the same time, never comfortable talking at all about sex or s-e-x, as she referred to it, or Beth's 'private-parts.' If it hadn't been for 'health' class at school, she'd not known about her menstrual period.

Part of her mother's obsession may have been, not only was Marie not shaped like Beth, but she was naturally conservative and shy. Also, Louise was going-through her own 'change-of-life' at that time. It didn't make matters easier for Beth's attraction to boys, and their obvious attention to her. Her mother showed little affection to her father, as twin beds replaced the full one, and then she later moved upstairs, once Mike moved out to get married at nineteen.

In many ways, Beth was oblivious to any sexuality she may have had, as she was usually more interested in fun with sports and activities. The years Mike worked at the golf course, he was always bringing home one thing and another to have fun with, so Beth was right there sharing in whatever she could. When he brought home the old, 1949 Harley motorbike to work on, she was with him getting greasy and dirty, to the bane of her mother. Once running, too small for Mike's six-foot-four-inch frame, but Beth could not ride it even on their unregulated roads without any sidewalks. So, the two of them cleared a track around the large backyard - avoiding the garden, grape arbor and four fruit trees. A back-neighbor had a sturdy, chain-link metal fence, but the other only a row of young, weeping-willow samplings across the property line.

After some very, basic instructions as to the peddles, hand accelerator and brakes, the ten-year old went zooming around the track. Beth, like Mike, was a natural to speed, so each half-acre turn around, he'd give her a thumbs-up to go faster. Unfortunately, going about thirty m.p.h, or so on the rough, bare ground, she hit a small-stump before the turn across the back of the property. The motorbike flew into the air, as her hand hit the accelerator, when her body raised-up. Flying through two, young willow-samplings, the wheel-axels clipped gouges in both, about four-feet off the ground. That 'wood-cutting' pulled the bike to the right, heading her for the chain-link fence, so she jumped off. Luckily, the bike died before running into the fence. Mike came running after her, yelling and laughing at the same time. Neither neighbor had seen it, but Chuckie did, running inside for their mother.

Mike was checking the two saplings for damages, when Louise started yelling at them. Ignoring her, he merely waved his arm up, and went on to get the bike. Neither it, nor Beth were hurt too bad. Both laughing and howling hysterically, she wanted to get back on, but he knew better than to push it with their mother. They slowly walked the bike back for him to check what Beth had hit, and was surprised they hadn't seen it before. By the time they got to the garage, Louise had given up and gone back into the house. Beth did get a lecture, as to the danger of the motorbike from her father, but Mike had left to go visit friends.

It was actually Mike who did talk to Beth about sex. Being eight years older, he saw how naive she was, yet with a body that he saw his friends noticing. She used to help him work on his old cars in the side-driveway, or garage when their father was at work. So, they built up a closeness, and she always idolized his independent ways. She'd also never forget how Louise totally dumped a pot of hot coffee on him for smoking a cigarette in the kitchen, when she told him not to. He never said a word, but jumped up, grabbed a kitchen towel to wipe himself off, then swooped up the pack and left. Beth started babysitting after his first son, Jackie was born, though his wife Barbara was sometimes jealous of his closeness to both his sisters.

One Saturday night, Mike and Barb went to a wedding, so when they got home, the slightly-tipsy Mike decided to sit his little sister down, and give her a drink. He wanted her to know what alcohol was, " . . . so no man can ever take advantage of you because of it." A whopping thirteen, he started her with screwdrivers to practice, as she got mellow. Time for her to learn the facts of life, since he knew no one else in the family would tell her. He doubted that Marie knew any more about sex than Beth did, but then she didn't have any of those physical attributes to worry about, though thirteen years older than her. At first Beth couldn't quite understand him, because he wasn't getting to the point. He began, "You see Beth, *we're both* very lucky people, some have it and some don't, and I'm positive you'll have it . . . that magic, sexual-magnetism!" Barb laughed, and shook her head, waving 'good-nite.'

Beth didn't know that Mike had started very young sweeping the girls off their feet with his 'sexual aura.' He truly looked like a cross between a lanky-John Wayne and a smart-ass James Garner. "You know, the first time I tried sex with the little girl next door, Mother caught me, and took my little, red wagon away." He paused to have another swig of his martini - he didn't drink screwdrivers. "I think I was eight or ten at the time," he laughed like it was yesterday. "It slowed me down a little, but it didn't stop me. I made sure the next time that Mother was not around." He laughed again, and continued telling her more of his young escapades, without any details, or awarenesses to have about her own life. Still it was fun being included in on his.

There wasn't one thing which could be pointed to and said, "That's it! That's what sexy about Mike." Maybe it was he really liked women, and comfortable joking around them, not segregating himself - only being with the other guys at functions. He'd inherited it from their father - which Beth learned was true, as Louise and Marie were not warm, gregarious women.

With Beth, maybe because she was comfortable being around guys from the sports, or she loved to joke so much. Her quick, impish smile, constant optimism and positive attitude of encouraging others made her seem older. But Mike repeated his concerns about her shape, which caused men to notice her for a longer, second-glance. The first time told she had 'bedroom eyes,' she didn't know what it meant. She could be devilish, yet innocent and vulnerable in her naivety.

"I'm just trying to tell you not to flaunt it around too much, . . . but not save it for posterity, like Marie is doing, either." He'd gotten up to pour himself another martini, as Barb knew to leave the canister on ice. "To abuse this appeal would be wrong. It's one of the greatest things two people can share, and should never be used as leverage." He sat there looking past her, more thinking of himself than her, with the liquor letting him slip away.

Beth confused again, but kept nodding her head, as if she understood every word. Some of this was lost on her, as he may not remember she was a church-choir-regular, and mother did require her well-indoctrinated with the strictness from Presbyterian beliefs. And, what the church might have missed, her mother insinuated the wrath of God and herself, if Beth ever even considered being *'loose.'* If she had to choose between her wrath and that of God, she was sure God would be more lenient and forgiving. She did take her faith seriously, teaching Sunday School, and talked of being a missionary with Dix, or at least joining the Peace Corps.

Beth already was someone who got involved in people's lives, thus many confided in her. She felt on an equal-par with most classes of people - though not the heavy-moneyed or the most popular - she wasn't in their league, she felt. But she did have many friends from both sides of the upper-middle-class town. This was difficult for some of her friends to understand, how she could associate with both. In the early '60s high school, there were the 'greasers' and the 'white-shoes.' Beth didn't consider herself either. Because she never did some of the things that the greasers did, she still didn't put them down for their actions - her brother Mike could have been considered one, years before. Yet, she never would have called herself a white-shoe, as she felt she had too much smart-ass-attitude about most things, usually doing only the things she was sure she could get away with.

But she did have to be very, straight-laced about sex, not only because of her mother, but her closest girlfriends were also straight and rarely talked of sex, much less did anything. Such as, any girl who went to the drive-in, probably *'put-out,'* which was one of their beliefs, without it ever being clearly defined. Beth did not live vicariously through her greaser-friends, though she felt they were more honest than some of the hypocritical white-shoes.

Still, she liked boys, and if she couldn't be their girlfriend, she could always be their buddy-friend. Muscularly built, while softly padded, she definitely was not the cutesy 'Shirley Temple' type or frail, feminine girl. Though in all honesty, she'd have enjoyed making-out with most of her buddies. Her first puppy-love was in eighth grade with a guy named Richie, who was a friend of her brother Chuck. He filtered in and out all through her high school days, and the first to teach her how to kiss - she liked his hands on her, too.

Richie joined her when babysitting for a neighbor, but she'd remind him they might come back any moment, so he never got out of hand, so to speak. He definitely was *not* a white-shoe, but was aware of her background, so knew the limitations. While she never spoke of it, her mother had pounded-in the necessity to be a virgin when she married, or God would strike-her-down on her wedding day, if she was not. Of course, if she had known of any of her friends having sex, it may have been different. She didn't want to be the first, or only 'bad girl' in the neighborhood. Beth had no idea that April had been screwing around since she was sixteen, nor of course, the molestation from her father.

Beth didn't realize, that since always around older people, she acted more mature and her figure reflected that, too. Add to that, she was always smiling, many older guys assumed she was interested in them. When fifteen, her girlfriend Sheri fixed her up with a blind-date who was twenty-one, he was told she was seventeen, and she told he was nineteen. This was all because Sheri had to double-date, but she didn't like to neck in the car. So, to avoid any heavy petting, she began telling her date how accident-prone Beth was, thus any pause of noise they had, there were details of her broken bones and stitches heard.

Sheri did have a wonderful sixteenth birthday party in the Spring, and that more than made up for it, as the first time Beth got swept off her feet. He was a tall, good looking guy from Sheri's high school. They danced all night under the magical, patio-lights, with him attentively kissing her frequently. Of course, shy Beth's fault it only lasted one glorious night.

Later, she went to summer school at his high school for extra credit, and he was there. But there always seemed to be a crowd of his friends around, and she was afraid he hadn't remembered her. She was too insecure to invade a strange group to talk to him. Her confidence was restricted to around her friends, as she withdrew simply nodding at him a few times. She found out later from Sheri, he was used to being pursued, and thought she wasn't interested.

Yet, summer school didn't prove totally fruitless, it was her first real pick-up. And, definitely not the type Mother would approve of, as he rode a motorcycle. Also, the first to take her to a drive-in movie. Since it was a double-date - his friend had the car and only *the movies* had been mentioned to Louise, so no problem. Though Beth was not his usual type, he liked going out with her, until she made it very clear that she did not 'put-out.' Very disappointed, he respected her, saying he'd check back later to see if she changed her mind.

Her mother still didn't like him, and said something about Beth's clothes being messed up, though she'd always made sure nothing was out of place. The last time he came by, was on his motorcycle, but no way would her mother let her ride with him. Louise began to insist on checking Beth's underwear, unbeknown to her why she'd do something like that. She'd have to strip down, give her mother her underwear - which she'd look at closely in the light, then give it back to her, with no comment. She asked one friend if her mother did that, and she laughed saying her mother was not a weirdo like Beth's.

Still confused from the *'sex-instructions'* Mike had given her, and not sure if premarital-sex was the 'flaunting' he had meant. She did wish he'd made himself a bit clearer in the details of 'not keeping it for posterity.' Did he mean marriage or what? Chuck didn't talk about dating, just occasionally went out with a few guys, who hung-out with girls, but she never asked him what all it meant either. Marie rarely dated, so she didn't have much to talk about before she got married at twenty-six. Beth was pretty sure Marie *was* still a virgin.

In her sophomore year, Beth participated in the talent show baffooning, singing and dancing behind an 'Aunt Jemima' costume to the pop song. A laugh or joke was the easiest way for her to communicate, and any school speeches were about something funny. Since her first time on stage with her girlfriends, though she'd sung with the school choir and did the chorus in several musicals. They had a great choir director, who got them Christmas and other performances at many places in Chicago, and even sang on television.

As always though, her parents never attended anything for her. Her father would've come, but her mother was either too tired and not feeling well. She was cooking dinner, when Beth sang on television, and didn't even come into the living room to watch her. On the other hand, Beth had to go with her parents to Chuckie's accordion recitals every six months, until he quit taking lessons. Since they had an old upright piano, she asked for lessons, but her mother said no, because she was still too much of a tomboy. She didn't understand, since Louise had already cut all her trees down the summer before, to keep her out of them. There was a realization that while her mother may love her, she didn't like her at all, still finding fault in everything she did.

By the time Beth started her junior year, she'd decided to go to college, with encouragement only from a couple of her teachers. She thought she had the brains for it, and knew it was the only way she'd ever *be somebody*. Somehow she felt there should be more to life than just being married - yet marriage meant sex was acceptable. Of course, a career like she contemplated was not quite pushed for a girl in 1962. Definitely split between school and career - but not wanting a secretary job like Marie, or her marriage.

She felt college would give her a little more experience in life. Her mother said *they'd* pay for college, only if she graduated to become a teacher. Beth doubted those precise words came from her father, but her mother tightly held the money. She didn't know a lot about scholarships, but didn't think she was smart enough to get one, so she got a cashier's job at the local-chain grocery. Her mother might be able to control her life in high school, but once she graduated, she didn't want her controlling it any more.

Those were the days - money, a license and a car - even if her mother's car was freedom. Beth was the only one who worked and had a car, so she took her girlfriends everywhere - Pollyanna, her sister Priscilla or Martha, her quietest friend. Beth loved to drive, and felt there was so much more than driving around hamburger-heavens in town, since they didn't live there anyway. Pollyanna and Priscilla preferred to drive downtown to Chicago's Lake Shore Drive if it was nice out, and they'd pay for the public parking, so they could walk around.

But O'Hare Airport called to Beth, as she wanted so much to travel and it opened only a few years before. It took her back to her young summers, when she'd lay on the back lawn, watching the planes fly-over to wherever and day dream. Until, her mother would yell at her from the basement window, to take out another load of laundry to hang on the lines. At O'Hare they could park for fifty cents, and the open-air, roof-top observation deck was only ten cents. So, she'd take Martha and sometimes a couple of her sisters, and off they'd go to dream. The observation deck was right next to an airplane, and they stared at the passengers wondering where they were going, and she 'd wish to be one of them getting far, far away. Walking through the airport, listening to the different languages, the girls would guess where they were from, and why they came to Chicago.

During her senior year, Beth met her first true-love, Tom. His mother worked at the food store, and she met him when he came to pick her up. Their first date was straight out of the story books, as he had an old-fashioned mother. He brought Beth flowers and candy, which no man ever did both again. Also a senior at another high school, and about as insecure about himself as she was. Their romance grew very slowly, but steadily. He was so nice, polite and good looking - about six feet, with light, brown hair and eyes. Beth was falling very hard for this guy, but was afraid of herself slipping, so made the mistake of turning him down when he asked her to go steady. Afterwards, she could only hope he'd ask her again.

After a movie one night, she suggested, "Why don't we just go to a quiet spot to talk, instead of going for a soda - it's such a pretty night?" Maybe once they started necking, he'd ask her again to go steady. Tom was a good boy, but Beth a good girl, who didn't want to be good. Sometimes she wondered why she even bothered being good, since her mother accused her of even being pregnant, and doing 'nasty things,' as she called it. Tom was probably not the one to go over the edge with, as he was maybe too, good. He did drive them to the park, and then the cops came by hassling them, though they had only been necking. One of the cops got mouthy, and accused him of screwing her. He jumped out of the car, and practically threw a punch at him, for saying such a thing in front of her

He obviously cared more for her than he did for just sex, and why they broke up. Tom felt they were getting too serious, and he respected her too much to take advantage. He then told her, he also decided to join the Marines once they both graduated high school, since she had set plans to go to the University in De Kalb. The weekend before their graduations was the last time they saw each other in years. They sat on her parent's front lawn to talk about the planned four-year separation. He would be out of the Marines, and she would be finished with college. They decided to not see each other until at least a year, to see if what they felt was real. The ultimate of best-laid plans of the young and naive - what could go wrong?

Beth knew her father was proud of her graduating with high grades, and going to college, but he never overly expressed his feelings. There was always a hug or kiss when she needed it, and he'd listen when she talked about some boys she liked, as well never questioning her virtue, the way her mother did. Most importantly, he encouraged her about the different careers she considered. She never felt anything wrong with his going to his bowling and lodge meetings, while Mother accused him of 'tom-catting' around. Why should he stay home, Beth thought, when she only picked at things he didn't do, or brought up things he did do twenty years before.

Living through the depression, John did not flaunt his money, and Louise was careful with the spending, yet when one of his children needed to borrow, he never said no. Mike and Beth learned the most of his responsible teachings, and would never ask for his help unless really necessary. When the day came for Beth to be taken to college, her father had a small surprise for her, to show how proud he was of her. He left the envelope on the bed, in her new home at the dorm. The plain white card simply said, "Elizabeth - Something extra for your spending. Jacques F. Cordeau." Enclosed was a twenty dollar bill. The thought made tears come to her eyes, and the signature cracked her up - he could be so formal sometimes.

Maura was Beth's roommate in the co-ed dorm at the state university, and quite different from Beth, except a virgin. Martha was at the university also, but no help about sex information, as she'd never even been kissed! Maura, a short, small, blonde was pretty. She taught Beth all about make-up and coordinating clothes. Louise made a lot of her clothes, so she didn't always have the choice, as to style or design. Maura was a little slow in her subjects, as she was more into socializing, so Beth tutored her in those things that came easy to her.

She introduced Maura to a wider range of friends, as she'd come from a higher income bracket, and Beth usually attracted a wider variety of people. Beth also worked in the kitchen at the dorm, though it didn't embarrass her, as she made a game out of it for fun.

Beth and Maura swung into a late, night routine of the other girls gathering in their room after hours - 10:30 pm. There was always a pot of tea, and some food from home to talk about boys, sex and their dating excursions. Most girls that joined them were as lost they were, learning from mistakes, and other's experiences how to have fun without any problems. Bobbie, from the Chicago Northside had only been kissed a few times, and anxious to change all of that. Martha, when she did join them, only sat in a corner smoking, and taking it all in. Another girl named Jane, actually from a town so close she could have commuted, just giggled when the others threw around their ideas about sex.

Undoubtably, Maura had the best stories, as she actually knew girls who had sex and told her about it. "This guy was screwing a virgin - now everybody take heed - they'd been going at it so long, that even after he had *'come'* he couldn't get out, because her muscles had locked." The girls were all on the edge, waiting for the conclusion, as very gingerly Maura picked up a cigarette and lit it. They screamed for her to finish the story. "So, he lit a cigarette and smoked, until she loosened up enough for him to get out." It was a wonder how naive they were.

Maura and Beth were on a double-date one night with two football guys in a Volkswagen, with Maura's about six-four, two hundred forty pounds in the front seat. Then Beth's was smaller by maybe an inch and about ten pounds. This foursome was not doing badly parked in the north-forty, when Maura and her partner broke their seat. A good thing they all had a sense of humor, and not really expecting a lot from the limited situation.

Beth started the school year off great, even if it didn't include the 'bang' she'd been hoping to receive. She'd been invited to Homecoming with another football guy, and since she'd never gone to any big dances in high school, truly excited about the whole experience. Having dropped a few pounds, away from her mother's carb-ladened cooking, and learning more about make-up with her general appearance, she began to feel more positive about herself.

Though she still hoped the guys would notice her mind also, she was glad for the physical attention. She thought this may be her big night, ending at the Holiday Inn, with her new, store-bought dress and everything. But like all the other nights, she ended up at the lagoon, except this time she let him go a little further than *he thought* she should have.

There was a part of her that wanted to get the whole virginity-thing over with, and what better time than Homecoming. She barely noticed that he'd stopped fondling her, when he said, "I can't go through with it." Seriously, she began thinking that something was wrong with her. She watched his face as he pulled up from her, and all he could say was, "You're the kind of girl I want to marry, not screw, . . . and I'm not ready to get married."

She didn't even know he cared much for her, and could only mumble, 'OK.' The rest of the school year had a lot of ups and downs, but unfortunately she had her clothes on throughout every session. The only real sex-excitement they had was watching the supposed *dorm-nympho*. She didn't look any different than some other girls, not that they thought she should walk funny, or be panting or something. The rumor had it that she'd been with ten guys, and there she sat in the lounge reading a book, like anyone else would have - and not even a sexy book! Oh well, what did they know as to a real *nympho* or not.

Even Maura and Beth knew more about sex than Bobbie, who had her heart set on "Joe College," a junior, a frat man and a very, good-looking playboy. He knew she was a virgin, and quite inexperienced, as well totally crazy about him. Just her first date with him, she practically fell into their room that night looking, as if the proverbial-truck had run over her and back again. Besides her hair and make-up messed, her clothes were in complete disarray with a bra strap and her zipper both broken.

The other girls stopped drinking their tea and stared, with a questioning look as Bobbie asked, "Why are my undies all wet?" At that point, Maura almost fell off the top bunk laughing. The majority who knew, howled for minutes over the divulgence of such ignorance. Bobbie was past naivety. The puzzled look turned to tears, when she added to her confusion, "Did I just lose my virginity, and not know it?" Funny how they learned from her.

Though Beth felt she was serious about her education, and not there to get a *"Mrs."* degree like most of the girls, though she did, of course, enjoy the boys. When she wasn't working in the kitchen, Beth joined the others in the co-ed dining room, and dressed with a little more attention to detail. One particular night, she was wearing a new v-neck sweater, but since it was rather low-cut, revealing too much cleavage, she borrowed a dickey from one of the girls. It wasn't a large dickey and it fit a little tight on her, so she felt she needed to keep adjusting it. Maura, of course, picked a table with a lot of cute boys, and Martha sat across from Beth at an angle, while Maura and Bobbie were on either side of her.

As dinner proceeded, Beth was vigorously talking with the boys, using wild movements of her hands for exclamation as usual. With slow realization, she noticed the boys nudging one another, and nodding toward her. Then Martha tried to get her attention, pointing to her chest. When Beth looked down, she saw the dickey had moved from her head-turning and arm movements, revealing her full breasts for all to see above her low-cut bra.

First reaction to cover herself with her hand, but unfortunately it still had a fork in it, and she poked herself. She began to laugh, so they all laughed, shaking their heads breaking the embarrassment. Afterwards, several of the guys asked when she'd wear that sweater again, and that she could sit at their table anytime. Others casually - not nasty - started joking, calling her 'big bod' and Maura 'little bod,' because her boobs were rather small. They loved the attention.

With Spring, Maura and Beth had their fifth-floor windows open, though the fertilizer smell from the farm-lands could sometimes be penetrating. The great view was of the far side of the campus, and they climbed up on the counter-ledge of the windows to dance to whatever music they had blasting on weekends. From this vantage point, Beth saw a Stingray-convertible pull into the circular driveway, and she called down to them, "Hey, Stingray!"

The girls, both in the bras and panties, thought no-one could see them at that height. The guys' reaction below blew that theory, as they stood up in the car whistling and yelling-up for them to come down. The girls, both on the floor by this time, were laughing hysterically. By the time they got dressed and down to the car, so had the campus cops. Some joy-killer turned them in for disturbing the peace, since they'd turned their car radio-up full blast.

Beth was becoming an expert on consoling broken hearts, which showed how desperate some people were, to get relationship support from a virgin! A guy she thought of as a platonic-friend decided he wanted to become more. It first started out after Christmas break, when Al came back with his engagement broken. Difficult for Beth, since she only wanted him as a friend.

Then, a week before Easter break, Beth went home to pick up her mother's car to bring all their winter stuff back. A real riot with Maura, Martha and Beth trying to stuff the car with a Spring, snow-storm blowing them down. Saturday night before Easter, Beth had her first real date with Dix. He'd also come home from college in Wisconsin. They hadn't seen each other since Christmas at church. Dix obviously had gotten some sexual experience, and seemed anxious to take Beth out, figuring she must have also. A shock to have someone she'd known through grade school, summer camp and his first shave to be attacking her boobs, like they'd just appeared out of nowhere. Even more riotous, that he picked their old, grade school parking lot to go for it.

This was the boy she wanted to save the world with through missionary work or the Peach Corp, and now found he was human, too. He truly was shocked, not only was she still a virgin, but she said 'no' to him, as if relenting was expected for old times' sake. In reality, Beth would have loved to, but not then and definitely not there. To top it off, next morning in church, he pretended they'd never been out, and went out of his way to avoid her. She then wondered how he would've acted, if she had said *'yes.'*

A beautiful, Easter Sunday after dinner, Beth went next door to visit their long-time, next door neighbors, Mary and her husband Bill with the four kids, she'd often babysat for them. Beth always liked them both, as Mary was a rather wild, free thinker and Bill a very funny country-boy from Tennessee. As they're sitting on the back patio, into the driveway came Mary's two cousins, Bruce and Jerry, from Cicero on Bruce's Harley motorcycle.

She remembered Jerry, who was two years younger, because they played together as kids, when his parents visited hers. She didn't remember Bruce though, because he was almost eight years older. After talking, and having a drink, Bruce was giving everyone a ride on his beautiful, older model Harley he'd recently gotten. Beth spoke up when he returned from taking one of the kids for a short ride.

"I'm going to have to finish packing, as my friend's father is coming to take me back to campus, but could I get a ride?" With her usual big smile on, as well a fitted top and Capri pants, Bruce was rather mesmerized, and could barely do more than nod, as he handed her the extra helmet.

So, Bruce took Beth for a longer ride, which she didn't hesitate to hold on to him closely, as she'd noticed him appraising her. They only talked at stop signs and traffic lights, but she managed to tell him of her prior motorcycle experience, expressing her love of it. He managed to tell her of being a journeyman typesetter, and he also had a car and a boat. She held on tightly even without any curves or sharp turns, thinking this was an older man from the city, so he must have lots of sexual experience.

Once she realized how far they had ridden, she cautioned him that she did need to get back, she didn't want her friend waiting for her. As feared, Martha's father was unhappily waiting in the driveway, so she quickly jumped off the bike, and gave Bruce the helmet. "Thanks, that was fantastic! I hope to see you around this summer." She gave a quick wave to Mary, Bill and the kids, "See you in June! Love ya."

Once in the car with her bags, after apologizing, Beth began to tell Martha all about Bruce, and what a great catch he would be. "He's got a good job, also has a car and a boat, so he obviously likes doing sporty things. Later that night at their gab-fest, most of the girls thought she was nuts saying crazy things, when all she did was take a motorcycle ride. They, of course, as well as Bruce, had no idea how the motorcycle had been such a 'seal-the-deal' on her feelings for someone. Also, Beth simply moved Bruce over to Mike's category as the same age, and was putting her attractions of him onto Bruce. She sat drinking her tea, and began to plot it all out, as she knew Mary would help her, because then they would be relatives besides being friends. *"Yes, he may be a challenge, being a 'bachelor' and all,"* she thought to herself.

By the time finals were over, Beth had an extra day before they girls went home together. She decided to join Bobbie, Joe and Al - who Beth thought she'd worked out the platonic-thing with. They were going to watch sunrise come up on the Mississippi, so they'd left in the afternoon by two cars, with sort-of picnics and drinks for all. She should have asked for more details, as to what all they were going to do around the Starved Rock State Park besides drinking.

Beth loved joining any group out in the cornfields for the drinking, but this was a little far to go to *just* drink. She'd not thought about simply agreeing to spend the night with a guy after drinking, and to have sex would've been an expectation. As much as she wanted to lose her virginity, she'd realized she wanted to care about the guy, in order to fully give herself to him. This night would be more than an opportunity, if it was still about losing her virginity, but it wasn't anymore.

When Beth got home the following day, she had no idea she'd never be returning to the university, except to visit friends there. She did find out Tom, her first love, had been home on leave, and came to see her. Louise, probably extending the last of her control over Beth, even though she liked Tom, said she told him, "She's having finals, and can't be wasting time on you."

Crushed, Beth had thought of him so often with such fondness. Her mother also, *couldn't seem to find* his contact information - phone or address. If she had it to do over again, she'd not have let him get away so easily, as she knew he still cared greatly for her, also. Her mother insisted on invading her life, from letting her nieces destroy her 'American Girl' doll collection, to giving away her favorite pink sweater to the church rummage sale. She was so mean to her.

Beth got a job working in Chicago from a temporary placement agency. The first two were bummers, but the third was a charmer - a receptionist for an art studio connected to a good advertising agency. The boss was old enough to be her father, but it wasn't his 'wing' he wanted to take her under. The other people there were a terrific, exciting, a very urban/urbane group. Only one other girl there, several years older, a very sweet and a talented key-line artist. Beth she was a real, class lady, so looked forward to becoming friends.

On the Fourth of July, Mary next door to her parents had a big, family get-together at her house. Beth was out sun-bathing on a lounge chair reading a magazine, so it wouldn't seem too much like she was waiting for Bruce. Mary made a point to let her know, he was invited, as well as herself, of course. When she heard the distinctive Harley-sound pull into the driveway, her magazine lost its appeal, until he came walking through the separation between the lilac bushes.

In talking to her, he invited her to the party, and out on his boat the next day. Totally delighted, she said she'd go in to change, and be over shortly at Mary's. She had a chance to visit with Bruce's parents, whom she called Aunt Sophie and Uncle Chuck, and Mary's other relatives she'd known since a child, from the family trips into the city to visit. She and Bruce were comfortable talking and partying, he'd also brought out some fireworks for the celebration.

The next day, Bruce being slightly insecure, brought along his brother Jerry for the day. It turned into a real scene, as the brothers argued and yelled at each other over all kinds of things. But somehow it seemed to be related to her being invited. Jerry acted quite jealous and childish, as if having to share Bruce's things with someone else. Though she tended to 'fry like a crispy-critter' in the sun, she put on her suntan lotion and hat on for the day-out in it.

She did enjoy the boat, but preferred the motorcycle. Despite Bruce's feuding with Jerry, they got along splendidly. Though only having been around college boys, she didn't notice how awkward, even being older, he was with her. They dated two weeks before he kissed her, and at first she thought it was nice, as compared to the college boys 'pawing' the moment she'd get in the car.

Beth saw Bruce almost every day, but there romance did not progress with any speed. By the time September rolled around, she decided not to return to the university, but take night courses at Elmwood College. This way she had school and her new advertising job, while still pursuing Bruce. In trying to encourage his dreams, *she* loaned him money to take flying lessons. Though he lived at home, he obviously wasn't as well off as she thought, as all of his possessions were on time-payments. And, it turned out, he still had several years of apprenticeship at work.

The fact that he spent an additional three hundred dollars for flying lessons, and still hadn't soloed should have given her a clue, but all her brain's warning signs were turned-off. By the time of her nineteenth birthday, she was sure she wanted to marry him, yet he was more of a challenge than expected. He'd been engaged twice before, the first one broke it off and the second one, he broke off. She thought being the third, a lucky charm to keep him, surely. Her birthday was also the first time he finally, really touched her body.

Bruce had never known a virgin before, and he gave her a complex about it. He'd ask her about her experiences, trying to find out how far she'd gone, without exactly asking. He began to tell her about his sexual experiences, at first trying to insinuate there were many, yet they all seemed to have negative overtones. Beth at first thought he didn't want to boast, yet he mentioned to her several times,

"It's usually disappointing and uncomfortable you know, not as good as in the movies, or how other people said it's supposed to be . . . especially if rushed." Not exactly a romantic thing to be telling one's girlfriend. If she hadn't been so naive herself, she'd have seen the problem. Now, she was beginning to feel like he was warning her, to not have some fairy tale dream or something. Many incidents should have daunted her feelings toward Bruce, but they didn't. She was 'Crusader Rabbit' when it came to the challenge of making him happy with her, and life in general. She'd always wanted to be a social worker, and save down-trodden people from themselves, by sharing her strength. If she couldn't save the world, she'd save this man.

As Bruce became totally comfortable with her, he revealed a hair-trigger temper over the dumbest things, which led to a string of cursing, like she'd never heard before. He used words she didn't know what they meant, but had literally seen them on public restrooms walls. She began to notice how different his parents were from hers, yet Uncle Chuck always had been exceptionally nice to her.

Sophie, as Beth got to know her better, she saw as a rather, strange woman. Not only an absence of femininity, but instead of teaching her three sons the ways of a woman, she molded her behavior to their male-activity. While she openly admitted to spoiling Jerry, her middle son John, less than a year younger than Beth, was rarely around, and had little to do with his mother. Sophie's *boys*, as she referred to them, never really learned to treat a woman kindly or gently.

It amazed Beth, Chuck knew how to do everything around the house, her father was lacking in most of those 'handyman' skills. Yet, Bruce had no interest to help or learn, which irritated his father to no end. Bruce moved rather slowly, and always preferred to read a magazine than help, unless his father really needed an extra hand. Sophie made excuses for him, for whatever it was he did wrong. Since Bruce was her oldest son, Beth learned she'd lost one baby in-between Bruce and John, so she acted like Beth was stealing Bruce away from her. After they had been dating a year, Sophie kept saying to him, in front of Beth, "Don't waste her time if you're not going to marry her. She's too young for you anyway." Hoping that they'd break up, and Bruce would settle back down into the house under her care.

Other differences in the families Beth never understood, was his family *never* celebrated birthdays the way hers did, as even her mother called them 'red-letter days.' Actually, the one time, Louise gave her a special, favorite dinner and cake, though the present, especially if a homemade dress, was usually delayed or late. As with Christmas, all his family did was exchange money instead of gifts. Beth felt the time and effort spent picking out the gifts, were part of the giving, how much you cared for the other person.

The attitude this family had about sex was also difficult for Beth to understand. Somehow they made it thought of as a dirty joke. Sex may not have been mentioned in Beth's home, but yet she felt it should be something private, between the two people sharing it. In Bruce's home, it was spoken of as 'hot-pants' or 'getting a little' by the boys, or his father with his mother laughing along. Beth tried to over-look these things, though they were more than tell-tales of what life with Bruce could be like, if they married.

In the mean time, Beth excitedly worked at a large advertising agency downtown on North Michigan Avenue, commuting to the city daily. She went out after work on a regular basis with many of the older people she associated with, so becoming more worldly, even if by osmosis. In February, Tom her Marine, was home again. When he called, luckily Beth answered, but she didn't know what to do. Not wanting to lose Bruce, but still something left for Tom.

She didn't tell Bruce about seeing him, until saying good night to him on Friday. "Oh, I almost forgot, I've got an old, high school-friend back in town a few days, we're going out to catch up and talk. OK, I'll give you a call on Sunday, to see if you want to do something together." He was stunned, and a little upset she hadn't said anything earlier, but he didn't show how much at the time. She didn't feel he needed to know her history with Tom, or how much he had meant at one time, as she wasn't sure if it was anything more than a high school crush or not.

By Saturday night, Beth was a basket-case, she even got diarrhea from her nerves. She knew she should do this, there was no going back, as she had to make sure it was over. When Tom picked her up, he seemed taller and better looking than she'd remembered him. The Marines had 'done him well,' and he seemed so much more confident that either of them had been before. They went to a movie and out for pizza later, with strange-shades of high school, not drinking alcohol, as she did with Bruce or her co-workers, *but they* were only nineteen. Back at her parents' house, they sat and listened to records, as her parents went to bed early to give her some privacy with Tom. He began telling her how he'd missed her, all that had happened in the year and a half, and also that he'd always kept her graduation picture with him.

With tears in her eyes, Beth told him there was someone else, who she thought she'd marry. Very politely, Tom said he understood and got up to leave. By this time, Beth was crying profusely, and apologizing for putting him through all this. He stoically stood there looking at his first love - maybe they'd both been too young. He then politely asked, "May I kiss you good night, and . . . may I keep your photo with me? I'm leaving for Viet Nam next week, and it might help to have a familiar face with me."

A vague name of a strange place, it hadn't been in the news much in 1965. Perhaps they should've started with a kiss, and maybe the evening would've gone a whole other direction, but it was fate and it was done. Beth would only hear of Tom one more time years later, but she'd never see him again. The kiss would stay with her, and so would he remain on her mind, especially when she heard more news about the Marines in Viet Nam. There would be times, when Beth would've given anything to hear from him, or see him once again.

When she saw Bruce on Sunday night, they had their first fight. She told him nothing happened over and over, and repeated she loved only him. Many events should have changed her mind, but she remained stubborn about loving and wanting to marry Bruce. She could see his *potential,* and he only needed someone to have faith in him, *with a push to encourage him.* She just knew she could be his 'savior from himself' and his family. She supported him to buy into an airplane, even though he still couldn't fly.

Beth continued to believe in him time after time, yet he continued to disappoint her. She'd not give up, because it was like admitting to failure and she couldn't do that. She'd marry him, and make a success out of him and their marriage, no matter what obstacles stood in the way. Even her brother Mike couldn't talk her out of marrying him, and God knows he tried every way possible. He remembered Bruce when they were kids, and how, "His mother would never let him play more than two feet away from her. It was pretty pathetic," he remarked. Yes, she knew his mother was the real problem, just not how much.

By her twentieth birthday, they had another big fight. Beth's associates at work decided last minute to have a party for her at their favorite bar, and a real humdinger, as they all loved her. She'd moved up to special assistant to the president and the bookkeeper so fast in the advertising company, they couldn't do enough to thank her. She'd also moved from safe screwdrivers to vodka martinis. They told her after six of them, she'd started dancing on the bar, with quite an audience applauding from her friends to strangers.

Her boss didn't want her taking the train home, so he had two account-executives drive her all way to the suburbs. He didn't trust just one, and it took the two of them to handle the party-girl. When they rang the doorbell, her mother about had a fit. Pollyanna and Priscilla waited an hour at the train station parking lot, while Bruce'd been waiting over two hours at Mary's. He did not think she was cute or funny, while she thought it was all so hilarious, especially the dancing on the bar.

After throwing her birthday card at her in the living room, he walked back over to Mary's. Not as if he had planned to take her for a big dinner or anything, he was jealous of her friends wanting to spend time with her. Bruce didn't have but a few friends, and they were not the type to throw parties. Bill and Mary's was a retreat for him, as well lack of imagination and being cheap, so always his favorite place to go.

When Beth pulled herself together, she went over to talk to him. Again, she apologized for her actions, and asked for his forgiveness. She felt she was so close to getting him to ask her to marry him, she didn't want to blow it. The following Sunday, they went to a realtor to look at houses. When they were about to give up, because Bruce thought they were outrageously expensive in the suburbs, they found a little, old one in great need of repair. He'd said they would get married, if they found a cheap house. He compared houses and everything to the inner suburbs of Chicago, the Cicero area where he lived. But Beth refused to live there, where all the old houses were on top of each other. His father promised him a thousand dollars as a wedding present, and agreed to loan him two thousand more for a house.

Technically, Bruce never did *ask* Beth to marry him. It was all taken for granted, once the house was found, as they planned on a wedding in March. Everyone was excited, and the time flew by with even Sophie being nicer to Beth. One night, Bruce, having some real hesitations, stood by the car before getting in to say, "You know, sometimes I think you're too much of a woman for me." Beth never would have believed how utterly true those words were *to become.*

The day of their wedding was perfect in every way, except Beth kept having the feeling she was doing something, she did not want to do But, she wasn't going to think about it now, she quickly put it to the back of her mind, and plastered a big smile on her face She knew she loved Bruce, really she knew she did, and everything - absolutely EVERYTHING - would be fine once they were married, and away from *his family and her mother*. She could *and would* make all of this work - wasn't love all you ever needed?

Except for the minister, who had known her all her life, no one had any idea Beth couldn't be happier. It was hectic, with the last minute pressing of the dress, which was usual for her mother and her sister, never getting anything finished on time. Yet, the dress was perfect, since Marie insisted on the French silk, and Louise sewing the lace appliqués on the veil and dress. Martha was her Maid of Honor, and Maura her bridesmaid, with Marie's two older daughters her flower girls, to make her mother happy. Paula and Pricilla got invitations since they disapproved.

The reception was one everyone talked about for over a year, being held at her father's lodge, with great live music and all the local catering being applauded. As they were about to leave, Bruce and

Beth stopped to thank both sets of parents. As they turned to go, his mother said, "Now, you two go straight home and go to sleep. You're both tired, and have the rest of your lives for that other stuff, believe me!" The fact she said it was shock enough for Beth, but that she meant it was absurd.

Bruce smiled and said, "OK Mom, whatever you say," Beth hoped he must be kidding, or it be the quickest wedding ever.

When they got to their little remodeled house, she was so excited she couldn't wait to get on her Grecian-style nightgown the girls had given her, and walk into the bedroom like she was doing her debut. Bruce waited in bed with his *Popular Mechanics* magazine. One of the times in her life she felt totally beautiful, and he hardly even took notice. He acted like this was the thousandth time for him, and completely bored. It did not seem possible after waiting this long, he'd not be as excited as she was. He finally tossed the magazine down, and she turned off the light as she got into bed.

Beth laid there waiting for 'it' to happen. After six-eternities, he turned and kissed her, "We'll wait for morning."

Beth blurted out, "NO. PLEASE, NOW! I've waited this long, please." She couldn't believe this was happening! She was begging him for sex on THIER Wedding Night!

Slowly he sighed, and said, "OK." To say it was nothing like she ever read about, was simply because most writers have more romanticism and imagination than Bruce did. She had such fantasies about how she'd lose her virginity, but this scenario was truly never one of them. The fact he had a slight problem with getting an erection, she was too ignorant of sex to know. When he finally finished, which was not long, he said, "See, I told you, it's not so great, or what it's cracked up to be."

Beth was not sure what he had expected her to say, or feel from her. But, not at all what she dreamed. It almost felt like he *read* from a copy of 'steps for sexual intercourse,' while he went about it. He'd not spoken a word, or told her how she looked, or any of the basics. Then the fact he should have known, to bring her to a climax through manual manipulation or something. If she didn't get one from the intercourse, perhaps he felt it'd be her problem. What amazed Beth most of all, was for someone who could hardly keep his hands off her body, especially her boobs, before their marriage, he practically ignored it and them when available. She tried not to act disappointed, but she didn't know what to say. She thought they had communicated before, what was the matter?

In the morning, they had sex again, though Beth wanted to think of it as *making love* to feel better about it all. He did tell her she looked pretty, and actually spent some time looking at her body, while appreciating her full breasts. Beth had to stop at her parents house to pick up her suitcase, which was embarrassing, although no one, not even Louise said anything to her. Bruce then insisted on stopping at his parents, to give his father the wedding money to hold for him - like they were incapable of taking care of their own money?

His family though did question Bruce about the sex, asking if *she* 'could walk without bowing her legs.' Beth couldn't believe they were saying all these lewd-things in front of her. Then he began talking like a Don Juan, telling how he had took her with slightly less aggression than rape. Beth didn't know if she was more shocked or hurt by his telling these untrue things. Was this the way it would be? Her begging for sex, and then him boasting like a high-school-boy about his conquest?

They finally left for the resort in Wisconsin, and Beth tried to talk to Bruce about him discussing their sex life with his family, but he ignored her. He took two books and four magazines on their four-day honeymoon. The fact that he read *all* of his reading material, said it all. Returned from their honeymoon, again they went through a 'sex discussion' from his family and relatives. Somehow their talks about sex, using what Beth called 'dirty words,' hadn't bothered her as much before she was married. How could they take something she'd always thought of to be beautiful, and make it seem so vulgar and ugly? Determined she wasn't going to let them get to her, she'd go along - to get along. But inside she knew, love with sex could be perfect and beautiful - and someday she'd have it that way.

Beth decided it was time to begin working on Bruce, to change him into the person he had the potential to be. He definitely wasn't stupid, but he rarely wanted to put out any effort, if less was acceptable. Between staying away from his family and some new clothes, he'd improve slowly from appreciating the benefits of a good life. Each new opportunity she found to expand him, he seemed delighted at the time, then bitch when the money was spent. He'd never understand you never got anything worthwhile for nothing.

The first year and a half went fairly smoothly, with the compensations mainly to be on Beth's side working to accomplish them, yet she felt in the long run, he'd be worth it. She still couldn't understand why he was so indecisive, and would rarely want to try new things. Always the same food at the restaurants he knew, unless she insisted on a new place, then he'd still order something familiar.

Beth had so much faith in him, enough ambition for both of them. Then he insisted she quit working downtown, so they could spend more time together, since he'd recently gotten a job in the suburbs. While constantly requested to stay for client dinners and promotions or just planning sessions, she felt she must be the one to sacrifice her career. She not only loved it, but was such a *natural* at coming up with so many creative ideas.

She quickly found another job in the suburbs for almost the same money, and none of the glamour, which suited Bruce perfectly. She'd learned to live with the mediocre sex, because she had no actual comparison. It did seem that her friends had a lot more thrilling, sex life to talk about. Once in a while, Bruce got a spark, and she'd feel bad about whining to herself. Though she'd picked up several new sex books, he had no interest in talking about it. Soon, she was regularly saying dumb things like, 'quality not quantity' or 'we don't need sex to assure one another of our love.'

They were excuses, to justify their *maybe* weekly sex, but she needed them to keep going, and couldn't admit that to herself. His jealousy was a real pain, when he felt she was spending too much time with girlfriends, and constantly asking who some man was that had looked at her. If he saw her talking to someone in public, like waiting in line, he'd do twenty-questions about who it was, and what they talked about.

As their second anniversary came up, Beth started talking about having a baby, and Bruce wouldn't hear of it. He had every excuse from money to not enough room. They argued several months with Beth always giving in. Finally she asked, "When can I get pregnant?" trying to stand her ground, on a subject that had great meaning to her.

He shouted, "When I'm eighty!" He sat in his recliner, as usual reading a magazine or studying the Sears catalogue.

Beth came out of the kitchen, as it was the last straw. "We talked about children before the marriage, and you agreed to three. So, what are you saying? You going back on your word, or did you just lie to me?" She stood looking at him, waiting for an answer.

Furious she cornered him, he was adamant. "Yes, I lied because I knew you wouldn't marry me unless I said 'yes.' I don't want any children, I don't want the responsibility and this is no world to raise kids in these days …" He headed to the basement, his retreat.

"Don't give me your bullshit-excuses. I'll raise the child, since you don't do anything around here anyway. Your father and I will do the remodeling, just as we did all of it before we moved in." He turned, shocked at her language. But constantly being around it from him, what did he expect, a 'Susie-sweet-breath' forever. With no reply, he went to the basement to sulk.

Beth finished her cycle, and didn't start back on the birth-control pills. Bruce always asked her if she had taken *her pill*, especially if he planned on sex that week. He didn't ask her, even though he saw her go right to bed without stopping in the kitchen for her pill. She figured he approved tacitly, he just didn't want to make the decision, or take responsibility for a baby, as even minor decisions he procrastinated about making.

Several weeks later, they left for a two week vacation out west. Already in San Francisco, Bruce asked her if she had remembered her pills. Beth put a surprised look on her face, "You know I haven't been taking them for over two weeks." The argument proceeded, and upset Beth, as she'd hoped this would be a 'better honeymoon.' She actually thought she might even be already pregnant, as there had been a *butterfly* in her groin for several days now. He slid back into his sulking, first about the pills and then bitching about what the vacation was costing. "It's already planned, and mostly paid for, so you may as well let it go, and have a good time."

Motels usually turned him on she learned, so made sure he had a few drinks each night, to be more palatable to having sex. In Las Vegas, it was the first time that she tried to get him to experiment with new sexual positions on one another. She referred to the books, which he was not happy about, as she realized that he had some real sex hang-ups. He could not imagine a *wife* doing anything like oral sex, as that's what a prostitute did.

In getting him to talk about it, she finally found out the only other sex, than his two fiancees, were prostitutes - particularly in Tijuana when in San Diego, his short time in the Marines. He kept asking Beth, "Are you sure it doesn't make you feel dirty and guilty?" As their talks went on, she found the real truth his mother told him, ". . . every time you have sex with a woman, you give your power away to her, and she's able to control you because of it." The problem was bigger than Beth ever thought.

Beth didn't get her period at home, and the pregnancy confirmed, while the happiest day of her life, was also the beginning of the end of her marriage. Bruce refused to touch her for the next ten months - not just intercourse, but any kissing or touching. He did everything he could, to make her feel responsible for anything which went wrong.

She soon had to leave her job, and take a lesser paying one, then he got laid off from his job. He didn't get another one for over two months, because he refused to return to working downtown or at night. His father was furious with him for not taking care of his family, and a pregnant wife working, but he wasn't.

The loneliness drew Beth closer to her unborn-child, talking to it each day about how she loved it, and would never leave it or give it up. At five months, she almost cheated on Bruce, as she wasn't showing, though she felt it was more wrong toward the baby than toward him. She had a perfect pregnancy, but nerves finally got to her with Jeremy being born five weeks early with an emergency Caesarean. They both almost died, and the shock of it did change Bruce somewhat.

Later, Beth began working nights as a waitress, at a very nice steak house. She spent daytime with Jeremy, then making good money, and didn't mind working on her feet. They argued, as he refused to help care for Jeremy, who developed several bad rashes from not being changed and cleaned properly. When his parents visited one night, his mother yelled at him for not changing Jeremy. He couldn't see why Beth worked so much, as they could *struggle-by* on what he made, though he refused overtime, and took unpaid time off.

Childishly jealous of Beth and Jeremy, he made no effort to spend more time with her himself. She tried to explain to him her work ethic, "Every generation should be better than the last. Your mother worked, and my mother worked, so that they could have more, and give more to their children. I only want the same for us and Jeremy." This seemed so basic to her, how skewed was his thinking?

He looked at her out of the corner of his eye, knowing where Beth worked were a lot of wealthy men, who would be looking at her, and could take her away from him. "Yeah, but my mother worked in a factory, not some fancy restaurant. I don't see why we have to be better than our parents." She didn't understand where his anger and negativity came from.

She could not believe what she was hearing, was this basic laziness or some weird belief thing or something? "Your parents are better off than their parents were, aren't they? What's the matter with being better, accomplishing more?" She was almost pleading now.

"I just don't see why we should have to," he said whining, like a spoiled kid.

"Do you mean to tell me, if you were born in a cave, you'd stay there?"

He thought about it, and how she'd cornered him again. "Yea, I think I would."

Beth realized there was no point in arguing any more, "Well, you can stay where you want, I'm working for better things for Jeremy! And, I'll do whatever is necessary to get there."

He did not expect that, and had to respond. "Don't let the door hit you in the ass, on your way out," he retorted, as if he had won.

"You'll never *live* to see *me* go out that door, buster!" She went to pick-up a crying Jeremy.

Things did not get better between them, they only got further apart. The lack of sex began to bother Beth, because she *was* around men all evening, and many at the bar paying a lot of attention to her. Her only retort was, if she started cheating she would get a divorce, and it wasn't over yet. Beth still loved Bruce, and thought he still loved her.

April had told her the story Sissy taught her: "When you're first in love, it's like two halves of your hearts making one heart of your union. Then, as time goes by, he does things that hurt, and it takes a chip out of that heart. You also do things that chip the heart. Little and big chips begin taking a toll on this heart. When there is no heart left, the love is gone." It happened to April, but she was holding on for dear life. Beth, too, was holding her marriage together with very, stale chewing gum.

With Bruce back working full time downtown, they had settled into somewhat of a marriage, and Jeremy was about to turn two. Beth wanted to get pregnant again, but Bruce refused stubbornly, until she threatened to leave him. But the pregnancy was not the same, and she felt something wasn't right. They'd also contracted to buy a big, new house further west. When it turned out to be a false pregnancy, Bruce was elated. Then he was even more so, when the doctor said she probably wouldn't be able to 'carry-a-child' again.

It got to the point where only when they fought would Bruce change his ways, but the length of the change got shorter and shorter. He was jealous of her girlfriends, as she went out after work for drinks and even dancing. When she'd suggest they go out, he'd only sit home and sulk in his recliner. They were never doing anything together any more. She'd buy him anything he wanted to try to make him happy, but still he'd sulk, and if she brought up sex, he got upset.

She'd gained some weight, and was afraid she was no longer attractive to him, yet other men were still making passes at her. Finally, he came right out and told her she was a nymphomaniac, wanting sex more than once a week, and she repulsed him. He then added, he didn't want anything to do with her. She thought of how many times she swallowed her pride, and begged him for any kind of attention and affection. Once she got her crying under control, she very cooly said, "Someday you're going to want me, and I'm going to refuse you." He just laughed.

They were in Wisconsin buying the lake front property that he always wanted, when he told her he didn't love her anymore. They'd had sex, and he was patting himself on the back for his performing when he didn't feel like it, as if some major accomplishment. Beth was so shocked at this revelation, she couldn't even cry, "So you honestly don't love me?

Bruce, in his 'tell the truth no matter how it hurts,' attitude blankly said, "Correct."

"That's all I wanted to know. Thank you." He had no idea what he'd unleashed for her, a release from the invisible chains, and a green light to find love for herself. She couldn't say she didn't love him, until he said it first. For the first time in years, she felt honest about their relationship. She wondered if she had really loved him, or if he'd only been a challenge to marry. Then the prize hadn't been worth the effort, except for Jeremy. He was her shining-singularity, who made it all worth while. She decided to check, "Do you want to get a divorce?"

Actually shocked, "How could you even suggest such a thing." The ignorance of his remark, told her he was happy to continue in the facade of a marriage. It was over for her. She knew she'd never ask him for sex again, and she didn't give a shit what he did with his life. There was a finer line between love and hate than she ever knew. Or, maybe she was tired of always being the 'good, little girl,' and trying to make someone *else* happy, or maybe it was revenge. The following week Beth began her affair with Rob Casey, a married customer from the Cafe' la France restaurant. They'd been attracted to each other since they first met, when she started working there. She found love and sex, the way she had dreamed it to be - even if temporary.

Bruce accused Beth of cheating back when she and her good friend-neighbor Sandy, worked together. She began to drink more, after starting at the French restaurant, but it got worse as her marriage did. When Sandy moved to Oregon with her husband and family, Beth started going out with Connie. When Connie got her divorce, Bruce didn't want her going out with Connie, as if contagious. Beth felt people had run her life long enough, so began to rebel.

Beth went to Connie, when she planned to have the affair with Rob, and she tried to talk her out of it, knowing her lack of experience. Her warning was simple, "It's like potato chips, nobody ever stops at one." Beth wouldn't believe it, no not her, she wouldn't do such things. It was funny though how true it was, as after the first man, the second and third were easy - no qualms, but lots of repressed-guilt feelings. When they surfaced, she drank, a simple problem solved easily.

Sure, she was in love with Rob, perhaps maybe, or she was in love with love. He was married with kids to a wife who didn't 'understand' him. But Beth was a real, sympathetic listener and lover, who showed her understanding of him - how cliched were they? And, if he was home with wife and family when she needed some love and understanding, it was her problem, wasn't it? Guess she could have another drink.

Beth's bad experience to open her eyes to what Connie regarded as 'on the loose with sex,' was when she ended up in bed as '#159.' The number she was to him, this twenty-two year old guy a pro-football player from Ohio, she didn't remember which team in town to play the Bears, who were regular customers at Cafe' la France. He kept track of his conquests, as he wanted to make a thousand before he was thirty.

Having had too much to drink as usual, she retorted, "And, what do you get then, 'Cock of the Year Award?'" Her language-repertoire had colorfully-expanded from Bruce and Connie. He didn't think she was funny, and even asked her to put up half the money for the Holiday Inn. Now, she laughed at him, almost calling him the 'epitome of a male-slut,' but he might not understand it was *not* a compliment. This ranked as the low-point in her escapades, and she later reminded herself of it often, to make sure she never repeated it.

Bruce tried four times the day after Christmas to have sex with Beth. He was sure she was involved with someone from work, with how he saw her act at their Christmas party. Now, truly afraid she was going to leave him, he thought if they had sex, she'd stay. He had failed each time because of premature-ejaculation. She at last said,

"Don't you think it's a little ridiculous for us to continue like this?" In reality, she could not have cared less if they had sex or not.

"Yes, I've had it," yelled Bruce, as he went out the bedroom door to the bathroom again. She giggled, as she thought, but he hadn't had 'it.' Amazing what having regular sex, more than once a week, had done for her own attitude-adjustment and confidence in herself.

When he got back to the bedroom, she replied, "I'll go see a lawyer about getting out of the new house, and this, too." Very point blank, so he didn't think she meant a divorce, yet he once again didn't question her in detail, as then the decision would lay on her shoulders.

After he came home from work, he was stunned as she calmly told him about her visit to the lawyer while serving dinner. He became enraged, screaming he didn't want a divorce. She then turned to him, not wanting Jeremy upset. "We'll talk about it calmly like adults, or not at all." She turned to walk away, and he jumped up to grab her.

"We're going to make this work out, I mean it." He was holding her shoulders tightly.

"It's over, . . . face it," she replied, again trying to pull away from him.

Bruce's hands moved to her throat, as he began choking and violently shaking her back and forth, while screaming "NO," over and over again. If Jeremy, almost four, hadn't come in between them crying, he would have continued. He went to the basement, not saying another word. Beth scooped up Jeremy to take him to the living room and calm him down from crying.

As soon as she fed him, she put him to bed. She ate something herself, and then also went on to bed, figuring he'd return having accepted the reality of a divorce. She didn't care, though she'd be more careful, considering he had tried to kill her. He came into bed a couple of hours later, and started arguing, but Beth turned away, refusing to respond to him.

Suddenly, he bounced out of bed, went to his dresser and removed something metallic. He then went to the kitchen, turned the light on, but all Beth could hear was a strange clicking noise. Bruce keep his gun and the bullets in his top drawer. Frozen in bed, with the realization he might be loading the gun, she couldn't move. He turned out the kitchen light and came back into the bedroom. He would shoot her, he was crazy with jealousy, as he didn't want any other man to have her. Her mind was going thousand miles an hour, but her heart was ten times faster. He was going to kill her, and she couldn't move off the fucking bed to defend herself!

He got back in bed and laughed, "Ha! You're not going to run up any charges on me at least. I just cut-up all the charge cards."

The relief was like a volcano erupting, as she laughed and laughed. "You asshole, you're the only one who ever uses them!" She rolled back over and kept laughing at his stupidity. But the following day while he was at work, she hid the gun, fearing in his condition he might go for it next. Her instinct was right, when he calmly questioned where it was, and she cooly told him he could have the gun back in the future.

January was one month Beth knew she'd never be able to live through again. Bruce became so erratic - one day sobbing, it was all his fault and he would change, really change if she would stay. She locked herself in the bathroom with Jeremy to keep out of his reach. Then the following day, he was cussing and yelling, it was all her fault and demanding to know who the other man was.

Seeing no point in involving anyone else, besides it was multiple men at this point. Beth swore to him there was no one else who she had set to take his place, which was true. Jeremy was again scared out his wits with all of his yelling, with him stomping back and forth across the living room. Once thoroughly exhausted, he'd take his exit to the basement, until later creeping into bed, with her as far to her side as possible.

The worst night, Bruce started confessing things Beth never knew about him, all the five and a half years married, and most she wished he hadn't told her. What hurt more than anything, was when he told her he had more sex from masturbation, than they'd ever had together. She thought of all those nights of lonely rejection. His massive insecurities, he'd actually been more afraid of failing at sex with her, so he thought masturbation would keep him from trying to perform.

Some nights they would sit and talk about so many of his personal problems, which he never divulged before. She felt sorry for him, but she now knew what a fool she'd been to think she could *'fix him'* with all his 'mother' problems and her negative indoctrinations. His umbilical cord was still *fully-attached,* and Sophie could jerk him back to her anytime.

Beth couldn't love him any more, he'd destroyed it long before with all of his cruel insecurities of rejection. She knew she had to go through with the divorce, simply for self-preservation. He'd held her down long enough, and she had to 'try to fly while she still had wings,' as they say. But, he wouldn't let go, honestly thinking since he'd told her all, she'd forgive him and all would be fine.

She knew when to throw in the towel, so her drinking got worse. One night after work, she got drunk with Connie and Cam at the restaurant, fell down and wiped out a row of glasses from the service bar. Cam drove Beth home in her car, with Connie following in his. He carried her up the porch, rang the door bell and fled when Bruce opened it.

At last, the colitis and dry heaves from her nerves got to her. She went to the lawyer, and said she needed the divorce *now*. Shortly she returned to the attorney's office with him, and the papers were drawn. He refused to sign until she offered him a nine thousand dollar settlement. Funny how his vows of love changed, as the money-offer increased. Agreed, she'd be in court the following week on Valentine's Day. How appropriate, like so many other special occasions, it meant nothing to Bruce. The night before though, it was different story. He brought Jeremy back from the weekend, putting him to bed, as she was still working and waited for her.

When Beth walked in, she knew something was strange, and she didn't trust him, as she knew how unbalanced he had become. After beating around the subject, he asked her to have sex with him. She could have been vicious, tell him to go home and masturbate, as he'd preferred it to her, but she didn't. At first she tried to give him excuses, and finally she said, "NO." As he was leaving, crying again, she said, "I told you, one day you'd want me, and I wouldn't want you. Well, I guess that day has arrived." There was no smile on her face, just the reality of what could have been, . . . but life would go on after divorce.

SECTION 2

LIFE AFTER THE DIVORCES

INFINITY

Time - where did it go?
What did we do with all our time?

When we were young, the time moved so slow,
now we are grown and the time moves so fast.

But love could make time stand still.
We had all the time in the world, when we had love.

There were no yesterdays and no tomorrows,
There was only today and the endless nights together.

But now the time is gone,
. . . just like our love.

Where did it go?

CHAPTER 5

September, 1971

Connie thought it quite appropriate her court date was on her seventh wedding anniversary, an apt way to handle serious "seven-year itch." George, in a last ditch effort sent her flowers, and now phoning to beg her not to go through with it. Beth, coming in the back door, heard Connie stiffly and coldly say, "Even if I break my leg going down the back steps, it won't stop me!" It took her a while to make up her mind, but once she did, there was no backtracking. Beth was babysitting Connie's two boys, as she drove off to become the first in the "Suburbanite Divorce Revolution" - not seen on any news - but it changed them all.

    Beth spent many an hour playing Scrabble with Connie, who was quite a challenge at the game. Once their boys were ensconced at the daycare, Beth spent less time playing housewife, before they went to work. Usually, during their Scrabble marathons, they drank wine, and talked quite openly about their lives. During one of these sessions, Beth dropped the bombshell about wanting to have an affair, with a particular married-man from the Cafe' where they worked.

    Even in her slightly inebriated state, Connie was the only one she could talk to, and know she'd get a straightforward, honest answer about the consequences. "My marriage, what there was of it, went down hill faster after I started running around. If you spend time with other men, eventually you will find one that you do care for, or even fall in love with." She took another swallow of wine and a drag on her cigarette, as she pondered her concluding sentence, " . . . enough to even leave, your supposed to be happy home."

    Enough was the key word here, which Beth would learn more about in the future. The difference between just loving someone, and loving them *enough* to do something about it. Connie was considering her own statement, as she thought about Cam. She knew he loved her, but not enough to divorce his socially-invalid wife, who was controlling him through his own guilt. There was nothing physically wrong with her, she simply couldn't/wouldn't cope with the outside world. She existed in their very nice apartment all day and night, day after day. Connie continued on with her verbal warnings, and advice from her own experience of being involved with a married man.

"You are restricted where you can be seen together. And, of course, you rarely see them on the weekends, and never see them on any of the family-holidays. In fact, the only extended time you have together is if he travels, and you can go along." But her words were falling on already deaf-ears, because she'd made up her mind. She believed that there was more to love, life and sex than she encountered with Bruce.

Yet, she had no intention of jumping in bed with the men that already asked her. If she was putting her marriage in jeopardy, it was with a man that symbolized her every ideal. He'd have a good sense of humor, she so missed laughing, like with her brother Mike. She wanted intelligence, since she accepted that she was, along with success, so he'd have the extra bucks to spend on her - that would be nice for a change. Looks weren't key, but always a compliment to be with a good looking man. Perhaps, she was using these 'qualifications' as challenges to keep herself from going over the fence, to those acres and acres of greener-pastures that surrounded her.

Quite interesting, once Beth started looking, she saw things that she'd been blind to in the past. So, it was with one of her favorite customers, Rob. Beth began to notice that his eyes were always watching her, and he'd sit at the end of the bar, near the service area, whenever in the restaurant alone. When he brought his wife in for dinner, he'd ask to have her wait on them. Especially then, there was something in the way his eyes watched her, and his quick smile when she looked at him. She knew he was *not* the happily married man that everyone thought he was. Perhaps, he was as good at pretending as she was, and covering it with a big smile.

One evening when Beth was getting off work early, she mentioned to Rob that several of the waitresses were going next door, to the discotheque to hear the new band. Since he'd mentioned his wife was out of town, maybe he'd like to join them, and he jumped at the idea. He'd been there several times before with his wife, so it wasn't so unusual, except for the noticeable enthusiasm he'd come into the bar alone that night.

They danced and talked, as they slowly sipped their drinks. Eddie, the owner hadn't been surprised to see them, because Beth brought lots of customers over from the restaurant. When the bar closed up, they were having such a good time, Rob suggested they go somewhere else for a drink. They drove over in his car to another place down the main drag. After several more drinks, the conversation got around to sex, and them both revealing how unhappy they were with their sex lives.

Later, as he was pulling out of the parking lot to leave, Rob said, "I hope this doesn't offend you, but you turn me on." Beth was dazed, and his adolescent-verbiage also made him seen vulnerable. Here was one of the best looking men she'd seen in her life - her list of requirements ran through her head, checking each off for him. It was hard to believe, though overly nice to her, but then other waitresses also. *She turned him on, really, seriously?* Silent so long, he was afraid he had stepped over the line.

"I'm sorry, I shouldn't have said it." Rob pulled back.

"No," Beth quickly said. "I mean, don't be sorry if you meant it." She turned toward him.

"Yes, I meant it. I just didn't want you to be offended by it, and I could have said it better, I suppose, but it came out that way." He leaned back toward her.

"How can I be offended by it, when you turn me on, too." He pulled over to the side and slammed the brakes on the car.

"Really?" He truly had a shocked look on his face.

"Yes, really . . . I mean it . . . I think you're super." He leaned over to kiss her, and before they both knew what was happening, they were in an amorous embrace, kissing over and over again, until a horn blowing from another car woke them out of the spell.

Rob slowly drove back to the Cafe' for Beth's car. They sat in his car for almost an hour kissing and talking about how to have an affair. It'd been so long since Beth had a man touch her so desirously, she could not let him go. She vaguely remembered him saying something about, *'an affair was always good for a sagging marriage,'* whatever that meant. She floated home that night, more drunk on infatuation than alcohol could ever make her. She crawled in bed with Bruce, but could only dream of Rob touching her. Bruce had told her he didn't love her, so what did it matter. In her mind, she had the green light to go find it for herself.

Beth didn't want to tell Connie who the affair was with, and Rob asked her not to. News like that travels so fast anyways. He was a friend of Cam's, and at this time he didn't want him to know. It was as if Rob felt he was better than Cam, if no one knew he was cheating on his wife. As Connie realized she couldn't talk Beth out of the affair, she told her about where to go and what to do. Funny, Beth wouldn't know what to do, but she didn't. She'd always been the 'good girl,' and so adaptive that she couldn't imagine herself having an affair.

The next time Rob was in the Cafe', they set up the date right in front of his wife, while she flirted with another man. Cam often said Sylvia, Rob's wife, did her best work in the dark-lights of a bar room, because the daylight would send any man in the other direction, when he got a good look at her.

Beth was taking the hypnosis classes with Martha, her old college girlfriend, and the night of her class was the perfect excuse for seeing Rob. They usually went out after class, since they always had so much to talk about. Martha was upset about Beth's marriage going bad. She liked Bruce, and had patterned her marriage somewhat after Beth's, marrying an older man, to help him to find himself, while she'd given up finishing college and her career hopes. Truthfully, Beth didn't like him, and never would.

As Beth walked into the Cafe' to meet Rob, Connie was walking out and stated, "You're late. I told Rob to wait for you." She laughed when Beth tried to pretend she didn't know what Connie was talking about, but it was no use. "I've been watching the way you two have been looking at each other. If anyone could tell about these things, I can," replied Connie.

"Then come on in and have a drink at least, so it won't look so funny if both of us are here," Beth commented. They went in and sat on either side of Rob, laughing about running into each other outside. Beth whispered to Rob about Connie knowing, and not to worry about her telling anyone, especially Cam. After two drinks, the three of them left. Connie had been right, Rob was about to leave when she told him Beth was on her way. He'd forgotten about her class.

Walking to Rob's car, Beth was flabbergasted when Connie called out across the parking lot, "Don't do anything I wouldn't do!" She was anything but subtle.

As soon as they got in the car, Rob kissed her several times to reassure and relax her. First they drove to the Holiday Inn, but with all the cars, decided there was too much of a chance of being seen. Rob thought of a small motel on the north of town.

When they got into the cracker-box room, Beth was visibly shaking. *Hesitation . . . he was everything Bruce wasn't or ever would be. Hesitation . . . she never wanted anyone as much as she wanted Rob.* She slowly began taking off her clothes. Obviously, the bulk of this motel business was by the hour - *did she want to join that group? More hesitation . . .* she stopped with her bra and panties.

Rob came over to kiss and gently caress her to give her courage to finish undressing. He knew what a big step this was for her. She had been so straight and raised so strict, no matter what love-tag she put on this, it was still adultery. Rob understood completely, being marvelously patient. "I'd rather have you this way, than someone who just jumps into bed with anyone at a moment's notice." He pulled the cover back for her, then slid over to her.

Finally they were in bed together, and his body felt so different, compared to Bruce. The skin, so tan from his golf, and texture so smooth, with his auburn, wavy hair, seemed more masculine. His touch was more tender, yet positive in his control, as more sure of himself, though he too, was nervous for he didn't do this everyday either. Soon the passion of the extensive kissing and exploratory touching, made them both forget how nervous they were, and brought them both to a new level. Rob surprised himself, at being more adept at what he was doing than he'd ever been with Sylvia. The intensity of the climax he gave her, was more than the rare ones she had with Bruce. Yes, this was how sex truly was meant to be. He made her knees go weak when he kissed her, and she'd never had this affect from Bruce.

The room was filled with such euphoria they seemed in complete suspended animation. They laid entangled in each other's arms, as Beth began to compliment Rob, and he answered, "I'm only a reflection of you. I've never made love like this before." They continued to hold each other and talked of their shared experience. Before either of them planned on it, they were again carried away with making love. One of them was going to have to keep track of time.

When Beth got home, in bed with Bruce her body still tingled from the afterglow. Her heart began beating at such a pace, her breathing became spaced - surely Bruce would know. She did not feel any guilt for what she'd done. It'd been so long since she had any happiness or affection, she felt that she deserved every bit she could get, even if it came from another man. Her mind went back over every moment with Rob, feeling his gentle, sensuous touch and the fire he'd so completely filled her with. She slowly drifted off into a new kind of blissful sleep, like none she'd had before. The next morning, she waited for Bruce to notice something different about her. He'd not have considered another man looking twice at her, much less someone of Rob's caliber taking her to bed. Bruce took her so for granted, something he'd soon regret.

Rob called two days later and asked if he could see her that day. They got to the motel about eleven-thirty in the morning, and he dropped her off at Connie's at five o'clock in the afternoon. She'd brought Jeremy back to her place after nursery school. Connie almost died when Beth came struggling in the door, as the marathon-sex did not agree too-well with her. She quickly fixed her a drink to pull herself together, and she finally got home five minutes before Bruce, yet he still did not notice anything different about her.

Connie suggested she wear her sunglasses, because her eyes were still glazed over. Beth avoided looking Bruce in the eye, as she kept telling herself that she did not feel guilty, since she didn't have a marriage to be cheating on. Yet, Beth could not bring herself to continue going to church, or teaching Sunday School. She called the director to say she'd be too busy with the impending move, and getting the old house ready for sale. She could lie to Bruce, and lie to herself, but she could not lie to God anymore. She'd lied when she'd taken her wedding vows, and that was enough.

Beth'd been seeing Rob twice a week during the day, when they decided to try for a night. They were going to celebrate her birthday, since Bruce never really did. She told him that she'd be meeting Maura and Bobbie from college in Chicago for lunch, then go straight to her hypnosis class, which Martha planned for them to go out after. Since she'd been celebrating her birthday before at several different times with her friends, it didn't seem strange to him. And, he didn't have to make any excuse for doing nothing for it.

A fairy tale evening for Beth with Rob - drinks before and after dinner, each at a different place in Chicago, as he was quite familiar with it. The weather was so wonderful for November, they even walked by the lake for a while. Needless to say, she'd fallen in love with him, and though at this time not mutual, he did care a great deal for her. It was also the best sex he'd ever had, and he was not shy to admit it. Maybe her brother Mike had been right, she did have that something special, it had just taken her longer to find and share it with a good partner.

Still for Rob, while totally present when with her, when she was 'out of sight, she was out of mind.' As their time continued into a rhythm, she could see how he was shifting. Totally with her, as the only person in the world, yet almost visibly change into that other detached-person, as leaving her each time to go back into his plastic, phony-married world. Maybe that was how he handled their affair, and what worked best for him - his life.

Beth discussed this with Connie, since she only got criticism from April, and she'd already been with Cam for three years. Connie'd even been out with him and his wife several times. Eventually, Rob's excuses for not being able to get out more often began to bother Beth. If he really cared, it wouldn't be so difficult for him to get out. He was clever, he should be able to think of some kind of excuse. It seemed all she got from Rob was one excuse after another when she wanted another evening. Yet, if he called with a gap in his schedule, she'd fill it for him as quick as she could get Jeremy situated. Yes, Rob had more concerns about being seen with her, or his being 'caught,' as the nice lunches were often dropped for motel time.

Then, he told her of Sylvia being out of town, but didn't call until almost nine in the evening after he'd been drinking, and she had rearranged her work schedule to spend the evening with him. It was too obvious for her to be home, and hanging around waiting for the phone to ring. Bruce kept asking what was going on, as she'd said she was meeting Martha to go to a movie. Still, if Rob needed to see her, as in horny, she'd be there for him. So, though he made her so happy horizontally, he wasn't giving as much as she gave, same with everything else, she usually gave over one hundred percent.

One night Beth was in The Place getting bombed with Connie, as Cam was out of town, and she couldn't go with him. Roy, the darling bartender noticed Beth a bit down, drinking heavier than usual, while Connie doing her usual attacking of Pete, the other bartender. She did sleep with other guys because she felt she didn't have Cam sewed up, and should always have an extra 'ace-in-the-hole,' so to speak. Beth felt it was one thing to cheat on her husband, but quite another to cheat on her lover, though he was married, also.

After several more drinks, Beth started talking to a good friend of Eddie's, the owner. Actually, if there was anyone Beth would've liked to have had sex with, it was Eddie. They had several brief encounters, but Eddie wouldn't consider screwing her because he felt she was above cheating on her husband. After talking more to Eddie's friend, Beth decided to go with him to another bar which stayed open later. Everyone was surprised when she left with him, but when they got to his car, he made the mistake of jumping her.

One thing she didn't like, or put up with was the rough act, it seemed too much like the college-boys in a hurry. Since he only had sex on his mind, she got out and went home. Beth, letting some of the Scorpio-sting out, told Rob about the incident in front of his wife Sylvia, when they were in together. Somehow she wanted to hurt him for not spending more time with her. Of course, he couldn't say anything in front Sylvia, and she wanted him to also know, he didn't have her one hundred percent any more.

Funny to Beth that before she started with Rob, Bruce always accused her of screwing around, yet now that she was, he never said anything. They had sex once since she first asked him for the divorce, and that was before her birthday. The only time Bruce was suspicious, was the night Connie invited Roy and Pete over to her house for a party, and insisted she came, too. A Friday, so she wouldn't have to get up in the morning for Bruce, which she did every day, no matter how drunk the night before. The four of them were sitting at the table talking, when Connie got up and lead Pete into her bedroom.

Awkward for a moment for Roy and Beth, but they were so bombed, they didn't bother to make a move toward one another. Roy was on the short side, so Beth felt gangly around him. Connie always teased that she was going to take him home in her purse. Later, when Pete and Connie re-emerged, they all sat around on the floor in the living room until they passed out. They were listening to music and occasionally talked to one another. Beth soon realized Connie went to bed alone, so she got up and crawled into bed with her, as there was no way she could drive even the short distance to her house.

Connie had no idea Beth was there until morning, when startled by her body close by. The guys never made it off the living room floor, and the four of them were quite a sight in the morning, having slept in their clothes. Real swingers they were not. About nine when Beth got home that morning, without saying a word, Bruce kicked her in the ass. She didn't try to explain any further than, she and Connie got drunk and passed out. There wasn't much else she could say, and she didn't care what he thought of her anymore.

Beth and Connie went to bars where they knew the bartender, and with Connie's bar-hopping experience, they never ran out of bars. It was good practice, because if they had a problem with a man, the bartender took care of it. Connie taught Beth never to accept drinks from a stranger, so no insinuated-obligation to him. She reminded Beth that screwing a man because he bought her dinner or some drinks, was a cheap-form of prostitution. So called, 'cheating' on Rob, had brought Beth into contact with #159 - such a beautiful, football-body, it had flattered her when he asked her. Somehow he reminded her of the football hero, that she let get away in college. There was no real excuse for her doing it except being wasted, horny and pissed at Rob - a lesson learned.

Beth had to admit Rob was there most of the time, when she needed him during her divorce. At first he was afraid, she'd expect him to get a divorce, but she never put pressure on him, and honestly she'd already realized he was not who she wanted for the long term. But, he'd listen, hold her close, as she vacillated between crying and outright-rage at how Bruce handled it. Especially bad, was the night she'd slept in the bathroom with Jeremy, the only inside door with a secure lock. Rob rarely made comments, only nodding or kissing her on the forehead while holding her. She told him the story of her wedding ring, which she moved to the right hand after the divorce, and then removed it all together from her hands.

Since Bruce did not officially ask Beth to marry him, she didn't want to bother with an engagement ring - also possible bad luck from the other two. But, she did want to design her wedding ring. Bruce gave the half-carat from the engagement ring he'd gotten back, and they got two ten-carat stones to go on either side of a lovely brushed, wide-gold band. She loved her ring until Bruce *had the need,* after compliments to her, to tell everyone the center half-carat was from his previous engagement. It not only shocked people that he'd say it, but embarrassed her as if a 'leftover.' He used the excuse he believed in honesty, even if it hurt, until she got furious at him repeatedly saying it. She said, If you bring it up again, I'll shove it down your throat." She came to hate the ring, as it related to so many little things he'd done to hurt her.

Just before the divorce, Bruce'd wait-up for Beth in the dark living room, then the moment she walked in the door from work, he'd start about what had gone wrong with their marriage. He'd dissect it the way he'd done their sex, until it was clinical. She tried to keep Jeremy out of the battle, yet he would invariably wake him up. With Rob, alcohol, and her friends, Beth numbed her way through the month before Bruce gave up, and moved back to his parents. She felt she owed Rob loyalty, as he stuck with her through the mental-torture. At that point in her life, she needed someone, even a married man to help fill the gap that friends and booze couldn't.

Considering everything, Beth pulled the whole affair off pretty smoothly. Bruce was convinced there had never been another 'single' man in her life. She did almost slip one night when she was drunk and horny. She rolled against Bruce in bed and started to seduce him, to his surprise. She was just about to call him Rob, when she realized who she had her hands on and stopped. He never said a thing to her about the incident.

And while, Beth would always be grateful to Rob for his support throughout the divorce, also her attorney Lou had been incredible. His speed, and remembering all the little things to get in writing for the divorce: insurance for Jeremy, child support and equal division of the property were just a few of the things that she had to learn. After much study and advice, she became quite an authority on a fair divorce, and there'd be many *men* and women she'd counsel and advise. She knew what it had been like, when she had absolutely no one to ask the questions of. The lonely, lostness that Connie, Beth and sometimes April might go through was something perhaps, they could share with others going down that long trail to freedom.

Soon they became almost legendary authorities on divorce, at the restaurant alone loaded with women who didn't know squat about their rights, and where a line should be drawn when dealing with a physical or psychological abusing-spouse. Almost, as if 'in the air' in the 1970s, everywhere they went seemed to be people talking about divorce, and the questions never stopped. Since they'd heard so many divorce stories, and shared experiences, the data became eclectic information to be doled out to those in need of it. It was obvious, there were a lot of women around their age, raised only to be submissive to their husbands, and give their lives totally to home and family rather than anything for *Self.* After you heard so many experiences, they tended to fall into categories. Also, there was no sexual preferences in helping, as the men friends - which there were many - had their sides to tell, too.

The consoling was given with sincerity, though sometimes there was a bit of hype or jive thrown in for the absurd or redundant person. Especially, if they thought they weren't going to listen anyway. Many women suffering their own insecurities, didn't know what to ask for in a divorce, and many attorneys were not prepared as the divorce explosion swung into full gear. The men, too, did not realize if they were being taken to the cleaners, or if the money-payment was justification for whatever guilt they had. Discussion and counseling on married boyfriends was a much smaller and more clandestine group.

And, though Beth and Connie occasionally saw other men, there was still a lot of time on their hands, because their 'main-man' was married. They needed support and reassurance of their lifestyle, and it brought the friendship ever closer together. Many nights Beth joined Connie and Cam in the bar, as he had a freer marriage than Rob. Cam always enjoyed butting heads with Beth, though sometimes he felt her newly-found independence influencing Connie to be more self-reliant of him, which he did not want. Still, Cam was a funny, clever man who usually made them laugh, and always good for all.

April still lectured Beth about Rob being a married, though she'd started going out on Wally. Unfortunately, she held onto believing the stigma that *'only another man'* in her life - both emotionally and sexually - would bring her back to life. April did not think she could get a divorce on her own, she needed a man to have the courage to change her life. She didn't want a 'sometime-man,' she wanted a new, permanent twenty-four-seven man, in other words without saying it, she wanted a new husband to take care of her. She really didn't want 'freedom' per se, as she had no real interest in working to support herself, much less her daughters.

This was how she was totally different from the others, they wanted a man, but more so their own 'freedom of choice as to the man,' *and everything else* in their lives. April only wanted to go out into the world for the opportunity to meet somebody, who could give her totally new life she wanted. As if he was simply going to show up at her door, like the Fuller Brush Salesman did. As much as she was studying her hypnosis, astrology and metaphysics, she was still looking *outside herself* for satisfaction of her life. Beth, Connie and later Michael, would learn the actions they took should be *their own choices, then learn from their mistakes*. Beth tried to remind April that anything was better than staying at home, and turning into a lump.

Connie always joked, "Be sure you get their first and last names to turn into the clinic, if you pick-up the wrong-someone." Beth reminded April to be very selective in whom she picked-up, as she did not have the excuse of drinking, as the others did.

Touch Me

Touch me - I mean touch me all over
and not just with your hands,
Touch me.

Touch me in my heart, my soul
and my mind,
Touch me.

I want to be alive - really alive
and that's what you make me -
when you touch me.

I feel brand-new and it's all because
of you, and the way you
Touch me.

I was hiding in my shell, you pried
it open, pulled out and
Touched me.

I said you were just a man
and there had been many before,
but none had Touched me.

The past is gone, like yesterday's news
with all its blues, because of the way
you Touch me.

Just Touch Me.

CHAPTER 6

Making a Sandwich

The week of Beth's divorce, she ran into Sam, the guy she'd almost slept with when pregnant. It had been four years since she saw him, and he still remembered her. The only thing he taught her: a man who talks about his sexual prowess usually doesn't have any. Beth was beginning to get a reference to judge some of the men by that she met, whether in a sexual content or other. She set up a scale of one to ten - Bruce at his best a three; Rob at best an eight. From the stories Connie told her, and what April was learning, Beth filed away details for future reference in grading for her scale.

A new idea, Connie and Beth talked about, was making a man 'sandwich.' Though Connie shared with another girl, a guy in bed, they'd never been with the man at the same time. The basic 'rule' for it to work was equal-equanimity - in other words, NO jealousy - that meant neither woman could be *more attached* to the man than the other - turned on, 'yes.' This meant pure fun or the newest term - recreational-sex. They hadn't thought of the French term - *'ménage à trois.'* The more they talked about it, the more exciting it seemed, especially to Beth. Truly anxious to make-up for all her 'lost' time when married. She'd try anything that seemed wild and fun. She simply wanted so bad to be almost-bad, if only for a while.

They constantly talked about a 'sandwich' to everyone, and tried to get Pete, Roy or Eddie from The Place, to be their first experiment. Of course, being the great-bullshitters they had become when drinking, they talked like they'd done it a thousand times. Eddie particularly, shook his head thinking, it had all been Connie badly-influencing Beth since her divorce. One night Beth was leaning over the service bar giving Roy a good night kiss - they rarely paid for their drinks, but did tip well. The big, beautiful hunk of a bouncer, named Don, gave her a swat on her butt, which was sticking up. The bombed Beth swung around and started attacking his body - she'd learned exactly what to do with her lovely, full-boobs. It took a few minutes for Don to remove the slithery body pressed against his. He'd only swatted her to get her attention to leave, since closing time. Which he kept trying to tell her, but she kept kissing him, as she rubbed her body up and down against his. "How would You like to be *our sandwich* tonight?" Beth perkily asked, as Connie came walking up.

"Sandwich? What are you talking about?" Don questioned staring, but intrigued.

Now with his attention, she purred seductively, "Haven't you ever had two beautiful girls make a sandwich out of you?" Beth's smile went ear to ear, as the devilishness came into her eyes, knowing Don couldn't believe what he was hearing. She coyly went on to explain, while Connie stood shaking her head 'no,' and her eyes bugging out. Before Beth realized, Don was ready, willing and able to follow them to Connie's house. Unfortunately, this began a long line of bad situations, where Beth's drinking too much - *'her mouth got her ass in trouble.'*

Connie was absolutely furious with Beth, "How could you have said such a thing?" Beth didn't understand, Don turned both of them on - that fulfilled the rule, what was the problem? After more talk, Connie agreed and at her house she said she'd join them in the bedroom. Having such a super time with Don, Beth didn't miss Connie until they'd both climaxed. She kissed Don, holding up her forefinger that she'd be back in a minute. She went into the living room to find Connie sitting on the couch drinking. Nude, Beth sat down to find out what was the matter, sometimes Connie could get self-conscious about something. She'd gotten a rash on her front chest and back, though it wasn't contagious, she didn't want any man but Cam to see it.

Beth didn't hesitate to argue, she simply rejoined Don making a weak apology, which didn't seem to phase him a bit, as he was having a great time. Recalling and adding to her scale, Beth decided that Don was her greatest lay so far! And, that young, fantastic body -

he wasn't an Atlas overdone, but perfect - so on the scale, a 'nine' - a perfect rough-cut diamond of the highest quality. If the edges were more smoothly polished, and they hadn't been pressed for time, he'd have been a 'ten' easily. Sandwich or no, she had gotten him, acknowledging she'd lusted over a year for him. Congratulating herself, only divorced a month and already had three of the men she'd wanted to try. The fourth one, really was number one on the fantasy list - the impossible list for just about every woman in the U.S.A.

Beth followed the career of Bobby Ryan, since his first, small part in a television series back in the early sixties. As his career advanced, from one series to another, with several "B" movies thrown in as he rose higher, Beth watched with more than intrigue. There was something about Bobby, maybe the same 'sexual aura' she knew from Mike, learning so well herself. Also, he had one of the wittiest minds, few people realized until on Johnny Carson's show several times.

She always noticed the smirk he'd had when delivering the drabbest lines, she really loved satire. Then, 'lo and behold,' Bobby was to perform a play at a big, theater-hotel in-the-round on the Northside. It was an opportunity to reenact his 'Tony' winning performance, and give his career an authentic/credible boost. Connie only recently followed his career, but was absolutely crazy about him. They decided to get several of the girls from the Cafe' together, to go see him during the week, as they agreed about him being the newest sex-symbol.

Always a great believer in fate, whether good or bad for the lessons to be learned, Beth felt she *could* control her future in many ways, but sometimes destiny was still up to fate - *And,* playing all the wild cards. She was recognizing, if it's meant to be, it will and everything good and bad happens for a reason - just don't let *any* opportunities be passed up. The date of their night out changed several times, with a couple of the girls dropping out. Carrie landed in the hospital unexpectedly, so then only Little Mary and her sister Jo joined with Connie and Beth. The seats were excellent, and Connie so thrilled she almost wet her pants.

She had never seen a live play before, nor a movie star that close-up. Exciting for Beth only because it was Bobby Ryan, as she'd seen many plays and met local stars when working at the advertising company. To say she thought Bobby was fantastic, put it mildly, but a bit prejudiced. She felt Bobby had the charming wit of Cary Grant, the sexual charisma of Clark Gable, the machismo of Steve McQueen, the satirical bite of Paul Newman, with a little-boy suaveness of Robert Redford. Even without sex, on her scale of one to ten, he'd have been a fifteen.

Since Bobby's nude centerfold just came out, there were hundreds in the theater foyer waiting for his autograph. Little Mary and Jo decided not to wait, so left to get something to eat and drink. Connie insisted on waiting in the bar till the crowd thinned out to get his autograph. Beth tried to talk her out of it, but gave in when she realized what excitement the night had been for Connie. So star-struck, only seeing and touching him would satisfy her now. When they returned to the foyer, Beth for lack of something better to do, stood in line with Connie - besides her enthusiasm had become contagious.

Women of all ages were still all over the place, taking pictures and kissing Bobby, as he was generous with his time and attention. By Connie's turn, she couldn't say anything, but Bobby noticed her full breasts immediately - the low-cut neckline helped. "My, what a *'healthy'* girl you are!" The sly smile spread across his face, as his job wasn't so boring now. "I like *'healthy'* girls." Connie, stunned he'd spoken to HER, mumbled her name, so he could sign her Playbill.

They were both wearing rather fitted pantsuits, Connie's blue and Beth's red. As Beth stepped up next, Bobby indicated his evening was definitely improving with two in a row, "My goodness, you are even *'healthier'* than she is! You two together?" They nodded, 'yes' as he added, "Quite *'a group'* you have there." Beth laughed, and told him her name. When they stepped away, Connie got so nervous she almost fell apart, not believing he'd really talked to *them*. Beth was surprised at his interest in them, as she'd met many phony-people when she worked in advertising. She thought of him as a great personality, but she never considered he'd be such a nice person to them. On the other hand, most of the women were considerably older, and not nearly as shapely, or showing it off as they did.

As they walked back through the foyer, Connie still didn't want to leave. "We've got to think up some excuse to go back and talk to him again." Beth could see her hopes were building like the 'star-struck' kid she was. It was funny to see her like that, men didn't impress her much any more, with all the money and some celebrity that came into the Cafe'. Suddenly, an idea struck Beth, and she picked up some extra Playbills saying, "We'll get him to autograph these for the girls that couldn't come tonight!"

When they returned, Bobby acknowledged them like long-lost friends. "Well, it's the *healthy-twins* again. What can I do for you now, girls?" Beth told him of Carrie being in the hospital, and Connie rattled off several others who couldn't come, and wanted Playbills.

Just as he finished, Connie said with the last ounce of courage and desperate hope, "Would you autograph me, here . . . too?" She'd pulled her scooped neck to the side, so he could sign on her chest. She barely kept from shaking, and feared his refusal.

Bobby chuckled with delight, as he signed away, "You girls are really something!"

Beth asked while the moment was ripe, "Would you like to join us in the bar for a drink?

Bobby turned to look at her, "I'll be in there in a few minutes." He smirked fully.

Connie's feet never touched the ground, as she waltzed back to the bar. Even Beth was actually excited. Connie sighed, "Wouldn't you like to jump *that one*. Talk about the impossible dream?!?" She picked up her drink with both hands, and put the glass to her forehead to cool her.

Beth calmly replied, "No, not at all. I heard him say on Johnny Carson, he really didn't have a lot of women, being so busy and all. I bet he's got extra time here to be interested."

Connie stared at her replying slowly, "Ss-hhit!" They quietly pondered over their drinks, when she suddenly said, "You've got to say something impressive or cool!"

Beth turned to look at her, as Connie supposedly was the experienced one around men. "What the hell am I supposed to say?" she snapped, as Connie often reminded her of lacking it.

"I don't know. You're the one that worked in advertising! Think of something quick, here he comes," she whispered.

After making the rounds talking with several people, Bobby walked over to them. "So, how are *My* healthy-girls doing?" The smirk was back on, with his eyes twinkling.

"Just fine," answered Beth with more confidence than she expected to project. "It was a superb play." She was giving him back, as much of the devil-may-care attitude as she could.

"Good, I'm glad you liked it," he seemed to be watching them both closely.

Connie leaned over, desperately looking at Beth to say something significant. Seeing her out of the corner of her eye, and feeling her energy, Beth asked: "Did you ever have a suburban sandwich?" It was more than a coquettish-smile that crossed her face.

"What?" Bobby asked, his ears almost perking at the remark.

Connie mumbled, "Oh, My God!" It was definitely not what she expected.

"A '*suburban sandwich*,'" as Beth pointed her finger from Connie back to herself.

Bobby just looked from one to the other, "Yea, I know what a sandwich is, what's the suburban part? And, are you serious?" He truly couldn't believe what he'd just heard.

"Yes, we're serious, and the '*suburban'* part is the extra '*mayo'* of the two of us." She was almost dead-panning it, as if he should have figured that part out. Her quirky smile was completely straight forward, waiting for a reply.

Bobby then quickly said, "Listen, you girls *don't* go away. I promised that group of *women* I'd have coffee with them. I'll be back in fifteen minutes." He quickly scooted off.

Beth reached the ultimate in excitement, while Connie was dazed beyond description, since she could not believe Beth had said what did. She looked at Connie, "Why the hell not? All he could say was '*no,'* and so far he hasn't. Don't you want to have sex with a famous movie star like him?" She brimmed with comic-confidence, as to what she'd said, and likely pulled off.

"Yea, sure, but it's all too unbelievable. This has got to be a dream, and I've drunk too much again." She ordered more drinks for them both, as if the alcohol would help them cope with the bizarre situation Beth created. She checked Connie's watch, and the fifteen minutes were up. Beth grabbed a cocktail napkin and wrote on the back, "Your sandwich is waiting." She sent the folded note over to him via the waitress. Bobby asked her to tell them, he'd be over in five minutes.

Before they knew it, Bobby was at their side again. "Well, where are we going to have *our little get-together?*" His eyes and smile elated, as if how lucky could one guy get?

Whether the alcohol or reality, Connie woke up, and told him at her house. "I can't make it tonight girls, I have a TV interview for one of the early-morning shows. I'm also tied up Wednesday, but Thursday is free. Why don't you wait outside the back entrance, at about eleven?" They were both in shock, not only had he accepted, but HE had set the date, time and place. After more formal 'goodbyes,' they all nodded. "Till Thursday, good night," as he smiled his famous smile, turned and sauntered to the elevator to go to his room.

At first, it would've taken a crane to move them. They were both so stunned, they had petrified onto the bar stools. By the time they got to Beth's car, they were both talking a thousand words a minute. For once Beth's new, big mouth turned out to beneficial - possibly. They decided at first not to tell anybody, as if not to jinx it, or have it get back to Cam or Rob. Also, they didn't want to broadcast it too much, in case it didn't work out for some reason. It was still almost Tuesday, though close to midnight, as they drove home - Thursday was two-light years away. How they lived those two days they didn't know - sleep became hard to come by.

At eleven o'clock on Thursday, Connie and Beth were right where they were supposed to be. Suddenly, Bobby came bounding out the back door, and over to the car only a few minutes late. After giving them each a kiss, he explained he'd be tied up about an hour with the autographs. He suggested they go sit in the bar, and he'd make sure he was out in an hour. Beth used the public phone to call April when they got to the bar, as it truly was going to happen - he promised to show up. She called Lynne, the babysitter, to confirm to her about staying overnight. She had the three kids at Beth's house, as planned ahead.

Sitting in the bar, sucking down their drinks, the tension and nerves building like a dormant-volcano about to blow its cool. They inhaled their second drink, while continuously glancing at Connie's watch. Without saying a word, they looked at each other and burst out laughing. Connie kept repeating: "This is all a dream. This could not possibly be happening *to me.*" Beth kept giggling, and nodding in agreement.

Back in Beth's little, bright-orange Super-Beetle waiting only a few minutes when Bobby again came running out to the car. When he said that he'd follow them over, Connie jumped out of the car to join him. Beth called - not too loudly after her, "You Bitch! It's not fair to start without me!" With Connie's directions, even though Bobby took the lead in his car, Beth was right on his tail pushing her Beetle. Connie wasn't going to lose her tonight, she had more experience, but Beth had shown she had more guts. She'd begged Beth to let her have Bobby alone, since she thought she could give him a more exciting time. Beth didn't care if she only laid next to him, and never got to do a thing, she wasn't going to be left out of what she'd engineered.

Connie had Bobby take a different way to her house, which she thought would be faster. He'd been speeding all the way, but Beth still pulled into the driveway just ahead of them. She then bounced out of the car with a new found agility, after working all night. "God, you're fast," Bobby remarked, impressed by her driving.

Not to let a remark like that go, Beth easily quipped, "Most men have trouble keeping up with me," snapping - trying to be both cute and worldly - the pretending built confidence.

"I'm going to try like hell," Bobby replied, constantly surprised by *his find*.

Connie, first up the steps to open the door, Georgie barked like crazy at the strange man. Bobby jerked back into Beth, obviously shaken by Georgie's huge presence. "Don't be afraid, it's just Georgie, she's a real pussycat. Come on in, for God's sake!"

Bobby thought Connie was nuts. "Georgie, she . . . Georgie is a pussycat. Georgie *looks* like a Great Dane, and *she* sounds like a he." He slowly entered the modest domain.

Beth and Bobby stood by the fireplace talking about the amazing statements in the book *The Human Zoo,* from the book shelf, when Connie brought in the drinks. He didn't quit surprising Beth with his realness - good looks, a great body, and now an enthralling mind. As the trio sat on the couch talking and laughing, Connie began to get the look of a deprived and/or depraved lioness about to attack a beautiful gazelle. Beth was cracking-up, when Bobby realized their small talk was a waste of precious time to Connie.

Suddenly, the room was filled with horniness. The trio became a three-ring circus, as they started disrobing and seducing each other's bodies. It was absolutely wild, that even without a single rehearsal, Connie and Beth performed like they'd been doing their 'sandwich-routine' on movie stars and other minor-men for years. By the time they adjourned to the bedroom, there was little left to take-off, since they were now only concerned with *getting-it-on.*

They all giggled and laughed till they cried, it was crazy-silliness. Every now and then someone would ask who's leg this was, or who's hand was that? With every question, there'd be another burst of laughter, no matter what anyone was doing. Bobby's sharp, comic mind, and witticisms amazed, along with his sexual talent. After the first incredible session, he asked, "Could I have something to eat? I mean if I'm going to last all night with you two fantastic ladies, I'm going to need something to keep my strength up."

Beth rolled off of him, laughing hysterically. Connie slid out of the bed, and pranced down the hall to the kitchen. Beth took the opportunity to delve into his mind. She loved the sex, but a fascinating mind turned her on - sometimes more. Connie soon returned presenting a peanut butter and jelly sandwich with a glass of milk. Bobby sat up against the headboard and devoured it like a rare steak. He'd hardly finished, when Connie once again attacked his body, almost obsessed, trying to accomplish as much as possible, before someone burst her bubble.

She'd kept saying, as much to confirm to herself, "It's really him, isn't it Beth? He's real, this isn't a dream? We're not making this up, are we?" Between two and three in the morning, the phone rang. Since Connie was busy giving Bobby oral sex, Beth answered in case it was Lynne calling regarding the kids. It turned out to be Connie's girlfriend, Marty, who wanted to know if Bobby was there. Apparently, Connie had told more people of their plot. She took the phone, as she couldn't pass up the opportunity to say: "Yes, he's right here! Where? At the moment he's under me. Sure, you can talk to him," as she passed the receiver to Bobby.

Bobby started talking in one of his funny, impersonating-voices, as Marty kept asking him dumb, typical questions, as if to verify it was him. Bobby's patience was wearing-thin, "I'm busy, busy, busy, so I'll say goodbye, because I don't want to stop having my fun." Connie almost fell off of him from laughing. Not satisfied, Marty called again, but then they took the phone off the hook - only so many interruptions were comical.

Beth again was surprised by how Bobby *was* making love to her, even with Connie's distractions, he *really was* making love, as if they were alone together. This was the tender side of his sexiness. His unbelievably sensual touch, with his mouth and tongue like they could spend hours exploring every curve, and hidden spot on her body.

His hand, slowly-barely touching, moved across her face and down her neck, all the time his mesmerizing eyes studying her. As if tracing, some magnificent painting only they could see. With bathroom breaks and drinks refreshed, they talked about both of their previous marriages, and what had gone wrong. One thing Bobby did say, that Beth would never forget, was his idea of total-love-making - "The before and after are just as important, as the in-between."

With this indicated respect for sex and love, as something that neither of them wanted to admit to jumping into for kicks, Beth had to ask why he decided to join them for this romp. Bobby slowly answered, "Somehow, deep inside, I knew you were both honorable girls, wth virtuous intentions." They all laughed at this one, though he added he knew, "You weren't some 'weird-kinky' type who'd tie him up or something."

Semi-joking, Connie asked, "You want me to go look for some rope in the garage, I think I might have some?" Now it was Bobby almost falling out of bed with laughter.

"I did know, more than anything that we'd have a lot of laughs together - which is also important in any good, sex-relationship. And, we certainly have." They all continued to laugh, with Beth's jaws starting to hurt from it.

Beth loved Rob, but also loved this man who had transformed from a fantasy to a real human being. Bobby became more man and lover than her fantasies could have ever portrayed him. Somehow, he was like a mutant of the Hollywood scene, that rare-bird who truly loved and enjoyed women, maybe that was his difference. Bobby brought more sexual excitement to Beth and Connie than either one of them ever experienced before. Concerned that Connie didn't have an orgasm, she assured him that he'd given her more than any climax could have. It was difficult to explain to 'the hero,' what satisfaction there was in hero-worship.

They'd almost destroyed the queen-size bed, and for a break, they moved back to the couch in living room. Bobby on top of Connie, while nibbling on Beth's boobs, when they rolled off to the floor laughing hysterically. Connie mentioned, at that moment, they *were* Bobby's favorite sandwich - a club with extra mayo. They all got rug-burns, as positions changed once again. Yes, one 'helluva' night, not only had he kept up with Beth, but also the insatiable Connie.

At six o'clock in the morning, Beth and Bobby were sitting on the bed getting dressed - exhausted, but obviously happy. Connie stood by with only her panty-hose and knee-high suede boots on, at the side of the bed. Bobby looked at the pose Connie had unconsciously struck - her glorious long, auburn hair almost framing her full, poised breasts.

At first, he called her the "Happy-Hooker," to which Connie replied, "Anyone for whips and cold oranges?" They all started laughing again, obviously Bobby knew the old joke. It had been almost six incredible, amazing hours of rollicking-sex and hilarious laughter, with jaws and sides aching, other parts merely numb. Connie had burned several candles and some incense, but even with all the showers they'd taken, the room still had the unique, lusty-scent of sex.

When finished dressing, Bobby turned to Beth and said, "I've been trying to think who it is you remind me of all night. If you," he lightly touched her face, "had a cute mole right here, you'd look just like Anne Francis. She's one of my favorite actresses and friends." Beth thought she'd melt right there before his eyes. He'd complimented them both, so many times that night Beth couldn't believe his sincerity. He'd proven her wrong about being jaded, as she'd earlier judged him before knowing him.

Bobby talked about Connie and Beth joining him in New York, where he'd be making his new movie. He also wanted to see them both again before he left the Chicago area. So Bobby would know if it was them that called, he said to use the nicknames of *Franny and Zooey*, from J.D. Salinger's book, that Beth had read. He also was going to say those names, when he said hello to them from the Johnny Carson show. Connie had explained that life for them would go on after he left, so they didn't want their boyfriends to find out what they'd done. Later, they laughed about taking out a full page ad in the Tribune, to tell everybody who they'd been to bed with.

Before he left, Bobby signed the magazine centerfold picture for each of them. He signed Connie's picture, "Franny, the world's greatest mouth." When Beth saw this she asked, "Make mine something a little less obvious, since I want to hang it where everyone can see it." Bobby signed, "Zooey, you're the most 'healthy' lady in the world."

Connie rode back to the Cafe' with him to get her car, and gave him directions back to his hotel. Beth stretched out on the bed and thought back over the entire evening. There was only one way to describe Bobby Ryan - SUPER! On the old scale, Bobby truly had turned out to be a fifteen. This would turn out to be one of the most significant evenings in Beth's life. From that day on, she would feel more than worthy of any man in the world. After having been put down for so many years by Bruce, she certainly had been escalated to the highest peak in one night. She felt like she was *'a somebody,'* and she could do anything she set her mind to do.

Time & Love

Time - There was a time
when we had nothing, but time.

Love - There was a love
that nothing but time, could destroy.

I gave you my time,
every minute of every day
you were on my mind.

I gave you my love,
like I'd never given it before.

And just like the time,
you let it slip through your hands.

We had something that very few
ever experienced in their lifetime.

But you didn't take the time to realize
what love had been given to you.

Love is like a burning fire,
that must be rekindled by more love,
to keep it glowing bright.

You let the light die out.

Chapter 7

Not Who I Dreamed

Over at nine o'clock the next morning, April wanted a minute by minute, stroke by stroke description. As usual, when asking how big he was, she wasn't asking about his height. Being more of a 'doubting-Thomas' than Marty, she wanted some proof to make sure. Why hadn't Beth thought to bring her Polaroid with her was questionable, as if she'd take nude photos of Bobby!. Beth began to tell the story which she would repeat a hundred times in the future. Of course, not quite so explicit as the version April insisted on.

Before she progressed very far, Connie came over. As she talked, Beth realized no matter how may times they'd tell the story, they solely had the real memory. Only the two of them to share and laugh about, till 'death do them part.' Like pulling-off the perfect crime - sharing it among their peer-group, but they'd never receive the notoriety they deserved for their performance.

Connie and Beth decided to go Friday and Saturday night again, to see Bobby after the play. He singled them out, and introduced them to some of his friends, but his schedule wouldn't let him get away. He also had an unexpected, famous-female guest come into town. If nothing else, this would be the world's greatest one-night-stand. Leaving for New York the following day, but Bobby remembered later to say hello to them from Johnny Carson's show. He'd gotten so much publicity from his centerfold, they were sure he'd forget them. The following Saturday morning, Bobby called Connie from New York. He said he was lonely, and would sure like Franny and Zooey to help keep him warm on those cold, New York nights. Connie said they'd send some Polaroid photos until the real thing could be with him.

It was Beth's idea for them to pose by Bobby's centerfold picture, which she hung over her bed. Just to be safe, in case they got lost or something, none of the photographs had their faces in them. One terrific shot was of Connie in her 'whips and cold oranges' outfit of panty-hose and knee-high boots. Standing on catalogues and phone books, balanced on the bed with her legs spread, so Bobby's head in the centerfold was between her legs. It took them all afternoon to get the photos, because of laughing so much.

Mainly the bare-boobs were photographed, so Beth thought a group picture of 'the girls' would be riotous. It took three photos of them together, before she'd gotten it right - arm-in-arm, boob to boob, they were jointly holding the camera at arm's length. They composed a letter, and sent the photos off to the lonely, cold super-star to help keep him warm. Apparently, someone got to him before and warmed him up, as neither one heard from him again. But Bobby would mention them in an interview for a *Penthouse* magazine and even in his own book about letters he received.

Connie and Beth weren't hurt, their fairy tale lasted longer and was better than any they'd heard of before. It wasn't exactly the kind of story they could tell their kids, or future grand-children. But over the years it sure brought back some funny, warm memories of one fantasy that came true. Beth often considered that she might meet him again at a different level, maybe more equal. Connie thought she was crazy, but then Beth always did have nutty ideas. Bobby saw something in Beth she'd never realized before, so who knew what the gods-of-fate might bring to her. Perhaps, she *was* capable of anything she wanted badly enough.

If nowhere else, Beth and Connie were celebrities at The Place. They were afraid to broadcast their adventure too much at the Cafe', with Cam and Rob coming in all the time. They told both of them, only that they'd been out drinking with Bobby, and others from the play. Most of the guys at The Place, now looked at them in a different light. The first time they thought of Beth as a swinger, and that Connie had real class. She wan't just jumping in bed with anybody these days, it was a famous movie star! The offers for a 'sandwich' came in from all over, even guys they didn't know before. Beth retorted, "We save the mayo for special occasions now."

Since Beth hung her autographed centerfold over her bed, Rob was jealous of it, to the extent he felt more than drinking had gone on. Any other guy who made a lewd remark about Bobby, either got kicked out of Beth's bed, or hit over the head. Connie followed everything Bobby was doing in his career and personal life. She wanted to go to New York to look him up, but Beth made her realize they'd all go on living their lives as they did before, only better. So, the trio became a duet without April. Connie and Beth went everywhere together, and tried to keep one another from getting into too much trouble. They'd cover for one another at work, and to Cam or Rob if there was someone else they were sleeping with.

They went through a period of having to prove to themselves that they were sexy to other men. Still, dealing with past feelings of their husbands rejecting them, they made sure they had that femme-fatale attraction. It became a game some nights, to see how many guys they'd excite and then turn down. Eventually, they hit a plateau, and it all tapered off. Funny, in their own way this kept them true to Rob and Cam. There wasn't another man either one was in love with, yet they didn't sit down in front of the television, because the 'boys' had to take their wives out that night.

Sometimes Connie'd almost had to hit Beth over the head when she'd get too wild. One night at The Place, she'd gotten quite drunk after work, perhaps if the booze hadn't been free, she might not have indulged so much. Beth's turn to drive, so closing time came, but Connie couldn't find her anywhere around. She remembered seeing her with some guy, but it wasn't like her to leave without saying something, or giving Connie the keys. She'd gone back to the car for the third time, when she saw Beth practically falling out of a nearby car - the windows all fogged up. She stumbled across the parking lot, when Connie called to her. Laughing she awkwardly climbed into her orange Bug, insisting on being sober enough to drive. Connie started to argue with her, when she noticed how disarrayed she was, "My God, Beth what the hell happened to your hair?"

Beth reached up, and touched her head, "My wig?!? It's gone, oh, SHIT!!" Before Connie could stop her, she was out of the car searching madly for her wig. By this time, the guy's car was gone, and no wig was in sight. Connie sat in the car laughing hysterically, as Beth plundered though the nearby weeds, and the parking lot wildly looking for her wig. The truly, staggering person was on the verge of tears. "You know how much that fucking wig cost?" Beth shouted to anyone who might be in ear-shot.

The drive home was enough to give the average person heart failure. Beth bounced from curb to curb barely missing cars, as Connie was ready to get out, when she barely missed skimming a tree. Connie's babysitter insisted on walking home, rather than ride with Beth in her condition. The next day Connie felt she should have a talk with Beth about her drinking, and acting like a swinger. "Time to cool it, Beth. You're going off the deep end. There's a difference between risqué and just plain tacky - the wig-incident last night was tacky, very tacky." Sometimes Beth listened, but most of the time she ignored Connie. She seemed to be cramming as much into her life as possible, using alcohol as her escape-ticket to do things that were not really her. She still rebelled against her mother with her strict, straight adolescence and her asexual marriage.

* * * * * *

The pressures of an inert life can make for unreal and unexpected happenings. If anyone ever thought that someone could have been a more devoted mother than April, they were wrong. The term 'smother-love' was invented for her. She might run around in jeans and a baggy sweatshirt, but her children were always dressed in the finest Marshall Field's had. Yet, when unadulterated-lust appeared on the scene as beautiful, bodily-formed Al, she tossed all notions of motherhood, the big suburban house, and a substantial income away.

April literally, flew to Al's side, seeing and enjoying the glory of it. Perhaps her subconscious mind knew that her brightly burning star, would soon burn itself out. For almost six months, she basked in the glory of uncompromising indulgence. Quite difficult for most of her friends to accept, yet Beth was glad to see her happy. Though she felt they were only playing-out a well- masked-charade, trying to convince themselves more than the outside world. Wally took advantage of his plight, to play the forsaken-husband with the abandoned-children to the hilt.

By this time, Al had turned from a reluctant lover into a real Don Juan. She told him so many times how good-looking he was, that he became intolerably-vain about his total appearance. Picking out his clothes very carefully, and grooming himself to the finest detail of trimming his beard daily. He had that certain smugness of a man, who knew he satisfied women sexually. Al *seemed* as much in love with April, as she was with him. Both were extremely jealous of one another ever looking at someone else, and constantly complimenting each other, like reassurance of an expensive possession. She didn't realize in bringing him out of his *insecurity,* she created a monster that soon would no longer be satisfied with only one prey, or such a limited audience. Now though, they were blissfully in love.

Beth invited them for dinner on April's birthday, and told Connie to drop in, since she had a large roast and homemade chocolate cake. April knew Beth's 'open door' policy, yet sometimes got unreasonably jealous of someone invading. Connie, anxious to see what 'super-stud' Al was like, happily accepted Beth's invitation. April must have been taking nasty pills, because she dove into Connie from the time she walked in the door. Jeremy finished his dinner, so Beth reset his place for Connie, while he went to watch television.

April's first zinger, "We were invited for dinner, but it's nice that you, could just drop in." Beth corrected April immediately, her birthday or not, it was still Beth's house and food. She'd invite whoever she wanted, whenever she wanted. When Al left the room to use the bathroom, April started singing the praises for his body, as if the only aria she knew. With all the malice she could conjure up, she remarked, "I bet you have to turn out the lights, when Cam takes his clothes off!" Before the stunned Connie could react, Beth jumped all over April for saying such a thing. She'd become very vain, and difficult to live with her weight loss, then worse with a lover who looked like Al. They were still very surprised, she'd gotten such a super looking guy.

These changes revitalized her in so many ways, but she still had her warped, opinionated personality. What no one could get over, was that April *wanted* to get out, and get a job to help support her new lifestyle. For someone who had *never* gotten up to make Wally's breakfast, she bounced out of bed at five-thirty in the morning, to go to her waitress job. If nothing else said it, that did, she loved Al like she had always dreamed of loving a man. It wasn't that she was lazy, because anything she wanted, she'd work like crazy at. But, working for money wasn't worth it, when she could get a man to support her. She didn't *need* the independence that a job brought.

They'd live together almost two months, and she knew very little about him. Then they left for California when April got her divorce settlement from Wally. She paid for the whole trip! No one believed April'd spend that kind of money on a man, but they never saw her in love before. The trip opened some doors on Al's shadowy-personality. Basically, he'd been married to a 'terrible' woman who didn't 'understand' him, and April never pursued him to tell the specifics of *terrible* or *understand*.

Beth didn't trust him as far as she could've thrown him, but she liked him on the surface. Her Scorpio ESP felt something strange, or off about him inside. A very personable man, he enjoyed women, but almost strange when he looked at her, he made Beth feel undressed. Somehow, when he flashed his mechanical smile, it was more than his smile he was flashing.

In California, April met his sister who gave her a small insight into his past. Several females Beth knew, had the fantasy of taking a virginal-teenage boy, and teaching him about sex. Al was the only one she'd ever known, that had it happen to him. He was sixteen and she was twenty-two, with her husband in Viet Nam. Not quite like *Summer of '42,* this had a lot more explicit sex. She only lived a few blocks from him, and they'd gotten to know each other when he'd run small errands and mow the lawn. 'Shirley' started asking Al to stop in after school for a coke, when she didn't need any work done. Very slowly, as to not scare him off, she started talking about sex, telling him anytime he ever had questions, he could ask her. She knew he was curious, because she noticed him watching her many times during the summer in her shorts or swimsuit.

Once they brought it out into the open that Al wanted to learn, she drew diagrams for him. She felt if he was to completely satisfy a woman, which she'd stressed was as important as satisfying a man, he'd need to have complete physical knowledge of male and female bodies. He'd see her almost everyday of the week, yet it was over a month before they had any physical contact. An excellent teacher, Shirley drilled him on every minute-detail until he had it perfect. There wasn't any sex training in schools then, and Al learned every erogenous zone possible on a man and woman. They'd have sessions where they'd lay nude, and take turns going over each other's body without having sex.

To say Al was very mature for his age was obvious. Also quite a quick-study learner - a child prodigy in carnal knowledge. Before they ever had intercourse, she taught him oral sex, to the point of tongue exercises, and how to apply pressure with either his mouth or teeth. It seemed it would've taken some of the glow out, if she was issuing orders while Al was performing cunnilingus on her, but apparently it didn't for her. He was never daunted by her criticism, because it was always followed by her praises, when he learned his lessons well. Besides, she wasn't creating a lover, she was *manufacturing* a sex machine. She had no intentions of replacing her husband, and he knew this. They were simply doing each other a great service. At the end of two years, her husband came home and she didn't see Al again.

The only problem was, of course, he was in the habit of regular sex and had no one else to turn to for it. Shirley created an adolescent-sexual-malaise in the interest of keeping herself satisfied. Since rape was frowned upon by the general female society, Al had to get a girlfriend he could screw. The only problem being that Shirley had never taught him to love, or feel love for another person in connection with the sex. He developed a puppy-love crush on her, but he hadn't received any in return. He never learned how to have an emotional relationship with someone of his own age group, yet too worldly experienced in sex to bother with progressing from holding hands forwrd. He wasn't a clod - "Hi, I'm Al, you wanna ball?" But he'd never learned there were certain things that must be said, in order to get into the pants of some young honey.

Unfortunately, April didn't know all this when she fell in love with Al, nor did she get the whole story at one time. What she got, she filed away, and was determined not to let it deter her from having a good time, while she had him. When they stopped in Las Vegas on the way home, April did have a time to remember for the rest of her life. If nothing else, Al could be a Ryan O'Neil to her Ali McGraw. The one thing which brought them closer was play-acting out a fantasy of being wealthy. They did strike quite an image of who they were trying to portray.

They'd park the old, beat-up car a block or more away, and walked into the Casino. Al had one super-suit, and April wore her thigh-length, fringe top, a body suit, colored panty hose and her boots. Her now long, black hair flowed in the breeze she created, as she strutted along. They talked, looked and acted like they had money. If there was any kind of an audience, they'd feed each other lines, one trying to out-do the other in their acting. One of the greatest things in the world to them both, was being in love and living out a fantasy, no matter how crazy it was to other people. For April, it truly would be an affair to remember.

Back home in the suburbs, it was another story. This Don Juan spoke with forked-tongue. She'd caught him several times lying for no reason at all, and then money disappeared, as well as her sacred, diet pills. There was no need for any of this, she'd have believed anything he said. He could've had the money, or pills if he'd asked. She was slipping very slowly from her magic cloud of love. Each step down to reality, was a painful hurt. Once again, a man she'd trusted was turning on her. April got some consoling from Beth, as an open-ear and a shoulder for her to cry on, though usually was a lecture attached. Beth turned to her when she needed someone to talk to, and April never turned her down, or hesitated in lecturing, either. Before they crashed completely, April made the rounds to her old friends to show-off Al. They spent many evenings with Tim and Michael, and even double-dated with Derek and Polly. Al got along fabulously, as he only showed them his superficial-side, the one he knew best.

Circles & Squares

    I would rather be wrong,
        than to hesitate.

           Not knowing what is around
    the next corner . . .

           It is better than just
    going around in circles!

The Real You

    You never miss
        whatever you've had.

    Yet, I miss you,
        because I never had
           the you I miss.

CHAPTER 8

Lost or Sober

Before April decided to leave her girls with Wally, she called Sybil. She'd gotten divorced several years before, and left her five-year old son with her husband. The best experience is first hand, so April asked her how she felt. Sybil was very honest,"It hurt, but it was the best thing for both of us. Now, when she saw Jimmy, it was because she wanted to, and she could enjoy him so much more, with no pressure of the responsibility of him. He adjusted well, too, especially since his father was remarried - so everything improved, even more."

She paused to take a long drag on her cigarette. "It hadn't been easy, but worth it for both of us." A very mixed up child/woman, Sybil had been in and out of mental institutions, as well having a drug and alcohol dependency. Her therapist said, she'd have a better chance on her own of finding what *she* was looking for, as well understanding herself. It sounded like it was better for Jimmy, too.

April discussed it with Michael and Beth, since she was insecure about making big decisions on her own. Simply, they both said if it didn't work out, she could always get the girls back. As mixed-up as she was at this time, she could do without two very needy, spoiled girls clinging on to her. Beth believed strongly that the girls needed to be exposed slowly to her new lifestyle, which would be quite a cultural change from the always-around mother.

Connie also thought seriously about the way she struggled with her two boys. She honestly believed some women were meant to be mothers, and some were not. Just because a woman had a womb, didn't mean being able to cope with the product of it. Connie loved being pregnant both times, though neither easy delivering. Definitely too young when she had Matthew, and not much older with Jeff. It wasn't a question of love, she loved her boys very much, she just never had much help in handling them - from George or her parents.

Connie never had much of a mother-child relationship with her mother, and felt lost developing one with either boy. There wasn't a school for parents, and never having babysat, those learning skills were missing. Honestly, she wasn't comfortable playing children's games, as she'd never done that either as a child. While, she loved to read, it was actually difficult for her to read to, or with her boys. Basically, she'd knew they made her nervous, and then she'd yell and scream without much antagonism from them. She'd felt guilty when she did, sounding like her mother. Yet to show them love, meant coming down to their level, and that was the real problem. It wasn't just sitting on the floor, it was what to do when she got there.

So for Connie, it was a big decision, also what was best for her and them. There was guilt of rejecting a role which society burdened her with, because she was the one that gave them life. Beth observed many times from close-up how upset and nervous the boys would get Connie. They both agreed the young babysitter got along better with them. Her child support was inadequate, but so was George's salary. He talked about getting married again, since receiving a draft notice, as a result of his new single status. After meeting George's fiancee, Carol, and having them spend weekends with the kids, the decision was made. Beth convinced Connie she was doing what was best for her and the boys. Perhaps when they were older, and she'd had some time for herself, she'd want to try again, if the boys were interested.

A few problems at the beginning with the new wife, but they got straightened out once the jealousy was gone. Beth ran interference for a while, because Connie wasn't speaking to Carol. The children adjusted better than the adults, as they always do in these situations. Jeremy would miss Jeff at nursery school, but there were many other kids, and he got along with most of them. So it wouldn't be such a shuffle for the kids, Connie moved out to let George and Carol rent the house from her parents. Now Connie could concentrate on if she truly wanted to catch Cam, not that he'd ever said much about the boys. She'd have more time and money on her hands, with it all being *her choice* how to spend them both.

A fun summer was had by the new couples - April with Al, sun-lover-Connie and Cam, and Beth had Rob, occasionally. And, the end of what was left for Michael and Tim. As they say, if it hadn't been for his running round, the bad sex and his not working regularly, they had a lot going for them. Also said: even a train stops and Michael's came to a screeching halt! At the same time, people always seemed to be in their house either for entertaining or counseling by them. Something they did well together, with Tim actually helping friends through their separations and divorces, as ironic as it was. What was happening to the safe, secure suburbs? Divorce was becoming more rampant than crab grass!

When Barb and Richard got their divorce, it truly surprised Michael, but she'd never known Barb's honest feelings about her marriage or her husband. It stopped Michael to evaluate her own, and where it was going. Since the one night stand with Derek never got anywhere, she hadn't gone looking for any other men until she'd met Donny. Her time was spent keeping Sybil glued together, or Polly and Derek happy. Sybil wandered back and forth between pills and alcohol, with so many suicide attempts Michael lost count. So many friends to help straighten out, yet no one noticed the continual daze Michael wandered around in. April wasn't much help with her own sandcastle falling down around her, no matter how many excuses she made for Al.

Men addicted to sex can only stay faithful so long, and then they're ready to move on. The first obvious clue, April couldn't ignore came with Al wanting them to join a 'swap club.' The other particular couple Al had in mind, were friends of his, naturally - Joe and Marnie. The mere thought of someone else having her precious Al was unreal. They got April to drink almost a full bottle of wine, yet she still wouldn't go through with it. She flirted with other men, including Joe, but could not cheat on Al. Basically, she was a one-man at a time-woman, she couldn't handle the juggling of sex with more than one man. One-night-stands were not her thing either, she liked having affairs. She still enjoyed talking and having relaxed time together.

April acknowledged the key sign - they weren't having sex every day any more - so she felt it only a matter of time till the writing-on-the-wall, would become clear to her. She kept catching him lying more often, then had to accept he was a kleptomaniac - she found twenty pairs of sunglasses in his sock drawer! Besides stupid stuff, he couldn't keep his hands-off her things. Feeling perhaps it was time to go to the nearest source, April started talking to his wife, who spilled more than just the beans on him. He'd done the same with her, regarding the swap-club, and showed April letters she'd found hidden after he left her.

Shocked at the language one woman actually wrote down, suggesting wild, sexual activities, along with obscenities, she questioned who this person she loved was. To her, it was one thing to perform the different acts, but quite another to write about them to a complete stranger. One passionate female sent Al a bunch of her pubic-hair. It was beyond April, why with a good, sex-life, he'd want/ need other women? They had put variety and spice in their sex, why did another woman need to be brought in? Controlling the appetite to not have to change partners, she thought was somehow basic in a good sexual relationship.

As quickly as her star rose to its heights, the crash went to unbelievable depths, with April not handling it very well. She controlled herself while he was packing, but when his other sister and Marnie came to pick him up, she got a bit rowdy. His sister, who she thought liked her, started fighting with her and pulling her hair. A real 'girl-fight' scene, with kicking, scratching and hitting. Al had enough affection left for her to pull them apart, and defended April, as the lies he'd told them about her had started the fight. Marnie left Joe to live with Al, and since she'd been a hooker, there might be a few tricks she could teach Al - maybe.

April had recalled, "Sometimes making love with Al, was like making it with a computer, as he knew all the right buttons to push." To her, that was part joke and part compliment. And yes, her most glorious sex was with Al, but she knew he never loved her the way she loved him - he wasn't capable of it. Knowing this, she still pined after him for months, never getting over him completely. Lost, alone and totally forlorn, April could not have survived without her friends. She stayed on her own about six weeks after Al left. It took almost three days to pull herself together, to keep going. During times like these, reminded them all how glad to have each other, and their friendship.

The distraction with Michael over Donny and Tim, kept April going as she felt needed, during the moving in and out of her home because of Donny. April went back to her old habits of picking men up in bars, for either sex or companionship, but put herself in a bad position by going to their place rather than hers. One night she'd brought a hockey player home with her, promising him the couch to sleep on, since for some reason he had no place to stay. She then became indignant when he tried to seduce her, and took him back to the bar where she'd picked him up. To say she could be unpredictable, was a safe bet.

Not being able to let go, and hoping somehow to fix things back up, April wanted to visit Al's sister. Since Donny was back in the hospital drying out again, Michael went with her. She'd made up with his sister regarding the fight, when she realized what an asshole her brother was. Part of April knew it was over, yet she wanted to be around Al's presence, or talk about him. It was a strange winter evening, because Marnie's ex-husband, Joe, was over visiting. He'd been off the wagon drinking a bit, which made his tongue sharper than ever. Though he teased April, it was Michael who fascinated him. Sober or not, 'Italian Joe' considered himself a *guru* of sorts.

He loved to listen to people's problems, then give them his great solutions. Surprisingly, he was right most of the time. He learned quickly what leverage it took to get someone to open up, or at least find their Achilles' heel. Of course, it helped him not to focus on his own problem, because he'd loved Marnie, and her leaving had been quite a shock. April always thought that the second reason - after sex- that Marnie left Joe was because she wanted to have a baby. Joe was twenty years older and had four children by his first marriage, so not inclined to cooperate.

Al on the other hand, thought it very virile to be able to produce a child, never considering he couldn't afford the two he already had. Marnie'd been a sixteen-year-old streetwalker when Joe picked her up, and taught her all the tricks of the trade in the big time. Though teaching her how to talk, walk and dress, a Professor Higgins he wasn't. It was his idea that if she was going to sell it, she may as well get the highest price, and *they* did. They'd been together quite a few years, and she'd only recently retired.

So, when Joe heard the background on Michael, he couldn't figure out how this sweet, young housewife from the suburbs, and its insulated protection could have gotten herself into such a mess. Was she still rebelling against the establishment, which she felt had held her down as a child? If she was, she sure seemed to be going about it in a 'self-inflicting' way. As April gabbed about Al with his sister, Michael and Joe were deep into discussions about freedom, life beyond death, independence and other mind-bending psychic ideas. When April was ready to leave, Joe asked if Michael would like to come to his place. She declined, but asked if he'd call her. He said he would, and it was the beginning of a long and unusual friendship. They'd spend many hours on the phone and at his place, rarely indulging in sex, but always delving deep into each other's mind and psyche. His favorite succinct term for it was *'mind-fucking,'* which he felt was usually more satisfying than *'body-fucking.*

* * * * * *

Ignoring Connie's protests one Friday night, Beth invited April to join them going down to Chicago's Rush Street. It gave them some variety and new blood to meet. Connie couldn't get over how crass April could be in wearing her little, hot-pants or flip skirts. They were getting tight, but she still wore them. Connie kept up constant zingers at her, but they rolled right-off her. Though Beth told her bad it was, Connie didn't realize April was clinging to a lifestyle that had given her the happiest moments of her life. Anything that reminded her of Al, she reenacted, as if he were with her. She'd gotten drunk the night Al left her, and Connie often commented she never trusted someone who didn't drink, or made snap judgments.

April would get to a bar, walk around to check out all the guys, and if she didn't see any that looked interesting, she'd turn to the girls saying she wanted to go. Since they paid to get in, Connie wanted her money's worth of at least a drink or two. She didn't like jumping from one place to another, especially when the band had been on break when they got there. April was obviously looking for a pick-up, but neither Beth or Connie were interested. If it happened fine, if not it was a good night being out, and listening to some great music to dance to if possible. Connie was on a "Black" kick at that time, and Beth helped her fix a semi-Afro wig, which she wore that night. She'd take Beth down to the Chicago Theatre to see all the new, Black-oriented movies like *Shaft*. If they came at all to the suburbs, they were gone in a week. The girls sat in the back row to not be seen.

Connie always wanted to try out a Black dude, so when a six-foot ten-inch one walked in, she almost feel off the bar stool. He walked right past the section they were in, even though the largest group of Blacks were sitting there. Beth laughed,"Maybe he's prejudiced." The fact that they were in the largest singles bar in Chicago, it was still not hard to find him. Since the girl's restroom was near where he was sitting, off they darted. April finally connected with someone, so she was taken care of for the time being. Again, Connie called on Beth's ingenuity to think up something to say, or do to get this guy's attention.

Beth walked out of the restroom first, just standing around waiting for Connie, glancing at the Black dude off and on. He noticed her right away, and motioned to her to come over. "I know this sounds trite, but don't I know you from somewhere?" He had a great smile.

Beth smiled, it had to be one of the oldest lines in town, so she decided to respond with her favorite line from *Charade* - Audrey Hepburn to Cary Grant, when he asked the similar question: "I don't really think so. I know so many men now, that until one of them dies or leaves town, I couldn't possibly know another one." Her smile beat his, as she added her devilish eyes.

He cracked up laughing, knowing she was putting him on, but definitely interested. "Oh, no, I didn't mean here, I meant out of state."

Beth was intrigued by the twist, "Oh, I've traveled all over, where are you from?"

Very coyly he answered, "L.A." Waiting how she'd answer his come back.

"I've been there several times," she answered with a bigger smile, turning closer to him. "perhaps I misspoke, maybe we have met." Lying through her teeth, she broadcast them. By this time Connie joined them, not too surprised that Beth made contact. "This is my friend Connie, he's from L.A. Connie, I was about to get his name." Thus they met Willy from L.A., in this case it was Lower Alabama, and his two 'white' friends. It turned out that the guy April was talking with was the roommate of Bob, Willy's friend! After dancing and carrying on, they lured the girls up to their apartment with the promise of Coors beer. Since only a few blocks away, they all ran over, the biting, cold Chicago-wind pushing them along.

April and her pick-up were already sitting in a corner by the fireplace. It was a snazzy, new apartment, hardly any furniture but a super, plush-shag-rug. They all snuggled with their beers, when Bob asked if anyone wanted a "j." Connie and Beth had tried grass for the first time a few months before, when they were following a rock group around the different clubs. It had been quite a mellow experience, and except for the one acid-trip Connie had six months before, she was clean and away from all the pills.

They wanted to try some grass again, as the band-boys turned out to be a fiasco, the guy Connie picked already had too much, and passed out before they accomplished anything. The one Beth got, seemed to have an 'aesthetic-fetish' and spent the evening touching her curves and valleys, going nowhere. One of those nights, details couldn't begin to describe, so the only good thing that came out of it was learning to smoke the grass.

Of course, April refused, as she believed if you ever got started, the next thing you'd be main-lining heroin. Connie bitched at her till Beth told her to lay-off. April went to the bedroom with her guy, saying she didn't want to associate herself with such people, in case the cops busted in - a rather slanted-sense of justice. For the next hour, or so, Connie and Willy were attacking each other feverishly, while Bob and Beth laid on the rug talking, and gently rubbed on each other. Several times April came prancing through, walking over bodies mumbling something about disgraceful, and asking when they'd be leaving. Connie told her to fuck-off, and April whirled-off, marching back into the bedroom When she came back again, she announced she'd called her father to take her home, out of this den of iniquity.

Connie, now highly pissed, laid into April so verbally, they were all rather taken aback. Beth told Connie what a weirdo her father was, besides the fact that he'd shoot a Black guy just for sport. Beth made April go and call him back, they'd leave. She quickly thought up the excuse that the parking garage closed at three, so they had to get Connie's car out. In the mad rush, they were passing out telephoner numbers. In the bitter cold, the three of them ran almost the whole mile back to the garage.

Connie had no intentions of screwing Willy with April around anyway. She didn't trust her to keep her mouth shut, and April wouldn't have. Beth and Connie saw Willy and Bob once more the following week. This time another Black guy was with them. When the bar closed, Willy offered to give them a ride to Connie's car. Two minutes after they got into the car, Chicago's finest pulled them over.

Being from total, middle-class white-suburbia, Connie and Beth never saw racist cops before. They demanded all the driver licenses, and wanted to know what they all did for a living. When Willy gave his license and business card, saying he was assistant sales manager for a very large, well-known company. As well, was his friend, an account executive there, and Bob was a teacher at the city college. They then didn't care about Beth, though Connie shoved her license at the one, wanting him to know she was from Elmwood. The cops never gave a reason for the pull-over, nor did they apologize for the harassment. The guys never caused a scene, as they were used to it. Beth and Connie thought how lucky to live where they did.

They never saw the guys again, but a real experience, with Willy keeping them all laughing. Connie still remarked how she wished she'd had a chance to try him, "Even if he'd split me open doing it. The bulge in his pants went almost to his knees, and you saw what long legs he had!" There were some things she'd always be curious about.

Glimmering Presence

While your presence gives me more than just smiles,
Your absence simply returns me to my times before you.
Do I miss you?   Sure.
Can I live without you?   Definitely.

Is life better with you?
Perhaps. Yet, I must ask, compared to what?
Do I lose sleep over you?   Not yet.
Are you in my dreams?   Yes, but they are not only of you.

Do I trust your coming and going?
I cannot say, for the investment has not reached that point.
Where trust is a pivotal issue . . .
It is a balancing act.

What I can say, I'm a strong woman who feels transparent.
I am filled with the Spirit of so many feminine voices before me,
Who mysteriously guide me, and support my inner strength.
Sometimes I believe there is a glimmering of kismet which enjoins us.

Where it goes, and what we do with it is Our choice.
That's some of the mystery of love.

CHAPTER 9

Comings and Goings

Not ready to stand on her own two feet, April devised a plan to get Wally to let her move back into the house. Without an amorous lover the reason of her being, April did not want the single-lifestyle pressure that Beth and Connie lived by being in love with married men - yet hanging out in the bars to occasionally pick-up a man. She tried it for several months after Al left, but one-night stands did not fit into what she wanted from a relationship. Working to support herself wasn't an enjoyable challenge to April, as compared to having Wally carry all the expenses. Guilt also mounted about leaving her two daughters in his care. If to get them back, meant returning to him, then that's what she planned.

The new seduction of Wally began slowly, as she felt it'd be worthwhile. Three weeks later she was back with him, but as they say, 'even the best *laid* plans of men . . ." It didn't work out quite the way planned - he didn't turn over the check book or credit cards, nor show his paycheck. Maybe he was dumb, but not totally stupid. Poor Wally *was* talked into an expensive engagement ring, and April planned a huge, church wedding with her daughters as the flower girls. Beth and Connie did not feel it was a clever ploy, just a sad one. He'd been hoodwinked, again.

Out of the goodness of her heart, April promised to have sex with him *once a month*. She lasted four months without going out at all. Michael had left Tim *for good*, and was living with April and Wally. She hadn't quite broken off with Donny, the first time April got desperate enough to go out. The fact that Wally accepted her going out was amazing. She soon started the same old pattern with her restlessness, that she'd done the year before. Wally, glad to have her back, was willing to let her go out - as long as she came home at night.

Naturally, she called Beth to join them, since she never said 'no.' Besides, she and Rob were falling apart *again*, so she needed an outlet. They made a cute threesome, but before the pregnant-Michael settled down, she called Donny at the hospital, drying out *again*. Always loyal, as long as she was in love.

It'd been six months since Beth saw Michael, she wasn't noticeably pregnant, though she wore her Levi's too tight for it. Fortunately for April, a friend of Beth's came in - he was married, but she made her usual play for any man. They only chuckled, as sometimes April thought she was Cleopatra floating down the Nile, collecting men to keep her amused. Fun talking and catching up, though April kept her informed of everything happening in Michael's life in living-color.

Michael was so much more intelligent, than her ridiculous situation indicated. April also tended to paint a bleaker-picture than it was of others, while adding whatever positive she could to her own situations. Love being the strange thing it was, Beth was not about to throw stones on Michael's situation, yet the pregnancy did blow Beth's mind as to basic prevention. Love can make almost anything seem right, at the time. April left to go neck in the car, as the other two talked until they closed up the bar. Having gotten a tease of going out, and having a man she liked be interested in her - even a married one - quelled April's taste for staying at home.

Beth and Connie regularly at The Place, always connecting to many friends of friends. One night they were invited to a super pot-party at Roy, the bartender's place. In Connie's words, it was 'un-fucking believable.' One joint after another was being passed around, with different bottles of wine following. It didn't take too long, for them to figure out what kind of a party it would become. Most of the participants were younger-singles, without any attachments, so a bit freer than they felt. Trying to leave, with most of their clothes on, but constantly attacked, they fought Roy and others off with little vigor. Still, they finally staggered out. After the shock of the whole situation wore off, they couldn't stop laughing on the way home.

They rarely missed going into The Place on Sundays and Thursdays after work, for the free drinks all night - though they rarely paid other nights. But Ladies Nights meant that the place was full of men, and a good band. So, with the two-dollar cover charge, they went to any of the four bars inside, and didn't have to stick to Roy, Kip, Chuck and Pete. They never knew when Eddie might hire a new bartender, they'd have to break-in as to their special status, as if.

One night Eddie made the mistake of coming into the Cafe' kitchen for some coffee, and began talking about the way they drank him out of business. He carried the joke a little too far, when he mentioned they sat with 'a bottle of Scotch and a long straw.' He might have had all the kitchen help in stitches, but Connie was highly pissed. They'd never gone in there and caused a scene, not a big one anyway. They decided when finished with work, they'd teach him a lesson not to open his mouth about their drinking habits.

At nine o'clock, they paid their two dollars and ordered their first scotch and water. Somehow Kip knew they were up to no good that night, so he cracked a fresh quart of Grants for Connie's drink. When they were ready for their second drink, Connie asked Beth to switch to Grants. She then had Kip set the new quart aside, and told him what Eddie pulled in the Cafe's kitchen, and Kip was more than willing to go along with whatever. Connie insisted they must do this with dignity, and be ladies while sucking-up the whole quart of Grants by eleven o'clock. The absurdity of it all was very profound.

Trying to keep it a secret from Eddie, everyone whispered and passed it on. Beth decided to keep her drink stirs for count. As the evening proceeded, they drew a crowd of onlookers. Since pulling this caper on Eddie, Connie wanted to pull one on Kip and the other bartenders. He had talked about playing the pin-ball machines with Roy, and they'd use up their quarters for it. That was it, since they always left a good tip for the guys, Beth decided to go buy a ten-dollar roll of quarters from the Cafe'. She also picked up some potato chips and Fritos Connie brought in earlier. On her return, Beth echoed, "Eat, Eat, they'll make you thirsty." Kip complained there was no dip. By ten o'clock Eddie found out their gambit, but with only a third of a the bottle left, no sense in stopping them now. The girls didn't care either what he said, as it became a challenge to see if they could do it, and not fall off their bar stools.

Actually, they paced their drinks well, with lots of water, and were doing beautifully. Connie kept asking Beth if she felt bombed, and it did surprise them how well they handled the booze. Their first and last mistake, was when a couple of cute guys asked them to dance about ten-thirty. Since they *were* doing so well, why not? A favorite rock song, who could resist? Besides the 'dancing' did make them hot and thirsty to drink more. What they didn't consider, it also made the scotch rush quicker into their blood.

Since, neither of them did anything in moderation, especially Beth, they didn't stop at one dance. The band was great and the night was young - go for it! When they returned to their bar stools, they gulped the watered-down drinks sitting there, ordering more refills. By the stroke of eleven, they finished the last drop of scotch out of the quart bottle. Eddie was practically pulling his hair out, while everyone else was cheering. Now, they were *wasted* - totally. Beth more so than Connie, as she kept telling Beth they had to pull this off without making absolute assholes of themselves. Everything started moving in slow motion, and them trying not to show how utterly drunk they were. If only they hadn't gotten up to dance, everything was dandy until then.

Before one of them passed out, they had the second part of the plan to present. Connie could hardly get the roll of quarters undone to dump on the bar for 'their boys' tip, as she called them. Beth began laughing uncontrollably at her, while starting to lean backwards on the backless bar stool. She promptly, and very unceremoniously landed on the tile floor with a thump. The precarious way she fell, still straddling the bar stool, it took three of them to pick her up. Connie stared down, then remarked, "You could've done that with more finesse!"

The drive home was never remembered by either one, as they stumbled up Beth's front concrete steps to its porch - her house was closest. When she couldn't immediately produce the key, Connie joined digging into her purse for it. She kept swatting her hand, sure she knew where it was, and finally produced it. After that, a problem finding the key hole to put it in. Connie began chortling hysterically,

"Oh my God Beth, I told you how many times you haven't got that much experience, see you can't find the hole!" Beth's little poodle was inside the door, barking like wolves were on the other side. Beth finally told Connie to shut up, when she kept repeating her joke, it was only funny so many times.

Then Connie decided that she was the more sober, or less drunk, of the two and she'd give it a try. When she also kept missing the key hole, Beth began guffawing herself, this time with almost convulsions. Two grown adults, and they couldn't get a door open. As she was bending over and straightening up, she backed right off the side of the porch, which had no railing. Beth fell spread-eagle into the evergreens with her open purse in her hand.

Hysterical, Connie rushed to the edge. "Oh, my God, OH, MY GOD! Speak to me Beth? Are you alive?" Then, she promptly fell on top of Beth. They both just laid there for a minute, so stunned they couldn't move. Once Connie found out Beth was living, she climbed back up on the porch to try the key again. Beth, in an uncontrollable state of laughter, was gasping for breath with tears rolling down her face. She also noticed a light go-on at the neighbors.

Beth didn't have the strength to climb up. But still roaring all the way, she crawled around through the bushes and up the steps, till Connie pulled her into a standing position. Now leaning on each other cackling so hard, they fell against the house, then rolled into the door, which popped open. After falling inside, they were only silent from the shock a few moments, and the giggles began again, with Beth's dog greeting them with face-kisses. They rolled off each other, snickering as they managed to stand.

Even as drunk as she was, Beth knew her house. Stripping her clothes off, she headed for the restroom. Though she'd already wet herself several times, she peed. She then staggered into her bedroom, and passed out in bed. Like any unreliable drunk, she left poor Connie to fend for herself, and her memory of the house.

Her profusely, barking dog awakened Beth in the morning. If it was the mailman, she couldn't understand why her dog kept barking so long. Why was he taking so much time? Upon rising from the bed, the sixteen tons on her head made her lay back down. Then, she had to get up to use the bathroom again, but not ready for the scene in the living room. Apparently, Connie hadn't remembered a lot of details of the house. There was a path through the living room that looked like a charging bull had been through there. A lamp was knocked over, as well the portable television, with the coffee table and several knick-knacks askew. The throw-cover from one of the couches was missing, as the room was dotted with underwear and top clothing scattered everywhere. Connie was no where to be seen.

Beth looked in her son's room to see Connie rolled up in the throw-cover on his bed. Thank God her son was at her mother's, she would've killed him when she crashed. Beth walked to the front door to let the dog out and get the mail. At first she just gasped, then she started chuckling all over again. Almost choking from laughter, she went to wake Connie. Dragging her out of bed, with only the throw-cover on, she led her out the front door. "You've got to see this for yourself, so you don't think I staged it or something." They sat down on the porch and roared - making quite a sight, Connie in her sarong-throw, and Beth in an old bathrobe.

Perusing the scene, there were several articles of clothing, plus one shoe strewn on the porch. Beth's coat was still spread-eagle on the ground, under the evergreen bushes. Her purse had emptied on the way down, with money and junk tossed into the bushes. Her torn panty-hose hanging from a bush was interesting, as no memory of pulling them off, but considering how shredded, she'd have been rather frustrated. The mailbox hung vertical by one screw, rather than horizontal on the house - probably from them falling against it before falling in the door. Amazed, Beth queried, "Why didn't the mailman ring the bell, or called the police?"

"Are you shitting me?" she cracked up. "He wanted away from this mad house as soon as possible." He'd probably seen a lot of crazy things happen at her house, but this by far the best.

"It looks like at least one 'roving band of gypsies' came through raping and pillaging," Beth calmly remarked. The more she looked around the more debris she saw from their actions.

"Wouldn't you know," Connie retorted, "I'd miss all the fun! I *coulda* used a fun-rape."

Thinking about the cops, they pulled themselves together to go back inside. If anyone saw them like that, with everything else, they wouldn't have to worry about the police, just the 'men in the white coats.' Beth grabbed the mail and went inside to dress to go out for something to eat, since it was almost noon. With seeing the porch scene, they couldn't say after a certain point, the night's memories were vague. It was all too clear, how truly smashed they both were.

They began comparing bruises, as Beth didn't remember falling off the bar stool - especially in quite the spectacular way Connie described. Yet, she never remembered a thing about the drive home. On the way out, she very carefully checked her new car, it didn't have a scratch on it. Amazingly also, neither one of them even got sick.

When they got to the restaurant, it was club sandwiches for both, with lots of milk for Connie. The waitress didn't understand why they both moaned, when they saw the potato chips on their plates. They chuckled lightly, wondering if they'd ever top this one. As long as they could live through it, it's always worth it, if for nothing else than the laughs in the retelling of it.

Not Enough

The perfect love affair was ours to make,
until we made just one mistake.
We became victims of our fate.

We fell in love so complete,
the kind of love, most never meet.
I never thought, that he'd retreat.

He said he loved me more than life,
but not enough, to leave his wife.

Now through my mind the memories leap.
How can you love so very deep,
yet not enough, for it to keep?

I question this behind my tears -
How can you love so very dear,
and yet not enough, to conquer fear?

So heed my warning of stalking fate -
And don't make my mistake.
Love a man who's free to return, all he takes.

CHAPTER 10

Breaking Up

Breaking up is not easy, whether you're sixteen or sixty. Beth felt it coming for a long time between her and Rob. Sometimes the only way to face something was head on. Even if it's the best thing for someone it can hurt, yet going on with it could make the hurt deeper, when the end did come. Many things contributed to the breakdown, but mostly Beth began to feel like a relay stations, emphasis on the *lay*. If Rob was simply traveling by, he'd stop in for a quickie. Even their luncheons-out had taken on considerable speed. Also, she changed.

Never a generous person, he almost ignored her birthdays, Christmas and Valentines Day. Yet, never hesitated to tell Beth what obligatory gift he got his wife, sometimes asking for her advice. She particularly resented the Christmas Rob purposely gave her the same, heavy-smelling cologne his wife wore, so *she* didn't smell her lighter perfume on him. Beth was heading to Mary's to give her babysitter Lynne, the cologne as a gift, when her clumsy niece, Cindy broke it on the driveway. At first furious, she then laughed, thinking Lynne wouldn't have liked it either.

Beth was concerned of him being caught, as he'd gotten brazen about leaving his car out front, rather than pulling it to the garage-end of her long driveway. She lived on a thoroughfare many people used as a short-cut, and his house was only a few miles away. She felt he almost wanted to be found out, then he'd have to make a decision about his marriage - something he couldn't do on his own. She had no intention of being his excuse, as she knew his two older kids. It'd been that sort of dumb affair, she being a sort of friend to his wife, and his older son actually working at the restaurant as *their* busboy.

Not as if Beth felt she was breaking up their marriage, or taking away from Sylvia's sex life, neither existed. She felt like Rob was holding her down, and she no longer had real guilt when she cheated on him, as she *was* the single-one. Yet, she knew he wouldn't have thought of her doing it. He had her on a rather high pedestal, knowing very little of her and Connie's escapades around the area or in Chicago. When he was recently leaving after a *'nooner,'* he said going down the steps, "I'll see you soon, be good now."

Standing on the porch in a light sundress, she couldn't help herself saying, "Good? Sometimes, I'm downright Great!" The big smile was more sly than happy, and he almost tripped on the sidewalk, turning back to glance, to see if she was serious in what she said.

The most glaring thing wearing away at their love was that she didn't *really want him*, like Connie did Cam, as she knew it wouldn't go anywhere anyway. This was one of those married men, who stayed well-hidden behind his family obligations to the 'little' woman, that bore him his children - *history together*, as he liked to call it. They were both rather comfortable in their clandestine relationship, yet it was starting to feel more like a rut to Beth. And, as they say: "The only difference between a rut and grave is six feet." Time to get out.

One night Beth was sitting in a bar with Little Mary, a waitress from the Cafe'. They were discussing there affairs with married men, as she'd recently broken up with her Texan of several years. Knowing each other also several years, they were honest in sharing. Mary was one of those rare friends that you never quite appreciated, until you didn't see her on a regular basis. Cute and perky, a miniature version of Mary Tyler Moore, although not quite as wholesome as the character she portrayed. This Mary took her birth-control pill with a vodka martini, rather than milk. Mary just wasn't the type you'd think of as having an affair, though honest about her 'nothing' marriage. She taught Beth the basics about married men - the truth about *enough* and divorce. "Sure they tell you they love you, but *not enough* to get a divorce from the old lady."

"Yes," Beth responded, "even Dr. David Reuben says (*Everything You Ever Wanted to Know About Sex . . .*) only about ten per cent of the women having affairs with married men ever end up winning them." The only consoling thought behind the break-up, it'd be more Rob's loss, as she would always find another man. He'd have his *'wifey-poo,' and* she's what drove him away. While she greatly appreciated Rob's support during her divorce, she didn't need it now, and no offers to her of any excitement, like trips even into Chicago.

The somewhat problem, if called such, Beth wasn't seeing another man regularly. The men she did see, had basically been fun sex. Sure, there were more men who'd be happy to be a 'regular' with her, but they were *about* as married as Rob. And, while most of the single guys she met in the bars, were happy to give her sex and maybe more, they didn't ring any bells with her. She simply wanted more, a more interesting character.

Learning to lean on herself helped her to make decisions easier, then if a mistake, learn from it. Her independence was growing in leaps and bounds, as to who she was *meant to be*. Beth still had her divorced friends to discuss things with - few of her married friends were *'allowed'* to associate with her. Divorce was a real social disease to most insecure, married men. Yes, Beth was ready for the affair to end, it was her idea, as all was *hunky-dory* with Rob. She felt she'd fulfilled any obligation left over from her divorce, but something niggled at her, feeling sorry for him at times. She wanted the release of the responsibility of being faithful to one man - that would come in the next marriage, which she was in no hurry to have.

She'd been lying to him so much recently, which angered her that he expected her to explain herself to him. She knew he'd never loved her as much, as she *once* loved him, so why was she feeling guilty about being with other men? Just saying she wanted to take a break, seemed juvenile, but not being as available was almost as if a slow drowning, but he'd be more appreciative of her in some ways. She knew there would be a certain love for him, for what they'd had in the past.

Beth reminded herself how she'd sat near a phone and waited for his promised calls, and he never gave any explanation for the delays. In their earlier times together, while never mentioning divorce to him, she'd let him know 'the second twenty years could be better than the first.' Of course, those mesmerizing beginning days, when she lived for the idle talks about anything he wanted to share, and the sound of his voice - he could have read the Yellow Pages to her, and she'd be satisfied. Those were the days of blood-rushing, just when their skin lightly touched, or they took time to ponder looking into each other's eyes.

Beth recalled the time she'd been a hair-model for her beautician friend, Caren who did her massive, full-head of honeyed-blonde into a Lioness Style - absolutely incredible. When she had a moment to catch him at the bar, and no one else around, she asked how he liked her hair? Without hesitation, and most seductively he said, "Tossed across a pillow." He really could be a *'silver-tongued dude,'* when he chose to, and knew it would get her quicker into a bed with him.

Sometimes, when she hadn't heard from him in a while, she'd rethink about his body - the touch, taste and feel of it pressed against hers, they certainly did know how to enjoy each other to the fullest extent. It wasn't as if she'd lived through him, as April did with Al. Beth was a stronger person, so when she did miss him, she reminded herself, it was just sex - she wasn't going to die. She was sure that in reality, he'd be missing her and 'the greatest sex he'd ever had,' because if there ever was a compliment he didn't hesitate to give, it was that one. It wasn't about being a survivor either, Beth loved life and the choices her freedom gave her - spending time with Jeremy, going to movies, reading books/magazines and her own writing or poetry. The classes she took at the county college were expanding her mind in so many ways.

Beth saw her growth into a multi-layered person, with slightly different personalities if she was in a bar, at school, with the girls or Jeremy. This was what she wanted - to never have a boring life of doing the same things over and over, with no choices or changes to make them different. Yes, sometimes she did over do it with drinking or men, yet she also had good times just talking with men or new women she'd meet at parties and get togethers. Then sometimes she'd reverse, sit home for the rarity to watch some television with Jeremy, or on her own.

There were those men at the bar, like John, who had always been so sweet to her - he helped her get her little Volkswagen, never asking or expecting anything from her. When he and his wife were retiring to move to Florida, they actually threw a great farewell party for him. Beth decided to have sex with him before he left. She didn't broadcast it, but didn't hide it either. There were many reasons other than just liking him, though she figured Rob would hear of it, or figure it out. Surprisingly, she got much more out of it than she expected - he had only ever dreamed of performing oral sex on her - nothing else. Beth felt truly worshipped afterwards. So, she knew the good guys were out there, and only a matter of time before she found one to be with, and talk to about whatever. Unfortunately, most of her male friends were too jealous to introduce her to other men. So, Beth was totally ready for some new friends in her life.

* * * * * *

Cam was doing more out of town business travel, as well recently acquired a run-about boat, and Connie excitedly joined him on both, so her head was not concerned with Beth's questions or looking for some suggestions regarding breaking up. Beth certainly didn't want to check in with April, as she'd get a lot of 'told you so,' since she refused to put the married-Al in the 'married-man' category - she did have her own set of rules. Michael, on the other hand, finished with Donny and her divorce at about the same time. It was natural for them to start spending time together, and Beth liked having new blood to discuss problems with one another.

Wally already realized April was only looking for temporary, bed and board with him in trade for occasional sex. He told her the wedding was off, and be out of the house when the kids were finished with school for the summer - the charade was over. He added, she should take the kids back, since he lost his built-in babysitter when she moved back. So, what April needed now, was a man to marry and support her with the girls, fast!

The one night Beth didn't join them going out, was when April met Alex. Michael had known him when he was seeing Crystal. They'd just broken up and he was sitting, sulking at the bar when April and Michael walked in. April practically pronounced on him, before Michael could introduce them. Though she complained her men were little boys, looking for her to mother them, if she didn't always pick-up 'broken-winged-birds' to her bosom, perhaps they wouldn't have the *mother-complex* problem. The trouble was the birds she got, were usually vultures, and the broken wings were phony.

Even if April did find a stronger man, she'd turn him dependent upon her. Somehow or other, they all had a weakness that affected their whole personality. With Wally, it had been the booze and Al the womanizing, so when she needed a man to lean on, he wouldn't be strong enough to help her. From what Michael said, Alex was more than ripe for marriage. Only twenty-four at the time - four years younger than April - he'd been ready to marry Crystal, and take on her kids. April figured if she worked fast enough, she could get him to marry her before June - it was March, 1973.

She turned on her *super-est* mothering-instinct, telling Alex what a sad thing that Crystal didn't appreciate him. This was not about Alex being some terrific catch, he was simply available, and her chid support from Wally was to be three hundred a month, which was not bad money to build on. But the way April looked at it, if the new marriage didn't work out, she could always get a divorce. If it lasted five years, that was enough. For a change, April didn't jump in the sack that first night - simply because it was too late, and she didn't want to piss off Wally.

She met Alex the following night, and started playing her usual coy little game of: "I've never done this sort of thing before." Alex didn't care, as long as they ended up in the sack. When they did, April found what she had always been looking for - a horny, young man who was well-hung. She fell 'in love' once again with sex. It was a whirlwind courtship, her working as fast as possible, to convince him marriage was the best thing for him. Actually, they deserved each other, since he was as anxious to marry somebody as she was. They saw each other every night, and the sex stayed ripe.

April fought constantly with Wally, so he'd be more than happy to be rid of her. Beth was the only one who was against the marriage, she knew April didn't love Alex, and she doubted if he was capable of loving anyone. There it was again, something about him she didn't trust, and she'd heard too much about his weirdness from the previous girlfriends. As corny as it sounded, she didn't like his dark-beady eyes, they showed a sick-cruelty behind them. No big surprise that April didn't listen to her, as she always thought she could change a guy, anyway - she never did succeed at that, but didn't care. They ended up having a huge fight, with April yelling and accusing Beth of wanting Wally, because of his money. Beth knew what tension she was under, so she didn't pay attention to absurdities.

April made up before the wedding, because she wanted Beth there. She was married four weeks after her first date with Alex. Beth attended, but refused to give her congratulations, as she made it clear she didn't condone the wedding, and wouldn't be a hypocrite. April wore a long, red terrycloth robe with moccasins on - so much for the expensive dress she'd planned on Wally buying her. Michael stood up for her, in a red, maternity-top with her Levis on. As previously planned, April's daughters in long, gingham gowns and the only ones carrying flowers. Then again, it was a church wedding, with her sad father giving her away - again, also.

April's dear, new mother-in-law bought most of the food, and the reception followed at the newlywed's apartment. The nuptial-night did not turn out as April planned, since her two daughters didn't want to go to grandpa's. Michael and Beth couldn't wait to leave, as Michael readied to move in with Beth. With a closer look at Alex's personality, she was glad April wanted him. He turned out to be a follower of Stalin and Hitler, so prejudiced against everyone. Michael gathered up her plastic bag full of clothes, and left with Beth. It was practically all she had in the world. There were still a few things left at the house, but she hadn't settled with Tim yet about collecting them. She fared the worst out of the four divorces.

Michael had no job, no money, no training and was five months pregnant, when she moved in with Beth - *until she got on her own feet.* Happy to babysit for Jeremy, who would be five the following month, and to keep the house clean. Beth worked lunches and dinners at the Cafe'. Bruce had Jeremy every other weekend, so Beth and Michael had a chance to go out. The arrangement was the best thing for both of them - and Beth was looking forward to the company, while Michael certainly needed a roof over her head.

They didn't go out immediately, with Beth usually too tired on Fridays with two shifts, and Saturday night she'd drink with the girls after work. Their first weekend was Easter, and Beth kept Jeremy since Bruce's family did nothing for any holidays. Michael planned on decorating eggs, then hiding them after he'd gone to sleep. She was not ready for Beth to come home in such a wasted-condition. She started tossing eggs around, and hiding candy in a very intoxicated state. Before she completely destroyed all the Easter goodies, Michael sent her off to bed and finished the job. A new experience for Michael, if nothing else Beth would be good for a laugh. She had tremendous patience with inebriated people, after so many years rescuing Sybil.

The following week was Michael's birthday, so Beth took her out for dinner with Connie on their night off. Though Beth told her that Michael was nothing at all like April, their first meeting really surprised Connie, as Michael was so nice and not conservative like April. She was also shocked that April and Michael were hanging out at The Basement. It sure didn't seem like their type of place, since neither of them actually drank. On Saturday night, with Jeremy at his father's, Michael was back at The Basement, and had a date with a guy she'd met during the week. He didn't show up, but Frank, the biker, was there once again.

They'd been out twice before while she was living with April, after he'd helped her get rid of Donny. Michael was crazy about him, but they did not mesh together too well in bed. It was not for the lack of trying, they tried several times. So, she decided he would be her big brother instead. At seven in the morning, Michael pulled in the driveway, with Frank right behind on his Harley. She decided, if she couldn't handle Frank in the sack, maybe Beth could. Besides, she knew that Beth needed a new man-diversion to take her mind off Rob. Beth only had a few one-might stands since they broke up. She couldn't find a man that interested her anymore.

Michael rousted Beth from her hung-over sleep to meet Frank. She'd heard much about him from Michael, so dragged herself out, perhaps more tipsy than presentable. Still in full make-up, wearing a long, silky-blue Grecian-style nightgown that hugged her boobs, she stopped to put on a robe. No idea where it was, so what the hell - *'take me as I am, or not at all.'* It wasn't as if he was the insurance man doing a reference check on her. Beth stumbled out and sat with her legs tucked under her, on the recliner across from Frank on the nearest couch.

What Michael thought would be a half-hour talk, lasted till noon. There was something electric between Beth and Frank from that moment. He'd never met anyone quite like her before, which within itself was not surprising. Still, feeling the affects of the alcohol, she rattled on about all kinds of crazy stories. Frank loved the story about Bobby Ryan, as Michael had related it, which surprised and impressed Beth. Obviously, *not* a man jealous or intimidated by much, he gave her kudos for the 'balls' to go for propositioning a movie star. He was also not the type of man that broke out into riotous laughter, but she really did crack him up several times, repeating some of the stories Bobby had told them about his most recent movies.

Quite a sight, shifting around, Beth sometimes rocking in the recliner, as Michael made them coffee, and found left over brownies Beth made for Jeremy. There was an allure of her loosely-tossed long, blonde hair, with a bit of smudged, eye-massacre, that only a freshly, awakened-female could have. Coming back into the living room with more coffee, Michael realized the chemistry transpiring, and if she could have dissolved at that time, she knew other things would have taken place. Frank had the mutual sixth-sense of a keen Scorpio, and it messed with Beth's triple-Scorpio accents, which often intimidated other men. As much as she laughed and joked with her stories, he felt something deeply bothering her, she tried to cover up.

But, it was her strange, satirical habit of talking with different intonations, accents and impressions - her Freudian-facade that she was more exciting when she talked in someone else's voice. About two hours of her jabbering dialects, Frank finally asked, "Don't you have a real voice of your own?" Beth was stunned. No one had ever been so outspokenly-honest with her, she was tongue-tied - a real rarity.

Michael almost fell off her couch with laughter. "She always talks like that, isn't it crazy?" Michael giggled, and so glad she'd stayed mostly quiet, as they were both intriguing to watch, she felt like a voyeur of verbal-foreplay. It took Beth several minutes before she could find her natural voice to talk with. He broke through the barrier, with his one question/comment. This strange, different man made the real Beth stand up, acknowledge herself and even like herself.

Michael continued to tell Frank how Beth used different variations of her name, when she was playing a different persona. Frank looked at Beth like she grew several heads, but quite fascinating heads. Michael rolled on, "You see, she uses the different names with the different guys, and they each represent a different person, she plays when she is with that guy." Beth almost posed, as if being photographed during an interview - or still the leftover booze.

"Like what?" Frank questioned with amazement, totally into the whole-ball-of-wax.

"Well," Michael paused, looking at Beth like maybe she was letting-out too much, and Beth shrugged her shoulders for her to continued, "she is Elizabeth when she wants to be sophisticated and worldly, using her New York accent, and speaking with her best vocabulary. Then she uses Liz for pickups, and says 'fuck' a lot. Liza is her 'little girl,' southern accent, acting like a dumb-blonde - usually on macho guys. The Beth or Bethie, when she is mostly midwest, middle-class or talking with the girls she knows." Beth began to giggle and snicker, as Michael had all of them almost down-pat.

Frank looked straight into Beth's eyes, and said like his words were to be chiseled in granite, "I only want to know Elizabeth and Beth, and don't forget it." It fascinated Beth this all meant so much to him. When Frank left, he never said a word about when he'd see her again, except for, "Catch your act later . . . " But Beth knew she affected him, and she'd see him very soon, the 'next act' would *not* include impersonations, and they both knew that.

The following Friday night, Beth joined Michael when she went to The Basement. She'd only been there once before, and it was the disastrous night she went out with Wally. Yes, she could have gotten him, he had always liked her, but she simply didn't want him. Beth was out of dress for The Basement, but she was not the type for *'holey'* Levis. The cast of characters down there was like no other, though it was much milder than it had been. There were many more *'citizens'* (non-bikers, gangsters or dopers) these days journeying in, as if to play their *'walk on the wild side'* role. Or just to observe the real bikers, as it *was their eminent-domain*. They had established it more than twenty years before, and still controlled it, when they had to.

Beth and Michael had not been sitting at the bar long, when Frank strode in with several other bikers. He came straight over to Beth, before she even noticed him come in. Michael felt him, but hadn't much of a chance to let Beth know - as she was busy talking to the cute bartender. Once Frank sat down, his presence silently-demanded the attention of everyone around, even Beth.

Basically sober, and mildly impressed, as Michael told her of his commanding aura, but she missed it the week before in her inebriated state, until he was leaving. His drink was in front of him without asking. Most noticeably, when his 'brothers' came up to talk to him, it was like paying allegiance. He did not introduce Beth to any of them, which she didn't understand, and they didn't ask. One of the younger brothers, not as well trained, asked "Who's the new broad?"

Frank snapped back, "That's no broad, that's a lady. And, I would not introduce her to the likes of you." Beth had visions of a middle-class, mid-western version of *The Godfather* - very low budget, of course. Though sure, some of these guys were capable of as much violence, as their leader would ask for. Almost everyone noticed when Frank *lit her* cigarette, and *bought her* a drink - *'a super no, no.'*

To the bikers, females were to be used for amusement. The girls usually bought the guys drinks, and even lit their cigarettes. When Frank then started leaned over to talk sweet to Beth, and even kissed her at the bar, it was too much for Michael. She nudged Beth to go to the restroom with her. Not knowing what was happening, and excusing herself from Frank, Beth reluctantly went.

As soon as the door was closed, Michael opened up, "What the hell have you done to him? I've never seen Frank, or any of the bikers act like that around a girl before. If it was anyone else, man, would they hear about it." Beth still didn't understand, she didn't realize she'd practically swept Frank off his feet. Michael encouraged her to go home with him if he asked, and as soon as she could, before he totally lost his *'cool'* to the gang. Beth said she had all the intention of doing so. She knew he'd be good for her, and she just might be good for him.

After a couple more drinks, Frank asked if Beth would like to cut-out and go to his 'crib?' Almost funny to her, to hear someone talk like James Dean would have, but she didn't snicker. She gave the car keys to Michael, and left with him. But, she was not really sure what she was getting into with this man, who was so completely self-confident himself - like no other she'd ever met. It had happened so naturally, that they both felt they'd see each other that night. Yet, she wasn't sure if she was quite ready for it all.

Dawn Rising

I watch your sleeping face
in the morning light.
I have long accepted the reality
of no permanent, or perfect lover.

Yet, I am not an entity unto myself.
You complete the last twenty-five percent of me.

Was it that good, or has it been
that long, since it was good?
Maybe it was just because neither
of us, had to steal away in the night.

A chill quivers down my spine as I watch you.

Your arm tightens around me,
as if you can read me in your sleep.
You nuzzle in closer, as I feel
the heat from your body meet mine.

My hips rise up to reach you, in their response.
My breasts are uplifted, to feel you closer.

I am like Alice falling through
the tunnel, after the White Rabbit.
But you are no dream - the real thing,
is better for a change.

CHAPTER 11

A Glimmering Presence

Frank drove a new El Camino for transporting his Harley around in to meets and stuff. As soon as they were in the car, Beth began to feel uptight. Only seconds later Frank felt what was going through her, and at the first stop light, he pulled her over and kissed her gently, "Relax Baby, anytime you want to get out of this, just say so, and I'll take you home." Immediately the tension was gone and she knew this was going to be one night she would remember for a long time.

The car flew home to his 'crib.' Once again, Beth was mildly impressed. Michael told her he had a snazzy apartment, but she still thought she'd be walking into a grease pit, where all the guys would be collecting to work on their bikes. It couldn't have been more of the opposite. First, the mirrored walls and ceiling struck her, as they walked through the back door, which was by the bedroom. The neatly made bed, was without a single pair of socks or underwear to be seen anywhere. She could tell the rug, which went up to the mirrors, was freshly vacuumed.

The kitchen was ultra modern, with a glass topped table, stainless steel chairs and not a dish in the sink. The living room was plushly carpeted, and his masculinity fulfilled with a black, nine-foot leather couch, stereo-tape deck-bar and a massive color television set. A combination of paneling, wallpaper and more mirrors set it off, yet not overdone. The sparkling-clean picture window looked-over the pool area, and his Harley chained right out the front door. An original design painted onto the kitchen wall, blended into the living room. Beth couldn't believe when he said he'd done the decorating by himself, with a little help from his brothers. Most impressive was the bathroom - done in one-inch square mosaic tile - floor, walls and ceiling. Frank casually referred to it as '*therapy,*' when he worked-through a few problems.

Frank told her to fix herself drink, and *asked* if she could get him a beer, while she was in the fridge for ice. Even that was spotless, and had real food in it, not the usual empty, bachelor's beer cooler. The only thing Beth noticed slightly-dirty was the humungous, glass ashtray on the plate-glass coffee table in the living room. This man, that lived outside of mainstream society, had more possessions that most hard-hats, and much cleaner.

He introduced her to Pink Floyd music, and she was leaning-in to truly listen, nodding with a smile of enjoyment. Not surprised he'd chosen well for her, as they settled into the massive couch to talk. And, talk they did. He sensed she needed someone to listen to her, other than her girlfriends. Beth began to get self-conscious talking so much, so he moved over by her. She'd settled into the safety of the couch-corner for some reason.

Frank gently shifted her around, so they were face to face, but he now had his arms around her soothing her neck, shoulder and arms. She'd worked two shifts at the Cafe' that day. Every once in a while, he'd lift her face up with two fingers and kiss her lips, ears, nose and neck. Finally, when it all drained out of her, and she began to respond more each time to the kisses. The tension slowly removed with each stroke of his hand and kiss from his lips.

Frank was an emotion-healer. He then asked how long it had been since a man had made love to her. Beth tensed her back-up for a minute, "I don't know, I don't write it down every time I screw!" She hadn't gotten him yet, and that he wasn't trying to control her, so a part of her tried to fight back by sounding like Liz.

Something she'd learn in time, she would rarely be one up on Frank. "I didn't ask you when was the last time you got fucked! Now, answer the question. I wouldn't ask such a thing if it wasn't important to me, *Elizabeth!*"

She couldn't understand why he cared, but what difference did it make, he cared. It had been so long, she couldn't even remember. She began to tell him about Rob, and how she *had* loved him. How he *had* been such a life-saver regarding her divorce, and how Bruce had been toward her. When she'd begin to choke-up, he'd hold her tight and kiss her tenderly. The vast range of his personality was almost mind-boggling. Frank began glueing back all the pieces of her broken-psyche, when she thought she'd never even find them again.

After she finished pouring out her feelings, he began kissing her again. But this time it was different, she could feel the passion beginning to grow in him. As he kissed her, he carefully started leaning her back down into the couch. Once again the panic began running up her spine, as she questioned herself, *"What am I doing here, with this strange man?"* Before her mind could answer the question it had asked, he moved from her lips to her ear and whispered, "I'm going to make love to you, the way a woman like you should be loved - from head to toe, and every inch in-between. I want to feel your body respond to me, the way it has never responded to a man before." He laid it out rather simply for her, *to try to* comprehend.

Not a command, but a release, so it seemed like Beth no longer had any control over anything. As she began to float, she totally let go, to enjoy everything around her. When he started kissing her waist, she knew not to resist, but relax and enjoy him. During the talking he gently undid her blouse, and released her full breasts from the confines of her bra. Her body became more agile and flexible, than she'd have ever believed possible.

Beth became more sensitive to every touch. His hands and lips were almost suspending her off the couch, as he touched and kissed down her neck, between her breasts and across from hip to hip. She was saying things, and responding like she never knew she was capable of doing.

She unbuttoned his shirt, to feel the texture of his skin against hers. He was squeaky-clean, like the rest of his surroundings, with only a natural smell of fresh washed. His body was amazingly cool, as compared to hers, as her fingers gently felt small scars down the middle of his chest. Not wanting to distract him fully, she slowly whispered, "What are the scars on your chest from?"

"A scattergun, a long time ago." Beth flinched from the imagined pain, but was not startled. Her curiosity was trying to get the best of her, yet his sensual touching rousted her emotions so, nothing else seemed very important. She'd simply file this latest information away in her mind, along with the total incongruity of this man, probably capable of the extremes of violence and tenderness.

Frank slipped her slacks off in one easy movement, while in the return motion he slipped her onto the thick, soft carpet. Her legs unfolded, as he began to kiss and caress the outside and inside of her thighs. Her body magnetically kept rising up toward him, seemingly uncontrolled by her. Before she knew it, he had her at such a high pitch, she was moaning to feel the fullness of him in her. He put her off, as he wanted to show her another new area of satisfaction.

"Nothing's going to be rushed," he whispered, "you've been rushed by too many men, and not fully appreciated. We have all night, . . . nothing but time to enjoy, over and over again . . . each other's body."

Beth's experience with having a man perform oral sex on her was limited, as compared to her learning the talent in taking care of a man. Connie, of course, felt it was the ultimate of what a man wanted, but Beth already found out from John spoiling her, that wasn't always true. Rob had never indulged in cunnilingus with her, or with the '69' position, perhaps thinking Beth wasn't into exploring new ways of satisfaction. Frank knew the greater pleasure a man had in satisfying a woman thoroughly. Beth began having the occasional, multiple orgasm, like little-blips building to a finale, with Rob at his best, Bobby, of course, and John.

But with Frank, a totally different saga - more than a simple story. He'd start over and over again, from her ears to go down one side of her body, and then the other, ending each time with giving an uncontrollable climax. Within a moment's notice when ever so slight a hesitation between these trips up and down her body, Beth grasped the chance to return the favor. It was the first time she'd ever been assertive, when making love to man in this way.

She'd waited for them to ask for something, but she knew this man could handle the changing-her and the situation. She held him, and kissed him as he moved with her when she rolled him over. Now it was her turn to show him, her experience might not be as vast, but her sensuality had never been so fully released before. She aptly removed the rest of his clothes, as she kissed and teased him with her hands and her mouth. She began also with his face and ears, slowly moving down his chest - tickling his nipples with her tongue, till he giggled to stop - and onto his abdomen, again teasing his 'short and curlies' with her fingers and tongue.

Ever so slowly now, she stroked his legs, and gently kissed his thighs, like she'd not noticed his enlarged muscle. So far, he had been quiet, but she wanted to hear him respond the way she had, so when he least expected it, she put her mouth on him. Even as she progressed, a few suggestions for improvements, which she followed carefully. Her hands continued on him, as his had on her. Then slowly the sounds of pleasure, she'd wanted to hear were coming from him, when he slowly pulled her up onto him, as he showed her in one easy move how to slip-up and mount him. It was an unusual position for her, that he soon made her enjoy, as he held her tightly to the flying end.

Several minutes disappeared, with body and mind coming back into existence, he then slowly rolled her over, reaching for her drink and their cigarettes. After inhaling, he joked, "You're not bad once you loosen up." Beth laughed, took a swallow of her drink, but didn't know what to say for a change. He was more than totally different than Rob, or even more so than the one-nighters she'd had since.

She'd said, she'd never compare another man to Bobby, simply because the whole 'aura of his status' changed the comparison. But, Frank was definitely in Bobby's league, and having him all to herself certainly made a difference. Honest and real were the words that kept filling her, as she sat completely relaxed and satisfied next to him. He took a couple of long swallows from his beer, and then kissed her again. "You're better than the beer." He responded to his own comment, by setting the beer back on the glass table, and dropped the unfinished cigarette into the ashtray.

Beth's heart started pounding in anticipation, before he'd even turned back to her. He gently took her glass and cigarette away, as he pulled her on top of him to stretch-out. They lay and talked and kissed, then once again he spoiled her with his time and leisure of the most thorough love-making she'd ever experience. Like a Picasso creating a new work of art, he found new and different ways to bring the orgasms on her. Sometimes, she could barely breathe from the energy that welled up inside, only to burst out uncontrollably.

As the dawn glanced into the picture window, a rainbow prism reflected through the beveled corner of the plate glass of the coffee table, showing from underneath their drinks and the ashtray. It was so totally surreal, yet still could not compare, as when he took her the last time. He'd given her a countless number of climaxes before, yet she could not believe what sensations he gave her now. It wasn't until he was positive she was thoroughly exhausted, that he leaned down and whispered, "Once more for me, so we can fly together." It seemed an impossible feat, which he made happen just by his asking for it.

Afterwards, Beth lying by his side, could feel the ripple of the sensations he'd given her. As if someone had thrown a gigantic rock in a small, still pond. The tingling-circles started from her abdomen, lead out to the tips of her fingers and the ends of her toes. They kept repeating, getting only slightly weaker with each ripple. She glanced again out the window, and the light-angle through the glass top was sending refractions all around the room, like some *"Midsummer's Night Dream"* whimsical decor or theater set.

She'd never walked, or sat on such a thick, shag-carpet, much less made love on it all night. Her skin liked its sensuousness. She glanced over at Frank, and the prism of light was glistening his long, dishwater blonde hair, and across his gold, muscular body. She slowly smiled, he surely accomplished what he had promised, and more. Bobby Ryan momentarily slipped through her mind, as she had a new, more glimmering-presence she'd imagine, when she wanted to feel good from top to bottom.

Frank opened his dazed, blue-gray eyes, and giving her a gentle kiss, he slowly got up, as he pulled her up with him. "Come on. Let's go to bed. I don't know about you, but I'm wiped-out." Beth's agility was gone, as she rose up to him. He kissed her again, and she followed him to the bed they'd never gotten around to using. Under the sheets, he kissed her once more pulling her toward him, and they both fell into a deep, very peaceful sleep. Even laying there drifting off, she saw the reflection of his body in the mirrors above, and still felt him covering hers

They'd had quick showers, as Beth reminded Frank she had to work. While he drove her home that afternoon, Beth couldn't help but keep smiling as she recalled the night before. But, they were not ready for the reception that was waiting. April popped over to join Michael. She'd have preferred to have Beth alone, to find out the details of their night before. But, Frank plopped down to observe the group. April also intrigued him, but in the complete opposite direction. He didn't understand how someone with her running-mouth would be let out unprotected. She didn't know how Frank felt about her, so he'd feed her lines and she'd swallow them whole.

She'd been bitching to Michael about hanging out with dopers - though of course, not herself, who'd been on *diet pills* for years now. Her best line was, "Dope is for dopers, isn't that right Frank?"

"Sure is," he said, "I never touch the stuff myself." Beth and Michael were about to say something when they noticed the smirk on his face. April never caught on to most of what any of the bikers said, it went right over her head anytime she'd been at The Basement.

Beth walked back into the room, as April started in about putting cream on her face, and setting her hair in front of Frank. She was so comfortable with him, she knew it wouldn't affect him. "April, I have to get ready for work, and he knows that. It's not as if we're in high school, and he just brought me home from the prom. The man knows what I look like, good and bad."

Alex then called, so she left like the good, little wife. April could be a real bore, when she did her sweet-facade in front of a man. Beth made tentative arrangements to see Frank again, knowing she could not pin him down. Frank had made it more than clear to her, that when he could see her, he would. His free spirit was one of the things that attracted him to her. But, she couldn't help herself, again falling love with a man who had thrown her a life preserver.

Michael began to go out with another biker, Don, but it wasn't as if they went double-dating. Rob heard the feed-back from going to the Cafe', that Beth had a new boyfriend. He'd always be jealous no matter what their relationship was, so he called her. Beth also heard that he'd been seeing another younger girl who worked at the Cafe', though she'd seen it coming. He wanted to see her for old time sakes, he missed her. Beth was anxious to see him too, not only to see if something was still there, but because she wanted to flaunt Frank at him. When she met him for lunch, the revenge disappeared as he began pouring his heart out to her. Without even knowing it, she had faired much better than he had. Rob lost his general contractor job, and almost became an alcoholic in those five moths without her. He'd never realized how much he'd loved her.

Beth showed her weakness by taking Rob back into her bed. But, this time it was different, for she had the upper hand. She still loved him somewhat, but never what it had been, he'd blown it. This time it was him needing her, and he kept apologizing all over the place for the other girl. He guessed he could replace Beth with her, but he rattled on, "She was terrible in bed, just laying there and not very smart, with nothing ever to talk about." Beth caught herself snickering and apologized, though he admitted he deserved it. He hadn't seen her in a month, and he wouldn't anymore. Beth agreed to see him, but he must accept that there were other men in her life. Rob knew Beth'd changed - again, but didn't know how much this time.

Strange but, Connie also was having qualms about Cam. A very influential and wealthy man, Stuart Cunningham, took an interest in her. Several years older than Cam, and more than willing to spoil Connie with his money. Very surprised that he was so young at mind, while having dinner one night at "The 95th" on top of the John Hancock Building, he turned the conversation to drugs. Not unknown that Connie indulged, but Stuart had no idea how often or to what extent. What surprised Connie the most, after spending almost a hundred dollars on her that evening, he made no quibble about just a kiss good night.

On their next date, Stu gave Connie a gift box the same size approximately for an expensive necklace. Excitedly, she opened the leather case to find enclosed a dozen, pure Columbian-joints laying on the velvet lining. A string of those expensive pearls, wouldn't have thrilled her as much. The price of that particular marijuana easily equaled the cost of the pearl necklace. He said he had it flown in that day for her. Stu taught her the foolishness of money - "It's of no use unless it's spent on happiness. Besides, *it's only money*."

This became her mantra from that day on, and they all heard it repeated whether appropriate or not. Of course, it was difficult for this hard-core, hard working Capricorn to believe at first, but as long as it was his money - OK. And, she threw the half-smoked joints out the electric window of his new El Dorado. *"There'd be plenty more where that came from,"* she thought.

In a short time, she'd probably thrown away more grass than she'd ever smoked. Because this was also the finest and strongest, it only took a drag or two for her to be flying. Stu still hadn't made any sexual advances toward her, so she began to feel safe with him. One night he was snorting some cocaine, and offered her some. She flatly refused. "It's only coke, what are you afraid of? Nobody gets hooked on coke, especially if you only take it once in a while."

He gave up trying to get her to snort the coke after several different times, then he said, "This is better, it's not just ordinary snorting, but through a hundred-dollar bill " - as if that made it better. Still not playing his game, as somehow all the gifts he gave her, and the luxurious dinners were becoming suspicious. Beth tried to warn her, it didn't matter about the grass, but if he got her hooked on the coke, she'd have to depend on him to supply it for her.

She'd never be able to support that kind of habit. Somehow those *vitamin* shots he supposedly gave himself were also suspicious. Could it be, one the suburbs finest, upstanding-businessmen was a doper of the highest caliber?

Cam began to hassle Connie about Stu, saying he didn't want her to see him anymore. Connie decided to do a turn about. A big fight ensued, with her saying she wouldn't see Cam any more, as she'd continue to see Stu. It was taking a chance, but it made Cam wake up. Yet, when he started crying, she told him she'd not see Stu anymore. She'd gotten Cam to say he truly loved her, and couldn't live without her. *Again,* he'd get rid of his other girlfriend, and in a fit of alcoholic-frenzy, he even said he'd get a divorce. Connie was elated, she was going to win after all, she'd known if she could hold on long enough, she'd get him. He did love her *enough* to get a divorce and marry her. If only she'd threatened leaving him before, perhaps they'd have been married by then.

Unfortunately, when Cam woke up in the morning, with his more than gigantic hangover, he didn't remember a thing he'd said, or done the previous night. Nothing said in a drunken stupor was legal, or binding to him. Connie held to her promise though, not to see Stu again. All for the better, since she didn't need to get back into the drugs once again.

Tomorrow

Why do I want to know tomorrow?
        Why can't I just enjoy today?
                I do not worry about yesterdays so.

        But, if I knew tomorrow -
                would it make me more prepared?
Or, would I then prefer to remain in today?

            What shall I do?

        I cannot change my yesterdays,
                nor know my tomorrows.

I must learn to accept and live with today.

CHAPTER 12

If I Only Knew

Driving them all crazy with her new *'housfrau'* image, sickeningly domestic, Beth was about to scream every time April called. It hadn't been that long ago, her world extended only as far as her next dinner-party-menu. All April ever talked about any more, was her needlepoint her wonderful mother-in-law taught her, or some delectable-garbage she was serving for *dinner* out-of-a-box. Before she woke up, the deception almost cost her the friendship of Beth, and maybe Michael. Whatever anybody wanted to say or do, was fine with Michael, as long as it didn't affect her, but April was getting to be a bore and lecturer. It wasn't as if they knew where they were going in their lives, they just knew what they didn't want to get back into. April reeked of *cop-out*, she'd opted for a quickie marriage, rather than stand on her own.

After their fourth month anniversary, April threw down the needlepoint and came marching over to Beth's house. The *love* had gone out of her blessed marriage - this meant she wasn't getting sex as regular. As per usual for April, she again made a mountain out of a mole hill. Beth felt she was never happy just to be happy, too much of fatalist. Not as if the sex had gradually slowed down, from the usual six times a night, Alex just quit wanting to have sex altogether. It dropped from once a week when she first complained, to once a month. She feared he was having an affair with a girl at his office, which made her even more upset. Then Beth asked, "Have you discussed it at all?" She didn't like playing 'Dear Abby.'

April shook her head 'no.' "I don't know him well enough."

Taking a line from her brother Mike, Beth yelled, "Are you shitting me?!?" She was beyond stupid. "Of course, April, I'd be the last one to say, 'I told you so,' about marrying someone you only knew four weeks." There was no making sense of April, or her problems.

She wanted some solution, and there wasn't going to be any, if he or she didn't talk about it, how could the problem be solved. What exactly was wrong with the relationship, he didn't want to acknowledge? And, if it wasn't an affair, but a sexual problem, like so many men, they figure it will go away, if it's ignored. When in actuality, most male or female problems can be helped with a few sessions talking to a good psychologist. The woman of yesterday never questioned her husband on his sexuality, or lack of it. For the woman who was from yesterday, it was fine, but today's woman wanted as much out of sex as her man. Maybe more, if she's capable of having many orgasms to his one, why not, the sky is the limit.

April wasn't miserable enough to get a divorce, and to do so the epitome of ignorance, if all they have to do is sit down and talk - like the adults they were supposed to be. It had taken eight years with Wally for her to go through with a divorce. Beth would not be very sympathetic - either do something about it, or quit complaining. If she would not talk to Alex, or divorce him - then suffer through with him, and keep her mouth shut.

They both put on such a front for each other before they got married, that neither one had ever shown any of his or her true feelings or thoughts. There were many things they were both interested in, but some things they never discussed at all - the real way he felt about kids and all of his different prejudices. They could sit and talk for hours, yet he always wanted to be right about whatever the subject. He was brilliant, but on some subjects he was fanatical. He'd sit and play songs to her on his guitar, but she had to give him her complete attention - she absolutely couldn't do anything else.

The next crisis came the following week after her discussion with Michael and Beth. Alex went to San Diego for a business meeting. He was supposed to have taken April, but he changed his mind at the last minute. When she called that evening, there was no answer in his room, so she kept calling every hour until she got an answer - at three-thirty in the morning. First he told her he'd been in all night, then he told her another story. When she questioned him about the noise in his room, he hung up on her.

Hysterical when she called, neither Beth or Michael could understand what she was saying. Sure Alex was cheating on her, and she had caught him in the act - over the phone. He started lying to her, the same way Al had, for no reason at all. After about an hour, the combination of them calmed her down enough to get some sleep. The next day, she again called and got a very flimsy excuse about him being drunk the night before. She was very suspicious and jealous person, because of her insecurities, as well her past cheating behavior. Added to that, of course, she never trusted any man. Yet, this time she may have been right. Still, she was quite delusional in believing every man she had was so desirable, that other women clamored for them.

While things did not improve between them, they still never communicated with each other about any of it. When April had sex, she was happily married, when she didn't, she yelled and screamed, saying she'd divorce the son-of-a-bitch. Sometimes Beth and Michael thought it was better having the phony, hausfrau-April than the screaming, complaining bitch. That weird Aries-personality: when she was good, she was fascinating, interesting, honest and enjoyable.

When she was bad, well . . . bitch was the only word. If any good came out of the 'cheating' incident, it was that April came to believe she did love Alex. No longer just a security blanket or meal-ticket she married, she was trapped in 'love' again. Now, at her most vulnerable, she sacrificed her own identity for his. It would be more difficult to talk to her, with no open-mind about getting divorced, or any other solution.

Despite April's domestic turmoil, it was a good summer for everyone else, including pregnant Michael. After Frank embarrassed her one night in The Basement, about taking lessons in oral sex from Beth, she decided she needed a guinea-pig to practice on. She developed an inflammation - from staying in the pool too much with Jeremy - that made intercourse painful. With this understanding, she got 'Crazy Don,' the biker, to be her practice-subject, since she also had a crush on him. Don practically lived at Beth's house that summer. He'd come and go even when they weren't home - if he forgot his key, he knew the back door was always open. They'd find his wet-trunks in the tub after helping himself to the pool. The only problem was, Don blabbed to all his friends about paradise found - he got to swim, was fed, boozed and gladly used for oral-sex-practice by Michael. In return, he freely gave Beth and Connie some good grass.

One Friday night, while down at The Basement, Michael and Beth were talking to some of the other bikers. Since Michael told them, - and Beth kinda agreed - they weren't really the 'old ladies' of Don and Frank, the guys thought they could move in. When Mike and Carmie offered to take them for rides on their bikes, it was all they had to say. Michael loved riding the Harley almost as much as Beth did. It was one of those perfect summer nights for riding - fantastic, just cruising around. At that time of night, there wasn't too much traffic to bother them. Mike was very careful with his very pregnant passenger. It seemed unbelievable that these men, who were almost frightening on the outside, were so considerate on the inside.

Beth and Michael heard, even knew of the things the bikers were capable of doing, yet they'd never been anything but nice and protective of them. In fact, Michael said many times later, if it hadn't been for the lot of them, she would've never made it through that pregnancy. They never once looked down on her in any way because of it, in fact, several of them respected her for going through with it. They knew she'd decided to give the baby up for private adoption.

At the same time, the guys never considered Beth or Michael, in the same class as the girls that hung out at the Club. Most of them were used by whomever wanted them. They were addicted to the Club, as well some of them supporting a habit, many also 'hooked,' to support their man. Because of their 'free-agents of any man,' before they knew it, Carmie and Mike were coming over to the house. Unfortunately, one of the brothers mentioned to Don what was happening, when he walked in The Basement. A little afraid someone was going to take his paradise away from him, he also headed for Beth's house.

As per usual, Beth was wasted when she hit the bed with Carmi. They had barely gotten started when Don pulled in the drive, and revved-up his bike. The surprise, and closeness of noise to her bedroom window, scared the hell out of Carmie - literally ending the sex. Beth was absolutely furious when he panicked, putting his clothes on. She started yelling and screaming at him, then Don pounded on the door laughing. Michael and Mike had finished before Don could interrupt them.

Beth came marching out of the bedroom cursing and calling Carmie a *'bum-fuck'* for not staying and taking care of her. She was telling him as he walked out, about sending someone over to finish the job. It was not one of her more ladylike-episodes. The fact that she didn't get her head knocked off, for talking that way to Carmie was amazing, and probably because of her relationship to Frank. Booze-speaking out of the mouth of a horny-broad was not too pleasant, but unfortunately very memorable. Poor Carmie was *'ragged-on'* by his brothers for weeks afterwards.

Surprisingly, Frank was not too upset. He called a week later and said he volunteered to finish the job Carmie started. But at the same time, without actually saying it specifically, he let Beth know, if she was going to play with his brothers, she wasn't going to be with him *at all*. He did not care if she was with other men, he just didn't want to have it be one of his brothers, or hear about it from them. They would talk about her in a different way than Frank wanted to hear. He cared much more about her, than he wanted to admit.

The summer breezed by with long, sunny afternoons laying in the pool - it was just a three foot above ground, but it worked well for them. Beth learned from Michael not to be so serious, and to stop worrying about bills and money. "They quit putting people in debtor's prison years ago." That was fine for Michael to say, but Beth worried about Michael, like a first-time father, with the baby coming any day. At the Cafe', anytime she'd get a phone call, the guys in the kitchen asked if she was a 'father' yet. If any unusual pain, Beth jumped, since this was Michael's fourth delivery, it would probably come fast. But typical Michael, showed no concerns about any of it.

In many ways, Beth tried to get back at Bruce for all the years he'd hurt her, and usually as soon as he was in her presence, she'd lose control and yell at him. He certainly brought out the hostility in her, while Michael kept telling her that revenge and hate were a wasted-effort. She slowly started to forgive Bruce, but her Scorpio wouldn't forget. She eventually quit plotting to find some way to get back at him, as Michael made her see there was only a lost-shell of a man left anyway. Beth's new language surprised Bruce, as she'd never heard the word *'fuck'* out loud before she'd met him, and though not common in her sober-talk, she wasn't afraid of saying it.

As Michael and Beth became closer and more involved in one another's lives, the new woman in Michael still had not quite emerged. Because of her pregnancy, there were many things she did not encounter, the the rest of them had - as they were put off until after the baby. But utmost importantly, having the messiest divorce, at least she'd never been alone. Though her mother was great in many ways, she didn't let Michael be dependent on her, but there when really needed it.

After one false alarm, Michael went in to have the baby. Typically, in the middle of the night, Beth was dressed, out the door and in the car before Michael got off the phone with the doctor. She'd bought a new Oldsmobile, when Michael couldn't to fit behind the steering wheel of the little, Volkswagen. She raced to the hospital in seven minutes, with her emergency-lights flashing. Beth fit the part of the protective-father superbly. Only a short while in labor, when they sent Beth to wait in the father's room. Thank God it wasn't crowded.

She practically ran out of the room when the phone rang, and couldn't hold back the tears, when she took Michael's hand. She remembered her loneliness when almost losing Jeremy, so she wanted Michael to know she wasn't going through this by herself. Assured by Michael to be fine, it hadn't registered that she mentioned the baby's sex. She said she 'just wanted to know out of curiosity.' Beth couldn't hold back the hesitant look, so she again assured her, "It's just curiosity, I don't want to keep it." Relieved, at that point Beth didn't need to take on any more.

Beth had set Michael up with her own excellent doctor, so she didn't have any blood trouble like before. The next day, she had a tubal ligation-sterilization operation. She more than proved, she didn't remember to take pills. Connie'd had the operation the year before, so encouraged her to have it - it was also part of the private adoption -

they paid for it. Michael *now* had a new life of her own ahead of her, more free than most people. April came to see her in the hospital too, and was happy to drive her home since, Connie and Beth were working. Totally ready, Michael couldn't wait to get started with her free life.

Just before Michael's delivery, Beth and Connie talked about how slow it'd been at the Cafe', and if things didn't pick up, the owner might close for a month or more. It was impossible to think how they'd live. Connie also worked a lunch job, but at the FireLite, since the Cafe' lunch staff was full. Supporting a house like Beth, although Connie's parents owned her house, but how long could she go without paying rent? The three of them sat talking of what to do, as Michael needed a job after the baby, too. Connie then suggested cleaning houses, as her mother told her about a cousin that was doing it for the summer, home from college.

By afternoon's end, the three of them had prices figured on what they would and wouldn't do, as well a name chosen. Beth'd be the head, since organizing was her forte, and such a penchant for responsibility. She thought it'd be a great idea to have other girls working for them, and collect a percentage. "Who knows," she said, "in no time we might have a franchise to become rich and famous." As usual, they thought Beth was nuts.

With Michael still at home, the calls came in for the jobs like wild-fire, but almost impossible to get help. Connie quit working lunches, to clean with Beth. A few customers took advantage, before every detail got worked out. Michael could hardly wait to get out to of the hospital to work. The Cafe' didn't close, but Beth decided to keep working at the housecleaning, while cutting back hours at the restaurant, and the same with Connie. It took a week or so to get used to the physical work, but then it was great money. Connie had a ball making so much money.

Michael worked lightly, a few days out of the hospital, and then she felt they hit the jackpot. For the first time in her life, Michael had money she could spend - any way she wanted. She had no expenses or bills, to speak of, so the money went through her hands like sand, never buying expensive larger items, but blowing it on crap-things she never could've splurged on before. It felt good to have money to spend on her kids, when she saw them. Now, with money she bought clothes for her new, slim body, to go out looking for a man.

Don came over the first weekend Michael was home, sitting on the front steps, while Beth mowed the lawn. He pulled in the drive, and before he even got out of the car, he was yelling over to Beth, "Who's the skinny-broad sitting on the steps?" Probably the best compliment Michael ever got from him. Yet, that was the last time she'd see him for months. She never figured out what happened, unless he felt she was getting too serious. A bad time feeling rejected, she waited so long to make love with him, then he disappears.

Michael went out by herself, as Beth moved into a regular routine with Frank usually coming over, or meeting her at The Basement to go to his place on the weekends Jeremy was gone with his father. The first man Michael got involved with was married, but she didn't find out until she started caring for him. It was a big, naive hurt. Beth was in bed with Frank, when Michael burst through the front door cursing and swearing. The two of them had fallen into a blissful sleep, not expecting to be bothered till morning from her. Frank thought it was hilarious that she'd be taken in, but he didn't understand, she'd just been released from her cocoon, still testing the wings, that had not been used on their own before.

Beth got up, and sat with her till she got it out of her system. Something she'd have to learn about men was that many of them lied, for various reasons to get sex. She felt nothing wrong with dating a married man, as long as he was honest about it, and your choice to invest time/emotions in him. The married ones sometimes treated a girl better, and if they didn't get any sex, they always had their wives. Beth told her not to waste time on any man that rushed her into sex, as they'd never be more than a one-night stand.

Michael pulled herself together, and went back out the next night, a little wiser. She'd have to learn for herself, and from her mistakes. She met another married man, David, but at least he was honest about it, and nice to her. He'd only be in town every month or so, and liked company for dinner, drinking and sex. He was good to her, and she appreciated that especially after the last one. At this time,

Michael decided to keep a record of how many men she had sex with. Since none of the other girls kept track, she thought it'd be fun. She wrote down his name, astrology sign if she got it, for the list to gain more meaning. Since she was now the least experienced, she wanted to go through all twelve signs of the zodiac. The problem with that, she usually didn't get their sign until after she was interested in him.

Michael was concerned when she got too many of the same signs. Yet, she'd begun to feel, it was *safer* to have sex with someone she *didn't* care about, than someone she did - so she wouldn't get hurt again. They'd all done this out of reaction to being hurt, yet somehow her method seemed more calculating. She also thought it would be fun to go back to some of the guys, she passed up before her divorce. The first one she called, of course, was Derek, since it was almost his birthday, she figured that was a good excuse.

It'd been over a year, and he still didn't want anybody to know about them, in case they'd think it had started before her divorce. After going to several bars, they ended up screwing in his car - again. He took her for granted, and basically was too cheap to spend the money on a motel room for a quickie. So much for the class-act she thought he was, or the nostalgia. Michael felt it changed between them, and she'd probably be free of his ghost haunting her - so, good for her to get him out of her system.

Next, she went looking for Stan, who she'd met the year before, and declined then to have sex with him. If she found him now, she felt she *owed him sex*. Beth, with her that night, tried to tell her *obligations* aren't paid with sex, but Michael'd made up her mind. When they found him, Beth figured him out in five minutes - he was the best looking and best dressed dude in a red-neck, hard-hat bar.

A man like this knew his limitations, and he'd never venture up to the swinging, big-city, moneyed-bars or even the classy, suburban ones. His glib talk, flashy clothes and smile impressed the 'hell out of' the factory-working women who fell all over him. But, he would've been laughed out of any bars where the competition was younger and hipper. He could bullshit these women, they'd believe every lie.

It took him a while longer to figure out that Beth was on to him, yet not blowing his cover completely. Each time he'd open his mouth with some smart-ass remark, she'd top him and leave him standing with his mouth open. She'd been around Cam and Connie too long, not to have picked up some of their lines. It got hilarious, the guy sitting next to Beth, kept buying her drinks, as he'd never seen Stan put-down in his life. "I'm proud to buy drinks for the lady who can do it." When Beth asked Stan to dance, he couldn't refuse, although he should've. She made a big ass out of him on the floor for more people to see, though making a floozy of herself.

While Michael went to the restroom, Stan admitted to Beth she was the winner. He said it would take a helluva of a man to handle her, and he was only a little boy, so Michael was more than enough. Beth was surprised he'd have enough guts to admit what a phony he was. She'd cut him down to size, something she always enjoyed doing to a man who thought he was something he was not. The way he bragged about not slowing down his sex life, even with a broken leg, was almost too much. She hoped he wouldn't be too bad in bed for Michael's sake. Beth knew from experience, most men who bragged on themselves in the sack, were all talk.

When Michael got back, Stan'd put back on his big front, and Beth couldn't help snickering. If he hadn't been so self-centered, there might have been room enough for a second person inside that narcissistic-heart. She finished her drink, and left the loveless couple. Michael began to lose the thought of caring about the other person, in her pursuit of more sexual experience. Maybe they weren't such a bad match after all.

The next morning at home, she admitted Beth'd been right about him. Not only a shallow and boring person, but lousy in bed, too. He was a perfect example of what they referred to as a 'plastic person.' He was genuine-artificial plastic through and through, so not capable of any true emotion, and self-satisfaction wasn't the end result. It was sad, a waste of what could have been a good man.

Michael promised to meet him the following night, though she didn't want to. It'd be a long time before she'd simply be able to say 'no,' to a man she didn't care about. She'd said 'yes' for so many years, she hadn't realized the freedom of choice she'd earned with her divorce. She finally called Stan with a trumped up excuse. Upset, but would forgive her this time, and said he'd see her the following night. Beth told her to tell him to just buzz-off, as she'd paid back her ridiculous obligation to him, why was she wasting time on him?

So, she didn't bother showing up or calling the next night either, she'd find another bar to go to. About four days later, Stan called back, saying "Out of the generosity of my heart, I'll give you one more chance to go out with me. I've punished you for three days by not calling you." Michael was awed, she couldn't believe he'd really think that much of himself. After a long silence, she blurted out to him that she would *not* waste her time on him, and to never call again, then promptly hung up. Beth applauded her for learning a lesson in having the upper hand. No man had a right to demand anything from any woman, or she from him.

Beth liked going out with Michael, though she was seeing Frank fairly regularly and Rob occasionally, so she wasn't really looking for guys to pick-up. She didn't want this to stop Michael, and it didn't. She explained to her, that one day she'd have her fill of different men, and be ready to settle down with one loving-man to make love with. Michael thought Beth was crazy, "Not me, not marriage and all that bullshit all over again." Beth could tell it was too soon to talk to her, she knew how she felt when she first got her divorce. Connie tried to talk to Beth the same way, but she had to find out for herself.

This was sort of a step-process for learning want they didn't want, and to believe who, and what they could become in growing up with their new, chosen freedom. Around them, they saw other women changing, most from going through a divorce, and a few whose husbands were more willing to change, than lose their woman. As always, it took women to make those first steps to initiate change, and some men would be supportive, while others would fight it 'tooth and nail' not to lose their power over women. Yes, they would falter venturing onto untread-ground, where no map or directions or how-to-help divorcees existed. Not really thinking of themselves as pioneers, but what else could they be called, if not 'strangers-in-a-strange-land,' figuring out how this freedom-and-choice-thing worked to their best advantage for happiness.

Unrequited Thoughts

The sweetest of anything -
is that which is out of reach.

The one we remember most -
is the one that got away.

If only - I had known
more and acted differently.

A second chance with the same love -
is never an equal one.

The grass will always be greener -
no matter how great our pasture.

Going back from whence we came -
nothing is ever the same.

CHAPTER 13

Learning Lessons

Connie decided to take Michael with her to Upper Peninsula Michigan to visit her relatives. Fall was the most incredible time of the year up there, with a zillion hard-wood trees in magnificent colorations, waterfalls and amazing, rock-formations surrounded by nothingness except nature in every direction. Beth was happy to handle the business for a few days, as they usually didn't have cleaning jobs on weekends, so Friday and Monday they'd be gone. She agreed that Michael truly needed to get away, she'd had nothing but bad luck with men since the delivery. She'd been surrounded by more willing men when she was pregnant. It'd also be good for her, because she'd never traveled for fun, so the change of scenery would be a good experience for mind-clearing. And, Connie's turn and chance to talk to her.

Beth knew no matter where they went, with Connie leading the way, two horny-people would find two *other* horny-people. The UP for short, was Michigan's back woods, there wasn't much to do but drink, have sex, hunt/fish or farm. Since the harvest was in, it only left the fun things to do. And, during the hunting season, men came from every surrounding state for the excellent and plentiful game.

For Connie and Michael, their game was to hunt for the *hunters* coming in from the woods. They went to town Saturday afternoon to bar-hop. The first one didn't show too much promise until two dudes walked in, that Connie knew were definitely not home-grown. Michael decided on the dark-headed one, and Connie on the blonde. The only problem was, nobody made any moves toward one another - the four of them sat staring from across the bar at each other. What was with that?

The guys walked out first, with the girls jumping up to follow them out. They were standing by their car not too far from the door. So, as to not seem too obvious, the girls turned and walked the other way, looking into the store windows, then back at the guys. When the guys got into their car and drove off, the girls gave up and walked into one of the shops. Later that night in different clothes, Michael and Connie were with her relatives back in the bar. After flirting with every man, and just before boredom set in, the two original dudes walked in. This time the girls weren't going to let them get away. Apparently, the guys felt the same way, as in no time Bob and Mark joined them. Mark asked Connie where they went that afternoon, when she told him, he couldn't believe it. The guys drove around town for almost an hour looking for them. What a waste of time.

The only problem now, Connie was bombed, and wanted to dance to the great music. She'd become so wound up, the manager asked her to sit down. She was attracting more attention than the go-go dancer. Mark practically carried her out when they left. The guys drove them up to their fishing cabin - the last five miles wasn't even a road. The 'cabin' had no heat or electricity, only light from a few candles. After seeing the condition of the cabin, Michael decided to stay in the *'Travelall'* with Bob in a sleeping bag. They proved beyond a shadow of doubt, that anything could be accomplished in a sleeping bag, if determined enough.

Difficult to imagine how they breathed, or much less what they must have looked like sharing oral sex in a sleeping bag. It should have been recorded as a miracle, or a world-wonder in the sex-annuals. Connie and Mark were doing just fine in the cabin, except for the frost-bite on certain parts of their bodies that got wet. If they kissed too long, their lips almost froze together. Connie soon passed out and Mark was exhausted. Michael and Bob kept each other warm, as well the friction of six-straight hours of the greatest-variety sex-marathon. Michael was satisfied more than thoroughly by this man. Her endurance record got back at her when she stood up. But, as long as she was horizontal, and him still willing, she didn't want to stop. Apparently, all the practice during the summer paid off, as no complaints this time.

They went into the cabin as the full dawn came up, and over-anxious Michael couldn't believe those two slept, and wasted so much time. She understood Connie had good sex at home with Cam on a regular basis, so she didn't need to do any cramming. Michael's attitude was get it while it lasted, as she never knew how long it would be till the next time. The guys were great fun. Mark came bounding out of the woods with a pine twig in his teeth, saying he'd been attacked by Euell Gibbons (of TV fame), so he had Connie and Michael in stitches. They'd never expected to have such a good time, out in the back woods.

Unfortunately, the guys were from Minnesota, with a very long drive home. Mark asked for Connie's address and phone number very enthusiastically. Bob asked, but not quite as interested. Connie could not believe Mark to be interested, between her drinking, hang-over and the way she looked in the morning, she was dumbfounded. Her hair kind of looked like it was combed with a half-melted candy bar when she got up.

When the two of them came dragging into her Aunt's house in the same, funky-clothes, a few eyebrows were raised. Connie dreamed up a story that they'd stayed with another cousin the night before. It wasn't believable, but acceptable. They spent the rest of the day catching up on sleep. The next day, they decided to drive over to see Michael's mother in Wisconsin - she had remarried and been living happily there. Though liberal, they didn't tell her their crazy story. After a good visit, they were anxious to be on their way home.

They couldn't wait to tell their story to Beth, she'd more than appreciate their woods' adventure. Connie decided to tell Cam the truth, since he'd never believe her. She made plans to see Mark again, but as those things go, with a few phone calls and letters, they never were able to connect again. As kind of expected, Michael never heard from Bob, but she'd remember him, and the night in the woods, that got her *'mojo'* back for many moons to come.

Back home things weren't too exciting, as Beth and Michael settled into Chicago's winter, but each caused enough scenes previously. One Friday night when out drinking, Michael wanted to return to her old haunt, where she'd spent so many hours with Donny.

She knew he was gone, so she wanted to see the bartenders, Joey especially always caught her eye. If not seeing Frank, and from working so much at both the cleaning and Cafe' on a Friday, Beth'd get drunk to unwind and relax. If she was on scotch, she wasn't bad, but when she drank vodka, look out, it just burned-a-hole in her brain. This time, on vodka and soda with lime - absolutely tasteless - but better than drinking the martinis. It made her unbelievably horny, and she'd 'fuck a snake, if you'd hold its head' as Connie said. The only problem, this was not the kind of establishment to get horny in. The guys here would screw a girl on a barstool, if she let them.

The drinks were free, since the older bartender, Frankie, was crazy about Michael, though Beth'd never been in the place before. Michael was circulating talking to old friends, while Beth drank, smoked and danced. Nothing in moderation as usual, "I'm Liz all the way tonight," she spouted. No one remembered when sex became the subject, but the next thing Michael knew Beth was passing out their cleaning-business cards, saying the cleaning service was just a front for hooking. Michael tried to shut her up when she started quoting prices. For some reason, Beth was arguing with Joey about being able to satisfy a man by oral sex. He kept saying it'd take an hour, or more because of his fantastic staying power. Beth, not to be out-done bragged, "Fifteen minutes in the parking lot, no teeth marks!"

At this Michael stepped-in again to tell her to shut-up, or a line would soon be forming. Beth didn't pay any attention, until the challenge was happily taken up by a half-dozen men, and Joey willing to be first. Beth laughed it off, until she realized the men were serious. She then added, "I'm not free, but I'm reasonable." She quoted fifty dollars for her performance, thinking this would deter them, and relaxed. Before she took another swallow of her magic sex-powered-liquid, four of them produced a wad of bills like she'd never seen before. Stunned, Beth didn't know what to say, she'd never backed down from a challenge, yet she'd never done anything like that before either. She prided herself in never taking money for sex. Talk about the ultimate of *'her mouth getting her ass in trouble!'*

Beth got up to casually go to the restroom, as she passed Michael, she said quietly, "I'll be leaving as soon as I get out of the restroom. If you're going with me, I'll wait in the car about thirty seconds before leaving." Michael didn't know what the hell was going on, but she knew Beth was dead-serious, and apparently, gotten way over her head again. She was absolutely pissed, but had no way to get home. Joey'd been too busy to talk to her, and there was no one else she was interested in being with.

Beth had the car-roaring to go at the side door when Michael jumped in, and she peeled away - loved how that big engine could move. She must have consumed a quart of vodka in the four or five hours they'd been out. It'd be a long time before Beth'd get herself in such a situation again. The skin on her teeth was wearing thin, as she more than learned her lesson. Connie laughed herself silly, when it was retold. Beth no longer thought it was too funny, since so sick, she just wanted to bury her head. That's it for vodka, never again - maybe.

Sunday was beautiful, so Beth decided to drive to her brother Mike's farm near Galena - he was a weekend farmer. She had Jeremy so wanted to do something outside with him. She'd never been to his farm for various reasons - mainly, Mike didn't like Bruce - but she wanted to go to rekindle her close relationship to her brother. The directions from her father weren't great - left turn at the old church, right turn at the two blue silos, etc. Connie came over as they packed up the car to leave. When she asked where they were going, Beth answered for a Sunday ride. Connie asked to join, since she wasn't doing anything exciting, but helping her parents at her old house. So, they took off not knowing exactly where they were going, or when they'd be back.

When Connie saw the sign for Dubuque, Iowa, she was ready to get out and walk back. They stopped for gas, and she called her parents to let them know where she was, although she didn't know. After driving around the hills and valleys for awhile, Beth realized the church had been torn down, and the farmer now had three blue silos. Just as they arrived at Mike's farm it started to rain. Michael was bored stiff, they'd been on these Sunday rides before, and it was never exciting. Mike sat around in his cut-off pajamas drinking, Barbara puttered-around in the kitchen cooking as usual. Barb was shocked by the braless-halter top Connie wore with her shorts, and also didn't like

Michael, because of her previous pregnancy situation. Of course, she didn't know either one, and her information came from her mother-in-law, who didn't like any of Beth's new, divorced friends.

Connie and Beth drank with Mike, as Michael had her usual coke. They both talked the legs off of Mike, with Connie relating Beth's latest escapade. Laughing wildly at her, though not surprised, he teased her, "You're *badder* than me." He continued to laugh while getting up to fix more drinks. Though they snacked when she gassed up, they ate a little not to insult Barb. A bit crowded in the old, mobile-home he'd modernized for their weekend trips out there, they went out to the picnic table as the rain quit. The sun was getting ready to set, and time to leave for the two-hour drive back, Beth called Jeremy. He'd had a great time as usual with Jackie and Jason, Mike's twelve and fourteen-year old sons. Though Michael hardly said a dozen words the whole time they'd been there, she'd also rarely took her eyes off Mike.

One night, sitting around Beth's kitchen table talking with Marie, who had dropped in - or rather escaped from the circus-den she called family. Beth'd been working on Marie since before her fortieth birthday, and she was slowly beginning to see the need for change. She'd been downtrodden for so long by her depressing marriage, it would take a lot of talking for real changes to make her into an energetic, if not vibrant woman again. Michael started picking up *Ms.* Magazine, and taking a class for women at the City College, from Beth's urging. While Beth had collected *Playgirl* Magazines since it's inception that past July, hanging up the centerfolds to join Bobby's in her bedroom - Frank was the only man who appreciated her decor. Beth loved it.

They gave Marie a list of books to read, in the order of from informative to explicit. First for the novice: Dr. David Reuben's *Everything You ever* etc., next his *Any Woman Can*, then *Sensuous Woman*, and of course, for details with drawings for the basically naive - which Marie fully qualified as at forty - *The Joy of Sex*. In order to understand men after learning to make love properly without hang-ups, Marie was to read Merl Shane's *Some Men are More Perfect than Others*. Not the best student, as she tended to sigh a lot, insinuating that it seemed too much like work, and the rewards not guaranteed or even great. She desperately looked for the magic wand, or magic pill or magic anything to simply make it happen. Truly, Marie waited for the White Knight to come and swoop her off her front steps. With much prodding she did start reading, how much absorbing or doing was another story-unfinished.

Beth then cut and colored Marie's hair. Though they were usually changing their hairstyles and color, she was not trying to make Marie into a clone - only to do the most with what she had with all the help she could. Beth convinced Marie to change her style of clothes, which were mostly leftovers from the 1950's, and most of all her outlook on men and the world. The books would help, but only if she practiced what she read. When all the changes were put together, including losing some fifteen pounds, Marie looked really good and not a day over thirty-five. She was ready for her first trial-run of new-wings, whenever the chance came. Michael and Beth decided they could start a school, considering Marie's results in, at least physically.

Marie's best friend from high school, Fran, was living in Oklahoma City and had invited her to visit for two weeks without her draining family, as a celebration of her fortieth. If anyone could help change Marie, it was Fran, as she'd always been the wildcat of their group. It was Marie's first ever vacation alone, so a frightened, but a determined woman when she stepped on that plane, with a brand-new wardrobe to give her that extra backbone. Beth told her, "Life begins at forty, if you play your cards right." They decided if Marie could do it, any woman could. She must've been playing with a few wild cards, because she had her first affair!

Beth while happy about Marie, worried about Michael, and whenever she could, she'd slip in a few of her 'don't do as I did, learn from my mistakes.' She didn't want to sound like a lecture, or God forbid, April, but Michael needed a regular or semi-regular guy, where she'd still have her free spirt, and not the constant one-nighters adding to her list. Where to find that man, was the big conundrum, as they didn't know where to look beyond the bars.

April in the meantime, still driving them all crazy with her miserable marriage, and of specific concern was her extremely-spoiled daughter Deidra. Alex didn't get along with her, and she constantly talked-back to him, as she felt he picked on her. He now started to knock her around, and they were amazed that April put up with it, but she wasn't miserable enough to get a divorce. Key-That meant she'd have to go to work and support them. She constantly complained about money, yet they were talking about buying a house.

She didn't make any sense vacillating, she'd criticize him for one thing, then she'd say how thoughtful he could be, like when she got his fish-hook in her ear. She went into this long dragged out story, as if he'd saved her life. She took a long drag on her cigarette, and continued, never noticing how shocked Beth and Michael were at how she justified her staying with Alex. When he had HIT her daughter.

"He was also considerate, when I was sick, ..." She stopped to take a long sip of her coke and noticed how they were staring at her. "In fact, if he was making himself a sandwich, he'd always offer to make one for me. That, and he always lets me work on my astrology, as much as I want, if he doesn't need me for something, of course."

To the others, these were supposed to be basic things any man would naturally do for his woman. Though she never had any of these things from Wally or Al, neither of them ever touched her daughter, who could be as bad a bitch as her mother, but still she was a child. Beth and Michael raised their voices in shock. And, April raised her hand for them to stop. "If you're not going to listen to me, I'll leave."

There was no way to get April to see her pathetic situation, as she constantly looked for the little things to keep her from having to leave Alex. If she considered him the best man she lived with, it didn't say much for her previous choices in men. At least, she wasn't antsy to go out, as he was home with her, except when he was at school. And, if she'd gone out and been caught, he probably would've killed her, and felt it justified. While she did complain about having to masturbate so much, because they still weren't having sex, she quickly added, she didn't want to talk about it. It was a drain for them to listen to her, and tired of being expected to make suggestions, which they knew she'd not listen to, or followed.

* * * * * *

In the whole independence scheme, transportation was a major part. Michael tried to think of some way to get some money, out of the old junk-car Tim gave her. It didn't run and cluttered up the Beth's back yard, so maybe parts could be sold or salvaged. No clue from Connie, so Michael got the idea to have Beth call Frank. Surely he or one of his group knew how to strip a car for the parts. Hesitantly, Beth called Frank, she didn't like to bother him, as she knew other women chased him, and she wanted to be different. If she showed that she cared too much anyway, he'd stay away for awhile because he didn't like a woman being hung-up on him. Besides, it was the night before Thanksgiving, and the guys were probably having a party at the club house. The party turned out to be over at Frank's crib. Vince answered the phone, and he wanted to know who was at Beth's house before he'd let her talk to Frank.

Once Beth mentioned Connie's name, Vince had to talk to her. He'd heard about her from Beth and Michael, and wanted to know if he knew her from before, when she'd come to The Basement. Soon it was forgotten why the phone call, the guys were on their way over to Beth's house. A mad rush to get the house picked up and cleaned before they got there. Marie arrived for a visit, and Beth asked her to take Jeremy over to their mother's, since they'd be heading there tomorrow anyway. She packed up some clothes for him quickly, as Michael and Connie finished the house. Surprising how fast they knew to clean, having the business. Beth laughed, she might not ever get the 'Good Housekeeping Seal of Approval,' but that wasn't something that kept her up nights.

Vince was thrilled Connie *was* the one he remembered, and was absolutely elated the he'd get a chance to have sex with her after all these years of pining. She definitely had other plans - so to leave before he made his move, she turned to Beth to think of something quick, as he was determined and gaining on her. Knowing Vince's weakness, Beth plied him with booze, and got Don to give him some grass he brought. Vince was soon happily getting it from both sides. It was Michael's first chance with Don since the summer. It seemed like she'd waited so long to be with him. Connie's luck was holding out as

Vince passed out before long. She carefully removed herself out-from underneath him and left them to whatever the night was to become.

Again, Frank and Beth were in a blissful, sound sleep when a horrendous crash raised them up-off the bed. Frank yelled to Beth, "What the fuck was that, a sonic-boom?" She had no idea, but grabbed her nightgown and rushed out of the bedroom. In the darkness, she heard Vince's voice, "I wouldn't go in the kitchen, if I were you, . . . especially if you have bare feet."

"What the hell happened, Vince?" Beth asked as she went to turn on the light in the living room. "What are you doing sitting in the dark for, anyway?"

"I'm not going to touch another goddamn-thing in this booby-trapped house," Vince replied, obviously afraid of what had happened. With the light on, Beth could see exactly what did happen. She had a metal mobile of owls hanging from the circular, florescent-overhead light in the kitchen. "When I woke up, everybody was gone and I was dying of thirst. You guys didn't even leave a night-light on for me."

Frank came out of the bedroom laughing at this last remark, "A night-light - which would you like Mickey Mouse or Donald Duck?" Really laughing, he looked at the mess.

"Fuck you, Frank! That thing scared the shit-out of me," Vince snapped back.

"Vince, you still haven't told me how you did it," Beth questioned, quite concerned.

"Simple," Michael said, "he was looking for the light switch, hit his head on the owls, the clinking-metal made him think it was a pull chain, so he pulled it. Only, the light didn't go on, it fell down." She'd just come staggering out of her bedroom with Don.

"Yea," said Vince, "that's what happened. You should see the knot on my head from that thing. It could've killed me." He still sat on the couch not wanting to move.

Michael stopped in her tracks, "Oh, My God! I'm beginning to think like Vince. I think they better get me to a home, right away!" Everybody was laughing now, including Vince. Beth and Michael started cleaning up the mess, which was in a million little pieces, Beth also bitched at Vince to dig up five-dollars for a new fluorescent circular-light bulb.

Since all up now, they may as well stay up. Michael set the table and made the coffee, as Beth made breakfast for the group. Michael rounded up several candles and put them on the table, with a couple for Beth to cook the eggs and bacon by. It was about seven-thirty, but a very, dark-gray winter morning. As they were eating, Vince remarked, "I've never had breakfast by candlelight, especially with the cook in a nightgown." He had a big smile.

Frank cut him off, "Enough said Vince. You don't want to get on *my* shit-list, too?"

Another wild and crazy night for all of them, too bad Connie hadn't stayed. The only problem was Beth and Michael had to work in the afternoon, so couldn't spend any extra time with the guys. It'd be another stretch before they'd see them again. Michael did have a good time with Don, and Frank said he'd get a tow-truck to get the car, and see how much he'd get for the parts for her. So, at least they got that problem solved. And, Vince gave Beth five-dollars, as he left.

A few days later, April was sitting with the other girls reminiscing. Connie brought up some of the crazy things they'd done and gotten away with. The time she tricked Beth into a double-date, that was a motel party. "Yea, that guy was strange, he only wanted to watch you two, he didn't want to do anything with me. The epilogue to that was Connie had to drive me up to the abortion clinic in Milwaukee, but thank God I wasn't pregnant. Needless to say, I went right to the doctor to get my IUD put in. That's one night I don't want to repeat."

Michael then said, "The way you got your color TV was a better story than that." Beth already started to laugh.

"That guy was so drunk, by the time we got to his furniture store, he never knew the trick I pulled on him. After having him chase me from bed to bed, which I was jumping around on like some kid loose in the circus, he passed out when I let him catch me with most of his clothes off. I rolled him off me, and let him sleep for awhile, so I could look around the store. When I heard him stir, I rushed back and started putting his clothes back on telling him what a dynamite time we had. He was so drunk he believed me, when he never touched me! And, most importantly, he kept his promise, my new TV was delivered the next day."

Connie started in on April the way she used to get into cars with the guys, or going to their apartments, then not giving them any sex. She was so lucky not to have gotten some *'freakoid.'* She even ended up at a motel once, with no intentions of going to bed with him. "He wasn't too mad, after he got his money back from the desk clerk," she calmly answered, "There's no law that says you can't change your mind. What about Beth, she did it after they were in bed!"

Beth laughed again. "Remember when I was drunk and Keith followed me home, without my asking him to?" Connie snickered. "Don't laugh, how was I suppose to know he was going to turn into an ape all over me? Anyway, we're in bed and he said some asshole-thing like, 'get it up for me, baby!' I thought to myself, I'm not that drunk or that horny to be ordered around. I got out of bed, got dressed, went to sit in the living room waiting for him to leave. When he asked me what was the matter, I told him I changed my mind. He was nice about, considering. I didn't know how to tell him, he was a klutz. Give me a break! I mean it blew my mind when he asked me, 'why is the hair on your muff a different color than the hair on your head?'" They were now all laughing, except April.

"It hurts me sometimes to think that my two best friends are becoming tramps." April loved to shock, but it also hurt that she'd say such a thing, even being totally self-righteous.

Connie asked her why she thought they were tramps and not herself? "Well," she hesitated, "you've all had more guys than I have."

"Oh," said Michael with fire in her eyes, "is there some cut-off point which makes the difference between tramp and good girl?"

"Yes there is." She'd gone this far, she had to follow it up.

"And, pray tell, how many men does a woman have to have, before she becomes a tramp?" Connie jumped in.

"I think about eight," replied April calmly. It happened to be the exact number which she had, since she was married. Of course, she never counted the ones before her first marriage, which only Michael knew about, then she'd also be a 'tramp' in her own eyes.

They continued to argue for several minutes, till Beth called a halt to the conversation, as the only one who had not contributed, pro or con. She knew April was partially right, yet numbers did not make a tramp, slut or any other name. It was what was felt inside. It was not that the girls had a hundred men each or something. They'd all gone through spurts of picking up guys, and then settling on one for awhile. Basically, not the sort of thing that April had a right to cast stones at, especially with her 'secret' sex partners.

She'd gained some weight again, and there was a certain amount of jealousy in the lack of sex in her own marriage which had to do with all this phony-chastising. None of them felt like they were following a sex-lined path into hell. Besides, it was no one's business what they did with their personal lives. Beth was very careful that her son Jeremy was never exposed to her sex life. He'd never been there when she had a man over. Besides, she reasoned to herself, how could they ever find the right man, if they didn't keep trying. At one time or another, they'd all thought each had done something a little too much. They were sometimes a reflection to each other, as they went through their different stages of growth and learning development.

Hell - growing up when you are already an adult was a real bitch. Learning not to judge someone on their actions was a very, difficult thing for any human to do, yet if it was only a stage, they would grow out of it, hopefully. They'd never gotten involved with the women's movement, but there were some new feelings stirring in them about the non-direction of their lives, and the role of importance that they were placing on the presence of a man.

Sure, they had a successful business going, and to them they were all making good money - though blowing it, too. Beth seemed to be thinking about the whole game, more and more lately. She didn't want to lose, yet sometimes the way she was playing the game, she didn't know if winning was so great either.

Dream People

Dreams - the playground of our mind.

Even tired wishes can bloom
into four-color dreams.
Live happily ever after . . .
Ride off into the sunset . . .
Have a sexual explosion . . .
Gold at the end of the rainbow . . .

All things to all people -
perfect, yet always human-like.
They walk, they talk,
they say what we want to hear.
They do the things we never would,
even if we could.

No one can take our dreams away -
not even the couch.
We pay no taxes and
receive no rebuttals on them.
Rich or poor - dumb or brilliant,
it can be Hollywood every night.

Even when freedom vanishes,
dreams can live on.
Practical men are dreamless,
dead men are empty of dreams.
I live through my dreams,
and also in spite of them.

CHAPTER 14

Where is the Love

Christmas came upon them before they knew it. Michael'd planned to visit her mother and step-father, but she didn't have the money any more. Since her first independent Christmas, she'd really blown it on her kids and friends. It turned out for the best, as Beth's mother finally adopted her into the family. It had to do with giving the baby up for adoption, and Beth telling how brutal her ex-husband had been to her. So, while Beth remained the black-sheep, Louise contended that Michael deserved a halo over her head. Beth hoped her mother never learned the truth, as to who Michael'd been involved with, but her pure, innocent baby-face helped convince Louise.

  The Christmas Eve tradition at Beth's parent's house only had Mike missing, as they were up at the farm snowmobiling on their new toys. Michael felt more at home, than with her own family, as she'd suffered through so many holidays with Tim's returning-ritual, and his crazy mother. It was a good feeling to be surrounded once again by love. New Year's Eve was another story, as of course, Beth and Connie had to work at the Cafe'. Beth'd been asked if she had some girls who could work a private party for one of their cleaning customers - serving drinks, and prepared food.

  Michael and Marie were given a crash course in how to be a bartender - simple mixed drinks, along with pouring beer and wine-opening. Beth told Marie, if she could make all her personal changes, and bring off her affair as well as she had, she could certainly make a believable bartender for these people. Michael'd be there by her side, what could go wrong? "Wrong-O Reindeer-Breath!" As Johnny Carson said so frequently.

  Beth became a great bullshitter, so there was no reason why Marie couldn't have the confidence to do the same. It was another step in her becoming an independent woman. She'd told her husband

Howard she wanted a divorce, if he didn't change, and he actually shaped up considerably. He came to pick her up when she finished, to return to a party he'd been at that evening. He was mildly impressed with how much she made, plus the clients' generous tip.

Michael came over to the Cafe' to join Beth, as Connie left to meet Cam and his wife, Janice, after she'd finished working. She didn't care if she spent New Year's Eve with his wife, as long as it was with Cam. Beth had fallen down her icy front stairs the day before Christmas, but she hadn't worked until just before New Year's, so she didn't know how bad the fall had been. She ended up with a cracked tail-bone, some pinched nerves and a pulled muscle. She couldn't let them down at work by not showing up, so she'd gotten some super-strong Darvon for the pain.

Beth took one before starting work, and by midnight he'd swallowed four more in order to function with the pain. It was a crazy night, Tom their super-chef was still in a good mood from Christmas, and even though they were jammed, everybody was having a riot, especially when the owner passed-out free champagne at midnight. Beth drank a full bottle by herself by one o'clock, then sang and danced for the customers still in the restaurant. When the girls were told they could have a free drink, she had George, the bartender, fix her one of his super specials - her favorite of Galliano and Courvoisier brandy on crushed ice. After all the customer left, the girls took over the bar.

By the time Michael got there, Beth was stuporous, so when she suggested going to the maitre d's house for an orgy, everybody knew it was time to close up shop. Despite everyone's protest, she insisted on driving her new car home herself, with Michael following behind. She bounced from one side of the road to the other, with only snowbanks and not cars that she kept hitting. She finally pulled into the garage with great pride of accomplishment. Michael was astonished, once more she'd gotten home without a scratch.

The most amazing thing, Beth did not have a hang-over the next day, which must have been from so many Darvon. They were going out for breakfast, and then over to Marie's for New Year's Day. Michael was waiting at the sidewalk for Beth to pull the car out, but in the cold light of morning, she could see the car wasn't put in too straight. As she started backing out, there was a funny crunching sound of metal. When she pulled up to straighten out, the wrap-around rubber-bumper hooked onto the side of the garage, so that she couldn't pull far enough up. When she backed up again, it crunched. Not a good situation - one car stuck in a two-car garage.

Beth went in and called for a tow-truck, and explained what she wanted done. Somehow he couldn't understand what she could've done that the car needed to be lifted-up and moved over. He kept saying the boom on the truck was too big and not moveable. She lost patience, and told him to please send the guy over, and she'd tell him how to do it. Afterwards, she felt she needed a second opinion, so called her brother Mike, the mechanical wizard who would know what to do. Beth said barely more than hello to Barb, saying she needed to talk to Mike. He was still in bed and slightly hung-over - also known for not doing anything in moderation. She began telling him about her prior evening and the results, so they laughed, with him saying his usual, "Are you shitting me?"

"No, that guy has a two foot boom-extension!"

"My God, you better hang on to that one."

Beth giggled, "Yea, but it's not moveable.

"Oh, then forget it, if it's not moveable it's not going to do you any good!" They were both laughing hysterically, and Michael, for the life of her, couldn't figure out what they were laughing about, but she knew it wasn't cars. He got serious, and said it could be done. Then he laughed remembering when Louise was learning how to drive at fifty, she turned the car around side-ways in the oversized one-car garage. Mike came over to get it out for her, they laughed and talked some more, as they'd been apart so long, though would always be close.

The tow guy never said a word about the position of the car. Beth explained to him what to do, and it worked like a charm. There was only a few scratches and a small dent. As the guy was leaving, he said, "You must've had one helluva night, I hope it was worth it."

Beth laughed, "As long as I live through it, it's aways worth it." She did feel bad about her new car, and her first New Year's resolution would be not to drink *that much*, and drive.

With the New Year, Beth also felt she needed to continue to expand herself, so it was time to take more classes at the county college. She'd been a psychology major, but now she wanted to pursue her creative-side in more writing, as even in high school she'd been told she had talent that should be developed. As if one direction wasn't enough, she thought about getting her Real Estate sales license to bring in some extra money. Her clientele from the business was ever expanding, so she thought she had some built-in referrals.

Truly being a private person, Beth soon found that she could express all those pent-up feelings in her writing, especially her poetry. She joked with Connie and Michael that one day maybe she'd write a book on, *"How to Be Happily Divorced."* Everybody else, with or without experience, was trying to tell them what to do, and she felt she'd heard just about every story.

As trite and corny as it sounded, about 'getting your act together,' it did feel like a necessary move in order to move on to something more and better. The men that Beth had seen go from one affair or marriage, to another sure did not seem like they had improved a great deal, if at all, in what they got back into. The more men she met, and became involved with, the more she learned, at least in what she *didn't want* in a relationship.

Observing others - men and women - she was learning from their shared experiences, too. At the same time, Beth rarely let something go by that would give a new experience, and most importantly, if it hedged on the previous formidable. The child-inside still wanted to express it all, and perhaps anything wild and wanton. There was great excitement in the trips she and Connie made down to Chicago most Saturday nights - a whole other world, as compared to anywhere in suburbia.

They were truly God-protected in all of their escapades, as they became groupies - probably the oldest of them - to a rock band, as it played in many singles-spots around the downtown area. They were careful in accepting grass, other than from their biker buddies, but took the leap occasionally. Beth then had fun, stepping back from the merry-go-round they were on, to analyze what was happening, and in the quiet hours, with a scotch in hand, she'd write. The three of them were obviously trying to do it all, playing as hard as they worked, trying so to get it all in.

She could visualize the White Rabbit running in and out of their lives crying, "It's late, it's late!" She pondered, how often they raced toward something, as much as running away from something else, and may not know the difference. It was a real curiosity, that sometimes brought them to a standstill, when they'd be shocked by one or the other's behavior.

Of course, they could depend on April to chastise them - through her own jealousy, sitting at home. Though Beth talked to Connie about Michael's vast entourage of men coming and going - she seemed totally un-selective; Connie talked to Michael about Beth's increased drinking, and Beth talked to Michael about Connie letting Cam still control her life and actions. Yet, they rarely chastised each other directly, since they felt they were going through some sort of phase, that sometimes changed in mid-course.

Beth attended her ten-year high school reunion, and though she sat with some life-long childhood friends, she felt completely out of step with most of them. She'd gone alone, since it was at the country club, and no way would Rob ever take a chance of being seen with her. Not quite the place you'd bring a biker like Frank, or none of the other men she involved herself with. It gave her a chance to talk and observe her old classmates without hindrance.

Many had changed so little, or became what she'd have expected. Though they lost a few in Viet Nam, the class was pretty well intact, and attended. The the red, hand-painted words on a back wall in The Place regarding the war, rung in Beth's head - "Care enough to be apathetic." Many attendees seemed to be in a cocoon, insulated against the outside world, protecting 'hearth and home.' There was nothing like a High School Reunion to bring back memories: first kisses, crushes, slights, hurts, rejection, praise and even some acknowledgments.

The post-war babies had definitely grown up, and many of them had something to say. Most of those in this group, it was about love, having a good time and music that would never be forgotten. Beth had a fascination with politics, but rarely had any one to talk to about it all. She considered herself one of the very lucky ones, to have heard in person the two most influential people of their high school days - Martin Luther King, Jr. and John F. Kennedy. Her church's young, Youth Leader had taken a group of them down to Orchestra Hall to hear King, and it changed how she would always feel about prejudice and discrimination.

Then during the 1960 election, Kennedy bravely took on the challenge to come speak at her high school, when it was a solidly-Republican county. She'd never forget the excitement in his voice, a manner-charisma that went beyond vitality, as he shook her soul, giving cause and reason for shedding any apathy about being able to change the status quo. She was touched into believing that she could save the world, by enlightening those less fortunate than herself.

Only her logical, rational mind had kept her emotional-self from joining the Peace Corps. And, such a rude-awakening these years later at the high school reunion to find that Dix, her childhood boyfriend, who also talked idealistically about the Peace Corps, now an accountant for Shell Oil Company. Still, even with the MidEast Oil Embargo going on, she could not throw stones, for she'd first found her niche in the plastic-world of advertising, and now did private parties for wealthy people. Though they both broke-out of their cocoon-shells, they certainly hadn't become beautiful, Earth-saving butterflies. But even a moth serves a purpose in society, and can still dream of higher things that might yet be accomplished.

It did Beth's heart good to see that some of those who had seemed to have-it-all, were now divorced, or didn't have so much any more. She looked forward to the thought that she still had the best years of her life ahead of her, and not behind, like some of them. Changing and growing almost to the point that she could feel it happening, felt really good. Yes, some of her choices might not have been right, but they were the best for her at that time, knowing what she knew, she learned from them.

And, yes, probably she'd make more mistakes which felt like she was going backwards, but those also to be handled as best she could. The fog was slowly clearing and the outline of a path for the best way to go. Beth looked at herself as an accumulation of the good, the bad and in-between, all lessons learned, as long as she didn't repeat the mistakes.

She did not feel it was wrong to want and do more, though Bruce argued against it. At the reunion, many people she talked to were rather shallow, how little they wanted from their life except for the material things, things they thought made them important. She recognized that with some of their well-off, cleaning clients, as everything was a great big "Whatever" - as acquiring another new car, or TV or 'whatever' they felt made a statement of who they were. Not for Beth, with definite feelings about everything other than the material things, she wanted to help people change their lives for the better. And, she knew she wanted to travel - see other cultures and unique places or museums.

* * * * * *

Michael and Beth were getting cabin fever-bad by the end of January. The weather usually made it a difficult time of the year for them anyway. Michael talked about her brother Webster now living in Ft. Lauderdale, and how great it'd be to visit him. Beth jumped on it immediately. "Why not, as long as we stay with him, we could surely afford the airfare, and spending money?" Michael was afraid of heights, and said she'd never fly, but for her brother Web, she'd do it.

In her opinion, he was such a cool dude, and it'd been two years since she'd seen him. She called him to set it up. The earliest they'd have enough money saved, would be the first of March. But, at least they'd have something to look forward to, when Connie found out she decided to join them. She'd never flown or been to Florida, but anything to get out of the horrible Chicago winter. She thought this might shake Cam up a bit anyway. He'd been stepping over his limit lately, taking her for granted.

When Michael called Web again, the three of them were all on the extensions with him, and his two friends. It was all set, each of the girls would have a guy to spend time with. They had over a month to plan and get ready. Sybil stopped in and said she'd like to go, too, but Michael knew that Web wouldn't want to see her again. She'd lived with him for a few months a year or so before. He had to kick her out because she stayed-stoned all the time, and wouldn't do anything around the apartment to help.

Friday night, Beth and Michael spent the last two hours bathing, getting dressed and putting on make-up. With only one bathroom, and quite small, they'd long ago given up being hung-up sharing the facility. Jeremy, sat quietly on the couch with the poodles watching television, and the fascinating-circus of the girls getting dressed. As they both ascended in all their array, Jeremy piped up with as smile, "You girls sure look good tonight. You smell good, too!"

Beth smiled at his understanding, and Michael laughed, "The kid has good taste."

She quickly gathered up his bed things, for him to go to her mother's for the night. As she was putting on the six-year old's jacket, he turned and gave her a big hug. "I love you Mom, and you have fun tonight. You deserve it." He was the greatest kid, and she'd worked to make him as independent as possible, so he'd never be emotionally-crippled like his father in standing on his own.

It concerned her, because her mother truly spoiled him, as if in spite, as to how she'd treated Beth. It was time to take him back to the Field Museum to see his dinosaurs, as she loved to make their time together educational, and not just a toy like his father did.

"I love you, too, Jeremy. And, sometimes we both don't realize how much. Would you like to go see the Dinosaurs, or the Science Museum with the submarines on Sunday?"

"Oh, the submarines, please." His smile even bigger.

"OK, the submarines it is. Now, you have something to look forward to." She kissed and hugged him again, she did so love their time together. Michael really wasn't into that sort of thing, and it wasn't cheap with three kids.

They went back down to The Basement that night, with new owners, who completely remodeled the place. They'd wanted to give the place some respectability, so they planned to keep the bikers out. With the new, eighteen-year old drinking laws, the teeny-boppers were drinking. Nothing was more embarrassing than to have a guy that looked twelve, put the make on you. The first time it happened, Michael cracked-up to see the stunned look on Beth's face. "When he said your place or mine, he must of meant his car, because he wasn't old enough to be living away from his mother."

Eddie, the owner of The Place, said it was ridiculous, they didn't know how to drink at all. The kids were passing out all over, and getting sick everywhere including the restrooms. Down at The Basement, they were glad to see the teeny-boppers, since they were easy money, and when the girls walked in, it was jammed. As they walked past the first bar, Michael noticed the cute bartender, all dressed in his mod-outfit.

Walking past the second bar, Beth noticed another good looking dude behind it playing bartender, things were definitely looking up, as he also noticed her. When they couldn't find seats, they walked back and stood between the two bars until seats were available. The good looking dude came over to Beth to take their order, "What are you having?" With a rather wide smirk on his face.

Beth couldn't resist, as her eyes twinkled, "Not a very good time, but I bet you could change all that." Beth took out a cigarette, and he bent over to light it for her.

When he stepped back, Michael snickered, "Looks like that Scorpio-magnetism is working tonight. Maybe you'll get lucky. What do you think of that one behind the bar over there?" Michael was smiling in anticipation of a good time herself.

"Not bad, but a little too young and modish for me," she nodded in approval for Michael. Later Fred, the bartender bought them a drink and introduced himself, and his younger brother Ted, the modish one, had finished working, so sitting next to Michael.

"The brother act," Beth laughed. "Do you do anything else together?"

Michael almost fell off the bar stool. "Jesus Christ, Beth, why don't you just come right out and say what you're thinking, and don't beat around the bush."

"Well, you said you liked him, and he's been sitting there for twenty minutes, and you didn't say a thing." Michael left with Ted, and Fred followed Beth over in his car. He seemed like a super guy when they talked. She couldn't get over how he zeroed in on her. When she wasn't trying at all, she was her best, and at least Michael was happy with her catch. When the two of them sometimes went out together, one or the other never got someone to talk to until the other one did. Michael enjoyed going out by herself, but Beth didn't.

They were both still gullible, as far as men went, but Michael didn't show her deep feelings to the guys, just a surface which showed that she liked them. She kept them in perspective, as far as not letting her feelings get hurt, if it was only a one-night stand. She always thought she cared more than she did, thus she had few one-nighters - that old Aquarius moon really helped keep her cool.

Beth, on the other hand with her honesty, always left herself wide open to get hurt. At the house, Michael was sitting on the couch with Ted. Beth had barely gotten a beer for Fred, when he went into the bedroom. Her *Playgirl* collection of centerfolds kept growing, though Bobby's was never moved from right next to the head of her bed. Fred was slightly taken aback with the photos when he first walked in. As usual, none of them annoyed men, but Bobby's picture, "What do you bother with that jerk for, when you got all the rest?"

"Wait a minute, sweetheart, I know how good he is, and I don't know how good you are. So, if you want to stay in this bedroom, you better not say another word about him."

Fred leaned over and read the inscription,"No Shit! Alright! I won't say anything else." Beth was used to men being jealous of Bobby, and she wouldn't put up with it. As it turned out, Fred wasn't nearly as nice in bed, as he'd been at the bar. His personality dropped from about a six to a two-and-a-half. The sex wasn't bad, but didn't have any emotion to it - it was just sex. She began to feel stupid about thinking some guy in a bar would ever be a good pick-up, or even if there was such a thing.

She got up and grabbed her robe to get their cigarettes. She was already in the living room before she knew what she was walking in on. Michael and Ted hadn't bothered to go into the other bedroom, and Beth hadn't realized what they were doing, with Michael sitting on his lap. The fact that she didn't have any clothes on, hadn't registered in Beth's head. They became very familiar, but never had sex in front of one another, like with Connie. She tried to make a joke out of it by saying, "Don't let me bother you, I'm just looking for our cigarettes." Too late, poor Michael so embarrassed she almost died.

Beth scooted back with the cigarettes, and closed her door before snickering to Fred. He suggested maybe the four of them should get together, on the queen-size bed. She told him Michael'd never go for it, she does not dig-on group sex. "Fine," he said, "How about playing switch?" Rather straightforward about it, like they'd been in this situation before.

While surprised at his coyness, Beth was honest, "Oh, I don't think she'd go for that, either." She began to understand the lack of emotional attachment on Fred's part.

"Go ask her, it won't hurt to ask her." He hit a nerve, but Beth didn't want to jump to any conclusions. Very reluctantly, she went to ask Michael if she wanted to play switch. She'd said something to Beth earlier about really digging-on this guy Ted. This was not something they'd ever discussed, or that Michael brought up out of curiosity regarding Beth's experience with Connie and Bobby.

Overtime, she thought she was learning to understand Michael, then she'd change. When asked, she responded, "Sure, why not?" She then turned to look at Ted, to see if it was OK with him, and he nodded, 'yes.' Beth was shocked, apparently she was the only one *not* interested in doing it. After Michael went into the other room, Beth mumbled something to Ted that she was too drunk, or something to do it again.

He didn't say much, just got dressed, but going out the door announced, "My wife'll be waiting up for me, anyway." A bit of a stunner, as neither brother had wedding rings on. Fred turned out to be on his second marriage, thirty-one years old and a real asshole. It was the first time Beth made such a poor judgement of a guy, when still fairly sober. Her real losers before had been when drunk. She came to find out that Michael only said 'yes' because it pissed her off that Ted said 'yes.' But she'd agreed, before asking him, Beth reminded her.

"But, he should've said, 'no.' I really liked him, and now I've lost any chance to see him again." Beth then told her he'd said his wife was waiting up for him at home. She shrugged her shoulders, like it wouldn't have bothered her much. C'est la vie.

A Woman on Women

We've changed. It didn't happen yesterday,
and it won't be finished by tomorrow.

We have put ourselves down,
as much as the men have.
For we have a needless fear
of losing our femininity.

We no longer need hide our brain under a new hair style,
and we are better now for sustaining one another.

For some, nothing can replace the love of a good man,
and yet women need women, as men need men.

There is an imbedded understanding of ourselves, that
somehow cannot be translated to the opposite sex.

We are women, and we make the changes now,
as we have for each millennium before.

CHAPTER 15

To Party Hearty

March at last roared into Chicago, and Cam was glad to see Connie taking a vacation, but not too happy where, or with whom she was going. So excited to go on her first plane trip, but Michael was an absolute basket-case. Her false-eyelashes kept coming off, and if it wasn't that, it was her false-fingernails. Connie teased her to make sure she still had the pads in her bra. Michael wanted to look perfect for her brother, Web, so thought she'd correct what Mother Nature hadn't given her. Though it wasn't Mother Nature biting her nails.

After a last drink in the bar, Michael make another trip to the restroom to glue herself back together, and they dragged her aboard the plane. In between them she felt safer, but they forgot the dramamine to give her. Michael repeated, "I'm doing it for Web."

Beth kept telling her, "Breathe deep, the nausea is all in your head." Connie held the barf-bag in case it wasn't. Michael calmed down, as Connie had her looking at the lights out the window.

They landed into seventy degrees, with Connie and Michael amazed over the palm trees. Web and friends nowhere to be found, Michael called, with his answer, she knew they were stoned out of their minds. He hadn't gotten their car, but they'd be right over to pick them up. After one in the morning, by the time they got to Web's apartment. His friend Chip, stoned on the couch sleeping. A fantastic apartment with murals and posters on the walls, huge tropical plants in the corner and black lights in the bedrooms. Roommate Phil even had a waterbed.

They started the first night off, getting stoned out of the pot-pot - a large, black-iron kettle they kept the grass and papers in. Anytime, anyone wanted a joint, they just fixed one out of the pot-pot. Web had built a seat into the corner, off the kitchen with a large, construction electrical-spool for a table - they all worked construction. They sat around it telling stories, and laughed till they almost fell over. Web started in on Michael, because she didn't drink or smoke. He was determined to at least get her to drink some rum in her coke. Soon they paired off, and went to bed. In the morning, they drove around after breakfast checking out the town. Michael and Connie were anxious to see the ocean, and more palm trees during the afternoon. They also cleaned the apartment and bought some groceries. After a fantastic Chinese dinner, they went to the movies - the girls' treat.

On Sunday, Web decided to make his 'special' spaghetti, and have his friends over to meet his sister. He cooked his sauce all day long, and they could hardly wait because it smelled so good. They lightly-toasted up some grass and put it in the sauce, since it looked and tasted similar to oregano, so wouldn't ruin the sauce or be noticed. The pot was about three times stronger when it was cooked. They weren't going to tell anyone to see what would happen. Most everyone knew to bring their own silverware, because he didn't have that much. They started pouring in about six o'clock, one group after another. Within an hour, there were a lot of smiling, giddy faces. No one had enough to get stoned, but everybody had a pretty good buzz-going. The crowds began to thin by eleven, until just the six of them were left around the spool-table.

This time, instead of dipping into the pot-pot, Web brought out some organic mescaline. He figured if Michael wouldn't smoke, maybe she'd eat some of the *'mesc,'* as he was set on getting her high on some thing. He did get her to drink rum with her coke, so anything was possible. Being organic, and Web knowing how much should be taken, they felt safe. Besides they weren't going anywhere, if they passed out, there was enough room for everyone. As it turned out, Michael was the only one remaining-straight, even after taking three tabs. Everyone else just watched the lights and posters spinning around. It was buzz-time for Connie, who kept laughing and giggling, "Thank God for a buzz."

Quite a night for the northern girls, with Connie the only one ever exposed to dope. The whole trip had been an experience in itself. Too bad, Beth wasn't her old-self. It appeared she'd been in a state of confusion since they arrived. Somehow, she didn't want Web to put her in the same classification as Sybil, so she kept running around cleaning up the place, and doing the wash everyday like a stupid servant. She also felt she should be available to Web for sex, every night, like included in her household duties.

The only problem, Web didn't feel that way, though they had fun. Beth also thought, she needed to show how turned on by him she was, since everyone thought he was great. She liked him, but she couldn't get comfortable, and it bothered her. Connie and Michael couldn't figure out what was the matter with Beth. As tension began to grow between the three of them, no one knew why, or how to talk about it. Beth went through such a state with herself, that even if asked, she probably couldn't explained any reason for her actions. She was trying to fit a role, imposed on by herself. She'd jumped in feet-first, not knowing how to tread water.

Beth never left Jeremy before more than a day or two, so she felt guilty about letting go and having a good time. Not the sort of thing the girls would've understood since neither had their kids. Only when drunk or stoned, was Beth more like herself, although at that time, though not sure who the real-self was. She was almost anxious to get on the plane and back to reality. Fantasy-land had been too much for her to handle this time - too used to having her feet firmly planted. Carrying a burden of responsibility was more comfortable, and she couldn't handle hanging-loose, as never done before. Besides, she thought she had to get back to her job at the Cafe' and her cleaning customers didn't need to suffer, positive about being indispensable.

Connie and Michael went the opposite direction, planning to stay an extra four days. They'd more than fitted-in well to the surroundings. The last few nights together, they went to Web's favorite drinking establishment, and got bombed on the rum and coke for a quarter a drink. The last night the girls took the guys for dinner at one of the nicest restaurants in town.

Beth had a crude awakening when she got home - not only had the Cafe' functioned fine without her, but her cleaning customers said it would've been fine if she'd wanted to stay longer. Jeremy, while glad to see her, hadn't missed her as much as she'd thought, as Louise, always over-indulged his every whim. By Saturday, she knew what a mistake coming home to all those people, to whom she was not indispensable. Life goes on, no one can't be replace. Another lesson learned, but she doubted she'd ever be a 'hang-loose' person.

For Connie, the trip was the best thing she could've ever done, since she'd newer left Cam in their five years together. He was insanely jealous that she was down there partying, and then that she stayed an extra four days, really blew his mind. Again, it reminded him how much he loved her, and capable of missing her that much. On business trips or vacations, he was never alone or gone for more than a few days, if alone.

Saturday night, he came into the Cafe' searching out Beth, like a tie-line to Connie. He'd just called her, but they couldn't talk, because of *another* party going on. "There's more people here than before," she'd laughed. Cam was besides himself, as he realized how much of his time she'd occupied. He truly was lost.

On Sunday, he picked up Beth to go to the airport to meet them. She couldn't believe her ears, when he told her that he'd decided to get a divorce from Janice. He was cutting off her allowance, and sending her back to work. Once she was self-supporting, he'd divorce her. Beth was flabbergasted, was this Cam talking, he even sounded honest about it. He practically ran to the gate, and kept pacing until the plane landed.

They'd been on stand-by for a 747 from Miami, and only one seat left, so Michael gave it to Connie, since Cam would be waiting. Unfortunately, she didn't know Connie was put in first class, so early off the plane. After watching several hundred sunburnt tourists get off the plane, Cam and Beth went looking for Connie. They found her on the pay-phone in the hall, calling to see where the hell Cam was. He was not quite ready, for the *'native'* standing before him, he'd not recognized getting off the plane. She'd left Chicago in a dressy pantsuit, and returned dark-tan in a braless-halter-top, patched Levis and sandals. She also still had a buzz going . . .

"You look like a goddamn-hippie," Cam wailed. It was some party the night before, as Connie smiled. She began telling how half the people from the party were still laying around, out-cold when they'd left for the airport. Cam wasn't too thrilled, when she talked about waking up in bed with a strange man there. She quickly mentioned he had 'most of his clothes on.' The funniest part, Michael in the same bed, had the same surprise waking up, to find another crazy friend of Web's had passed out on the bed.

Back to the airport bar, to wait another two hours for Michael's plane. She'd probably gained the most from the trip, in that she was reunited with her brother. Having left home when sixteen, they didn't have much chance to be close. He never got along with Tim, in fact, mutual-hate described it best. Web'd never known Michael except as a housewife and mother of three kids. He never gave much reaction when she divorced Tim, and gave him the kids. She'd always been so straight, he couldn't believe his older sister getting *'nerded'* on quaaludes at the last party.

Michael by this time, drank like a trooper and put the make on several of his friends. She'd not known how deeply he loved her, or so thrilled she'd come down to visit him. He'd never told any of his friends that he even had a sister, yet by the time she left, so glad they'd all met her. Of course, she thought of him as the 'greatest living-free spirit.' And, he thought Michael a pretty cool-head, too. They both knew, no matter how far apart in distance, they'd have a closeness. Web made other influences on her changing, as her false-appendages went, since not needed.

All in all, it was one of the best things the three of them did, since getting their divorces - a revelation and experiential-trip for them all. The morning they got up early to watch the sunrise over the ocean, the three of them would remember a very long time. They were feeding the seagulls cheap donuts, while Connie took pictures of the progressive sunrise. There'd been some bad moments, but they'd remember most - the good times, as always.

April was anxious to hear about everything, as she didn't have much excitement in her life lately, so was living vicariously through the others. It didn't take her long to realize, something was the matter with Beth. As usual, she wouldn't leave it alone until it all got flushed-out, which was good to a point. Beth still hadn't gotten her head together very well, so it was hard to explain what was the matter, when she wasn't sure herself. Basically, she'd no longer be able to do things she didn't want to do, just because the others were doing them. Anyway, it was sort of settled, and the air fairly cleared between Beth and Michael. It would take time for two, very different people like them, to work out a balance. Beth was slightly better for the talk, and April felt terrific having settled all the problems, she thought.

Michael'd been going out with a nutty, married guy, everybody called Irish. They had a super relationship, very sincere in its own way. He was very much in love with his wife, as the second time around for both of them, but time he spent with Michael helped him unwind. It didn't make a lot of sense to Beth, but Michael didn't want any commitments, so fine to her.

Irish and two of his friends, Ray and John, were trying to bring off a super-coup. With business in Toronto, it seemed the perfect excuse for a weekend with the girls. Since Ray's regular girlfriend couldn't get away from her husband for a weekend, Irish asked Michael if she knew anyone who'd like to go. Beth didn't say 'no,' though it took Michael a few minutes to convince her. She'd blown enough chances at having a good time in Florida.

Somehow, these guys were more what she was used to, and that was the difference. So, determined to go and have a good time, she put her smiley face on. Still, not that easy to be so carefree and blasé, with her mother making her feel guilty, and *she* didn't even know the men were married. Beth'd have to take another weekend off from the Cafe'. She and Michael looked super going up to Toronto with their Florida tans, although there wasn't much left for Beth.

Having never flown before Florida, Michael was getting experience fast. It'd be her first time out of the country. A real fun group, they started laughing from the time they left the FireLite for the airport. Beth felt a little uncomfortable, since she'd only met Ray once, but he soon helped her relax with his jokes. Sheri, the third girl, was a stranger to both Beth and Michael. She'd been going out with John, off and on for over six months. The three women clicked pretty well, considering Sheri had a slightly professional-side about her, with definite dollar-signs in her eyes. She'd recently gotten her real estate license, and mentioned a few times about hoping to 'rake-it-in.' She also turned on the charm, to any man that might be of some benefit to her. It didn't take Michael and Beth too long, to figure out she wasn't going for the fun, like they were. She likely had other arrangements wth John, the oldest and wealthiest.

Amazingly, nobody had a hot temper when the luggage got mixed up, the rented car wasn't the Cadillac it was supposed to be, and the rooms had to be changed because they weren't connecting. It was a classy hotel, but the Canadians didn't hustle like Americans. And, almost impossible to get ice in a drink in this cold country. They weren't that quick about serving another round either, and these people were drinkers. The guys ended up picking up a couple of bottles and mix when they came back from their afternoon meeting. They left the girls to pick a restaurant for the evening, and decided on seafood.

When they walked into this exclusive restaurant laughing, everyone turned to stare. Sedate didn't begin to describe the wealthy Canadians, who were obviously not ready for the rowdy Americans. The nice maitre'd made the mistake of putting them in the middle of the restaurant. The tables were set into different-level cubicles for privacy, yet no wall for a sound barrier. The poor waiter didn't even speak English well. Besides not understanding the jokes they were constantly making, he became the brunt of several of them. He didn't have trouble with the drink orders, but with the food order, he stood there nodding his head.

Irish thought it'd be easier if he ordered for everyone, except no one knew what they wanted. He kept repeating three escargot, until the waiter informed him he had ordered fifteen of them. After the appetizers, the waiter decided to offer to make his own special salad for them. He figured, if they could order the food and wine that they had, they could more than afford a special made salad. Beth tried to impress them all, when she suggested the wine for dinner. But these guys were not the type you impressed, because they didn't take anything seriously. By the time dinner arrived, they'd almost emptied the place. They all laughed so much, their jaws ached. Ray had a dry, subtle-sense of humor, Beth kept believing him when he was putting them on. He absolutely drove the poor waiter crazy about the sour cream not being on his potato, just because he hadn't asked for it.

After dinner John suggested drinks, but he wanted something different. Beth suggested a "Root-beer," one of the drinks she learned from a bartender friend. She'd suggest it to customers at the Cafe' when they wanted something different. She explained to everyone, and the waiter the ingredients: one shot of Kailua, one shot Galliano over crushed ice in a tall glass, and filled to the top with club soda. When stirred well, and sipped through a straw, it tasted like root-beer with a kick. The guys enjoyed it, but Sheri and Michael didn't. By that time, everyone was bombed.

When ready to leave, they'd been there over three hours, and the place completely empty. The waiter buzzed around so fast, Ray said they could've had their shoes shined by him. He probably got one of the biggest tips in his life by his reaction, and even the owner was holding the door for them. Back to the hotel, the bombed-people were now horny-people. All the way driving back, they'd been attacking one another. Somehow the frozen-north hadn't daunted their passion. You could tell these men were used to being around each other in intimate situations.

Still another drink, after the girls put on their nightgowns and the guys got more comfortable. Sheri'd brought some grass with her, not that anyone needed any help, but it was nice to get mellowed-out. Michael, the only one close to sober, since she didn't smoke and back on just coke - with Irish, they were the first ones to break away. Ray and Beth got the mattress off one of the beds for the floor, while Sheri and John had the other room.

The next morning, Irish called room service for rolls, juice and coffee. The night before was a vagueness to Beth. Every part of her body was sore, from her hung-over head to her stubbed toe, she'd gotten during the night. In the bathroom, Michael asked her what the hell they'd been doing last night. Beth giggled, "Everything I've ever done before twice, and things I've never done, once. I think it was about six o'clock when we both collapsed. He's absolutely unbelievable." This was more fun than she'd expected.

"You woke us up a couple of times," Michael said, "When I looked at you, I couldn't figure out what you were doing, or the weird noises you were making. One time you woke Irish up, and he asked me what the fuck you two were doing. I didn't know, so I just said, 'fucking.' He asked, 'really?'" They both laughed, shaking their heads as to the adventure.

"Well, Ray is one hell-of-a-stud, but I sure couldn't take that kind of sex every night, I'm sore all over," Beth added, smiling.

While the guys went to their meetings, they gave the girls a hundred dollars for expenses, so they went shopping and toured the local castle. It was a bit of a bore, but the taxi driver was a riot, he thought they were all hookers from Detroit. When they told him from Chicago, he spoke to them with greater respect, like high-class call-girls instead. What a hoot, they laughed and laughed, not insulted at all. Since the Canadians had no gas-shortage or speed reduction, the driver drove between eighty and ninety all over town. One of the scariest rides they'd ever had, as they barely missed three cars and he kept talking without missing a word. It was a relief to get back to the hotel, and take a nap before the guys got back. They didn't have dinner reservations until nine, so plenty of time.

They were all sitting around, half-dressed and drinking in the larger side of the suite on the beds. This time Michael was bombed, while laying in Irish's arms and Ray started teasing her. Pretty soon, he was kissing and fondling her all over. He'd start at her boobs, that were falling out of her low-cut, push-up bra, and worked down to her bikini pants. At first, Irish and everyone laughed at the spectacle, as Michael sucked down the rum and coke, like dying of thirst.

She began rattling on using Connie's words, she'd never say without the booze. "Don't stop now, I'll write you a check," every time Ray'd stop whatever he was doing. When she said, "I'd fuck a snake if you'd hold its head," the limit was reached. Irish said he didn't think she better go out in pubic as she was. Not so funny, when it looked like Ray would take her right there, in front of everyone. Michael seemed willing, not caring about Irish or the others thought.

Irish finally put his foot down announcing, "It's time to get dressed to go out to dinner." Once everyone was ready, Michael'd sobered up a little, and the incident somewhat forgotten. All laughing and joking again walking into the restaurant, the guys were slightly pissed when a half hour wait for their reserved table. Beth and Ray game-played to see how many different glasses they could rip-off.

Water was served for the drinks in a little, side-glass bottle, which was rather unique. When finally at the table, the girls had three glasses and a water container. Dinner was a little more subdued than the previous night, but everyone was pretty tired. Still a lot of fun, and good laughs, as the guys complimented the girls for the choice of restaurants for both nights. They had a wait for the food, too, but again it was excellent. This waiter wasn't fun at all, but the place was very busy, even that late.

The return to their rooms was almost a repeat of the previous night. The guys decided to put something all together, so pushed the two beds next to each other, as the six of them piled on. No one seemed to accomplish anything with all the giggling and laughter about whose leg was whose, and hand was rubbing who. Ray cracked them all up with his *Nanook of the North* jokes. They broke back-up into pairs again, Irish taking Michael into the other room, as he wanted a little more privacy and quiet when they did get around to sleeping.

Beth and Ray were back on the floor with the mattresses, as the best place for them, since they indulged the most in the pot and booze. The stuff loosened Beth enough, that she was game for about anything, and this was one man who could perform that way. Between the sex, laughing and some general groping with ice cubes left over from their drinks. When he got up for fresh ones, Beth had no idea what he'd do with them. He did stop long enough to throw some at Irish and Michael, then returned to Beth. They laughed and giggled and titillated each other's genitals till they were worn to a frazzle. When one ran out of ideas, the other thought of something new.

Then, finally falling into a deep sleep, the fire alarm went off. A horrible, frightening sound they'd never heard before, a deafening blast. No one knew what to do, if it was for real, God forbid, or just a mistake. Crazy Irish went streaking through the halls, with only his sports jacket on yelling, "The Russians are Coming, the Russians are Coming!" But Ray went down to the office to find out what was happening. The alarm rang on for about fifteen minutes, when Sheri woke up John. Unbelievable, he could sleep through the noise and all the lights. Not good if it had been a real fire. Needless to say, the guys were *not* at the hotel they'd said they'd be at. Everything settled down about four o'clock.

On Sunday, they had a fantastic French, buffet-brunch. It was very impressive with a strolling guitarist, and every kind of specialty one could imagine. Afterwards, they decided to drive into downtown Toronto to get a look at the city. On the way back, a blizzard was blowing up, that looked absolutely frightening, with an afternoon flight-out, that could not be missed. Time to go back to the rooms, and pack to leave. Irish and Michael wanted to go for a quickie, since the maid hadn't done the one room yet. They were hilarious, as Ray kept knocking on the door to the other room, while the maid was cleaning the bathroom. Somehow as usual, there was more to pack than before. Irish wanted some of the beer left on top, so they could have a brew while waiting for the plane. In the midst of everything else, he and Ray had a snowball fight, with the fresh snow formed outside the windows. Really a crazy group!

The plane was delayed an hour on the ground, so Irish had Beth break-out the beer for them. For some reason, there was a row of people between the girls and the guys. With nothing better to do, so they chattered back and forth over those people, quietly sitting in their seats. First they were passing the beer back to the guys, then John passed the doggy-bag from the night before up to the girls. It must have had a pound of meat in it! Irish had even stolen a knife to cut-it-up with. They were going to have it for a snack later the night before, but it'd been left in the car, and almost froze. John found it when he returned the rental car. The stewardess came back to scold them, for bringing their own alcohol onto the plane. Irish told her, he'd be glad to buy hers, but she couldn't serve till the plane was off the ground, so he kept drinking his.

The people in between them got quite an education, as Irish yelled to Michael, "I hope your husband won't be at the airport?"

Michael laughed, and not be out done with the jokes, answered, "He'll probably be standing next to your wife." It cracked up the guys, and made the little, old lady in the middle-row gasp. After-wards, the stewardess came back again, to scold them for being so noisy, and disturbing other people. Finally the plane was able to take off. It turned out to be one of the most beautiful sunsets, with all the glistening snow, it looked like a pink blizzard.

Back in Chicago, it was cold and rainy with the usual bitch getting out of O'Hare on a Sunday night. Michael teasingly asked Irish for the airline tickets for a souvenir. When he gave them to her, she said she'd sell them to him for a hundred dollars a piece, as the evidence to hang-him with his wife. She explained, she was trying to save up enough money to move down to Ft. Lauderdale, and bribing married men was a start. Irish laughed at her, but grabbed them to throw in the nearest trash container. Everyone, as tired as they were, could still laugh at each other. With all the numerous-glitches over the weekend, these were the easiest-going guys Beth ever encountered. Somehow, it would've been easy to get used to having anything she wanted simply in exchange for sex, especially this, fun-kind of sex.

Sorrow and Joy

One cannot have joy
without sorrow.
For the essence of joy
would be lost without the comparison.

The depth of happiness, like wealth
can only be known after traveling
though the heights of sorrow, or being broke.

But money does not bring
the joy of life with it.
Some of our happiest days we spend time,
never missing the money.

As joy brings me happiness,
sorrow gives me wisdom.
For the next joy will be cherished,
as the fragile thing it is.

Joy cannot be sought after,
it is merely a small reward of life.
Sorrow, contrary, cannot be escaped.
It patiently waits its turn.

CHAPTER 16

More Lessons Learned

Beth called Connie, to thank her for bringing her car over to the FireLite, then she said she had some bad news for Beth. "I'm fired from the Cafe'."

Connie was shocked, "How did you know?"

"I just felt it, I guess. What was his excuse?" There was no real concern in her voice.

"There actually wasn't one. He said, since you liked taking vacations so much, maybe you should stay on one. A lot of little excuses, but that was the main thing. I don't know what he's going to say to your customers that ask for you." Beth had been there over four years, and did have a following. When she finished talking to Connie, the rest of the conversation faded away.

What was she going to do, it was at least a hundred dollars a week from her income, and she couldn't be blasé about it. Used to having cash all the time, to blow on whatever she wanted, so it was usually gone each week, unless saving for something special. Of course, there were her payments and bills coming in every month, and Michael had yet to contribute directly to them. Yes, she bought groceries often, and other extras, but the normal electric, water, phone, as well the mortgage, no - nothing given. Part of that was also Beth's fault for not sitting down and talking to her, and maybe now might be a good time.

Jeremy was registered out of her parent's address for his grade school, so there was rarely a time that Beth asked Michael to babysit with him any more. Beth dropped him off at school, he went for lunch to her mother's and Beth picked him up after she finished with her housecleaning jobs. She even invested in having the attic partially finished off for Jeremy, so Michael kept the downstairs bedroom. She was usually out every night anyway.

Yes, there was always another waitress job, but maybe time to learn how to better use the Real Estate license she'd gotten. Then she thought of how being confined to one office got to her, when she'd tried it for a few weeks, months before. She'd been the organizer of their cleaning business - going to the houses to do the pricing and go through the cleaning routine with training the new girls as hired - over fifteen now. Maybe that was it, start pushing more into the private parties and expanding them into the easier, more lucrative side of the business. Then she could start taking a percentage or fee or something for her cleverness - didn't she deserve it?

Perhaps she could concentrate on her idea about franchising the business. A headache sometimes dealing with the girls, as they were never as dedicated about doing a really good job as she was. But there was also a good sense of accomplishment when the compliments came in. Maybe Michael was right, she'd worked hard long enough, it was time to relax, to enjoy staying home evenings and weekends to do whatever for herself, extra time with Jeremy. A blessing in disguise, as she probably would never have quit. She'd pick up a few more cleaning jobs, and see where the other ideas went. Beth had to recognize that the more she made, the more she did spend sometimes, so learning to budget was a new goal.

There were so many friends at the Cafe' - both employees and the customers, that Beth would miss, even when they'd sometimes been a pain in the ass. Super-chef Tom, not only shared a lot of jokes, but he'd also taught her many of his personal recipes, when she'd come in early to pick his brain. Connie sometimes joined them, though she was more for playing jokes, like when they had a whipped cream fight early one Thanksgiving, that was a riot. Even though they'd donned giant plastic bags, they were both covered from head to toe. They only stopped when the maitre'd came in screaming, and got whipped cream on his tuxedo.

Wild Selso, the Puerto Rican assistant-chef, could throw them a curve when they least expected it, with his crazy temper and free-sex talk. One slow Sunday, with nothing better to do, Selso carved a perfect replica of a penis out of a large carrot. He and Tom then hid it everywhere, scaring and shocking some of the more conservative waitresses. They put it on a covered customer's plate, so the waitress didn't find it till she got into the dining room, and took the lid off. But the best one, was when they hid it in straight-laced Virginia's purse, so when she went for her cigarette break she screamed loudly, and a dozen people came running.

The jokes they pulled on Nadia, the Russian-born waitress, were the best, though not very nice sometimes. She'd complain no one would talk to her, so she was told she had a message from a phone call, and the number to return was actually Dial-a-Prayer. Connie loved to tease Tom, and asked him if she could make his apron stand out, when she'd talk very sexy to him. His face turned bright red. She also made sure that one of her dinner checks always had the number '69' on it, and when she'd come in to pick it up, she'd have some joke, as to her favorite sex position.

When Connie gave Selso a pair of her bikini panties for his birthday, he hung them up right over where he worked. When slow, he'd do everything unthinkable to them, from putting a banana in the crotch, to putting them over his head. Even Theo, the new assistant, though not as wild, would do silly things like put notes in the mouth of the heads cut off the trout, and then leave them for a waitress to find. It was amazing what the owner put up with out of them, yet he knew his success depended on them being happy.

Dorothy was probably one of the wildest 'old ladies' they'd ever known. If she knew they called her an old lady, she probably would've beat the shit out of them. She might have been in her fifties, but old she wasn't, a swinger she was. Everyone called her Mrs. Hungry, because she was always eating. One time Connie was teasing her about eating some chocolate cream candies. Without the slightest warning, she shoved one at Connie's mouth, and rubbed it all over her face. She couldn't get mad at Dorothy, because it was so funny. Another time when she was carrying hard candy in her pocket, she offered one to Connie. She'd been talking about oral sex, so Dorothy said casually, "Want something hard to suck on?" Everyone fell down from laughter on that one. She was some swinging, old lady, telling stories of her boyfriends and all.

Connie and Beth had a few good times with the maitre'd. He'd gone to a big motel party with them one night, and let it all hang-out when he got bombed. He could really be a lot of fun when he wanted to. The owner knew when they did work, they were all the best, and even joined them over at The Place when they had an exceptional band. There they'd be dancing and getting bombed, still dressed in their tuxedos and uniforms.

A tight-knit group, with many of them being there as long as Beth. They'd been a real family to her during her divorce, and probably wasn't one of them she hadn't gotten drunk with, or told about one of her boyfriends. They all enjoyed sharing the experiences of her and Connie's crazy life. Most of them didn't believe one hundred percent about Bobby Ryan, yet they knew if anyone could've pulled it off, Connie and Beth would've been the ones.

One thing Beth wouldn't miss were the men who thought, because of their low-cut French uniforms, that they were available to feel-up whenever they wanted. It had been bad enough when they'd have the Black Hawks or the Bears in on a regular basis, whenever they were in town after their games. The owner was such a big fan, he'd never say anything to them and tell the girls to laugh it off.

"They're relaxing after their work-out on the field," he'd say. But Beth's favorite story was the obvious, well-off, young businessman who had automatically assumed Beth was available for a price. When she'd still turned him down after a fifty-dollar tip because of his arrogance, he directly asked, "So, what is your price?"

Beth turned and looked at him with all the glee she could fake, "I don't know, what was your mother's?" He almost knocked the table over getting out, and shouted at the owner he'd never be back.

When he asked Beth what happened, she simply said, "He thought our prices were outrageous." She smiled and went to tell Connie how she'd handled him, as he'd been hassling her for over an hour to have sex with him.

There was no reason she shouldn't still see them all, if not working there, she could be a customer. They still had the best French food in the suburbs. She decided she'd go meet them after work on Saturday to drink and talk with their little group. The first week was so strange staying home, Jeremy was happy having extra time with her and watching television was almost a pleasure. It had been years since she'd seen any shows, so it was a novelty.

Michael'd been going out at the beginning of the week when Beth was home anyway, so this expanded her free nights. It was still mainly Frank and sometimes Rob, so there were no new love interests, and Beth was fine with that. Connie then thought she'd fix Michael up with her old flame Jerry Asher, as he was still looking for new girls to meet, and he didn't mind spending money on them, which was nice. At least Connie knew he was good in the rack, and Michael wasn't looking for a permanent relationship. Jerry still called Connie from time to time, but she said he'd have to get a permission slip from Cam before she'd return to his bed.

Michael went to meet Jerry at the bar in the Cafe', so if it didn't work out, she could always talk to the maitre'd to help her get out of it. Connie said he was one of the best looking men she'd ever been to bed with. But Michael almost passed him up, it was funny how everyone had a different opinion of good looking, or sexy. Jerry was in construction, so Michael began revealing all she'd learned from her brother. He surprised her, he could actually discuss books he'd read, though they were a passion to Michael, so was sex, and she was ready to leave with the small talk done. On the way back to her car from the motel, she still kept attacking him.

Not to leave a good thing alone, Michael invited him back to the house for some more of the same. It wasn't that she was greedy or horny, she hated to see a good hard-on go to waste. Jerry insisted he had to go home and change into his work clothes. Sex was one thing, but he didn't want to miss work. It was about five-thirty when she came dragging in.

Frank had stopped by, and was still there in the morning, and unfortunately, Michael wanted to talk with Frank and Beth. Since she felt she'd become so adept at oral sex, she'd been wondering if Frank might give her another chance. When she mentioned this to Beth, she was furious, but never said anything directly to her. Frank wasn't just another guy she'd picked up and screwed anymore, they'd now been together almost a year, and she knew she was in love with him. It didn't matter if he had other women and she had other men, they did't count anymore, even Rob. Since Beth was mainly working days now, Rob had been gutless about going out with her at night.

Beth knew marriage was an impossible thing between her and Frank, but not what she wanted from him. Ridiculous to say, she loved him too much to marry him, even if he had wanted it, which he didn't. Marriage would change his free-lifestyle, which was a basic part of his attraction. They came from two different worlds, and she knew she could never truly fit into his, as he could never fit into hers.

Frank loved her mind, and the fascinating things Beth could get wound-up talking about. Whenever she used a word he didn't understand he'd stop her and ask her what it meant, never embarrassed by his lack of a larger vocabulary. Yet Beth knew she could talk to him also about basic problems, because he had such profound common sense, which she was usually too emotional about things that bothered her. Frank said once that, "He could screw any broad, but when he wanted to make love, he came to Beth."

Frank was the only man she ever had a completely honest relationship with. Somehow when he'd lecture her about letting the house go till it was a disaster area, it did affect her. He was glad she'd done something more about her weight problem, as she gained easily when she got too emotional.

He wasn't like the rest of the men who just kept saying what a pretty face she had. She could say or tell him anything about herself or others. When he'd ask about Michael, she'd tell him all of it. For some reason, because he'd known her that year before when she was such a novice, he now considered her rather loose. It was the 'keeping track' of the men that bothered him the most. Although Beth'd probably had more than Michel, he'd excuse that. Frank also realized that Beth changed too, and she was still changing, but in his opinion it was for the better, as he could see she actually was learning from her mistakes.

Not even seven in the morning, and Michael was drinking a rum and coke, more than half rum. Slightly bombed from the night before, she kept singing the praises about how great Jerry was in bed - it reminded Beth of April and Al. Beth didn't care for Jerry, because he thought he was so great, and said so. As usual, if a man had satisfied Michael, she was on his defense. Then out of the clear blue, Michael asked Beth, "What all were Ray and you doing that night in Toronto?" Stunned Beth couldn't say a thing, but tried to give Michael a look, so that she'd shut up, as she felt Frank tensing up. She was too bombed to notice anything, so kept rattling on. Michael then started telling Frank all about Toronto, and what all they'd done.

Beth tried again to cut her off by saying, "I told him about it, Michael." And then as she started to speak again, she sternly said, "He stopped by that weekend, and wondered where we were." Even with this, Michael continued, then Frank stood up, and said he had to leave to get to work himself. When Beth stepped back into the house from saying goodbye, she began to jump all over Michael. "What the hell are you saying all that for?" At first she didn't know, or pretended to not know, what Beth was talking about.

Then as if her brain changed gears, and she knew Beth was really angry, she apologized. "I was just wondering what all had been so different." She then admitted, "I guess it was a bad choice of timing in front of Frank." Yes, sometimes Michael could be very thoughtless.

Michael not only would not a get a chance to try Frank again, but he'd not even want to be around her anymore for a long time. He was still very protective of Beth for some reason, and he'd not excuse the fact that Michael was drunk, either. Some how he liked her better before she'd gotten the sex experience and started drinking. Frank felt Michael was trying to make Beth look bad to him. Since he'd actually kicked one woman out of his apartment, throwing clothes after her, when she'd spoken badly about Beth. Michael was lucky he'd left and nothing else.

Michael kept adding to her circle of men to keep her occupied. She went to a pub near by where she'd lived before. One of her old neighbors, Betty and her husband Richard, went there regular on weekends. During the week, Betty met her boyfriend there. Michael'd had a crush on Betty's husband, too, while she was married. She then figured, what the hell, if Betty wasn't going to use him, she would. So, Michael started getting up at three in the morning, to be ready when he stopped in at four o'clock. As long as Richard got home, before his family got up in the morning, Betty wouldn't know he hadn't worked some overtime. It was one of the advantages of working nights. They had great sex, and a good friendship. They'd known each other quite a while, so they had good and bad old-times to talk about. He'd call some nights to gab, like 'one of the girls,' as he got a kick out of her new free-life. He understood how she felt about sex, and was never jealous of other men.

Joe was also back in Michael's life, as he'd gone for the winter, retreating in Minnesota to completely heal all his wounds from the Al and Marnie fiasco - who were now married to each other. He'd called April to find that Michael was living with Beth, and that calling there would be like getting two-birds with one stone. He'd met Beth under the same circumstances, as he'd met Michael, with April dragging her along to meet Al's sister one night, when she was still hung-up on him.

Though Beth turned down his invitation at the time, he thought she might be fascinating to know better. Not too surprised, the Michael Joe now talked to, had certainly changed more than her maternity status. The winter and spring, saw her grow up, but also get rather hardened about men and life in general. Now more interested in sex than she'd been in the talk. She said she'd pickup some Chinese and head over to his place before he'd even invited her.

Soon Joe became another one of the regulars dropping in or calling, talking to either Beth or Michael. Though nothing could have set Joe back on his ears or shocked him, he knew Michael had gone a bit over the line, and needed to be taught a lesson. He'd gone with her to meet Betty and Richard, along with Derek and Polly. Michael didn't want to make a fool of herself in front of Derek, yet she didn't want to show up alone.

Joe could always be counted on at the last minute as an escort. During the evening's conversation, after everyone had a few drinks, they'd turned the talk to, of course, sex. Basically, they were discussing *'lines'* which people used in bed between each other. Not knowing that Michael had been to bed with both Joe and Derek, Richard dropped the *line* that she'd frequently used on him, knowing that his wife was never suspicious of him. Michael almost swallowed her glass. Joe watched Derek smirk at Michael, and then nod at Richard, following the acknowledgment to her, that she'd also used *the same line on him.*

Joe did everything possible to keep from breaking out in uproarious laughter, what the two unsuspecting girls obviously missed, in the silent conversation. Richard said it as an endearment to Michael, like it was *their* private little secret. He never knew how wrong he could be. Michael gave Joe a swift kick under the table, when she realized he'd caught the whole thing. She'd make sure not to have *her men* together at the same time again. She must also do something with her repertoire, and Joe reminded her of that also.

Later while Michael and Joe were in bed, he really gave her a lecture, "Do you have even the foggiest idea of where you are going with your life?"

Michael sighed, as she knew he was right. "Maybe I'd slow down, if I met someone that could make me care."

Joe retaliated, "You think picking-up guys in bars, is the way to find someone who cares? You better start *caring about yourself first!* Those guys are looking for the same thing you are - just sex. When you stop wanting someone *just* to jump your body, you'll start getting men who are more interested in you, than in just the sex."

Michael was silent, and then responded, "I guess I don't know what I really want yet, but I'm certainly learning what I don't want." It was a big step they all had to reach on their own.

"Listen, Babe, we all prostitute ourselves . . ." Michael started to vehemently deny it, when the cool-Joe continued, " . . . Listen, prostitution means exchanging one commodity for another. You might not be selling for money, but you're certainly giving away a part of you every time you are with someone, that you really have *no reason or feelings* to be with."

He looked at her childlike face, so innocent. "Many married people do it day-in and day-out, until one of them dies. Most people who have routine jobs do it, too. I know you're trying to make up for lost time, and get back at your husband and father and God knows who else . . . " Joe took a drag on his cigarette, and slowly continued as he cuddled Michael to him, in a very protective stance. "It's just not really going to *affect any of them* . . . only you and how you feel about you!" Joe's message not immediately applied, but it wasn't forgotten.

Not expecting Beth home till late, Michael had taken Joe into Beth's big bed. They'd been finished talking a little while when Beth came stumbling in the door, bombed out of her gourd. When she found them in her bed she said, "That's OK, don't get up. I'll join you." She proceeded to remove her clothes. Knowing she was serious, Michael and Joe scrambled out of the bed. Neither the time, nor inclination for a *menage' a trois* - Beth rolled in and pass out.

Michael got smashed one night at the FireLite with Sybil, who was always bombed whenever possible. First Michael attacked the day bartender, who was a good friend of Connie's. When he managed to get away from her, Sybil suggested they go with the two guys who wanted to buy them dinner. They weren't regulars at the bar, so it wan't like Michael to accept. They ended up at the worst, expensive Italian restaurant in the area. Not knowing what she ordered, Michael asked for the fettuccini alfredo. When the dinners arrived, already drunk, loud and obnoxious. But when the plate was put in front of her, she said, "That's nothing but fucking macaroni and cheese!" The two guys, and even Sybil wanted to crawl under the table.

Later at the motel, Michael was getting nowhere with the guy she was with. The first time was so fast, he must have broken a record. It looked like Sybil was all right with hers, though. When she didn't want to switch, Michael knew she must have a live one. Though, at Michael's car to go home, Sybil said,"I'm glad one of us had a good time, mine was a real bummer!"

The empty evening made Joe's words come rushing back to Michael's mind. "Shit, I'm not going to worry about it now," she thought, "The deed's been done."

Michael developed a crush on a bachelor she cleaned for. His name was Daniel, and they talked a lot, but had never been to bed together. They were afraid they'd get too involved and neither one was ready for it. They also didn't want to loose the friendship they'd built up, if the sex didn't turn out. They'd been on the phone five hours when he talked her into letting him do it over the phone. It was quite a masterful feat, she even had a climax while he talked to her. Whoever doesn't believe sex is ninety-five percent mental is crazy.

About a week later Beth talked Michael into going over to Daniel's place for the real thing. Unfortunately, he was better over the phone than in bed. From working two jobs and drinking, he was a little too rough for Michael in the rack. It was amazing, that it seemed to improve their relationship. Since she no longer had a crush on him, she could be more open with him, when they talked. Very lucky, she had an aura about her that made men want to take her under their wings, and play big brother.

During this time Michael was still seeing Irish. They would always do something crazy, like pick-up fried chicken, and eat it in bed at the motel room. One night she met him and Ray at the motel bar. When Ray's girlfriend couldn't make it, Michael volunteered to take them both on. Irish didn't think she was serious, but at least he was willing to share her this time.

This was what Michael was hoping for, a reverse-sandwich. She'd always had a sexual-fantasy of two men - one kissing her on the mouth, while the other giving her oral sex. Everything she thought ever dreamed it could be. Perhaps satisfying the fantasy, and the fallacy men couldn't be good friends, Michael realized more of what she wanted in a relationship. She also acknowledged, she not only could have it, but *she deserved it.*

The Magic Land

You made me love you -
when I had no intentions of doing so.
I thought you would only be -
another one night stand.

But then you called me -
just like you said you would.
You took me in your arms -
to hold me and nothing more.

You saw beyond the facade -
to who I could become.
I felt myself slipping -
but I would not stop it.

I took your hand reaching out to me -
as you guided me to the Magic Land.
There we found happiness -
and all my dreams came true.

If we should end tomorrow -
I would accept and understand.
No one is promised a permanent stay -
in the Magic Land.

But as I spend each day -
lavishly here with you -
I realize how few
even get a glimpse inside.

CHAPTER 17

Is this Love?

Beth and Marie decided to have a surprise birthday party for their mother, Louise's sixty-fifth birthday, as it was a good excuse to get the family closer together. They didn't have much contact except Christmas, and Mike's family wasn't there the last time. Because of his absence, Louise dragged out the old family album to show her new favorite, Michael photos of him. Out of curiosity, rarely looking at the album, Beth stuck her nose in, and saw a newspaper clipping of Mike she'd not remembered before.

Just nineteen, he'd been hired in a new program the regional electric company started for training their fleet-mechanics. With his head in a truck's engine, he'd turned his smiling face to the camera. "He'd be given opportunities for growth and development, as high as he chose to go," the article said. Their father told Mike to take advantage of everything they offered, every class, every school and never say 'no' to any job. This was his chance to really make something of himself. He did, now in his mid-thirties, already night-supervisor of the largest city division, over several dozen mechanics.

But the article, or Louise talking about her son's accomplished had little notice on Michael, as she gazed upon this tall, good-looking hunk with the slicked, black hair and dark eyes. Perhaps, that was what got her attention on that fateful trip out to the farm, almost six months before with Beth, Connie and Jeremy. She was looking forward to getting to know this 'god,' they'd all put on such a pedestal. Maybe Beth was the more realistic about him, but she also thought he was a pretty cool-dude, with his 'shit all together.' In many ways, he couldn't be more opposite than Web. So, exactly what was so great about Mike? Base-line, Beth knew he regularly cheated on his wife, so perhaps he was looking?

Michael's chip on her shoulder toward him at the party's beginning, was almost visible. Thus, Beth seated Mike between herself and Michael, - in many ways they were both true, free-spirits. Truly, he'd meant so much to her growing up, she wanted him to have some real fun in his life. Michael couldn't help but stare at him, though his thick, black hair was thinning, and the high, Indian cheek-bones had weathered from working outside at the farm so much. But those solid muscles covered the six-foot-four-frame, and that hearty laugh so full and real. What he did have, that she recognized was a sureness like Frank, a man with confidence in all he did, from the experience-earned in doing a job well. The masculinity came natural, and it didn't take long to see that sexual-aura, comfortable around both men and women.

Mike'd been talking about his latest project out at the farm - a bridge over the creek, which was a small tributary of the Mississippi - so the concern of a proneness to flooding. He had to get his equipment from one side of the farm to the other to care for the crops. Michael, fighting not to fall under his spell remarked, "You mean you don't walk on water?" with no naivety on her face.

Mike, hardly taken aback, but amused at her final outspokenness, but since Beth's friend, so almost expected. "The bridge is for the farm equipment, not me." He later leaned over, and brushed each of Michael's shoulders. "There, the load should be much lighter for you." His smile was beaming, as he had felt her vibe, as he did from most women.

"Touché," was all Michael could say. Like Frank also, he'd read her too, well.

After dinner and the gifts opened, Beth suggested Mike showing some of his home movies, particularly of the bridge being built. The on-going project, since he only had weekends, vacation and summers to work on it. There was a method to her madness, as an excuse to get Michael and Mike alone together. Somehow, she knew if she could get that spark between them going, it might roar. Mike'd been doing side-games in his marriage to Barbara from the beginning, though he wasn't ready to throw in the towel on it. But, his sex life sure wasn't what it had once been, or what he'd like it to be.

Before coming to the birthday party, Beth said to Michael, "Listen, I did enjoy my little tryst with Web, I thought maybe you'd like to give my brother Mike, a whirl." She didn't jump on it, so Beth added, "One thing for sure, he isn't like any of the other men you've been with, but maybe Frank." She put the word into Mike also, and he was always willing to check out somebody, to see if they clicked - her red hair and the feisty attitude, was an attraction.

Taking the ride back to his house for the movies gave them some time, as Beth hoped, and Michael no longer being shy about it, jumped in for a little necking before heading back to the party. The movies gave her a chance to see him in action, as well stripped down to his Levis, bare-chested working on the railway-ties, they were using for the bridge. This was no flimsy bridge, or simple project - the engineering skills were a challenge that he studied up for.

Since they hit it off after the a rather tenuous start at the party, Beth asked her if she'd like to have him come over some time. The next step was getting Mike over to the house on a date, where they'd have an excuse to be out, and he'd be able to get off work a little early - he worked the night shift. Beth got theater tickets to see *"Grease"* for Michael's birthday, as the James Dean-style she was really into.

And, the old photo of Mike at nineteen embedded in her head. Jeremy stayed over with Louise, for their special birthday evening out. Besides dinner and the theater, it'd be the best birthday present to get Michael would be Mike. As it turned out, they both got a surprise when they got home. For Michael it was Mike, and for Beth it was Jim Rayburn, Mike's old friend and Beth's childhood-crush. The guys best friends from high school, through thick and thin for almost twenty years, including both their marriages.

After drinks, Michael didn't hesitate to take Mike to her bedroom. They were off to a great start, with acknowledging 'sex for the fun of it' and anything goes, but the 'whips and cold oranges,' as the running-gag. Beth and Jim also had a great time, but it was nothing like Michael and Mike, there was something more happening. Mike was the only man Michael ever met, that called when he said he would. It could be a painful thing to have them say they'd call, with no intentions of doing so. Some men felt they had to say it, just as some women said they had a 'good time,' when they didn't.

By the second time Mike could see Michael, she'd gotten her period. Since his wife had some weird-sex hang-ups regarding it, as Tim had, Mike picked these up also. Most of the other women he'd fooled around with were in the same mid-thirties age bracket, with the same sex-training. Michael's younger years and current lifestyle, as well as Donnie, released her of that. She knew it'd take time to break him of these ideas, if they kept seeing each other. But he'd come over anyway, just to be with her and talk.

Jokingly, she told him none of the men she'd screwed with her period had died. Still all night long, he held her in his arms, and kissed her while they talked. Since they were both bonkers about kissing and making out, Michael turned out to be more than satisfied in a much different way. She'd never spent an evening with a man in bed *without sex*. A surprising change for her, to have a man want her for the comfort and cuddling. Suddenly, Joe's quote jumped back in her head, and she smiled, maybe *this was love*.

By the time a month passed, already several changes in Michael and Mike. She no longer went out every night, and if she did, she'd be home in time for Mike's call. Contrary to what she'd always said, 'no man'd put her on a schedule, and no intentions of sitting by a phone waiting for him to call - a free spirit didn't let any man hold down her lifestyle.' But, Mike *always did call* when he said, and those things became irrelevant, or didn't count where he was concerned. Since seeing him so often, Michael wasn't even anxious to see any of the other men to keep her occupied and satisfied. If not so tied up with his farm, he'd have spent every night with her.

Mike changed, too, not only about sex. She gave more meaning to everything, he soon became more lenient with sone of his employees, where he'd been too strict before. He didn't push a job, simply because he didn't have anything better to do than work. As the sex went, she taught him that nothing about the body was ever dirty. The smell, touch and most of all the feel, of all of sex was exciting and sexy. They kept telling one another that neither one of them were getting hung-up or hooked. It was *just* fun sex.

Mike planned to set up a weekend for them out at his farm when he'd be working alone. Since he couldn't set up anything with Jim for Beth, he talked to Bret who lived out there. He'd mentioned him several times to Beth, so she was more than willing, if Bret was. A big step for Mike, as he hadn't gotten this involved with a woman since his marriage, over sixteen years before. He'd been telling himself that this affair wasn't that important. Somehow, if Beth came along, it'd be more like 'just fun sex,' as they kept referring to it.

One weekend while on his own at the country club by the farm, Mike came right out and told Bret his plans, "My lady friend and my sister, Beth, are coming up for the weekend. If you're interested, I've paid for a motel room for Beth. Whether or not you'd care to join her, is up to you. She wanted to meet you, Michael is going to be staying with me at the farm." Without any questions or shock, Bret said he'd like that very much. Mike told him they'd be having dinner about six o'clock at the farm, if he'd like to join them and meet Beth.

Michael was so excited she drove Beth crazy, and then a nervous wreck as they arrived at the farm. Preparing the food for dinner was a snap, considering all they really wanted was to attack each other's body. So happy, to have uninterrupted days and nights together - like two high-schoolers knowing they're going to get lucky. When Bret arrived, Beth was pleasantly surprised, as not a country boy at all.

He'd brought a very nice bottle of wine for dinner, so they were all quite *snockered* when dinner was finished. Bret couldn't get over how Mike acted with Michael, he'd never seen him like that before. In the few years he'd known Mike, he was always so straight and business like. Beth and Bret decided to go to the country club for a few drinks and dancing, as well leave the two lovers alone at last. They were getting horny, just watching them attack each other.

Bret followed Beth to the motel to leave her car. He wanted to stay then, but Beth insisted on going dancing, as she never liked to pass it up. They both got unbelievably drunk, and she talked about him getting some grass. To her surprise, in the car on the way back, he lit-up a joint to share with her. The last thing she needed in her state, so the rest of the evening was fuzzy. Except, she blew his mind starting to unzip his pants, while they were driving to the motel. Apparently, neighbor girls or the local college girls, had never been like her in the rack. The alcohol and pot-combination made her bananas in bed. Unfortunately, Bret was tied up the next day, as he managed the golf course. So Beth spent the day between the farm and the motel. It could've been a great weekend with Bret though, but the rest was nice.

For Michael and Mike, it was no 'could have.' Beth and Bret were barely out the door when they headed for the couch to curl up and watch the sunset. They'd promised each other not to mention the time, or rush because of the precious few hours they'd have together. But, they each had a clock ticking away in their heads. Michael sat curled up, with Mike around her cuddling and kissing, as the vibrant pinks and purples moved from cloud to cloud across the sky.

Mike loved this land from the deeper-reaches of his soul, yet his wife never shared in the serenity it gave him. Now, he was sharing these feelings with Michael, like he'd truly found a soulmate. Her eyes were wide open, as each new view was a vista she'd never even imagined before. She'd not considered herself a nature lover, but then at no time had she been exposed to a nature-setting like this, or this natural-man that surrounded her.

The sun almost gone, they saw a young deer come to the creek and drink. They watched intently, until the night completely enveloped the scenery. A cold chill went down Michael's spine. "Chilly?"

"No," she answered. "Just think how peaceful their days and nights must be, except during the hunting season. Oh, Mike hold me real tight, and protect me from that world out there." He pulled her toward him, as he held her and kissed her protectively. Though she'd slowly changed, he'd not seen her protective-shield dropped-down before like this. She made herself totally vulnerable to this man, with the pure, honest-feeling that chipped away the enamel, she'd so carefully laid around her heart. He felt the real innocence of the child-woman, burying her head in his chest. Like he'd found the other side of her, never tarnished by a bad marriage or pseudo lovers.

He picked her up, with her arms clinging sound his neck, as he moved the couch to snap it into a daybed position with his free hand. He gently laid her down, like a fragile piece of crystal, carefully wrapping himself around her. He began by running his fingers through her curly, long-red hair, and down her back to the end of her spine, and slowly back up again. All the time repeating, "Don't worry, I'll protect you, I'll save you . . . you're always safe with me."

They were entwined for an hour or more kissing and holding each other, softly talking as they rose to peaks, then ebbed back still not removing any clothes. Somehow, it'd been more fun to play underneath their clothes. Eventually, shirt and blouse discarded, as they continued to titillate each other for fun and ecstasy. Though Michael had already been given several climaxes, she was ready for the full power of him. First she undid her jeans, and then Mike's. She laughed when he almost popped-out of them in his anticipation.

Their bodies free at last, she climbed on top of him to kiss him all over. Like the child in her, she bounced-off saying, "I've got an idea that will make you even tastier." She went to the kitchen and grabbed the bottle of wine off the table. Though her eyes became accustomed to the dark, she managed to trip on her way back. Mike still laughing at her, she slowly dribbled the wine across his body, and soaked his crotch area. She playfully jumped back on him, and began licking the wine off his body.

The sensation was wild for both of them. She was getting turned-on, just by his own excitement. Against his protests, she insisted to bring him to a climax with her mouth. It was almost a war-hoop that he gave out, as she finally collapsed him. She fell on top of him, grabbing the wine bottle for them both to finish.

He'd gotten his breath, taken another swallow of wine, and announced, "Now, young lady, I'll show you how it feels to be completely wiped-out." His eyes sparkled with glee.

"No, Mike, let me catch my breath, and you yours." Hesitant.

"OK, you've got one minute," he said, as he rolled over and began kissing her. As he completed the kiss, his hands cupped under her buttocks, and raised her to meet his mouth. He'd barely begun, when she grabbed the edge of the couch, to hold on for dear life. Time after time, the waves kept pouring over her, with the sex turning her into a rag-doll. Her rippling body began to perspire from the heat it generated. When she was about to blackout from all the hyperventilating, he released her, and wrapped her legs around him. He soon filled her, and brought her back down to a more basic lovemaking. They'd driven their senses to the furthest point, between his imagination and her playfulness, they'd never be bored in bed - that weekend or afterwards. More than the sex, they'd found and nurtured a comradeship to hold them fast.

The next day, they acknowledged the fact, they were madly in love with each other. Now, what the hell were they going to do? The 'fun-sex' not only backfired, but mushroomed into something neither one of them was ready to handle. There'd have to be a lot of thought about this. They talked inside and walked outside, covering almost every inch of his fifty acres. Beth joined them for meals there and at the country club, while they talked and laughed.

Beth and Michael left out at six, Monday morning to drive back. It had rained all night, with early fog, and dew still heavy in the deep, lonely valleys. This isolated northwest corner of Illinois, had the only 'almost' real mountains in the flat state, so it tried to do the most it could with them. They came up on a high ridge, and Beth stopped the car to look-over the breathtaking-countryside.

The slightest, glistening rays of the rising sun were coming through the mist. The scattered lights from the houses were sparkling-up from down-below. She turned to Michael and said, "Doesn't it look like *Brigadoon* is appearing from its hundred-years' sleep?" Michael quietly sighed and smiled, as Beth continued, "And, only a powerful love will make it appear again, before the next hundred-years pass."

Beth reflected in her audible thoughts. Then to herself, she thought how nice if only Mike and Michael had a *Brigadoon* to disappear into. It would keep these new lovers safe from the outside world, and the 'Witched Witch of the East.'

She thought, Barbara had her chance and blew it, because of her selfishness. She never appreciated this tremendously, caring-man, but only took him for granted. Mike told Michael they'd had some good years, but the recent past ones together were so bad, the good ones could never make up for them. Beth put the car in gear to fly them home, wondering what this new future would hold for them all?

Fly Away

We touched the sun when it was shining.
We touched inside the moon's silver-lining.

We never touched on land,
when we touched as woman and man.

Where is he? Has he gone traveling?
Where is he? I feel our love unraveling.

We touched the stars, and knew them all by name.
We touched on Mars and Venus the same.

Our world knew no bounds,
now I'm stuck on the ground.

Where is my traveling man? Did he fly away?
It wasn't supposed to end this way.

CHAPTER 18

Brief Chance of Love

With Mike, Michael decided to drop-out of circulation altogether, and it cut into Beth's going out also. She didn't like to go out alone, unless over to the Cafe' or The Place, if Connie joined her. One night, Beth got Michael to go out for dinner, and over to a small lounge where Rob worked part-time. They sat at the bar and she was next to a good-looking dude, dressed nicer than the usual crowd that came there. She told Rob about some new customers they got for her cleaning business, and how well it was going. When the stranger asks her about it, she quickly presented him with a card. He was in the process of a divorce and could use some cleaning help himself.

Beth hadn't noticed prior, but at the end of the bar was a guy from her past, who was drunk. One night he'd gotten drunk at the Cafe', and followed her out when leaving. He began attacking her, and she didn't know what to do, as she'd thought of him as a friendly customer. Just then, the Cafe bartender came out and broke him off her, she quickly jumped into her car to drive home. Now, he'd seen her, and was calling to her from the end of the bar. She froze, and said, "Oh, my God, what the hell is he doing here? He's drunk again." Michael leaned over and asked if she wanted to leave, but Beth knew he'd only follow her.

The observant-stranger leaned in from the other side, "My name is Bill. If I can be of any help, please don't hesitate to ask."

"Thank you," Beth answered, if you could dance with me, to the next record, maybe he'll get the hint that I'm with you." She asked Rob for another drink, but before she could say anything else, Bill told him to put it on his tab. He hadn't noticed that Rob didn't charge her for her drinks, she merely had cash sitting in front of her. Beth looked up to see Rob flash a look at her like, *"What the hell is going on?"* To calm him down, so he wouldn't get jealous, she told him that Bill was going to pretend to be with her, to save her embarrassment from the drunk. If Rob had gone over to the drunk, and said something after his outburst, she wouldn't have needed Bill saving her, but Rob hadn't.

Suddenly, the drunk was beside her, and she froze up. She tried to be polite, but cold to him. At last a song Michael put on came on, a slow one. Bill leaned over and said, "I think this is our song, shall we?" Beth slid off the bar stool and into his open arms. She was trying very hard to smile, when she realized she was having a good time.

She looked up at Bill, smiling even more, to say, "I'm glad you're smiling, we're both supposed to be having a good time."

"I am having a good time, you're an interesting woman." He had a cute smirk on his face.

Beth danced even closer to him talking away, when she noticed Rob staring at her. She'd never seen him so jealous before. A strange feeling, since she was enjoying Bill and didn't really care. After a while, the drunk gave up and left, but they waited until the song finished before sitting back down. Right after, Rob's wife Sylvia came in. Of course, she came over to talk to Beth, and she introduced Bill, as if a long-time friend. Shortly, she moved on to other people she knew, Michael then said she was bored, and wanted to go home to get ready for Mike. Beth gave her the car keys saying, "Go ahead, I'll get a ride home from someone."

"Don't worry about the ride, you've got it." Bill surprised Beth that he'd speak up so quickly, so wanted to reassure him.

"Thanks, I only live a few blocks from here, as long as you don't mind." She looked at him more closely, as they sat and talked for another hour. Since she couldn't have Rob take her home with Sylvia there, she might as well enjoy this interesting man who appeared in her life. It'd been a long time, since she'd met a man that intriguing. She couldn't get over the fact that he'd rescued her without any questions of what happened in the past with the drunk. She called him her 'Don Quixote,' for saving her from the two-legged dragon. So later, even with Rob's glare, she innocently smiled and said good night, as she left with Bill.

When they pulled in her driveway, he made no move or advancement on Beth. This was a gentleman. While Bill continuously complimented her, he'd not forced his attentions on her. She invited him in for some wine, and he gladly accepted. They sat in the living room drinking and talking about astrology, of all topics. Michael then came out of Beth's bedroom to read, but soon realized Beth wanted to be alone with Bill, so returned. As the time for Mike drew near, Beth knew she'd have to decide if she'd ask him to stay. They were having such a good time talking, she decided to ask him if he'd mind moving his car out of the driveway to the street. She explained Mike was coming, but not staying the whole night.

Bill headed back in the house, as Beth stood inside the door hoping he'd gotten her message. She waited for a sign that he actually wanted to stay. He comfortably walked in, and pulled her straight into his arms in one easy move. As they were kissing, she felt her knees go weak. Yes, a long time since she'd been with a new man, who truly romanced her. Lately, Rob was in such a hurry, and it often seemed, she never got comfortable as he moved on, not wasting any time. Frank also, didn't spend too much time with the romantic stuff, as at first. It was super to have a man slowly caress, kiss and hold her like he had all the time in the world.

As her feet settled back onto the floor, he led her into Michael's bedroom, and it suddenly became awkward. Beth hesitated, "This is Michael's bedroom . . . I've been giving my bigger bedroom to her, on the nights when Mike comes over that . . . uh . . . I'm alone. There's only a single bed in here."

Bill did the cute smirk again, "It doesn't matter. We'll only be taking up the space of one person anyway." With that clever comment she relaxed and thought, *"What the hell, who needs sleep anyway?"* She lit the candle and closed the door.

This was certainly going to be a new experience for her. The moment Bill joined her in the small bed, she knew he was going to be great. A man that loved making love to a woman, yet she felt it had been for her *only*. He covered every inch of her body, like only Frank had done that first night. He knew a woman's body as completely, as he knew his own. His timing was also perfect, and Beth felt like they'd been making love together many *life-times* before. One thing she did appreciate with Rob, he did know what she liked - he didn't expand much from there, but hey. What truly surprised her now, was how relaxed she was without being drunk at all.

They fit together well, which amazed and delighted her. He was a big man in every way, yet she never felt being smothered or hurt. She couldn't believe what all they accomplished in that little bed. They talked like they had old times to share. After, he totally took her, they fell asleep completely-entwined around each other.

Beth woke when she heard Michael saying good night to Mike. She woke Bill, to see if he wanted to switch over to the big bed. She got up to tell Michael about the change, and asked her to wait for her in the bathroom. She was quite surprised, she'd no idea that Beth wanted to go to bed with him. "Neither did I, it just happened." Her smile spoke volumes.

"Is he staying the rest of the night?" she asked, just curious.

"He could stay the rest of my life, as far as I'm concerned!" Beth giggled.

"What?" Michael's voice raised. "What are you talking about?" Now totally shocked.

"I think I just fell in LOVE!" Beth said, as she walked to the other bedroom where Bill was waiting. Michael stood with her mouth open. It was NOT like Beth to fall for some guy, just because he was good in the rack. She couldn't imagine what had happened in the little bed. For that matter, neither could Beth.

As she slipped into bed, Bill welcomed her again into his loving arms. She thought he couldn't improve on their first time, but he did. As they laid together, she once again told him how fantastic he was, and he calmly responded, "I'm only what you make me. I thought you'd be good when we were dancing, but I had no idea you'd be this great." After their loving, they drifted off into a dreamy-sleep holding onto each other.

Bill swung his legs out of bed, and said he couldn't stay for breakfast, so Beth found her nightgown to put it back on. Michael'd left right away for her cleaning jobs, so they could be alone to talk. He was putting his shoes on when the phone rang. It was Rob calling to check-up on her - he probably drove by and saw the car sitting out front. He mumbled he wanted to make sure she'd gotten home all right. Beth stood there lying to him, while she watched Bill. She didn't know what to say afterwards, as she was a terrible liar. She awkwardly tried to explain the situation, but afraid he read it like he'd been second choice for the night.

Without sounding too serious about him, she tried to say what last night meant in bed and talking. Beth blurted out, "Listen, uh, not just the sex, but talking and dancing - I've never had such a connection before. Not sure what to say." The nerves were pouring out.

Bill then tried to explain, as last night must have also startled him in the same way. "I told you last night, I'm getting a divorce . . . and I'm not . . . shouldn't be ready to get serious about another woman." He was avoiding looking at her, as he gathered up his things.

Beth interrupted, trying to save a slippery situation. "I don't want to get married. I just want to see you again." She wanted him to look at her, and when he did, it was fear she saw.

He detailed it with total honesty. "Hey, this isn't my first divorce, it will be my *third*." In shock, Beth didn't know what to say. He then went on to explain what happened in the previous marriages, and after she heard his side, it was understandable. "I just can't and . . . *should not want* to get involved again." His eyes looked so sad, she wanted to cry.

Almost desperately, "We don't have to *get involved*."

Bill then took her in his arms straining, "You silly girl, don't you realize a man couldn't help but get involved with you, unless he didn't have any feelings at all. You're exactly the kind of woman a man *should* marry. I've jumped into too many marriages. I'd like the next one to last." He then kissed her with more passion than even before, yet somehow Beth knew it was a farewell kiss. He hesitantly added, "I'll call you. I have to go out of town this weekend, but I'll be back Sunday night." He reluctantly released her, heading out the bedroom with Beth behind.

"I'm going to my brother's farm, but I'll be home by Sunday, nine o'clock at the latest." She continued following him to her front door, and watched him walk down the steps, out of her life. He stopped for a long look at her on the porch, then got into his classic, Shelby Mustang. She could only think of what could have been. He was the closest thing to perfect she'd ever met. Of course, with time he probably wouldn't have been, but still nice to remember him the way he'd been last night. If she never saw him again, she'd have much to reminisce about.

It'd be great for Beth and Marie to be at Mike's farm, as they'd not been able to be close to their brother, they dearly loved. Marie had a ball driving the tractor up and over the hills, Mike wanted them to see his dream farm that a neighbor had. Michael busied herself tromping with his boys Jackie and Jason, through the fields and woods. Such a kid at heart, her marriage never gave time to enjoy her teenage years. She got along better this time with Barb, as they were on their way to becoming best friends. Michael ensconced herself into Mike's family, simply to be close to him, even if having to control their sexual feelings. But Beth couldn't take her mind off Bill, as she thought how she could be sharing this great outdoor fun with him.

There was no phone call from Bill, Sunday night or ever again. Michael was surprised, as he had all the earmarks of being a winner. This was one time that it was difficult for Beth to swallow the adage that 'everything always turns out for the best.' Her inner feelings were being wrenched around, as if there was anything she could've done differently, or if there was any chance of running into him again.

In all honesty, Beth couldn't call it rejection, in the normal frame of things. They had both reacted to feelings, and he was the one that felt he couldn't 'move past his past.' Part of her understood - other than celebrities, who goes for a *fourth* marriage? Yet, why not if you did find someone you truly loved. Yes, it would take time, but she'd survive, she'd *risk* loving again - wasn't that what she was doing with Frank? They loved each other, but both afraid to move forward. She did believe in hope, more than any fear of future rejection, and never a lag between an experience, and her response to it. No regrets.

Beth laughed at herself, she wan't just involved with her own clandestine affair with a married man, but those of Connie and Michael, too. Since they were both somewhat out of circulation, it gave Beth a chance to explore on her own some different types of men. She felt she wanted to do some 'loose'-girl image-changing. She'd also realized pushing thirty, with the drinking age lowered to nineteen, the competition not only was getting younger, but they were brassier than she'd probably ever be. She pondered the scary possibility of becoming a burned-out bar-fly. They, the 'girls' were all beginning to look the same, as those people that were in the bars.

Beth took some time away, to travel to Oregon with Jeremy to see her old neighbor-friends who moved there. Then she and Connie made a trip up to northern Michigan to visit Connie's relatives. It was a nice time away, and Beth questioned Connie if she ever thought about where it was all going with Cam. Connie'd thought about it, but had a great fear of starting all over with another man. The occasional one-night stands were fine, because she was detached from them, and usually never saw them again.

After a long silence driving, Connie spoke, "Sometimes I think I'm hanging on to Cam because of our mutual friends, and to see if he ever will have the balls to get a divorce from his wife."

Beth quickly asked, "Would you marry him then, Connie?"

"I don't know . . . sometimes it is what I dream about most, then other times I realize what an asshole he is, and I think I could never do it."

In the meantime, Michael and Mike had an almost perfect affair. They'd already given so much to one another. She'd taught him how to live life-freer, and he'd taught her how to maintain it. He'd found the woman that had been hiding inside her all her life. She'd brought out the man in him, that no other woman fully appreciated or wanted. His sex life sat on a shelf for many years, during his marriage. A very sexual man, he now found the perfect match. The sex never tapered off for them, it only got better, which they would've said was impossible. They not only fit-together perfectly, but completely fulfilled one another's wants and needs. Michael had no need of another man, and Mike no interest in another woman.

He was tied to his wife through his two sons, and felt he needed to stay married until they were on their own. Thus, he felt the obligation more to his sons, since he believed divorce would be a stigma on them.

Beth disagreed, and felt he should pull out now, especially if he loved Michael so much. She believed the kids would do better with one happy parent than two unhappy. What a price he put on his freedom, and happiness, but Michael said they didn't look at it that way. Beth then talked to him about getting his finances overhauled, too. She questioned with all the money he made, Barb must be doing more with it than paying the bills. If he didn't have his farm, his life would have little meaning, and it was the only thing that Michael could never replace. Not only that, but it was a future for his children, not just his life and freedom that was important. If Barb hated it so much, he needed to make sure it was protected, Beth felt Barb was undermining him on it.

Mike may no longer care for Barb, but he deeply loved his two sons, and without the farm as his legacy, they'd never know or appreciate what happiness and freedom he'd given up for them. Beth tried to remind him, that they were still individuals passing through his life, on to becoming adults on their own, and he surely wanted them to pass through smoothly. On the other hand, Michael believed a rocky-road built character and taught survival, but she well knew that Mike was not of the age or era, that could believe in doing 'your own thing.'

In reality, Michael knew she was not ready to live with a man on a full-time basis. Being honest with herself, she'd have to be one full person, before she could be part of two. She still hadn't lived by herself - on her own, and that was the last step of completing herself as an individual. This she knew she had to do, and their future relationship could only be better for it. She acknowledged that for her to become more responsible, she'd have to take charge of her life, and run it rather smoothly, also.

Reflections

Only people who care enough,
   seek to find the answers to
      their own questions.

They realize you only get to know
where you're going, when you've learned
    from where you've been.

Sure Sign of Hope

I stand proud and smile,
    I am a woman.

I know love is hard to find,
    but not impossible.

Fate can play some wild tricks,
    but I like the challenges.

I can learn to play well,
with the cards I've been dealt.

I guess I'm a realistic optimist,
maybe because I've never folded.

CHAPTER 19

Not the Usual Status Quo

Connie's love life wasn't going the greatest lately. Cam hadn't gotten a divorce, of course, and wasn't even talking about it anymore, but he was as jealous as ever. One night, she sat at the bar in the FireLite waiting for him, late as usual. A very big, drunk man that she briefly knew was trying to make a pass at her. Since he was known as a harmless flirt, she didn't get upset, besides he was too big to tangle with, if she was nasty to him. She was wearing one of her low-cut halter tops. The character was about to reach over to touch her cleavage, when Cam came in and observed what was taking place.

Rather than say something, he thought more direct-action would be quicker and teach him a lesson, also. Because the guy was standing with one foot on the bar stool, and leaning over the bar, it was easy for Cam to grab him by the balls from behind. He quietly said to the guy, "I wouldn't do that if I were you," with a gentle, but firm squeeze. The guy jerked his hand away like he'd been burnt.

"Hey, man! This your woman? Sorry, I thought she was alone. I was just leaving." She was proud of him for not causing a big scene.

Cam hadn't been easy to live with lately, because he'd been out of a job. "Old and lonely was one thing, but broke, too, was *too, much*," Connie teased Cam, to cheer him up. Now, at least he was working, if only at what he felt rather a degrading job, a car salesman. They'd been having a great time on the boat lately, except he could hardly afford to take it out. They had sex on every space in and around the boat, which included all twenty-three feet of it, in every lake they put in.

One night while they were on a diet and *not drinking,* Connie got him to try some grass. He'd never believed that anyone could get high on some weed. They both got so stoned sitting at the kitchen table, they had to crawl on their hands and knees to find the bedroom. Neither one of them remembered what they accomplished in bed, but they were both so worn-out the next morning, it must have been good.

Another night Connie's very strange, straight-laced girlfriend, Linda was over with a guy named George, Connie fixed her up with. Now George knew Connie was a little kinky, he'd been to bed with her himself a while back, even so, he wasn't prepared for her next shot. Since she had only two chairs at her small kitchen table, Linda was sitting on George's knee, while she was on Cam's leg. Connie lit up a pipeful of powerful grass, and when she started to feel real good, she started bouncing on Cam's lap. She then proceeded to slide off his lap, unzip his pants, and wrap her mouth around him.

Since they were on the other side of the table, Linda could not see what she was doing. So stoned by this time, Cam couldn't even get shocked, he just sat there with the shit-eating grin on his face. Linda kept asking George what they were doing. He figured it out, and if she didn't know, he certainly wasn't about to tell her. Finally, Linda stood up and leaned over to take a good look. She yelled and ran out of the room, with one hand over her mouth and the other over her eyes. Connie looked up, laughed and continued enjoying herself. Cam didn't change his position, or the look on his face.

Connie was famous for her one-liners, which she'd learned mostly from Cam. Michael was one of the best targets for Cam. When she was pregnant, he referred to her as 'Frick and Frack.' One night Connie and Cam met Michael and Beth at a nightclub. Connie danced with Cam after he'd been dancing a slow dance, close to Michael. She asked him how Michael's boobs felt to him, since it wasn't a sarcastic question, he answered, "Fine, why?"

"Because they're my boobs, dummy. I gave her all my old padded bras."

"Well, I'm certainly glad Beth's are the real thing, cause it's not nice to fool Mother Nature three times in a row!"

Not that Connie never got embarrassed, on one of her first business trips with Cam, she was sitting across from him in the motel dining room having breakfast. When she finished, she looked up with a smile, "You ready to go back to the room and screw?"

Cam wasn't the only one who heard her, the guy at the next table started choking on his scrambled eggs. She turned bright red when she noticed him. If she could've crawled under her plate, she would've. Cam took his time finishing, thoroughly enjoying her embarrassment.

* * * * * *

Mike's Fourth of July celebration was the christening of his three-year bridge project. Proud he's built it with only the help of his two sons and a few friends. It would have cost over ten thousand dollars, if he'd had it done by a contractor. As Mike remarked, "Not too shabby!" It was a four-day celebration of drinking, good food and lots of laughs. Plans were then made for Mike, Marie and Beth to go up to Beth's lake property in Wisconsin - also the perfectly-planned excuse for a weekend with Michael. Beth was trying to decide if she should still hold onto the property with the high payments, or sell it.

Since both Marie and Mike never saw it before, they fell in love with the area at first sight. They thought she needed to keep it, and started clearing the virgin timber, for a path down to the natural sand beach. That night they enjoyed their steaks cooked on an open fire, with a little unwanted sand. The light rain sprinkling down didn't dampen their feelings about the hauntingly, beautiful lake area. They sat around the humongous-bonfire drinking the Cold Duck. It was becoming a tradition to use Cold Duck for celebrating. They sang songs, hearing only their own echo in return for company, coming across the lake.

Probably one of the happiest times in Beth's life, without a lover-man by her side. She was dancing and singing, as she ran around the fire, then in and out of the water, with the bottle of Cold Duck in her hand. Mike said, "What a shame, she doesn't have a man who could share this with her, she has so much to give in so many ways."

It was true, all the men Beth knew, she couldn't find one she wanted, who wanted her, always one-sided, one way or the other. But, she was happier than poor April, stuck in another bad marriage that she didn't want to get herself out of. Or, in reality even Michael and Connie being in love with men who were not totally free. They all had their problems, all different, yet all not totally happy. But the fact, they always had each other that kept them going, when a man let them down. And, it was better than their first marriages, by a long shot.

The next time out to the lake, they took the whole gang - Mike's family and Marie's family. Fun continued while clearing the brush and trees with, of course, drinking. After lunch, they wanted to look around at some of the other properties. One of the lots, the land was a straight drop to the lake with no beach, so the owners hung a rope for swinging-out over the water. Beth and Michael argued to see who would get to go first. Since Michael couldn't swim, Beth went to to see if the rope would hold. There were some boys playing near the edge of the water with their row boat. Since it was late autumn, everyone was bundled up against the cold.

Beth stepped back with the rope, and took a running leap out over the water. Just as she reached the furthest point, her hands broke-loose and she plunged into the deep, frigid water. Mike was about to go in after her, when she popped up and started to swim into shore. She was laughing so hard, she could hardly make it. When he pulled her up onto the shore, he told her she missed crashing into the boat by about a foot. She figured it must have been so much booze, and working with her arms too much that made her loose control. She started stripping, putting on clothes from the others, while Mike ran back to get a fire started.

Michael and Marie held up a blanket while Beth changed clothes, as none of them could stop laughing. Beth hung her tennis shoes on a branch over the fire to dry, while she was drying. Naturally, she forgot about them until the toes were all stringy, and melted like pizza cheese. The day not going at all well for her, later that night, sitting in a lawn chair inclined toward the lake, for the greatest warmth from the fire, she fell over. Obviously wasted, when she started falling, she barely called out, "I'm f-a-l-l-i-n-g," then plopped into the sand. Everyone else was also bombed, so they just watched. Always good for a laugh, she'd given them plenty that day. She sleep like a log in the motel, but the next morning her mouth felt like the bottom of a very old, very dirty bird cage, and so stayed a little more sober.

Beth felt better to make people laugh, than to let them know what a confused state she was in. The turmoil she'd been living through, so lost lately, she didn't know which way to turn. She felt like on a treadmill, that kept going faster, as the angle was increased. It seemed she'd be keeping up with it, when it would tilt and she'd fall off. She didn't know who was the real person inside her anymore. She had so many fronts to keep up: The good, clean-cut hard-working mother image for her cleaning customers; the loose, sleep-around tramp-aura for some men, the 'I'm usually not like this' with other men, and at all times acting like she was flowing in money.

If she only had a real career goal, something to look forward to, some purpose she was working toward, other than getting her bills paid and getting laid occasionally. Marriage, or having a permanent man, did not seem to be the answer, whatever the question was. They were all neurotic, but now she felt like she was going over the fine line, which she could not do when the others so depended on her to be the rock, and have all the answers to *their* questions.

Time to go see April, to have her do a complete astrology update for her to have some clue. At least there was something April could be helpful at, and that was the astrology. They sat for hours going over all the points of her chart, it was a very difficult one, and April hesitated to admit at first, that it was the most intricate one she'd ever done. Even when she compared it to famous charts in her training books, Beth's amazing details she'd not seen before. April was becoming well-versed, and invested in a teacher that was nationally known. She so loved learning the infinite details of astrology.

It certainly looked like things would be great in years to come, if only she could get through the times now. Beth talked about the book she wanted to write on divorce, and how she wanted to finish college. April told her that she'd shortly get the motivation to do all of it. Going through what was known as her Saturn Return, which everyone did between the ages of twenty-nine and thirty, keeping occupied would be the best thing for her right then.

Funny, she couldn't talk about her confusion, and questions in her life with Connie and Michael. They all got involved with each other's problems, but there were certain things that they couldn't talk to one about, they could always talk to the other. If they didn't have all four, through their rough and tumble lives, none of them would have lasted very long.

Michael'd been more open recently with Beth, than she'd been with April or Connie. But she'd always kept a certain part of herself totally private. A solo-person anyway, she didn't give out opinions, or advice the way Beth and April always did, even when it wasn't asked for. Something Beth had a hard time accepting, was when Michael said she didn't care one way or another, she didn't, but only if she truly did care about it. She must have strong feelings about something, in order for her to be decisive about it at all.

Yet, Michael bared her innermost-soul out to Mike. They told each other things, that they'd never said out-loud before, much less to another person. One thing that frightened her, if she ever lost Mike, what would she do? Almost afraid she'd never get her soul back, once having shared it so openly.

Michael survived all those years with Tim, because she always had that secret-hiding-place in her mind to escape to. The sexually-degrading things he'd done to her at the end, she wiped-out because she hid them away. She honestly told Mike, how she felt about the baby, which was not at all as blasé, as she ever acted. Now, that she shared all these things, the shell she climbed into when things got to be too much for her was gone. Somehow, revealing it to another person dissolved it. Totally vulnerable, she only had Mike, and she had made him the *oasis of her life*.

This was something which worried Beth, since Michael only thought of today and tomorrow with Mike, not much else mattered to her anymore. She'd never been impressed with much in life - "This is all there is." Her attitude was a statement, not the usual question. It didn't seem possible that she could see no more in life than what was immediately before her. She said, "It was like I watched my world change from black and white to color with Mike, so there was no need for anything else." Yet, she still hadn't lost all of her unique individualism, what he'd first fallen in love with. Beth knew if she became a 'yes' woman, she wouldn't be that different from his wife, or other women he'd known. He wouldn't want a woman, whose only interest was him. Still her own free-spirit, she was going to have to watch it closely, if she filled her life up with Mike, there wouldn't be any room left over for Michael.

The fact was, the only thing she wanted was him. Sure, there might've been a few things they differed on, but nothing earthshaking. They were so good for one another, she couldn't deny that. Michael knew how to bring him around to her way of thinking, as he so capably knew how to do the same with her. Beth'd been hurt very little by Rob, but he'd never made promises, and she never really asked for them, or shared so much. So there was no real comparison, as their relationship was never the same. It wouldn't be easy for Beth, but she'd have to stay out of it, no matter how difficult to voice her opinions sometimes. It was Michael's life, and she was going to live it the way she wanted, since prior she had people telling her what she should or should not do. Then again, at twenty-eight, Michael should be ready to make her own decisions.

No matter what they all had in common, Beth, Michael, Connie and April were still four very individual people, who were grabbing at whatever happiness they could find in life, without hurting anyone else. If Michael was happy, it's what counted. Strange, the greatest loves of each of them was a man not totally free to marry, or be with them all the time. Time never changed the way April felt about Al. Such a small piece of her life spent with him, yet when she looked back, she remembered it as being much better than it was. No matter, since the effect it had on the rest of her life had been phenomenal. He'd touched her soul, and she'd never be the same again.

Also true with Connie, she'd given Cam a seven year limit, and they were starting their sixth year of being together. If they never ended up even living together, another man would have a tough act to follow. The sexual awakening that he'd given her, was only the beginning of their sexual experience. She kidded him that he was six years older than Elvis Presley, and four years younger than Paul

Newman - what happened to him? Yet, she wouldn't exchange him for either man then. Life itself was more enjoyable with Cam around.

Although, Beth no longer loved Rob the way she had, she'd never hate him because of his weakness of not being able to assert himself. He'd always be a suburban, middle-class married man, staying in his marriage until the last of his three kids were grown, and on their own - because it was the *'right'* thing to do. Yet, if she hadn't known him, she'd have never known what real love was like, which lead to being confident enough for Bobby and Frank.

There was that scary-chance, she could've still been married to Bruce, because she didn't know any better man was out there, who also wanted her. Of course, these few years later, she'd have dried up like a prune, or been covered over with green mold. Beth laughed at her analogy, or how life - hers and the others - had been like Dominos. Once one is set off, all the others fall from being touched. None of them would be where they were, without the *first one being released.* They may not know where they were going *now*, but they did know *they were an accumulation of growth,* which brought them this far, with all the changes they'd had in their lives.

So, it was Michael, who at long-last found the *'perfect'* love - man. They'd only begun, yet they'd already given so much to each other. They both gave more meaning and purpose to their life by becoming one - he made her feel brand-new, and she made him feel reborn. Everything took on more perspective, because they *now did have* each other, and some day they hoped it would be *'forever.'* Their time was coming, if only they both could last until it came.

A Friendship

No one said friendships were easy.
And, no one said they would last.

Some people come into our lives
for just one purpose,
and others return again,
and again to share with us.

Is there a line or border if crossed,
an acquaintance becomes a friend?
Or, is it by time or bonding,
we judge or measure a friend?

I don't know the glue that works for us,
because at times it's cracked wide open.
But, I do hope - and I'll always hope,
we'll be stuck together in times to come.

CHAPTER 20

You Got A Friend

Beth started taking an architectural course at the county college. It was only for house planning, but it made her feel creative, and hoping one day to build a dream house. This was to play with regarding her lake front property, as she had no idea where the money would come from to build it - but a girl could dream. With no restrictions as to money, it had everything she ever wanted in a resort home. It had to be big, open and spacious for all the entertaining that she'd want to do, if she had it.

Suddenly feeling so vital and alive, April was again correct. She started the book that she'd been thinking about, and planning on *'How to be Happily Divorced'* as its title, as it was more than *'You've Come a long way, Baby.'* She felt it all happened in small or sometimes giant steps, with no 'mother-may-I' help along the way. All the small ideas about changing were grouping together into a big idea, which spelled: GROW UP AND CHANGE! This *'getting your act together'* was not easy.

Most of her cleaning jobs she was alone, and a great time to do what she considered her *'mental-writing.'* She probably wrote and rewrote the beginning of the book a dozen times in her mind. To her customers that were home, she talked to them about it, and her house plans. She felt that many of them were sort-of-friends, not just customers. Likewise, many of them would ask her opinion on one thing or another. Michael and Connie also became very close to several of their customers, and a few that were divorced, too. So, between the book and the house plans, Beth was busy and happy. There were a few new men in her life, but no one special. She even saw Jim Rayburn a few times for quickies, and though a close friend of Mike, he hadn't realized how involved they were. Beth liked Jim, but she knew she couldn't depend on him if needed.

When she did have a bad time, she knew who she could run to, if she didn't do it too often. The last week of October was one of those times. She'd almost been raped on Monday night - a man that promised to help her with the book. She'd decided at its inception, she wasn't going to screw anybody to get the book published. If he'd wanted to be her friend, talk with her about it and so forth, it would've been fine. And, if he hadn't rushed and pushed, she'd probably would've gone to bed with him later. But he had, and he did, and it scared the hell out of her.

On Tuesday night, he called saying he knew her married name, which she never used and her home address, which she never gave out. This scared her more, as he must have been obsessed not to be able to take 'no' for an answer. On Wednesday, Beth's beautiful, pride and joy, her shiny, new car was hit by a truck. The front end was totally demolished. She was stopped at the time, at a traffic light with no place to go, to get out of his way. She just sat and watched the big headlights come pounding down on her. It was not until afterwards, that she realized if he hit her broadside, he'd have killed her.

On Thursday night, she was late getting out of school, which made her twenty minutes late for a first date with a new guy. Thinking she'd stood him up, he'd left. She sat and talked for an hour with some woman, who had obviously been hiding in a cave somewhere. Her husband left her a half dozen times, treated her like shit, and she always took him back. Now, he kicked her out. Beth gave her a lecture on everything from women's rights to changing her clothes, make-up and hair style. By the time the woman left to go to a friend's, she was standing completely erect, and had all the intentions of telling her husband to go fuck-himself.

It's what Beth liked to do - talk to a down-trodden woman, and show her how to stand-up in this world. She could always talk a good line, even when she had trouble living it. She finished her drink and left to go home. Half-way there, she noticed a car following very closely behind her, with a sole figure in it that looked like a man. She thought twice in one week was too much to get attacked. When he pulled alongside of her, and motioned her over, she didn't know what to do. She figured if she kept going, he might follow her home, which was worse.

A busy highway, so she pulled over. When he came over, he was surprisingly nice. He said he'd noticed her in the bar, and asked if she wanted to go for a drink or cup of coffee. She politely refused, saying she had to get home, as a babysitter was waiting. He put up no fuss, and never asked a second time. He thanked her for her time, but never asked for her phone number, though she should have thought to give him one of her business cards. Who knows what would have happened - maybe one she should've accepted.

Friday night Beth went to meet Cam and Connie for a drink at the Cafe', Connie wanted to go to another bar, and Beth felt they wanted to be alone. So, she had another drink by herself before driving home, then on the way she turned around and drove to Frank's apartment. Already in bed when she came to the door, there was a girl in the living room reading a magazine and listening to the stereo. Frank told Beth to get in bed, as he went to ask the other girl to leave. Beth was hiding under the covers, when the girl walked out the back door. If she hadn't been sort of drunk, she would never have pulled such a stunt.

Frank knew immediately something must be really bothering her, since he usually went to see her, or they came to his place after The Basement. She'd never come to him before. He was so calming to her, as she opened up to talk to him. He understood after she told him about the *'week from hell'* that she had, but he still felt it was no reason to drink too much. He didn't like a drunk woman, and she knew it. Lecture-time again, since he was one of the few people she listened to, maybe she needed it. They talked and made love all night.

In the morning, Beth kept thinking about the discussion they had about his association with his 'brothers' in the motorcycle club. She'd felt that he didn't need them because he was such a together person, but then she didn't know how serious he was about it all. "How many friends do you have?" Frank quietly asked, drinking his coffee slowly.

"Three - good friends," Beth responded, "As you know, Connie, Michael and April."

Frank smiled and said, "You've got two or three more than most people. But would they be there when you needed them night or day?"

"Yes, they have and I have for them," she took a swallow of her coffee feeling good.

"You mean they would drop anything if you called?" He looked at her closely.

"If I was desperate, and I asked them - yes." Her mind churned, thinking it over.

"Either I was wrong about them, or you're giving them more credit than they are due."

"Frank, they would do it - I would do it for them. We've been through the worst and best together. I wouldn't ask unless really desperate, and they probably wouldn't either."

"Would they kill for you, or die for you?" With it said, he took a big swallow.

"No, unless to save my life - that's absurd. I wouldn't ask them to. I'm sure if I was dying, they'd try to save me, even putting their lives in peril." She was holding her cup tightly.

"Well, I have twenty-one brothers, who are *all my friends* and would do *everything* I said, if I asked them to. My own family wouldn't do it." He sat still, quite serious.

Beth responded with surety, "Neither would mine - it's why we *choose* our friends, and why they are sometimes closer than family." She smiled releasing her grip on the cup.

"So, you think I'm better than my brothers and don't need them, . . . and I think you're better than what I've seen of your friends, . . . But we both want them and need them, or we wouldn't have them, would we? So, if your friends are so great, why didn't you go to one of them last night instead of coming to me?" Frank leaned in as he spoke to her.

Beth leaned over and kissed him, as she was getting ready to leave. "Because they can't comfort me the same way you can, . . . since you are my friend *AND* lover. Thanks." She rose and turned to go out the back door, truly feeling like a new person, even if there was some asshole out there screaming and yelling, she'd blocked his car. Nothing was going to bother her today, or for a long time.

As Beth's birthday rolled around, April was more than anxious to have an excuse to go out. The walls were coming in on her, and she needed an outlet. She worked for Beth for a few months cleaning houses, but it wasn't her bag. Beth also had a few complaints on April, which rarely happened on any of the girls. She tried working in a small factory, too, but quit when Alex quit his job. She probably would've been fired because she started organizing the workers into a slowdown, or strike against the working conditions.

This was also the first time Michael would be going out with the girls in a long time. April started getting ready about noon, so got very irate that they didn't want to go out until ten that night. Even then, the first two bars were dead, or only had teeny-boppers. Michael wanted to check out her old haunt the Longview, since it had been over a year when Beth had shown her ass so badly there.

To their surprise, Carmie and Vince were at the bar. It was like old home week. There was a whole different crowd there, thank God. The only one who didn't have a guy to talk to was April, but she had feelers-out checking all the guys sitting around. There wasn't too much female competition. Vince was dressed-up, fit-to-kill in 'citizen' duds, and Carmie looked great in his usual leather, biker-outfit.

When they got bored, they all left for another hangout. Michael rode with Vince, which was taking her life in her hands, but she knew she was safe with him sex-wise. Beth drove her car, and Carmie rode in between Beth and April, so he could cop-a-feel whenever he felt like it. He talked to Beth about their fateful night, when he failed, and she'd ridiculed him so, in front of his brothers.

She never knew how much she hurt him by all that. He liked her, and he wanted another chance. Beth apologized profusely, but then made it clear to him, that she was still not having sex with any of Frank's biker-brothers. She was more than happy spending time with him, and them enjoying themselves, but nothing more. Carmie thought about it, and agreed he'd not to hold a grudge against her, and they'd have a good time, which made Beth feel better.

April was trying very hard to get along with Carmie, but her personality was not even close. At a stop light, Carmie reached out and grabbed Beth's boob, giving it a gently squeeze. He then did the same thing to April, as if to be fair, and teased April that her's was not nearly as firm as Beth's. She almost drove-off the road from laughing, then expected April to come-out with some sarcastic remark, but she managed a laugh. Carmie carried on for a few minutes, then gave April a kiss, so as not to hurt her feelings.

At the new bar, they ran into Crazy Don, with a 'buzz-on' which was about perfect. April got nervous, as she had no intentions of getting-lucky with '*the gang.*' She got up to go look around, after some encouragement from Michael and Beth. It wasn't like April to drink, so they didn't know what she might pull, since she'd swallowed-down a whiskey sour like a coke. Two more of the bikers then joined the group. Most of the gang was there now that they knew, except Frank. They all drank, danced and laughed till they were about to fall down. When Michael and Beth couldn't get the guys to dance any more, they asked some strangers. One time, when Michael came back from dancing, Vince gave her a swat on the ass. "What's that for?" she yelped.

"That's for your dude. He wouldn't like you dancing that sexy-way." She nodded, he was right. Crazy Don introduced a new guy named Crow, a trial member in the club. He was really cool, and turned both Beth and Michael's heads. He went with Beth when she took Carmie back to his car to go home. Beth almost accepted, when Crow asked her if she wanted to stop at his apartment, before going back to the bar. She would've accepted, if she'd thought it wouldn't get back to the other guys. But that was impossible, because everything always got back. Besides, a quickie with a guy like that was a waste for both of them. And, she felt that she wanted to get away from that sort of thing, now.

Later they were still all laughing and drinking, even April, when Vince asked Beth what the weird-rock was around her neck. She'd actually picked it up on the coast in Oregon, the previous summer. But she decided to see if she could blow Vince's mind. Answering him as straight as possible, "That's my ex-husband's ball.

He only had one, and I had it petrified when I got the divorce." They all burst out laughing, at her outrageous statement. Vince said nothing.

Michael hung her head in her drink saying, "Oh, my God." over and over. She'd never get over the gems Beth could come out with in public. The three girls got up to leave at closing time. They all had offers from almost everyone of the guys, but turned them down. It was one group that they could have fun with, yet know there were no problems about not having sex with them. It wasn't so much that they respected the girls, but they did respect *their right* to say 'no.' Giving each one a kiss, Beth thought how she would've reacted a year before. She probably would've gone to bed with several of them, especially Crow. A huge realization of how much she had changed.

Out at the car, they talked about how they felt like it was the end of an important chapter in their lives. Michael now knew she could last through any kind of temptation. She also knew that she could have fun without sex, and without Mike. Sure she would have more fun with him, but it was fun to go out with the girls, too. April thought about what could've happened, but didn't. It had been a big decision, but she'd made it. She wouldn't have any guilt to live with. She went home to Alex. And for Beth, she had her one and only - Frank, the Biker. The guys had been fun in the past, but just that - the past. It'd been quite an experience that night for each of them, and they knew it could never be repeated to come out the same way. They had each been given a choice, and because *they'd changed,* the decision was different than it would've been before.

As fate would have it, Jim Rayburn came to see Beth on Sunday, he'd called to say he was in the area, and if he could stop in. He didn't know it was Beth's birthday, but OK, since no way he would have. And, Beth was used to being disappointed, as she'd learned to expect it. What she still needed to learn, was how she contributed to it.

Retake

Sometimes, I think all the great words
have been written or spoken before.
If not in this life, maybe the one
we had in the days of yore.

If I say, "I love you" and
it doesn't last forever;
I'll do a retake and
move onto the next lover.

If that doesn't work out
I'll know it was a mistake.
One, that doesn't take
long to discover.

Etcetera... Etcetera...

So, my dear, when I say, "I love you"
I hope you'll understand,
just why I've lost my spontaneity
that once was so grand.

The face and the body
may have changed;
but all the great words
were spoken before.

CHAPTER 21

Surprise! Surprise!

They were trying to make it through another holiday season. Connie, as usual, getting her 'rocks off' more by counting her money, since working lunches and dinners, besides doing cleaning. Beth and Michael were spending as fast as they made it, per usual. Beth got her head so deep in debt, she had to come up with a thousand dollars by the end of December, or her ass-was-grass. She tried a loan company, but was refused because she'd just signed for a car loan for Michael. She went to her bank to see if she could have it added to her home-improvement loan, she'd gotten for Jeremy's new room. They turned her down needing an evaluation on the house, which could take weeks.

Very down, Beth had no idea where she'd get the money. She didn't have anything worth that much to sell, that was completely her own. It was then that she realized her wedding ring was gone. She'd left it on the dresser, but didn't want to think some guy had taken it, but between her and Michael, a lot of men had come through. Another lesson learned, she no longer like it, but could have made money off of it. When the banker called her back to say they'd changed their mind, she was elated. They'd be depositing the thousand dollars in her account in the morning. Beth was singing and dancing around the house, as she was going to make it yet! That was close, as already the twentieth of December. Beth prayed she wouldn't need money for any emergency, since she wouldn't be able to get money from even a loan shark, at this point.

Since the first New Year's Eve that Beth hadn't worked in five years, they had a party. At Marie's house again, since she had the extra space, and getting better at parties, as her third one since August, but not exactly overwhelmed with style. Michael thought to invite Sybil, since she didn't have anything exciting to do either. She'd just gotten back from Synanon in California - the famous rehab place. For Sybil a real bummer, not at all rehabilitating, just degrading. She overdosed again while drinking, because she broke up with her married boyfriend. She always seemed to have something throw her over-the-wire, rarely going more than a few months without attempting suicide.

Sybil wanted to become independent, which was something she'd never been before. In all honesty, quite emotionally unbalanced, so never been able to find that person inside trying to get out. Escaping through drugs and alcohol always quicker and easier. Not easy being a Gemini, as every road she traveled had a fork in it, and she usually took the wrong one. She talked to Beth about wanting to be her friend, which was a change for Sybil.

Ever since Beth came home from waitressing one night at the Cafe', and found Sybil passed out in the middle of her living room floor, she hadn't been too tolerant of her actions. She'd also emptied two of her liquor bottles. Beth told her she'd never been through the things Sybil had, but she could understand her feelings of lostness. Beth talked to her about her same feelings the past summer, and learning to survive an affair, when she thought it was good love.

Sybil felt at last, that she was going to make it. She'd learned how to be a survivor just from being at Synanon. When standing on the beach in California, with nothing but her name and the clothes on her back, she decided if God got her home, she'd never let this happen to her again. After many telephone calls, her mother finally wired the money for her airfare.

Then, while waiting on a bench for a bus to the airport, a good-looking, well-dressed guy sat down next to her. He told her not to look, but there were two guys sitting in a car across the street watching her. He said they were pimps looking for *'fresh blood.'* They always waited outside the bus station for young, naive girls, which he thought she was. He said he'd sit with her until the bus came. She wanted to know why he was doing this, after she saw the guys, and knew he was right, but why trust him either? He laughed, he thought she knew, he was gay, and modeled in a gay magazine. Because he didn't dig girls, he still didn't want to see them used. It could only happen to Sybil - God watched over her in some of the strangest ways. No matter how low she fell, she'd always bounced back eventually.

Out of shear boredom and searching for something to do, Sybil and Beth left the New Year's party to go for cigarettes. Also, a ploy to get away to visit some old haunts that Sybil knew, they stopped in four different bars, starting with the sleaziest one first. She knew someone in each bar, so they didn't have to pay for any drinks, and usually walked out with the glasses. Beth also started collecting crazy hats, horns and leis as they went along. At the last bar, they left when the cops arrived. They got back to the house, and had something for everyone to make noise with, and wear. It livened up the party, and got a longing out of Sybil's system to look back on her past. She was ready to go forward, and to not look back again. She was coming to the point in life, where this time when she turned over a new leaf, it might take root and grow. None of them had been as desperate about life as Sybil, and Beth hoped none of them ever would be.

The following weekend, Michael and Beth took Sybil out to get her mind off the old boyfriend, as meeting someone new was always the best medicine. The first place they went was dead, naturally and Michael bored, she drove them crazy with her deep sighs, coming all the way from her toes. She only thought about being with Mike, since no diversions. Beth got them to leave, as she knew a swinging bar with live music. One of those places, if a girl couldn't get lucky there, she may as well turn in her boobs.

Jumping as expected, they settled at the end of the bar where Beth knew the bartender. She got the drinks ordered, while Sybil started checking out the guys, at least Michael perked up with the fantastic band. Beth noticed a super-looking dude sitting next to her, who acknowledged her in a very interesting way. She couldn't figure out, if the woman around the bar corner was with him or not. She wasn't that pretty, but who knows as Connie'd say, "Maybe she screws like a mink." She obviously had money, the way she dressed, so she could have brought him.

By this time, Sybil made contact and progressing nicely. If she only didn't get too drunk or sharp-tongued, everything would be perfect. Michael was dancing and having a good time, so no more worries there. Beth said something to one guy, it went nowhere, then another guy asked her to dance. After dancing with several guys, she still couldn't get her mind off the one sitting next to her. Since he continued to keep glancing over at her smiling, she felt maybe she should push it. She'd thought if she ever got up the nerve to make a pass, he'd probably be gay, but what would he be doing in a bar like this? He seemed like he was interested. Now teasing Peter, the bartender about his age, while paying his bar bill, Beth thought she'd say something.

"You shouldn't be picking on Peter, cause he's my secret lover." This cracked them up, especially Peter. The mysterious guy got her into the conversation, and after a few minutes, the woman got up to go to the restroom. Beth and the good-looker took the opportunity to get to know each other better. She noticed the slight southern accent, so jumped on it to let him know, she dug-on guys who said 'darlin.' "Well, you silver-tongued, Southern gentleman!"

He again cracked up at this, saying "I'm just from Springfield, and not a bona fide southerner." His smile full and genuine, he sat back down to talk.

Surprised they both owned their own business, and anxious to get so much said in the few minutes the girlfriend was gone, neither noticed when she was back. Beth pulled back as she sat down, so it wouldn't be so obvious, and thought this was one of the strangest situations she'd been involved in, and that was saying a lot.

Beth danced again with some other guys, and then asked the bored lady if she'd mind if she danced with her talkative-male companion. For some reason, she still hadn't asked his name, and he'd not mentioned it. When dancing, Beth questioned, "I hope you don't think I'm too forward in asking you to dance?" She watched his face, trying to figure him out.

The melodious voice replied, "No, I was hoping you had gotten my signal, that I was interested." Beth couldn't believe what she'd done, he smiled again and went on to explain. "She's a girl I have been dating for a while. I work so much and . . ." he hesitated, . . . "I'm not the type to go to bars to pick up females." Then he asked, "Could I see you some time?"

Quickly Beth responded, "I'll get my card to you." Beth never caught the incongruity of the conversation with his actions, since she was being carried away. When they got back to the bar, he excused himself to go to the rest room. Beth got a card out of her purse, and asked Michael if she'd give it to him. With suspicion toward both of them, the girlfriend watched their every move. When the good-looking stranger returned, he knew immediately things weren't too cool, so waited awhile before again talking to Beth. It became a cat and mouse game, as Beth danced with someone else, he'd dance with his girlfriend, then moved his chair closer to Beth, when he sat back down. The girlfriend went to the restroom again, so both talked at once. Both Michael and Sybil noticed something going on. The guy Sybil met was super, but she was acting like a real ass. She had this new attitude to show her worst side first, and if they could handle that, she'd be nice to them. Michael tried to tell him underneath she was terrific, but he could see something more bothering her than a night in bed would take care of.

Meanwhile, the estranged lady-friend made noises about leaving, while practically throwing daggers at Beth, when the mysterious gentleman included her in the conversation. Suddenly, Beth felt a hand on her knee, and couldn't believe the brass-balls this man had. She moved so that he could continue, without the girlfriend noticing. Beth hoped she hadn't seen her almost inhale her drink when he started. This continued for about five minutes before they left, only stopping when he helped her on with her coat, but also winked at Beth. She tried to keep a straight face, while talking politely with the girlfriend. He then hesitated just long enough before they left, to give Beth a pat on her butt. Michael and Sybil almost fell over at that one, as they'd never seen a guy pull such a thing with a girlfriend-in-tow.

Beth quickly called Peter over, to ask what the dude's name was. "Don't waste your time, they're a regular couple in here." He smiled, wondering why she'd ask.

She then gave her devilish smile, telling him "He's asked me to go out, so I have to know what his name is!"

Peter's jaw dropped, "Beth, you're unbelievable, how did you pull that one off?"

She shrugged her shoulders, and smirked. He told her his name was Gene. She hadn't been so excited about a man since she'd met

Bill the summer before. Maybe this could be a live one. As the night preceded, Beth danced and had offers from three other men, even the one first interested in Sybil. Michael got pissed that Beth was dancing with him so much, but then Sybil'd been dancing with other guys, too.

Beth loved to dance, especially with a good, live band and the guys weren't bad either. But she decided if she couldn't get the one she wanted, she'd go home with Michael and dream about Gene. She hoped he'd call, but Michael reminded her, "Don't bet on it too, heavily. The guy's taking a chance on losing a regular girlfriend, for someone that might not work out." Gene never called.

Back to Ft. Lauderdale for Michael and Connie, this time for the whole month of February, which of course, set Cam and Connie back to fighting on a daily basis. Being ridiculous, he dragged up one excuse after another, but she was determined to go. He made no promises this time, but she figured a week or two without her, and he'd be singing a different song. The bad weather and the jobs got to them both, as well Michael felt a break from Mike would do her good. They'd not been apart for more than a week before, so a real test for them both, and giving Mike time to think about so tightly holding on to his marriage.

Beth sometimes felt like she was getting closer to meeting "Mr. Perfect," yet something always happened. The ones head-over-heels for her usually were heels, and the ones she thought had some potential couldn't handle her independence. One *actually* told her she *was* too smart for him. Times like this, she was glad to have the extra time to spend with Jeremy, as he was the real love that kept her going. In between it all, she continued to see Rob and Frank, with Jim Rayburn popping in from time to time.

In reality, though all were good fun as a sexual pastime, none of them a serious 'marriage' consideration. Beth wanted more out a man, and the relationship to bring marriage into the mix. She understood that men in general weren't changing as fast as the women, with all the new beliefs of equality, respect and acceptance. Then, still so many men openly resented the-hell-out-of the women who had changed, almost before their eyes.

Beth looked forward to some peace and quiet for a while, as sometimes it felt like she had a revolving door at her house. She'd frequently been trying to write on her book or poetry, with Jeremy watching the blaring television, Michael with the stereo blasting some rock music and Marie pounding on the electric typewriter, at the other end of the kitchen table. Certainly a pleasant change from how hectic before they left, with snowmobiling at Mike's farm, Marie's appendix surgery and April's big blowout with Alex.

Yes, it finally came to an actual, physical fight, as he not only hit her daughter Deidra, but April, too. She decided to teach him a lesson, so had him put in jail. But, being April, after four hours she had him released, as he agreed they would see a psychologist. Things slightly improved until he quit going. Yet, it was a great help to April to have an objective-someone to talk to as she'd been holding so much inside for so long.

As April told about her childhood and adolescence, the psychologist was amazed she'd turned out as well as she had. At last, she didn't dwell on feeling sorry for herself. Slowly she shared her many revelations, "It was all in the past, and I'm not going to use it for a crutch any longer . . . as the reason for my weakness." Suddenly, she too, was developing an inner strength to go and make something of her life. Tired of being a loser, from now on she'd learn to be a winner. Beth was amazed, having a professional tell April worked - maybe.

Once again, April turned to her astrology to help keep her mind off Alex. And, once again she became rather cold and calculating, as with manipulating Wally, figuring how long it would take for her to be able to support herself on her own with the astrology. Basically it would take years to build up a clientele, and become well enough known - at least three or four years she'd have to mentally, gear-herself to survive living with Alex. With her priorities set, she'd not give up the unencumbered freedom of her studying freely, the minute details of astrology, to gain the credentials she needed to make it on her own. So, for now she'd live off Alex, rather than give up her talent, and take a nondescript job to support herself and the girls.

Soon, April was doing terrific with her students at the county college, and new clients on a regular basis. Since using Beth's chart on a regular basis in class, she got excited about so many big things that would be happening for Beth in 1975. In fact on her following birthday, the biggest once-in-a-lifetime point would hit on her ascendant, and continue to make major changes in her life for the next seven years. Uranus only happened every eighty-four years, so most people were never lucky enough to be alive, or at an age to appreciate or get full use from it. Beth, beginning the prime of her life - she'd be thirty in November. Beth could learn to control her life, and April knew how to get the most out of every special aspect.

April also wanted to write a book about her theories, so she'd need to keep track of everything that affected Beth at these special times. She doubted that she'd know another person that had so many important things happening in her chart in one year. It gave them both something to work on, and to think about together.

Glad about the changes, Beth truly felt like she was finally coming into her own, with more security on the inside, as well the outside. She'd always put up a strong front, but now she had stamina like nothing was impossible for her to accomplish, if she kept working at it and had faith in it. Yes, someday she might have everything she wanted, and be able to do the things she wanted for everyone who was close to her. She learned her opinion really counted most to herself. Who knows, she might see Bobby Ryan again, and he'd probably not recognize her. The changes in her physical appearance were nothing, compared to her growing self-assurance. Maybe she wouldn't even need booze to talk to him.

February 25th, April said was first big date in her chart, so Beth brought a bunch of lottery tickets, and waited for something exciting to happen. About to give up, when Jim Rayburn stopped in. In reality, having one more fantasy-fulfilled, the satisfaction factor was declining. Since Beth'd made her New Year's resolution of no more married men or one-night stands, she'd not had sex with a man. Which blatantly told her what kind of a sex life a divorcee could have when she set-down scruples for herself, and stuck to them. Being selective and saying 'no' did have its price tag. Oh well, so much for resolutions - they lasted almost two months.

Her whole body was still tingling, as she watched him get dressed in the morning. Beth didn't know if from being sexually satisfied, or just glad to be with Jim. That tall, magnificently-built body was still tan from his recent trip to Florida. Yes, maybe her luck was changing. He'd continued to return to see her, and he did care for her, to what extent she didn't know. She didn't understand what April meant her 'reward' would be reaped, according to the 'Saturn' she'd earned - Saturn being the teacher. Well, she earned Jim and she'd worry about the rest later.

Independence

You walk a path that is well trodden,
to an end that was long ago begun.

The woman who walked ahead of you
is now stronger.

The person by your side
is a better one.

Those behind are best
left forgotten.

What Price Freedom?

No matter how we earn it,
the price of freedom is very dear.

Stand on your own two feet
and move forward.

Meet the challenge of the everyday,
every year alone, on your own.

Something for nothing,
is a most expensive item.

Retribution is, and should be
God's great equalizer.

Hell is a very cold and lonely place,
here on Earth.

The bonds you held me with,
left more scars than chains ever could.

CHAPTER 22

On the Move

Connie and Michael returned earlier than planned, without any real explanation except they had enough. Somewhat disappointed, Beth thought she'd get a lot more done without their distractions at home. But in Florida, nothing really changed there - Web still into drugs, though the guys were working more in construction. And, neither of the girls got sexually involved with any of the guys this time, which surprised April, but not Beth. The cleaning jobs kept rolling along and growing, with their jobs being turned back over to them. The calendar was almost full with more party-servicing, which was a very fun and lucrative addition.

Beth also came up with the idea to sell her house, free herself and make some other changes in her life. Though she'd mainly been a weekend or party-drinker, she definitely was cutting down. She resurrected her decision about no sex with married men or one-nighters, which that one stopped Connie in her tracks, "No shit! Way to go, girl!" Beth'd been writing more poetry, and her teachers at the college were quite impressed with it, encouraging her as she pointed to the stack of poems on the kitchen table, available for their perusal.

The last kicker came, "I've been helping my cleaning-client Lori, with her own art-lecturing business. Since I did a lot of public relations stuff at the ad agency years ago, it's been fun." Beth looked at Connie, "You know, I kinda have a natural knack for the bullshit, even when not imbibing." No intentions of working in Chicago, but the way Elmwood and other high-dollar towns were popping up with malls and such, who knew what work she might get. The beginning of an awareness to get back into the mainstream, where she'd receive some recognition for her creativity. The bottomline, unspoken, meant finishing her degree some way in something.

Still confused, Beth wanted to concentrate on her writing, yet she felt tied down - responsible to everything and everybody. She felt her life a sham, and the life of a divorcee not nearly as happy as it was suppose to be - like there'd been a promise, once a certain point met. Getting out from under the house, meant it would no longer be their gathering space or lay-station. She wanted a more private life, and Michael only contributed limitedly, not as Beth expected. If she was really to change her life, she needed to rid herself of the old memories, that while fun, kept pulling her back to being the life of the party - the 'good-time-charlie' keeping it all going.

Beth wanted a man to be her friend, to talk like she did Frank - without judgment, and not just that good time in the rack. So, this meant all new men, none of the men she knew took the serious side of her in a conversation. And none of them, girls or guys understood her burning desire to finish her college education and *be somebody*. Yes, she definitely needed to change all areas of her life. Connie and Michael, not sure of what Beth wanted, began to feel that to better herself, perhaps Beth was putting them down. Adding new friends, did not mean Beth'd get rid of the old ones, she just wanted more variety, especially those who understood her creative interests. The girls loved her writing, even when they didn't understand it, and had no clue as to what was involved in creating it.

Only April seemed to understand the turmoil that Beth went through, as she encouraged her to pursue her dreams. Yet, she had a definite problem in supporting Beth the way she wanted her to. April felt Beth was going off the deep-end, and it ended with them having a big blow-out. She was so insecure, she didn't want Beth to move anywhere, as the house was so convenient for her - April. She fell into her old whining complaint that, Beth was 'not as good a friend to her, as she was to Beth.' This never made since from the school days, and certainly didn't make any now.

Hesitant to push Michael out before selling the house, Beth was happy for her to stay, as Michael'd been thinking about moving out into the world on her own. This would give her the nudge she'd never give herself. She'd been living with Beth for two years and it obviously got a bit crowded with choices of things to do and food to eat, etc. Beth added, "There's no hurry, of course, I want to get the house fixed up, as best I can afford. It's a great opportunity to clean out all the leftovers from my marriage, and start fresh."

Many of Bruce's large things were still in the basement and garage, it'd be quite a job to get the house ready. Beth thought about being divorced three years - 'my how time flies when you're having fun.' Cleaning-out always gave direction in what to keep and what to throw away. The business had been a fun challenge for a while, but Connie and Michael weren't interested in expanding, though their attorney thought it had the potential of a great franchise business. Beth never got anything extra for running the business, or hiring and training the girls, so perhaps letting everyone do their own thing was the best way to go.

Michael had also been thinking of what she wanted to do with the rest of her life, as she didn't want to be cleaning or waitressing another ten or twenty years. She'd always enjoyed teenagers, and had a rapport with them that most adults never understood. Maybe that she was so fun-loving like a kid herself. But more than fun with them, she could talk to them - they would listen, and when they talked to her, she'd listen. She felt maybe if she'd had someone taking time and interest in her when she was that age, she might not have run off and gotten married at sixteen. Beth and Michael talked about it several times, "If you're serious Michael, I'll talk to Ellie (her cleaning customer that was a social worker). I'm sure she'd know about some agency or something, where they're looking for volunteer help. Then if it works out that you like it, you could see about going to school to get certified or something."

"Yea, the college has courses in working with juveniles." Beth was thrilled to see her interested in expanding her world. She'd taught Beth so much about freedom of expression, and not worrying so much about what other people thought, or letting everyday pressures get her down. Though Beth would never be as free as Michael - or as irresponsible - she loosened up her life a great deal, since her living there. She taught Beth how to do things *just* for herself, instead of always for others - though she didn't apply it often. Beth soon got the information from Ellie, and Michael called to find out what was involved, and how soon she'd be interviewed for the volunteer program. She had so much to give, and wanted also to be needed.

Michael came in that evening from her first interview absolutely elated, this was just what she had in mind to give her a feeling of how she'd adapt to such a job. There would be two more interviews, then if she passed those, she'd take some training sessions. "The two assistants I talked with are my age and younger. They're more involved with the teens, than like a Big Brother or Big Sister programs. They want you with them almost daily, especially to start out. Most of them come from one-parent homes, or where there was abuse or something. They are in juvenile-homes or wards of the court now. I think I'd be good at it," Michael resolutely stated.

"I know you would!" Beth staunchly responded.

The second interview was with the director, and Michael's early return to the house was full of resentment and bitterness. "The director was a full-fledged, civil-service-dedicated to the book twit! You know, very different from her younger, sensitive assistants I talked to." Michael shook her head, "I decided at the beginning to be completely honest about my background, and my own shitty-teen years, which was not easy to do." She hesitated, because recalling it brought back so many bad memories, and pain regarding her father.

"Well, the director in her-wiseness, felt that I would *not* be a good example to these easily-influenced teenagers, with my own teenage-marriage, giving up my three kids to asshole-Tim and the clinker - the baby I gave-up for adoption. I tried to explain that I was an excellent example of 'don't do as I did - do as I say.' I don't know why I kept wasting my breath, but I tried to tell her I learned my lessons, though I was *not* apologizing for anything I'd done in my life. I felt that I could relate to these troubled teenagers, having been through so much myself." She sighed with great restraint, "But, of course, the director had the last word, and it was that they, she, preferred to do things by the book, and not by experience."

Beth was incensed by the absurdity of the director. "This is 1975! For God's sake! I thought by now they were acknowledging the fact that no book, or classroom-study can replace valuable experience. Because of that stupid-woman and her prejudice standards, some kids are going to continue on struggling, and be lost because nobody cares *or understands* the conflicts they have in their lives. That blows my mind, that she would think, like you're going to teach them to run-off and get married, or pregnant or God knows what else."

Michael tried to write-it-off, like it didn't matter that much. "Hey, listen, don't worry about it. I should have known, that I'll never fit into the mold, the establishment has for leaders of any sort. I mean, first of all I'm a woman, and most men *and* some women will tell you, that a woman can't lead. What's worse, on top of that, I'm a divorcee, which means that I've already *failed* at something that *is an institution*. I've broken the code of 'hearth and home' by giving up my kids, not that it matters that it was the best thing for their behalf and my sanity.

Then the list goes on, with such notables on it as 'adultery,' illegitimacy,' etc. etc." She paused for a moment of realization. "I probably wouldn't have been able to cut-it with all the paperwork and reports, you have to do every time you have contact with your subject. You know how I procrastinate." She tried to smile as she continued, "I'll just keep cleaning - no red tape involved there."

Beth watched her very slowly, pull herself neatly, and tightly back into her shell, so other people wouldn't be able to step on her, her lifestyle or her past. But Beth knew by now, that Michael's give-a-shit attitude wasn't always what it seemed. It was one of her many ways to protect herself, from acknowledging the pain that was coming at her. There was nothing more Beth could say, she'd learned when Michael closed a subject, it was dead, and she would *not* discuss it again. As long as they'd been friends - through laughter, tears, men and the kids - she would never know and understand all of Michael. But maybe that was what made her such a great friend - she was never boring, and there was always something new to learn about her, but only when she felt like revealing it.

Michael soon found a reasonable studio apartment in a very old building in a nearby town, so she'd still be close enough to do her cleaning jobs. The building wasn't quite quaint, but it did have some unique, old character to it. Michael needed more than ever to have something different and challenging to take up her spare time, and refurbishing the apartment was the answer. It worked out perfect, Beth was ready to list the house at the same time of Michael's planned moved. Beth painted, paneled and carpeted all the rooms to make the little, old house look its best. Lovingly, she took down Bobby Ryan's picture, and the rest of her nude-males, storing them carefully in a small box. Symbolically, it was the end of the wildest chapter in her life, and the close of a lifestyle. Although April predicted that Beth would move before the year was up, from her astrology chart, no one paid much attention, or remembered.

April brought-out they'd no longer have a place to escape to or meet at all hours. Beth's doors had always been open to male and female, who wanted a place to roost, or drop in for a talk. Marie would also miss having some place to escape from her family, if only for a few hours. But Beth had to think of her own needs, and it seemed like getting out from under her house, and all the attachments that went with it. Though Bruce put up a big stink about getting all his junk out, Beth reminded him that he'd get his pay off, once the house sold.

With Michael moved, Beth felt like the mother-bird watching her fledgling take flight. It gave Michael and Mike more freedom, since no concern with other people being around them at the apartment. Though Beth permitted men in the house when Jeremy got his room upstairs, she preferred not to have him exposed to the different tangents Michael's lifestyle took.

Beth took Jeremy on several vacations around the country, and up to the lake property several times, but still felt she missed the daily part of his life. And, afraid that her mother had too much influence over that day-to-day growing. Beth'd stress for Jeremy to be strong and independent, while her mother and Bruce spoiled him, letting him have his own way. She sometimes felt it would be best for him to be completely away from both of them. They overindulged Jeremy, she'd complain, then out of guilt of not spending enough time with him, she did, too.

Beth sent-off her book on divorce to the publishers in a flurry. When there was no immediate response from them, April said, "You still have to earn your *Saturn,* before your writing is accepted." Beth didn't understand, so she started channeling her feelings in the direction of her poetry. In fact, her poetry became therapy for her. All her deep-seated feelings about Bruce, and subsequent men in her life were best released through these words, sometimes bittersweet and sometimes quite satirical. One of the revelations that she discovered in her own writing was that, it was the man she *wanted* Bruce, and the other lovers *to be* and not *the men* they *were* that she had loved. It made it much easier to forgive and forget, when she accepted the fact of seeing their potential and *she turned the men into her fantasy roles,* that they could never have fulfilled.

With this concept in mind, Beth jokingly said to Michael, "Sometimes, I really believe all our problems, and those of most of the women of our age, were caused by Walt Disney, and his believable fairy tales." Michael laughed, then kind of nodded, as she pondered the influence.

The four of them had been raised in the in-between-era of too young to be members of the innocent 1950s age, and too old to see the point of the 1960s radicals. Beth felt she had a generation gap with people only five years younger. She couldn't begin to keep up with what they were protesting against now - it was like they belonged to the *Protest-of-the-Week Club,* and they got together and marched somewhere. The war was far away, and hadn't really touched her, except when she thought of her old, high school sweetheart.

The women's movement didn't really move her, since she felt she already was an independent, divorced woman, so she didn't need to be liberated. Granted, they made a few steps into that world, the 'younger' generation was promoting, with free-love and hallucinating drugs, but they were short, quick steps and not often anymore. Beth didn't know which was worse, the fairy tale world of Disney, or the one around her, that she also felt didn't quite fit.

Connie felt like it was time to take some direction in her life. Eddie sold out his interest in The Place, building a bigger disco in a new, growing area of the county. Connie thought she'd take her money out of the house her parents bought from her, and invest it into turning the old disco into a modern new one. Since a whole new, disco-sound was coming out, she'd be getting in on the ground floor. She worked day and night getting her new place, The Glass Onion, ready for business. She spent a fortune on a sound system, lights and dance floor, along with new decor for the old building. It was dynamite for her, both physically losing weight and mentally realizing her own worth, accomplishing something on her own initiative. Cam was impressed, with how much she took on herself, and the correct decisions she made.

After one, such long, arduous day with the remodeling that Connie stopped in to see Beth. They just settled down talking with a bottle of wine when the telephone rang. Almost eleven, Beth hesitated to answer, but then thinking it might be one of their cleaning girls cancelling for the next day. It was Rob, and he'd been drinking, a lot. He'd not called for several months, and Beth'd only seen him infrequently, for some quickie-sex, like she *was* some lay-station. He had another fight with his wife, and mumbled, ". . . just couldn't go back to her."

Beth calmly asked, "Do you mean, that you're leaving her for a divorce." Though she already knew the answer, she had to ask, to stick-the-knife in a little deeper.

"No, I'm just going to teach her a lesson, . . . by not coming in till late."

Beth laughed, "Some lesson that will be. So what did you want?" As if she didn't know.

"Just some love and understanding," he slowly and sadly replied. Beth tried to explain Connie was visiting, and she hadn't seen her in several weeks. Besides she was a tired, messy-wreck. He replied he didn't care what she looked like. Beth laughed, and Connie grabbed the phone to give Rob a few zingers, and tell him not to take up *her time* with Beth.

With Connie talking to Rob, Beth thought about all the times he'd not been there when she needed some comforting. Or, the times he'd disappointed her with his 'married-excuses,' like it made everything excusable. But for Beth, no excuse *not to* see him. She got back on the line, and tried to set-up another time when he would be sober, and she'd be more in the mood.

"But you used to always be in the mood for me, " Rob whined. She knew he'd not handled her growing independence, since she started the business. She'd always respected the importance of his job, yet he'd not take the seriousness of her writing, or the cleaning business they built.

"No, not tonight."

"But, what am I going to do?"

Very cooly Beth replied, "Take it home to your wife!" She hung up the phone, regretting it slightly, but feeling stronger afterwards. The first time she'd chose a female-friend over a man. Not the way she wanted Rob to exit her life, but his choice she never heard from him again.

Beth raised her glass to Connie cheering, "Here's to the future - yours and mine - may it always be better than the past!"

The Support Searches

Some think there is a fine line between love and fear,
And while sometimes there may be, it is much more dear.
It is similar to the relationship between black and white -
One the absence of color, and the other having them all.

What must the moon think, knowing it cannot stand alone,
For it gets all of its light from what the sun has shone.
It is much like understanding the difference between
Wishes and dreams, or why prayers seem unanswered.

What can one do when looking inside reveals buried pain,
But looking for answers from the outside makes you insane.
Of course, I want peace for me, but also for others to know.
My Soul realizes and believes the promise my smile shows.

The gift of love must start with me, for me, not wait for another.
There is then a silence, as letting the fear go, the love covers.
It is no mystery as my Soul, my heart are filled deep through,
Since love has always been the answer, and reason I'm renewed.

It is more than believing in miracles, or promises along the path.
It is the lessons learned from the interactions from people met.
You now know who you are, and why you're here without fear.
The shadows are gone, and the wandering has ceased my dear.

CHAPTER 23

Moving On Out

Michael was not really frightened, as much as exhilarated to see if she *could* make the move on her own. At eighty-dollars a month for the single room, there was no reason why she shouldn't be able to handle it financially. Old Mr. Johnson hadn't raised the rent in twenty years, *Thank God*. Though her key reason for the move was for Mike, as most reasons for doing anything. Though she knew being on her own was a good for her. She had some great plans for decorating, yet it seemed like she'd never finish, as with so many of her other grand-intentions of change.

While Michael wanted her own apartment, and came to need it, she first thought of it as only temporary, as if she and Mike would soon be planning there own place together. Admittedly, she'd not made any decisions beyond the patching and painting, since she daily came up with something new and different. Somehow, final decisions seemed like just that - if one color was put on the wall, it could never be changed. Unfortunately, this same rule-of-thumb applied to everyday-life, so the only way to avoid *not* being able to change the decisions, was *not* to make them. The basic excuse for the decorating was, "If I have the time, I have no money, and vice-versa." There was no excuse for the rest of her non-decisions except, "That's just me, what can I tell you." Eventually, Beth's two nephews went over to help her get the painting finished. It fit well into her grand scheme of getting closer to Mike's sons.

Mike was not overly accepting of Michael's new lifestyle to still be so *free-style*. He expected her to become *domesticated,* when she moved into her own place. Also, he didn't understand the concept of a 'studio' apartment. So, nothing as he anticipated - like a living room, dining room and bedroom, per se. Her studio had a kitchen alcove, dressing area off the bath, and the rest one big room. Even the furniture, he'd envisioned to look like straight out of a showroom - one couch, one easy chair, two end tables and two matching lamps. Michael's *living-plant* collection - he referred to as a jungle, and her used furniture from her grandmother, as attic-leftovers. It was not that he expected her to live in a high-rise, with all new furniture. Yet, he'd not contemplated her to be so happy in this 'bohemian' atmosphere. Mike loved the 'wild-child,' but also wanted 'homeyness.' He had no idea of the money she made, and how badly she handled spending it.

Actually, Mike doubted that she could hack the little step of independence she took from Beth, more the emotional part than the financial. She felt it somewhat of a challenge to show him, that she could. Again, if any problems arose, she simply put them out of her mind, as "I'll worry about that tomorrow." or "Somehow, we'll work it all out." So much easier than facing it head on, or quite the ostrich-syndrome. After a few weeks, and falling back into their prior sex-pattern, Mike soon accepted the apartment, as well Michael's adjustment on her own.

The summer and fall went on, with Michael and Beth helping Connie out at the *The Glass Onion* doing I.D. checks, and other miscellaneous odd-jobs. She got several young girls to be waitresses, since the drinking crowd always got younger. Michael felt completely out of her element in the disco. Nothing fit her anymore - the music, the smoke and the young-age of the crowd. Adding this to her cleaning work schedule and seeing Mike, some nights were almost twenty-four hour days, so she '*zombied'* through many routine-evenings she worked at *The Glass Onion*. But, a good chance for Beth to get out to see Michael, as they didn't much any more. Even April dropped in from time to time.

Though Beth still had the house, it wasn't the drop-in center it had been. April talked about expanding her teaching at the college, and Beth was excited for her, so helped her do the required lesson plan, to get the final approval. It would be good for her to get out, since her marriage stood in name-only. At least being busy with her astrology, kept her from running around and cheating on Alex. That kept peace in the family, and a roof over their heads, which she felt made it all worthwhile. Deidre complained to no avail. In the back of her mind, of course, April might meet someone new to love. Not out chasing, but she still kept an eye open for Prince Charming.

Out of the clear-blue one night, Vince came strolling into *The Glass Onion* wearing 'civilian' clothes, and his hair cut so stylish that Michael almost didn't recognize him. It was a highlight to her to have old times and friends to talk about, even if it was from another era.

Things went along fine with Michael and Mike, as his marriage seemed to not be interfering, and he talked of being free of her soon. Though they talked more positive about a future together, Michael still occasionally found some kink in the plans. Sometimes it might be as trivial as the design of their dream house, and other times it might be serious, as concerning her children. She'd see them as frequently as possible, yet Tim still moved all around. His new wife had two kids of her own, yet he still drifted from job to job from Texas back to Illinois and so forth.

When in the area, Michael spent many weekends with them, and had them for several weeks during the summer. She felt there *might* be a possibility when teenagers, they *might* want to come live with her. Michael'd not want to turn them down at that age, because she was always able to associate so well with Mike's teens.But, a sore-spot with Mike, since his kids were almost grown, and soon on their own. She was stunned when he said, "I don't want to be tied down with some kids, when it's going to be a carefree world for just the two of us. I'm so close to my own independence, I can't comprehend you're willing to take on something that tied us down."

Michael couldn't believe what he said. "These are my children - MINE! I gave them up once. I'm not about to turn my back on them in the future, if they ever want me." Mike stared at her in disbelief. They finally agreed that it was a big 'if,' and when the time came, the right decision would be made about it.

He then added, "I'll be open to the possibility, as long as you don't pursue it, but take a wait and let's see attitude." She hesitated, then agreed. She made more small-compromises in her life because of him. So much good in their relationship, she never tried to think about the constant adjustments *she* seemed to be making, so that *he* wouldn't have to make any in his.

Connie was finally having a party almost every night of the week, except now her 'friends' and strangers were paying for their drinks, and she didn't have to worry about the clean-up, or counting beer cans. Though the business was slow getting started during the week, she always managed to have a good weekend-crowd. Beth thought that she'd be the first to make it big in some business, and Connie's success made her very proud of herself. Cam did*n't* handle Connie's success at all. He'd insisted on helping, by tending the side-service bar, when in town. If Beth and Michael felt a little old for the crowd, Cam was really out of his league. His bar jokes were a waste on these kids, since they only wanted their drinks, and get back to the dance floor.

Connie felt it was necessary at the beginning to fraternize with her younger employees, so that they'd handle an 'older' woman boss, and build some loyalty. She also enjoyed going out with them to the bars in Chicago. One night Cam called 'enough' on her going out with them, and ordered her to stay home with him, when she replied a very definite 'no,' he walked out. When she got home, he'd cleaned his personal belongings out of the bathroom. At first Connie was relieved, but then she realized she had no one to replace him, and still insecure on her own. When Cam called the next day, she was more than happy to take him back.

Another Friday night, that Beth opted for staying home, rather than continuing her long-running role of barfly. About eleven-thirty the doorbell rang, and Frank had his back turned when she opened the door. "You think my bike will be OK, parked right here?"

"Sure. You locked it, no problem." Beth held the door for him to come in, as she added, "I mean this is suburbia, crime and unhappiness don't happen here. Besides, they wouldn't know what to do with a bike like yours." she snickered, so glad to see him.

"Yea, that's why last week that doctor's kid in Elmwood, stabbed his mother and her lover to death." Frank made himself comfortable on the couch.

Beth hadn't thought Frank even listened to the news, but then she remembered he said he watched television 'just like all the rest of the nerds in this country.'

She returned from the kitchen with his beer, adding, "Like I said - happiness personified. Don't you wish you lived in upper-middle-class Elmwood?" While she lived in cheaper Villa Glen.

He finished a swallow, "Are you shitting me? Elmwood has nothing but a bunch of rich, tight-ass bitches and rich, impotent-men."

Beth laughed out loud, "You put that rather succinctly, talking about my wonderful hometown. Some of them aren't so bad. There's a few redeeming characters, as I have some very nice clients." She'd sat next to him, thinking how fun this was to have him there.

He leaned over and gave her a big kiss. "You're the only smart-broad I've ever known that I liked, and could fuck-fantastically." Now, he was beaming also.

She almost choked on her wine, "Compliments, sir! Are you trying to turn my head?" Frank kissed her again, as they sat cuddled watching the television, like a married, old-couple.

When *Midnight Special* came on, their featured rock star was David Bowie. Beth was fascinated with him, since she'd not seen him perform live before, and he was so different in every way. Curious, she asked, "What do you think of him?"

Frank shrugged his shoulders, "Nothing, why?"

"I mean the makeup, clothes and all, as well his music is very original." She watched his face watching the performance.

"Hey, it's his face and body. If that's what he's into, fine. That's cool."

"I've heard that he's bisexual or homosexual or whatever." She wasn't sure why she wanted to know what he thought.

"Beth, there's a lot of people who don't care for my lifestyle, as a biker. I do my own thing, and I don't bother nobody unless they bother me." He took a swallow and added, "He's smarter than I am. He's making money off the way he dresses and acts. That's cool, as long as he pulls it off."

"I guess I was wondering if gay-guys bother you?" She knew he was an enigma.

He turned to look at her, "No, I've never had one of them bother me."

She cracked up, "No, no. I mean does their interest in other men get you upset?"

"Hell, no. It leaves more women for me to enjoy." Beth laughed and poked him.

"Frank, I'm serious. You're the absolute-symbol of macho, and most macho or other *men* get very uptight about the gay-guys."

"Beth, I'm not worried about any of them turning me on, or trying to convert me. I think it's only when a guy isn't sure of himself, you know, how well he makes it with a broad, he can't stomach the *gay-gays*, as you call them. They only get uptight because maybe they've had some of those feelings about another man and it scares them, because *being-queer* is supposed to be wrong. The only thing that's wrong, is when you *don't do* what you really *like to do*. So, if you want to screw a man or a woman, it shouldn't make any difference, as long as it's your choice."

Once again, his depth of perception blew her mind. She thought about how right he was, about the fact that usually only sexually-insecure men resented homosexuals. Their basic reason was probably that they feared their own sexual inadequacy, was probably a sign that they were latent-homosexuals themselves. Rather than trying to work out their own problems, they projected their fears and hatred of what was lacking in themselves onto the gays.

Beth slipped herself around Frank, so her arms were around his neck facing him, with her boobs purposely grazing his chest. "You know, my dear, if you were gay, I would still love to have you as my friend, because you never cease to fascinate me, with your understanding of people. But . . . since you're even better at being a lover, I'm glad you're not gay." She very slowly, and very deeply kissed him.

He smirked a little. "I have a feeling that besides that compliment, you have something else on your mind, and I'm not going to get to see the rest of this program."

"Only if you insist." She smirked back at him.

"Well, since I'm so *'suavey' and 'debonner,'* as you say, in your smart-ass way," he quipped, "I wouldn't think of refusing a lady, which you are to me." He kissed her again very tenderly, then gave her butt a swat for her to move, so he could get up. "Let's hit the sheets then."

Beth laughed, "Yep, 'suavey' and 'debonner,' that's my biker!" He got her play on words.

* * * * * *

In a fit of depression and frustration, April called her long, lost-love, Al. She'd always been one to trace-down where people were, so she had his phone number. She managed to get him when Marnie was out, and used the excuse that she wanted to do his astrology chart. Al considered it to be a compliment, and being so vain could not pass it up. Enough time had passed that the bitterness was gone, but the hurt was only softened for April. They talked again, and then set a date to get together for 'old times sake.'

She made it almost a monumental decision, as she did not want to start back running around, and lose the roof over her head, yet she was starving for some attention and affection. She knew that she could never recapture the past, yet. Michael and Beth both warned that her memories would always be better than her reality, still April insisted.

The night for their rendezvous came, and she was more than apprehensive. When Al walked into the bar, somehow the Adonis-aura was gone. He'd gained some weight, and the clothes which always fit him so sleekly, now had a shabby, worn-out appearance. His hair and beard, which always immaculate, looked as if they'd been hastily-trimmed. April smiled, since she'd changed, too, gaining a little weight, and cutting-off all her long, black hair.

They were like two retired stars that once shone brightly, when they had each other's reflection. But, the magic of their togetherness had lost its power. They left the Holiday Inn to get a room at a cheap motel - April offering to pay half. Al was guilty as April, at trying to recreate something which had been so good at one time. But, too many of the magic pieces had been lost. It turned out to be a mutual-disappointment, only because the expectations were clouded-over by memories. April learned later that Marnie was pregnant and absolutely elated to be having her first child, though Al's sister said he wasn't quite sharing the enthusiasm. Perhaps the responsibilities, or the restrictions were becoming more real.

Around midnight, April came pounding at Beth's door, whining and crying. "Tell me to get a divorce, I'm no good. Tell me to get a divorce, I've committed adultery, again. I just can't make it *'married.'*" Beth sat her down, got a glass of wine and stuck it in April's hand. She was drinking it before she realized, she was consuming alcohol, not coke.

"Now, let's talk about what happened, and what you should, or should not do about it."

"Before it's too late, I better call Alex and let him know I'm still here, and I'll be home soon." Beth shook her head, as she thought once again it was April being overly-dramatic, but she would sit up, and listen, and talk, because she'd done the same for her.

"Now, first of all, you know I'm not going to tell you to get a divorce, since you only get a divorce for one reason, and that is when you're ready. Besides, April, you'd always blame me for pushing you into a hasty decision." April curled-up back on the couch, after giving Beth her usual complaint about not having any coke in the house.

She slowly sipped the wine, which she'd added several ice cubes to, and listening to Beth. "OK, let's look at your situation here, and let's be honest about April. You left Wally for Al; three weeks after Al left, you went back to Wally - a man you didn't love, but would put a roof over your head, because you didn't like living alone, one-night stands or supporting yourself."

"I also wanted my kids back, and it was six weeks, not three!"

"I'm not going to argue with you over the time, because you did spend several weeks just getting Wally back." Beth joined her in both wine and the couch.

"Yea, my kids should appreciate what I went through, to get back to them."

"April, it wasn't just for your kids. You know that, and we all know it. You couldn't hack it out on your own, getting up at the break of day, going to work when you didn't have a sweet-honey to come home to at night, to make it all worthwhile. You still haven't learned the value of working for your own self-satisfaction - accomplishment. I doubt you will, until you feel you are worth doing it for."

"That's not true!" The truth hurt, and she'd already lost much of what she learned from the time spent with the psychologist.

"April, you married a man, Alex who you hardly knew. Wally was kicking you and the kids out, *and* you did not want to find a job to support yourself and them. I mean, let's face it, you were pretty lucky to find a man who *would* take all of it on. He might not be perfect - far from it. But, when you are ready to go out into the world, and get a job which supports you and your two daughters, then maybe, you can talk about divorcing Alex. Otherwise, try what you can to keep your sanity and your roof, since they both mean so much to you." Beth poured a second glass of wine for April, as she mellowed with the first, and ready to accept her plight in life, though hopefully, only temporary.

"It does mean a lot to me, he gives me a free-hand in working on my astrology. He never says a word about how many classes I go to, or how late I stay out at the lectures or over here. He never makes me get up in the morning to cook breakfast, or fix his lunch. He will eat just about anything, if I get around to fixing dinner, or even fix sandwiches for all of us, when he knows I'm involved with a chart. I just wish . . . " she started to cry softly, ". . . he would make love to me once a week, or once a month even. He likes to cuddle sometimes, but if I start to make a move at all, he gets up and leaves the room." They obviously still had not talked.

"April, be grateful for what you do have, because the last year with Bruce, I didn't have any of the good things you mentioned, and you know I didn't have any sex from him at all." April took a big gulp of her wine, wiped her eyes, and started talking about how it had been with Al, not so much about that night, but when it was good. By the time she left Beth, it was almost three in the morning, and she'd be able to plod-along in her self-created rut for another few months, getting by on her memories and digging deeper into her astrology.

Again, Beth got herself into an unbelievable financial bind. The house still not sold, and she seemed to keep getting further behind in all her bills and payments. There were payments for the car, the lake property, home improvement, and of course, the mortgage. She wasn't making bad money, it just went. Now, it was the astronomical heating bills, even the occasional money from Michael would have made a difference. Her depression came from the money worries, and the pits of her personal life, as she also became almost celibate.

She continued writing her poetry, but could not face the looming cynicism of her upcoming thirtieth birthday. A scary-milestone of non-accomplishment. It was supposed to be this big turning point in her life, but where was she going with her life?

Beth thought about one of the girls who cleaned for them, who she talked to about her book. The girl, divorced with two kids, lived on welfare prior. She told Beth that if someone wrote about her, the title would be: *'Shit: The Story of My Life so Far.'* Beth did not want to take that attitude about her own life.

Granted, she'd made some mistakes in her rush to make-up for the time she wasted in a love-less/sex-less marriage, and being a dumb virgin when she did marry. At least she learned from those mistakes, and was not repeating them. As Frank always said, "If you learn from the mistakes, and not repeat them, they are never a waste of time." She learned to respect that person she was getting to know better - herself. And, almost more importantly, Beth acknowledged her creative talents, with her poetry and her other classes at college. Still, the illusive future - where was it all taking her, and exactly when was she going to get there?

Back to April and her astrology, who again explained that the stars were not fortune-tellers, but guidelines of our destiny and what could best be done with it. That wasn't enough for Beth's wanting to know, how soon this turmoil of her personal life and her financial mess would be over. She didn't have the patience for April's generalities, but at least knowing things would be better in the Spring, pacified her awhile. She could endure almost anything, as long as she knew it wouldn't last forever. It did seem like one more mountain to climb, over and over again.

Loneliness best described April's life, and while not totally unique, being married and lonely, somehow they should be incongruous, antonyms, not synonyms. Supposed to be the divorcees who were lonely. Married is supposed to be having another person by your side, and that was not spelled *lonely,* except for April. She tried to fit into the other's lives from time to time, and even Connie was nice to her, in her pathetic marriage. It'd been worse for April when Michael was still seeing so many different men, and having one exciting time after another. And, Connie had the boat and trips with Cam, before she got tied up with the bar, but even that was more exciting than anything April had. Then Beth, who was supposed to be the stable one, the one she could go to for talks on deeper things, but Beth was so pre-occupied with her writing, and whatever else she squirreled away her time on. April didn't like having so little to contribute to their conversations.

April's focus and solid concentration was for surviving, to keep her head from going under, how many different ways could her astrology save her? She'd never been good at making new friends, and alienation was all she could conceive of, what she felt from the ones she did have. She chastised herself for rarely doing, or saying the right thing at the right time. Aware of her track record, she hesitantly tried with new friends in her astrology connections she'd made, hoping that they would also, be as loving and forgiving as Beth and Michael.

Finally, April pushed herself to go one Friday night in early December, to an astrology lecture on the north-side. Since she hadn't had anything but surface talks with Beth in the past few months, she'd no idea of the state of confusion Beth's life had taken. Her only happiness in turning thirty, was that her thirties had to be better than her twenties had been. Picking Jeremy up after cleaning sometimes, she wasn't so sure he was better with her, than her mother. She was so depressed, feeling her life being wasted and the future didn't hold many prospects. Into this quagmire, unsuspecting, insecure and lonely April was about to descend.

As long as she was out, and would almost pass Beth's house on the way home, April put in a call to Beth to see if she was at home, and *sans* a man. About ten o'clock so, if alone, would be fixing a snack or something before Johnny Carson came on. She was sure that she dialed the wrong number, when a recording said that number was disconnected. The phone was Beth's second-right arm, she would not have it disconnected, unless she'd already moved and no matter what, she would've called.

April asked the operator to check the number, and proceeded to argue with her, regarding the disconnection, "There must be a mistake, that's my best friend, and she wouldn't have the phone disconnected without calling me. There's some mistake . . . " April stared at the pay phone, like it was going to give her an answer. "Shit!" She rushed to her car to drive to Beth's, hoping she'd be there.

Beth answered the door surprised and happy to see April, but before she could get more than two words out of her mouth, April started. "Did you know your phone is disconnected? I was just horribly-frightened, at what I might find here. I mean you'd think they'd fix it or something. You - you of all people without a phone. I'm so glad you're all right."

But Beth was not 'all right.' As a matter of fact, she felt *all wrong*. She plopped on the couch barely listening to April, though it was nice someone cared. She sure didn't. Beth looked around at her tacky living room, with its tacky furniture and how it all fit her tacky life. No wonder the fucking-house wouldn't sell. She wouldn't have bought it, if she was looking. April'd finished talking, she obviously waited for an answer. Beth took a deep breath, "It's not broken April, I haven't paid the fucking-phone bill." She stared at April, not really caring what she thought.

"They don't turn it off when you're just a month late," absolutely clueless.

"I haven't paid it for three months." Still looking blank at her.

"Three months! Didn't they send you a warning notice, or anything?"

"Yea." This all seemed so redundant to Beth.

"Why didn't you pay it?" To April, it was as if she'd left the time-zone, because this conversation couldn't be happening - not with Beth, anyway.

"I hadn't opened them all till I realized today the phone wasn't working."

"You mean . . . you didn't open your mail in three months?" April's voice was beginning to get tight, the fear coming back.

"Yea," Beth answered with almost a continuous-monotone in her voice. "You want some wine? Johnny Carson will be on in a few minutes and . . . "

"Beth!" She almost screamed, with a definite shake in her voice. "What the hell is going on?"

"I've only got some red wine, is that OK?" Beth called over her shoulder, heading for the wine.

Trying to control herself, April could only think *she* must have neglected Beth, but she didn't know what the problem was, or if she could have pushed herself enough to help. In total shock, as she sat sipping her wine, watching Beth laugh at Carson's monologue. Beth was a very responsible, sensible person. To see her so irresponsible, as to *not pay* her phone bill, and *not care* about it at all, blew her mind.

Beth 'cared' about everything - details-organizing always her forte. If Beth didn't give a shit - something was grossly wrong - Michael had always been the irresponsible one - NOT BETH! April's mind raced a thousand miles a minute. Something was wrong - this couldn't be the Beth that had seen everyone else through crises and trauma. April was going to have to play 'Crusader Rabbit' to Beth, but she didn't know where to begin.

She got Beth to turn off the television, and start talking about the whole situation. As April listened, she could only comprehend the shortage of finances, since Beth couldn't really explain the basis of her real depression. Since the financial end was the easiest for April to help with, she volunteered to go to the grocery store and buy Beth some 'staples.'

Beth repeatedly refused, then reluctantly went along to get April to shut up. Saying groceries weren't the real problem, as she'd been eating mostly at her parents. But, it was the only one April felt she could handle, so insisted. They came back to the house with such 'staples' as soda pop, ice cream, a fresh baked blueberry pie, etc. totaling a little less than twenty dollars. If nothing else, they'd have oral satisfaction - basic to most people who had a tendency for emotional weight gain.

After indulging with Beth, April left feeling she'd done her civic-duty. The next day, she called Connie and Michael to see what they could do to help Beth. Since, they both had a greater sense of what was going on with Beth, they saw no reason to help Beth. Her financial bind had been self-created by Beth's depression, and ignoring the bills. Connie said. "April, would you cool it! Beth is just all fucked-up right now, and if she wanted to borrow money, she would have asked. She'll be fine, once she sells her crappy house. You're making a mountain out of a mole hill, as usual. She will work this out herself, eventually, like she always does."

The crux came, she wanted credit for what she did. "Well, I spent twenty dollars on *groceries* for her *to live on.* I think that's the least you could do, if you cared for her as a friend."

"Don't give me your 'friend' bullshit, April . . . " Connie rattled on some more and then hung up. Michael, on the other hand, was shocked that Beth was quite so bad off. But as for helping financially, she was always broke and didn't think Beth really wanted money from her friends. Frustrated at not being acknowledged for her helping, she felt she'd done the right thing, though she'd not delved into Beth's problems even after the 'groceries.' She convinced herself, she'd tried the best she was capable of.

Beth was very upset and embarrassed when she got the feedback from Connie and Michael. She felt April made her sound like a sniveling-idiot, about ready to hit the soup-line. The money situation wasn't that bad, she could've easily paid the phone bill, but didn't since they wanted a seventy-five dollar deposit, plus what she owed. After having the phone for over ten years, them wanting a deposit rather pissed her off. And, since she was moving shortly anyway, she figured, "Screw you, Ma Bell."

The hassle of owning the house, and the cliche-ridden suburbia choked her badly, since the divorce. She liked her older, divorced-neighbor on the one side - she never gave her any problems. But the pseudo-Bible-banger woman on the other side drove her crazy. She almost walked the legs-off her dog, trying to see what was going on when Beth had company, especially when the bikers.

Yet, the good 'religious' woman could walk-around with clothes which looked painted on her 'Dolly Parton' body. How could Beth tell April, that she was just tired - tired of the hassle of the house, tired of the pettiness of people and tired of life in general. She was burnt-out, and had no idea what it would take to get her *'love of life'* back. Granted, she'd have a little remission once in awhile with Jeremy, or Connie or Frank, but basically her smiles and laughter were surface. The occasional glass of wine and television, rather than her usual interacting with other people, became her passive-pastime.

Crossing & Burning Bridges

Which bridge to cross and which to burn,
a decision only life can teach us.
I only liked the smell of smoke
if it was old wood, or dried leaves.

If the bridge is over troubled waters,
I'd need to know when to row, wade or swim.
Also, if it's a babbling brook or a roaring falls,
one can entrance you, while the other can kill.

Illusion is a pleasure we hold dear.
But is disregarded, once it's out lived its usefulness.
Which means it has not given us pleasure, or become reality.
By crossing the bridge, we leave the illusions behind.

I must risk, or nothing is worthwhile to have,
but the empty risk has no meaning.
Yet, just because things are different,
it doesn't mean we have really changed

The talent is knowing how to play the cards fate deals.
Choices may be from a conscience or just cold feet,
in that we can covet or compete for what we want.
A burned bridge can be rebuilt, but will not be the same.

In the cold-dread of night, even an atheist
hopes there is a higher power to help guide them,
through the new territories of life.
So, savor the illusion, but live for the change

There's so much more to it,
than just women's intuition.

CHAPTER 24

Choices for Change

Just before leaving the old house, Frank came by one evening. It'd been a while since she'd heard from him, since they weren't hanging out around any of the biker's bars. Not exactly elated, as she'd usually been with his appearance, as he was more into chemical drugs like *'crystal'* which sometimes made his behavior erratic. Beth gained weight with her anxiety and depression, as well not being out dancing it off. Frank gave her an unexpected whack across the side of her head. "Now, that's for letting yourself go, and I don't want to see any 'old lady' of mine looking like that again." Frank picked up his beer and walked into the living room. He'd never hit Beth before, and only given her a few good shoulder shakings, when she was very *'nerded-up'* drunk, and mouthed-off in front of his Brothers.

    She was not about to put up with any physical abuse from any man, no matter how much she had loved him. She also didn't feel like hassling with him about her being a 'liberated-woman.' It was quite simple, she was moving, and she'd leave him behind, with the other memories she wanted left with the old house. She walked into the living room trying not to show any smugness on her face, yet not intending to mention the incident. "What do you mean 'old lady?' I don't remember you ever wanting to *tie yourself down*."

    "Who said 'tied-down?' I keep coming back for years, so maybe we should make it on a more regular basis." Beth couldn't believe what she was hearing. Why was it when she was no longer 'in love' with a man, they *then* wanted her. Irony, was the story of her life.

    "What about my son? I can't just go live with a man. I have to think about my son, because his father would never put up with it." Beth stared at him with a very straight face, but Frank just looked at his beer. "We're a packaged deal, Frank." She was not like the others, she'd never, ever let Jeremy go. Frank'd never met Jeremy, so had no idea what a great boy he was.

"Hey," he laughed looking at her like she didn't understand the offer he'd made, or it was not negotiable, or a counter-offer expected. "What can I say?"

Beth then responded with *Frank's usual retort*, in an almost sarcastic tone, "Wear a long coat, and it won't show. Let's talk about it later, right now I just want to hit the rack, and get some sleep." There were a few seconds of hesitation, in him rising after Beth got up off the couch. Frank was *not* real happy with her attitude.

Beth didn't know if it was her attitude, or Frank's condition, since she had no idea how much, or what kind of uppers or downers he'd taken. All she knew, it was the worst performance he had ever given her, and her response hadn't been much better. It didn't feel like she'd been made love to, merely occupied. Well, she wouldn't worry about it. He was asleep, and she may as well, too.

When he left in the morning, he only gave his usual, "I'll see you, when I see you." Only this time, Beth knew that would be never again. He'd known since the spring that she was moving, but he'd never once inquired where, expecting of course, that she'd contact him. Once again, a man was wrong - taking her for granted - changing again, and they'd have to run to keep up with her. When she closed the front door the last time, she thoroughly taped a sign on it which read, "Elizabeth Doesn't Live Here Anymore!"

* * * * * *

The move was on - Connie moved to the old apartment building that Michael lived in, and Beth regrettably moved to her parents. The house still wasn't sold, as the market collapsed, but Beth couldn't take the depression the house seemed to lay on her. Connie'd been living in a new, expensive high-rise with her straight-friend, Linda. With Connie putting in the long hours at *The Glass Onion*, and rarely home except to sleep, she didn't feel like she needed all the luxury and expense if she was never there.

Other than the front door sign, Beth, very unceremoniously, moved out of her house that had been such a big part of her married, and unmarried life. The leavening closed a large chapter of her life, and one that, thank God, would not be relived. Moving in with her parents, she gave up much of her own freedom, while concentrating on finding out what she wanted to do with the rest of it. No one thought Beth would last very long at her parents, as she'd never gotten along very famously with her mother. And, though she loved her father, John was fanatical about locking-up the house every night at bedtime. But Beth was determined to stick-it-out, until she made some kind of career change. With everything else in her life hanging in limbo, she did not want the hassle of all the little bills, and maintenance of her own place. Besides, it was no big change for Jeremy, as he'd been going to the school by her parents since he was in kindergarten.

* * * * * *

Beth got herself entangled in another web, involving cleaning clients - a very wealthy, older, unmarried couple. Helene worked at a travel agency - for something to do, and Harry was a commercial business-park developer, semi-retired and did most of his business over the phone from Helene's exclusive townhouse. Harry knew Beth when she worked at the Cafe', and had made it a point to find out more about her. Little by little, as Beth came to clean every week, Harry'd have her sit and he'd name-drop some of the well-known men that she and Connie had been known to 'associate' with. Beth wasn't sure what his ploy was, though most likely she knew the bottom line would be him wanting her in the rack.

He seemed to get a kick out of the stories of Bobby Ryan - which he never doubted happened - and other escapades, so Beth didn't mind giving him a thrill listening to her. She was amazed, though when he said, "An enterprising-woman like you, I'm surprised you never got into the business of selling it. You could sure make more in one day that you do in a week cleaning." Beth's only remark was that she liked to choose her partners. "You still can . . . if you're interested in my plan."

Beth listened, as he began to describe his obviously, well-thought-out scheme. "I have this farm a few miles west of here with a big, remodeled farmhouse with lots of rooms. I also know a lot of businessmen and politicians, who are looking for a 'good time' with no strings attached, with some sharp ladies like yourselves. They're willing to pay top dollar for their company. Now my idea," he paused to see how intently Beth was listening, "is for you to head this up, and make sure everyone is happy. If you'd like to partake of any of the men, of course, you would have first choice. When we got this thing rolling, you could make a thousand dollars a week, or more depending on how much time we had it open, and how much participation you had." He smiled.

Beth was astonished, she sat and stared at him. "Don't answer too quickly, because you should talk it over with the other girls. You're in a financial bind, so you'll get paid for something, I bet you're very good at." His smile personified exactly what one expected from his remark. "It's what we call in the business-world, 'taking full-advantage of all of your assets.'"

Somehow to Beth, with the acceptance of money for sex, came all kinds of other hang-ups, most of all the name attached. But Beth did not say 'no,' she would discuss it with the others. Maybe it'd be just her, and her middle-class straight-background that would say 'no.' That evening she told Michael and Connie, and as he'd said, "If not for the money, maybe they'd be interested in the sport of it." Michael responded first, "If it was before Mike, yea, maybe . . . No, I don't think I could do it. I'm not putting-down hookers, if that's your calling, fine. But, no, I wouldn't like doing it with someone I couldn't stand, because he paid me to."

"Yea," said Connie, "the whips and cold oranges, and chains might be boring after awhile." She chuckled at her cleverness, thinking Cam would be proud of her quick-quip.

Michael gave her a swat, "You ass!" They relaxed and laughed.

"No, Beth, I couldn't do it. Years ago, sure, I'd jump at the money. So, what's he getting out of all of this - pick-of-the-litter at no charge, or something?" She really giggled at that one.

"Oh, I'm sure he'd expect a percent to cover expenses, but other than probably a few sessions at no charge, and all the benefits which come from satisfying these businessmen and politicians. Well, I'm glad I wasn't the only one not interested. I almost had myself convinced if you guys said 'yes.'" They continued to discuss it, but the decision had been made, and they would stick to it. Money was a lot, but it wasn't everything - besides, 'it was only money,' as Connie usually reminded them. They never felt they had ever put a price-tag themselves, and weren't about to start now. Besides, they'd begun to realize their own self-worth, and it was more valuable than paid-sex.

Beth continued to clean for Harry and Helene, and his attitude changed about her considerably. He'd never known someone to pass-up money so easily earned before. He'd also kept at Beth about the sex with him, yet not in a pushy way, but kidding and teasing. Since he wasn't married, and not a one-nighter, she wouldn't be violating her rule. Then, one day in a more kooky-mood, Beth threw down her cleaning rag and said, "OK, Jocko, let's see what we can put together." She not only blew his mind, but she almost gave him a heart attack.

From then on, unless he had a business meeting or someone over, they'd jump in the rack sometime during the time she was there every week. It became almost a game to her, as to when and where they'd have their encounter.

Beth came walking out of the bathroom, putting the rest of her clothes on when Harry, who was still lying on the bed said, "You know, you're really something else."

Beth laughed, "Yea, I've been told that before, they haven't been able to categorize me."

"No, I mean you - you grow on a person." He swung his legs down slowly off the bed.

"I'd rather you say I got under your skin - leeches grow on a person, and I've never been a leech." She picked up her glass cleaner, and proceeded to do the mirror while watching him.

"That's just what I mean, you have never asked me for a thing, and I'm sure you have an idea of what I'm worth." He'd long ago informed Beth of the million and half settlement, he'd laid on his ex-wife with the divorce, and generous trust funds for each of his grown children. Yes, Beth knew he was worth somewhere in the nice neighborhood of ten to twenty million, which not a bad neighborhood - especially in the mid-1970s.

She looked at his reflection more closely, wondering where this was all going. This man had been a fighter-pilot during the war, before she was born. He'd also made his first million, and been awarded "Man of the Year" before she'd gotten out of grade school. He'd fascinated her with *his* stories, though he always seemed so nonchalant about his life, knowing if he tried to impress her, he'd have turned her off. She came to look forward to their clandestine-romps since they perked up her currently, depressing-life. Somehow, she had a vague-feeling that because he now cared about her a little, too much, it'd be the beginning of the end. It truly saddened her.

"So, it's just because of that, I want to do something to help you. You have told me of your financial plight, I want to give you a few thousand dollars to tide you over, until the house is sold." She swung around instantly and glared at him.

"We can make it a loan if you prefer, with signed papers and interest and all that shit if you insist . . . " Perhaps Beth's independence was a stubborn downfall, but she still believed that she'd been the one who got herself into this money-mess, and she'd have to be the one to get herself out. Yes, she felt sorry for him that his money was a necessary factor in their relationship.

"No, Harry, really. It is very kind of you, but I'm sure it will be sold soon. I just need to put a push on the real estate people." A flat smile, but he did understand.

"Why don't you let me do it - I know them all - who's handling it?" He perked up.

Beth hesitated, then told him the realtor's name, and somehow it all became very simple, her house was sold two weeks later. How much he helped, she'd never really know. They wouldn't close till the end of January, but it was a tremendous load off Beth's mind. Things had gotten so bad, and soon it would be over. She wouldn't have to worry about money for a while. When she saw him next, Harry tried to get her to invest her house money into a new townhouse project, not too far away. The developer went broke, and he bought-it-up for the first mortgage. "I'm going to be moving in there myself. I'd prefer to give it to you, but I'll have them sell you one, for whatever amount you *insisted* on paying. There's a vacant two-bedroom next to me."

Beth smiled rather graciously, he was still trying. "Yes, I'm familiar with them, but I really don't want to get back into the hassle of my own place right now. I want to get away from work, and everything to travel, then concentrate on my writing for awhile. I appreciate what you've done for me Harry, but I really need complete-freedom from entanglements, to find the real me, I've been searching for the last year. I know it sounds *hokey*, but that's the way I feel. In fact, I hate to mention it now, but I should let you know I'll be leaving the cleaning business altogether. The first of next month, I'll bring in one of our girls to train on the job."

Harry was silent for a moment, as he watched the smoke dissipate from his little pipe-dream she'd dissolved. "Does she fool around?" he asked, trying to put a joke into the remark. Beth laughed, he'd made it easier for both of them. She knew now, whatever else happened, they would remain friends. She picked up her can of furniture polish, kissed him on the forehead, and proceeded to the living room to finish cleaning.

* * * * * *

Beth was at Michael's with Connie, when April called to see if she might join them. Just before Christmas, and April came bearing gifts with exuberance for all. Since the first time Beth saw April after the 'grocery-bit,' egged on by Connie, Beth planned to tell her how upset the whole thing made her. Connie and Michael left to pick up a pizza. Beth started to talk to April, feeling a little guilty, with April giving her a Christmas present - something she rarely did, not expecting one in return. But, the underlying hostility, for April's expounding her 'good deeds' was greater. Also a momentary-scapegoat for the rest of Beth's problems. Unfortunately, Beth did not finish before the girls returned. Up to this point, they had been rational in discussing what happened, and how they viewed it from completely different directions. Connie, perhaps feeling some score to settle with April from the past, started in at her usual, rapid-pace of dialogue, "Who the fuck do you think you are, April . . ." When Michael also started shooting verbal-shots at April, it was too much for her. Crying and trembling, she gathered up her coat to leave.

"I was only doing what I thought she wanted, and needed at the time. Don't worry, I'll never offer my help to any of you again." Beth'd not meant it to turn out that way, yet she'd not opened her mouth to control the others, like before. Beth drank more wine than usual, trying to drown the guilt. She felt she'd watched April take a public-whipping, and not lifted a finger to stop it.

April got into doing house cleaning on her own with a rather, heavy-work schedule. Teaching classes and taking in clients for charts, she tried to busy herself to the brim, to keep her mind off the break-up with her friends. Still, she'd sometimes be on her hands and knees scrubbing someone's floor, and break down sobbing over the loss of her allies. Through all the trauma she'd gone through with her father, the disappointment with Wally's drinking, loss of Al and disillusionment with her marriage to Alex, April always had her friends to fall back on.

They'd been there, no one knew April better or longer, than Beth and Michael. Now, they were gone, more lost than if they died. She mourned that loss for almost a year, blaming them in crying almost everyday about it and how it had all gone wrong. Then, she reverted back to the only defense she knew, to turn hard and cold, to turn-it-off, and to forget the pain to go on surviving. The answer was to gather up her strength, try to make new friends, turning again to her astrology to develop the new friends she wanted and needed.

* * * * * *

Though Michael had a continuing friendship with her cleaning customer, Daniel, Connie never got involved with any of her customers. Oh, she had a few offers and in particular one might have been interesting, if she didn't know his alcoholic-wife was at home, and how they lived. One thing about being a cleaning lady, there was nothing you didn't know about the people you worked for - from what they ate, how they dressed, to their sex life or lack of it, and what possessions had meaning to them. Sometimes it was fascinating, even with the routine, and felt like a psychological-study with the subject never knowing they were being observed.

Sybil appeared on the scene once again, as the unpredictable comet she was, dissolving out of the dark, and disappearing back into it. As Michael talked about her client, Sybil was interested in meeting Daniel, though she kept saying, "No ties that bind, just a cool, casual live-in is all I'm looking for." Michael timed her cleaning, so she'd be at Daniel's when he was home between work and his evening classes. She told him about Sybil, when he went in to take a shower. Just finished changing the bed when he came out, still drying himself off, Michael began again about Sybil. Daniel tried previously to get Michael to return to bed with him, but she said she'd not cheat on Mike - no reason to. This, of course, seemed like the perfect time to pursue his quest, with him nude and the bed in-between them.

Michael managed to keep talking, ignoring the body in front of her, and watching his face only. Daniel then bounced down on the bed, and pulled Michael onto him, before she could move out of his reach. In utter frustration, Daniel gave up when she continued to not respond, but only repeated, "No. Now, can we finish talking about Sybil?" Michael caught her breath, and continued. "She's a bit erratic, but I think she'll stabilize with you in a routine situation. You know, she could cook and clean for you . . . "

"No, I want you to keep cleaning." She looked directly at him, giving a futile head-shake.

"OK, I'll clean, you'd have separate bedrooms, unless of course, things work out better."

"As long as she doesn't cling." His face was very stern regarding this.

"On, no. In fact, it was that you're not a clinger, that she thought it might work out." Daniel quietly listened as Michael rattled on about Sybil's many good points, which there were, but she ignored, or quickly passed over her problem with alcohol, pills and almost regular suicide attempts. He agreed to meet Sybil and they hit it off from their first flashes at one another. Maybe Michael'd been right, miracles did happen. So, Sybil moved in with Daniel on a strictly platonic-relationship with her staying in the spare bedroom, and both leading independent lives, yet occasionally sharing one bed. Sybil got a job at a local flower shop she could walk to everyday, and she'd have money of her own - happier than she'd been in a long time.

Then, as fate would have it, after Michael, Beth and April took turns talking to her, Sybil promptly fell in love with Daniel. She saw every kind gesture and mannered compliment, as an example of his dying-love for her. All of her own, small accomplishments she began to attribute to him, and that if not for Daniel, she'd once more be out on the street somewhere, or waking up next to someone, that she neither knew or wanted to remember. Instead of taking the credit for any of her changes herself, Sybil lauded the praise on Daniel, how she owed it all to him, and how much she loved him for it, and loving her.

Michael felt what the next step might be, but she tried to talk to Daniel, to see if they couldn't work something out. Thinking that bringing home a girlfriend might clarify his feelings, Daniel didn't know he put the last straw on a broken-down camel. Sybil ran to the nearest bar, and no one ever found out where she got the pills, but somehow managed. He was not prepared for the lead-weight body piled by his front door in the morning. Michael had to tell him of the many previous suicide attempts, she managed to help Sybil through, but again she did not learn.

Daniel welcomed her back in the apartment after the hospital stay, and he was, of course, feeling as guilty as Sybil wanted. He came home that first night with flowers for her, only to find her passed-out drunk in his bed, with his gun in her mouth. He'd seen a lot guys crack-up in Viet Nam, but he was more perplexed by this mixed-up woman-child. He grabbed her limp-body up in his arms, and again carried her off to the hospital, but this time it was the mental hospital. Michael would be the one to visit, as Daniel washed his hands of her.

Sybil was to stay six weeks, but since she'd signed herself in, so to speak, she signed herself out in three weeks. Michael told her that Daniel boxed up all of her things, and left them with his apartment manager. When she went to visit Sybil, the hospital attendant told her she'd checked-out with another patient earlier in the day, and, 'no,' she'd not left a note for Michael. The apartment manager said, Sybil picked up her things earlier that day with a young, long-haired man. Michael decided this was the last time she'd play 'Good Samaritan' for Sybil, or try to fix two friends-up with each other. It'd been an unnecessarily long, tiring nightmare.

Connie invested twenty-thousand dollars in *The Glass Onion*. Now, having problems wth stubborn Emil, who owned the building property, and the Cafe', she'd worked in for so many years. He felt after six-months, there should be more profits than Connie produced. She argued that it took time for a bar and disco to get a following. It was losing money, and he felt time to cash it in. Connie argued to let her try some live-bands for weekend variety. Even with the big upsurge in the attendance, Emil countered the additional band cost, did not offset the increased sales. Being European, he was not used to an outspoken-woman like Connie, and it became a power-play for him to prove he was right. Still, she wouldn't give in, until he hit her where it hurt the most - her pocketbook. He simply locked up the building and closed down the business.

Connie basically lost five-thousand dollars on *The Glass Onion* business venture, but she could not hold a grudge again Emil. She earned a good salary, which consisted of both hard work and having fun. It was a great experience, and she was a *'somebody'* for that period of time - *an entrepreneur*. Almost a relief to Cam, as he came closer to losing Connie during that time, than ever before. But, since she'd *gone-down* unsuccessful, he once again had full and complete control of the reins of their togetherness.

With the Christmas Season in full swing, Connie decided to get a small job in a catalog warehouse. She had plenty of money in the bank, and just wanted something to do, until she came up with what she wanted to do next. Not a big decision, since she was not interested in waitressing, when she could make as much money and be off weekends, if she went back to the cleaning. Come January 1976, Connie returned to being, *just* a cleaning lady once again.

About #30

There was a time,
when thirty was considered old.
Speaking of the body,
it was the official end of youth.

But the mind has just begun to realize,
there are no limitations.
The searching for one's destination
should be an important question at thirty.

I have been known to jump into things feet first.
Yet, I am no longer drowning in the sea of my indecisions.
Instead of sinking,
I learned how to tread water.

Keeping my head above it,
has been the greatest challenge.
Learning to be a long distance swimmer
is an easy trick . . .

The more difficult one is knowing
in which direction the shore is.

Being thirty is like finishing the first volume
of life's trilogy;
Not the beginning of the end,
but the end of the beginning.

CHAPTER 25

Crossing Borders

A bittersweet end, Beth turned over the keys of her customers' houses to the girls she trained to take over. Most of her customers she had since they started the business - two and half years before. They'd all been very generous to her, and treated her more like a friend, or one of the family, than *just* the cleaning lady. She'd alway been there when they wanted, and always felt they'd gotten their money's worth. Though the job might have a stigma to some people, to her it meant freedom and independence. The mental and emotional changes she'd been through, she knew that she'd not have been able to take the routine, pressure-politics of an office job.

Waitressing, a fun, challenging experience at the beginning, but toward the end, she felt more like her tips were left to the whims of the customers, than what she rightfully earned. With the cleaning paid by the job, she could pace herself, listen to the stereo, read a magazine, work on a poem or sweep-through like a tornado to finish as quickly as she wanted. Her work was consistent, so her time was her own variable. She really enjoyed the quiet of the empty houses, or the ladies that were occasionally home, the conversations they got into. She was glad that the other girls felt much the same way.

Yes, an enjoyable business and job. Though she'd dreamed of turning it into a career, expanding or franchising, that was not to be. She thought at thirty, she'd 'get her shit together,' but it was at thirty that she knew how far she had yet to go. The experiences of her twenties were behind her. Though not forgotten, they'd not be repeated. A new woman, with some financial freedom and time that she put some *'class into her act,'* and get started with a career.

More than anything, Beth had to get away for awhile, to breathe some different air and be around different people. She and Lori became better friends, as they expanded their mutual interests. Beth's lifestyle changed in proportion to the amount of time she spent with Lori, and her acquaintances in the creative-arts. She helped Lori with some advertising and promotional items, while also enjoying personal-outings to the theatre and museums. These people were sensitive and more responsive to her writing and poetry. She found real empathy and indulgence for her personal-quest of finding herself, and what direction she wanted to go. It wasn't as if Michael and Connie hadn't been understanding about Beth's turmoil, they just weren't going through the same thing. Their lives were filled with their men, and the problems that came with them being married.

April usually a good listener to Beth, as she had tried to explain why she was not satisfied with where her life was going. Yet, April's solutions would be something as innocuous as 'get a good job, finish the book,' then start telling Beth about *her own* problems, that were *so much more* pressing. Beth hadn't realize that when, they weren't sharing the same problems as they had in the past, the door of communication was not always open. Beth not being involved with any man, made her part of the conversation lacking, when so much of their discussions were *based on* the men in their lives.

Beth recalled her past relationships, which didn't have the viability as when an active involvement. Though she kept her eyes open for a new man, in the back of her mind, to be strong she should be a *total person before* she tried to have another serious involvement. Beth looked for something more permanent than an affair, yet she wasn't ready to say the word 'marriage.' That realization alone, told her that she needed this time to fully-develop Beth, so she wouldn't lose the little bit she'd found, by changing to suit some man's preference. New people around her would be new blood, a source of new ears and new suggestions for her to listen and learn from.

So, it was off to Mexico. Beth talked Lori into going there for a week, the beginning of February. It seemed like a far-enough trip to give them the sensation of getting away, and yet familiar enough, so comfortable on their own. Beth'd forget about the money she lost on the old house, the cleaning business and all the unanswered questions in her life. She was going for fun and relaxation. She'd been to border towns on vacation, but neither of them to the interior of Mexico. They both felt something was drawing them to this country and together.

Adopted when she was two, Lori felt her parents had kept her name, Dolores. She thought possibly, she had some Spanish blood in her. Though not on a quest in Mexico, she wanted to see what *vibes* she felt surrounded by these warm-blooded Mexicans. Armed with their *'lomotil'* prescriptions and guide book, they were off to discover Mexico, the Mexicans and each other.

They wanted to stay at an older, grand Mexican hotel, rather than a new, flashy-American one. As much as they could, they didn't want to take the *'tourista-route.'* They wanted to get the *real* feeling of Mexican life, granted the higher-class life, but at least not the pampered-American tourist-way. So, their choice hotel in Mexico City was the Del Prado, with the Diego Rivera murals, unexpectedly-accosting them, after the grand, marble entrance.

Their first experience of cultural-shock, with so much old and new within and surrounding it. A terrific view, their rooms overlooked the fifth-floor terrace pool, and across from a small park. Their five days in Mexico city, they scheduled a trip to the pyramids, the Folkloric Ballet, the Polyforma and, of course, the famous Anthropology Museum. They wanted to leave room for added side trips, shopping and whatever else might come along. First, they'd relax, explore the hotel and then choose a restaurant for their dinner.

A five star, highly-recommended by the guide book, and several of Lori's friends, was their choice. A little after seven, and though the middle of the week, they'd expected more people to be dining. Neither of them were aware that Mexican people were on a much later schedule, and the few businessmen seated were probably left over from a late, lunch meeting. Trying to be as elegant as possible, they ended-up making several faux pas. Beth, sure that a restaurant like this, there'd be no problem with the water or food, yet Lori wanted the maitre'd to reassure her. "Aqua, purificata?" she carefully asked.

He did not laugh or scorn her, but as a perfect gentleman, he smiled and said, "Si."

The dinner was exciting and delightful, with all the different taste sensations. Three gentlemen, sitting several tables away smiled at them through dinner, and stopped to talk to them as they were leaving. They had attended universities in the United States, and spoke English.

Being one of those lovely, balmy evenings, Lori and Beth walked to the Zone Rosa to window shop. Along the way, they passed an art gallery with a show being-previewed. It was there that Beth first discovered and fell in love with the work of Zuenga. Lori, familiar with him, but had not seen such a collection before. They walked and talked along the Reforma, as they paused to look in the exclusive shops of the 'Pink Zone.' They then took a taxi back to the hotel, for the next day would be busy and full, with the trip to the Pyramids.

In the heat of the sun, surrounded by architectural-feats, they could almost feel the pulse of the people, who'd once so mysteriously lived in these ancient ruins. They were both anxious for their next day's visit to the Anthropology Museum. The little background they'd been given at the tourist center, wetted their appetites for more information about this land and its various peoples. Beth had several visions there flash through her brain, as a past life perhaps.

Although, fully aware that Mexico City was an international, sophisticated city, Beth still thought that a park, was a park. And, when she went to a park, she wore Bermuda shorts, a T-shirt and sandals. She brought her warm-weather clothes, and saw no need to wait until Acapulco to wear them. Lori did not feel authoritative-enough, to tell Beth not to wear them, nor did she know her well enough, to feel that she could dictate to her. So, as they proceeded to the subway, a few blocks away from the hotel, Lori noticed the hotel-people taking longer-looks. Lori's spring-pantsuit, contrasted to Beth's Paul Newman T-shirt, shorts, white sandals and a big, white straw hat, to protect her from burning.

Wearing that T-shirt over her full-bosom, set off by her long, curly, very-blonde hair created somewhat of a neon-sign to the men. Lori noticed right away on the crowded street, that Beth was drawing more than their usual attention for being *'blonde-Gringos.'* The real culmination came, just before they arrived at the entrance of the subway along a thoroughfare. A pick-up truck, with several men in it honked, a second one slowed down and a third, had to slam on its brakes. They were all whistling and waving. Just ahead of them on the sidewalk, a man coming down the steps from the subway, stopped in his tracks when he saw Beth, and stared till she'd passed him by.

Then even turning, to watch as she ascended the steps into the building. Beth was embarrassed, but all Lori could say was, "My God, I wish the cracks in the sidewalk were big enough to crawl into!" Beth tried to convince Lori and herself, her apparel would be acceptable once they got to the park. She then quickly commented to Lori about the beautiful mosaic tiles and artwork, all around in the station.

Lori truly had never known anyone quite like Beth before. She pushed and practically packed her into going on this trip, convincing her how much she, too, needed the vacation. Upon making all the reservations, tour arrangements and depositing Lori into the seat next to her on the plane, Beth felt she'd done her part of the trip. She promptly left the planning and navigation up to Lori, who got several local-type maps from friends, who'd traveled to Mexico.

Lori liked having the choice of where and how, they'd go around the city in-between the tours. The subway was modern, with its intricate, colorful mosaic-murals and very clean. It was also very crowded, and a heyday for lechers, but it was fun. There always was four or five times more males on the street, and the subway was no different. As usual within the culture, the young men were *'copping-a-feel'* so not considered rude or vulgar. They were *merely* taking advantage to more closely-admire, what so-conveniently pressed by them. About a fifteen-minute ride to Chapultepec Park, about half-way, Lori turned on one young man, who had more than his share of feels, and said, "Stop it!" There were a few laughs and snickers, to let her know her message had been understood.

Beth was still the most, casually-dressed person at the park, but she was there now. What her clothes might have distracted from her, her new Polaroid SX-70 camera attracted. Only out in the States a short time, it was virtually unknown there. People loved to have their pictures taken, and to see them right away, made it even better. In front of the Anthropology museum, taking pictures of some school children, they met him. With excellent English, he introduced himself as Carlos. Beth, so intrigued with the excitement and innocence of the children, kept taking their pictures, while trying to talk to them about it. He began talking to Lori, telling her he only recently returned to Mexico, from living in the States for three years. He then asked Beth, "Do you want to take my picture?"

"No, it's OK, I just like the beautiful, little children." Turning back to the children, he quickly interpreted for her. Several minutes and photos later, the children went skipping and giggling away. Lori and Beth started for the main entrance, with Carlos following behind. Lori'd read that some young Mexican men would do favors, and then expect the vulnerable, woman-tourist to not only pay their way, but also pay them for being a guide. Beth said, they could simply ignore him and he'd go away.

Carlos then asked, "Do you mind if I go with you, so I may use my English? I do not want to lose what I have learned."

Beth coolly, but kindly responded, "It's a public place, but we do want to concentrate on the exhibits, not just conversation." So, Carlos followed them in, paying his own admission, and only talked to interpret some of the Spanish for them, or make a comment about some object or display. He politely divided his time between Beth and Lori, as they wandered in awe, from every room and display.

The far building held an original, Aztec stone-calendar which for some reason, Beth felt drawn to. It amazed her, they had this great stonework in the open, available to be touched and experienced. And, she did, until she'd covered almost every crevice of it with her finger tips. She slowly sat down on the bench, provided in front of it and absorbed all she'd touched and seen. She'd been there at least twenty minutes, before Lori and Carlos found her.

"Here you are!" Lori exclaimed. "We couldn't imagine where you went off to. Did you see Montezuma's head dress?"

Beth nodded and replied, "But nothing can compare with this." Lori and Carlos sat for several minutes looking at the stonework, with Beth telling them in detail all about it. This had definitely come from those visions at the Pyramids, but she didn't know why.

Carlos was quite amazed, "Did you study about that? I did not know some of that."

Beth looked perplexed, "I don't know, it sort of came to me." She turned to Lori, "Like yesterday at the Pyramids, I felt they were talking to me." Lori was the art authority, not Beth.

"Well, you've become an amazing student of Aztec artwork. Ready to move on?" Beth continued to stare at the stone calendar, then reluctantly followed them, turning several times to see once more the magnificent art work, that invaded her system with its presence. Later, they stopped at the outdoor restaurant to have a late lunch, before leaving the museum. Carlos turned out to be very warm and charming, never asking them to pay for anything for him. Lori wanted to go shopping at a Mexican market, and Carlos said he'd like to go along to help them bargain.

So, it was back to the hotel, to change into shopping-clothes, suitable also for dinner. It was a true Mexican-market, and not a tourist rip-off. They got many bargains, but Carlos insisted that they must leave before dark, to be on the safe side. He stopped and bought a couple of cans of beer and some lime, to show the girls how to drink beer 'Mexican-style.' They stopped in a liquor store to get Kahlua for Beth, and a bottle for Connie. Then Carlos got them a taxi, and they were off to a Mexican nightclub. Lori wanted authentic, and that's what they got. It was a marvelous, older building with meticulous-tile on the wall, a glorious mahogany bar and trim.

The noisy crowd almost-quieted, as the three walked into the big room. Beth and Lori looked very blonde, very white, very female and very affluent. The waiter showed them to a center table and took their drink order, and Carlos ordered the appetizer, while the mariachis came over and began playing. It was an amazing place, with the decor mainly consisting of toreador-outfits in glass cases, of the most famous fighters. Once again, there were few women in evidence.

They were on their second margarita, when the dinners arrived, as they quaffed their first drinks quickly with the spicy-nachos. A very long, and busy afternoon between the small lunch and dinner, Lori was getting giddy. Beth thought it hilarious, as she'd never seen her really lose-it before. Her whole image had always been quite proper, yet not too-stuffy, and very much the lady. Lori, taken by the trumpet player, as once again at their table blowing his heart out, as she swooned. They'd become the center of attention, and following dinner several of the men joined their table. After several hours, many margaritas, and much beer, Carlos felt it was time they should be leaving.

Getting a little rowdy, with someone accidentally breaking one of the Kahlua bottles. Besides, there were too many young-men hanging on Beth and Lori. He became very protective of them, and felt he should see them safely to their hotel. It'd been a great day, made even better with Carlos showing them a part of his world, *they* wanted to see. He said, he could join them the next day to see the University, San Angel Inn and shop. This time, Carlos brought his cousin along, so Lori and Beth had two, young men escorting them around the city.

That evening was the Folkloric Ballet, a fast-paced, colorful and exciting experience. Even without Carlos, Beth and Lori became completely at ease with the Mexican men. If they stopped at a corner to look at a map, it seemed within sixty-seconds a gentleman would appear out of nowhere, say he spoke English, and asked if they needed directions. So, when the young man approached them, as they were walking down the steps of the Fine Arts Building from the Folkloric Ballet, Beth and Lori did not hesitate at all.

"Excuse me," he said to Beth, "I know this sounds strange, but I lived in California for awhile, and you look so much like someone I knew there." He appeared very earnest.

Beth smiled, "No . . . I'm from Chicago. I just have one of those faces, that looks a lot like others." Beth kept walking down the steps, as the young man pursued the subject.

"Are you sure, you're not somebody from Hollywood?" He was almost pleading.

Beth cracked-up, and Lori responded, "Oh, brother! That does it! I don't believe, what happens with you!" She went marching ahead, feeling a little left-out.

"No, really, I'm not, . . . but that's nice of you to say." She couldn't help snickering.

"Well, could I ask you, and your friend, to join me for a drink?" He urgently asked.

Beth kept walking to catch-up to Lori. "No, thank you. We've had a long day, and will also tomorrow." She shook her head, and tried to keep from laughing out-loud.

"Could I at least, give you a ride to your hotel?" He seemed desperate for more time.

"No, really. It's only a few blocks, and we'd rather walk." He finally gave up, and went the other direction. Beth didn't want anyone to ruin, her good feelings about the Mexican men.

Their last day they spent several hours at the Sequoias Polyforme. Most happy to have the oval-shaped, three-dimensional mural all to themselves to enjoy it. Lori even laid on some chairs to soak-up the elliptical-sensation of being part of the Mexican Revolution, that was surrounding her. Beth never saw violence portrayed, or unadulterated-hopelessness, so truthfully-depicted.

They'd been in the room about half an hour, dissecting each section of the mural, slowly to grasp Sequoias' meaning of it all, when three, American-tourists journeyed up the stairs and into the room. They spent about three minutes looking-around from their entrance spot, mumbled a few words, pivoted and vanished down the stairs. Lori turned to Beth and said, "Now, that's what I call tourists!" They both laughed, and shook their heads, returning to indulge in the mural.

Afterwards, Lori and Beth leisurely walked the fountains and courtyard, as they left the Polyforme, to view some of the lovely homes of the surrounding neighbors. Along the way, the mouth-watering smells of a small bakery, pulled them inside to try some unknown delicacy. They not only spoiled themselves in something for the present, but also the future - of course, chocolate for Beth and gooey-cream for Lori. Not a proper lunch, but it was obscenely-delicious. Afterwards they sauntered for almost an hour, then back to the hotel for an afternoon swim. They'd been invited to diner at Carlos' father's house. His mother died a few years before, so his sister and brother-in-law lived there, also. Lori and Beth bought some chocolates for his father. Putting complete trust in Carlos, they followed him to the subway and the long trip to his father's house.

An experience they wanted, and one they'd never forget. His family was waiting for them, as if Carlos told them he was bringing home two celebrities. The house was small, but very clean and reminded Beth of some the bungalow-type houses in the older, suburbs closer to Chicago. The dinner was simple, but presented with the finest grace. Carlos was the only one fluent in English, and you could tell he was very proud of that fact.

Beth took several photos for them, and after dinner they drank Mexican beer, while Carlos played Spanish and English records. His cousin, and another male friend, joined them as they danced in the small living room. A warm and loving evening, like Beth and Lori had not known before.

Being welcomed into a strange home, given kindness and affection like they were long-time friends, was something they'd never have dreamed could happen in a foreign land. They kissed them all goodnight, when they got out of the car at the hotel. They'd sadly be leaving Mexico City in the morning. Carlos made their time there better, than ever thought possible.

With the morning sun, came the last-minute packing, and they were on their way by tour-car to Cuernavaca. They only had a few hours, to see the city with the lovely hills, and town square, with a band playing in the gazebo. The country got hillier, as they arrived in Taxco, the Silver City, as it was referred to. The countryside they passed by, revealed a people that had changed very little in the past several hundred years. On every hill in Taxco, the view was grand, but when they got to the top of the highest hill, with their Holiday Inn perched into the hillside, the view was breathtaking.

The Inn was brand new, but built in a hacienda-tradition, with all the rooms overlooking the city far below. Beth and Lori were happy to see the Inn was run by an all-Mexican staff, so they wouldn't lose the flavor they enjoyed in Mexico City. They relaxed on their patio to watch the sunset and shadows, creep across the sky and hills.

But it was the town glowing-alive below in the tiny-lights, that became enchanting. No gaudy, giant-neons or flood lights to affect the mesmerizing beauty. Just small lights flickering in the dust, through the black night. They had fun touring the city, and all of the silver shops, as Beth found out she was allergic to silver after wearing it for a few days. Oh, well. Lori really felt in her element, and enjoyed it all.

The last-leg of their trip was Acapulco, and exactly what they'd expected - flashy, expensive and loaded with American tourists. With the busy week they had, laying on the beach and picking restaurants, seemed like a wonderful past-time. The real fun came playing the game with the hundreds of urchins, who were hawking their wares everywhere. If you didn't take money to the beach, you missed a good bargain, and if you did take money, you spent it.

The sunset-cruise and their carriage-ride on the last night, were the highlights of Acapulco, the tourists were sometimes an embarrassment, how rude they'd be to the soft-spoken Mexicans. Beth did sunburn to her usual 'crispy-critter,' but then, how else does one enjoy the beach. She saw no reason to go home with any money, so after buying souvenirs for everyone, she didn't have any left-over to worry about. Until, they got to the airport, and found out there was an extra, five-dollar exit-charge, which Lori lent her in order to leave Mexico - another irony of Beth's life.

The whole trip could be recalled in memories, but the closeness that they shared had begun. Lori was in a married-man-syndrome as well, which Beth could understand completely, so tried to give her suggestions on coping with it. Like many relationships, they followed basic development paths of either improving or eventually dissolving. With the married-man, the steps were almost identical, to the point of being almost cynical, regarding any real success. Since it was usually the single-person in such a relationship, that never rocked the boat, at this point, Lori was almost content with the way things were going. Though she went through the usual pain of him not being there, when she really needed him, because family came first.

The most recent painful experience, Beth had shared with Lori right after she had her hysterectomy. Lori went through the common depression following surgery, when she called Ted to come stay with her, if for even a few minutes. His rejection and refusal, with a very, flimsy excuse simply confirmed her feeling of her lost femininity. She'd finished crying, then became calm when Beth came bounding into the house to clean. She checked to see how Lori was feeling, and said *'fine'* with such a far-away look in her eyes and sound in her voice, Beth knew something was definitely amiss. She sat down on the bed beside Lori, and asked very strongly, "How are you, *really*?"

Lori looked at her like she'd seen her for the first time, and started to cry, showing very, little emotion. "Really? . . . Well, I was trying to figure-out the easiest way to commit suicide." Beth slowly put her arms around Lori, not knowing what all to say, but knowing that she needed someone to show that they cared. Beth held and talked to her for about twenty-minutes, until she felt she was ready to be left alone, while she cleaned the house. She was glad that at Lori's lowest point, she'd been there to help her, and Lori never forgot the gesture.

Ted was very, supportive *financially* of Lori's career with the art lecturing, and she had no qualms of taking money from her lover. He couldn't envision the unlimited-horizons that she had, but he knew the career was very important to her. Like most, playing the 'other woman,' the lovemaking was satisfactory. The friendship-part of the relationship was lacking, as that took an investment of time. Once the wants between his legs were satisfied, he didn't usually have time to listen to her thoughts, much less any problems or generalities of life. Lori still had a lot of anger and hostility, left-over from her marriage, so often acquiesced to the role of 'being used.'

There was always the rub, their rendezvouses were at his convenience, because of course, his job was more important than hers. And, his reputation the one to be guarded, so that he wasn't seen with her. The only reward for juggling a schedule, making excuses to the kids why the dinner was late, and re-arranging her own appointments, was simply having the pleasure of his company, which after awhile wan't as pleasurable as he thought.

When a liaison with a married-man runs on for years, as with all, there were plateaus that last for months - sometimes bordering on stagnation. Though Ted never made any reference to getting a divorce, like Cam always did to Connie, he tried to pacify her with an expensive gift, or taking Lori on a long business trip, to some place he knew she'd like to go. Needless to say, most married men have to make a pretty, good-dollar to keep two women happy. Because of this, they sometimes let the money take the place of the time, they spent with either woman.

Beth could not see Lori involved with an unemployed, uneducated man, since money was very important to her, as was status. Because of this, she attracted men, who not only had it, but they were also generous with it. She *was* expecting of money, unlike Beth, in fact it did play a part in the investment of her emotions for the man, and the money he spent or gave to her. At this time, Lori had no interest in marriage, and Ted's better points, still outweighed the bad ones, which was the balance to any relationship.

Upon their return, Beth began to feel more separated from Connie and Michael, partially as she appeared to be traveling in a separate circle. Connie's move into the apartment across the hall from Michael, and them mutually sharing their relationships with married men, brought them more into context with each other. Beth's moratorium on men, was probably the wisest thing, since she didn't need any additional fuel to feed her mother, regarding the company or hours she kept. Beth's main concern was continuing to build a solid relationship with Jeremy, she didn't want to lose him. He was still, the best thing she'd gotten out of her bad marriage.

Beth had no reason to turn her back on her long time friends while she expanded herself, yet her almost-daily contact with Lori continued. She did expand Beth's quest for more knowledge regarding art-appreciation, and she was also there for whatever support Lori needed. Beth really valued that she relied on her opinion, and listened to her suggestions, to the point of rarely seeing her therapist any more. Beth asked for Lori's ideas, so no more social, faux pas, and much polish was added to her overall presentation of herself. Still, when Connie or Michael reached out to her - usually as a pair - Beth didn't refuse, *if* she didn't have some function or something with Lori. She didn't want to lose them.

While rare, Connie and Beth managed to spend time at their Scrabble, with Beth diligently gaining, so she might win once in awhile. And, with Michael, those mind-bending hours discussing books - more read by Michael - or movies, like no one else saw what they did. Of course, April's dabbling in metaphysics - particularly world religions captivated Beth and Michael into their own studies. They saw the religious dogmas so many people, especially women, got caught-up with and assumed. Thus, all her friends contributed to Beth's expansion, to keep her diverse in many ways, and she shared these to whomever wanted to learn.

Into the group, also appeared Beth's sister Marie, them trying to educate her into grasping the importance of independence, or Connie's very straight friend, Linda, or still, crazy Sybil. Everyone basically welcomed, as they made them either appreciate their own life more, or see how they could grow, change and keep moving forward. The truth was, they could say things to each other, they couldn't say to their men. They learned camaraderie was not something *only men* knew on the battlefield, or sports field. It meant human-beings who'd been through some kind of trauma, and together survived by pooling their strength to support one another as needed.

If the Shoe Fits

Would you do for me, what I've done for you . . .
if you were in my shoes?

Could you be best friends to my husband . . .
if I were the married one?

Would you give up your children, and be best
friends to mine?

Could you listen to my husband talk about me . . .
and our sex life?

Would you console him, if he thought there was
someone else I was seeing?

Could you watch me flirt with other men . . .
and still believe I only loved you?

Would you still want me as much, and as often . . .
if we were both free?

Could you lie, and do whatever else was necessary . . .
just, so we could be together?

Some shoes you would have
a hard time filling . . .

no matter how big
your feet were.

Chapter 26

Little Lies Become Bigger

Recently back from a snowmobile trip in Wisconsin, Michael felt they'd never been closer, and not just because Mike was away from work and his wife. They spent several days with her mom and step-dad, which left Michael feeling closer to them, also. They stopped in a few times before when up at Beth's lake property, but never had the leisure of several days. Michael spent much of her spare time with Mike's sons, Jackie and Jason, as they now worked with her two nights a week cleaning the city offices of a near-by town. Wanting to be closer to Mike, spending time with them, as her kids were out of state, and she enjoyed the teenagers, reliving what she missed.

This brought her closer to Barbara, though from opposite-camps and generations, a friendship developed with constant proximity. Michael felt she helped Barb break out of her rigid mother-housewife role, she made for herself. She'd worked for several years, yet kept the boys and Mike dependent upon her to feel needed. After several months, Michael saw Barb had no true hobby or expression of herself - there was no Barbara Cordeau - individual person, woman or separate human being - only *Mrs.* Mike Cordeau, the mother of Jackie and Jason. Almost twenty years, she patterned herself into only living through her kids and Mike's needs.

Being ten years older than Michael, Barb was a product of a generation which did not produce many independent women. And, those women with grown children and a husband that no longer needed them, rebelled for all the years that they *kept themselves* in their own captivity. Michael went out to the farm almost every weekend with them, so soon an accepted part of the Cordeau family. A method to her madness of being 'best' friends to her lover's wife, the quicker Barb became independent, the faster they'd get a divorce. This left the field open for Michael to be ahead of the game, already friends and accepted by Mike's sons.

Michael started opening her mouth, giving her opinions on how Mike and the boys treated Barb like a servant. Many times, Barb deserved the treatment they gave her, since constantly placing herself in the position of *wanting* to do for them, to still be needed. Yet, Michael defended her, and fought her verbal-battles on the principle of no-one should be used or taken for granted. She became a thorn in Mike's side - if speaking up on Barb's defense, she lectured him on how *he lectured* his teenage sons.

They pulled off a spectacular trip to Yellowstone for snowmobiling, and it seemed like things could not get better - as long as *Michael was willing* to compromise. Then, in May, with much aggravated help from Beth, Mike pushed Barb enough for her to get a divorce. A tedious situation, as Michael built-up a false relationship with Barb, to spend time at the house with Mike. When it came to love and sex, she definitely had no scruples. It took a good memory to be a great liar, and Michael, one of the best, for them to get away with it all for so long.

Since Mike and Barb's love/sex disintegrated years before, and apparent to many people, they were merely staying together until they boys finished high school. From basic remnants of her own marriage, Michael told Barb to leave them, "Since they use and abuse you, and the breakup imminent, why not get out now to start building a new life, before you get any older?"

Michael had no idea Barb was listening over the past few months, much less had the guts to do it, until she came pounding on Michael's door one morning about six o'clock. Barb drove around town most of the night, after a big fight with Mike and decided to leave. She came to Michael's because she really didn't know where to go, or what to do next. Michael stood with her mouth gaped-open. Mike'd been there only a few hours earlier. Within a week, she helped Barb move out, and into her own apartment.

Beth, Jeremy and Michael joined Mike, with his boys at the farm for Memorial Day Weekend. Barb gone a month, with the divorce court date two weeks away. Everyone so changed, Beth could not get over it, especially Barb happy as could be. Although, Mike found out several little *'shitties'* Barb pulled with money, but he wasn't going to make a big stink, since soon to be over. Beth was amazed at how Michael took over organizing the boys and Mike. She did some unbelievable cleaning-out when she helped Barb move, and followed with cleaning both at his house and the farm. Beth thought what good therapy for Michael, cleaning the wife right out of her mind - and his.

Beth walked into the kitchen at the farm, to see Michael giving Mike a lecture about something with other than therapy at work. She rattled off words in almost rhythm, with her finger poking his massive chest. In the twenty years Mike was married to Barb, she never talked to him that way. In complete disbelief, Beth saw a smirk on Mike's put-on little-boy-face. He glanced over at her and replied, "Ain't she cute when she's all fired up!"

"Goddamn it Mike, would you pay attention to me!" Michael obviously serious.

"Oh, I am, I am." Beth saw he was, much more than either of them yet knew. They were like so many scenes out of John Wayne and Maureen O'Hara's movies.

"You are hopeless, absolutely hopeless!" Beth thought, so was Michael - both hopelessly in love. One week after his divorce, Mike made his move on Michael public, as they *started* going out. Beth, not surprised when Michael didn't resist one bit about the quickness, nor caring what everyone, including Barb and Louise, would say.

* * * * * *

Beth became active in a local writer's club. She enjoyed not only sharing what she'd written, with the constructive-critique, but as well as the writing of the other members. She found a comfortable niche with them, as several earned money with their writing and were rather serious. Yet, it was the rejects from publishers, Beth didn't think she could handle. She wrote several things, what she and others thought were clever, short stories, but the magazine publishers didn't. Going to the meetings, also kept her writing poems, though she knew rarely a market for them. They made her feel better, to get all her emotion out.

The writers' club brought her back into contact with her former attorney, Lou, who was now a judge. She'd not known of his interest in writing, and they spent many hours drinking after the meetings, talking over their experiences with a few of the other members. What Beth needed most of all, was some knowledge on how to get published, or some connection to show her the magic key, *as if*. So, when one of the ladies told her about the summer-workshop at another local college, she was off to sign up. The course promised lectures by a variety of people in the media, and awards at the end of the eight weeks for best poems, stories, etc. Beth's expectations, as usual ran-away with her, feeling her impending creative discovery was, obviously, just around the corner - if she could be at that right corner.

But, Beth was lucky enough on the first night of class to meet, a lithe, dark haired, slightly older woman, coming in late, to slip into the chair next to her. Without her saying a word, Beth felt this a lady of style, understated refinement and class. At the break, Beth not yet forward in a strange crowd, complimented the woman on her unusual, clay necklace. They started talking, and Anne introduced herself, as an artist that wanted to expand her writing. Soon, to Beth's delight, they were sharing many common-interests, including the same birthday.

Anne was also in the process of a very long, drawn-out divorce, which Beth jumped on to see if there was anything she could suggest. But, Anne *had* her act together, pretty much with the worst of it behind her, having considered suicide at her lowest point. By the second class, Anne, as promised, brought in a watercolor, she'd told Beth about. She was awestruck. She'd never seen anything exemplify her own current search for herself. This painting had women-posed in stages of thought, on the limbs of a giant tree, nude in the moonlight. Beth knew, if she could, she'd one day have that painting. As Anne and Beth became friends, they looked forward more to their own conversations, than the in-class lectures. Anne wrote in the vein of Erma Bombeck, having five kids of her own, ranging from younger than Jeremy, to a high school senior.

After listening to relevant lectures, none lit any fires, until Beth heard one speaker say, "If you believe in your work, especially poetry, have it printed yourself. Sometimes it's easier to sell when it's a packaged deal." Yes, Beth thought. She had the poems, and some money left-over from the house sale, she'd do it. She told Anne of her plan for her poems to be printed, as soon as possible, and Anne agreed, offering to help if needed with the artwork. It'd be Beth's first time investing in herself and poetry - believing she was worth it. Anne did the calligraphy, as Beth thought it'd make an unusual style for her poetry book cover title.

She wanted a whimsical title to belie the seriousness and satire of her poems, with a cover-sketch in mind. Then, she saw Lori's son, Tommy, doing a cartoon-type frog, that she knew was perfect for what she wanted. The cover was set, with Anne's title, Tommy's frog and Lori doing some lily pads with cattails for the background. Beth used the local college copy services for the insides, after she won an award for her poems. Spread out in her parents' basement, she collated the pages, with occasional help from her nephew Jason and Connie. It was a slow, tedious job, but eventually the books were ready for the binder.

In the meantime, Lori discovered a source to do her lecturing on a regular basis. It was a women's group that offered regular eight to ten week courses, in a variety of subjects during the day and evening. Perfect for some of her longer-series lectures, and perhaps gave her an outlet to larger, more lucrative lectures. Lori'd been especially helpful to Beth in locating the printer for her book-covers and a binder. She had much faith in Beth's poems, and sure this would be the start of something good for Beth. She then helped Lori write and layout her pamphlet for her lectures, which once again showed another side to Beth's creativity. They both had something new to work towards.

Michael, who always found good, unusual books to read, gave Beth a copy of *Some are Born Great,* by Adela Rogers St. Johns. Beth, so impressed with it, told everyone she ran into, about these great women. Lori thought Beth a great story teller, so suggested she join Lori for the interview at the women's group. Beth never lectured anyone but friends, yet was more than willing to try anything once. By the time of the interview, her ego had grown, that she came up with two other subjects to lecture on. So, besides "Great American Women of the Twentieth Century," she had "Women of the Letters - Writers and Poets," and because she'd become a rather, creative-gourmet cook from Tom's lessons, a class on "Gourmet Cooking Simplified."

Beth could not believe how well she did in the interview. So sure about what she knew and confident, like she had many years experience. She truly, *'baffled them with bullshit, and dazzled them with dialogue,'* as Cam often said, and it flowed well that day. In reality, she didn't have a word written about any women to talk about, or a single recipe ready. The important thing was, they believed her, and signed her to give two lecture series - on the great women and the cooking class. Then perhaps, the other women, and another cooking class the next session.

Beth's life was busy, and full with getting her poetry printed, doing research and writing of her lectures. In between, her free-lance writing and advertising picked up, too. She also met a couple of interesting men, though not unattached, she was happy to have their acquaintance and interesting conversations. These were the life-savers that kept her from letting her emotions go from the heights of success, to the pits of depression from the pressure of living with her parents. While her brother Mike, in the midst of his divorce, their mother constantly gave Beth flack about being the instigator of it. Though Beth could not deny the charges, she reminded Louise, no one forced Mike to do anything. Soon Michael also became Louise's target, as changed in her eyes from a sweet, innocent girl, to 'out and out tart,' castigating her to anyone around.

Unexpectedly, because Beth was so nonchalant about advising Mike, Louise backed Barb instead of Mike. Even after Mike found that Barb had not made the payments on the farm, and forged his signature on a loan at the bank, their mother still supported Barb, hoping Mike'd change his mind. He did not, so Beth received a constant, daily-hassle-barrage from her. Beth tried to escape, since arguing was detrimental to her mother's health, with her high blood pressure and stroke-history. Besides, to give logic where her mother's emotion-prevented any want of understanding. Louise simply would rather see Mike married unhappily to Barb, not a product of failure and divorce, than happy. Similar to what she did to Beth during her divorce, which frustrated her beyond belief. Their mother lectured them there had never been a divorce in the family, and she'd not allow it to happen, though Beth knew it wasn't true.

She truly felt Louise was trying to drive her crazy, and often succeeded. Whether Beth escaped to Lori's or Michael and Connie's, but it was the alcohol that eased the tension quicker, than the company. It got to the point, wherever Beth visited, usually with Marie in tow escaping from her family, a bottle of wine or scotch was available to her, or brought with her. It took Beth back to her divorce, and how in Louise's eyes she'd always been the black sheep of the family. It didn't matter that job and education-wise, Beth had accomplished more than Marie and Chuckie. But then, perhaps her mother resented that she broke-off her umbilical cord so early in life, whereas theirs were still fully-intact. It was also acceptable for Mike to have his independence from their mother, but she'd not accept him doing so from Barb. Maybe she just did not want him free to roam the countryside, as she felt Beth did.

Beth still feared her mother's recriminations, or her weakness to do what she wanted, hoping to be liked and loved. She had waited till her parents had left on vacation the day after Christmas, before she went to the attorney to file for her divorce. She figured if all the wheels were rolling when they returned a month later, Louise could not stop it. Unfortunately, her father's heart attack on New Year's Day changed it all.

Since he'd always been her source of strength and support, Beth felt the one-leg she stood on, had been knocked out. Once strong enough to be moved, Louise brought him back to Elmwood by train. When Beth told Louise about the divorce, she glared at her like a flashing sign marked FAILURE had appeared. She then said, "You have to be the one to tell your father, and any resulting consequences will be on you." Thus, expecting John, her father would die from the divorce notice.

Beth's father meant more to her than anyone, except Jeremy. He'd always been there, and though, since his accident before her wedding, she knew he was human and vulnerable. Yet, still on somewhat of a pedestal, she walked into the hospital room with a big smile on her face. After she'd given him her usual big kiss and hug, she tried to talk. At last, looking directly into his eyes, she told him of her pending divorce. John was the kind of man, that had no enemies and knew no strangers, truly they were people he'd not met, yet.

He loved everyone, and never had an unkind word for anyone, since he always found some redeeming good point about them. He was quiet for a few moments, knowing Beth usually put a great deal of time, and thought into what she did. Also well aware, that she'd not been her happy-self for a long time, no matter how much she'd tried to cover-up in front of him. Her father tried to get Bruce involved in his lodge, and got several printing jobs for him, but he rarely followed-up, or followed-through on them. He looked at his baby, which Beth always was, right back in the eye to speak, "Elizabeth . . . I could never understand how someone as ambitious as you, could have married such a lazy man."

Beth started to cry, as she threw her arms around him with kisses. "Thanks, Pop. I needed that." So relieved to have his support.

"You're young and have your whole life ahead of you, so don't let your mother or anyone else tell you what to do with it. I know your mother talks about no divorce in the family, but I have to tell you . . ." Her father went on, and told Beth that he'd been married before coming to Chicago, and that the woman he sent money to cheated on him, so he divorced her. He also told Beth, not to ever let her mother know, he'd told her, as he'd promised to never tell anyone. But it was important that Beth knew the truth, to not let her mother get to her. When Beth needed him, he was there, and she could not say that about other men then, or even now that she'd been on her own for four years.

When the Fourth of July came, Beth skipped going out to the farm, because she didn't want to be in the middle of a family squabble. Why Mike wanted to put himself through it, when he knew their mother would do nothing but bitch. Nothing he or Michael could do then, or in the future would ever be acceptable to her. Since Jeremy was with his father, Beth instead went out on Cam's boat with Connie and another couple. The family confrontation was coming, but she wanted to put it off as long as possible. As it turned out, her father feigned not feeling well enough, as he knew what Louise had planned, so they never went out to the farm.

Michael wanted only for Mike's kids to see him happy, and as the man he could be with a loving woman by his side, that was as anxious to do new things as he was. She was right in there with Jackie and Jason tubing down the tributary from the Mississippi, that came through Mike's farm property. They hiked together, biked and previously even snowmobiled, all around the farm. Barb always stayed back at the trailer, and kept the home-fires burning with the food waiting. She rarely participated with her three males, like the kitchen was a greater need.

Michael felt they could always whip-something-up, when they came back in. She'd rather be out having fun, and interacting with *her* three 'boys.' Though Jackie and Jason called Michael by her name, they were accepting of her being a figure of authority and discipline, since she had the role for some time doing the cleaning jobs.

Michael did not expect them to move in together or get married. She felt they were all free to do their own thing, because everyone was happy. She was hopeful some day, Louise would accept her as the new woman in Mike's life. At least, they had the farm to go to, and her parents welcomed them with open arms when they traveled up to Wisconsin. Michael tried to live her life, with as much of it as possible being shared with Mike, and the boys. So, she tried not to let Louise's remarks, or Barb's lies drive her crazy, like they seemed to be doing to Beth.

Far and Away

There were those summer days,
stretched out on the back lawn
watching the planes from O'Hare
fly-high overhead to somewhere.

It was the recurring day-dream
of going far away on one.
Then, mother called to come
get another laundry-load.

Dutifully, hanging them on the lines,
it was rote-work, as if planted.
Mine was a stuck-life in suburbia.
Things didn't seem to change.

I did what I had to do to keep
peace, and maybe get to visit friends,
whose lives weren't much different than mine.

More than gravity pulling me, as there was no
magnet to attract any opportunity for a different
identity. There was no choice to equalize power.

My truth was knowing my character
was shaped by everyday numbness.
There were no real challenges,
or results from making an effort.

There was a wish to be passionate
about something, almost anything.
They were the 'tween years,
not old or experienced enough.

Without being told, I knew we were a family
being held by unchanging, daily habits.
Getting far away was the only answer.

CHAPTER 27

Family Matters Hurt

The family confrontation between Beth and her mother, Louise came on her father, John's seventy-first birthday. Her mother insisted the whole family be together for the celebration (as if she cared), which would be held at his lodge. Louise had relatives from Alaska visiting who were, of course, expected to join before leaving. Almost a soap opera, with Beth knowing all the skeletons everyone had in their closets. Connie laughed, "This whole mess makes *Peyton Place* look like Disneyland!"

Mike was not concerned, as he felt he could endure a few hours with any words said. But Beth was a nervous wreck, that *someone* would say or do something and she, as usual, would get the blame. She actually had cause to celebrate, because her first hundred books went to the binder that morning. But, as usual, if Beth couldn't escape physically from the party, she escaped mentally. If she got bombed, no one could blame her what she said or did - as if.

Her Uncle Eddie, Louise's youngest brother, who himself, in the process of divorce for several years, offered to buy her the first drink. Beth smiled, she knew he had *a thing* for her for years, but had substituted Barb, *just before* her divorce from Mike, when Beth refused. Barb confided the affair to Michael, who told Beth, not knowing about Uncle Eddie's *emotional attachment* for her. When Beth told Mike, he hardly flinched, since he'd occupied himself-sexually other places long before the divorce. His only comment was, "Is that right? Now, I won't have to worry about her bothering me. I should call Unk and thank him." Michael, had no intention of being at the festivities, as Louise made a point to Mike, she wasn't welcomed.

Beth smiled, as she told Uncle Eddie a very, dry vodka martini would do her just fine. By the time Mike arrived, Beth was on her third drink. She'd even been smoking, which upset Louise even more. Beth couldn't wait for dinner to be over, to move back into the bar. She'd tried talking to most of the relatives at the table, but was too upset. She simply continued on the vodka, because she knew nothing would get her gone quicker - a pure psychological-binge. In trying to strike out against her mother, she did it in a masochistic way. The gears of spite and revenge in motion, well-lubricated by the vodka.

Beth sat at the bar between Mike and her uncle from Alaska, rarely talking, but drinking the vodka before the ice had a chance to melt. She asked no one in particular, "Am I having a good time yet?" Mike left at midnight, but Beth didn't walk him to the door with her condition. Across the bar, Barb and Uncle Eddie pretended to be 'just good friends.' Beth thought she'd call 'a spade a spade,' since tired of being the only acknowledged 'black sheep' in the family. Barb expected something from the smirk on Beth's mouth, but not what she blurted out. "So, Unk, how's second choice there?" He almost dropped his glass, trying to put it on the bar. "Oh, come on, now," Beth continued, "it's OK, if you tell everybody you're screwing her. Your wife won't find out." It took both of the uncles to get her out to her car, to drive her home.

About five in the morning, the crash woke-up Louise and John. Beth was lying nude at the bottom of the stairs, with arms and legs going all directions into the living room. Before doing anything else, Louise in her propriety need, got a nightgown to dress Beth. Her ignorance of whatever physical damage she may have incurred doing this, was of no concern. She then woke up her visiting brother, who told her to call the fire department. With their arrival and rescue squad, came neighbors. An enterprising soul could have done a bang-up concession business, with the two dozen people Louise had assembled to view the display. Of course, Beth never did anything halfway, so a crowd would've been encouraged Louise. She made coffee.

Beth swayed in and out of consciousness during the whole episode, either from the fall or the vast amount of alcohol she'd consumed. After she'd been taken to the hospital, most of the people stayed to get a closer look, at the nine-inch hole Beth left in the wall at the bottom, where the steps turned into the living room. It was a tremendous force that drove her right elbow into that wall, as if she'd *not* tumbled down the steps, but flew to a crash landing.

Being Sunday, the orthopedic surgeon asked if Monday would be all right for Beth's operation. The wrist was broken in several places, other breaks just above the elbow, but worse triangular breaks in the upper arm. The doctor felt that a metal plate would be necessary to hold the pieces together, beside clearing out the bone fragments, and straightening the muscles and some nerve damage. Beth didn't want to hear any more. She'd really done a *bang-up* job this time. Not only had she almost destroyed her right arm, but the whole episode would be written off as a product of her drunken-frenzy. Her well-laid plans of promoting her poetry book herself dissipated, since she didn't even have a hand to write an autograph with.

Before she could concentrate on her future problems, the pain in her arm was a very present. She called for the nurse, who informed her another hour before the next pain pill. Though usually a high-threshold for pain, tears welled up in her eyes. "It's supposed to be a shot, not a pill. You give me a pill and I'll throw up from the water. I drank vodka, and it doesn't mix with water the morning after." Trying to be funny to forget the pain, she mumbled after the nurse, "My mouth already taste like the bottom of a bird cage, I don't want the aftertaste of vomit, too." An hour later the nurse appeared with the pain pill and water, ten minutes later Beth threw up. It took three nurses to change the bed, and the charge-nurse then gave Beth a shot.

It would be late afternoon before she felt human again. Having to repeat the story each time the phone rang, made the absurdity of it all too painful. Maybe, she learned her lesson about booze, but coping with her mother would take longer. April called after the operation, and Beth asked her to just bring a pad of paper and pen. She planned to practice writing with her left hand.

Being a believer in fate, Beth was sure there'd be a learning experience from the accident. She then questioned the whole validity of it being an accident. The kind of state she was in, she might have attempted-suicide under the guise of drunkenness. Though she always felt above that, being a strong person, the level to which she'd let her mother relentlessly badger her, Beth more than relished the escape of suicide. Consciously with the pain, pure hatred welled-up for Louise, yet subconsciously Beth knew, only one person could be blamed for her problem - herself.

Beth thought back to the year before when Lori contemplated suicide. At first shocked, she felt it was a weakness of character like Sybil, that would do such a thing. In sitting and talking to Lori, telling her how much she had to live for, and no man was worth dying for, Beth realized how battered her psyche was at the time. And, now she knew even a strong person had a fragile-side that got uncovered once in a while. Pretending to have self-esteem seemed to be the expected role for a divorcee. Beth understood that contemplating suicide was not a sign of weakness or insanity, but a point to which someone was driven out of sheer frustration.

She didn't remember all she said to Lori for her to believe her life was valuable with purpose, but now she had to convince herself of those same things. Connie had been on too many drinking binges with Beth to want to believe the suicide theory, but Michael and Lori did believe it. Connie'd, never been on the receiving end of Louise's accusations, insinuations and negative rants. Her castigations reviled them all, as the lowest of despicable people to commit adultery.

Lori's mother, never satisfied with her accomplishments, in a subtle way, let her know what a disappointment she'd been to her parents, most especially after her divorce. For Lori, it was she owed her parents more, because they had adopted her, and given her the advantage of the finer things in life. They never understood that it was love, appreciation and attention that she wanted, not their money, though she accepted it almost for spite.

Michael, on the other hand, knew Louise's wrath directly, as the sweet girl with a halo, to the fallen angel almost over night, with her participation in Mike's divorce. Though neither image was quite correct, in Louise's black and white world, she only saw people the way she wanted. Michael knew how Louise could take the simplest statement or incident, turn it around, so everything or everyone was what she said they were.

Louise was difficult and narrow-minded before the stroke, but after she was erratic, as it truly afflicted her mentally. Once Beth could it into her head that nothing her mother said or did affected her, possibly she'd be alright. She simply had to *'consider the source'* of the statement or action, and remind herself that her mother did not fully know what she was doing. Only other choice, she briefly thought, was to physically remove herself from Louise's presence.

So, onto life after the 'accident,' as she called it. Beth accepted she had at least six months in multiple casts, so adjustments to learn to do everything with her left arm. It'd take time and patience - the time she obviously had, the patience once and for all, had to be learned. Her sense of humor would be her saving grace, and looking for the irony in most everything foremost.

It started with inserting a Tampax with her left hand, and almost going through the ceiling in pain. Slow practice, as it was not quite something, you could ask another to do for you, and she refused to wear a pad. Then shaving her legs, put forth as a comedy routine, when the hair-remover removed more than hair, and so slippery she almost stuck her ass to the floor. But the safety razor made her look like a total-accident victim.

Connie came to pick-up Beth from the hospital, and got there early to help her get dressed. She was learning how to carefully wheel-around the bulky-cast, that went from her fingers to her shoulder. It was sheer frustration to Connie, "I don't believe you, this is unfucking believable!" She slipped off the hospital gown, leaving Beth in all her glory. "Now, how are we going to do this?" she asked, holding Beth's underwear. "You want to hold the arm or put on the underpants?" Beth thought a moment, she knew how far the arm could be moved before it hurt, and Connie'd seen her nude body before.

"I'll hold the arm," Beth slowly responded, started giggling with the thought of the extremes they, put their friendship through.

"Don't start, or we'll be here all day trying to get you dressed." Connie pulled the underpants over Beth's hips.

Beth was bending over so Connie could get her full boobs into the bra. She had to say, "Remember the time we did the nude-boobs for Bobby Ryan's photos?"

Connie too, laughed. "Yea, and when we got drunk and fell off your porch? My God, I'm surprised we haven't had something happen sooner. I hope you've learned regarding vodka."

When Beth got to her parents, her mother planned to make sure she remembered her lesson. Louise had *not* had the hole repaired, and had no intention of doing so. Connie laughed, "Yea, you can hang a wreath around it during Christmas." Louise pretended not to hear her remark, as she'd done so often in the past. The tension was high as she, as subtle as ever, reminded Beth what all *she* was doing for her.

Being around her so much more, Beth observed first hand, how Louise managed to spoil Jeremy, until he'd pout or have tantrums when he didn't get his way. She now tried to make Beth dependent on her. Not being able to drive with her arm, Beth was stuck, until one of her friends came and to rescue her. Only home a few days, she knew she'd have to get away before Louise drove her over the brink again. She had to have enough time away from her, to get her mind cleared completely to handle her mother's constant-manipulative abuse.

Beth almost clung to the wall, as no railing, every time she came down the stairs, with the hole at the bottom waiting to engulf her. She was resting on her bed, when her mother's evil-cat pounced on her, giving her such a start, the pain from jerking her arm, brought tears to her eyes. She had to get out, away from everybody, if only for a few days.

She staggered down the stairs to call her brother Mike. She hadn't even finished explaining, when he offered for her to go out to his farm for a few days. Her nephews wanted to go to a rock concert that weekend, and she'd let them have her car if they took her out to the farm. Beth informed her parents, ignoring their protests about the danger of being there alone. She could think only of the sanity of *being alone*. She threw some clothes in her weekend bag, and some food in a paper bag.

Her nephews turned on the water and electricity, then made sure everything was working before they headed back for the city. They'd be back Sunday evening for her, Beth had three and a half days to sort out her mind and feelings, regarding the whole 'accident' thing. The boys were gone about fifteen minutes, when she realized she'd forgotten to ask them to undo her bra. "Oh well, I guess that'll be the challenge for the evening, and I'll go braless the rest of the time."

She walked all around the farm, and through some of the rows of crops, before she settled on a hillside to watch the magnificent sunset, as it caressed the wide-open hills of the country scene. When she listened to the echo of herself, she turned the FM on, and picked up a magazines to read. She put the cooked steak on her plate, sat at the table, and realized she'd not use a lot of forethought in bringing it.

After several messy tries, Beth figured she could balance the fork with the cast-hand, while she sawed the steak with the left hand. She finish with the knife, reach for the fork, and the cast-hand fell onto the steak, with almost a splash in the juices. After the third adjustment, she laughed, then picked up the steak with her left hand to eat it.

The next day, Beth walked more to explore the fifty-acre farm. She lay on a blanket underneath the giant, old oak tree, listening for the sounds of nature. Once in a while, she heard a jet so very high in the sky, trailing across the clouds. She never felt so infinitesimal, or close to nature and God. With pen in hand, the words of her feelings began to pour onto the paper, as the tears fell from her eyes. All the hurt of others, and her self-inflicted pain, flowed from her body with every drop. She'd not hate her mother for anything she might have done, as Beth understood Louise did what she felt was best for her, in her own warped-controlling way.

Louise wanted Beth to be like her, as she had no understanding of her beliefs or interests, as they were so incomprehensible to her own. As Beth comprehend more, she saw her mother also had difficulty showing her love. And, she often had the same problem showing love to Jeremy, in her fear that he'd be spoiled and weak, like his father. They were both caught in such an ugly-cycle, perhaps Beth could break hers, her mother's probably was indelible.

As all these realizations unfolded one after another, Beth dissolved her anger to look for secondary emotions affecting her. These were the results of her conflicts with herself, and other people about *them* not doing the 'right thing,' as stuck in her own perfectionism. The more she kept opening her mind and her heart, the more awarenesses came to her - it could have been *her neck* that was broken, not her arm. Whether she tripped going to the bathroom or what, she had been flung down the stairs, as she hit nothing until the wall at the bottom. Whatever caused the fall - subconsciously at the last second, she put her arm over her face or forehead. These mixed realizations accepted, she *must* have a purpose, as she lived, albeit with a multi-fractured arm.

Beth was never so happy to be alive in her whole life. There truly was something healing about going back to nature. She felt warmth from the sun, as she rolled back and forth on the grass. Loving life was the first step on her recovery, and a giant step forward to begin loving herself more, no matter what any one else said to her.

She also would work on finding more direction in her life, with a definite goal to work toward, instead of her vague pie-in-the-sky hopes, with not many actions and changes. No matter these setbacks, she'd be determined to do whatever was necessary to find that special person - herself. Then, she'd be able to find a man heading in the same direction of positive change. She'd hit the pits, but could only go up from there. She was that Scorpio-Phoenix-Bird rising again, to create and rebuild herself.

As the number of people getting divorced increased almost exponentially, Beth wondered how many of them went through this search for themselves. Divorce, within itself, was disorienting. That was one thing she could say about marriage, it seemed to have an order, boring but orderly. So, everything and nothing was the same.

One thing she did know and learned was, she'd not fear life or risks, just keep rolling along with the flow - one well-placed foot in front of another. It was OK to feel lonely, as she knew the loneliness would not be forever. It was good for her to get in touch with herself, without somebody else's influence, or trying to fix her. It came to her, rather adamantly, that she'd not be feeling guilty about herself.

* * * * * *

Things were going along fairly well with Mike and Michael, though he was afraid that she'd be worried about this new freedom. But she felt secure in that the future was basically sewed up, with the threads of their love for one another. Not worried about when they'd be together, she knew it would be as soon as his boys were out of school. With great enthusiasm, Mike very neatly laid out the plans for them both. It'd be a while, before Michael understood that no matter how excited he might be at the moment, he merely verbalized his feelings *of the moment,* and two days hence, who knew how they might change and a week after - God ONLY knew.

To this point, she felt unbalanced to where she stood, when she'd repeat his plans, and he'd offer, "Well, that's a few years from now, and you never can tell." Beth had no idea Michael ever felt insecure with Mike. It didn't seem possible if two people loved the way they loved, it simply had to work out. In somewhat of a fantasyland, Michael thought their love could see them through anything. Although, once again, he did not care for her kids, though they were crazy about him. This brought old resentments to her, and not easy to ignore.

Connie, in a sudden decision to make a career change, wanted to take some courses in court-reporting at the college. She'd heard they made fantastic money, and her mother was willing to foot the bill. Michael also thought going for more classes would be good for her, and found a course she liked on the same night, so they rode together. "New Directions for Women," seemed made for her, as it covered women out of high school, who didn't know what they wanted, older women reentering the working world, and open to others wanting a career change. Aptitude Testing to show numerous careers which might be of interest, was first on the agenda. The teacher, very pro-women's lib and assertiveness, gave reading along these lines to back up the classes.

Mike couldn't be bothered by details, and same with Michael, yet she'd do small things for him. Through this course, she began to tire of these 'secretary-things,' she'd been doing for him. With no intentions of taking Barb's place, he greatly balked when she said, "No. Nobody does it for me." Rather than relating it to the course's influence, he felt it was her basic independence and *inconsideration*, which he'd felt exempt to.

With the course also, she became cognizant of how much she'd cut herself off from other people - women or other couples she knew prior. Her excuse at first, related to his night job - 'what could she do attitude,' rather than seeing the reality of things. One of the main people, she realized she'd lost was herself. As Mike became her whole life, she acknowledged the process was *her* doing. But, in her basic insecurity, she could not fathom anyone wanting to become submerged in her life.

Habitually, Mike reinforced the 'insignificance of Michael' feelings. If she wanted to talk about anything serious or 'heavy,' he immediately countered with, "Let's keep this light and airy, alright?" The rare occasions they sat up with his older son Jackie, to talk deeper subjects, her opinions to Mike were far-left. She soon saw a polarity in most things, with only sex being a common-ground. He felt he must follow the rules of society - the 'establishment.'

You did what you were supposed to do, because that was what everyone expected you to do. Yet, Michael knew, deep-down inside he was NOT a 'herd' person, but thought he should be - much from his mother's subliminal diatribes. Michael's constant resistance, and proving the fallacy of these establishment ideals, kept poking holes in his long-created facade. So, if they were horizontal, and not verbalizing, everything was copacetic. The moment feet hit the floor, the arguing began.

His favorite complaint was Michael's attire, or better yet, her lack of it. While she went to great lengths to get him in new and fashionable styles for his management promotion. Opposite, she felt herself as a nonexistent person, so what covered her body didn't matter, as long as clean. With a closet full, Michael only wore jeans and a top. With an immense hate for her body, though not overweight, no reason not to liked it. Contrary, Mike's raved to Beth or anyone who listened. He might not like her mind, but he almost worshipped her body.

The clean, soft skin, always smelled so delicious, plus the supple-breasts and slimly curved legs, were his absolute delight. No man ever savored-himself more in a woman's body, than he did in hers, yet her persona did not change. She clung to her rebel-James

Dean or biker-look to keep her feeling young, and slightly-vain to remain younger-looking. Men's long-sleeved shirts, from Goodwill, Michael rolled up the sleeves and put-up the collar. Clothes held no importance to her, and cut-down on decisions to make on a daily basis. Though for Mike, she twice wore a dress for parties they attended.

Work was the same, she took the non-decision easy-way out. The cleaning jobs, first taken as temporary, were easy, if not a boring way to make several hundred dollars-cash a week, without being tied down. Michael felt she could not spread her wings while tied to Mike, yet she'd not taken any evening career classes, which the new class challenged her to. It also made her acknowledge, she was capable of doing anything she truly wanted. She simply had to get started at it.

A View From the Past

My mind takes me back to the days of old,
when I struggled against the cold,
across the campus bold.

The wind was ripe, with the smell of farmer Brown
feeding his precious ground,
so there was plenty of food to go around.

The sun was falling behind the level plain,
around the golden grain
and bouncing from the window panes.

My mind was wandering even back then,
to a future destination of when,
not knowing what was around the bend.

Nothing came easy, as the wind wasn't at my back
but I seldom missed what I lacked,
yet I never accepted that fact.

Sunrise

When the hopes and dreams
begin to fade with the morning light,
I wonder if I will ever see
the fame which once was promised me.

It is not money or power
for which I claim,
But only that the world
will remember my name.

Chapter 28

Education Versus Learning

There was a new astrology bookstore opening with weekly lectures and discussions that would not only expand April's knowledge, but help her get some depth. Now, a most-welcomed guest, since teaching two astrology classes at the college, and her students would bring much business to the bookstore. Still, not easy for her to push herself every week, to overcome her anxiety of meeting new people, but she did it. She hoped to replace the camaraderie she once so relied on. She went alone and came home alone, though they'd all been friendly and talked to her.

   She had no one to share her self-inflicted plight of loneliness with. Alex had no interest in her life, except general chatter. Heavy conversations were as foreign to him, as they'd been to other men she'd known. Besides, he couldn't comprehend the loss of friendship, since he'd never had any. So, Friday night she'd shower, dress with intention and put on her makeup to go to the lectures. She'd get home around midnight to a quiet house, and delve into her books for solace.

   Closeness of feelings began to spark between April and Gina, the owner of the bookstore. In her wants and needs to again be fulfilled, she began to push for more intimacy. Gina, who liked her, sat down one night to explain the problem with her *wanting and needing* friendships. "April, you have two personalities. You are either all-together, cool and professional, or you're an emotional invalid. I like you, I think you are a good person, but I can't stand your 'needing' that sticks out all over you." Knowing that she, must care to say that, April asked what she should do. "Bury 'needing' April to be the cool and distant, be professional. Be like you don't need anybody, and things will work out, take my word for it." She got the message, and was not hurt, because she knew Gina did her a great favor.

April thought about it at length, and realized whenever she'd been cool, aloof and non-emotional, everything seemed to work out better. Then practiced, she gained the friendship of a student named Lee. She'd given-up her kids with her divorce, so they had a common ground to work from. She was also what April's insecurity felt she lacked, a complete antithesis of herself - an ultra-feminine woman. Lee had great respect for April's astrological knowledge and her interpretations, so felt insignificant in her presence. They balanced each other's need, with Lee holding up a mirror to April, so she'd fully see and acknowledge her true self-worth.

Lee told April to reward herself for her accomplishments on a regular basis. She'd buy Lord and Taylor clothes for her girls, but rarely for herself. Lee suggested she buy something frivolous as a fifteen dollar ashtray, if the beauty of it made her happy, and reminded her of her astrology. The friendship grew, though Lee became jealous of the phantom Beth and Michael, that April constantly talked about. As the tightly held hurt released slowly, the happy memories shared, became a regular part of her conversation. Unfortunately, also some of April's needs began to creep in, so her friendship with Lee began to disintegrate. As well, Lee tried to see April as a mother-figure, so they both needed to pull back to reassess it.

April made friends with another student, Steve, but he'd dated Lee a few times. That added to Lee's jealousy of April's friendship to Steve, which ended their closeness. Though April never admitted it to Lee, she had a brief, but unemotional affair with Steve. Alex told April if she wanted sex, to go out and 'get fucked.' In retaliation, she had a few one-night stands with some students. None of them were anything great, but did help her through some rough spots, on her rocky-road of self-esteem. She and Lee tried to patch-up their differences several times, but the affinity once there was gone.

Beth told April, shortly after she married Alex she would have left Alex as soon as she found out about his experience in Viet Nam. Most men who fought there, couldn't wait to finish their one year tour of duty. Alex, signed up for a second tour, as he'd been a helicopter-gunner, which was a perilous position. He told April, with apparent pride, that when shooting at the enemy, he'd rather shoot them in the groin to maim them, instead of direct hits to kill. When April did Alex's astrology chart, to her horror his Mercury - the mind - was in the same house and degree as that of Hitler's.

Alex therefore, had a great a sense of power and satisfaction from inflicting pain on those he felt beneath him. So, while going through all of her loneliness and friendship problems, she was still under the threat of actual, physical violence, that he reigned over her and her daughters. When she threaten to call the police again, he struck the future fear of his promise to burn the house down around them. April did not have the greatest faith in the court system of being able to put him away permanently, and their lives were on the constant edge of fear.

Most of April's beatings came from her voicing resentment about the lack of sex she received, while he openly-masturbated in front her. Her older daughter followed her footsteps of being vocal on her opinions, and was the object of his regular physical abuse. More than once, April placed her body between Alex's fist and her daughter. Her younger daughter was shy and demure, so only received the other side of his feelings. Yet, still a witness to the happenings around her, and sometimes got hurt being in the firing-line.

The sound of silence became a game, which they all played, to keep the volatile situation down to a minimum. April eventually turned her emotional and sexual feelings for him completely off. She again perpetuated the semblance of rigidness, as she had to Wally at the end of their marriage. Also, never help from her father, since he'd gotten Alex into the iron workers union at her request to buy the house, and felt a man bringing home a big check made up for anything else.

The only benefit April had from not having her time or emotions taken up with an active friendship or marriage, was her astrology career growing in leaps and bounds. On the go all the time - lecturing, workshops - either leading them or participating, private students and teaching more classes at the college, April built a wide circle of professional friendships. They didn't have much depth, but filled what she needed as to always having someone around to talk to, or be on the phone with. Her success was keeping it professionally-cool and never personal. None of them had any knowledge of her vacillating home situation, but Alex was still enthusiastic about her career, so welcomed her students and clients.

* * * * * *

Beth was in desperate need of a job, with only the cooking class having enough women signed up for her to lecture. Her broken arm, of course, slowed down planned promotion of her poetry book. She had as usual, expected fireworks, but the response was slightly more than lukewarm. Lori and Marie drove her around to some of the local independent book stores, and it didn't take long for her to see that she wasn't the first to print her own poems, and there were better produced books. Though her friends helped, buying extra copies of the book to give to others, it wasn't the fantasy of being discovered that she expected or hoped for.

 As she became depressed about the non-success of her writing, she tried not to ignore the compliments that she received from a much wider range of people, than she thought would be interested. Beth wasn't writing just for women of divorce, but she was surprised when some very, married housewives said they often felt the same way, though never able to put words to those feelings. From young never-been-married singles to retired women, and even a few men being honest, told Beth what her poems meant to them.

 Even a friend of Mike's, who'd never taken anything seriously, gave her a compliment, left-handed, but still good. "The first time I read it, I thought it was real dumb, then one night when I was drunk I read it again. And, I realized how true it was about my own life." The high point came from Lori's friend, the school district superintendent. As part of his annual address to the several hundred teachers of the district, he read her opening poem.

 None of the compliments brought more than a few dollars to Beth, as the sales of the book barely went over one hundred. She'd accepted that fame and notoriety passed over her, so she needed to be realistic about future poetry writing. Right now, though she needed a job to carry her through. She only received her weekly child support, which she turned over to her parents for room and board. She was wiped out financially, what the printing of the book hadn't taken, she spent on medical bills over and above her insurance, with more coming in.

Beth sat in Connie's apartment while she scrutinized the want ads for something that Beth could do, while her arm still in a cast. "Here's one," Connie exclaimed, "phone work, no sales, part-time, work your own hours from eight in the morning till eight at night, six dollars an hour to start. It's right here in town. You can answer a telephone and talk can't you?" She sat there drinking, starring at Beth.

"I won't do phone-sales, " Beth insisted.

"This isn't phone-sales. Call the number and see, ask for Mrs. Martin." Beth didn't want it, but Connie was already dialing the number, and asking for Mrs. Martin. Hesitantly, Beth spoke to the woman, and made an appointment to see her the next day. She did get a job description which was sorting, filing and manning the phones for a collection agency.

When she hung up, Beth complained, "Oh, Connie, how could you do this to me? I mean, a collection agency, that's the pits!" The reality of her life really sucked.

"Beth you've got to have a job, and this is better than nothing. I mean you're not exactly the prime example of the most-wanted employee." She always knew how to put it right on the line. "You remember last year, when Cam quit his job to go with that new company, and then it folded, well he thought he'd sunk to about his lowest, when a car salesman. It's not forever, you know. He lived through the next three months, though I thought I was going to kill him, he complained and whined so much. You'll be out of that cast in another month or so, then you can get yourself a real good job." She was being supportive.

"But Connie, you don't understand. I don't want a job. I want a career. I'm a writer, a creative, intelligent person. I don't want to waste my talents in some job." She said it, and Connie glared at her.

"You think you're so damn great, or better than we are? Well, what the fuck? I don't see anybody lined up wanting to pay you money for all your smarts and talent. So don't go to the interview, just stay a broke, in-debt writer because you don't want to lower yourself to join us peons, who work for a living. I think you've been hanging around Lori too much, and she's been filling you with all this creative-garbage. Well, you better start taking money from the men you fuck then, like she does. Come to think of it, you even think you're too good for any of the men you used to go to bed with. Well, I hate to burst your bubble, but you ain't such a great prize!"

"Connie, you're not being fair. And, that's not right what you say about Lori. Ted helps her out financially, because he knows she is struggling to get her lecturing business going . . ."

"RREEALLLY!? Beth, there's only one name for it, and it's as old as the hills - call a spade a spade. Give me a break!" She shook her head, and took a swallow of her drink.

"We're talking about me, and you're right. I can't get a super job because I don't have a degree, and having a few poems printed does not make me Emily Dickinson. I guess I haven't been able to accept my current fate. It's just, I was expecting so much from the book, and the lecture series." Beth paused to collect herself. "I'll go to the interview, and I'll take the job and I'll accept it the best I can. You know that was a cheap shot about men. You know I've lost a few pounds I gained, and I'd love to find a man, but I won't go back to one-nighters or marrieds."

"Listen, I'm sorry, but you need someone to break your rose-colored glasses. You have been tough to swallow sometimes, since you quit cleaning. I'm not saying for you to go back to those men, but I have a feeling Lori wouldn't even date a guy who didn't have a degree or make twenty-five thousand dollars a year, and I think she's made you categorize men the same way."

Beth laughed, "Why do you pick on Lori so?"

"She makes me feel like she's patronizing you, and looking down on us because we're cleaning ladies."

"That's not true, and not fair that you feel that way. Besides, Cam has a degree and makes over twenty-five thousand dollars a year. I bet there are very few, if any, of the men you guys hang around with that don't." Beth got up to leave, "I'll make it yet. I might go down a few streets the wrong way or dead ends, but I'll find something yet. By the way, you were right, I do think you are too good to be wasting yourself as a cleaning lady. I was, you are and so is Michael." She gave Connie a hug, "Thanks for the help, and I do mean it."

The tears came again, as Beth got into her car to drive home. She cried so much the past few months, she wondered what, if anything, they helped. Later that night, she was up reading a book about Dorothy Parker. Since two of her older customers, who bought copies of her poetry book told her, that her work reminded them of Dorothy Parker's, she'd read her complete works, and now a book about her.

Beth felt vibes, this woman had been through more struggles, than she knew existed. She thought Dorothy Parker was one of those story-book cases, of one day stumbling into Vanity Fair, and the next writing all her witty, clever words with the world applauding at her feet. Surprised to learn Dorothy was in her thirties, before any of her poems were published. She went over some of Dorothy's simpler poems, and could see some of the resemblance, but she'd never dare to compare herself to the great Dorothy Parker. She dreamed of the height she accomplished, at a time women struggled to achieve success in any field.

Beth stretched out on her single bed, with her head at the foot, so she could have the greatest benefit of the light from her desk. There was a soft, deep laugh. She looked up to see the small figure, of a dark-haired woman sitting in her chair smoking a cigarette. A cold chill went down Beth's spine, as the apparition began to speak.

"So, Kid, you think you've had it rough. Ha! You haven't seen nothing yet. And, that's the only way you're going to get the character to write. You gotta suffer, to enjoy the good. You have to experience all the emotions, to write the way you want to. Yea, you're good, but you're not great yet. Are you going to make it? Well, I'll leave it up to you. If you can take the struggles, and the setbacks, we'll see."

Beth bravely asked, "Am I going in the right direction?"

"Yea, you'll make a few wrong turns, but you gotta wanna make it." Before Beth could ask anymore questions to the spectrality, it dissolved away, as quietly as she'd come. It was two-thirty in the morning and Beth thought to herself, if she'd dreamed it all, that still didn't make the advice unacceptable. Everyone said that the poetry she'd written since the accident took leaps and bounds in depth and meaning, over what she wrote before. She'd not take this visit lightly from Dorothy Parker, whether it was a figment of her imagination or not. Beth told herself that she'd keep on pursuing, believing and not feel sorry for herself that success eluded her. Funny though, she could still smell that strong, cigarette smoke.

They were off to night school, Connie taking the court-reporting and Michael back in another women's awareness course and Beth with writing and psychology. Even Marie braved Howard 's repercussions and her daughters complaining, to return to fashion design, her first love. Beth's satire writing course took her beyond any prior expectations. Connie became diligent doing her homework practice, and Michael very surprised how well she fit into the awareness group.

Several women revered Michael, as an independent-pioneer and free thinker. These were women on their own, either widowed, divorced or separated. Even a forty-five year old, though married, wanted to do something with her life, since her children were grown and gone. To them, Michael was a veteran, but she honestly admitted she needed guidance, too. And, first to acknowledge she did not have the answers, or even understand all the questions.

But listening to how those women struggled with what Michael considered everyday problems, reminded her how far she had come on her own. The books the instructor had them reading were opening up her eyes, ears and mouth, too. She saw she'd allowed Mike to govern too much of her life, from strictly his preference. Now, voicing more independence, and not always home for his call, or being taken for granted to agree to every plan he had.

Unfortunately, as Michael expanded her horizon, Connie limited hers. She felt after the fourth lesson, she wasn't grabbing onto the knack of the court-reporter. She gave up, while she could still get her money refunded. Beth encouraged her to try a few more weeks, but she said it made her nervous to not be able to compete with others.

Beth on the other hand, found a teacher that not only encouraged her, but was willing to help her expand herself. The last one in the cinema writing class, expected perfection out of her, because of her age and experience. He'd compliment her on the one hand, by quoting her poetry to her, and then turned around crossed out an "A," giving her a "B," because he felt she was capable of doing so much better. He'd been pure frustration.

In the satire class, Bill, the teacher divided the class in half, to do a radio show on the college station. It could be a take-off on any show they wanted, and he put Beth in charge of producing and directing her side. What she decided on, was a jocular-version of a news show, complete with commercials, and herself doing zany-interviews as a character she created - "Ms. Kitty Litter, Hollywood Reporter."

Bill later worked with Beth, to have a joint-poetry reading between the college and the writers' club. It was during this time, Beth decided if she really pushed herself, she could take several courses, and get her associates degree. Because of working part-time in 1976, she also qualify for a student grant, which financially enabled her to go to school full-time. She became so excited, with something big to work towards.

The job at the collection agency was not as bad as Beth imagined, but she still felt it a real come-down. Though the other ladies there were very nice to her, she tried to do the job the best she could, and go home to work on her writing. As with almost everything Beth did, she just wanted to get it done, so the time passed to moved on to whatever was next.

It took six weeks for her grant to come through, and she had all the classes picked out. She simply wanted to get on with it, and get it over with. It seemed like her whole life really dragged lately. She came in from work to find her mother sitting with Auntie Adele - Mary's mother from next store - and her poetry book in from of her. She smiled up at Beth, "Your mother was just telling me how much she helped you with your book, that's really wonderful. I'm sure she's really proud of you." Beth shot a look at her mother, *'how could she lie about her book?'* when she understood nothing about her or her writing. No point to say a word, she smiled and went to her room.

The winter was depressing and cold, as the weather broke-records for the most days below freezing. Her arm, even with the physical therapy, was constantly sore from the bitter, frigid-cold. The doctor said she was developing arthritis, and it would only get worse if she stayed in Chicago's damp, cold climate. Everything was a drudge, and everything was the same day after day. The only excitement that weary January, was celebrating her artist friend, Anne's divorce. It took three-long, dreadful years, but she at last got it over with, and kept her sanity. Beth brought Marie to the party for encouragement, as they dressed in their best, and gave Anne a divorce congratulations card with a bottle of Cordon Bleu to do her own private celebrating. Anne brought more meaning to 'chic,' as she filled her house with the many artist and writer friends.

At last, the notice came for Beth to check at the college financial office. Her anticipation level at one hundred percent, she froze in her tracks when the girl at the desk said there'd been a computer glitch, and she'd not be getting the loan. The counselor told her the college loan program-funds had not been extended, and they ran out of money, two names before hers. She knew she couldn't say a word, because she'd break-down sobbing. Somehow there wasn't any consolation, knowing that she was not alone in losing. For one fleeting moment, she hated everyone connected with the government. She knew it was all to no avail, as she sat in her car crying and writing a letter to the President, letting him know that bombs and weapons were more important than a college education for somebody struggling to get ahead.

Beth wanted to run away, as her life was going no place - fast. Every time she tried to expand herself, her *great-laid plans* fizzled-out. She went to her sister Marie's for tea, sympathy and to make new plans. Marie's house was on the way to Beth's job, and she'd been stoping in on Marie's days off to talk. Since at last, planning on divorcing Howard, many conversations could not be done over the phone, or in front of their mother. Marie was going to visit her close friend, Fran, living in Oklahoma City, on quarter break, which was the following week. When Fran was back in Elwood the past fall, for their twenty-fifth high school reunion, she and Beth got into several discussions about where Beth was going with her writing.

Fran, a LVN-nurse, had several friends who were in the advertising business. She'd gone on and on about the jobs Beth could get in Oklahoma. Maybe that was the answer - start over in a new state, where maybe competition wouldn't be so tough, and not having a degree wouldn't be such a drawback. Fran sure made it sound easy, and the weather was much drier and warmer for her arm, too

Beth sipped the herbal tea, "So, I guess I'll move on to Plan B or Plan Z, considering all the failures I've had the last - how long? My whole life?"

"Oh, Beth," Marie sneered, "so dramatic. You've had more accomplishments than me."

"Sorry, Sweetheart, that's not saying much! Anyway, I thought we could drive down to Oklahoma, then we'd have a car, and we can both check out jobs. If it looks promising, I'll stay to get settled, before Jeremy joins me when he finishes school. He needs to get away from Bruce and mother. Then, when you get the divorce and move down there, I can ship all my stuff with yours. I'll take enough clothes to last awhile, and whatever other necessities."

Michael and Connie, of course, did not have Marie's enthusiasm of Beth's moving to Oklahoma City. Marie hoped to have as many familiar-faces around her there, as she could. Connie reminded Beth, she was moving off to someplace she'd never visited, with no real guarantee of a job. Not be put off, she was going, and she didn't want Connie with her logic.

Difficult for Beth to say goodbye to Jeremy, then eight. They had long talks while she packed, but Beth was afraid he wouldn't understand, she was doing it for both of them. She tried to explain to Jeremy, her need to make it on her own, without her parents pulling the strings. Independence for both of them, reminding him to be independent. She'd seen it eroded by Louise and Bruce, and countering them, she sometimes got too strict. Beth told herself, as well him, it was the best thing for them both.

She held Jeremy close, as she as she calmly spoke, "I can't be everything to you. I can only be your mother, and in order for me to be the best mother I can be, I have to do some things that are best for me. That way, as I get better . . . happier, I can be a better mother for you. We will both benefit." She held him at arm's length, and looked him straight in the eye. "Someday, you will understand. I do everything because I love you, and that will never change." Jeremy wiped away his tears, and nodded.

"I love you, too, Mom." He stood straight and tall, making her feel so proud of him. One last hug and kiss, she sent him off to school. She got into the car to leave the home, she'd spent almost her whole life in. As she pulled out of the driveway, Louise and John came out onto the sidewalk for one last wave goodbye. Funny, how through her tears, the house seemed so much smaller, and her parents not at all domineering.

Almost Always Counts

To attempt the climb, but not make it -
lessens neither the mountain nor the climber.
The mountain will always be there,
and the climber better prepared.

To attempt love -
and be alone in your falling
does not break the fall,
or lessen the love.

The hope of love
shall always be there,
not as an impossible dream,
but the practical illusion that it is.

To attempt life,
is to live every day to its fullest.
For only existing,
is not really trying.

Almost always counts in life,
for we are not perfect, nor is the world.
Experience is the reward,
and the force makes us keep going.

CHAPTER 29

Your Basic Farmer's Daughter

Once upon a time, there was a very young, very sweet - like saccharin - country girl - your basic farmer's daughter. She came to the big city to further her education. She met a struggling, young man who *seemed* as honest and hard working as she was. They soon married, and as expected, she gave up her education to work, so he'd have an easier time of finishing his. Once he became a rising young executive, they promptly had three kids - a latter *unexpected* fourth - and settled into a Chicago-suburban tract-house. As known, Suburbia has been hermetically-sealed, and insulated against any woes that befall the big city, and those city folks.

Some say, a curse from the 'Wicked Witch of the West,' put a crack in the seal that let the ill-wind blow in, and happiness slipped-out. While her youngest, barely a toddler, her husband left for a less responsible life, with a girl from the secretarial-pool. After the initial shock wore off, our heroine realized it wasn't from something she ate or temporary-insanity, so pulled herself-up by the proverbial, 'Chicago boot-straps,' and went on, as the 'sun would rise tomorrow.'

At times, she tried to examine herself and what went wrong, since under the auspices protected by living in Suburbia. She'd done everything right, she'd won the 'Good Housekeeping Seal of Approval' three years running, the Betty Crocker Award in 1959, 1962, and 1965. She faithfully attended all neighbor's Tupperware parties, and had regular visits from her Avon Lady. Just everything the good suburbanite-housewife should do, including never sweating in the noon-day sun, in the middle of July or getting a speck of dirt on her, when wearing white.

She held everything together with white-knuckles showing - devoting her life to her children, by working sometimes two jobs for ten years, and watched her ex-husband go through his third marriage. After that, she decided to be selfish and take some time for herself. Through the marriage, divorce and struggling, her best friend-neighbor and her husband stood by her side. The husband was *there* when a pipe needed fixing, or furnace repaired, or bigger jobs that somehow could not be repaired *alone*. She hesitated to ask, though he *insisted* on helping, however he could to save her money, *too*.

So, when ready to get involved with men, it was not her ex-husband's image she measured her dates up against. Not until Cathy suddenly married a man six-foot-four, big build, with dark brown hair and dark eyes, everyone got a clue it might be Mike Cordeau, she wanted to duplicate. He'd been divorced a few months himself, *after* Cathy married the clone. She never wished Barbara the divorce, but when Mike was free, naturally after all those years she expected *them* to finally be together. He'd done *so much more*, than just repair the furnace for her.

The 'instant' love between Michael and Mike was too much to swallow. And, no matter how seemingly-perfect some clones were, they're not the real thing. So, Cathy accepted she couldn't make a *frog* into the prince-charming she wanted, admitted the mistake and got a divorce. Now, available for Mike, when he came to his senses, and was ready for a real-woman of his age, that truly *knew* what he offered, *they'd* live happily, ever after.

Michael planned to go to New Orleans with her mother and Connie. They'd be staying with her brother, Web, who now lived there. They may as well go for Mardi Gras, which was the middle of February in 1977. This, unfortunately, coincided with Mike's birthday - not just any birthday, but his *fortieth*.

Michael spent the past birthday with Mike, while Barb was still there, and he'd not made a big deal about it, so she didn't think he'd be upset for her to miss it for Mardi Gras. She had her thirtieth birthday last year, and no body made a big deal about it. So, she was off to New Orleans to party, while Mike went to the farm with his boys to sulk being by himself at such a monumental occasion. To him, she seemed again, not to care about his feelings, only herself.

Sitting with his morning coffee, enjoying the snowy-view of his farm, a familiar car pulled in - Cathy, with a couple of her kids and a birthday cake. Since her son was best friends with Jackie and Jason, it was easy to know the comings and goings of Mike. She knew her trip to the farm would not be questioned, since she'd been a welcomed guest for years. Practically-part of the family, her *divorced, lonely* years Louise and John invited her over as part of their family dinners. (Michael wasn't the originator of the *'friend of the family'* ploy.) Of course, Cathy remembered his *fortieth* birthday, and came to celebrate it with the kids, *all weekend*.

Little did Michael know, while running around with Mardi Gras craziness, Cathy started building onto a cornerstone, she and Mike *laid* many years before. Without saying a word, her *responsibility, sereneness and organized, competent actions,* Cathy removed - kicked aside - the few stones that Michael put in place, to support the sand that held her and Mike together.

* * * * * *

The middle of March, Oklahoma City was green, and blooming-colors everywhere. The weather mild and breezy, so Beth could see no reason why she wouldn't like Oklahoma City. When Fran came home that first evening, she gave Beth the first reason not to. "Well, you're two days late for the job in the advertising department, but it involved a lot of travel, so maybe that's for the best. Tomorrow I'll call a few friends, and see what they come up with. My neighbor that was with one of the biggest agencies, transferred to Tulsa last December, but don't worry, there will be something for both of you."

Beth's heart sank, as she watched Fran bubble-around, so excited they both came to visit. She tried to gather some of Fran's optimism, but she didn't know how many disappointments she could handle. And, her pride wasn't going to let her go back to Chicago with her tail-between-her-legs. Fran insisted on Marie and Beth staying in a motel, at her expense, because her son unexpectedly moved back in with her and her husband, Mac. It was generosity that was very rare, as far as Beth was concerned, yet Marie took it all for granted, since Fran always treated her like a queen, whenever she visited.

Marie's vacation time was up, and it seemed she spent more time on her pre-occupation of looking at houses, than seriously looking for jobs. She got a vague promise, in a job with a fashionable department store, while Beth got nothing. One after another of Fran's leads dead-ended. Even when her sister Rose, gave Beth a contact at the television station, it went nowhere. But Fran and Mac wanted Beth to stay, to help her find a job. Marie flew back to Chicago, and Beth concentrated on the job market. "Surely," Fran optimistically replied, "with your experience and qualifications, you'll have one before the week is over."

The last week of April, Beth was out of money, even the two hundred her father sent, and out of hope. She'd been on one wild-goose-chase after another. Most jobs she was 'over qualified' in their terms, since she had owned her own business, and the better jobs didn't like the fact that it'd been eight years since she worked in an office. There were a couple of good jobs - one starting at fifteen thousand a year - she was a contender for, but came out second and third when they went for the people with degrees. She accepted the fact, if she didn't have a job by the end of the week, she'd go back to Chicago. The grand notion of starting over a certified-flop.

No matter what Beth had done for others, it was difficult for her to accept what Fran and Mac were doing for her. Almost six weeks she'd been there, and though at first when she had money, she'd buy some groceries. Now, she felt like receiving charity, though Mac reassured her she was great company for Fran. She cleaned and cooked dinner everyday, when she returned from job interviews, but she felt it was such a small thing to do for them.

So not to intrude on their lives, as they never knew when their son would be there, Beth stayed in their camper, Mac put-up in the garage. Beth lay in the bunk-bed after they'd gone to work, and wondered what the hell she was doing there, and who was she kidding? Even the low paying jobs didn't want her, as they figured she'd only stay till she got a better one. She felt so lonely and afraid of life. She remembered a man telling her, he never met someone so compassionate, yet lacking in humility, as her.

"Well, he should see me now, in my humble-abode without money, or a job. I don't know how much more humble I can get. 'If only my friends could see me now' - The Grand and Glorious Writer - waiting to be discovered, in the camper parked in her friends' garage, in the illustrious-Oklahoma City! Boy, they'd laugh their asses off." She pulled herself together, and rolled off the bunk to take her shower, and called the employment agency, *again*. She walked past the mirror without looking, not wanting to see what a failure looked like.

Beth finished with the want ads, when the agency called back with an interview for a one-girl office job. She didn't bother with the details, as she took down the address. They were doing repairs on the Interstate, so decided to drive across town, as the job was in the industrial-southeast, and her coming from the northwest. Still miles from the address, stopped at a traffic light, Beth noticed smoke coming out from under her left tire. She immediately pulled into the service station, not paying attention that it was a Black neighborhood. So frustrated, she could've screamed when the nice owner told her she needed a brake-job, but he could do it later that day.

"I have a job interview in thirty-five minutes, that I can't tell you how desperate I am to make. Now, I can borrow the money for the brake-job from the friends I'm staying with, but there no point in fixing the car if I don't get a job. I've been here six weeks, and I can't begin to explain to you all the things that have gone wrong." Beth knew she was whining, but she'd held it in for so long. Sometimes it was easier to complain to a complete stranger. She prided herself on her independence, and not needing other people, but somehow since coming there, one person after another helped her in one way or another, that she truly never expected.

The man smiled, trying not to chuckle. "Take it easy, no problem. Sonny, take my car and drive this lady to her job interview, and bring her back." Beth had not noticed that several men stepped out into the parking area, checking-out the loud, blonde, white woman.

Beth was jubilant. "Oh, my God, thank you. I mean, so kind of you. I'll give you a check for half when I get back. It's an out-of-state check, but it's good. Thank you, really." All her honesty, her accent, as well pulling into a station, in a Black neighborhood, he knew she wasn't from around there, and just kept smiling. The young, Black man, named Sonny, came driving up in a *red, Corvette convertible.* She barely shut the door, when he whizzed off with her.

They eventually found the large pipe-yard, and Beth dashed inside the portable-building, hoping she was in the right place. Quite a few men worked around the yard, which looked like still getting set-up. Inside the building a young, good looking man with dark, curly hair was on the phone. When he told her she was at the right place, she ran out to tell Sonny, while Terry, the boss, finished his phone conversation. Out of all Beth's interviews, this was the strangest.

Terry was obviously in desperate need of organization - he didn't even have an application for her to fill out. They talked - her telling him what she could do, and he spelling out his requirements. They quibbled about money, but Beth relented to five hundred and fifty per month, with a raise within a month, if she did well.

"What about the placement fee?" Terry asked.

Beth hadn't thought of it because in Chicago, the employer always paid, but in Oklahoma it was mixed. "I'll split it with you," she volunteered to have it done with.

"OK. How soon do you want to start?" He watched her closely, feeling her desperation.

"Now is fine with me." When he nodded agreement, she added, "Then I'll let my ride go, and see about getting a ride later to pick up my car."

"No problem, I'll take you." Terry said as he got up to follow her to the door. He watched as she went out to thank Sonny, and told him to tell his boss she'd pick up the car later. Sonny quickly whizzed back out of the pipe-yard. As Beth walked back to the building, about a half-dozen men had watched the whole scene. Apparently, they didn't see many young, Black men driving around blonde, white women in a Corvette. "Is that your boyfriend?" Terry asked.

Beth got busy straightening out what she could. Back to business, so very organized, and it was good to have a job. Though Robert Ringer wouldn't be proud of her, as she misused the whole point in his book - *Winning Through Intimidation*, but he'd never met Terry. There's definitely a difference between showing up hungry, and being desperate, she *was* the latter. When she left the advertising agency over ten years before, she was making the same salary she'd accepted. The cost of living *was* lower in Oklahoma City, but ten years behind Chicago was ridiculous. Still, it'd been that long since having an office job. Her skills were rusty, but she had the know-how.

When she finished totaling the tallies, she gave Fran a quick call. As usual, she could only talk a minute, but she said they'd go out and celebrate. The job had many drawbacks, including the lack of restroom facilities - only port-a-potties - but no problem would be insurmountable, now that Beth had a job. She'd make a go of it in OKC, and soon have her own apartment, and Jeremy joining her. She could take the trailer living, knowing it'd only be a matter of time before being out. Fran and Mac did so much for her, she could never begin to repay them. Fran again reminded her how much she'd helped others, so her turn now.

The apartment Rose helped Beth find seemed perfect and reasonable. Beth spent more time with Rose, as Fran was on a leave-of-absence from work-exhaustion. She put too much of herself into her nursing, and warned Beth was heading for the same thing. Taking all the overtime she could get, her nice apartment filled with everything borrowed: daybed, couch, lamp and a folding table in the dining room. They'd got together to loan her the basics to live, since her kitchen stuff were packed, waiting in Elmwood. Beth hoped to get it all replaced by new before Jeremy came.

Established with a job, and a two bedroom apartment, Beth started the ball-rolling on the legalities to get Jeremy moved down with her. The night before she left Elmwood, she met Lou, (her last attorney - now judge) for a few drinks and talk. Though, since last summer he told her, he felt for her the same way she did about him, they never got together. After the fall election, and he hadn't gotten the new office, he stayed on with his wife. He was not strong *enough* yet, to leave her. His fear of what it might do to his political life, made him hesitant. Beth's leaving, they only had a few clandestine-meetings, that *never* got beyond raising temperatures.

But Lou had always been good for her ego, as a great fan of her writing, especially her poetry. At one of their writers' meetings he had a story idea that he could use his legal experience. Beth loved it, and quickly showed him how to expand it into a novel, with a bigger audience. They laughed that she could write it, and he'd be her legal advisor on it, but he was not a 'doer.'

"Besides saying goodbye, I wanted to ask, how you'd suggest I handle moving Jeremy out of state, without Bruce throwing a leg-out?" She loved how they cuddled so easily.

Lou softly rubbed the back of Beth's hand. "We could have been really great together."

"I know . . . and maybe we will," she paused. "You were the one who never took the initiative . . . you were afraid she'd catch us. Beside I wasn't going to push you, she bosses you enough." She sipped her drink. "You do occasionally have to go to Springfield, I could meet you in St Louis, Lou," she chimed, giggling.

"Don't laugh at me," he teased, and kept kissing her cheek.

"I'm not laughing at you, but you forget, I've been through this married-man syndrome before." She lowered her voice, "And, you turn them upside-down, and they're all the same, a chicken." She laughed and he snickered. Lou then explained the necessary steps and information she needed to send to the court, to get its permission to move Jeremy out of state. Though he could not handle the paperwork for her, or advise her directly, he felt she'd be able to do it on her own.

Beth was in the midst of typing the letter, when Mac called to say she'd gotten a registered-letter at their house. She didn't have to open it to know the contents. School was almost out, and Louise obviously touted to Bruce she and Jeremy would soon be leaving for Oklahoma City. He got the jump on Beth, and what could have been settled with a few phone calls or letters without attorneys, would now be a court battle. ". . . and I really need the aggravation and expense," Beth said, when she hung up the telephone.

My Son

My son is eight going on forty-three,
but that's the way I raised him,
and that's the way I want him to be.

I felt like it was just the two of us,
from his first inception;
I tried to say there was love,
but the world wouldn't be holding a reception.

Independence was what I pushed,
he wasn't going to be a mother's son.
Sometimes, maybe, I went too far.
I might have lost a few battles,
but I think the war was won.

I always talked to him like an adult -
he has understanding beyond his years.
He has learned so much other children won't,
but then he has big ears.

We are good friends, so promises are kept
and lies are not told.
I ask his advice now,
and know he'll be there when I am old.

CHAPTER 30

The Judgment & the Judge

Beth got Scott, her girlfriend Caren's husband to be her attorney for the child custody case, and the date was set for the first of July. It worked out for taking several days off, to visit everyone while back in Chicago. Beth'd made Caren the group's beautician, so was always up to date on what everyone was doing. Though Beth four years older, they'd been childhood friends - her parents living across the street from Beth's. Also, Caren had a son only four months after Jeremy, and they'd been close, she'd frequently been Caren's hair-model for the big shows in Chicago.

Apparently, Bruce was not interested in total custody, he simply didn't want Jeremy to be moved out of state. For his convenience, he thought Jeremy should stay with Beth's parents, so everything remained the same for him. Beth was confident the court would see her parents were too old and not in good health to have permanent custody. Also, Bruce did little for or with Jeremy in the five years they'd been divorced. She'd been gone four months, and though she wasn't some rising copy-writer in an ad agency, she wasn't doing so badly for herself. She got two raises, and the job was a terrific challenge since she knew absolutely nothing about oil pipes before hand. Besides, she hoped yet of some career-breaking chance.

Rose was the co-director of the OKC branch of a national action group, sponsored by the CBS-TV affiliate there. They needed new TV-spots written, and the station didn't have the extra time to work on them. Rose had the idea, if Beth wrote the spots, maybe she could promote them, and if accepted, she could do the voice-overs - as she'd done them for the ad agency. It might be the start of something. Beth had the knack of talking with different dialects, and intonations, so she sounded better than many of the local commercials, whose quality was that of the fifties. She wrote the four - thirty-second spots, which everybody thought were clever. But Patti, the co-director with Rose, worked with the station adjutant, and just wasn't promoting them or Beth.

Rose didn't know why, and she didn't feel she could push Patti on it. Still, she'd opened up some doors for Beth, though no jobs available at the station, but Rose tried to drop her name as often as possible. She did get another volunteer group interested in having Beth do public relations work for them, but not much money. At least a small toe-hold in the door, Beth found more reason than her job and her arm for moving to OKC, to convince the court in her favor.

Lori picked Beth up from the airport that rainy night. The flight seemed forever with the bad weather, and O'Hare's traffic kept them circling. They embraced, "You got your hair cut, I like it." Lori had a broad, positive smile on her face.

"Oh, you know me, I used to change my hair as often as I changed men, now I just change my hair. I like yours, too - a little lighter and curlier?" She was happy to see her.

"Thanks, Caren gave me a casual-perm, she said it'd loosen up." She watched the traffic.

Beth laughed, "I hope we all do when this is over." She didn't miss the heavy traffic.

Lori'd been steadfast in her phoning and letters encouraging Beth in her efforts. She now knew that her leaving was a good thing for her, too. Before she left, once again, she'd worked up a promotion for Lori to lecture on King Tut's Treasures, that were soon to arrive in Chicago. As she came to rely on Lori's praise and enthusiasm for her creativeness, so Lori also responded to her, as a sounding board for her new ideas, and belief that Lori could make a career with her lecturing business. But Beth knew, she could not grow in someone else's shadow, and Lori'd never completely believe in herself until she succeeded alone. A difficult part of Beth's leaving, because there was the chance that Lori'd fail, and she never wanted to see that happen. Yet, the time came in order for them both to grow to their potential, they must be on their own.

On the other hand, Beth knew the time passed for Michael and Connie to have their mutual-daily-assurances from her, as they had each other more than ever. Besides, living across the hall, they shared most of their jobs, so only missed Beth, not really needed her. It became the same with her to them, talking or sharing her poems, but they weren't into bolstering her ego, or other creative efforts. They weren't geared the same as Lori, nor the real interest. Connie didn't like to 'blow any air into anyone's pipe-dream,' and believed she'd never know anyone who became famous - other than Bobby Ryan, of course. As for Michael, she'd always told Beth that 'she expected too much from everyone and everything, and that's why she was often disappointed.' Beth learned to take one day at a time, and tried not to make too many future plans.

April still needed Beth, and called on a regular basis to tell her absolute mundane things that were going on, as if Beth were in a foreign country, not just OKC. She called sobbing that Elvis died, and didn't understand why Beth wasn't more upset. She wore Beth out, and definitely tired her of the whole life April insisted on living, so Beth rarely gave any suggestions on anything. She knew when it got bad enough, April'd leave, and she hoped she'd soon find the strength to divorce Alex to make it on her own. She wouldn't acknowledge the delaying affect it had on her girls. Through talking to Michael, April's time was entirely buried in astrology and teaching. Michael was closer and more sympathetic than Beth.

Happy to be surrounded with friends and loved ones, as Beth'd been such a nervous wreck the past few weeks over the prospect of what might happen in court. "I don't know Lori, somehow I have a feeling Bruce is going to pull some shot. I'm glad you're going to be my character witness, if I need one." They were coming into Beth's parent's old neighborhood.

"Beth, I can't believe any judge would be cruel and dumb enough, to give custody to that ass!" Lori slowly turned into the driveway.

Beth laughed, "I don't know, nowadays anything can happen. I'll just be so glad when it's all over." She took a deep breath, getting ready to face her parents and Jeremy.

The reunion with Jeremy made Beth feel guilty all the way down to the pit of her stomach. It seemed he'd grown, and very, obviously now overweight from her mother spoiling him with food to console him. It upset Beth to think that he did as she had, in her emotional states. Bruce tried to convince her that Jeremy didn't want to go back with her to Oklahoma City, but after talking with him a few minutes, Beth knew that was not true, but his father had made him feel guilty if he left him.

"Mom, Dad says if I leave him, it means I don't love him anymore."

"Jeremy, don't you think he's being a little silly? It would be the same as, you saying I didn't love you anymore because I didn't buy you an expensive toy. We'll only be two and a half hours away by plane, that's not so far, now is it?" Jeremy looked up at her and tried to smile, then nodded his head.

Beth hugged him tightly, "I missed you so much, and I love you so much."

"I know, Mom, me too." She'd taken him so for granted, until he was out of her life did she realize how much he'd been such a big part of it.

Lori dressed simply, but dignified, as Beth had also, for her court appearance. She felt like she was in the eye of the hurricane, at any moment to be tossed off her feet by the wind that would be blowing. Before walking into Scott's office, Lori offered Beth a valium, "No thanks. Drugs like that usually overreact on me. I better be in complete control of all of my faculties."

"OK." Lori said, as she popped the pill in her mouth, "but I'm not as brave as you are."

Scott reminded Beth, "You must control your feelings about Bruce in court, and come off as a very solid, earnest mother and career person. I will try to bring out the reasons for the move, and that Bruce was well-aware of the planned move several months ago, and not just recently. He is accusing, that you were going to remove Jeremy from the state without anyone's permission."

"Scott, I have an excellent memory, and I remembered the night he was returning Jeremy to my mother's, he almost tripped over my luggage parked near the door. When he asked, my mother told him. I mentioned the possibility of moving there before to Jeremy."

"When was that?" Jotting down the details to use for his questioning.

"Right after I got back from the doctor, he told me the arthritis was imminent. He was right, after all the rain and cold last night, my arm's killing me and it hasn't hurt for months."

Sitting in the courtroom, Lori was on one side of Beth and Louise was on the other, with Barbara at her right hand. Beth learned to be nice to Barb, who'd already realized she made a mistake in divorcing Mike. Barb went out of her way to help Louise with what ever she could for Jeremy. John was in the waiting room with Jeremy. Scott had no intentions of putting him on the stand, but be available.

It seemed the case would never be called as one after another, the judge was hearing divorces. They were much quicker now with the new no-contest law, you didn't even need two witnesses. Beth commented to Lori, "Bring back any memories?"

"It's sad the dirty-laundry, still has to be done in public."

Scott whispered to Beth, "It'll still be a while until your case, and Lou is in his chambers on the next floor. It wouldn't hurt to talk to him, and clarify how much you can say about writing to him and his advice. I mean suggestion. A judge, remember is not supposed to give *advice*." Beth quietly slipped away, and went to Lou's chambers. Before the secretary could come back out to tell her to come in, Lou had come for her.

"Beth!" he happily exclaimed. "What are you doing here? Given up Oklahoma?" She went in and he closed the door.

"No, I'm here for the child custody upstairs." She's stood smiling at him.

"Oh, yes, Judge Burham?" He beamed at her, as a true wish.

"Yes, I just want to clarify some things with you, so I do't say the wrong thing."

"I'm sorry I didn't get back to you sooner, but I've been in quite a turmoil myself." He gave her a big kiss, "Sit down, you're not going to believe this. Jane and I are separated, and I finish moving out tonight, and I'm having a party. How long will you be in town?"

"Well, through the weekend, Sunday if I can take Jeremy back with me." Irony, again?

"Listen, let me give you my address, and if you can come by, I'd love to see you." He quickly ran over the details of what he said to her before, and how she should say it.

She gave him a kiss goodbye, "I'll try to come by tonight." All too funny of the timing.

Beth dashed up to the courtroom. Jeremy was reading a dinosaur book, and she gave him a hug and a kiss then turned to her father, "Thanks Pop, you're so patient." She gave him a quick kiss, and slipped back in with Lori, giving her an 'A-OK sign.' Finally at eleven, their case was called and Bruce was first on the stand.

Beth couldn't remember him looking more pathetic. He remained thin, after dropping the sixty pounds he gained during the marriage, quickly after the divorce. Lori whispered, "He looks like a survivor from a concentration camp."

"I know, it's supposed to make you feel sorry for this man, his wife must have been a very mean person. I've seen men fifteen years older, look better than he does. His thin hair, and the ridiculous way he combs it. Honest to God, I hope the judge can see through him."

"I don't know, he didn't respond too much to the divorces."

Bruce very nervously began to answer the questions. To try to be more effective, he kept turning to talk to the judge, and over-explained everything like he was up for murder. It began to annoy the judge, since he'd look down at his papers right away to avoid all eye contact. His attorney, who was well-know for his flamboyant remarks, was trying to prove what a terrific father Bruce had been, because he'd always made his child support payments, and leading somewhere with it. Beth wasn't sure, but then thought maybe he tried to paint Bruce pure, and then bring up Beth's past with men or something. She whispered it to Lori, and her eyes opened wide. "I hope they can't do it, if Jeremy was never exposed to any of it."

When it was Scott's turn, he tried to show the only thing Bruce had ever done for Jeremy *was* to pay the child support - which was conservative, for his income and for enforcement purposes paid through the court. Scott pointed out though Bruce received four weeks vacation a year, he'd never taken Jeremy anywhere, but for camping trips in the five years. Bruce's living quarters were another point he made, a man with his income living in a two-room apartment, in the industrial section with Jeremy sharing a sofa-bed, when he stayed over. Scott pressed at the age, and ill-health of Louise and John, showing it would be a detriment to them and Jeremy for permanent custody. Bruce simply inferred, he wasn't aware of either their age or poor health, this did raise the eyebrows of the judge.

Then, Scott moved onto why Bruce did not want Beth to have custody, now after five years. Bruce hemmed and hawed, "I thought we weren't bringing personal-stuff brought out here . . . " he looked sadly at the judge.

The Judge responded, "If you have something to say, say it."

"OK, Sir, uh Your Honor. I, . . . I don't know how to say this." Beth was holding her breath, she couldn't believe after all this time, he'd still be so vindictive. ". . . she has a drinking problem," Bruce spoke as if wild-horses had dragged it out of him.

Beth gasped and her mouth dropped open in shock. Lori grabbed her hand and squeezed it. Beth was only grateful Scott had Louise leave the room before he started the questions. There was no telling, what kind of a scene she'd have caused. She may not like Beth, but Bruce truly disgusted her. Now gloating, Bruce was in his glory of the pain he so cunningly poured on Beth, knowing she could not respond at the moment.

Scott wan't quite prepared either for Bruce's statement, so he tried to continue the line of questions of why this revelation now after five years. He did manage to cross Bruce up, at the time of divorce, he'd felt she was capable and fit, though he testified the 'problem' existed before the divorce. When Scott felt he'd left Bruce and his statement confusing, he had no further questions at the time. It was recess for lunch.

Barb took John home, so he could rest before going to his bartending job at the lodge. Beth took Jeremy, Louise and Lori to lunch. Scott said he wanted to do some research, so he'd meet them back at two o'clock. "He obviously laid a bombshell on us, but it is one of those gray-areas of personal opinion. You've never been arrested for drunken driving or public behavior, so it's what we have to prove, you don't have any such problem." At lunch, Beth barely picked at her salad, as she tried to explain to Jeremy what was going on, without discussing the details.

Beth sat on the stand smiling and composed, as she calmly answered the questions Scott put to her. She talked about her job, the details of importance and her creative work she hoped would get her a better job and more fulfilling career. He went into detail on the apartment she acquired, how spacious it was and she made the school district her prime prerequisite for choosing it.

Despite the objections of Bruce's attorney, Beth began to explain why she went to Oklahoma first for the health of her arm. Scott carefully avoided the events prior to the accident, but Beth describe the intricacies of the operation, and at the final moment lifted her sleeve to reveal the six-inch scar. At all times, she kept her eyes on Scott so the judge wouldn't think she was appealing, like Bruce did.

Beth then told how she first tried to talk to Bruce about wanting to move to Oklahoma City, "As usual, he didn't want to talk about anything, which might make him have to change his routine, he simply said, 'No, I'll see you in court.'" To give it even more authenticity, Beth could recall the date, since it was right after her last visit to the doctor, and he'd given her the information regarding the arthritis. She then repeated how Bruce even tripped over her luggage, the night before she left. Scott now asked her to explain how she was about to contact the court about the impending move. Carefully, watching her wording, though trying not to be obvious about it, Beth explained how Lou, her former attorney, discussed it with her, and she was following his instructions when she got the court notice.

Scott smiled at her, "No further questions at this time."

Beth lasted an hour, but she knew the worst was to come from Bruce's attorney, who was rather frank about his dislike of women. He paused longer than necessary, and then never even rose from his chair to pursue the questioning. Beth tried to control herself, but this prejudiced, sick-man got her back up. She transformed from the composed-woman who was sure of what she was saying and doing, to almost a defensive bitch. If he'd not give her the courtesy of a lady, then it was the sardonic-Scorpio he received in return.

Her voice changed a whole octave, as she slid back in her chair, and responded curtly to his questions. As often as possible, she answered the questions in such a way as to make them, and him look ridiculous. The more sarcastic he got, the more contemptuous and clever she answered. At one point, she even got several contained snickers from the filled courtroom.

He was not prepared for her at all, and kept 'x-ing-out' questions on his legal pad. A few times, Beth noticed Scott rolling his eyes and she tried to pull back, but then this insult-of-a-man asked her another absurd question, like 'wasn't it very damp and rainy in Oklahoma?' Over and over, he tried to get her to use the word *'advice'* when speaking of her talk with Lou. Even though he knew, she knew it was illegal for a judge to give advice, he kept trying to trick her, until the judge reminded him he'd asked the question previously. Beth contained herself, as she wanted to use Connie's phrase, "Watch my lips, dummy, maybe you can understand this time."

He then tried to insinuate there was something between her and Lou. Beth got very cool and said, "Being a friend of him and his wife for several years, I felt he put some light on the subject, since he knew the difficulties I had in the past with my ex-husband." Suddenly, he had no further questions, but Scott felt he should clear the air about the drinking. He had not wanted to bring it up, but since Bruce's attorney ignored it, Scott wanted the record cleared.

Beth stated though she rarely drank now, Oklahoma was a *dry state*, she did have a problem while going through her divorce. "Just like my colitis, it cleared up with my divorce."

With no further questions from either side, the judge called a recess and asked the two attorneys to join him in his chambers. Beth was on the stand for over two hours. She felt her perspiration went all the way to her knees. Now it was over, Beth hoped her big mouth had *not* once again gotten her in trouble. She felt the judge open-minded.

"Don't worry, you should've seen some of the looks he was giving the attorney. I don't think a weaker woman could have held up to those terrible questions."

"God, Lori," Beth shuttered, "he's such a worm. He made me feel so dirty and stupid. He must really have a problem with women. Only Bruce would pick an attorney like him."

The judge came back and handled two more quickie divorces, before giving his decision. He'd emptied the court of every case but theirs. Beth was anxious, as Lori slipped her hand over hers and squeezed it. "You're not alone, remember." Slowly the judge began to explain Jeremy would spend the school year with his mother, and a maximum of two and a half months at summer with his father, who had to acquire an apartment which would have a separate sleeping facility for Jeremy. Beth held her breath. The judge continued saying she must put up a five-hundred dollar bond, to guarantee Jeremy be returned at the specified times, including one week at Christmas break. Bruce would have to pay airfare at summer, but Beth would have to split it at Christmas.

So, neither of them really won or lost, and Beth still in slight-shock, as they started to leave the courtroom. Scott suggested they go and talk, so he could explain it all to her. Barb had returned to take Louise and Jeremy back home. Scott said, Bruce told him he would not take Jeremy until after the holiday, so Beth could visit with him while she was here. "Ain't that white of him!" Beth snipped.

As they walked through the lobby of the court house, there was a young couple with friends all dressed for their impending wedding. Beth stopped in her tracks, "Honest to God! You know, if they had a day in the courtroom upstairs to see what can go wrong, not only the divorces we saw, but a child custody like mine, maybe they'd hesitate to get married." She kept shaking her head, in all of *her naiveté* thinking, she actually had thought she could have made it work.

Scott laughed, "I doubt it," as he walked out the door, holding it for Beth and Lori.

"Look at them, barely twenty, if that . . . " She sucked in her lips to not say anything more.

"You don't get cynical until at least twenty-one." Scott chuckled again.

"They're young and sure that it won't happen to them," Lori sadly added.

"Listen, ladies," Scott asked, "I don't know about you, but after today's day in court . . . I could use a drink - how about you?"

Beth and Lori laughed. "Well, if the judge can't change his opinion," Beth retorted, "I'd love to have a drink"

Though Beth had known Caren since childhood, she'd not gotten to really know her husband Scott until this whole mess. It meant a lot to her, in her frustrated state to have him take the time to explain what it all meant, while she sipped her scotch and water.

"Beth you have to realize we came into today with a lot against us. I mean it was only your word-of-intention, you were going to inform the court of moving Jeremy. Besides, look at it this way, during the summer, you won't have the expense of a babysitter. The only problem I foresee is getting the five-hundred-dollar-bond. It only costs fifty dollars, but these cases have a high-risk, so it's hard to get a bond. If I can't, you'll have to deposited the money with the court.

"Well, I hope you can get it, since I sure don't have that kind of money, after what this has all cost me." Scott went on to explain other parts of the case to Beth, so she felt she had accomplished much of what she'd come for.

Beth barely hit the bed to rest for a few minutes, when she heard the phone ring below. When she heard her mother start walking toward the stairs, she knew it was for her. Michael was calling to see how she survived, and what time she wanted to be picked up to join her, Cam and Connie for dinner at the Cafe'. After a shower and change of clothes, Beth was ready to go party and definitely laugh. Since they were all going to be gone for the Fourth of July weekend on previously made plans, it would be Beth's only time to visit with them.

Short of cash as usual, Beth had only been able to bring a few small things back for her friends. Michael collected miniatures for her old, type-case they'd swiped from Bruce's printing supplies, so Beth brought her a little, bronze adding-machine which worked. Connie, always teasing Beth about the size of her boobs, she brought two Texas-sized grapefruits. Walking into the Cafe' bar was not quite nostalgia, but certainly brought back memories of many evenings spent trying to fill a void.

Funny, how differently Beth now looked at it. She began telling Michael the condensed version of the day, and then began all over when they were joined by Connie, Cam and other old acquaintances. Connie, already well on her way to flying, so she appropriately added at intervals her interjections into Beth's dissertation, a few expletives like, "Fuckers, the asshole," and her usual "unfucking believable." She could still crack Beth up, with her succinct way of saying them all, more funny than vulgar.

When Beth got to the punchline about the drinking problem. Connie chirped in, "Did he happen to mention he had a 'fucking problem,' and it's why you started drinking to begin with?" Everybody howled, even Connie. "At least his wonderful attorney didn't ask you what caused you to fall down your mother's stairs." Ironically, as she sat sucking-down her drink.

"God, Connie, I've never seen such a weasel of a man, in such a position as him."

"Rreeeaaaally?! What else do you think that ex of yours would hire? I hope it cost him a fucking-fortune, trying to dump your kid on your mother, because it's *more convenient* for him." She stressed the *convenient* part.

They laughed and talked over dinner, catching up on the past four months in things not covered by phone calls. Beth passed over the bad times, like they never existed. Her friends might not have understood why she stuck it out, when it would've been so much easier to come back to Elmwood. But to Beth, it was the whole point. Cam and Connie would be leaving in the early morning to take his boat up to Lake Geneva with some other couples. Michael said she'd drop Beth off at Lou's party on her way back to the apartment. She'd be packing, to meet Mike out at the farm in the morning. She gave no indication of any changes between them.

Lou with his usual style, had chosen one of the modern-new apartment complexes. His college-age son and several buddies were moving his boxes in. Other than his grandmother's bed, which was an antique, he rented some furniture. For a man who always made over fifty-thousand a year, he didn't have much to show for it. His first wife got the house, and now Jane, the second got the rest. He only had his books, which there were many, his few personal possessions, his clothes and the few things Jane didn't want. Beth thought it was sad he didn't have more to speak for being forty-five years old, yet at least he now had his freedom. Beth helped him celebrate, though she no longer had a future-interest in this man, so slow to make decisions.

Michael came in to say hello, as it had been a while since she'd seen Lou. There didn't seem to be any other guests, so she stayed to talk to Beth until Lou had some time after the moving-in. Beth began to tell her about her job, "Well, Terry's good looks are only outdone by his ego and vanity . . . " she turned her head to kiss her shoulder, "you know the type." Michael laughed. Beth rattled on about the different people, and what all she did. "It's really kind of interesting, and everyday is rather a challenge.

"But you'd think being the only woman with thirty men, I'd meet someone. The only one who interests me at all, is engaged to a girl who lives at his house in Houston. So, I content myself to be friends with him. He really is super and certainly perks up my day, when other things get to me. I'm surprised how much I've learned to like living alone, I'm getting to know a person I haven't known before - me. I can understand your enjoyment of your solace. Rose and Fran have tried to fix me up several times, but it was really pathetic. Either I had a headache, or they did."

"Well, everything kind of runs the same here, with customers. Ellie asks about you all the time. We've had a few weirdos we dropped right away, but the money has stayed good, so far this summer. We've gotten a good range of customers now, so we pretty much clear two-hundred a week for a six or seven-hour day." Beth could see why they stuck with the cleaning, but they weren't getting any younger. Not in the mood for lecturing, since she'd said it all before.

Michael continued, "Everything seems to be going great with Mike, still dominates me a little, but it's going along." Somehow it sounded like all was *not* perfect, but if Michael didn't want to discuss it, Beth'd not pursue.

Lou came in to give Beth a kiss, "So where's the party?"

"I don't know, we can still have one, I have plenty of champagne," he smiled.

"Well, Michael wants to get back home to pack, but if you can give me a ride, I'll stay."

"Terrific. I must be living right, the night I move out from my wife, Beth, my love, comes into town." Still smiling, Lou left to get some more boxes.

When they'd brought in the bed, Michael said to Beth, "I'll help you make it, since it looks like you might get a chance to use it."

Beth laughed, "It's not quite anti-climatic, but last year I'd have given my eye-teeth for this. Now, well . . . it just sounds like a fun time, and good idea for something to do."

"Beth, you mean you're not horny?" Michael couldn't believe her ears.

"Not really, it passes after it's been so long. I've been busy discovering new facets about myself, and trying to make a go of my writing, so I really haven't missed it that much. Don't get me wrong, I'd love to have a good man to share some time with, but that's just it, good men will aways be hard to find, but I think I'm worth the wait.."

"Boy, Jane was really generous, these sheets don't even match, and they're also torn."

"Here, " Beth added, "help me put up the extra sheets for drapes. At least in Oklahoma, the apartment comes with lined drapes." They finished, and started unpacking the other boxes of miscellaneous bed and bath things. "You know, this apartment is almost identical to mine, with the walk-in closet and bath. It's so nice to have my own bath. I nonetheless wonder how we lived so smoothly, all together for that couple of years. It doesn't seem like you're on your own two years already." Beth paused again looking at Michael, thinking of their times together.

"And really, I love it. Sometimes I even question my want to get married. The freedom spoils you." They'd been moving back and forth placing things in the linen closet and bathroom.

"I know, Scott reminded me many women would trade places with me to have freedom from their kids for a few months every year. I've learned to do so many things by myself I never would've considered." Beth paused folding the towels, "God there's not one which matches. I go to the movies by myself, the friends I've met down there, just aren't into movies the way we were, and you have to go right away to see something more liberal, cause they just don't have the audience there.

Of course, no foreign films, except once in a while over at the University - Lina Wertmueller or a Bergman. I know you and Connie didn't like the subtitles, but Lori and I got to enjoy them without difficulty. I've gone out to eat by myself - usually just lunch, but for me these have been big steps to find out what good company I am."

She stopped to open some more boxes. "I make almost a regular-routine going to this one pond close by, to feed the ducks day-old-bread and watch the sunsets. I have to admit, it is so flat there, you can see the whole sunset, and they are spectacular with the dust creating pinks and purples. I like not having all the crowds, buildings and traffic, I feel like I'm living in the suburbs because there is such a little downtown. I think Oklahoma has been very good for me, because I have learned to really depend on just me. Fran and Rose have been great, and Mrs. Porter, too, but they're not you guys."

"Well, more power to you," Michael said, as she sank down on the floor with her back against the wall, "I moved enough when I was married, and never new what kind of a job, if any, he'd get. I kinda like my simple, little life with eighty-dollar rent, and no one to worry about but me, and if it's Tuesday, I know who I'm cleaning, and how much I'll make every week. We can schedule our trips and weekends, and for us everything is fine, just the way it it."

"If you're happy," Beth sunk down, "that's what counts."

Michael had been gone only a few minutes, when Lou came in with the last of the moving, and some supplies from the store. His son and his friends quickly devoured the pizza and beer, then discreetly departed. Beth and Lou sat down on the rental chairs at his rental table. Beth laughed, just telling Michael my apartment is almost identical to yours, including the elaborate furniture."

Lou gulped his martini, Beth made and laughed, "Yea, ain't this terrific. The great judge can't hold his own marriage together."

"Oh, honest to God, Lou, you know it was doomed from the start, because she pressured you. I feel the same way when I've helped friends with their problems, and my own life has stayed so screwed up." She watched him and smirked at his naiveté.

He laughed again, "Doctor, heal thyself. How about some champagne?" They went into the kitchen, and he took the Korbel out of the refrigerator. "I even picked up some glasses!"

Beth laughed, "Lou, you're a stitch - plastic glasses for good champagne - well, why not?" She'd forgotten how quirky he could be.

He'd already started taking off his shirt, as they headed for the bedroom. Beth had a slight hesitation of nerves, she hoped would go away with the liquor. They toasted and kissed as they finished undressing, Lou released Beth, trying not to get over-involved. "Let me shower first, and get this sweat off, then we can uh . . . "

"No, no," announced Beth "It's been a long time since I've been around a sweaty-man, and it makes me very horny. Let's have a quickie, then we'll both shower, and have some more fun after." She was now giggling, and pulling him toward the bed.

"You're crazy, but you won't have to . . . ask me twice."
Coming out of the shower, Beth called to Lou, "Don't put on any cologne silly, I have something better," waving the champagne bottle.

He put the cologne bottle down, without even bothering put the lid on again. She'd refilled their glasses, and sitting in the middle of the bed waited for him. "Now, take a few swallows and lay back and relax . . . if you can." His eyes were popping out of his head.

"What are you going to do?" he asked with a grin on his face, and the devil in his eyes.

"Monsieur, you are getting, " she started with a terrible French accent, but kept giggling, "le champagne special." Beth began dribbling the champagne on his chest, and licking it off.

"Oh, God, you are nuts! You are really something else, you're crazy . . . you're fantaaaaastic . . . don't stop now."

Beth laughed out full, "It's true what they say, it is just like riding a bicycle, you never do forget, and I won't hurt myself if I fall off." They were both laughing loudly.

Later Lou said, "I'm sorry it wasn't longer."

"Longer, hell," Beth retorted, "I waited a year and a half for it." They both then laughed, and continued to party all night.

To Find Me

It was a long time coming
and sometimes I thought
   I would never make it at all.

  But I kept searching,
    moving to wherever I felt the call.

I knew I could never find you,
       until I found me.

I knew I could never be free,
       until I found me.

We were both worth waiting for.
  Now, I'm ready for love,
    and whatever else is in store.

Because I now know, the secret of being free,
    and finding you,
      was to find me.

CHAPTER 31

New Opportunities in OKC

Saturday, Beth invited Caren to join her and Jeremy at Lincoln Park Zoo, as her two kids always got along well with Jeremy. She told Caren how much Scott's interest in the case meant. The day gave Beth a chance to spent time with Jeremy, without him feeling the pressure of alone or concentrated time with her, after being gone so long. Later, Beth was then ready to have a quiet time at Lori's with Marie, and a bottle of white wine.

There was so much to talk about new in Lori's life, that they'd not had a chance to discuss. The new man in her life spelled business and romance. When she'd been the head salesperson at Manson Galleries, Lori met the famous Mexican artist, Ricardo, at one of his phenomenal shows. Quite taken, both with Lori herself and her quality to sell people, Ricardo asked if they could keep in touch. Since this was prior to their trip to Mexico, Beth pushed her to contact him, and perhaps he could show them some special points of his city. Lori hesitated not wanting to bother the busy artist, who created sculptures as well as, free-flowing modern paintings.

At Beth's persistence, Lori had written, but too late to get a response. She didn't even want to bother him by calling, when they were in Mexico City, and now she was working for him. He'd called her the day they returned from Mexico, and was very upset she hadn't contacted him sooner. Ricardo needed someone with Lori's art knowledge and ambiance, that could be his representative to the United States' museums.

Though his shows did very well at the larger galleries, he was very interested in being established in the museums. He was already established in Europe. Lori traveled to NewYork to meet with him, and made several contacts there. So, in between her own lectures, she was contacting museums on his behalf. It gave her income a boost, and also her ego, to have the capability of handling such a creative artist.

Ricardo was definitely a continental man with his dark, good looks, sensitive eyes, flair for the elegant and a dry, quick wit. Easy to see why Lori was falling in love with him, so full of élan. Her voice filled with exuberance, as she talked about the places he'd taken her and the exciting things they'd done. Though she'd heard Lori tell the story before, Marie soaked up every word, she loved anything that sounded like a fairy tale. Beth couldn't have been happier for Lori, yet their distance apart and dedication to his art made romance difficult.

Beth then had a brainstorm. "Maybe Oklahoma City might be interested in something of his, if he'd like to build an audience there. I could even get some television coverage through Rose's connections. If you'll ask him, and if he's willing, I'll pursue it from my end."

"I'll be talking to him after the holiday, so I'll see how busy and interested he is. He's very anxious to meet you, and I sent him a copy of your poetry book. He really liked it."

Beth smiled, rather surprised, "That's an amazing compliment from someone of his artistic stature." Beth enjoyed the expressionistic flowing lines of Ricardo's work for sometime, so she was thrilled that he was interested in meeting her. She remembered 'Real Estate Harry,' her wealthy customer/lover, having several of his paintings.

The next day, Beth was once again with Lori, this time Jeremy playing ping-pong with her sons, as Beth helped with some of the business-end of things, that Lori relied on her assistance. Beth pushed her not to let her lecturing slide, while occupied with work for Ricardo. "Lori, you have to remember that he could vanish from your life, and you have to go on making a living." It was a hard fact to swallow, and be realistic. Ricardo was also married with four children.

Bruce picked up Jeremy, and Beth tried to make sure that there were no teary goodbyes, after she explained to him what was happening. She wouldn't have the triumphant return that she'd wanted, but maybe this would give her the added time to get her life in more order. With some new things to think about, Beth was on her way back to Oklahoma City alone.

She felt a slight separation from Michael and Connie, but the ties that bind were still there. April had called, but they'd not been able to get together either. At least the phone call made Beth feel that April was surviving, and progressing slowly. April also tried to persuade Beth to stay, since she wasn't doing that great in Oklahoma City, but Beth stubbornly refused, saying she'd conquer it.

Fran picked Beth up at the airport, and anxious to hear the case details with everything else. They made plans to go the following Saturday to the Art Center, to talk to them about Ricardo. Fran dabbled in water colors, while she was off work and her walls were covered with some favorite paintings.

So, excited at even the prospect of Ricardo coming to OKC. At the Art Center, the director, Adam, had recently been to New York and seen some of Ricardo's work, so he was quite happy at the idea and appreciative of whatever art piece he presented to them. Beth noticed the Art Center sponsoring a trip to New Orleans to see Tut's Treasures.

"I worked on publicity for a lecturer-friend of mine in Chicago, but I left before Tut arrived. I'd really like to join your group going." She couldn't believe the opportunity.

Fran in her effervescent-way, said, "Oh, you should get Lori to lecture for your group on Tut. She's terrific. I went to Chicago to see the exhibition, and her lecture set-it-up wonderfully."

"As a matter of fact," said Adam, "we're hoping to get someone to lecture to the group for it."

Beth jumped on the band-wagon quickly. "Well, we could maybe put this all together, since she is Ricardo's representative. If we're lucky, we might be able to get the dates to jive, and have him give the presentation and her to lecture. Let me send you a brochure, and I'll call Lori to let her know, then she can take it directly from there." This was unfolding wonderfully.

Adam smiled, "I'll present it to the board this week, since October will be here before you know it." He was totally amazed this was all being so generously presented to him.

Beth threw in for good-measure, "I have a connection at the television station, so I'll try to see about some special coverage." She couldn't believe how many bases she was covering.

"Sounds good to me," Adam's eyes lit up, "this has certainly been a pleasure."

Floating as they left, "Now," Beth said, turning to Fran, "if I can pull this off, maybe the station will take notice of me. Thanks for coming with me, and bringing up about Lori. Since you've heard her, it validated what I said about her. This could not have gone better."

Within a week, Lori called, and said Ricardo would be happy to do a large painting suitable for the Art Center. So excited, Beth could hardly stand it. Lori was getting the dates set for her to lecture, so they'd both be coming to Oklahoma City the middle of October. Lori had given Beth a copy of a large book on Ricardo's work, with other publicity, she was ready to forge on to the television station, to see if they'd interview Ricardo and Lori. To Beth's surprise, Tut fever was sweeping the country, even conservative OKC was being affected.

In a flurry, over all the frenzy about to happen in Beth's life, she felt she needed to write a poem for Ricardo, to thank him for sharing the wealth of his talent in her new home. Beth was so proud to be the instigator, of bringing both the modern art of Ricardo and Lori's descriptive words about the ancient beauty of Tut's world there. The Art Center had some excellent western art, but definitely lacked in anything from the modern world.

Rose was most helpful in presenting Ricardo's book and the information on him, to Lou Ellen, who did the local interviews. Beth then followed with phone calls, and wrote the basic outline for Lou Ellen to be familiar with Ricardo's background and style. Beth received a lovely thank you note from Ricardo for the poem, and he casually mentioned that he was sending her a small watercolor in gratitude for it, and saying, *". . . how I wish I had your talent for words."* A chill went down her spine, as Beth mumbled to herself, "I don't think I can handle a great man like that, giving me such a compliment." She slowly sank-down in the folding chair, clutching the letter to her heart. "Soon, maybe someday soon . . . " She felt recognition was getting close.

Marie at last got her act together and her divorce done, so proceeded to move to OKC with all her furniture, boxes and Beth's few boxes left in her parents' basement. Marie drove down with

Louise and her eldest daughter, Sheri, who'd graduated high school the year before, and currently a nurse's aide. Fran found a lovely three bedroom apartment for Marie and her three daughters, who would be joining her soon. Louise was staying with Fran and Rose's parents, the Porters, so they could talk over old times.

Marie insisted on staying with Fran, even after Beth told her she could have a relapse from the strain. Marie could be so into herself, and not considerate of people who helped her so much. Beth especially asked Fran to find an apartment for Marie not too close to her own. "For once in her life, she needs to learn to make it on her own," Beth said. "I'm really tired of her leaning, she has three, grown daughters to support her, and they should now learn to work together, not fight all the time like when she was married to Howard."

Beth's speech was in vain, since Marie decided she didn't like the apartment Fran got her. Beth's apartment complex was much nicer, so she wanted it also. To break the news to Beth, Fran invited her for dinner, so Marie could explain. Rose didn't want Beth to have cardiac-arrest in front of the others, so she called Beth before she left work. The furniture was arriving in two days, and the new apartment wouldn't be ready for five days. Beth was upset, but could live with it, as long as Marie got it all out by mid-August when Jeremy arrived.

Beth smiled through dinner, as Marie began to explain why she didn't like the other apartment, and why she wanted to move into Beth's complex. It made no sense, she just wanted what Beth had, as usual. "It'll only be a week, and then we'll move all the stuff over to our apartment." Marie and Sheri had now been with Beth for several days, and they weren't easy to live with even in her empty apartment *without all the boxes and furniture*. Beth learned to be very conservative, since she paid the electric bill, but Marie and Sheri never had to worry over any utility bills, since Howard always handled all the money.

Beth came in from work, to find the patio door wide open, with the air conditioner running and every light on, though it was still bright outside. Sheri took half-hour showers and washed her hair everyday, even after Beth told her that she paid for the hot water. Neither of them ever picked up after themselves, and they'd taken over both bathrooms, freely using all of Beth's things. She never realized how much her privacy had come to mean to her. The past three months were the first time in her life, she'd ever lived totally alone doing as she pleased.

Beth put her fork down. More than anything else, she'd do this to please her mother, to show her how she'd changed. Once more it was Beth, who'd be helping her *older* sister, not vice-versa. "OK, Marie, but you have to promise me you *will* have everything out by the fifteenth, when Jeremy arrives. I want to have his room fixed up, so he'll know how much I want him here." Beth looked over at Sheri, who just kept shoveling food into her mouth.

"Don't look at me," she talked wth her mouth full, "I'm flying back to Chicago next week." She was the most lazy, insolent child Beth had ever been around, except for her two younger sisters who only got worse in the categories of: impudent, ill-mannered, discourteous, rude and disrespectful. Marie was a totally, non-participant parent, with Howard always yelling and throwing things around. Truly, Beth did not blame him, yet the girls could not be reached, since they'd learned to just shut everyone-off around them.

Beth glared, "You can still help move the stuff. The apartment will be ready before then!"

Sheri glared back at Beth, and then over to Marie, "Mother you know I don't have anything, but my own things, and that's all I will move and that's final. Teri will be here soon, and she can help you move." Sheri shoved the last forkful in her mouth, stood up from the table, taking another roll, as she walked away.

Fran called after her, "You're welcome, and it really wasn't a bother to fix the dinner. I only worked all day at it!" Sheri plopped into the recliner-chair, after turning on the television. She never gave a 'thank you' to Fran, or even acknowledged her. Marie made absolutely no comment to Sheri, or to Fran for her behavior. They were truly embarrassing to be around, so totally undisciplined, and above reproach on any correcting. Oblivious Marie, so spoiled by Louise, that she was incapable of disciplining her daughters. Beth should have known better than to trust her.

Beth turned to Marie, "Don't you ever accuse Jeremy of being spoiled, when you have yourself an A#1 Bitch right there. And you better be moved out, because I'm no more Mister Nice-Guy with you. I've been through too much, without taking advantage of anybody here. You are so incredibly ungrateful."

Marie had not wanted to leave *any* of her possessions, she'd gathered in the past twenty years of marriage, including her hundreds - truly hundreds - of boxes of scrap-material for all the clothes she was *going to* make for herself all those years. The boxes were actually piled to the ceiling in the living room, dining room and what was to be Jeremy's room. Beth had the movers put all of her things in her bedroom, walk-in closet and the kitchen. There was now half a hallway, a small path through the living room to the patio and barely breathing room around the card table in the dining room. Beth trying to control her temper, as this was not necessary and hideous on her sister's part.

"Marie, my God, I thought you'd have gotten rid of some of this in a garage sale or something." Beth only thought of all the time and energy she wasted on her twit-of-a-sister.

Sheri laughed, as she walked to the refrigerator for more food, "She did!"

"Marie, did you have to take *everything* from a ten-room house, I mean really?"

"Don't yell at me," she started to whine, "It's all I have to show for twenty years of marriage." She was more than pathetic, she was disgusting in her little-girl-helpless gig.

Beth blew up, "Oh, fuck! Don't give me that shit! What do you call the forty thousand dollars you get, from your half of the sale of the house - peanuts?"

"It's for a new house, Sheri a new car, and her nursing school."

"You're hopeless, absolutely hopeless. You make me sick."

Sheri did exactly as she said. She moved only her things, and nothing else. Beth gave up yelling since Marie and the girls were so totally immune to it, from so many years with Howard. Marie started working at the department store, rather than wait till after the move, so she only got a few boxes moved everyday. She unpack them, putting the glasses and china through the dishwasher, and putting them away before she moved another box. Day after day Beth came home to see barely a dent in the mess. It was Friday and Jeremy would be there on Sunday. As usual, if Beth wanted something done, she did it herself. Louise had flown back with Sheri, so Marie continued to stay with Beth, not wanting to be in her apartment alone, beside the fact that she'd not moved any of the furniture.

Beth was ignoring Marie's complaints about how tired she was, needing to rest, and how heavy everything was. "You should have thought of that when you let that damn-bitch sit by the pool day after day without helping and you're giving her a car and nursing school? And, don't give me that shit that you're just trying to make up for all the years that Howard mistreated them." Beth put down her end of the table, she was carrying up the stairs. "The past is just that, and you are only letting them take advantage of your guilt." Beth knew she was only wasting her breath again on Marie, like she had for so very long, but at least it vented some of her anger.

Jeremy bounded back into her life with mixed feelings of his new surrounding. One day he'd be full of excitement at exploring the new and unknown, then the next he was sullen, pouting and giving Beth absolute hell. Rose's step-son caught a mountain-boomer lizard for Beth, when she'd been up at their farm. Then Mr. Porter built her a cage for it. Beth caught grasshoppers to feed Zoomer, as she called it, so that Jeremy had a pet when he arrived. He like Zoomer, but his curiosity would not leave it alone, and always letting it out of the cage, beside not wanting to catch the grasshoppers himself.

Beth came home from working overtime, tired and hungry, only to have to search the apartment for Zoomer, before it got stuck somewhere and died. Jeremy rode the bus, and had a hot lunch at school, so she didn't have that worry. He became so spoiled with Louise always fixing him special meals, Beth was going crazy fixing dinners. She'd rush to fix the dinner, feeling guilty at leaving Jeremy alone, only to have him turn his nose-up at most of what she fixed. She said fine, and told him eat peanut butter and jelly if what he wanted.

It didn't help she didn't have extra money to do more things with him on weekends. He always wanted to go play video games.

Rose spent much time wth him before school started. She even offered to pay Teri, Marie's youngest daughter and Jeremy ten cents for every box they moved to Marie's apartment. Since there were still plenty to move, it was quite a challenge. Even then, much younger Jeremy would move faster, to get more done. Rose told Beth, "I tried everything with Teri. I bribed her with McDonald's and money, and she still only works for a little while then quits. She's sure like her mother, and I never saw two sisters more different."

"I know. The only good one out of the bunch is Cindy, and they pick on her because she's so much like me," Beth retorted. She couldn't stand it any more. It'd been almost a month and she wanted her apartment back. Marie was barely making an effort to get everything out. There was still furniture and dozens of boxes, mostly filled with her scrap material. Beth decided on a compromise, so she called Marie.

"OK, I want this out now, and you say you can't afford hired help, and you're doing your best. I figure what you say I owe you, for the gas and motel for our trip down here is equal to my phone, electric and food expense, when you and Sheri were staying here. Not to mention what it would've cost if you had to put all this shit in storage. I mean, if you were paying for this space, maybe you'd move it quicker. Now, we are even-steven, right?" Marie responded with a vague 'yes,' so Beth continued.

"My plan is I'll pay a couple of Teri's high school friends to move the rest of this stuff out of here, then when you have the money, you can pay me back, OK?" Again, Beth got a vague 'yes.' The boys had everything moved in a few hours, and except for the heavy credenza which Beth had the room for, and didn't want to take a chance on them scratching it. Beth paid them forty dollars, Marie then refused to pay her. So, they were no longer speaking, after all they had been through together. It made absolutely no sense to Beth, but she'd had it with her twit-of-a-sister, who just expected people to take care of her, and Beth wasn't going to any more.

Now rid of Marie's things, Beth could plan on how she'd fix up the apartment for Ricardo's and Lori's impending visit the next month. First of all, with plans to have them for dinner, she'd need a new table and chairs. Beth took the watercolor from Ricardo, to the finest art gallery in town to get it properly framed. In talking to the assistant there, Beth mentioned he'd be interviewed on television. He was familiar with Ricardo's work, and asked if she might be interested in him doing another television show, that his friend did on arts and crafts. Beth got the names and phone numbers so she might call them, and found out what it was like or if it would be well suited to Ricardo.

Beth was once again on the phone with Lori, explaining her new idea for bringing Ricardo to the public's eye. Soon it was all set. He'd stay over another day, and do a watercolor to demonstrate his technique. Beth was so excited in anticipation of all that was soon to happen between their visit and her trip to New Orleans to see Tut's Treasures. Her life was definitely taking on more fun and meaning.

Too quickly, Lori arrived and Beth was stuck at work, so she took a limousine to the Hilton. They had several hours to talk before Ricardo's plane was due in from New York, and then more time when it was delayed. Ricardo'd asked Lori if Oklahoma City would have a brass band at his arrival, but the best Beth could do was a plastic horn she'd picked up for fun. Meeting Ricardo for the first time, Beth felt like an old friend arrived. He was shorter and slighter built than she expected, yet he definitely had that Scorpio charm and magnetism. Back at the hotel suite, they enjoyed champagne before going out for Mexican food.

"Beth . . . " he asked in his charming Spanish accent, "where have you brought me to? I hope it is not the end of the world - so flat, we might fall off! In New York my friends asked me where I was off to next, and when I say Oklahoma, they say 'Okla-what'?"

Beth and Lori laughed, "It's not for everyone, and I sometimes wonder if it's for me. Between you two, I think it will have more class this weekend than it's had in a long time."

At breakfast the next morning, Beth prepped them for there preliminary, run-through for the half-hour arts and crafts show, Ricardo would do on Tuesday. Beth then began to tell them the menu for the dinner, she was preparing that evening. Ricardo halted her, and said he'd not have her going through so much trouble for him, and he insisted they go out for dinner. "Beth, really, there must be a restaurant in town you would like to go to." His endearing smile melted Beth.

"But Ricardo, I want you to meet my friends Rose and Fran, who helped so much with it all. Their husbands are off deer hunting." She really wanted to pay Rose and Fran back for their help.

"So bring them along, and your son, Jeremy. I want to meet them all." Upset at first, Beth remembered that sometimes letting someone do something nice for you, is the nicest thing you can do for them. "OK, but I insist we come back to my place for dessert. Now, there is this place . . . " The dinner, and Beth's famous chocolate mousse, all went superbly. Fran and Rose were delighted to have special time with Ricardo, while Beth was happy for Marie not to.

The Art Center publicity hadn't had the best coordination with the newspaper, and there was a small group at the presentation. Ricardo did enjoy a saunter around the sculpture garden, which made him feel that it needed some addition from him. The after party, at a patron's house, was very well attended by some of the more notables of the city. In sketches of conversation, Beth heard Ricardo talk about his early days, striving to receive recognition for his work.

He struggled for several years, even while he did have the advantage of not coming from a poor family. Later, he again stressed that Beth should not be wasting her talents in the job she had. She tried to explain she needed the job to support Jeremy and herself, but he seemed to only comprehend that she was not writing, and her job did nothing to promote her writing.

"Ricardo, I cannot afford to be a starving writer now. Someday, maybe. I have not forgotten it. I've just shelved it for awhile. Working on the publicity for you and Lori was a challenging and exciting experience, and I was grateful for the opportunity. I hope that the interviews the next few days go well." On the way home, they stopped for an obscene ice cream concoction, and then for more childish fun, they went to see the movie *Star Wars*.

They laughed and talked until Beth's jaws hurt, and she couldn't remember how long since she'd been so happy. Topping the perfect day, Ricardo said, "Beth, if there was one person I would choose to be on a deserted island with, it would be you. You are never boring." Beth was so astonished, she almost drove off the road. Ricardo then realized he'd forgotten Lori, so he quickly added, "And, you my love, you can me make me so happy, too!"

Beth had been the extra person with a couple for a while now, and she always felt comfortable until a small scene like this, then it reminded her that the other woman had the man. She had no sexual interest in Ricardo, in fact, a long time since she had a sexual interest in any man. The need was there, sometimes, but Beth tried not to think about it, as her much larger *want* was a permanent relationship - marriage. Still, she knew she wasn't quite ready yet, and when she was, they'd find each other.

The television interviews went well for both of them, and Lori had a good crowd at her first lecture. It was Ricardo's first experience at having Lori in the spotlight, so he was quite impressed with how well she carried herself and held the audience. Ricardo took the opportunity to give Beth a check at this time, as a token of his appreciation for all the effort she'd put forth for his visit. He knew in public she'd not cause a scene, though she tried to tell him her watercolor had been too generous to begin with.

"Please, Beth," he said, "the little watercolor was nothing compared to your words you sent me. I wish I would have had time to buy you a more mindful present, and money is, as you say, 'tacky,'" he laughed. "Please accept it with my love and appreciation of your friendship." Beth relented, and placed the folded check in her purse without looking at it. She'd known few people as generous and loving as Ricardo, as well she treasured his friendship dearly.

Lori surprised Beth by paying Anne the balance for her watercolor, that Beth wanted for so, very long. Lori stayed an additional few days after Ricardo left, to visit with Beth, relax in the sun and see if she could sell some art he'd given her. When they were both gone, Beth remained in a state of flux, unhappy with the void their leaving made. Ricardo stirred up Beth's hopes about her writing, while at the same time made her resentful of her job. To top off her frustration, Beth got a letter from her attorney, Scott, saying that he was unable to get her a bond, and she'd have to forward five-hundred dollars immediately for the court to hold. Beth planned to spend the two-hundred dollars on her New Orleans trip, Ricardo gave her, so she was lucky to have the company credit union to fall back on.

Beth enjoyed herself immensely in New Orleans, meeting some terrific people and taking in all the fascinating sights, since they stayed in the French Quarter. Finding a rare buy on a miniature Goddess Selket of Tut fame, it gave Beth a chance to repay some of Fran's generosity, as she wanted one so badly. Beth was happy, but circulating her insides, the turmoil abounded.

Female Knowledge

Inner strength was growing, knowledge of surrender's value.
Move easily with the wind, it can't blow you around.
Dominate your own choosing, not a whim come and gone.
A gift of mutual enjoyment, he'd never realize she'd given.

The initial time a woman truly sees her power, it's bloomed.
It's a different point to each, and regrettably never to a few.
A transient moment looked back upon, not noticed till then,
But things changed, and would be remembered succinctly.

It's a learning curve, how/when used for maximum success.
She's not treated as another female variation of her age.
He had known her long, and knew she was not a facsimile.
Fads, passing styles, or flavors of the month, wasn't her.

More than a woman of substance, she used her intuition.
Unlimited passion, she approached the unknown fearlessly.
Rarely the same twice, she took on new ideas feverishly.
Her belief: poems to write, bridges to cross or dances to do.

It was her life, she loved it as it was, without compromise.
Taking a while to get there, she was not changing her stance.
Acquaintances might come and go, but friends stood the test
accepting her as she changed, and felt was better for them all.

CHAPTER 32

It's Not Over, Till It's Over

To say it seemed like a good idea at the time, would be the only way to explain Michael's moving in with Mike, and his two boys for two months, during the summer of 1977. Her brother, Web, and his girlfriend, Cindy came up from New Orleans to help Mike construct his implement building. Since Michael stayed with them in New Orleans, and her studio apartment was just too small for the three of them, Mike thought it'd be easier for her to move in with him. Michael actually had no other place to go, Connie's studio would not be conducive to a third person with Cam there so much of the time.

Michael questioned it all, but Mike could not be happier. Now, he had sex every night, and Michael got to do her cleaning jobs all day, then come home to clean up after the three 'boys.' How much fun, and lack of privacy was that? The shit hit the fan. The guys were basically messy, and she wanted the place spotless for Jackie's graduation party.

The topper came when Cathy, mother of Jackie's best friend, had his graduation party without Michael being invited. Cathy did, however, invite Barbara and Uncle Eddie, who was still married. So, Barb's married-boyfriend was good enough for an invitation, but Michael, who was single, but currently living with Mike, was not. Mike defended Cathy, in that 'she'd never hurt a flea' - be conniving enough to make it miserable and crazy for Michael, yes.

Mike then said, he'd probably not go, because some neighbors who'd hassled him during his divorce, would probably be there. Michael blew up, "I wouldn't go anywhere YOU weren't wanted or invited, and that would be my *first* reason for not going, because YOU weren't welcome. And, since she wouldn't hurt a flea, I must be lower, because she just hurt me." She was, in his opinion over-reacting and making a mountain out of a mole hill, so no further discussion.

Insult on top of injury - Louise refused to come to her grandson Jackie's graduation party that Michael was giving, saying she was having one of her spells. But the walls did not come tumbling down, till it was vacation time out at the farm. Also, Web and Cindy's wedding, to which Michael put-out-the-word, that Cathy was neither invited nor welcome. Cathy very simply went over Michael's head, and asked Mike if she might come out to visit *after* the wedding, and being the kind of man her was, Mike said, "By all means."

Michael figured she'd survived the two months of complete loss of privacy, and almost sanity at Mike's house. So she surely could make it through a weekend with Cathy at the farm. It wasn't, as if she was competing with Cathy for Mike - Michael thought, surely not. As Mike helped Michael make sandwiches for everyone, the pressures and lack of sleep got to her.

Thinking Mike must realize, as she'd put in so much time and effort for the wedding, she said, "Let's not make all of it up into sandwiches, let's leave some of the meat out, for them to make what more they want." Cathy and a girlfriend, who'd come up with her were sitting in the living room. In the kitchen, Mike absolutely exploded at Michael for such a *stupid* suggestion. Michael was speechless, not only for the outburst, but the fact that he'd do such a thing to her, in front of Cathy or anyone else.

Everything that Michael had been though with Tim, her ex, they NEVER, until the last, horrendous-week they were married, *ever* argued or bitched in front of anyone. It was an unwritten-law, and with all of the rest of the rules and regulations that Mike would follow, how could he not adhere to this one? Michael was so crushed that she didn't begin to know how to recover. After serving the *made-up* sandwiches, Michael retreated to the bedroom to pull some of the loose pieces back together. When she emerged later, everyone was sitting around the bond fire, and Mike sitting next to Cathy. Michael sat down across from them, never saying a word. She watched Mike trot back and forth several times, bringing fresh drinks to Cathy. It was not unusual for him to play bartender, except that he neglected each time to ask Michael if she'd care for one, or anything at all.

That night as they got into bed, Michael was still livid with the anger and pain. It was a good thing that he was too drunk to even want sex. She put up with petty remarks trying to pit her against Cathy, as if he wanted them competing for him. Michael very coolly stated before turning out the light, "I'm not kidding, Cordeau, the tone around here better change by tomorrow, or you're going to make your choice this weekend." The next day Mike pleasantly continued, like a warm can of beer-shaken well - it wouldn't have taken much to pop his top.

Michael hoped that things were worked out, yet nagging at her consciousness was the fact that Mike never physically touched her while Cathy was around. Trying to ignore this factor, would be like ignoring neon-signs and flashing red lights. Michael felt a certain amount of restlessness in Mike, which was common in any newly divorced person. Though it'd been over a year now, had he been repressing these feeling simply because he did love Michael? The only previous time they cropped up, was at Beth's autograph party the August after his divorce, when he most flagrantly-flirted with Lori and Anne in front of Michael.

Strange also, that these women and Cathy were all closer to Mike's age. But he did not realize, the only way to rid oneself of restlessness was to experience whatever it was, and get it out of the system. To repress it, was putting a cork on a rumbling volcano. Mike told Michael about his dalliances over the years with Cathy, and many of the other neighbor ladies. And, he'd made jokes about the sex being so straight and missionary-only style, so absolutely no comparison to what he knew now, as real uninhibited-sex with Michael.

So Michael tried talking to him about going out with other women, as she felt secure in his love of her. He wouldn't admit the feeling, or the need for a change, or even taking a break or time-off from seeing Michael. Yet, their constant verbal-exchanges between them, of resentment and antagonism continued. As Michael left on Monday morning for work, she reminded Mike that they were going to have to talk about this, as it wasn't going away and sex wouldn't be able to cover it up any more.

Michael learned that Mike, once again, had a very convenient memory. As he'd only remember the daily-sex when Michael was living with him. Jackie and Jason unfortunately, remembered well the daily fights. She was cursed and blessed with having a memory of both. She knew if there was anything to be continued, what caused the fights was going to have to be settled. After Mike returned home, things were almost back the way they'd been when Michael felt almost comfortable enough to bring up the subject once again. When she proposed this to Mike, very blasé as usual, he said, "Let's not rock the boat." She wasn't looking for an argument, so she dropped it. Then they mutually agreed to see each other *more often,* rather than less, like the sex was going to soothe everything over.

The only problem with this was that with Mike working nights and Michael working days, she was not getting any sleep. She had to be up at six-thirty, since Connie liked an early start of seven-thirty or eight. Michael tried to sleep when she got home, but invariably there were interruptions and things like laundry and shopping to be done. After a few weeks, Michael started falling asleep anywhere, any time she was still for more than five minutes. Mike started bitching that she was always sleeping in the car to the farm, or to her Mom's. He never bothered to correlate that she lacked sleep because of her schedule with him, and didn't clarify. He made her life completely surrounded by him, and she started to throw minor-nags, breaking the hold.

More and more Michael acknowledged, that they had little mutual conversation. He wasn't interested in the books she read, or the movies she went to with April or Connie. He only liked to talk about his farm machinery, the farm or some problem or another at work - always about him and his life. The frustration began to make Michael resent her *non-personage,* that she'd allowed him to create. Sex remained their *only* mutual interest.

So, the night came that Michael went to see Frank Sinatra with her mother and Connie. Michael got home five minutes after Mike got there, and though he'd been late on occasions, there was still a slight-feeling that he was ticked. When they got to bed, Michael had put in another nineteen-hour day, since he'd been over just the night before.

She turned to him and asked, "Look, I'm really wiped. Could we catch this in the morning?"

"No problem," replied Mike. In the dark, she could not see his hurt, puppy-dog face. He wasn't getting his way.

Michael slept about an hour when Mike's tossing and turning woke her up. "What's the matter?" Her frustration with him, and lack of sleep on her part, made the situation unreal.

"Nothing!" he raised his voice at her. Hours later Michael had only dozed off and on with Mike's restlessness. Once again, she asked what was the matter, with his same reply. At five in the morning, he was up slamming around making obvious noise to wake her.

"What the hell is going on? What are you looking for?" she called out to him.

"I'm leaving. I can't be expected to lay in bed with you all night, like this." He slammed out of the door like a depraved man, that had been taunted and tempted all night. When Mike called later that night, Michael was *still* irritable since she'd *still* not gotten any sleep. When she asked what prompted his grand-performance in the morning, he became defensive and soon was as pissed as she was. One word let to another until he said, "Well, see you around sometime kid."

"That's just fine with me, Mister!" The sex that had glued them together, broke them apart. The realization of it all, did not hit Michael until she finished work that day, which was Friday. Her rebelling against a man's control, and her independence released once again put her in a state of shock. When she went to bed that night, she did not leave it until Monday morning when she went to work. Michael hadn't adjusted till her mother called on Tuesday, with her water pump trouble in the car. Since her step-dad died that past spring, Mike told her he wanted to maintain her car for her. Not wanting to give her mother an excuse, she called Mike to ask for his help.

He was very surly over the phone, and when Michael thought about it afterwards, she got pissed, and called him back spurting off how could he be such an S.O.B when they'd been through so much together. After they both cooled-down, he asked if he could come over that night and she said 'yes.' Still, it was never the same, and they knew it never would be. Though they continued to try for about a month off and on. In October, Mike started dating Cathy.

He was seeing Cathy and several other women as agreed, but Michael was not seeing other men, though she told Mike that she was. Michael told herself that it was logical for Mike to see Cathy, since they had such a long friendship, beside the interspersed sex and other involvement over the years. Then, when Cathy married the man that looked so much like Mike, she more than admitted her feelings for him. At the same time, Cathy epitomized his complete ideal of the acceptable-presentable woman to the establishment - especially meaning his mother.

Though Mike openly stated to Michael and Beth, his contemptuous-dislike of his mother, for trying to control and punish him. But, like any child, he still wanted her acceptance and love. And, to Louise, Cathy would be the perfect wife and mother - never tainted by anything untoward. Of course, no one knew how well Cathy *covered* her tracks. Well known to Mike, and everyone who knew Michael, the last thing she wanted was acceptance by *any* establishment.

The big problem/question, if Cathy didn't really satisfy Mike's sex urges *before* Michael, how would she ever do so *after* her. Cathy could not have changed that much. Like so many men, what was between his legs, sometimes influenced his actions. It dawned on Mike that he could see Cathy, and when he really missed the tantalizing-sex with Michael, he'd return to her.

It never occurred to him, that he was doing both women an injustice, not that he ever put their concerns first anyway. Cathy knew she'd never get to build a rapport with Mike - sexually or otherwise - if he continued to see Michael, so she began to give him flack about his continued liaisons with Michael. At first Michael didn't see the problem, until she realized Cathy was building to take their relationship into marriage. Since she never pushed for it, and still doubted if she wanted it, then aggravating Cathy with seeing Mike became a game.

Thanksgiving rolled around, and Mike promised to spend the night, as well all day with Michael. The boys would be with Barb, and they'd all leave together for the farm Thanksgiving night. When Mike appeared that Wednesday evening at the apartment, he simply announced there'd been a change of plans - he and the boys would be leaving first thing in the morning for the farm. Michael quickly knew that she was getting the crumbs, as Mike spent the holiday with Cathy and her children also, at the farm. To say she once again fell apart, was putting it mildly. Her emotions ran the gamut of screaming to crying, till the sunlight appeared.

She knew she wanted him back, and though she never knew jealousy, it was exploding out of her. Not only her imminent-aloneness on the holiday caused the hurting, as much as the fact of his having a good time at the farm without her. At his return on Monday, they decided to only see each other until December first, then nothing until February first, to see what decisions would be made with the separation. For the next few days, of course, they saturated themselves with sex.

Michael only made it through a little over half of December, before the depression crushed her, and she called him. Mike, on the other hand, had been content seeing several other women and Cathy. This got Michael's back-up, so she started rattling off pseudo-men that she saw, so he'd not know of her loneliness without hm. He did not offer to see her, and she did not ask. Beth was coming in for the holidays, with Mike having her and Jeremy out to the farm for Christmas Eve, so Mike called to invite Michael. She knew it was a gratis-call, he really didn't want her and she felt she shouldn't intrude on Beth's limited time.

* * * * * *

Though perhaps contagious, and definitely ironic, discontent also brewed with Connie regarding Cam. on the same topics of independence versus control. She'd known Greg for several years, as his second home was also the Fire-Lite. The only difference was that Greg was a bartender there, who had realized his drinking problem several years before, and joined Alcoholics Anonymous to stop. Many a night, while Connie waited for Cam to come in, she'd talk with

Greg. In the past few months, he became a rock to Connie, that she could cling to while she dumped out her hostility about Cam. The longer Connie had to wait, the more she drank and the more she talked to Greg. He listened quietly, with his sober-patience sometimes making comments, but mostly teasing and cheering Connie-up with his jokes, or witty remarks. He usually kept a running commentary with the other customers, that would always get some kind of a rise or laugh out of Connie.

Probably the same age as Cam, Greg was about fifty or fifty-one. He was also about as tall, but his build was a little tighter, with dark hair and soft brown eyes. The greatest difference was probably, that Greg had a soft-face with a very, easy smile. It resembled his way of life, that he rolled with the flow, not concerned with building or maintaining a facade to anyone, or for anything.

Cam, always on guard, to *always* be first with the zany-remarks and clever witticisms. It was almost as if, always 'on,' or a part of his image that was so important to maintain. Cam was concerned with his age and being 'with it.' It was his way of running from the foreboded, increasing age number. Greg just took it for what it was, a number that was going to increase no mater what he did, so why sweat it or worry over it.

Sometimes, becoming comfortable with someone was another extension of the friendship that had built-up. With Connie, being comfortable also meant that she could say or do almost anything, and the friend would accept it. She'd been this way with Greg, as over the years talked about a vast number of things, and he always listened to her, never chiding or making fun of her the way Cam would, to put her down. Yet, he didn't always just agree, but argued when he felt she was wrong, and almost applauded when she had any original ideas. Cam usually didn't even listen, or if he did, he'd automatically put Connie down, no matter what stance she took, and finding some joke in it for him to boast about.

So, Connie began to look at Greg in a different light, as they joked and teased about sex, though he never made a direct pass at Connie, in all the time that she'd known him. Greg was married, and Connie was aware that he did play around, but he was not an open flirt. Connie'd even seen him pass up obvious invitations when she was there, as if he preferred talking with her to indiscriminate sex. Cam was out of town for several days, when Connie thought she'd fulfill her little game plan, that she'd been toying with for some time. She came into the bar as usual, and at the beginning of the conversation, she let him know that Cam was out of town and she had no plans for the evening.

When Connie came back from the restroom, before she could change her mind, she passed him a note on a bar napkin while gone. As soon as she gave it to him, she wanted to erase the whole scene. Greg opening the note, which said, "Why don't we go to my house - smoke some grass and fuck our brains out?" He burst out laughing, tore up the note and dropped it in the trash.

"I'm sure you're kidding, but that's still the best proposal that I've had all year, or even longer." Smiling, he intently looked into Connie's face and eyes, to see if she was joking or not. It was an uncomfortable minute for them both, since this really was no joking matter. Greg knew that Connie had not played around on Cam in years. Looking down into his club soda, he asked directly, now serious, "Are you kidding?"

Connie still silent and thinking, but didn't want him to think she proposed marriage, jokingly said, "No I'm not kidding. Nothing the matter with a 'friendly-fuck' between two buddies now, is there?" Greg was just finishing his shift, as she knew, and arrangements were settled, and she finished her drink. She sat at her little table making odds with herself, that he'd not show up and how embarrassed she'd be, the next time she saw him when the knock came at the door.

Greg said he hadn't smoked any grass since the old days, when very young and played with a few boys in the band. There was no miracle, or great explosion of ecstasy for either one of them, yet there was something more to this evening, than just another one-nighter. Even without the grass, she would have been loose and easy with this man, but with the grass, they'd been giddy, able to say and do all kinds of foolishness.

Connie in her buzzed-state, noticed Greg let go himself much easier with the grass, than Cam did. Greg called before Connie left for work in the morning, and then again from the Fire-Lite. The phone was ringing, as she came in from work. The following two nights were almost a repeat of the first one, except that Greg brought dinner for the two of them the second night, and Connie fixed it the third.

Neither one of them brought up the subject of Cam or Greg's wife. Before any promises were broken, they were not going to be made, until they both had an idea where this was all going. Connie soon noticed that on her own, her drinking had almost stopped when she was in Greg's presence. He sent her a card almost everyday, sometimes just funny, and sometimes very romantic.

Even the romantic ones Connie would chuckle over, since he signed a different, unusual name to each one of them - male and female. The day after she told him where she kept her spare key, she came home to a gorgeous bouquet of flowers. The note attached said, "Hope you didn't work too hard. XXX Hortense." Connie just shook her head and laughed.

It didn't take long before she was comparing Greg to Cam. Maybe Cam would've made some attempts at changes, if he'd known that he was being judged and rated for his past nine years. He still took Connie totally for granted, and noticed no changes in her. When at the Fire-Lite, she was very careful not to talk too long to Greg, or avoid talking to him, either. She did become very aware of Cam's drinking, and that he obviously did have a problem.

Someone who had a minimum bar-tab of two hundred a month was not a light, social drinker. Connie also noticed she still had to drink when she was with Cam, as he appeared now almost obnoxious to her sober-self. She began looking forward to Cam's trips out of town more and more as things between her and Greg only got better.

There was no pushing or prodding from Greg for Connie to break off with Cam. On the other hand, she noted that Greg dropped all of the other women he'd been seeing. Trying to give Cam the full benefit to change before he lost her completely, she began asking him why he never romanced her anymore with flowers or cards, to confirm his feelings for her. Cam could only laugh at the notion, and then asked,"Why?"

She looked him square in the eye, dead serious and said, "Cam, if I have to tell you why, then you can just forget it." Unfortunately, for Cam, he did.

Connie was out for dinner with Cam, when she stopped to call Greg on her way to the restroom. She told him how much she'd have preferred to be with him, when he interrupted to say 'I love you,' Connie was dumbfounded. They both had avoided any words of commitment in the past few months. Now it was out, and *now* she could also acknowledge her feelings, too.

"God, Greg, I love you, too. I've been so afraid to think it, much less say it, but I do. I love you . . . " That was the moment Cam rounded the corner, saying he'd come to look for her. She quickly recovered, "Yes, Michael, don't forget to call Mrs. Thompson about the job tomorrow. I'll talk to you later."

Cam started in, "My God, Connie, your dinner is getting cold, and . . . I thought maybe you've been raped by a band-of-marauding-gypsies. I mean, I hate to interrupt a good time . . . "

She didn't know how to tell him, his clever jokes and sarcastic remarks lost their humor. She simply walked past him and back to the table, never bothering to give any further explanation to the phone call, other than the part she made up for him.

Connie knew well enough if Cam had heard the previous remark, he'd have said something. Now, of course, it was up to her to decide exactly what her next step would be. She knew she was incapable of loving *fully* two men. She had over nine years with Cam, and though it had not all been roses, she'd not done badly with him. Cam was right, her dinner was getting cold, and the decisions she had to make would not be done in one evening.

Déjà Vu

My heart is almost keeping pace
to the beat of the second hand,
as it sweeps around
the face of the clock,
ticking off the moments
of my remaining life.

My mind is flashing slides
across the prism
screen of my brain,
reflecting visions
of what I must have done
in some previous life time.

We have a destiny
to fulfill with each other,
as surely as spring green
will follow winter brown,
and all the inevitable
things of life slipping by.

Karmic ties bind us together
in a groping understanding.
Is it that we know
the concluding chapters
having read the words before,
or is it simply that we wrote them?

Chapter 33

Picking Up Life's Pieces

Beth was doing very well in Oklahoma City, considering her self-imposed celibacy wasn't being threatened by the likes of the male population. She had more raises, was putting in lots of overtime and been able to pick up several free-lance advertising jobs, including some promotions for the Art Museum, following through after Lori. The more important thing Beth learned, she could become good friends with men, without being sexually involved with them. They were really interested in her opinions on things, and just talking in general. This job had given her an opportunity to meet a vast variety of men, from very wealthy oil clients to truck drivers coming in and out to pick-up shipments.

Technically, Beth was the Assistant Manager - as Terry the Manager, was frequently gone out to do field inspections. An older gentleman came in wanting to see him, and she said he was out and could she help him, as she was the Assistant Manager. He looked at her like she couldn't be serious, and said he'd wait. She then told him he wouldn't be back in for a day or two, would he like some coffee for his wait? "Where you all from, Girl, … you sure is uppity?"

In no mood for his local-yokel crap, "I'm from Chicago, and no one's called me a 'Girl,' since I was twelve." He got up and walked out. Beth never asked his name, and he didn't give it. Typical of many of the lease-holders, so she mentioned to Terry a 'weirdo' came in and wouldn't leave his name. He just laughed, saying he had a lot of them out there.

Beth continued the routine of being the third person with a couple. As she worked with these men, and had no desirous interest in them, the wives were also comfortable with her company. It gave Beth something to look forward to on the weekends, as Oklahoma being a dry-state for liquor service. Beth actually lost interest in going to bars to hang out to meet someone. Spending the time with the couples, began to renew her faith in marriage, and the possibility of some really good men still out there.

Perhaps the move had been most beneficial in realizing that getting away from Chicago, she met people who had some very basic beliefs in caring for each other. How did the saying go, "Even if you win the rat race, you're still a rat." Beth felt she was no longer running so hard and fast on the treadmill, that never got anywhere. She was finally getting to know who she was, and even beginning to like what she saw. Maybe there was something to be said for this "Me" decade, as the media had begun to refer to it, with all of its "How To" books, and jargon of 'getting in touch' with yourself. But, it was beginning to make sense that she'd not be able to relate to another man or woman, if she couldn't relate to herself.

Beth liked men for friends, especially when all they wanted from her was the friendship. Clarification of what she wanted in a man and a relationship, came the more she was around them. But there was still no hurry, since Beth was liking this time to herself, as she knew she still had a ways to go. She attended church with a couple and even found that it seemed not to be condemning or chastising. It gave her a good warm feeling, to know that though she felt she had left God when she got her divorce, He never left her.

Beth's birthday came and went without the fanfare that the girls usually celebrated for their birthdays. Her biggest thrill, perhaps was that her brother Mike called, reminded by some prodding from Michael. The aloneness for her birthday helped Beth to decide, that she'd return to Chicago for Christmas.

The time and distance healed some wounds and resentments in the past. Her parents were old, and not in the best of health, so she'd have to make the trek back at least once a year, while they were alive. Beth hadn't been thrilled that her mother shipped much she didn't want - old, broken and worn, but then it had been a big task to ask of anyone. One thing that Beth was not happy about, was Louise riffled through her stuff, and pulled out all of her Playgirl centerfold men, and most sadly Bobby Ryan's autographed one. At least her father paid the movers, and with her tax refund the first of the year, she planned to pay him back.

Since Marie and Beth still weren't speaking, Rose invited Beth and Jeremy to the farm for after Thanksgiving. Marie and the two girls were there for Thanksgiving Day. Rose's brother Mark, had come down from Chicago with his son, Johnny, and once again Rose was trying to play cupid for Beth. Mark was recently divorced, and a few months younger than Beth. They hadn't seen each other since maybe they were twelve-years old.

At first Rose told Beth Mark was interested in moving to Oklahoma. She said, "He's tired of all the snow, and also needs the change . . . you know. Such a long-hassle before they finally got divorced." In the far reaches of her mind, Beth'd been considering returning to Chicago. If things worked out with Mark, maybe he could make the difference. If he was interested in Oklahoma, then it would give her more purpose for staying.

On the other hand, if he wanted to stay in Chicago, it'd give Beth more of a reason for going back, rather than admitting she was not *that* happy in Oklahoma. For a fleeting moment that independent side said, *"Don't let a man be the basis of your decisions . . . "* Beth ignored it, as she trudged into the living room to say her hellos to Mr. and Mrs. Porter and Mark, with a big smile on her face.

Mark'd grown tall and good looking, but was slightly conscious of his thinning, black hair. It didn't bother Beth, as it seemed to be a chronic problem with men these days, as she wished she dropped a few more pounds. Johnny and Jeremy got along great playing outside, as Rose tried to get Beth and Mark together as much as possible. Mark was more on the shy-side, and Beth was nervous, because it'd been so long since she'd been in this sort of situation. The word 'dating' still sounded so juvenile.

When Beth asked what food she could bring for the weekend, Rose simply asked Beth to make her great lasagna. "It'll show Mark what a good cook you are."

"Rose, really, you make me feel like I'm a spinster, who needs unloading on the first eligible-man." Dinner ran almost smoothly, with Beth having to play referee once between Mrs. Porter and Rose. After their parents left to return to the city, Rose started pushing Mark and Beth should go into town for a few drinks with David, her stepson. Her husband John, made a remark or two they didn't need David as a chaperone. But Rose ignored him, as she knew they'd all feel more comfortable with it being the three of them.

Beth insisted on sitting in the back, because of David's long legs and the bucket seats of Mark's car. Besides, she didn't want Mark to feel like she was pushing herself on him. He was a Gemini, and hard to tell what his feelings were. When they got to the first bar, it was only beer and pool, but it was some place to start to break the ice. They each played a game, and soon the beer was going to Beth's head, as she hadn't drank in so long. She needed to change to scotch, if she was to last the night, between getting giddy and peeing every twenty minutes from the beer. The waitress told them of another place, so they were off for the atmosphere to warrant talking.

They settled into a corner table in the smoke-filled room, with the loud music far enough back to not drown, but cover, the talk. Trying to include David into the conversation, while they both talked openly about their divorces, Beth reminded David he could learn from what they were saying. "David, "don't do as I do' routine is still the best information. We were both too young when we got married, and both had a slight case of hot pants. You have to wait till you're at least twenty-five, so you are thinking with what's above your shoulders, and not with what's below your waist." Mark almost choked at Beth's bluntness. "Well, why beat around. He's twenty-one, and no virgin. He should be talked to straight!"

Mark laughed. "Yea, I guess you're right. You're really something else." Beth then laughed, as she told him she'd been told that before several times, as a matter of fact.

When they got back to the house, Mark put a few more logs on the fire. Rose turned down the sofa bed for Beth, and the two boys were tucked in their beds for the night. Beth sat on the end of the bed, with a blanket around her, as she watched the fire. David felt his presence wasn't needed, so he said good night. Beth turned to Mark, standing by the fire. "Why don't you sit down." She motioned toward the end of the bed, since there were no chairs close by the fire. "Warm yourself. The fire is sure mesmerizing." Mark slowly slid onto the end of the bed, being careful not to let Beth think he was moving up on her. As cool and collected as Beth tried to bring it off, she didn't want any fast moves to her freeze up.

They talked about the divorces some more, as Beth could see him relaxing with letting it all out. He probably didn't have a lot of people he could talk to, who understood or listened. Beth experienced similar herself, or someone she knew had been through the same type of things he had - it made her realize, once again how much she learned. They talked for over an hour before they said good night.

Beth stayed awake for a long time, going over in her mind the definite good points of this man, and trying not to emphasize the bad points - as usual for her. There was something calculating, about the way he was able to turn his emotions off and on, but Beth tried to equate that with the effect of only being divorced six months, after five years of on-off separations. She was going to see what she wanted to see, and that was all there was to it.

They did not have much more time to talk, as he left at two o'clock the next afternoon, to drive back to Chicago. It was something Beth couldn't understand, since he made such a good buck, why he'd put himself thorough such a long drive, when the weather could become treacherous that time of the year. Even when Beth couldn't afford it, she flew because she felt her time and patience were worth more, than she could save money-wise.

Before he left, Rose managed to set-up their next meeting, "Since you'll both be alone Christmas Day, why don't you get together - talk over more old times or new times - whatever."

Beth halfway-laughed and said, "If you don't have any plans, Mark, my parents would love to have you for dinner. I'll be at my brother's farm Christmas Eve, but I have to have Jeremy back by noon. Call me if you want, and we'll set it up from there."

"That sounds good to me," Mark nodded., "I'll let you know."

Though Beth had the urge to kiss him goodby after Rose did, she didn't want to put him on the spot, so she simply said "Drive carefully." Consciously and subconsciously, Beth was already plotting if this man could be *made to fit* into her life. What she wouldn't acknowledge, of course, was her loneliness and wanting to be in love again. Shortly after returning to the city, Beth wrote Mark to tell him how much she'd enjoyed the atmosphere of the farm, and their talk by the fire. Without sounding too pushy, she tried to let him know she had feelings for him, and looked forward to seeing him again in Chicago.

With his Christmas card, Mark enclosed a letter also, saying how much he'd enjoyed the same things. So far so good, thought Beth, as she began to plan how she could spend more time with him, during her short time there. Beth kept talking herself into stronger feelings, as she pointed out that he also only had a son, who was just a few months older than Jeremy, and they'd played well together. She kept going on, over all his good points - intelligent, quiet, but dry sense of humor and a good job. She tried to ignore any of the bad points, as only hearsay from Rose, or things that would change once he was back into a marriage. She was tying everything up into a neat, little package, she'd make him fit into it.

Rose then thought she'd have Mark pick-up some sausage, she couldn't get in Oklahoma from their aunt in the city, then have Beth bring it back to her. As a joke, she offered Beth's body to pay back the favor to Mark. She now brought the sex out into the open, making Beth look compromising and more than interested. Mark called and Beth nervously laughed at the whole thing, not wanting to let Mark know she was easy, yet not wanting him to think she wasn't interested at all. Trying to cover all the bases, she failed at covering any of them. She really hadn't made up her mind and before she knew it, the time had come and she was in Chicago.

Their flight was delayed coming in, because of a union work-slow-down, so Beth had already lost her evening with Connie and Michael. She'd gone with Lori the next night to see *"Side by Side by*

Sonheim" at the dinner theater in Chicago. Beth wasn't ready for the total family confrontation, so she took Jeremy and went out to Mike's farm for Christmas Eve. Beth thought that the trip out to the country would help, and it did to a certain extent. Mike got a bottle of her favorite wine, and after all the non-drinking in OKC, she still consumed the whole bottle.

She then went on to scotch when they went out to the local bar, to see some of Mike's friends. Beth was sliding right back into her old self, with the booze, getting loud and obnoxious. Maybe it was because she wasn't sure if the others would accept her changed, so she accommodatingly reverted-back to the one everyone knew.

Beth paid for it all in the morning, by throwing up and having a head like she couldn't remember. She then had the long ride back to Elmwood, borrowing her nephew's car. At least Jeremy had a good time snowmobiling, and rough-housing with Jackie and Jason. Beth also had Jason take her out on the snowmobile, when she was well-oiled and not worrying about her arm.

Even with the snow and icy roads, Beth flew back to Elmwood hitting seventy and eighty most of the way, figuring the police would be resting Christmas morning. She got Jeremy ready to go with Bruce, and then returned Mark's call she'd just missed. She was glad to hear, he was about in the same condition she was, and a two o'clock dinner would be fine. He would pick-up the sausage before coming over.

There was a slightly awkward moment, as Mark moved his red Monte Carlo for Bruce to leave in his brown Gremlin - it certainly typified the two men. The dinner was pleasantly quiet, as Beth insisted to her mother not invite any of the straggling-family, she always seemed to gather in for holidays. Her father didn't ask too many questions of Mark, and Beth was grateful he also didn't ask him if he wanted to join his lodge. Anxious to leave when they finished dinner. and her head was much better. She even looked forward to a walk in the snow-covered woods. As long as she didn't get nervous, she could retrain herself to be the person he'd known at the farm.

She'd asked him to drive over to an old, popular ice skating place, they'd known as kids. The cold was refreshing, but much too bitter for a leisurely stroll. Their mutual love of nature was a good feeling, though Beth was grabbing at any connection they might have. Back in the car, it was where-to next. Mark suggested a movie and Beth stridently said, "Have you ever been to a show on a holiday?"

Mark looked at her questioningly, while he shook his head 'no.'

"Sorry, I didn't mean to pop at you, … the crowds are big."

Mark hesitated, then suggested, "Well, maybe if you want, we could go to my place and we could talk, or just watch some TV."

"Fine," Beth responded, "I can see how today's bachelor lives." She felt unbalanced.

Not as if she was going into a web she couldn't get out of, Beth just didn't want them to both feel the pressure of the situation. She was overcompensating, and worrying about everything, *and* she really didn't know why. The evening flew by as they listened to music, talked and laughed. Maybe Beth talked too much about her past loves, as honesty filled with titillation wasn't part of what she wanted to portray, yet what poured out of her mouth. They had a little bit of wine, but not more than a glow to mellow them. Beth stayed as nervous as Mark, as they both sat in the corners of the couch. She tried to inch nonchalantly toward him, and did some light hand touching, but he still did not make any great response.

Finally, it was after midnight, and they'd been together over seven-hours talking about everything from God, to work and politics. Mark came in from leaving the car to warm up, since it was now one of Chicago's famous bitter, cold nights. Beth's natural response was to put her hands on his face to warm his bright, red cheeks.

Slowly, looking at one another, they slipped into a kiss, with Beth hesitating and breaking it off. Why, she never knew, but the moment was gone, and she rejected Mark when that was the last thing that she wanted to do. Her tongue now tied, and not thinking of a clever thing to say, or do to recapture the moment to start it again.

They reverted back to general conversation, and he soon helped her on with her coat. Maybe Beth didn't feel worthy of him, and if she did let herself go, that he'd not want her. A long drive back to Elmwood, Beth kept talking to Mark about coming down to Oklahoma. Although he made it clear, he was not interested in moving there, and he was a lot more hung-up on this stock-car racing and building, than she previously realized. Not just a hobby, but a passion.

Somehow with pulling in the driveway at her parents, Beth began to feel like she might not see him agin, and she really wanted him to know how much she enjoyed the day and him. They sat for a few minutes talking, when she finally decided it was a right time to kiss him. Since she was showing feelings, he also responded with feelings. It began with passion, but ended-up being stupid. Two grown people in a car, trying for sexual stimulation like s couple of teenagers. They both let their glands take-over, and now they were almost embarrassed at the results. Somehow what had at one point, been beautiful was now tacky.

There was no way to say goodbye, and Beth couldn't help but ask, if she'd see him the next day before she flew out. "Maybe we could put this together the right way, and be a good time." It was almost as if she was pleading, even after the evidence was in.

Mark hesitated, then reluctantly said, "I'll call you if I don't have to work too long." Beth knew he wouldn't, but she wanted a thread to hold onto. Top it all off, she couldn't find her keys, so rang the doorbell, to wake her father up to get in. All in all, she'd literally screwed up, when she hadn't pursued him at his place, since she had the perfect excuse of weather to stay over.

Mark did not call the next day, so pretending to be the liberated-woman, Beth called him. He talked about needing a getaway weekend, and Oklahoma was as good a place as any to come for it. Beth felt like she was politely being put-off and rejected. He couldn't see where he had time that day working on a car, but he'd call her to let her know if he'd be coming to Oklahoma.

She tried to keep the conversation light, but the situation the night before made it off. Some people seal a relationship with a kiss, she tried to seal it with sex. Someday, she'd be secure enough within herself, that she wouldn't feel that the sex she could give a man was the only thing she was good for. He'd be a good one that got away, because she used the wrong bait.

Beth got back with Michael and Connie when they both took her to the airport. Since Jeremy would be staying on with Bruce for the week, they had plenty of time before her plane took off. It was the first time that Beth had as chance to talk to Michael, about her tentative break up with Mike. Beth had more than heard his side of it, when at the farm. It was still all too new and raw for Michael to go into details, but she definitely was a basket-case. One minute admitting they might yet get back together, and the next just wanting to kill him.

As always, how could something so right seem to go all wrong. They still had the sex, but what eventually Michael had to learn was that as much as they both changed, and tried to change for each other, they could never be the person the other one wanted. Beth had a feeling that it would take a lot of pain, for them both to let go and start again with new people.

Connie hesitated to tell Beth about Greg, because he was another married-man, so she just related her problems with Cam. She said the fun was gone out of everything he said and did, only leaving her with a feeling of *'living a rerun-life.'* Even now, he was seriously talking about divorce again, Connie questioned if this man was the one she wanted to marry.

It had been nine years, and she could only talk about the hassles he was constantly giving her, and she him. As Beth listened, she felt that there was somehow part of the story missing. She knew Connie for six years, and the only times they ever lied to one another was because of a man. In time, if there was another man involved, she'd tell Beth, so she didn't push it.

"Listen," Connie was saying, as if to convince herself, as much as the others, "by the Fourth of July, Cam should have his divorce, and we're going to get married on his boat. Everybody will be invited, and we'll have a great time." After Michael said that she felt Connie would only be trying to prove a point by marrying him, Connie retreated and started spewing out more complaints about his most recent bullshit.

Beth started laughing and pointed out, "More than anything Connie, you've definitely outgrown Cam. You'll turn thirty in just two weeks, so you're not the gullible girl of twenty, who'd been grateful, he was more than a one-night stand."

Beth finished her drink, as she realized she wasn't the only one battling the changes, attacking and tearing her life into so many pieces.

"This growing up when you're already an adult, is a real bitch. Hopefully, like everything else that didn't come easy, it will be worth it in the long run - that is if we can make the long run!" She chuckled at herself again, "It's nice to know at least, if we've outgrown some of them, we've not outgrown OUR friendship."

The flight back was long and lonely, as she tried to rehash her rushed, long weekend. It didn't seem like she accomplished much, but she learned a few lessons. Beth would not share any of the details of her time with Mark, as she knew that Rose felt that the sex should have taken precedence over the talk. Beth thought she would have slipped into the sex easier with Mark, if Rose had not made such a point of it to begin with. Still, there was no one to blame but herself. Beth hated the game-playing. Everybody did it, but why? Was life really so hard to play as it was? The New Year could certainly hold some changes that had to be improvements - but then, she said the same thing with great hope, every year.

For weeks and even months later, Beth'd be driving down the road, think about Mark and all she could say was 'Shit' - over and over again. Somehow, she had the feeling that he'd been a very, good lesson to be long-remembered, and hopefully the last one along that vein. Beth wrote to April to see what she thought about a match to Mark - somehow in Beth's stubbornness, she wanted to make sure in no-uncertain-terms it wouldn't have worked out. A simple, direct answer from April - NO. Beth was too emotional for a flighty Gemini.

To keep herself out of the pits, and from feeling sorry for herself, Beth decided to invite a few friends over for New Year's Eve. She'd become close with Vic and his new wife, Brenda. He had truly been the only interesting person Beth worked with. Now married, his wife joined him in Oklahoma from Houston, and Beth was anxious to know her better. It was Vic's second marriage and Brenda's third. After six months of marriage and living together even longer, they were *still* blissfully happy, and in love. It gave Beth hope that someday she might also find who and what she wanted in a man with marriage.

Brenda was very honest with Beth about her past with married men and others. At lunch one Saturday, Beth asked her how Vic handled her past, since they'd been friends for several years before becoming lovers. She easily answered, "Just that, Beth, it's my past and my future is with him. He's a very special, understanding man and I know how lucky I am to have found him. Men are changing, not as fast as we are, but then they don't have as much to catch up with as we do." This key phrase about the past, Beth would long remember.

The other couple Beth was having over was Tricia and Dick, she'd met through friends of Fran. Married almost ten years, although theirs was not a blissfully-happy marriage, but one in which they both respected each other's individuality. Dick had been in the Air Force, and now in civil service, while Tricia returned to college to finish her degree and masters. Beth enjoyed visiting their home because the conversations were always lively, yet deep, with many of Tricia's student friends - male and female - freely contributing their opinions, no matter how controversial the subjects. For Oklahoma, and its majority population being so conservative - like living in the 1950s - these two were truly a rare-find for the liberated and liberal Beth.

So, once again it was friends who saw Beth through the hard places of her life, and opened up the new vistas, she wanted in leaving Chicago, Elmwood and her past behind. With the New Year, Beth had many plans to put into action - the changes she so wanted in her life.

The Conversation

My ears
are trying to hear
the words
you are not saying.

My mind
is filling in the blanks
of your empty
conversation.

My eyes
are trying to see
if the there is a different
meaning behind yours.

Your lips
are moving,
yet the words
are now foreign to me.

I try to smile
and nod agreement,
but the salt from my tears
leaves a bitter taste in my mouth.

CHAPTER 34

Cold Turkey and Lies

The holidays were almost a relief to have over with for all of them. If nothing else, the New Year, 1978, would certainly bring some changes and hopefully those would be improvements. April noticed simple, memory-lapses and becoming indecisive with basic decisions. She'd been on her diet pills from the 'good' doctor for ten years. Her sleep became more erratic, as she realized what was happening to her.

She already started her master plan of how she'd get out from under Alex, but she knew she'd never have complete faith in herself, until she gave up the pills. She already accomplished so much, so quickly with her astrology career, but she feared greatly the imminent, weigh-gain and loss of the false-energy the pills gave her.

April tried 'cold-turkey' in the past, only to sink quickly into a chemically-reacted-depression. She made up her mind, if she was going to try it again, she'd plan a time of strength from her planets-inner chart. When the day and the time planned arrived, she ceremoniously threw the remainder of the pills down the toilet, and tried to keep herself from falling apart, by reminding herself how much better she'd be once they completely cleared her system.

Three days after disposing of the pills, April went into heavy withdrawals. She became suicidal with only a thread of reasoning left, to tell herself that it was only the withdrawals and it would soon be over with. Still, she'd never conceived that they'd be as horrendous as they were. If she had done it at a weaker time, she'd most definitely have killed herself. Even with the vomiting and dry heaves, she tried to maintain a small shred of sanity, reminding herself that it would surely pass soon.

Late on a Friday night, with Alex gone and the girls at their father's, that the worst pressure hit. In between the diarrhea, shakes and chills, April tried phoning for help. She just couldn't seem to get anyone home, or even no answer at the crisis-line, when she felt like she was slipping over the edge, feeling that death would be her only relief. She still had the consciousness of pride not to call any of her professional friends. Instead, she finally called Michael, she'd seen Sybil through this, and came right over, never asking why.

Michael held April tightly, as she softly cried-out her fears of not wanting to die, yet the racking pains of the withdrawal, made it seem the only way to escape. While April was vomiting again, Michael tried desperately to get through to one of the crisis-lines. She finally gave up trying to track-down an antidote, so just sat and held April, since it seemed to have such a comforting effect. By the time Alex got home, April was able to go to bed, with only some chills and shaking left. She knew that Michael was not comfortable with Alex around, so she insisted that it was all right for her to leave.

When April woke in the morning, the affects had left her body enough, that she was now in control of her faculties. Michael called her in the morning to see how she was, and if she needed any help of any kind. April never fully comprehended that Michael, or the others ever realized what they'd done to her that night, over a year before, when they turned on her. They just thought that April was squirreled away with her astrology, and her bad marriage.

At first April was cool to Michael, since she'd not expected the phone call, and she no longer needed Michael or anyone else. The strength of the wall that she'd been building up around her was once again under full power, and now hers with no help from any pills. Still, April listened, and she heard Michael reaching out to her.

April could not refuse Michael's need, so she reluctantly went over to talk to her. Michael had written off April's coolness on the phone, as still under the influence of the withdrawals. When she saw April, and talked to her with very little emotional response on April's part, she knew something had very differently changed in her. "April, for God's sake, what is the matter with you? I have just poured out my feelings to you, and you sit there nodding!" Michael was very taken aback by her actions.

Very dryly, April responded, "I don't let myself feel anymore, about anything or anyone. I have absolutely no feeling. I do not even listen to music, because it might stir up some feelings."

Now it was Michael, who was in a state of shock that the emotional April, who always surrounded herself with everyone else's problems, and then with hers could sit there like a deep freezer, reciting out her excuse. As April once pushed herself to block Michael out of her mind, she now had to make the effort to get back into Michael's life. It was a strange period of adjustment for them both.

The icy-April sat and listen to Michael, though she knew how distant April was. Still, April could not refuse Michael's needs of friendship, since she came when April was at her very lowest point. Yet, everything they talked about was an effort on April's part, as her *wall of needing,* so well built around her.

With time and Michael's patience, April slowly unfrosted, but stopped before she turned to 'mush' again. Then, she personified the cool, confident-career-oriented woman, who could still be human to her friends and others. Michael had a problem accepting this new April, because *career* to Michael was so far away in the distant future. April never went into her problems unless Michael directly asked.

With the change of April's personality, and not being able to be hurt by any remarks anyone might say, she was able to get along with Connie. Once Connie got all the zingers-out of her system that she'd been saving up for April, they became *somewhat* of friends. It had always been April's whining and bitching that pissed-off Connie before anyway. Now that April had a stiff-upper-lip about everything she lived with, Connie gained much respect for April and her complete professionalism.

Since Michael's affair with Mike was on the skids, and she fully knew what it was like to be in love and losing that love, she had greater understanding of what pain April went through with Al. Michael also began to gain respect for April's strength, and was listening a bit more intently than she did before. April kept her friends she'd built on her own, and was soon integrating Michael into them.

Though Michael had problems with the intricate math of astrology, she still struggled to learn, with taking April's classes at the college.

Seeing how April was with her new friends, Michael also got a different perspective of the professional-side of April. She never pushed Michael into the astrology, but she did let her know that it was open, if Michael wanted to learn it. April had a slight apprehension about letting Michael fully into her new life, with all of her professional friends that only knew the new April. She gave Michael the ground-rules of what was *not* to be said in front of these people, and Michael had no qualms about following her requests.

The middle of January, Jackie, Mike's older son was taking a course at the college, and Michael stopped in to drop off the information, since she was also taking one. She picked-up the registration forms for them both. Mike was home, and asked Michael if she'd like to take-in a movie. As fate would have it, the movie was sold-out, so they picked up a bottle of wine and came back to Mike's house. With the bottle of wine gone, it was an easy-enough excuse to hit the rack together.

It didn't take long for Cathy to find out, and once again gave Mike an ultimatum of choosing between her and Michael. The meetings between Mike and Michael once again became clandestine, Michael never knowing fully the reasons behind it, and never asking.

* * * * * *

In all of Connie's experience, and all the men she knew, she never really had a man who totally romanced her. Since it always seemed, that she was more interested in the sex, it was assumed that she was not then interested in being romanced. She just had her thirtieth birthday, and Greg surprised her with a beautiful, hand-woven wool cape. Connie did not know how to respond to such generosity, when he also gave her a dressy, pants-outfit for Christmas. Not really the difference in money, she was thinking of when comparing them to what Cam gave her, but the fact Greg's gifts were more personally chosen. She had dictated to Cam what to give her.

Connie became the non-participating-member in sex with Cam. As he had to have someone to blame for this, he chose Michael. Connie laughed when he said that she was cutting him off in sympathy to Michael and Mike breaking-up. Cam, of course, did not know that she started with Greg the same week of Michael's *original* break-up with Mike. Connie hadn't really cut Cam off, as much as she was not responding to him with the sex. At first Cam thought she was pulling a joke or putting him on, but when it continued for months, he could no longer find any excuse for her behavior. Sometimes she made sure that either she had too much to drink, or kept him at the bar so long, that he couldn't have gotten it up with a derrick.

More and more, Greg was showing her another way of life. They'd go for walks in the woods, or strolls along Lake Michigan. Since they were avoiding both Cam and Greg's wife, they were spending more time in Chicago, rather than the suburbs. Sometimes he took her to the jazz-spots, since he still knew some of the older musicians, or just go through the shops in Old Town or New Town areas. With these things, Connie could see the vast difference in the two men.

If she asked Cam, after putting up a fuss, he'd have said, "Can I get a drink there?" She began to realize how many things she missed. From inside a saloon you cannot see the leaves turning, or a breath-taking sunset. She also missed many vistas, while sitting in front of the television every Sunday watching a football game.

Cam finally began to focus on the changes, which had been taking place in Connie for the past six months. Perhaps, maybe it was time he do something before it was too, late. He started pushing Martha to get out and get a job, telling Connie once again, as soon as Martha was financially independent, he'd proceed with the divorce.

By now it was such an old tune that her only response was, "Sure Cam, sure." She never asked Greg about a divorce, since she still wasn't sure this was what she wanted. It was going on ten years with Cam, and she didn't make any changes too, fast. She knew she had to be sure about this one. She did know she was tired of watching herself grow old, looking into the mirror behind some booze bottles. It would not be long before she woke up and be forty. If Cam's one-liners sounded worn and used at thirty, she could not imagine hearing them then.

* * * * * *

April now felt in total control of her mind and what direction she wanted to go. She fully realized she needed money to get away. She gave up the cleaning as too strenuous, when working so many hours in her astrology. She tried several jobs, finding none that would fit into her schedule with the classes and clients. April gained the weight as she expected, but she didn't expect Alex's reaction. Out of the clear blue he said, "You're fat and ugly and I'm ashamed of you."

During all the time April had been married to Wally, he'd seen her fat, skinny and all sizes in between, and he never said, or let her know he ever felt that way about her. It was a blow to April's ego, but not because it was Alex who said it. When Alex won an award for outstanding apprentice, he'd be honored with a banquet, and knew about it weeks in advance, so had time to think up something to keep April from going, as he didn't want to be seen with her.

April made plans for the astrology convention, which was being held in Atlanta. She'd been saving her money for months, when Alex said, "Well, it'd cost you a hundred dollars to buy a new outfit for the banquet, so why don't I give you the money instead for your Atlanta trip?"

April, knowing what Alex was thinking said, "Fine with me." It also completely opened up her eyes, that this man must really be embarrassed by her appearance, which meant he'd no more true-feelings for her, if he ever did. This was probably the biggest thing that would happen in his life, and he didn't want his wife by his side? That said so much to her.

Off to the convention, April made her decision about Alex when she returned. She wasn't going to let worrying about his feelings stop her from having fun. And, that she did, fun at every chance she had. She soon realized, not only how many prominent people she'd gotten to know, but also how many knew her, or of her. Maybe someday, in the not too distant future, she'd be one of the keynote speakers. As expected, following her return home, they fought. For a change, April packed up some bags, dropped the girls at her father's and went to Michael's. But she wasn't ready, willing and able to take that big-step out on her own. Almost feeling like it was a rehearsal, terrified and unorganized, April went back to re-group, get better direction - planning.

* * * * * *

Happily enjoying the times Mike gave her, Michael felt it *a coup* that she spent the weekend of Easter alone with him out at his farm. Connie called Beth on Easter to see how she was doing, only to find out that Beth just talked to her parents, also. It was mutual shock when Connie said that Michael was with Mike, since her father happily informed Beth, Cathy and Mike would be getting married shortly. Beth didn't know what to think, since when she last talked to Mike and Michael at Christmas, they'd both sounded like they were recovering from their break-up, and would *not* be seeing each other again.

Connie knew there was only one way to tell Michael the bad news, and to come straight out with it. Michael laid her life on the line, Mike would not EVER lie to her, no matter what. She dropped Connie off at the house to be cleaned, and went back to her apartment where Mike was just waking up. Michael came straight out with what Connie said about his impending marriage to Cathy. "If you are, *fine,* she'll probably make you happy. All I ask is you let me know, because I'll be damned if I'm going to be part of a triangle - again. Or, if I'm going to be the one you come to *only* for sex."

Mike could only say, "It's not true. I never said that. My father has been listening to my mother, and is merely what she hopes."

This was quite acceptable to Michael, because she knew how Louise felt about her, and Mike never lied to her. They continued for another month under heavy-secrecy unknown to Michael. Mike continued to relay to her how Cathy kept at him about not seeing anyone else, especially Michael. "Where does she get off with that?" Michael asked in all innocence.

"I don't know," Mike responded. "For some reason, she thinks she owns me."

Michael once again asked him if he ever discussed marriage to Cathy. Again, he denied any mention of it. "Mike, what bitch does she have? She's the one you take out to nice steak dinners, and visit your parents and friends. She's the one you rush back to on Sunday night from the farm - something, of course, you never did for me. I get the Kentucky Fried Chicken-bucket and drive-in movies, with the horizontal refreshments. What is she bitching about?"

Again, he only shook his head. "I just don't know."

Michael's ears were once again closed to the constant flow of facts from Connie and April. "Are you nuts, Michael, the writing is on the wall. He's using you, like he always has. He's lying to you!"

Michael would only shake her head 'no.' "Mike Cordeau and I have been through too much together. We might not have a lasting-future together, but *he would not lie to me*. I just know he wouldn't."

The Spacial Experience

As Midas had the touch of gold,
you have time and space in your control.

Time is irrelevant and stands still,
as minutes stop ticking-by at your will.

You turn any where I can name,
into a place of Shangri-La fame.

I am lost in your colors, shapes and design,
as your presence in all, boggles my mind.

Tell me you are more than just a man -
for you have made me, truly Alice in Wonderland.

CHAPTER 35

Escape the Mundane

Beth taught Sunday School for twelve years, before and shortly after she was divorced. She was thinking about that, when she decided that being involved with a church again was one of the things that was missing from her life now. When she'd first committed adultery with Rob, Beth stopped going to the church of her childhood. More than just the act of sin, and the hypocrisy of continuing it, was the realization that Beth lied to God when she'd taken her marriage vows. She'd known somehow, deep inside that marriage to Bruce would not be a lasting thing.

A couple Beth met on the New Orleans trip told her about the church they went to, with the freedom of individual-belief and love it gave to *all*. It also had a very large, active-singles group which combined discussions with social activities. As Beth was no longer into the singles' bar scene, it was not easy to meet singles. She also really wanted to meet those men who were more interested in her as a person, than a one-night stand. She gave the couple a call and planned to meet them the following Sunday at church.

Afterwards leaving the sanctuary, Beth never felt so surrounded by so many strangers that didn't seem to be strangers, because they cared. She said for the past couple of years, as she'd been changing, she belonged to a congregation of one. Now, she knew she was not alone. As her family, except for Mike, always made her feel like the black sheep, her childhood church always made her feel God was there to reprimand and punish for the slightest wrong. Yet, she always felt that God was not like that, but loving, forgiving and most understanding. It only stood to reason, He didn't save her life twice, or give her back her sanity after the accident, *without* some purpose in mind for her. Beth definitely found a niche she was comfortable with, for growing and understanding where her life was going. She knew now, she might have left God for a few years, but He never left her.

The next Sunday, Beth joined one of the adult discussion groups, who were starting the book, *Your Erroneous Zones* by Dr. Wayne Dyer. Though she read it before, with the dissecting and listening to the other people's opinions, it began to sink in more and differently. She had so many of her own *erroneous zones*, especially the guilt of her past, she needed to erase, after squeezing all learning-out from the experiences. The most remarkable expounding of the group was *guilt was a man-made emotion,* and not one to give any energy to. When she got home, she called Brenda and Vic, to see if they'd want to join her for church, since they often talked about religion and how much their minister in Houston counseled them before their marriage.

Starting from a small glow, everyday Beth seemed to find more joy in her life, and soon began acknowledging, if only to herself how much God was behind all the fate in her life. She'd still made mistakes, but then she was human and she'd not hate herself for them, since she was accepting and loving herself - all frailties included.

It'd been the worst winter in Oklahoma in seventy-five years, so it was great news when Lori called to invite Beth to go to Mexico with her, all expenses paid, compliments of Ricardo. Lori'd pulled several great-coups, and had been able to place some of Ricardo's larger, metal sculptures in some prominent museums. With his generosity to Lori for her hard work, he invited her to get away from Chicago's snow and come to Mexico. Because not being able to spend much time with her in Mexico City, he suggested she have Beth join her, for part of the time.

Once again, Beth got a college girl to come stay with Jeremy, and a substitute to take over at her work, as she flew to Mexico City for a much needed getaway, on this Valentine weekend. Lori's friend, Nancy came down with her for the first week, which they spent in Cozumel, trekking through the ancient ruins of the Mayans. Anxiously, that Friday night they shared their experiences wth Beth, since Nancy returned to Chicago the next day. Lori's generosity in sharing her wealth from Ricardo with both of them, was a positive turn in her feelings about money and need for it.

Beth and Nancy went shopping the next morning as Lori scheduled a business meeting with Ricardo, and some of his supporters. Beth loved Mexico City with a passion, and a comfortable feeling of the familiar with the unexpected. The lovely, small hotel on the Reforma in the Pink Zone was absolutely perfect, for the relaxing atmosphere that they all wanted.

A tearful-goodby for Nancy, as she left for the airport, thanking Lori for the opportunity of the total-experience. Beth and Lori had a quick lunch on the balcony, never running out of conversation, or acknowledging wherever they were together for a good time. Beth was then off to Chapultepec Park on her own, and Lori looking forward to some private time with Ricardo. Though Lori, no longer *madly in love* with him, it had taken on the proper-perspective of a woman who is in love, with a prominent married-man. She always had that great joy of sharing his work and accomplishments, which few other women had with him. That, she was learning, had longer-lasting satisfaction, than the sex ever could.

It had been almost two years to the day Beth had been at the Park and Anthropology Museum. This time, not only dressed more appropriately, but she was also aware of young, Mexican-men noticing her. She decided not to go back through the museum, but just buy some postcards and a book for Jeremy.

She then took her time to stroll over to the pond to feed the ducks some corn chips, and contemplate while soaking up the great sunshine, though beneath her wide-brimmed hat. Soon a young man by Beth's side, literally cracked her up when he said his name was Carlos. Beth tried to be very nice to him, but firmly made it clear that she was not some *Americano* looking for a Latin-lover. She thought she'd walk back to the art center, since Lori said there were some interesting pieces on display. On the way, she stopped to buy a yellow balloon, and laughed when Carlos told her she'd given the old man too many pesos. "The joy I receive from the balloon, is worth more than whatever I gave him."

After relaxing in the sculpture garden, she took a taxi back to the hotel, where Lori had left her a note to meet them at a restaurant around the corner. Beth decided not to change, but go as she was with her sun hat, and yellow balloon-in-tow. Ricardo as always, greeted her with great affection, and loving her always doing the unexpected. They sat and talked, laughing when Beth related her story about Carlos at the duck pond, as it reminded her of the fun times she and Jeremy often had feeding the ducks at a pond, not far from their apartment.

"You are so mean and cruel," Ricardo teased, "not to give this young man the love and affection this pour country needs. I mean you have so much to share, and we are so lonely and poor down here."

Beth laughed, "He'll have to find himself another American-divorcee, which I'm sure he will." There wasn't enough time for Lori and Beth to visit his studio that day, since he was having some buyer up later, but they'd be able to come over on Sunday, to see the new tapestry that he recently got back from the weavers in Spain.

Until that time, Lori and Beth contented themselves with dinner that evening, and a trip out to the market square the next morning, and then back to the park. They toured through the palace, but enjoyed the view more than the remnants of a bygone-reign. After having seen the Diego Rivers murals the day before, of the struggles of these oppressed people to free themselves, the riches of the royalty left a bad-taste.

Beth wanted to return to the Polyforme to get a Siqueiros print for herself. They didn't feel they needed to experience his three-dimensional murals again, but Beth was surprised that the print she once wanted, was no longer how she felt. This time, she chose a single-child walking into a sunrise-image. Even dressed in the ragged clothes and no shoes, she felt that he symbolized the eternal hope of all struggling people.

Later at Ricardo's studio, Beth felt like Alice in Wonderland, with every room jammed with his paintings and sculptures. If she had to choose, she couldn't have, because there were too many for her mind to separate. The experience of the tapestry was even more mind-boggling, as Ricardo rolled out the wondrous, woven-design. He never simplified his paintings for the weavers, and so intricate were the color-combinations that only one or two stitches would sometimes be used for a color. As Ricardo would jokingly say, "I don't do paint-by-numbers."

Beth and Lori were both awestruck and speechless, as they saturated themselves into the tapestry. Finally Ricardo said, "You're not saying anything. . . You don't know how to tell me that you don't like it?" In shock Beth and Lori laughed, and began lauding him with all the superlatives that he and his great tapestry deserved.

Later, while they were talking business, Beth again wandered from room to room, exploring and feeling like she was at a private showing. In the one room filled with sculptures, she felt as if in a forest of metal trees and onyx plants. It was great, because everything could be touched, without harming its presence.

Ricardo walked in on her experiencing a small, ivory wisp of onyx. "Oh, Beth, the way you are touching that is turning me on." As Lori was behind him, she slipped her hand underneath his jacket. "Oh, I'm not jealous any longer." He wanted to show her something new he'd been working on, to see what they thought. Beth almost reluctantly left the sculpture, to follow them into the other room.

As they were getting ready to leave, Ricardo said to Beth, "Wait a minute, you've forgotten something." He went into the sculpture room, and came out with the wisp she so lovingly fondled.

"Oh, Ricardo, I couldn't" she protested, unbelievably shocked at his generosity again.

"But you may as well, it is only a reject, a mistake." He put on a serious face.

"Ricardo, you do not create mistakes." Beaming in amazement.

"I know, Beth, but maybe you'll take it anyway, since you have now so spoiled it. It will never be happy with anyone else." He had such a great smirk on his face, she giggled.

Too generous of him, but Beth knew he only gave from the heart, so she said "Thank you, so, very much."

"Well, since you are going on to dinner, and you only have reservations for two, I will send your new-found-pet over to the hotel in a box, suitable for your flight home."

Beth give him a big kiss, "What can I say Ricardo, you are too much for description."

Their final day, Beth and Lori walked around the Zona Rosa window shopping, talking and leisurely enjoying the atmosphere. Lori decided to stay on a few more days, and though Ricardo had asked Beth too, she had to return, as she promised Terry and her sitter. She packed before their walk, so they could enjoy one last margarita on the terrace in the sun. Lori surely brought out the creative and intelligent side of Beth, making her realize she had only scratched the surface of her potential. With the marketing course she was taking at the college, she once again began to think in terms of getting herself out of her job, and into a *career* that would give her full potential to bloom ad grow.

On the flight back to Oklahoma City, Beth was seated next to a talky-hardware salesman. It cracked her up, because Lori mentioned on her last flight to Chicago, she had some executive who was interested in purchasing some of Ricardo's art. Beth tried not to think that *hardware salesman* would be her recurring fate, but somehow she thought 'chic and elegant' would not be adjectives used to describe her, as they were Lori.

Communication had become a problem wth Jeremy, and though the babysitter was very good, she was not adept at his cleverness. Since his bathroom was the hall bathroom, he told the babysitter he took care of it, and she should only use Beth's bathroom. Why she never opened his bathroom door to check it, or the fact that she never smelled it, as she walked by amazed Beth.

When Beth walked into the apartment, she smelled something, but then it had been closed up because of the cold. When she went to use the bathroom, Beth noticed the door closed on Jeremy's. As she walked back past it, she opened the door and the odor almost knocked her over. She started scolding him for not flushing the toilet, as she did so, it began to overflow. She then knew, that he was aware it was clogged. Beth's temper flared, as she yelled at him for not telling the sitter that the toilet was stopped-up, and why had he been so stubborn *as to keep using it?*

Beth then found out that he also told the sitter that he could take Zoomer, the lizard out, though he knew that he was trying to hibernate. But he wanted to show the sitter and play with it. Of course, Ginger, the cat, thought he was some, new toy for her to play with, and she promptly chased Zoomer and massacred him. Unfortunately, when they pulled Ginger off, Zoomer was still alive-enough to hide, but they had not found him yet.

"Terrific," Beth yelled again, "Besides a bathroom overflowing and stinking with crap, I have a dead-lizard decomposing somewhere in the living room. What a three-ring-circus I came home to!" She really didn't know what to say to Jeremy, as she'd told him before to tell her things, as it would only get worse, and she eventually found out about the situation, that could have been fixed.

Work wasn't quite as much of a mess, but Terry had not wanted the girl to do any of the reports or details of the business. She was there basically to type invoices, total tallies and answer the phone. The catch-up didn't take too long, but it was always several days to sort out some details. With everything considered, the trip was still worth the aggravation at the return.

Beth almost became religious about school, realizing it would be her ticket to a better career. There was a lot to do, to complete all the changes she felt were necessary in her, that getting all her priorities in the right order, so she wouldn't be going off on different tangents. She finally paid the doctor off on her arm, so she could afford some new medical expenses, namely a tubal-ligation like Michael and Connie had several years before. Certain for some time that she was not interested in having any more children of her own, yet Beth hoped to marry a man with his children. She would leave the baby-producing to the younger set.

Rose recommended her gynecologist so Beth took the step. Though he foresaw no problem with the operation, he did wish Beth could lose some weight. "I have lost some," she defended herself.

"Well, Beth, I recently lost fifty-pounds on the new Weight Watchers program, and you should try it." He wanted to help her.

"Oh, I'm a three-time dropout on that." Frustrated about the yo-yoing of her weight, maybe she did need some structure to her crazy schedule.

"The program has changed, and it did work for me." Beth thought about it. She read an article in the Wall Street Journal about companies being very weight-conscious of their rising, young-executives and how being overweight cut-down your chances at interview time. Considering everything else, Beth had going against her to change jobs, she called to find where a Weight Watcher's meeting was by her house.

Only on the program a month, when Beth had the operation ten-pounds lighter. She was on her way, and she knew she could make it this time, because she wasn't losing a few pounds to capture some man she wanted, but doing it for herself, and that made it more important. She had all new cooking and eating habits to learn, and the program was forgiving, because she could always start again with the next meal back on program, when she did cheat.

Jeremy put up a fuss at first, because it was no more of the breaded pork chops and fried chicken. Eventually, Beth turned into a quasi-health nut, cutting out all sugar and taking vitamins, minerals, kelp and lecithin, etc. As she said to Fran when she bought some candy for her sweet-tooth, "Fran, don't bother eating it, just stick it on your left thigh, that's where it's going to end up anyway!" She even cut-out her occasional glass of wine or scotch, unless she was out with Brenda and Vic.

As the emotional layers she collected, began to slowly melt off, she had new hope about getting a job in the marketing-field. With help from her teacher, and an excellent reference letter from Lori in her hand, Beth went to a placement agency knowing just where she wanted to get a job - Dallas. It was vibrant, growing, yet not too big. Somehow she felt, since she was a young, impressional-girl reading Edna Ferber's *Giant*, that Texas was in her destiny. She'd been drawn to the southwest, and she knew now that Oklahoma City wasn't for her. Somehow fate would pull the strings, and get her where she should go - it felt like Texas.

Lori came back down to Oklahoma to do one of her lectures for the Arts and Craft show to tape and show during Christmas. While there, she and Beth went down to Dallas to check out some museums for Ricardo, and get the feel of the town for Beth. It was much bigger and sprawling than Beth imagined, but then she'd been away from Chicago a while now.

The interview went well with the employment agency, the marketing company Beth was interested in was not hiring at that time, but he said to feel free to follow up on her own. In the meantime, her resume' and reference letter were forwarded to their Dallas office to check out any other possibilities. Beth felt an impending move would be very beneficial to her psyche. If nothing else, as Oklahoma City had begun to get to her, with its reluctance to change snd grow as quickly as she thought it would. Beth wrote to April to see what she thought of a relocation to Dallas would do to her astrology chart. Her response back was kind of what Beth expected - Dallas would be better career and person-wise than Oklahoma City. She then added, that even Chicago held less conflicts - Come home!

But Beth knew she'd have to find her own space to call home, and that would not be Elmwood - it was her past and she left it all behind her. There continued to be no response from Dallas, and Beth was again reminded that her lack of a degree and no recent experience in marketing and advertising were detrimental to her. In a different vein, Beth felt the stirring of something in the wind at work. Even with Terry's secretiveness, she knew something was up, and after she overheard a dozen different conversations, Beth figured out it was a new project in the works in the San Antonio area.

Since she'd only heard good things about San Antonio, Beth waited to see if he would ask her to join in the move. She was getting ready to leave on vacation with Jeremy to the Grand Canyon, when Terry finally talked to her about it. She learned enough from before, that it would not be as large or complicated a project, so Beth was glad she'd asked for her anniversary raise before it had been settled. She'd give Terry an answer when she returned from vacation, so she'd have that extra week or so, to hear from Dallas, since it was her first choice.

Beth looked forward to the trip with Jeremy, since they still had a communication problem. She hoped the hours spent in the car, they could talk about his interests in astronomy, space and rocks, as well the dinosaurs, while she tried to install some of her feelings about their relationship. Beth put several hundred dollars into the car, to make sure they'd have no trouble, since it was just the two of them. With the cooler packed with as much of her Weight Watcher foods and drinks as possible, they were on their way.

As always, Beth didn't accomplish as much as she expected, but Jeremy did share many feelings with her as they hiked trails during the day, and learned about the stars at night. Jeremy was proud that Beth kept up with him, as they climbed and crawled through Mesa Verde, Painted Desert and the Petrified Forest along the way. On the North Rim of the canyon, they played in the snow and Beth enjoyed the solitude of the sunrises and sunsets of the awesome views.

Since Dallas hadn't contacted her, Beth told Terry that she'd join him in the move to San Antonio. Things became hectic, as she and Jeremy packed up for his summer return to Chicago, as well she had him pack his stuff that would be going to San Antonio. She packed everything at work and home, so she was packing both places.

Jeremy finally liked Oklahoma City, so now he started rebelling about the move. The school had been so atavistic, she had quite a run-in with his ancient, backward-teacher, after he'd been in such a wonderful progressive school before in Elmwood. She at last got the principle to accept that Jeremy bring his own books to read, after he finished the classroom assignment, so he didn't act up.

Beth came home from work to find the apartment a wreck, from Jeremy and his friends having s fight with sandy, wet towels from the pool. It was the last straw, "If you're going to be so inconsiderate and irresponsible of where you live, and what I've done for you," Beth was almost shaking as she yelled at him, "then you can just stay in Chicago with your father, because I can't stand you not cooperating with me.

Now, I've told you I can't get a job here at the same money I'm making. I've worked too hard to get to this salary, where we have the extra money to do extra things. And, if you think I'm kidding or I won't go through with this you're wrong. If you don't have this room and your bathroom clean when it's time to go to the airport tomorrow, you can stay in Chicago. I don't want a son who is going to fight me on everything."

Beth walked back into the living room, sank down on the couch and started crying. She didn't know where she'd gone wrong, but she certainly had. She was tired, the tension at work with Terry gone so much to San Antonio was getting to her. She'd been alone for so long now, trying to do it all by herself, and she just wasn't cutting it. She'd wanted a man to lean on and help with Jeremy, as well life all the way around. She also wanted a career, but they didn't want her, so the more she thought about their life at that point, the more she cried.

At last, Jeremy came out of his room and put his arms around Beth. He'd rarely seen her cry. "Mom, I'm sorry about the sand. I'll wipe it up."

"Why, Jeremy, why must you be so destructive?" He couldn't answer, so he slumped off to get a rag to wipe the walls. The phone started ringing, so Beth pulled herself up to answer. It was Brenda inviting her to join them for dinner after Jeremy left for Chicago, and before they left to move back to Houston. Beth didn't want to pour her problems out on her friends, but she really needed company to take her mind off Jeremy's being gone, so the invitation was perfect.

In the morning Beth began to worry because Jeremy stayed in his room, and not done the cleaning of it. What would she do if he decided it would be an easier new life with his father? He meant the world to her, though for so long she held back so many feelings not wanting to spoil him, or her ultimate fear of him being a mama's boy, like his father. If he did come back, they both had a lot of changing to do. Sometimes more than anything else, Beth had expected too much out of him - he was only ten.

Jeremy must have made the decision to come back, because like a whirlwind he began to clean his room and the bathroom. He pushed it to the line, because they were late for Rose's brunch, and almost just eat and run to the airport. Waiting for the plane, they played a card game, neither one talking about the problem or a solution. Too soon, it was time to board, so Jeremy only had time for a quick hug and kiss. Beth stood by the window, and cried about all the weight she had on her shoulders, then all the weight she put on Jeremy. She could only say, "God, please give me some strength to *not* screw this up with him. I just love him, too much."

Underestimating Women

We are not the women of twenty years ago,
Much less those of fifty or one hundred before.
Our sense of humor has buoyed us,
As we've changed radically, men have rarely.

Resilient from surviving so much,
And letting go of those small minds,
Who have been shocked and rocked
After underestimating us so often.

It is more than basic education
That has made us less innocent,
Or no longer ignorant of the world;
Nor myopic of who we can become.

We're 'the Queens of multi-tasking,'
As we run family, career and
Even contribute to the community,
While barely, breaking a sweat running.

We are neither fragile, nor afraid
Of taking on the issues of adulthood,
While looking to embrace age . . . as
A gift to use our experience and wisdom.

CHAPTER 36

Why Does Starting Over Hurt So Bad

Mother's Day weekend, and Jason joined Michael to go up to her mother's. Jason had more of a problem getting along with Barb, his mother, but always a closeness with Michael. He sometimes also tired of the trip out to the farm, so the drive up to Wisconsin was enjoyable. In the car, barely on their way, Jason started his dissertation.

"Michael . . . somebody has got to tell you this, I guess it has to be me, cause you got to know." Jason again hesitated, drawing upon all of his strength. Michael glanced over wondering what could be so horrendous, that the usually verbal-Jason had trouble coming out with it. "Dad and Cathy have been talking about marriage since Valentine's Day, when he gave her a ring." It was a heavy sigh he released.

Michael's hand squeezed the steering wheel of the car, until her knuckles were pure white. She'd only gotten a card for Valentine's Day, but it had been signed, "All my love. Forever, Mike." Jason then continued to relate all the other presents, mostly clothes, since Cathy was the *'perfect size'* and needed clothes for her job. Jason went on for awhile about the marriage plans, but Michael only heard him vaguely.

When she got to her mother's house, Michael went straight to the bathroom and threw up. Without saying one-word to her mother, Michael once again relieved her hurt when she was alone. Very, slowly now, so she could comprehend it completely, she went over all Jason said. There was no other answer - MIKE HAD LIED TO HER - not once or twice, but over and over again in the past few months.

On the way back home, Michael put the hurt away, as the anger began to surface. She promised Jason she'd not let Mike know that he told her. But Michael had to tell someone, but she knew right then, she could not begin to discuss it with Mike - even if some way to do so without incriminating Jason. So, she had Connie and April come over, and she slowly unfolded the story to them. Connie, needless to say, said, "I'll hold him, while you beat the shit out of him."

April, though prone to some violence in the past, said, "I'd *have to* make a phone call to Cathy, and let her know what he's been doing to the both of you. It's not been you playing games with him, but him playing with both of you." She was a little smug for being correct about him.

Michael seriously considered it. The only thing which stopped her was the possibility Mike would kill her, and definitely Jason would *not* have a home to come home to. Michael decided to keep it all to herself, and give Mike a chance to redeem himself by confessing, or keep taking on enough rope to really hang himself permanently. Two months passed without Mike taking the former out, while Michael kept giving him the latter.

Finally, one night while they were talking on the phone Michael said, "Before you just keep burying yourself with this 'ultimatum-shit' from Cathy, I think I should let you know that Jason and I had a long talk on Mother's Day. I've seen the light of day, Sweetie," as she repeated about the personal gifts, ring and marriage talk - "You don't need to do this to me or yourself any longer."

Mike still could not confess, "Now wait a minute. One person talking about marriage does not mean two people, talking about marriage. The ring was a friendship-ring and nothing else . . . " He continued on, but he was no longer convincing to Michael.

Now it was Mike who was talking into her deaf-ear. He tried to explain that the color TV he, and the boys gave Michael the *year and a half before*, more than made-up for any ring. Like that should be a sufficient-gift for eons to come? When Mike realized he could not explain his way out of it, he ended the conversation saying, he had to get back to work. Michael knew he needed time to rethink a new strategy not to lose Michael or Cathy.

Mike called Michael again when he got home from work. "I've been thinking about this, and Jason really, kind-of shot-me-down . . . "

Before he could finish Michael said, "If you feel like he shot you down, then you must feel you did *something* wrong. If you feel like you have done *nothing* wrong, and you have nothing to be guilty about, then what Jason told me shouldn't matter to you one bit." She paused, and when there was no response she added, "I'll tell you what - I think you better steer-clear of me for awhile, since I'm in the mood to bring your whole-world down around your ears. I *can* do it with one phone call to Cathy, and you know it. Besides telling her what's really been going on the past year almost, I think I might even tell her some of the small-details you've been bitching to me, about your sex life with her, especially."

Psychologically-heard, the gagging on the other end of the phone until Mike responded, "Don't threaten me!"

"I ain't threatening anything Sweetie . . . I'm PROMISING you!" Michael knew it was really too late for Mike to come down on Jason, and it accomplished nothing since Mike was no longer in control of the ballgame. She hoped Cathy and Mike would be happy, yet she felt a little sorry for Cathy, since she'd become a willing victim of Mike, as Michael once had. The sex they had could never be replaced, and the corner of her heart would always love him. They were the only redeeming factors she had to console herself for the years they'd shared.

As Jason repeated to Michael about Cathy, 'Mike alway knew he could count on Cathy to say something nice, no matter who she was around. That was something that he never knew what might come out of Michael's mouth.' Cathy filled-out the roles of appearance that Michael never could, or would. In retrospect, Michael realized that she-herself, couldn't have lasted the next twenty-years, sitting around every weekend and vacation on the farm talking about machinery.

In the long run, he'd have made her just as unhappy as she'd have made him. Even Michael's mother, who had always liked Mike, couldn't imagine them continuing forever. She could see the compromising-effect he had on Michael, which was completely against the grain of 'doing your own thing,' which she raised Michael up wth. Mike always thought Michael's values were shit, and she thought his values were everyone else's, not his own. That was the crux of it, and Michael knew no matter how good the sex was, she could not swallow the rest of it.

The pain was as much physical as emotional, as Michael fully, finally accepted it was over between them. She functioned at her cleaning jobs a robot, and dreaded the weekends, as the vacuum that they'd become, almost watching the clock, until she could escape once again into the routine of work. For months, this continued as she could only repeat to herself - *"I will never love like that again, because I will never hurt like this again."* At last, one day she realized that was not it at all. She then began to say, *"I wouldn't love like that again, because I couldn't do that to another person, much less do it to myself."*

She really thought about it in depth. *"I can't imagine anybody loving me like that - that's got to be an enormous responsibility, and weigh on you about two thousand pounds. It's also got to become goddamn-boring, because then you have no one to interact with but yourself, because this other person has become you!"* BINGO! Giving too much does't enhance love, it produces resentment, a feeling it *must* be repaid. Many people, particularly men, can't live with someone and have feelings of obligation to them.

To become herself again was a very horrible and tediously, slow process of almost finding one piece after another of herself, and then putting it back in place - where it once had been. There was almost nothing to build on, since Michael the woman, the individual drowned years before in the persona of Mike. By the end of six-months, she almost reversed the flow out of her, to completely within her entity. Now, almost jealous of her weekends, and cherished them as the precious time for her, and her only to dispose of as she wanted.

Looking back on the years with Mike, she smiled and remembered how much they'd given, grown and changed each other. She accepted her responsibility of its ending, since those things not done for herself, but as part of a couple. She'd never trade anything, but she'd also never repeat it, and everyone should maybe experience a *consuming-love* once. Yet, it was the ending and in the subsequent time-healing, Michael realized how she grew and expanded in absolute-leaps and bounds.

* * * * * *

Connie wanted to go on a new diet. She tried Weight Watchers like Beth, but did not have the patience for the weighing and limits of keeping track of everything she had to be eaten. The few weeks she'd tried, Connie even cooked for her and Michael, since it seemed easier when there was more than one person suffering with her. Connie saw an ad for a medical clinic, where you pay two-hundred dollars, and they guaranteed you one year of weight control, supplying the special food at additional cost. The way Connie figured, in how she felt about money, for sure she'd lose the weight, because she was *not* about to blow that kind of money seriously. The diet also forbid any alcohol, which with more and more time with Greg, Connie came to realize she did not need it anymore.

Connie started on the diet a few days before the Memorial Day holiday. Cam bitched and moaned, it would foul-up their usual rollicking, booze-filled time. Connie very calmly told him, he could eat and drink as he wanted, and she'd not try to convert him from any of his needs. Once again in Connie's sober state, she saw Cam's weakness and need for alcohol to make life more stimulating and livable. In a few months, Connie lost thirty-seven pounds, getting back into those clothes of ten years before.

The sex had constantly gotten better with Greg, but then it was not their focal point, as it had been at one time with Cam. He kept up the flowers and the daily-cards, which Connie hadn't expected. All she could say, "He's *unfucking* believable. I think he is solely supporting Hallmark, and surely doing his bit for the post office, too."

What a great feeling to have someone madly, and totally in love with her. She just loved it, and had never been more happy in her life. Greg told her that he'd spent his whole life cheating on some woman, and yet he'd not once cheated on Connie from the first time they started. He'd been searching all his life for someone like her, and he couldn't believe he'd found her. He told Connie it was like finding a twin, because they could read each other's mind so well.

They managed to get away for another weekend together. After dinner, overlooking the Mississippi from a high ridge, Connie thought how she'd be very satisfied with her life, if she should die right then. She was sipping her tea, while watching the little-lights from the riverbarge move, ever-so-slowly by. With Greg's touch on her hand, she felt the tingling warmth move up her arm, so that she slightly raised it off the table. It seemed, as time went by, she became more sensitive to his touch, rather than used to it, as a common thing. "How about a walk around the balcony, before we go to our room?" Connie nodded as she'd already noted the high setting-in, and her breathing starting to skip. She never considered herself sensual, but with this man, sensual was only the beginning.

As they walked around the terrace in warm summer moonlight, Connie thought of all her experiences, and all the men she'd been with. Satisfaction, total satisfaction, could not be connected to any of them, but him. Greg closed the door of their room behind them, and automatically started unzipping Connie's dress, as he languidly kissed her neck and shoulders, adding little licks with his tongue. One thing Connie had a hard time getting used to with him, there was no such a thing as a 'quickie.' If they did not have the time, to spend at least an hour on each other's body, he would not start.

Connie's breathing was once again very spaced, as she began to get lightheaded, slipping into this dreamworld with Greg. Soon, as they were both nude on the bed, the sounds of the outside world became very distant, and the time-suspended. Connie was only aware of her heightened-sensitivity, all over her body, even parts not usually aware of existing. The arousal was almost an end in itself, like they were skimming the best of the sex-act.

With the long, deep-kissing, she became aware of the exquisite tension - almost an ache and hunger, as her breasts got tight, for them to be touched. And when he did, she felt like fainting from the tingling warmth and dampness, that now waited for his fullness. An awakening, or the beginning of life as she became conscious of her vagina. Its beckoning for a longing-feeling, Greg had almost trained in her. In this very intense state was so good, Connie could not even dream it could be better.

After he covered her entire body with his leisurely kisses, and circular licks with his tongue, she was again on the edge of an earthquake, following several small tremors from previous orgasms. Their entire bodies were urging forward, toward the complete merging of them and suffusion. All during the act, even with the changing of positions, Connie desired to kiss and be kissed, over and over again. With his acute senses, he kept kissing her mouth, neck and breasts without her saying a word. There was a definite, electric-current flowing through her body, every touch setting-off another shock wave.

Greg was now holding Connie's hands, as she was grasping on, almost for her life. As if she were being thrown-out of the gravitational-pull, using every ounce of energy to keep from flying-off into space. It built-up like the small blip on a radar screen, until it was gigantically magnified, as an UFO, flying right overhead. She said before of previous times, "Indescribably-delicious, and yet elusive, because every time it seems new again." Now it was her pelvis and hips, which were generating the sole-control over her body. Suddenly, her back-rose-up like an arched-cat ready to jump and attack, as she pressed her body hard against his. She held on so tightly, with such a rigid tenseness of almost rigor-mortis.

Greg continued kissing her mouth and breasts, longingly in between the orgasms, while giving her a chance to catch her breath, then continue on for the next one. Connie laughed, as she breathed deeply, "For someone who an orgasm used to be a 'once-in-awhile-thing,' I think I could compete in the 'Orgasm Olympics,' and win the gold medal." They continued until he was sure her energy was about zapped. With the final build-up, she had the sensations of a dam breaking, and rushing away with the powerful currents, enjoying every moment of the delicious-orgasm. As the heat had fused them together, slowly melted, they both limped back to a flat position again.

The release of tension starts as the toes uncurl, that she never remembered curling, and the life slowly flows back up the body, through the legs, thighs and abdomen, like a puppet let-go and now all the strings being drawn back, from being extended so tautly. Her body became soft and fluid, so weak as if she were lying in whipped cream. Connie began drawing up almost in a fetal position, as the only way to calm her body back to normal use. Greg whispered, "Are you all right?" She turned her curled body toward him, and he gently stroked the hair off her face.

After almost an alarming silence, Connie's face, with still closed eyes, was covered with a smile. Not in her usual voice, she said, "No . . . I died."

Greg, now fully smiling, as he watched her body physically change color, as it cooled down, "Well, I hope you will rise again in three-days."

She laughed, and reacted like it hurt, but a very good hurt. "Listen, Mister," she started, "if I ever thought I was a bottomless pit, well, I'm not, because you found the bottom."

"And, how would you rate this one, Lady?" he asked in his deeper voice.

"Oh shit," Connie moaned, "there ain't no number that high." Greg howled, and rolled over to kiss her once again to continue.

Connie planned to go on vacation with sone friends to Florida and the Keys. When she returned, Cam was waiting with a long face. Martha had served *Him* with divorce papers. All Connie could say was "Shit," over and over again, and not for the reason Cam thought. Now, she *had to* make the decision, she'd been putting off, for so very long. She waited almost ten years for this man to get his divorce, and now she was very definitely in love with someone else. *"Ain't that a kick in the ass. It couldn't happen to no one else but me. SHIT!!!"* She was so confused, and really didn't know what to do next. How could she no longer want, what she'd wanted for so very long?

Cam began giving her constant pressure to move in with her. He even began talking about them getting married, before the divorce was finished. She told him he was nuts, and it would also be bigamy. Obviously, he was panicking, since Connie was not showing any enthusiasm about his impending divorce. Greg never gave Connie any pressure to even break-up with Cam, nor talked about getting a divorce himself. There was almost nothing left to do, but break up with Cam. At first Connie, asked for some time alone, so she could completely diffuse everything out.

Absolutely unbelievable, the sexual avoidance Cam put up with in the last ten-months from Connie, and yet he *still* thought she wanted him. He'd not let her go, or respect her wanting some time alone. Relentlessly, he continued to pursue her whenever she was in the Fire-Lite, or calling her at home, begging for her to see him. She didn't want to tell him there was someone else, since she realized he truly did love her, like he'd loved no one else. Granted, it was a sick-love, which would be reignited when she'd leave him, or threaten it.

Almost a month after the breakup with Cam, he came plodding into the Fire-Lite. Seeing her at the end of the bar, he pulled himself together and sat down next to her. Once again he started his whining-shit, and Connie stopped him in mid-sentence. "Listen, if you are going to sit here, we will talk about the weather, or anything else, except us. Have I made myself clear?" Cam silently sipped his drink, watching her drink her club soda.

"All right, but I just want to ask one question. Is there somebody else?" He pleaded.

Connie thought for a few moments. They'd been through too much together, for her to be cruel and vicious. She knew if she told him there was somebody, it would literally kill him. Besides, he'd then not leave her alone, until he found out who it was, and he considered Greg a friend over the years. Then, she said, "No Cam, there is nobody else." He sat there silently, and she got up to go to the restroom.

When she returned, she started again, "No Cam, I am wrong. There is somebody else . . ." He swung his head around, and looked at her intensely. "You're looking at the somebody - ME! For once in my goddamn-life I come first, not you. So, if you want to consider me somebody else, fine - then there is somebody else."

Trying to understand, and not really comprehending, Cam asked, "Was it my fiftieth birthday, was that it?" He pathetically watched her.

"No, Cam, it was *my thirtieth birthday* that did it to me. I wake-up, and I'm thirty-years old - I'm not going to wake-up at forty, still hanging out here, and listening to Martha stories. It's like she's the only woman in the whole-fucking-world who had ever been through a trauma. And, the poor woman this and that. I'm going out working my ass-off to buy what I need and want, and I have to listen to you bitching about her buying a pair of sixty-dollar boots - she never even wore last year's style, because *she never goes out* of the fucking-apartment."

He started to make a reply, only to have Connie start in again. "And, what do I get out of it all?" She took a deep breath, and a swallow of her club soda. "Cam, I'm just tired of answering to you - tired of being under your thumb. I don't need a father anymore . . . "

He shot a look at her, that made her realize he'd taken the remark age-wise. "No, Cam, age has nothing to do with it. You just don't understand what I went through with *my father,* when I was growing up. You're trying to control me the same way he did. You just don't get it. I feel like if I stay with you any longer, you will *turn me into another Martha.*"

"What the hell are you talking about?" He raised his voice.

"Cam, you have taken away more of my self-confidence, and made me feel less of a person in the past ten years. In the last ten months, I've been pulling away from you, I feel beautiful - I like myself. You are selfish, Cam." Now shaking, pouring out truth-serum.

Grabbing at words which had been building-up inside her for so long, Connie couldn't get them all out in the right order to make clear sense. "You want everyone and everything your way, and under your control. Well, you're not getting me, ... not any more." She grabbed up her purse and left. Ridiculous to try to go on, Cam would probably never comprehend her past. Not as if he did it all consciously, but he'd made her dependent on him for decisions, and felt whatever she did on her own was wrong.

It was why he preferred to pluck-her-out of the bar when she was so young, and impressionable. He could, and had shaped her - honed her into his perfect role-model. When she did things on her own, and shown some independence he couldn't handle it. Lucky for him, these little tangents were not usually successful, and Connie came back into the fold - under his control once again. But he was wrong this time, he'd taken her for granted for the last time. And, he'd totally underestimated how she had changed.

Ode to a Man Unknown

I see in you the reflections of myself -
        the me that was, and the me that is to be.

So much that I have done -
        so much I want to do.

These are the same wants and needs
        that you have also dreamed of.

I feel that there is a part of me
        that is a part of you.

I can think the way you feel -
        having felt those thoughts before, too.

The words you speak I understand -
        having spoken those once myself.

I've climbed the hill to make me strong -
        I've endured the lonely valley.

We will be our own oasis - protecting us,
        in the middle of the man-eating desert.

I will take your hand as we pull each other up,
        to the highest mountain to reach the top.

I will be your friend,
        confidant, cohort and comrade -

As you want and need me,
        as I need and want you.

CHAPTER 37

New Men - New Lives

Beth had only two weeks to get everything packed and settled. She didn't have the time or patience for a garage sale. Rose gave her the name and address of a community worship group that would take any kind of donations. Fran had a friend that Beth could give all her good clothes to, that were now too big. So, what she wasn't giving away she still had to pack, though many things like her books, china and crystal had never been unpacked, so that was a few steps ahead. She weeded through Jeremy's things she'd not sent to Elmwood. Much of the packing for the office had to have boxes left open, until the last shipment went out. It was amazing, they completed at six-thirty on Friday night, and were to open on Monday morning in San Antonio.

Beth finished the last-minute things she was taking in her car and the apartment cleaning, so she at last pulled out about eleven on Sunday morning to drive nine hours to San Antonio, with only Ginger, the cat in Zoomer's old cage for company. As she left the city limits, Beth remembered not to look back, "So we won't turn into a pile of shit, Ginger." Oklahoma City had very definitely been a learning chapter of her life, glad it was over, and hoped she'd not repeat it. The manager had all the instructions for Terry's movers, and keys for her.

Beth could't remember ever being so tired, as when she pulled into the apartment complex Terry had picked out. She was happy he'd gotten her apartment early, with the rental furniture until hers arrived. As Beth brought in the necessities, she felt like her bad arm was going to fall off, and her back was already broken. She finished the rest in the morning, before Terry came over to show her the way to the project. She ate her Weight Watcher dinner, took a shower and collapsed in the bed.

Thirty-seven miles one-way to the project, but with the company paying for the gas, Beth wouldn't worry about it, as long as the old car lasted. Their building had been set up, with the phones and electricity in by the second day. There wasn't much unpacking, as most of the boxes from the the Oklahoma City project were sent on to the corporate headquarters of the oil company in Houston. Beth loved it in the country, all green and rolling hills. She'd gotten so tired of being flat and brown, except the colors in spring. Though Beth knew virtually no one in San Antonio, she was determined to get to know the city and see the sites.

Ricardo was right - the prettiest city in Texas, The Riverwalk was a romanticist's dream with quaint shops, restaurants, boat rides and lots of trees with bridges to loll around by, on a lazy afternoon, or watch the stars at night. San Antonio had all the good things about a big city and none of the bad, so far. She loved it - maybe she'd found her place.

When the furniture came, Beth took her bike to ride around the neighborhood, or drove to the bike trails. She called and wrote Jeremy regularly, but usually he did not write back. She was lost and lonely without him, but once again the time on her own became somewhat of a blessing. She had so many things to straighten out in her mind, just to begin with, where was she going from here? Terry said that the project might only be six or nine months, and she knew she didn't want to spend the rest of her life, or Jeremy's following Terry from project to project. But what was she going to do? If she was gong to think about that tomorrow, 'a la Scarlett-baby,' she still had to get her act together, since she learned tomorrow came quicker nowadays.

After a few weeks things settled down on the job, and without all the different processing to worry about on this project, Beth was sometimes finished by nine in the morning with her reports for the day. If there were no trucks going out, she only had the incoming tallies to look forward to. Terry stayed out in the yard, or at the pipeline-take-up site. Beth was about to go nuts, she could only write so many letters, and no one else had her extra time to write back.

The middle of July, when what Beth had been dreading happened. Even after pouring several hundred more dollars in her car, it was still acting up. When she pulled over on the interstate coming home from work, what she'd thought was steam, turned out to be smoke and fire. For the next six weeks Beth went through utter-frustration, as she poured more money into the car, to try to get some out when selling it. It was one time that Terry did come in handy, as he tried to set up one deal after another.

Once more Beth's stubbornness caused her grief, and much money. Terry had gotten the local dealer by the project to look at the car, and best wholesale price he could offer was eleven hundred. Beth was furious, thinking that this man was just some country-hick, and didn't know what he was talking about. When following Terry back to San Antonio that evening to another dealer, she blew a rod.

In the meantime, Terry's brother in Houston found a Buick, just what Beth wanted. Anxious to quit driving the company pickup truck, Beth agreed, and the company paid the down payment of twelve hundred, with her hoping to sell her car for that much or more, once it was repaired again. In the middle of all of her own problems, Connie drove down to see Beth.

"Honest to God, Beth, why don't you face it, the car is now a piece of shit!" If nothing else, Beth could always depend on her honest opinion. She wasn't laughing, as she'd gotten very attached to her car, and could not just junk it. There was also the money factor. "And, I wouldn't sell it to a person yourself, either. Sell it to a dealer or wholesaler, so you don't have to worry about them coming back after you when it falls apart." Yea, Beth thought, Connie was objective and honest. With Connie's help, on it's last legs, she sold her car for eight-hundred dollars to a wholesaler. Between what she'd put in it for repairs, she lost about five hundred dollars, since not taking the eleven hundred from the dealer by the project. Maybe he wasn't so dumb.

So down in the dumps, Beth couldn't even be thrilled about her new car, as they got into it with the eight-hundred dollar check in her hand. "Come on," said Connie, "you've been in worse money situations. Let's eat, then go see Bobby Ryan's new movie."

Beth tried to smile, take a deep breath and forget about her latest royal screw-up. "Yea, you're right. Besides you've got to tell me all about Mr. Wonderful, and how it's all going."

Connie needed the time away from both Cam and Greg to clear her head, to see exactly what she was going to do next. Greg had already called since Connie got there, sent flowers and a card, he must have mailed before she even left Chicago. Beth had never seen Connie so alive and vibrant, when she talked about him. She truly loved being in love, and the glow was from head to toe. As they walked along the riverwalk the next night, Connie continued how much Greg would love it because he was such a romantic, and had turned Connie into one, too. "Once he gets his divorce, we'll probably leave the Chicago area. I'm so tired of all the rain, snow and general shit up there."

"This is a great town and area to come to, I mean this is the Sunbelt, baby, and it's really growing fast. San Antonio is really a resort, almost a party town. In his line, I'm sure Greg wouldn't have any problem. There is practically a restaurant or club on every corner."

"Well, we're talking about traveling first, and then deciding where we want to settle." Beth was so happy for Connie, that she didn't know what to say any more, except that she certainly deserved it. She reiterated what she'd said at Christmas that Connie had sure outgrown Cam, and there really was no going back.

One day while Terry was out of town, Beth had Connie come out to her office, and they played Scrabble for several hours. Beth was supposed to get a few days off while Connie was in town, but once again, she had to change her schedule because of work. They talked about many things, catching-up on the big points, and small details, even the cleaning customers and Beth bitched about her buying into the franchise again.

In the evenings, they drank wine and laughed about their old 'wild' days together, when they'd try just about anything. Beth felt that maybe now that Connie made so many changes in her life, she'd understand why Beth had to leave Elmwood when she did. Beth, talking about both of their weight-losses and so many other changes, when she said, "I sometimes wonder if the old, bar-group would even recognize us any more."

"Yea," Connie chuckled, "just as soon as we started laughing. You know we can't be together without laughing for very long."

Beth was a little concerned Greg was still a married-man, but Connie seemed to feel his wife would soon give him a divorce. Since he'd changed so much in the past year, he'd been going with Connie. Soon her week was up, and she was planning to make the twelve-hundred and fifty-mile drive straight through. Beth thought she was nuts, but if she had a man whose wife was out of town, Beth might do the same thing. It made Beth feel great the closeness she and Connie had once was again there.

Connie came home to more than free-time with Greg. She dropped off her things from the trip that she didn't need, and picked up some clean clothes to go over to Greg's. When she came in the next day, Cam was in her apartment 'supposedly' picking-up the last of his personal things. Because Connie was very neat and orderly, she knew immediately that Cam had been ransacking her apartment. She didn't say anything, waiting for what he might reveal.

As her eyes glanced around the apartment, she realized in one year it now reflected Greg, with all the small mementoes that he'd given her. Cam's presence had been totally removed. Maybe it was easy to do, because in the last ten years, he'd not left a lot of himself around as evidence. Connie put all the cards that Greg sent her while in San Antonio in her train case. Cam obviously found them, because he threw them down on the table, where she was sitting waiting for him to go.

Connie picked up the cards, got up to put them away in a drawer. As she did, she said, "You know Cam, it's very rude to read someone else's mail."

He stood there demanding, his face very red, "Who is it?"

"First of all," Connie calmly said, "it's none of your goddamn business." Almost a relief, so she decided to tell him the basics. "It's a friend I have known for several years, and we've alway talked, but it then grew into something more, because he made me feel special and he didn't take me for granted." She continued to tell him that it was just not the cards, but flowers and the walks and talks. He almost cried when she asked him for her key back. Connie felt she'd have a few more scenes with Cam before truly over, but then as if this man was now going through two divorces instead of one. He didn't let go easily.

* * * * * *

Time can invariably make or break, the affinity and building of intimacy between two people. About a year and a half before Michael's divorce from Tim, she met Will. Not remembering how Tim would've known such a type of character as Will, she remembered him appearing at their house one Saturday. He'd just returned from doing the motorcycle-run at Baja. Completely intrigued, she'd listened as he told of the experience. She'd been so totally engrossed with him at the time, with all the variety of travel and interests he had, she retold his stories several times to April, Beth and whoever else would listen. The man personified her alter-ego, which at the time had yet to emerge.

As Will left that day, he'd thought, *"What the hell is she doing surrounded by these kids in suburbia, married to that asshole?"* He thought if he'd said to her, *"let's go,"* she'd do it. But he did not, and for the best since that Michael simply wasn't ready to chuck it all, even for an alter-ego. When Will found out later she got a divorce, he spent the next two years looking for her.

One Saturday, he pulled into the parking lot behind her old building. He tracked down the street where she lived, and was in the process of going from building to building, looking for her name on a mail box. Physically, he was an opposite of Mike, as only a few inches taller than Michael, with sandy-brown hair and magnetic, baby-blue eyes, which could mesmerize easily.

Michael was getting her three kids into her car to go shopping, when she noticed him pull up next to her. She, or course, instantly recognized him, and was flattered he had remembered her. When he told her how long he'd been searching for her, Michael was stunned. She thought she could never have been so important *to anyone* to find. If he had found her sooner, she'd have still been hung up on Mike.

Since she was taking her kids back later that weekend, she made arrangements to see him after they left. Still, he called several times, and they talked for hours on the phone. He took her up to Lake Geneva, and it was non-stop talk. He was interested in her passions of astrology, reincarnation and her in the archaeology he experienced in his trips to South America and Mexico. She couldn't believe it - she found a man she could not only talk to about everything, but he listened and respected her opinions. Before she knew it, they were in bed, but it was to be expected, since he was a Scorpio, like Frank. She didn't quite remember how they got there, but great, so who cared?

On Tuesday, he left for Hong Kong for two weeks. She was very nonchalant waiting for him to de-board the plane, but as soon as she saw him, her heart started pounding. She couldn't believe herself. She'd only spent two days with him, and now he'd been gone two weeks. She could not comprehend how excited she was to see him, and how much she missed him. It was bliss, like she'd only known at the beginning with Mike, with the big added plus that she found a man that she'd not have to change to her way of thinking and doing. He'd been on that wavelength, most of his forty-one years.

The only problem, that slowly arose was the decrease of sex. Since Michael felt she'd been the usual initiator of it, when she stopped, the sex stopped. Will was driving with her to Peoria to pickup her kids for the weekend, when she wanted to broach the subject to him. She felt maybe they'd been seeing too much of each other. "Are you bored?" she carefully asked.

Will glanced over to her, and said, "No."

A little uncomfortable, but Michael was not going to be April - she wanted to know, so she continued, "Are you unhappy?" This time Will took a much longer look at her.

"No. As a matter of fact, I'm probably happier than I've been in a long time - maybe even years. Why? Are you unhappy?"

Looking directly at him, Michael said, "In some ways, yea."

Will turned off the radio. "What's the problem?"

She was astonished by his action, and direct questioning with no evasiveness, as Mike would have. My God, she thought - he *turned-off the radio for us* to really concentrate on talking. She slowly began to explain what she felt was their dilemma with sex.

Will quietly listened until she finished. "You had one man who came to you for sex, I didn't think you wanted a second one for sex." She was totally surprised regarding his actions.

She couldn't believe his compassion, as she began to detail, that as true as it was, she still didn't want him *not coming to her* at all. "I think you don't want me . . . if nothing."

"That's not it at all. I thought you knew how much I want you." He was very relieved.

"No, I didn't. I guess that's my screwy-head. I still connect overt-sex to caring."

"Yea, it's your screwy-head. I don't want you here to service me." Michael was so impressed that they could not only talk openly, but have it completely settled, and then both comfortable with it.

Will's next trip was to Egypt, and wanted her to join him on it. She was so excited as she told Beth and Connie. "I mean, Egypt - the pyramids, crypts, the desert - I mean Egypt. God, I can hardly wait."

They weren't going until October, and still Connie had to take Michael down to the post office, to get her form for the passport filled out, before the ten-day deadline. To get her on her way, Connie loaned Michael the spending money, since she insisted to Will that she wanted to take some of her own money with her.

Unlike Connie getting used to all of Greg's generosity real fast, Michael could not let go to let Will spoil her, though she knew money was no problem to him. She still didn't feel worthy of being treated well. With Mike, she'd always been concerned with any expenses, and had always picked up at least half the tab, even when it wasn't necessary. To Mike, she'd also been expressing her independence, since Barb cheated him out of so much money, but that was not necessary to continue.

They were soon off to Egypt. Michael was completely at ease, simply because Will was. He'd done so much worldwide-traveling, his confidence was comforting. She couldn't wait to do all the tourist things like riding a camel, climbing the pyramids and seeing the Sphinx. Not having any children of his own, Will was also interested in Michael's, which was another big change from Mike.

In a small shop in Cairo, when the proprietor asked him how many children he and his wife had, Will never hesitated responding, "Three." He then proceeded to buy them each something, that their individual personalities would enjoy, rather than some generalized gifts. It meant much more to Michael than she could say.

Will even thought about Michael's kids sometimes when she didn't. Dumbfounded when he asked her if there were any snowmobile trails in Peoria. "Why would you want to know that?"

Will looked at her as if it were obvious, "Well, don't you think your kids would like to go snowmobiling?" In a million years, Mike wouldn't have offered and Michael simply accustomed to not asking for favors for her kids, since his answer would deeply-wound her.

Still, Michael rebuilt somewhat of a friendship with Mike, so they could talk on the phone and see each other for coffee from time to time. She was still very close to his boys, and would probably remain so. When she returned from Egypt, she was so enthused to get her pictures back, and share the excitement of the trip with Mike.

Even though Cathy forbade him to see her anymore, they continued talking only until his marriage. Michael talked to him several times since she started seeing Will, but this would be the first time seeing him in several months. Confused at first, if she should lie to Will or come out with the truth, demanding to see an old friend to share her trip memories with. It was not necessary for her to make any demands, when Will told her that one of the things he really dug about her, was that she never questioned him where he'd been, or what he'd been doing when she hadn't seen him for several days.

Freely and open then, at least for Michael, she saw Mike to share her trip experience. Unfortunately, he also took the opportunity to 'stroll-down memory-lane.' Michael was past that point of the conversation, since Mike took it upon himself to only remember the good times. He'd obviously not grown, to the extent that she had. Part of her heart would always love Mike and remain so. But she was so much happier with herself, and personal-worth since their break-up. This was something Mike never understood, since she was more a 'loss of sex' to him, than anything else. He'd lived a fantasy of sex and fun, that most men his age could only dream of. And, he just didn't want to let it end.

Michael didn't have to worry about that with Will. He didn't want her to be attached to him like another appendage, or her only answers to him, "Yes, dear. Whatever you say, dear." She teased him sometimes and said, "Stick it in your ear!"

Will laughed responding, "That's great! I want to hear your independence."

Sometimes it was almost spooky to Michael, because she still would occasionally feel she didn't deserve a man like this. Then she'd remember some of the previous men, and what she'd been through to pay her dues, and she'd just sit back and say to herself, *"Hey, Dummy - enjoy - enjoy!"*

Blossoming

Congruence - all of the parts
fitting together exactly,
and working together
in harmony.

The day came to risk -
when holding on
was more painful
than to blossom.

Beauty encapsulates the essence
of opening my soul.
It wasn't broken-open,
but surely blossomed.

Intuitively I sensed its expansion.
I breathed deeply into life,
allowing life to breathe
deeply into me.

A willingness to step
wholeheartedly,
into the power
of the moment.

You allow your consciousness
to expand,
and your horizons
to come to you . . .

CHAPTER 38

Escape and Return

April oldest daughter had seized on the thread of hope they would soon be out from under Alex's fist, so she'd not relent at nagging to make the move. April at last, chartered out the move, so she could give the girls an approximate date they'd do it. She still had no idea what she'd do about a job, but she was sure providence show her through.

One Sunday afternoon the girls were playing in the front yard, when it started to lightly drizzle. It wasn't even enough for April to call them in. Suddenly, Alex jumped up from the couch, and got hysterical, screaming as he was going up the stairs to the bedroom. "Those goddamn girls, left their fucking-windows open again. I'm going to nail them shut." After slamming each window, he ran back down the stairs, got the nails and hammer, then ran back up. Still raving on, as he nailed the windows shut. April stood at the bottom of the stairs, too afraid to go where she'd be within reach. She just kept pleading to him, not to nail the windows when it was summertime.

The realization could no loner be ignored, no matter what she did, said or felt would not make any difference. Since she was not dealing with a sane person, it did not matter. Still, when he came down, she tried once again to beg him not to, and he started to come at her with the hammer still in his hand. She had to back off and shut up.

On Monday, April was reading *Atlas Shrugged* at Steve's suggestion. Thinking about the book, and how it applied to her situation, she decided to take out her Tarot cards to ask them what she should do. Very simply, the cards told her to get a job, not using her body as before, since the physical wore down so quickly, but with her mind, since it was her best asset. Once the wheels were rolling on what to do, the Aries began searching for where she'd go for this job.

The college was where she worked the longest teaching her classes, so she went to them to see what kind of openings they had in the administration. She knew so many of the people there, it would not be like totally new and alien to her. April then figured that she'd be better off having someone introduce her, so she contacted the man she'd worked with on her radio-interview show for the last year. He said he'd be most happy to take her over to personnel, and put in the good word for her. By the time he finished, April was filling-out an application only for formality. They even gave her a choice of which job she wanted. The one she picked out, the girl would be leaving in six weeks, which was fine, since April needed almost that long to make all of her moving arrangements.

The next day, she went apartment hunting. Not immediately finding an adequate one for them, she put the word out to her friends with instant success. By Saturday, April made a hundred-dollar deposit on a three-bedroom apartment in a converted-farm setting. The fundamental ground work laid, she went to see an attorney to complete-out her game plan. This time around she was going to walk away with more than just her freedom.

She figured, she more than 'earned every dime she could get' from the rounds of knock-down, drag-outs with Alex. April calmly told the attorney. "I'm going to take all the furniture, clean out the bank account and charge what I need before I leave. Anything else after that is gravy, so go to it." She wanted alimony since through her father, she'd gotten him the job in the iron-workers union

She carefully watched when Alex sent the payments in on the department store and bank charges. The following day, she carried bag after bag of household goodies into Michael's apartment for safekeeping. In four days, she charged twelve-hundred dollars. She reserved the truck for the move, and once again recruited her father's help to move-out on a man. Connie and Michael were now by her side in support and physically helping.

Alex came home just before they finished loading the last bits into the truck. He stumbled in and asked, "What are you doing?"

April tried smiling, like she had it all together, "Leaving!"

Incredulously, Alex asked, "Why? What have I done?"

She gasped for the words, which would not come. How could she put into a sentence the abuse she and the girls suffered physically, emotionally and mentally the last five years? With April still staring at him in absolute wonder, she reached into her purse and pulled out *his* gun, she'd carefully hidden. "You are not going to stop me, or hurt me, or the girls any more." He swung around and marched out.

With the combination of relief and guilt, she sank down and cried. She was closing the door on another ugly part of her life, and he was behind it now. Here she was doing a rerun of her life. Maybe this time she got it all acted out right, since she was doing it for just herself, and not for some man. April still had several weeks before she started her new job.

Being alone in the new apartment, she started to cry almost out of habit. This time though, she knew there was no turning back - she had to make it on her own. Alex was not 'a Wally' that would welcome her back with open arms, if she changed her mind. The two weeks until working, she was a nervous wreck, and hardly able to sleep. Once she made a decision, she couldn't stand the waiting. When she called Beth to tell her, they both laughed and then cried.

Once the job started, to her own amazement everything was fine, and she even liked it. Soon, everyday things got better and she got more confident. As April fell into the routine of work, and the pure enjoyment of her freedom from hostility from Alex, everyday became an expectation of no anticipated-fear. The independence she always had deep within her, bloomed and grew. She could almost joke now, about her fear of being on her own. She'd finally joined her friends.

April began to think back about the men in her life, and that the only one she had real love, not infatuation filled with sex, was Wally. Even then it dissolved, when she became so disillusioned with him. She'd known 'cloud-nine' more that once. Beth was right, 'life happily ever after was only Disneyland or Hollywood made for the big screen.' Knowing that the total commitment-love that April wanted and needed never really existed, so she said she'd never look for it again. She found a very, important special-person - herself - to give her love to, as she grew to know her better everyday. Her individuality-spread its wings, never to be clipped again. They each had to learn it in their own way, and in their own time.

Cam began sending Connie flowers and cards. Added to this, he called her over and over again. He now offered to pay rent on her apartment, or even a new one if she wanted to move out. She could have had anything she wanted from Cam, just so she came back to him. Connie tried to tell him that it was too little, too late. He still didn't understand. Greg took her to the circus with Will and Michael. Will learned to give Michael explicit instructions *not* to bring any money along, so that she'd not try to spend it. Connie began relating to Cam about what a good time she had at the circus.

He began defending himself, "Well, I could have taken you to the circus!"

"Cam remember when the circus came last November? I asked you to take me then, and you said 'no,' and a lot more words. Well, now I have a man who will not only take me to the crazy places *I* want to go, but he thinks up a whole bunch more on his own."

"Well, you're going to be sorry, burning your bridges."

"No, I don't think I am, Cam." There were no feelings left.

The next week would have been their tenth anniversary together. Knowing how sentimental Connie was about the anniversary, it was a last ditch effort on Cam's part. He got a shoe box and filled it with gravel from the parking lot of the factory, where he'd first made love to her in his car. Included also, was some of the food product that the factory produced. He wrapped the box in beautiful foil paper, and attached the most romantic card he could find.

Connie almost slammed the door in his face, when she saw him standing there. Reluctantly, she let him come in. Before she opened the box, she asked Cam why he'd taken all of his money out of their joint-savings account before his last trip to New York?

Being afraid of ruining the moment he'd so prepared for, he hesitated, then said, "Well, if anything happened to me, Martha needs the money more than you do."

"It's funny Cam, you never let it bother you before. I figured you didn't trust me anymore. Just like when I wanted to get the fifty-thousand dollar life insurance policy for you. It's like you want to be selfish in death, like you were when alive. I mean, Cam, what would it have hurt for me to have the things I wanted after you died, that you never gave me when you were alive? Well, Martha can have you and your money - dead or alive."

He began again, by saying he was trying with the flowers and all. "Yea, sure, Cam just like George did to me when I divorced him. It's too late. Stay out of my life - I'll write it down for you so you can look at it once in awhile to remember. STAY OUT OF MY LIFE!"

He began to slump, "Don't cut if off altogether."

"I already have, Cam. I've grown up, I've changed. You're the one that's got to change, and give me up. I've outgrown you emotionally, and the whole rest of your game." With his head hung down to his chest, he left the apartment a defeated man, as Connie had not even opened the box in front of him.

She sat down and lit a cigarette, as she slowly opened the box to see what trick he had planned to use on her. She sat there shaking her head, as she ran her fingers through the gravel. That was exactly where her past with Cam belonged, neatly tied up in a little, shoe box. She knew Greg had helped her find herself at first, but now she was discovering the rest of the iceberg, and enjoying every minute of it.

* * * * * *

Beth became friends with another married couple through her job. Gene was the company controller, and his wife Paulette was shortly going into her own business. Beth only met Gene once before coming to San Antonio, when he came to Oklahoma City to check-out the office system that she had set-up. He was very impressed with her at that time, and began to wonder what someone like Beth was doing in such a mundane job. At the same time, he was more than grateful to have her, since Terry was the epitome of disorganization. When Beth went to Houston to pick up her new car, Gene brought Paulette with him to join Beth for lunch. Gene and Beth had only talked on the phone for the last year and a half everyday, and those daily phone calls had consisted of as much personal matter as business.

Beth hit it off immediately with Paulette, as she was another Scorpio who really knew where she wanted to go. Since they had old friends in San Antonio, Beth urged them to come visit as soon as possible. She'd love to spend more time with them that day, but she was also looking forward to the rest of the weekend in Houston with Brenda and Vic. Beth continued to see both couples from time to time, and through their friendship she began to feel that there were many more people happily married, than she'd recognized before only hanging out in bars. She had her hopes of joining those happy ranks in the near future.

Through her Weight Watcher's class, Beth then met a recently divorced woman named Mary. She reached out to Beth, when she was so frustrated with losing her car, and they continued to see each other when Jeremy came back. He got along very well wth her two kids. Beth gave Mary a copy of her poetry book, and began telling her about the book she'd written on divorce.

With Mary's urgings, Beth decided to take it out again, and start working on it again. Not only was it great for Beth's fill-in time at work, but it began to give her new hope of developing her creative talents. When Lori called to say she'd just been talking to someone about the divorce book, it gave Beth great pleasure to tell her that she was active once again with it.

In doing the writing, Beth began to feel a new closeness to her friends in Elmwood. Going back over all they'd been through she knew now whatever held her back before during last Christmas, was now gone. She still truly loved them, and wanted to continue sharing that love with them again. With the long distance phone calls all made, this time covering more than just 'the news from home,' Beth told them that she'd be coming back for Thanksgiving, and there were more changes in her than just the weight loss, that she was so proud of.

Beth then became friends with another divorcee was in her apartment complex. Barb'd been divorced almost as long as Beth, and she'd also had many difficulties making it on her own with her two kids. After Beth met Princella in the laundry room one day, it seemed that her new circle of friends was complete. Being Black, Princella helped Beth to comprehend the struggle for divorced-independence was not just a white, middle-class revolt. So, these new friends helped shape Beth's attitudes, as she once again tackled writing her book on divorce. She now looked at it from a very different perspective, everyone had their own story to tell, about how they rose step-by-step into independent women, now looking for men very different from their past. What still surprised Beth were those who did not choose independence. And again, reminded herself that it was their choice.

The day before Beth's birthday when Roy walked through the door at her office. He simply stared at Beth, as she tried to ask him how she could help him. Terry was out in the pipe yard, and Roy said that there was no big rush to call him in. It'd been a long time since Beth had sat and talked with an eligible man. Though she enjoyed talking to their contractor, and a few other men, that came through the door, Beth had not been able to meet any single men. When he asked her to go to lunch, Beth explained that she usually ate lunch at her desk, because someone had to be around. She mentioned Terry would be gone the next day, if he'd care to join her then.

Roy called her later, and they talked on the phone for several hours. He was separated from his wife, but had made sounds like he was not sure if he wanted a divorce or not. Beth mentioned that the next day was her birthday, still she was not expecting him to come in for lunch with a single red rose in a white bud vase. He gave her one of the best birthdays that she'd had in years. They had four days of wonderful talking, and one exquisite night before Beth realized this man was not capable of falling in love with one woman, when he was still hung-up on another. She figured it was still better to have loved and lost, etc. At least, she knew she was ready to have men in her life.

Beginning to accept the fact, she felt more positive about herself, and her future, she was drawing in to her similar types of people. It certainly was a wonderful change from all the negatives she had prior. It was as if the more she accepted that she deserved the good times, the more they were brought to her. Beth decided to have the plate removed from her arm, during the week between Christmas and New Year's, while Jeremy was in Elmwood with Bruce. It would be as much an emotional removal as the physical one. No longer any pain, reminding her of what she inflicted upon herself in the past.

The trip to Chicago for Thanksgiving would give her a chance to visit everyone. Beth was slowly following the holiday crowd, through the jetway to the plane bound for Chicago. It would always be returning to her roots, but home would now be the domicile within her, since she made peace with her past. She knew that she and Jeremy were enough of a family, and no rush for an addition. She put her hand tenderly on his shoulder, "Easy, honey, don't push. They won't leave without us, we already have our set-seats."

Jeremy looked up and smiled, "OK, Mom."

Yes, the homecoming would be different this time, so many major changes in each of their lives. With Beth, it was as if the metamorphosis of herself was about complete. Yes, Michael said so aptly, "You are what you've been - the good, bad and the in-between." Only now, it seemed Beth somewhat succeeded in how to put all the ingredients together learning from, but not repeating the bad, to expanding the good. She knew she couldn't have gotten to where she was, without having gone through where she'd been in her past. Beth stepped on the plane. The great thing about this new-self was there was no limit to where she could go with it.

Days later, Beth looked out the window at the snow, she really didn't miss, living in San Antonio. She joked to Connie about the current eighty-degrees temperature there.

"Rrreeally? Fuck you," she laughed. "It's your move." She sat back and drank her wine. They were having their reunion with a Scrabble game, as usual.

As much as they changed, some things stayed the same. Beth finished her play and picked up her wine glass, as she lit a cigarette. She took a swallow, as she watched Connie ponder over some triple-word-score. "Remember the night we spent with Bobby Ryan?"

Connie cracked up, "Remember?!? My God, I hope to remember it in minute-detail, until we're old and sitting in our rocking-chairs at the home for Wayward Waitresses!"

There was nothing like friendship.

SECTION 3:

THE FOLLOWING DECADES

Mystery of Secrets

Sure, all my friends, we all have secrets.
If we had no secrets, we'd have no mystery.
About us, or who we are, even in our dreams.
How can life be mysterious without secrets?

So without secrets we're without mystery,
And without mystery, we'd certainly be bland.
Actually, we'd be boring, the kind of beige-person
That no one sees, or the mind ignores noticing.

Secrets can raise eyebrows, as to shock or why?
They are that personal, even unfulfilled, or just dreams.
Is thinking about illicit, as secretive as being so?
Just as a sin of omission, being as wrong as commission.

It is not always the quiet ones who are deep.
Some talkers do so to cover up their secrets.
Is the showing of secrets required to trust one?
Or believe honesty? Or, rendering of disillusionment?

Must we all be stripped-naked to prove our reality?
It is back to the cookie-cutter for those too different.
Yet, we search for the mysteries of life, not knowing,
They may simply be secrets, we have yet to fulfill.

CHAPTER 39

Rushing Into the 80s

April's life could not have been going better, yet at times she still could not let go of the loss of Alex, as if she might still change him. Similar to Michael's not being able to totally and completely be unattached from Mike. Perhaps, as Beth used to believe, April - consciously or subconsciously - loved and needed drama, and would set herself up for it to be created. On her Thanksgiving visit from San Antonio, Beth told April how well things were going since the oil job finished, and she'd been continuing with her college courses. Not to be outdone, April proudly announced how much she was now earning between classes, full time job, the couple hundred she was getting from alimony, and her child support.

Beth was truly happy for her, so couldn't understand why she felt she needed to contact and see Alex. With no real justification that April knew she would accept, she just blew her off. She instead, bitched about Wally getting remarried to a woman with a son, so he all but stopped seeing the girls, yet she made sure he paid the child-support. Beth noted, though didn't say anything to April, the girls were still quite spoiled, and everything was always about money. April contended the weather was wearing, so maybe she'd join Beth in the warmer climate. Beth immediately thought she better not paint, too-bright a picture, as the last thing she wanted was for April to come piling-in on her like her sister, Marie did in Oklahoma.

Lori was making another trip to San Antonio, and had asked Beth if she could come up with a title for an upcoming exhibition in Chicago at the Museum of Science and Industry for Ricardo. Very excited, Beth responded back shortly - she had gotten really good at titles - with: "The Creative Spheres of Ricardo . . ." Lori was astounded once again, Beth did much of her job for her. Though she offered no promised-financial remuneration, Beth wasn't bothered much about it, as the joy of being associated with Ricardo meant so much to her. When in San Antonio, Lori took her out for dinner and then confessed, wanting Beth to hear from her, before she might find out on her own.

Lori had been arrested at Saks Fifth Avenue for shoplifting a hundred dollar scarf. They talked about her bouts of kleptomania, warnings she'd been given in the past, and now the arrest - which cost her a lot of money to keep from going to jail. She talked to her therapist, and it came from her feelings of deserving more than she got and not - in her opinion - being given the love she deserved from her parents. While totally shocked, Beth stayed open about her being honest about it, yet it also answered many questions of how Lori was regarding money and being paid generously for things.

Once she returned to Chicago, Lori called to mention she needed to find a good photographer to go into the Museum to record every one of Ricardo's pieces for his portfolio, for her to use in future presentations to other museums. Beth immediately suggested her nephew Jason, who had already won several awards, and he'd be honored for the opportunity. Once the job was finished, Lori and Ricardo both were joyous over the results, Lori then ended up stopping payment on the three-hundred twenty dollar check she'd given to Jason. Her only excuse was, "He's too young to make that much money for only a few hours work."

Beth had seen the incredible photos, and was furious with Lori. In this case, 'blood was much thicker than water' for more reasons than just him being a relative. Jason had incredible talent, and this would be a big acknowledgement of it, which Beth did not want to see go unrecognized. She immediately sent a letter to Ricardo, but he simply said, 'he was sorry, but he paid Lori, and it was her discretion as to how she paid the money out.' It broke Beth's heart, yet Jason was totally mature about it, being grateful for the experience. Beth would never speak to Lori or Ricardo again for her action and his inaction.

* * * * * *

Unlike April, Michael could not have been happier with Will and their relationship, as he took her so many places, as well treated her children like his own in his time and generosity. Mike, on the other hand, fulfilled his guilt-obligation and married Cathy in late 1980. He then - amazingly - inquired if Michael would like to see him sexually. She made it clear, she'd never be the 'other' woman again. If he didn't push it, they could still talk, but their sex-history would remain that. Her real problem was her health, as her back started to really give her a lot of pain. In her usual, non-prevention or ignoring getting any medical consultation, Michael searched out alternative - non-active jobs she might do, as she cut down on her house cleaning jobs.

Having learned to do basic bartending with all of their party-servicing jobs, Michael added that to her income at a nice local bar, and a chance to meet many new people. Like Beth, she was more gullible and accepting that 'people were who they said they were,' and really didn't question, or ask for lots of details. Connie and April were the ones to be more paranoid, or questioning of unclear information. Of particular curiosity, which they continually asked Michael was, "What did Will *really* do for a living, that he traveled so much, and had so much money?"

Her response was always the same, "What difference does it make, he has a company that makes children's bicycle-handle-bar-grips - with the streamers. They're made in China, and I think some other simple, plastic-products for children. I don't know or care, whatever?" Will bought some bicycles for her girls, Kristen and Jenny, as well the grips. He got a bike for Travis also, but he was too old for the grips. In the process of receiving the grips, they sat around for sometime, as the kids were once again out of state in Florida. Connie noticed them and picked them up out of curiosity. There was a strange, but familiar smell that wasn't just that 'new-plastic' smell as Michael said. When she talked to Greg about them, he agreed, China and the handle-bar-grips were the perfect 'vehicle' for smuggling cocaine.

One thing lead to another, with Michael's confrontation to Will, his honest-admittance of smuggling drugs, and though he used children's toys, he did not sell to them. "I'm only full-filling a 'need' for those who chose to use it." As she learned, since the final break-up with Mike to compartmentalize more and more of her life and feelings, she was done with him, no matter what he said. She simply acknowledged: "He was *Not* who I thought he was - another mistake made, and another lesson learned." It was another hurt, but she processed it easier this time.

By 1981 Michael stopped cleaning all together, and her mother moved back to the far-western suburbs to be close to her. As fate would have it, later that year she died, but at least they had some great times together, to mend any fences that needed it. Now, it was just her brother Webster and his wife Cindy that she could call family, as Tim refused to bring her children back up to Chicago for the funeral.

After Beth finished in late 1979 with the oil company, turning down their offer to work in Houston for the corporate - she really didn't like the city, sprawled similar to Los Angeles and an absolute humidor, weather-wise - she found work with a large employment agency in San Antonio. Most significantly was the meeting up with Una, who became an incredible 'like-minded' friend and party-goer. Originally from Temple, Texas, she knew everyone in San Antonio, as she a typesetter and marketing-whiz to many businesses. Immediately, Una got Beth connected into a 'Women in Business' group, and together they did the newsletter and other marketing in all areas. She loved Beth's creative writing and helped her get many side-line jobs, encouraging her to create her own business for them to work together.

Beth's dating was mixed until she connected with a very open and accepting Methodist church that had a large single's group, basically run by a therapist named Glen. They had regular Friday night get-togethers with a variety of mostly, divorced people. Beth also got involved in the church Sunday morning discussion group, with unlimited topics and even speakers from time to time. This was where she met Harry, the Reformed Rabbi, going through *his second* divorce. Always fascinated with Judaism and Jewish men, they quickly got involved. Harry was quite brilliant, and had as much appreciation of Beth's mind as well her body. Though a bit older, he had his two, teenage children from his first marriage living with him, so they split their time between his home and her apartment with Jeremy.

Usually a fascinating time for them, as she learned about Judaism and participated in his serving a small reformed-group as their Rabbi. Harry really acknowledged her poetry, as well her creative, quick-mind and wit. He also introduced Jeremy to the local Mensa group in San Antonio, and he got along well with his children, though he was gone during the summer to his father's. During their ten months together, they had a very active sex-life, which Beth later learned was the downfall of both his marriages. Beth invited Harry to join her and Jeremy, as they were going back to Chicago for the Christmas holidays, but he declined.

When Beth returned, it was actually his very upset daughter, who told her, that Harry cheated on her with some other woman. He admitted to being a sex-addict, and thought he'd done quite well, as he'd stayed faithful to Beth longer than to *either* of his wives. Using the adage of 'variety being the spice of life' his excuse, and why there was '31 Flavors of Ice Cream.'

Beth merely responded, "I'm not vanilla, never have been, and if you need variety to satisfy you, then I'm out of here." Beth learned later when Harry joined her little, morning-running-group, of several of her divorced-female neighbors, he'd propositioned three of them. They hesitated to tell her, as they knew how much she'd cared for him. It was a great lesson for her, *once again.*

With her association to many of Una's friends, they became hers also, and one night about a half-dozen of them were out celebrating a 'Bachelorette Party' at a recently opened *Male-Stripper* joint. It was a first for Beth, and she thoroughly enjoyed it, especially when one of the taller, really good-looking men did a dance on the table in front of her. She gingerly went to put her dollar in his shiny-jockeys, as he bent down to kiss her hand - their eyes met and they both beamed. *"How fun,"* Beth thought, as he squatted down to tantalize her with his assets. The other women were squealing, while she simply kept smirking to him. One of the ladies, now rather booze-wasted, offered the darling, valet-parking guy five-dollars to 'cop-a-feel' of his penis being displayed under his skimpy outfit, and he accepted. Beth laughed herself silly, as sober this woman would *never* have even said the word *'penis.'*

The following Monday morning at the employment agency, Beth was called to the front lobby to handle a 'walk-in' applicant. She picked-up the application and called the name, only to have her 'stripper-friend' be the one to come smiling up to her. He recognized her the moment she came into the lobby. Controlling herself from laughing out loud, she led him into the private, interview room, where the moment she shut the door, he began kissing her. Not to let the situation get out of hand, and get fired or worse, she laughed, "Is this providence, or what?"

Once she got him to sit down, they talked and Beth learned this young man - nine years her junior - had basically been a gigolo in Hawaii, when he was in the Navy. He had to resign or be court-martialed for 'entertaining' too many of the officers' wives - though none of them would testify against him. Beth thought he'd do well in sales, especially in something women would be interested in buying - truly, he was that good.

As Jeremy had already left for the summer, she gave him her address, and they spent almost every free moment, that both had available together. It was the best month that Beth would ever have, truly no strings attached, and not much time spent vertical. She did get him a job that took him away, so she went back to the Friday-night singles-group to see what newcomers had gotten involved.

They were organizing a Fifties-Style Sock-Hop, so she was exited to participate and be totally in it to dance her buns-off, she announced. There were three men very interested in her, and they were sort-of friends, so the dating of them was a bit convoluted and complicated, not to mess up the friendships. She'd also started dating another older man she'd met before in the group, who was a retired, Air Force air-controller who was quite fascinating, but had a serious drinking problem. This led her to drinking more when with him, and she really didn't want that.

Once Jeremy returned for school, she had to consider a baby-sitter when she was out - either for her college classes or dating. She came home one evening to find Jim, the tall, well-built guy, with the male-pattern-baldness and glasses. Not as good-looking as the others, but certainly was the most attentive to her. He'd dropped by to visit, and the babysitter told him she was at school, so he decided to wait on the steps of her apartment till she got home. She'd noticed his new Harley parked close by, which was a big attraction, as her love of riding them.

Beth didn't feel it was stalking, though she told him, "It would always be better to call, before making the drive over," she invited him in, and she paid the babysitter as she left.

Jim spoke up, "I understand you're 'dating' several different men," - he did not ask for clarification as to what-all that meant, simply assuming it was her euphemism for having sex "and I've got no problem with it. I just wanted to know when we could go out?"

Beth liked his directness, so informed him she had classes twice a week, and tried to be home with Jeremy the other nights during the week, but was available that Friday night. Jim immediately volunteered to babysit for her on her school nights, and that certainly impressed her. She also informed him that she didn't have men at the apartment when Jeremy was there. After their Friday night, he wanted to join her on Sunday at church, and then take Jeremy to the park.

It didn't take long after, she'd later been to his place for sex, that she started to drop-off the other men and concentrated on Jim. He seemed to know what to say, and how to listen to her and definitely seemed comfortable around this independent woman. Not being as good looking, he wasn't continually looking at other women, or having any kind of arrogant attitude.

He seemed pleased she liked him, and being a mechanical engineer, he wasn't familiar with her writing or poetry, but open to learning. So many years around Mike, she had enough of the 'technical' vocabulary, that she enjoyed listening to him talk about his job. But what impressed her most was, this six-foot-four-inch man was happy to sit on the floor and play with Jeremy, regarding his '*Star Trek, Star Wars*' stuff, as well as his dinosaurs and planets in the Milky Way. His father had never, ever done that, and it meant the most to her. He'd been married before, but never had children, so the idea of a son meant a lot to him.

Beth was happy to go to East Texas to meet his mother and grandfather, who had raised him, and then another time to his father's ranch, where she met his step-mother. Honestly, only his father appeared 'normal' and the others were a bit strange, but Jeremy was intrigued making the trips, and loved the animals on the ranch. By the time, holidays were coming, Jim, unlike Harry, was most happy to join Beth on the annual trek to Chicago to meet the family. Rather than be uncomfortable at the house, Beth suggested a motel close by, though she knew her mother would make a *stink* about them staying there.

After meeting her family, including Marie's now ex-husband, who still hung around for any free-meals he could get from Louise, Jim asked her to marry him. Beth felt a bit rushed, as it'd only been about five months they'd been dating, so said she wanted to wait for marriage until the end of May, or six months into 1981. Jim agreed, but wanted to move in with her, once they returned to San Antonio. Beth felt that was a good idea, to make sure they could work out any kinks that might come up before the marriage.

Hearing the great news of Beth's engagement, and upcoming marriage over the phone when she called, April popped in at Beth's parents to see her, before they left to go out to the farm for a few days with Mike. Almost visibly taken aback, that while Jim was tall and well built, his ordinary looks surprised her. She had Beth walk her out to the car to talk alone when she was ready to leave. "My God, Beth, couldn't you get a better-looking man than that?"

Very shocked at April's shallowness, speaking even more crass than usual in her opinions. "Not too, rude are you? I've had enough of the good-looking guys in the last few years, who are more into themselves than me. And, before you ask, 'Yes' he happens to be very good in bed, he's great with Jeremy, makes good money, dotes on me and a very good mind, not that *those things* were ever at the top of *your* list." She was pissed and not hiding it at all.

There was no erasing the words she'd spouted out, so she got defensive. "Well, you always got the best-looking guys cause you're the prettiest, I just wanted to know what happened." She went to give Beth a hug and kiss goodbye, but it was all rather cooly-received and reciprocated. "I'll call you in a week or so, to let you know what's happening here." Beth did not respond, and truly wondered why she continued to put up with April, and her mouthy-jabs.

Mike enjoyed talking 'machinery' with Jim, and Beth was glad Cathy had not come out to the farm, only her nephew Sweetie-Jason, who spent time with Jeremy. They had a fun time snowmobiling, and playing in the snow - Jim had only been in snow once. They had a few days back in San Antonio alone, while Jeremy stayed with his Dad through the New Year. Beth felt it'd been a good decision, but Jim did seem more possessive, now that he knew she was *his*.

They had some great rides on the motorcycle, both alone and with other couples up to the Hill Country, or as far as South Padre Island. But it got s little rockier, the closer to their wedding date, as Jim when attending any of Beth's women's functions, got tired of being referred as "Mr." using her last name, rather than his.

They'd talked several times with Glen to work things out. The only *significant* incident, while Beth was in the laundry room, Jeremy and one of his friends were running around playing in the apartment, instead of outside. When Jim said something to them, the friend mouthed-off at him. Jim released his temper, and slammed his fist into the table, which was a 'butcher-block' thick wood, so the fist broke, not the table.

The neighbor boy went home and Jeremy was in his room, when Beth returned to the scene of Jim with ice on his fist, sitting at the table. She said simply, once the story was told by both Jim and Jeremy, "I will NOT put up with any violence, whatsoever, for whatever excuse. It better not happen again." Beth went and talked to the neighbor-mother, before she took Jim to the emergency room with Jeremy. She had a deep concern, but felt she could deal with it, as she'd been working to eliminate Jim's insecurities regarding her growing, public-persona.

Beth changed jobs, to working with the Drug Awareness Association, as their Public Information Officer. They did several seminars, conferences and programs for groups and the public, working with other larger organizations. She'd been the spokes-person, including the Public Service Announcements on television and the radio. In fact, she'd won an award for the best PSAs for her writing and performing with a well-known radio disc-jockey. The wedding was a success, though a hurricane had come far enough in-land to really soak the wedding, which was done at the Brackenridge Park, and the reception followed - supposed to be outside at Glen's house, with all of the Singles' group people attending. Irony included, they'd be putting-off the 'honeymoon' until Beth finished doing a 'Domestic Violence' conference for the regional area.

Una also got Beth involved in "The Mayor's Committee for the Status of Women," as well working on the forth-coming, 1982 State Treasurer's campaign for Anne Richards. But when their Women in Business group joined with Ginger Purdy, and her Network Power/Texas II Conference in 1981, it was the big one. They had over a thousand women at the San Antonio Convention Center, and it featured Maureen Reagan, as a Keynote speaker.

This involved them in the leadership of numerous, support-groups for women, with the purpose of promoting equity and self-sufficiency for women through educational programs, activities and services. As the Marketing Chair, and best known speaker, Beth gave the opening, welcome and introduction for Maureen Reagan. Also Beth's job to be at Maureen's side every minute, which meant having the Secret Service at their side, since her father was then President. It was a benchmark for Beth, who would not surpass the experience for almost ten years.

Beth noticed Jeremy seemed to have more spending money lately, and working for Drug Awareness, she sat him down to talk. He openly said, "Well, some of my friends can't afford to rent the video games, so I copy them for a couple of dollars." Beth explained, as nice as that was of him, it was illegal, and she didn't want him doing it any more. She knew he was becoming quite the whiz with computers, but when he came in all excited, she almost had cardiac-arrest. "Mom, we don't have to worry about how much money is in the ATM, I've figured out how to read the black magnetic strip, so we can have as much as we want!" She then explained the F.B.I., frowned on such things and would put her in jail, since he was only fourteen.

Though things mellowed between Beth and April as the months again past, a few weeks after Beth and Jim returned to San

Antonio from their honeymoon, April called to say, "The girls and I will be moving down to San Antonio the 4th of July weekend. I'm having too many problems with Alex, so a move out-of-state is the best thing." Shocked, Beth made it more than clear she had no room for them to stay with her, but there were plenty of cheap motels all around. She did not want to be drawn into April's bad decisions any more than she had been. Michael related a rehash of when April moved out on Alex, as she helped her to pack up a truck once again. Connie, out with Greg, wanted no part of her stupidity in moving.

One could say, April learned to finagle, manipulate or maneuver, especially men, from her early years of getting 'guilt' money from her father, regarding his molestation of her. Unfortunately, she expanded to whomever, friend or just acquaintance, she could use to get whatever she wanted. Right there, eying and learning was Deidra, her smart, resentful and conniving daughter. In her own mind, April justified *whatever* she did to better herself, as she deserved it, for all of the bad things she'd suffered in her life - though the person she was using had little or no connection to those things she suffered. Regarding Alex, she felt she got him the *highly-paid* ironworker's job, so he '*owed her*' more than the court-set alimony.

April found out as much information about San Antonio as she could, regarding what she considered best '*zip codes,*' area-suburbs, etc. And, that was the wealthy, small town of Alamo Heights, surrounded by San Antonio. Not just for the best schools, but so her daughters would be surrounded by money, to associate with money and to eventually *marry* money. She hadn't been educating them in the 'finesse of marrying-up and well' for nothing - they'd be her 'ace-in-a-hole,' so to speak for her old age - if she didn't find another man to marry and support her.

One mess and situation after another, April would pull Beth into, with her old saying of "I'm a better friend to you, than you are to me - or you owe me." The most factious was April's dryer that didn't work after the move, and Jim couldn't fix it. Pissed at his *ineptness*, as she called it, she placed an ad in the newspaper in Beth's name, with her address and phone to sell the dryer for $100, with promise of delivery, since Jim had a pick-up truck. She even had the gaul to say it worked. April ignored all of Beth's complaints, especially those regarding it from the people who bought the broken dryer - even when Beth gave them her phone number. Beth would enforce another 'break' from April, but she'd always finagle her way back.

The next big hurdle for Beth was finally graduating from the university in May 1982, with a double-degree in Psychology and Marketing. In her mind's eye, she made it with no-limitations in what she could do. Shortly after her graduation, Beth got a job at the San Antonio Housing Authority, the fourth-largest in the country, as Public Information Officer. Beth and Jim had already moved from the apartment to a small rental house, and now to a larger house that was a lease-to-purchase. The marriage had it ups and downs, but she was determined to keep it together, whether it was with chewing gum, super-glue or duct tape. He didn't seem to be as communicative as he had been, and not always handling her spotlight growing.

* * * * * *

Back in Chicago, Connie was at last ready to marry Greg after so many trips, and gifts and continued attention to her through his divorce, feeling she made the right decision. Valentine's Day, 1982, on a cruise to the Bahamas, they had the Captain marry them. She was thirty-four and he was fifty-five, and though a very active person - he had gone sky-diving to prove how young he was, and ended up breaking his back. Still, Connie figured maybe she'd have twenty years with him before he died, and that would be enough. She'd be young enough to remarry if she wanted, or just enjoy her own life. They already had several, really great years together, so she wasn't going to worry about it.

Also in 1982, Beth's older nephew, Jackie graduated from DeFry, was hired by Ford Motor Company, then got married and bought the family house. Meanwhile Jason, her younger nephew, now without a roof, moved into the old, apartment building down the hall from Michael and Connie. He'd graduated from Ray Vogue's Art School studying his love of photography, and worked at the largest photo stores in the area. Jason ran into Michael's son Travis at her place, also living in the area, whom he hadn't seen in some time. As Travis was quite talented doing a lot of artwork, Jason became a mentor to him, as he had no supportive-male to bond with.

Jason continued his close relationship to Michael, as he became a real 'sounding board,' as well supportive friend to her, laughing and talking about all topics whenever possible. Once back into dating, she began to date a wider variety of men, most much younger than she was. It was all about having fun and not getting tied down to any of them.

An opportunity came up for Michael to manage a small group of condominiums, of which one was rented by her son, Travis and Connie's younger son, Jeff, who had become friends. As she moved into bar management, Michael was completely out of the house-cleaning business, and actually doing well for herself. The next time Tim had the family back in Illinois, she approached him and the girls to see if they wanted to come live with her. Since Travis, already on his own, and the girls were in high school, Michael felt the time was right for them to live with her.

She rented a three bedroom house, and once again took on parenthood. It took her a while, as they'd had little discipline from Tim and his wife, but since Michael believed-basically in them 'doing their own thing,' it would all work out, she felt. Almost out of nowhere, to the surprise of even Connie, in 1984 and less than a year with her girls, Michael married Jack at the courthouse, a guy she'd met in the bar she managed. For her, the big bonus was to have her family around the dinner table once again, at least on Sundays, with a man she thought she loved.

To celebrate, Beth and Jim drove the trek up to Chicago, for the experience. They stopped in Oklahoma City to visit Fran and Rose, stayed-over there and then on to Chicago. Since Michael became quite the collector of all things 'strange and old,' Beth found what looked like a small-sized, old trunk and filled it with things - including an old pair of boxing gloves for them to 'do battle with each other.' It was a wonderful reunion with Connie also, and somewhat thankfully without April, though Beth brought a wedding gift from her for Michael. April started a new job working in phone-sales for a bottling company, taking orders for stores and restaurants. She put Deidra through beauty school to become a manicurist, as the big fad was the acrylic-nails. April wanted to make sure that they all knew, of course, Deidra worked in a salon in Alamo Heights, though that meant nothing to Connie and Michael until Beth explained.

April would not comprehend or accept, she could not just come barging into Beth's house, as she had back in Chicago. Jim may not be fully-dressed, or them preoccupied with each other. By that time Jeremy wanted to live full-time with Beth, and she began locking the door to keep April from walking in anytime she had some trauma, or something she wanted to drag Beth into. Now April was trying to control Deidra, who was employed and practically on her own.

The very first thing Deidra purchased with her nail-money was a Louis Vuitton handbag, and April was so jealous she wanted Deidra to start giving her money for living with her. Deidra more than vented on her, "How dare you ask me for money, when you allowed that S.O.B. to constantly physically and verbally abuse me, so you didn't have go out and get a job. *You owe me,* and I want nothing to do with you." Deidra proceeded to pack her things, and moved in with her new boyfriend. At least, she had enough sense and '*moxey*' to not marry him or get pregnant.

April was shocked, as she later cried to Beth, "I was only trying to keep a roof over her head. She just doesn't understand how hard it was for me, to have her suffer the way she did." They were her usual giant, crocodile-tears. Beth blew her off, agreeing with Deidra. Then the problem was with Teresa, her younger daughter, who'd never been on the receiving end of Alex's cursing or physical beatings as Deidra had. But also had great resentment for her mother putting them threw it all for five years.

Teresa never had any weight problem, as April and Deidra suffered with, and became a cheerleader, as well femme-fatale observing how her mother was around the men she toted home, or stayed overnight, changing as regular as possible. Jim regrettably introduced her to a friend, who she soaked money out of, after a few turns in the rack. When Teresa turned her young wiles onto Deidra's boyfriend, and she practically caught them in the act, Teresa accused him of trying to rape her. The poor, shocked-boy went running out of the house. Teresa turned out to be the real-brains in the family, and on her way to a total scholarship at several Universities - any one would do, yet preferred one as far away from April as possible.

Beth showed no remorse when she responded, "We all thought you were wrong to make the girls suffer so long under Alex, and now you're not even using your astrology, that was your main excuse for not working." April screamed at her as she ran out of her house. Beth was happy, she didn't have to put up with her for several months, until she called and said she'd forgiven Beth, so she wanted to come over and talk. When she came in, Beth jumped right in. "Talking about forgiveness, did you ever forgive your father before he died. I mean, I remember how pissed you were, as you tore his house apart looking for his money, . . . you were sure he'd stashed it away. Really, after all he'd done to help you and your men, . . . did you forgive him? You really shouldn't hold onto that old crap, it's going to make you crazy." She smiled slightly.

April started screaming at Beth again, "How can you ask me that? You know I don't talk about that . . . you know I've put that all in a heavy, metal box, covered over with concert inside me. Never, never, ever would I forgive him for what he did to me! He owed me, everything he did, he owed me." She was crying, totally upset. Beth said nothing.

Jim came into the kitchen to see what all the noise was, "Hey, what's going on? What's all the yelling about? You don't have to be so loud." He stood there looking concerned.

"You shut up! This has nothing to do with you!" April then turned around, and left.

"Hey, this is my house, you don't talk to me that way . . . " He turned to look at Beth.

Once she heard the door shut, she started laughing. "Wow! I should've learned to do that years ago. What a great way to get rid of her." A month later April called regarding her Uncle Artie dying in Tucson. She said she'd pay for the round-trip airline ticket for Beth to come out there with her, to deal with it all. Which Beth did, thinking she needed her support, but was wrong. April planned to drive his car back, and couldn't wait to find out how much money she got from it all. Once she was back and had the money - she never would admit how much - she bribed Deidra to go with her and Teresa to Disney World. She promised to buy them anything they wanted, and they did. She never saw the point in saving money, when she could buy material things to fill up that giant-black-hole inside her, that made her feel good momentarily.

Beth really was not happy at work with how the Director controlled the Housing Authority, and Una was talking to her about starting a magazine for career women. Through a community conference that Beth was speaking at, she met the man who invented the patented recycling machines, which were used around the world. He wanted her to write his biography for young people, and was willing to pay her fifteen thousand dollars to do so. With that, also came a trip to Washington D.C. to interview a couple of Senators he knew, and check out the the whole Medal of Freedom, which he had received. So, she and Jim went for the 4th of July week, 1984, and did the research and interviews, as well as enjoyed seeing the Beach Boys perform on the National Mall. Sometimes her writing was really worth-while to have for the bonuses.

Beth and Jim were invited by a friend to another friend's house to see some slides regarding their two years they spent in the Azores teaching. Totally amazed, by it all, they talked several times before about being able to work overseas, once Jeremy was set with college. They checked out an agency that handled all kinds of jobs, and Jim with his mechanical engineering would be easy to place, and the trainer said it would be best if Beth got an ESL - English as a Second Language Certification - or even Graduate-work for teaching English.

Since Beth left the Housing Authority, she'd gone to work for the Dale Carnegie Courses as a Training Advisor. She worked with them over three years, while she attended classes at the University for the Bi-Lingual/Bi-Cultural programs, with linguistics along with the ESL. One of her professors she got along well with, had taught in Japan for several years, and gave her some contact information. The timing would be perfect, as Jeremy was to graduate in 1986, and she'd finish her graduate studies within a year and half later. Now, they had a goal of something to really work for, that brought them closer than they had been. They agreed that whoever got the job offer first, the other would follow, of course, it was expected that it would be Jim.

Christmas of 1985, Beth felt they could afford to fly back to Chicago with Jeremy, not really expecting that Cathy would get Mike to stay in from the farm. Still, it was a good visit until as dinner finished, Mike had to help their father, get up to use the restroom. He'd already had a couple of small strokes, so when he didn't return after about five minutes, Beth asked Mike to check on him. Sure enough, he had another stroke, and the ambulance called. Once in the hospital, the doctors also found a mass in his stomach, so he was operated on to have it removed.

Beth went to visit her father several times before they flew out, and he knew his time was coming soon, so insisted that Beth make-up with Marie. "You're the smarter, stronger one, it's your job, and I want you to promise me you will. That good-for-nothing husband of hers was only good for mooching, but he was organized, she never has been." Beth promised, but John wanted more. "I want you to bring her to my funeral, because it will make your mother happy."

Beth now hesitated, "You know I can't stand being around her, she's so whiney." He looked at her with those eyes which said 'don't disappoint me,' and she relented, hoping the day would be far away, or maybe she would be, too. Her mother, Louise had been slipping with dementia, and Mike thought it best she not take care of him at home, so John was put in a nursing home in Elmwood. At least with the shock of it all, Mike realized how he'd taken his father for granted for so long, and began visiting almost daily before going to work.

Beth called every few weeks to talk, but invariably ended-up crying, as her father had always been her savior from Louise. He wanted so bad to come home, but eventually settled in, yet only lasted until May, when another major stroke took him. When the call came from Mike, Beth was more than devastated, at least her father had seen her get her degree and be rather successful. She got Marie's phone number from her mother, and called. Arrangements were made to pick her up in Oklahoma City, where she now had a house and her little retail sales-clerk job at the store. Beth decided not to put Jim or

Jeremy through it, as Bruce's father had died, just before Jeremy was to leave and come back after Christmas.

Beth arrived at Marie's the next evening after the nine-hour drive and, of course, Marie was not organized at all. "Marie, I will not put up with your ineptness or stupidity. I will be leaving at seven o'clock in the morning, whether you're with me or not. As far as I'm concerned, I've fulfilled my promise to Dad by offering the ride, you can get there however you choose." She could not have been more disgusted with the absolute-filth in her house, with neither her or the girls ever picking-up anything or cleaning anything.

Beth at first thought the shower had black trim, until she realized it was mold. At least she'd been given clean sheets to make her own bed. She set her travel alarm for six, and managed to scrounge up some breakfast for herself, and moved to get herself ready to leave without any more warnings to Marie. She'd been doing the laundry the night before, and as Beth packed the car for the thirteen-hours to Chicago, she gave only the five-minute warning. When Marie started whining, Beth put up her hand to stop, and then moved it across her throat to knock-it-off.

Beth was literally backing out of the driveway, when Marie came running out with her suitcase, and her youngest carrying the cooler with snacks and drinks, as well a bunch of other stuff which didn't get packed. While Beth forgave Marie for the past-histrionics, she felt no obligation to be around her at all. It was obviously not a pleasant trip, and Beth had Marie drive very little. She was such a cautious driver, having no assertion, and a constitution weaker than milquetoast. All Beth could think of was how Marie had been so spoiled by their mother, and so glad she'd been strict with Jeremy to not be. She thought of how very proud of him she was, and how well he'd done, as he was about to graduate from high school with an opportunity for a scholarship. Marie's three daughters were almost as much worthless-twits as she was, granted Howard had not helped with all of his constant yelling, instead of some support.

They arrived too late for the huge ceremony John's Lodge had given for him, the largest attendance ever. Beth barely made it through the funeral on Saturday, the crowd almost two hundred. Sunday was

Mother's Day, and Cathy made all of the arrangements for everyone to be together at a restaurant, including Barbara, she was good for handling details. While Michael and Connie had come to the funeral, and Beth visited them later, as her time was limited. That Sunday morning, Beth took Marie up to the grocery store to pick up some supplies for Louise, as she didn't really drive much any more. Beth picked up some fresh rye bread from the store bakery, and mentioned it to her mother as they came in the kitchen with the bags.

Louise looked at her and said, "I never really liked the rye bread, it was because your father liked it so much, that I ate it." Beth was stunned. They'd been married fifty years, and John would buy several different kinds of bread every week, but Louise playing her stoic-role, 'only trying to make you happy' persona, never saying what she preferred. It truly showed what a pathetic person she was, as if in not acknowledging-herself made her a better person.

No wonder Beth disliked her mother so much, and always felt her mother had guilted her into doing things she didn't want. They left early Monday morning for the long, drive back. Beth turned on the radio, and informed Marie she didn't care to listen to her whine or carrying on, so unless she had sometimes important to say, 'just look out the window.' They're only stops would be for gas, which included potty-breaks, and they had enough sandwiches for lunch and dinner.

Fall of 1986, Connie's father succumbed to lung cancer and died. She immediately quit smoking. With her inheritance, she and Greg decided to buy a Subway franchise, as he was ready to retire from bartending. Unfortunately, during the same period Matt had gotten heavily into drugs, and his father felt he couldn't handle him, so Connie took over and got him into rehab. Once she got him cleaned-up, she talked him into joining the Navy, figuring they could straighten him out better than she ever could. He ended up learning how to be a cook, and became chef to one of the Admirals. When he got out, Connie made him assistant manager of their second Subway. The money was rolling in and she couldn't be happier.

After graduating high school in 1986, Jeremy no longer wanted to go to the University, which had already accepted him. Instead, he wanted to stay in town with his cutie-pie, that he'd met at the laser-tag game-place, where he worked doing the repairs to the ray-guns. Beth through up her arms, and said 'fine' as he went off to live with Bimbo, earning a whopping two-hundred dollars a week, and eventually going to the community college. He had to learn, as she did about college and what better way than with a girlfriend who went to college and screwed-his-ears-off.

After their father's death, it didn't take long for Mike to realize Louise, could not be left alone. She'd opened the door to the basement and fell down, not realizing where she was. Only because her neighbor came over to visit, was she found. Mike talked to Marie, who lost her job, about coming back up to Chicago to live with their mother, and take care of her as needed. He offered to get her a job, and whatever else that was needed to get her settled in. Her middle daughter, Cindy was working out in the western suburbs for a bank, said she'd come in to help, if she didn't have to pay any rent - why was Mike not surprised? Marie had to sell her house, and get herself organized, so it was almost six months before she moved back in to the family house.

* * * * * *

Beth realized, just seeing the 'potential' in Jim and encouraging it, was not totally working. She and Glen discussed that he had some self-destructive tendencies. He had an *'accident'* with his second motorcycle - the Harley was stolen, when he *forgot* and left the backyard gate open, and then not put it away in the utility room. The accident was him *'avoiding'* a woman, who he was *sure* would hit him, so safer to go over the curb. Loaded with excuses, his leg was broken in several places, which took a long, healing-process.

Determined to full-fill *their* dream of working overseas, Beth kept going to finish her courses in graduate school. The following February, 1988, after applying to jobs in China and Korea she ended up not wanting, she got a job offer in Japan, she did want. Beth flew out to San Francisco, with Jim to follow several months later, once she got settled in Nagoya, Japan, and got him a job. N*ot* a happy-camper, but 'a deal was a deal' and he'd *not* gotten a job offer, though 'he was the engineer.' This would be the pivotal-growth-point in Beth's career, as she found her niche in teaching non-native English speakers, not only how to speak the language, but also to become comfortable working in foreign cultures.

Beth started teaching the engineers going to Kentucky for the new Toyota plants. As she got acknowledged for her skills, she moved to the Prefectural College, and became head of the Adult English Program. Then, sponsored by a company, she used her graduate-thesis training-plan, combining her Dale Carnegie experience with her ESL. Her team trained mid-level managers being sent overseas for many major manufacturing and trading companies. Beth also did voice-overs for training, testing, and advertising.

She even used her cooking-skills to teach Western-style cooking classes on television, sponsored by the local gas company. But the extensive-traveling in the three to six weeks off between work-sessions - around Japan, and eventually to thirty-six countries - was what she loved most, fulfilling her dream of 'flying-away.' Jim savored the deluxe travel amenities, though it was Beth's six-figure income paying for it. She'd gotten Jim a job at Brother Industries, regarding materials for workers in English speaking countries. But he wasn't happy not working as an important engineer - as if, when he spoke no Japanese.

Changing Lifetimes

I was sometimes caught
      between the smoke I created
      and the mirrors I used
to hide it all conveniently behind.

I filtered other people's lives
      thru my own collection of experiences
      - dismissing those not plausible,
or acceptable to me at the time.

But real life has no such handy filters,
      and some people truly choke to death
      on the grit that comes gusting in
from the storms of living every day.

I thought I knew love as well as life,
      and knew a man's moods and seasons -
      what he wanted better than himself,
with his changes prepared for in advance.

Yet, I admit that time veiled my vision,
      for the man I divorced so desperately
      wasn't the man I married so willingly
nor, I the woman he had loved so wantonly.

Chapter 40

Chasing the 90s

In 1990, shortly after Michael divorced Jack, she collapsed at the bar - hemorrhaging blood in gushes from her female reproductive system. The local hospital felt they couldn't handle the expected cervical cancer, and shipped her to Presbyterian St. Luke's in Chicago, which not only had a special cancer-ward, but took indigent patients. Michael had no health insurance or money whatsoever.

Taking into account all the years of avoiding her health or any check-ups, it came back with a vengeance. Not out of choice, but circumstance of being indigent, the hospital used her as a guinea-pig, with not only extensive radiation, but actually placing isotopes into her, rather than simply doing a complete hysterectomy. Connie contacted Beth in Japan, who was devastated, not knowing if there was anything she could do. Pray for Michael's survival, was about all anyone could do and she offered to send money.

The end results, more known in the years to come, was the extensive damage done to Michael's out-lying organs. The bladder, pancreas and liver, from the highly toxic radiation and the experimental use of the various isotopes, were as if *fossilized*, no longer working. Realized more in later years, would be the scaring damage to her vagina from all of this, making intercourse painful. Michael was confined for months, and then almost a year for any kind of recovery. So, it was survival, but at what price she'd pay in the years to come? Her daughters had both helped with the bartending, as prior they'd done house cleaning on their own and for Connie's franchise. Once she got home, they helped as they could until later in the year, she was able to get back to managing the bar, with little physical movement required.

Just prior to Michael getting sick, Beth and Jim visited Chicago in early 1990. They were actually joining their Japanese landlord and his family in San Francisco, and then going on to Los Angeles for more touring, since Jim had never been there. Beth wanted Jeremy to join them all to go to Disneyland, so they weren't bothering to travel to San Antonio. April was really pissed at being ignored, and took it personally. It was a good visit with Jeremy, and he was intrigued with the Japanese family, as he'd been studying the language in college.

Jim and Beth, then stopped in Hawaii for a few days on the way back to Japan. It was there that Beth met Barbie in the laundry room, and struck up a conversation. Beth noticed the accent, since they'd already been once to Australia the prior year, so soon both husbands had joined them, and they spent most of the rest of their time together. Her husband Paul loved to deep-sea fish, and they traveled to Hawaii usually once a year for him to do so. Since Beth and Jim were soon planning another trip to Oz, as they called it, they had new friends to meet there.

The height of Japan's expansion - nine of the top ten banks in the world were Japanese. Beth's private company sponsorship came from her first Japanese friend, Kazuyo. The company had numerous contacts, and Beth already worked many times for Toyota, her biggest client for training their mid-level managers they were sending overseas. They received one hundred-fifty to three hundred hours of training in all areas of business and cultural understanding, so they'd be able to step off the plane to start doing business. When Beth's team of four got them, they didn't even know how to make decisions, since only CEOs did that. She explained, they couldn't be calling Japan for answers to make their daily decisions. She started them from square one - deductive reasoning to teach them decision making.

Giving presentations was another huge part, and she used video tapes of them speaking, so they could see their progress to being able to do a twenty-minute presentation with three visual aids, only using six notes cards. When she first presented the finished tape to the Vice

President of his four manager-participants, he accused her of 'dubbing' it. She laughed, "I'm not that clever with the equipment to do it. That's your employees, and what they've learned from me." Beth was soon booked solid with a waiting list, as this was the 'Golden' era for Japan's internationalism. Her unmitigated success was amazing to her, as other jobs for voice-overs continued, also.

In reality, Jim was not handling Japan well, especially since Beth kept excelling while he floundered, even on their trips he'd find reasons to complain and not truly be happy. He did love Australia, as it reminded him of Texas in the 1950s, and definitely wanted to move there. From several Aussie teachers in Japan, Beth made more contacts, and they saw Paul and Barbie on their next trip. As busy as Beth constantly was with her work, when on vacation she didn't want to deal with Jim's pouting, or catering to him as she always had. When he got into his jealous moods of men talking to her, she began ignoring him and continued to do what she enjoyed, even if he chose to not participate. When Jim saw she was no longer *really* trying to make him happy, his rebelling got more extensive. He was also upset that he did not have as much time off work as she did, so he became jealous of her traveling without him.

Beth had just gotten back from three weeks in China, which he truly had no interest in going to. But she'd stopped in Hong Kong, going and coming, which Jim loved to get new suits and shoes there custom-made. She brought back a fax machine, since they were less than half-price to what Japan charged, and had it totally set up while there. He'd met her at the airport, and been very affectionate in the taxi, so she thought he'd gotten past his jealousy and pouting. Beth really wanted a shower before joining him on the futon for lovemaking, so when she came out with the towel wrapped around her, she'd not expected him to be involved in taking the fax machine apart. This was another of his passive-aggressive moves, to rile-her-up.

"What are you doing? I told you that I had it all programed in Hong Kong?" Perhaps Jim felt redundant, or whatever, but blew up, throwing the fax to the floor. But it landed on a large, throw-pillow, so whatever damaged he planned to incur didn't happen.

Nothing he was saying was making any sense about " . . . being tired of them all and they're always staring at me . . . " - ugh, yea, at his height - He wanted to get out of there. He was tired of living under her shadow . . . and now it was coming out. Even though it was a cushy-job, he'd realized that he'd never be made President of Brother, so what was the point.

Beth had enough of his spoiled childishness - and a good portion of this was her fault for always building up his ego. "Fine, you want out, you can leave whenever you want . . . " He came at her with his hands around her neck before she knew what was happening. She began kicking at him and actually got his groin, as *he taught her* to do in self-defense for her. Jim quickly broke away, not saying a word knowing he crossed the line. "OK, Buster. This is no longer a choice situation - you are out of here. Get your shit-together, and get ready to exit." She could certainly do it, because she was his visa-sponsor.

He went into the kitchen and sat down at the table, as she picked up the fax, put it on the shelf next to the phone to connect it up. She then went into the tatami room where they slept, removed two of the four futons, along with a couple of covers they used, and threw them into the living room. "Here, these are for you, we'll not being sharing any more." She closed both sliding doors, put on her nightgown and crawled into the covers.

Jim sat up and drank for a while, then came and knocked on door connected to the living room. "Can we talk?" Part of Beth was wiped out, as she felt her whole-world crashing down, along with her marriage and the 'happy-face' she had put on for so long, around all of her Japanese and *gaijin* - foreign friends.

"I have to be up in the morning to teach, as you do also. We'll talk tomorrow night, now leave me alone." She could almost feel his fist curl up, but Jim had enough control to not hit anything. In the morning, she heard him talking in the shower arguing with himself, as he'd done more and more lately. It was early April, the beginning of the work year in Japan, so a very busy time for new classes. The end of the month was one of the biggest holidays - Golden Week, and Beth had already prepaid for a week in Bali, as all trips needed to be scheduled far in advance since of the travel-jam. They sat and talked like two-adults dividing up a business, and what best to do with the least financial loss, or more important in Japan - 'loss of face.'

Jim wanted to stay until the end of June, so he could get his bonus from Brother, and he'd be going Oz. A business friend there had said before he'd sponsor him, once they'd left Japan to emigrate, to start an air conditioning business. It had been one of Jim's specialties, and they really needed it in northern Oz, where it did get very hot. She said he could join her in Bali, but better not give her any problems, and definitely no more sex. They then agreed that his exit-story would be his mother having a heart attack, and no one to take care of her.

So, now it only meant staying-civil with each other over the next few months. Beth said she'd support his move to Oz, and as they opened a saving account there from their first trip, and he'd been sending most of his paycheck there. Jim had more than enough money for his half of setting up his business. "So, you'll no longer be in my shadow, as you said. And, if it works out, maybe we'll get together to see if we're staying together or not." She looked at him wondering how it all went wrong, especially with the communication that he'd been so good at in the beginning. "What happened to all of your communication skills and concern for me you had when we first met?"

A big smirk came across his face, as if he may as well be honest. "I had sat and read all of my mother's and my wife's magazines - *Redbook, Journal, Cosmo,* and more to practice how to sound caring and concerned to get a woman. I simply wanted to screw you, and that was the quickest way to get you. I didn't know you were going to continue to be so independent and successful" Jim was quite satisfied with himself having out-smarted her, but maybe not in telling. The shock on Beth's face was instantly replaced with determination to show how wrong he was.

Still later, Jim could not have been nicer, and she was also in return. Then one night he asked, "So, if you're supporting me in my move, then we're still friends, right?" Beth answered, 'yes' having an idea of where he was going. "So, if we're friends, can't we have sex once in a while?" Beth answered, 'no.'

In Bali, it was really going well, they were having a wonderful time, platonically sharing a bed, and he offered to give her a back rub after an arduous hike. Soon, they were making love, and he assumed all was erased, so he started acting up and lying to impress the staff. Why?!? Beth, royally pissed off at his ego, with more of his haughty passive-aggressive actions, got up and walked out on dinner. When he came to their bungalow, Jim tried to deny everything, and realized he'd screwed it up. No more sex, no more Ms. Nice Girl, as she made him tow the line.

The end of June came, and while some of her friends could see right through the flimsy-excuse, Jim made his goodbyes to the landlord, that he considered a friend, and the few gaijin that had put up with him for Beth's sake. She took him to the plane, reminded him to give Barbie money for his stay. Paul had died, so she only expected him to stay a day or two before he headed up to Townsville, where their restaurant-friend waited to help him get started with the new business.

There was almost thirty-thousand Aussie-dollars in the savings account, so should be sufficient to get it off the ground. "Best laid plans, and all that BS." With absolute-freedom and more money than he'd ever had on his own, within three weeks Jim had almost drained the account. The bank sent Beth a registered-letter checking if their bank card was lost or stolen.

Beth asked her good friend Kazuyo, who was a simultaneous-translator, to go with her to her bank. All use of her money was tied to her bank card, which she had given one to Jim, though he opened a separate account for himself, to have money available locally. She tried to get the bank to cancel the card in his name, that was attached to her account. She'd be leaving shortly for a six-week European trip, and as one friend she'd been honest with said, "Do you really want to get to Rome, and find out your account has been drained, if he's already gone through almost thirty-thousand dollars?"

Neither Beth nor Kazuyo could get the bank to remove *her husband's name* off of her account. Beth finally said, "Fine, close the account and I'll open one across the street in my name only." As Kazuyo finished the translation, Beth stood up and started to walk to the teller. The Banker jumped up and removed Jim's name. It had taken almost two hours.

About a week later, just before Beth left on her vacation, that she got a call from Jim in Oz, saying *his* card had been refused. Beth reminded him it was *her* account card, and she didn't care what he did with the savings money, as he'd never get another dime from her. He was still talking when she hung up. She spoke to their friend in Townsville, as he'd called asking what happened to Jim, and she told him. Eventually, Jim made it up there, but the friend said 'no-go' if he didn't have his share of the money to invest. She never did find out how he left Oz to get back to Texas. They'd been married ten years - twice the first marriage, so an improvement.

Beth decided to have Jeremy come for three weeks over the Christmas holiday, and told him, "Get a passport and buy your own round-trip ticket to Japan, I'll pay for everything else - tour around Japan, go to Hong Kong, Thailand and Vietnam." Jeremy had been through some rough times, and she wanted him to know how much she missed and loved him. Besides, she wanted him to see the tremendous value in traveling to other countries and cultures. Another teacher, Patty, asked to join them in Hong Kong, and fly onto Thailand together. A riotous trip, that Beth said they'd have to write about it sometime, as not your typical, tourist-venture, of course.

* * * * * *

Connie joined Michael in becoming a grandmother - Travis was the first to produce progeny - something he continued to do with a variety of women - either married to them or not. Connie's younger son, Jeff married a wonderful girl named Sharon, and though they were only eighteen, she felt it was real and good, so the following year welcomed her first grandson, David, that would change her life. They were about to have the second child that April of 1992, when Beth returned to get her divorce finished, including her name changed back. She laughed about Jim asking for alimony, and her telling the attorney he'd already spent it. Also, it was her mother's birthday, so Beth had to deal with her sister Marie again, as well her pouty, niece Cindy.

Connie called all excited, and came bounding over as her new grandson, Eric, came a couple weeks early and she had photos. Beth certainly appreciated the reprieve from her sister and niece, while her mother's Alzheimers was not easy to handle. They treated Louise terribly, and Beth seriously thought they's knock-her-off soon, as neither of them had any patience with her, though they were both living there for free, spending all her money. They went outside to talk privately, and Connie noted how dirty the house was, since neither Marie or Cindy ever cleaned.

Beth would be leaving the next day to return to Japan, as a new session would be starting soon, and reminded Connie they didn't celebrate the coming Easter there. They had their reunion dinner with Michael a few days before, so not many other things to catch up on - the cleaning franchise and the two Subways were all rolling along fine, so Connie still happy with Greg and the money flowing in. Now, with a wonderful, second grandchild, how much better could it get?

The following Saturday morning in Japan the phone rang, Michael shocked Beth with the surprise call. "My God, Michael, what's up?" Something told her it was not a happy surprise.

A rather shaken Michael, began the horrific story which would change all of their lives. "Jeff, Connie's son - who just had the baby - was murdered . . ." It took several phone calls over several weeks before all of the pieces were put together by the police, when they caught one of the culprits. It was Good Friday, and Jeff had the day off from his job, and was out near this field picking up some rocks he noticed before, for his new patio. He drove the new company van, and parked off the road loading the rocks in back when two guys pulled up behind him. It had been raining a lot and all very muddy, so everything was very slick.

The two guys were high on drugs, and the one with the gun approached Jeff wanting money. He reached in his pocket and all he had was a five-dollar bill. The guy expected more money with the new van, though Jeff explained it wasn't his. Still, he demanded more money, but Jeff had nothing on him. The guy then shot him five times in the face - equal to the five-dollars. He fell into the mud, so when a policeman found him, they originally thought he slipped and fell, until they rolled him over to see he'd been shot.

Apparently, these two had been terrorizing the area beating up people, and even raped and murdered an older woman, simply wanting money for more drugs. It took years for any justice, as when Beth finally did get to talk to Connie, the devastating-toll on her life made her an empty-vessel. The most telling - poignant thing she said, regarding losing her twenty-four year-old son: "It would have been easier to have died myself, than to have been left behind to suffer the continual, daily loss of him."

Connie still tried to be there for Sharon, alone with a brand new baby and a toddler, but she could barely function herself. Running away seemed like the best answer, so as summer came around Connie wanted to go back to the Upper Peninsula of Michigan, where her mother's relatives were. The land was filled with millions of trees, clean water and kind people. More than just a simple life, it was a quiet life. Greg supported her how he could, but there would always be a part of her that was void and dark that she'd slipped into.

The next phone call Beth got in Japan was in October, six months after she'd been to Chicago for Louise's birthday. It was Mike, and Beth knew immediately it was their mother. She had *not* been wrong in feeling that Marie and Cindy were anxious to get rid of Louise. Mike explained it: The three of them sat eating dinner in front of the television, as one of Marie and Cindy's favorite shows was on.

Louise had started gasping, and they ignored her until the commercial, but she still was having some problem breathing. Just as the program was coming back on the doorbell rang and it was Aunt Leona, Ernie's ex-wife. They went back to watching the show, but Leona realized that Louise was having a heart attack and started screaming. *She* finally went to the phone to call 911, while they were still glued to the TV. The paramedics revived her in the ambulance and at the hospital several times, but she finally died.

Beth's dilemma was two fold - she could only return to the States thirty days a year, or be fined by the IRS. On the other hand if she returned, she'd probably choke-the-shit-out of Marie and Cindy. Beth mentioned to Mike the Will had never been acknowledged after Dad died, and now as he was the Executor, it needed to be settled.

Beth was shocked when he said 'everything had been turned over to Marie by Louise after she moved in.'

As Beth questioned, Mike said Cindy had it all done by the Trust Department in the bank where she worked. Beth yelled, that he knew there was no way that Louise was cognizant to sign any papers. If she hadn't been officially designated with Alzheimers, she certainly did have dementia and that would not be a legal document. Mike did not want to deal with any of it, especially not now, and was Beth coming or not? "I swear to God, the mood I'm in, I'd shoot them on site." Beth thought what *vulture-people* Marie and Cindy were?

* * * * * *

The pure nature of the land did have a healing quality to it, so Connie kept returning, even when Greg didn't want to, as he'd stay back and make sure the businesses were running. Delay after delay kept the trial from going forward, as the one guy pleaded-out on his part in the murders and assaults, but the actual-shooter kept dragging it out pretending to be mentally ill, etc. It had been two years, and Connie decided they'd move to the Upper Peninsula or UP, as they called it. Greg didn't mind the trips, but his life was in the Chicago-area. Still in such pain, she was going and he could join her or not.

She sold the cleaning franchise first, and began looking for a house on a lake in the UP. It all fell into place, but Greg questioned, though he loved her and understood this was what she needed - wanted then. Perhaps in time, they'd come back. The summer of 1994, the house was sold, and they were about to close on a wonderful house in the UP with five acres on a beautiful lake, about ten miles out of town. Matt visited often, but not quite ready for the total move up there, but when she sold the Subways, his job went out from under him.

Beth returned to the States, heading for San Antonio to see how Jeremy was doing and also visit April. Now, herself manicuring nails - not at an exclusive salon - as well as making things she could sell to her customers, like little decorated throw-pillows. Her daughter was getting married, and April pleaded to Beth - since she made big bucks - to buy her the Mother of the Bride dress.

April said her money was all going into building her 'toy collections,' which would be worth a fortune in a few years, and she felt like a big investor in some Ponzi-scheme. It wasn't until the dress was purchased, that April confessed that she wasn't even invited to the wedding. She'd put up such a stink about the pitiful-groom Deidra was planning to marry, she didn't want her there. Seriously, April was planning on crashing the reception, figuring Deidra wouldn't cause a scene. Beth truly questioned April's sanity in her conniving schemes.

She'd never really gotten back into her daughter's good graces after Alex, yet she still tried to tell her how to run her life. He was 'just as cute as he could be,' but he was a five-dollar an hour security guard, and that was all he wanted to do - like it or lump it. On top of that, he'd been involved with an older woman who convinced him to have a vasectomy, so April would not be seeing grandchildren any time - if ever, as he didn't want to get it reversed.

Teresa was off at college, but April rarely heard from her - by phone or mail, as she didn't return any messages. April would not acknowledge that having put them both through such ordeals with Alex, she was now 'paying-the-piper' in their disowning her. It was a sad state of affairs, that April still refused to contend with it all her fault. She'd never done well herself in choosing men - her current being a pen-pal with a man in prison for killing his wife - which she immediately became defensive about how innocent he was. Truly, where did she find these men? Beth was glad she was getting away to take Jeremy to Kennedy Space Center and Disney World.

* * * * * *

Back in Japan, Beth was involved with a few gaijin men, and as time rolled on she needed to make some decisions regarding knowing when to leave Japan. She loved her students, the teacher/trainers working with her program, and many of her Japanese friends. But she'd seen others stay too long, and not be able to fit back in, once they returned to the States. She'd been doing a lot of research into the American Occupation of Japan, and interviewed many survivors who had incredible stories, which she was writing. She also got back into community theater, with a great group of participants, so not without personal activities to explore. Even the local video store had English dubbed movies to enjoy the Japanese directors. The tradition she started that first year of Fourth of July and Christmas Parties - both scheduled for before all the gaijin left the country - was still the best mix of any around town, as she became rather well known.

Beth was on another Christmas holiday trip to Oz, visiting with friends at the downtown, Brisbane-Sunday Market. A group of people were parading by for some charity when it hit her. She shocked her friends, as she began crying and said, "I'm going to have to leave Japan." Beth told them that if in Japan, the group would all be dressed identical, while the Aussies didn't even all have the T-shirts on, because they're so individualistic. She realized she'd begun to lose her individuality, as she'd been adapting more and more every year.

So, that moment the decision was made, after the incredible Sakura - Japanese Cherry Blossom fun-time - she'd leave. Also the beginning of the business year, so she'd close out everything the month before. It had been quite a run of seven years, with so many trips in and out of Japan, and so many friends both Japanese and gaijin she'd made. This time - the experiences would be the pivotal, reference-benchmark for her next twenty years. Almost twenty people came to the airport to see her off, telling her how she'd made such a difference in their life. Kazuyo, her first and best Japanese friend, and teachers Susan, Chris and Patty, would continue to meet up with her over the years.

Beth chose San Francisco to be her new home, as she always wanted to live there and it was the most Asian-International city. She took a year off to write, volunteer and explore, before taking on her working life there, as no clue what she'd do. But it was a city most people loved to visit, so she knew there would be lots of new adventures. With the whole 'New Age' rampant everywhere, the first of her Metaphysical classes had to do with relationships and learning how to be better at them.

The idea was to start with one's parent/guardians being key to all following relationships, and forgiveness the basis of clearing out the old garbage. Beth felt so good after doing the 'forgiveness letters' to her deceased parents, that she decided to do the same for Marie. Unfortunately, Marie was not so enlightened, about what Beth's forgiveness-letter meant, and had her attorney send Beth a letter to *only* contact her through him. And, if she made any more accusations or 'threats' against Marie, he'd take out a restraining order against Beth. WOW!

At last in 1995 the murder trial began, and Connie made the six-hour drive back and forth to Chicago, like it was a commute to the grocery store. She also began talking to Sharon about moving to the UP after the trial, and that she'd help her however she needed. Going back to her roots, Connie did waitressing and bartending at one of the local bars, getting to know people and be accepted. She knew the rules and non-acceptance of 'Big City' people invading their country. Each step was also taking her mind off the loss of Jeff, and into living-life once again, in a new place surrounded by new people. Greg settled into fishing and working with the local AA group. It became home.

Though Beth had plenty of money in the bank and invested, she could not get even a studio apartment in San Francisco without a full-time job, so she contacted Connie to co-sign for her. It was a laugh to Connie that the 'big-time' corporate-trainer needed her help. November, and close to Beth's fiftieth birthday, thinking she might go visit Jeremy in San Antonio, then she got a late-night call from one of his close, older friends she knew.

Jeremy had an accident at work, falling off a ladder fixing some cables - *not his* IT job - to impress some girls, and shattered his ankle. He didn't want her called, but when he almost died because of a blood clot, his friend insisted. Beth was on the next plane to be with him. If the doctor hadn't decided to do another x-ray before the surgery to put a pin in his ankle, a blood clot would have killed him instantly. So, he was on crutches and taking blood-thinners until they could do the surgery.

His friend Alex drove Jeremy and Beth to go out for her birthday celebration, and they all had great fun. Jeremy impressed Beth in how he'd grown in his own New Age Spirituality, as he began to tell her about this great book, *The Celestine Prophecy*, that he not only read, but took a series of classes. She was sure there would be similar ones in San Francisco, so she'd let him know. Jeremy also got interested in fencing and acting lessons, with hopes to perform some Shakespeare as a goal.

Perhaps he was becoming more like her, with community theater before and during her time in Japan, but never Shakespeare - she was impressed. Nothing could have made her happier, as they were getting closer with more things in common. Partially out of guilt, Beth let April know she'd be in town, but telling her the main purpose being Jeremy, but the next night they'd have dinner together. April added, Beth'd have to pay, as she was short money.

Without even exiting the parking lot of Jeremy's apartment complex, April started in on the fact that Beth chose to have her 'birthday dinner' with Jeremy, instead of her - Beth's oldest friend. Beth lost it, wondering why she bothered to call her - didn't she ever learn? "April, he almost died, does that not penetrate your insecure, jealous brain? What do you want, a fan-club of me? And, don't give me your usual crap of you 'being a better friend to me,' bullshit. You even had the nerve to ask if I would pay for dinner, and then you bitch about not my birth-*day*! No wonder your daughters don't want anything to do with you! Pull over." They hadn't gotten two blocks from the apartment when Beth opened the door to get out.

April yelled, "OK, OK. What are you doing? There's traffic."

"What I should have done so long ago, *Good Bye,* and I mean that in the sense of don't *ever* contact me again. I want nothing to do with you. Nothing is ever enough for you. You're truly nuts, a real sicko!" Beth stepped up on the sidewalk, and went down to the light to cross-over to the apartment complex. April finally drove away. Beth rang the bell to Jeremy's apartment-gate to have him let her in, as she proceeded to tell him all about April and her craziness. She had a lovely couple of days with Jeremy before she left. April tried many times through Michael and even Connie, to get Beth to accept her apologies to talk to her. But this time, Beth was adamant about April truly being crazy, and totally done with her.

The end of the trial, even with the guilty verdict, brought no closure, just an ending that would have had, so many more wonderful, happy chapters, had not his life been cut so short. Connie had become familiar with many people in the UP small town and they, with her, as well her story of tragic loss. When a long-time bar-owner decided to retire, Connie thought she was ready to step-up and create a new bar out of the old setting.

A disco it would not be, but she learned a lot from building and operating *The Glass Onion,* back in Elmwood. Greg could not have objected more about going into the bar business. He wanted nothing to do with it, which Connie simply said, "Fine, don't." Most importantly, nothing takes your mind and emotions off pain, than the hard work recreating and building the largest bar in the county. More than ready to go back to work, by 1996, her UP Bar and Grill would be opened to establish her new life. Sharon, and the two grandchildren, shortly joined her in the move up to snow-country.

As animals had always been a important part of Connie's life, it wasn't any different in the UP. When she tracked down the county, animal shelter to get a new dog, she was shocked and disheartened at the conditions, as well lack of care. The animal-control men were known to prefer to shoot the dogs, than keep them around. The shelter was located in an old, dilapidated school house with few volunteers, and rarely a visit from a veterinarian. When Connie had time, she came to put her organizing skills to work, and began searching out where they could get a new building. She soon adopted more dogs, and left Greg to contend with them, as he stayed home while she worked the bar.

Connie would usually leave him a meal or two in the refrigerator, or supplies to make himself a sandwich. When Greg started bitching about the arrangement, she replied, "Fine, get your own then, you've got nothing better to do around here." He let his age disgruntle him, and though she loved him, she was not going to wait on him. Soon, Greg was driving into town to pick up KFC and donuts, thinking the bad diet would guilt-out Connie - it didn't. It was like him driving his car out to the mailbox - they had a very long driveway - instead of getting out for the exercise to walk. It was his choice for his life, she felt, though she could have given him more of her time. She installed an electronic fence around the large property, so he didn't have to complain about walking the dogs - they could run safely anywhere they wanted.

Sharon's happy-blooming as she grew, was a totally different story. She went from working in a doctor's office, once the boys were in school full time, to starting to take courses for nurses' training. Over the years, she continually advanced in her career, as she raised her boys alone in a very, positive-atmosphere, never taking the 'poor-me' attitude. After many successful years as a surgical-nurse, and her older son headed to college, she competently finished her Masters in Nursing Administration to become the manager of several of local clinics connected to the hospital. Connie could not have been prouder of her incredible daughter-in-law, and how she overcame such a horrible life-situation of being left alone, at such a young age to raise her two boys.

With snow 'up the wazoo,' usually starting in October and going through April, the next logical thing - snowmobiling. Actually Mike and Michael got Connie hooked on it, but truly living in 'snow-country,' and one cannot ride if one does not have trails. After learning how disorganized it all was, that was the next group for her to organize and pull together some volunteers to improve the whole trail-use for fun. What she began to see was how her bar could become a community meeting place, and function in some fund-raising support with snowmobile-runs. Little steps, getting Matt involved in the bar and other things in her life she enjoyed pulled together, as she rebuilt her life with new friends that supported her well.

Though Michael totally understood Connie's need to completely restructure her life, and while she returned frequently to Chicago, the moving-away left a rather gaping-hole in Michael's life. Yes, she had her daughters and Travis, sometimes, he had his father's wander-lust for Florida and irresponsibility to family. So, in not having a regular man in her life to cater to or plan around, Michael sought out Marie and Cindy, since not many people wanted to associate with them after Louise died rather suspiciously. Truly, the two only had each other in their craziness. The oldest daughter, Sheri eventually did become a nurse. Though she lived about forty-miles straight west, she and her husband wanted nothing to do with Marie and Cindy. Tammy, the youngest, lived in Kentucky and the only one with children. She did not want to see them either, so Marie never saw her grandchildren.

Michael in her best 'rescuing of the down-trodden,' had Marie and Cindy join her and daughter Jenny's family for most holidays, as Michael didn't have much room in her small apartment. Marie and Cindy would go anywhere for a free meal, and even better when they were catered to, as if needy and helpless. It was an arrangement that Beth and Connie didn't learn of for years, and yet Beth was not surprised when informed. She reminded Connie of that incident when Michael was still living with Beth, and had stopped to help a young woman that she saw a man beating up in a strip-mall parking lot. Typical of those situations, once Michael had pulled him off the woman and hit him herself, the woman started in on her to stop. Michael could be a real *Crusader-Rabbit,* yet not ever maintaining herself well.

* * * * * *

A teacher who had worked for Beth in Japan, kept in touch since she'd left. About fifteen years younger than her and fluent in Japanese, Jeffrey had a real attachment to her. They'd spoke on the phone several times, and since Beth wasn't tied down with any big job, he wanted her to consider moving to Hawaii. He said he had financial backing to set up a school for teaching English to Japanese, and vice-versa. Beth felt that going back to teaching was one thing that she really didn't want to do anymore. But he was persistent, and talked to her about his new, very innovative methodology, and with her management expertise they could do very well, creating books, as well as teaching. He insisted on coming to see her in San Francisco, as he was in Washington, outside of Seattle. Fine, she thought no-big-deal and a distraction would be nice.

Within a few weeks, they were on their way to a seminar in San Diego to meet one of his investors, and then onto Hawaii to start setting things up. There was no doubt Jeffrey was brilliant, and his new system even more so, as well his affection for her definitely. While they were still trying to get their English books published, Beth returned to Japan to speak at the International Language Training Conference, and met up again with so many of the teachers she'd known over the years in Japan. She convinced several of them to try-out their new training system.

What was not realized by her, nor acknowledged by him, was he was becoming Bi-Polar. This major miscommunication became a disaster of enormous proportions, as she'd taken much of her money earned in Japan, and put it into the company that was desperately going so fast-down the tube, not even a swirl was seen by her. He had lied to her regarding investors.

To say there were other lies and deceit, those were only on the tip-of-the-iceberg. Of most concern, Jeffrey's addiction to older women - especially while Beth refused for them to be involved - and he preferred the Japanese women, as they were so easy to manipulate, as he spoke their language. The crux came, as Beth was to sign a two and half-million-dollar-deal for book distribution in Japan, when the *wife* of the Japanese man behind the deal *admitted to him*, she'd had sex with Jeffrey, and begged his forgiveness. This way - per Japanese culture - she was guaranteed no recriminations, as if he'd found out, she'd have lost everything.

In Japan, the head of the company - Beth - was responsible *for any and all* actions of directly-associated subordinates. So, even though she knew nothing of the affair, *she should have,* and the deal was off. Beth ended-up filing for bankruptcy to the tune of two-hundred-fifty-thousand dollars. Amazingly, she landing on her feet, solely because one of the clients she developed a good relationship with, hired her to work for him to do marketing, promotion and customer service training. And, to him she did not say *'no'* to. He was the most exciting man since Frank, the biker - though very married with several complications, but worth it. With him, she traveled to all the four islands, doing training for the largest retailer in Hawaii, as well his company. They had a fun year, seeing and doing so much marketing at numerous trade fairs.

Yet, before the 'shit-hit-the-preverbal-fan' regarding Jeffrey, Beth had lots of visitors come to Hawaii. Connie the first, with a trip over to Kauai, as Jeff took Sharon there for their honeymoon. With sixty percent of the island inaccessible by car, Beth suggested they take the helicopter tour over the Waimea Canyon. The tropical rainforest covering the incredible, dramatic cliffs and pinnacles of its Na Pali Coast. They were both excited, until Connie said, "Beth, you have to sit next to the window, I'm afraid of the heights." Beth thought she was kidding, until she saw the fear in her eyes, as Connie passed her camera over, for Beth to take the photos, but they still had a great time. Connie also was quite thrilled to run into someone from the UP, as the odds of someone from such an obscure area of the States would be rare on the little island. Back on Oahu, Beth learning her way around, happily shared her exploring it all with Connie.

The next important visitor was Jeremy, and it wasn't just for her, as his high school buddy, Alex who joined the Navy, and now stationed at Pearl Harbor. Caren, beautician to the group, had asked to visit, and brought Beth her Teddy-Bear Cookie Jar, her father had given her as a child. It was the one thing that Marie was willing to let go of, as she still had not settled the Will after Louise died.

Since turning twenty-one, Jeremy had inherited 'male-pattern-baldness' through his grandmother Louise, as Beth had warned him when he used to tease Jim about his. Caren suggested to him to let her shave his head, as it was so perfectly shaped, and he thought it'd be cool with all the acting he was wanting to do. It looked incredible, and Caren also said Yul Brenner sexy-cool, as she taught him how to shave it. He never let it grow out again, as he embraced his new, slick-look.

But most importantly, Beth took the time to really talk to Jeremy, and even-out some misconceptions about a lot of things regarding his father, who died just as Beth arrived in Hawaii. They did get closer talking through it, as Jeremy couldn't understand why a woman like her had married him. "I wasn't *this independent-woman then*, and your father wasn't *that man* who died, when I married him."

A long lesson on a short marriage, of how people grow and change. Jeremy, still the most important person in her life, was now a man she was so proud of. His importance to her, he still needed to learn and believe. He returned for a second visit, with more closeness-developed, as to why her raising him to be so independent. She then took him to the Big Island for the helicopter ride over the volcano, and its unbridled power impressed them.

The next important visitor was Jason, her nephew, he had mainly come to play stadium-football. Being six-foot-five with a sixty-inch chest, he'd finally gotten to play the game in 1982 through DuPage Eagles - Team USA - arena style. He had never been able to play regular football in high school, as he and Jackie were made to go to the farm almost every weekend to work, to help Mike get it all up and running. He loved his football, and they were really good, as they became National League Champs in 1992. Unfortunately, the Samoan players *'ringered'* on the Hawaiian team out-weighed even their biggest people, so they were pretty-much hammered.

Jason contacted Beth in early June of 1995, before their National team went to Graz, Austria for the 'World' Championship against the Olympic team - they were trying to get recognition to play in the Olympics. She gave him some suggestions as to what to see and do in his free time, "Don't miss seeing the Clock Tower, and that's *real* Pilsner beer that tastes so much better than in the U.S." His National Team truly trounced them, but no Olympic-bid ever came out of it. His second love, photography was well-served by all the endless mountains, rain forests and water-vistas of Hawaii. Beth cherished the wonderful eight-by-ten photos he gave her, staying part of her permanent-collection wherever she moved.

Having Mike join him for the second football-go-round, gave Beth a chance to spend time getting to know her brother again. She wasn't surprised to learned that it didn't take but a few years married to Cathy for him to return to his 'cheating-ways,' especially since she didn't like coming out to the farm - what better excuse and cover? Yet, it was Mike's being alone out at the farm one late, hot July-day in 1992, which almost cost him his life. It concerned Beth and everyone else who loved him. Working his 'in-loader,' pushing-down small trees for clearing more land on the other side of his bridge, a tree snapped-back to flip the in-loader onto Mike, crushing his leg into multiple-fractures. A weaker man would have laid there and died, but he crawled the hundreds of yards to the gravel road - passing-out several times along the way - then waited at the side of it, until someone came by to see and rescued him.

These years later, he still walked with a slight limp, but eternally grateful to be alive. He was one, who when life was tough or sometimes downright mean, he found strength and wisdom to overcome his struggles. Beth also wasn't surprised, how often Mike and Jason dropped into the bar Michael managed - sometimes picking up pizza from next store to make a party of it. Michael and Mike would always be in each other's blood with much love. Mike looked forward to retiring, and Beth felt it included being done with Cathy - upon having served his twenty-year-term of indebtedness to her.

Then, as her last job on the island, Beth also served as the Director of the largest non-profit for the islands, specifically hired to organized it, as well get rid of the excessive corruption. She learned how to direct, her now-acknowledged mild OCD - Obsessive-Compulsive-Disorder. Her new friend Diane, had it much more severe with cleaning lists, as well other lists for everything. Beth saw how she'd always found her challenges, and usually success from failure, along with again making life-long friendships.

She began to realize her innate-resilience, a revelation of who and what she was, and more could be. So, after three and a half years, the pace of work was too slow for her. Though she'd come to understand the Hawaiian Pidgin-English, and their need to take-off to surf at whatever opportunity that came to them - 'hang loose,' the Island-motto worked for them. It just wasn't for her Type 'A' personality - workaholic style, she needed more than sunshine everyday with eighty degrees.

This wasn't giving up, but facing life with courage and acceptance, while allowing her wisdom and intuition to guide her forward. At last an understanding of the concept of 'letting go,' as there's a need to accept the futility in pushing against dead ends or brick walls. As so succinctly learned in Japan - 'the peg standing-up, must be pushed-down,' to fit in with all the others. Beth was still, too independent in thought and action. Her dogged-determination had seen her make progress in life. Yet also tripped her up, left feeling frustrated and downhearted at times, when life hadn't panned-out as she hoped.

Little Barometers

We all had those lists,
mental probably more than written,
of things that made us happy.

Different lists for different times and places.
These were our little barometers of excellence,
recording our inner-climate of wants and needs.

Few of us ever grow up to be what we intended.
Few of us also fulfill our own expectations,
Much less even fulfilling our 'potentials' as set.

At some point we stopped making demands on our selves,
and settled for what we felt life had set for us.
Enjoying became more important than stressing over it.

It had become too constant a pain to try endlessly,
to be what we thought, we should become.
Besides, others were no longer expecting more of us.

You can't miss what you don't know, can you?
Maybe that's why occasionally we all have
that funny little streak of sadness, from time to time.

We are missing something,
and we don't even want to know what it is,
or whether it will ever be revealed.

And they say life is too short,
but maybe not for some,
as they expected so little, and fulfilled even less.

CHAPTER 41

Acknowledging the Millennium

Before she left Hawaii, the beginning of January, 2000, Beth got a call from Jason - hoping that he might return again, she happily greeted him, "Hi Sweetheart, what's the good news?"

He paused, not prepared for her happiness to be doused so completely, "Well, Aunt Beth, it's not. . . Uncle Chuck has been killed. The school van, it was empty, he was driving this morning, got pinned on the commuter-tracks and . . . " As he went on with the full story, Beth's questions answered, then she knew it was no 'accident.' Crying, when she told him, 'no' she'd not be coming back for the funeral, no real point. She said she needed a break, and went outside to enjoy the little park with the incredible flowers - 'yes,' a real bonus of Hawaii.

Beth thought back all Chuck had been through, with Louise holding him back every step of the way. Once he graduated high school - though two years older, it was the summer *following* her graduation - there was little waiting for him. Before Beth left for college, she'd influenced him to join the Navy, as Louise had turned him into an absolute-sloth with zero ambition, nor interest in anything. Beth knew the Navy could straighten him out, though overweight, at six-foot four-inches, he could become quite a specimen for them.

Viet Nam was soon in full-force and his job there was loading - unloading ammunition wherever needed. Though a huge target himself, the snipers seemed to be proving their skills in constantly shooting the smaller guys-off the other end, carrying the containers with him. Chuck came back with a lot of PTSD - post-traumatic-stress-disorder and survivor's guilt.

But little was acknowledged for years - a really, useless-wife, three, unruly-kids and a job at the post office, did not improve his outlook on life. Louise's firm-gripped-attachment to him was a crippling-addiction he'd never let go of, especially since he had no appreciation or love from his family. Retired for health reasons, he drove the day-care bus to keep busy, yet once Mother had passed, he had little sympathy or support for his existence. Chuck had ultimately given-up, so when the express-train-opportunity presented itself for him to exit it all, he did.

Beth talked to him maybe a half-dozen times over the recent years, as the only one who listened, and knew to get him into group therapy, if nothing else. Obviously, it couldn't make up for the rest of his life. She'd learned herself years before, that life may not be as we want it, with pain, struggle, unhappiness and challenges, but these *are* always the contrasts that make up life. Happiness is not a default setting, nor is it a result of being 'fixed,' it's a power to be cultivated, nurtured from inside and believed to be possible, if we're ever going to experience it. Chuck never learned how to create it on his own, he'd never developed that gumption.

At the end of August, through Patricia, a good connection made prior in San Francisco, who also visited Beth in Hawaii, got a great job referral. It looked like a perfect-match for all of her people-skills, with a huge business-event planning company in San Francisco. Once again a teary-goodbye, covered with flowered-leis from Diane and several others who joined Beth for an 'aloha' dinner before she took the 'red-eye' back to San Francisco. She had several interviews with the top-people on a Wednesday, and was 'hired,' only waiting for the background check and other details for a Monday start. About four o'clock on Friday, the woman who was to be her immediate-supervisor called - regarding the on-going 'Dot-Com Bubble Recession,' of which eighty percent of their clients were. They'd just been bought out by another company. Not only was her job gone, but also Beth's.

A real slap-in-the-face, Beth floundered for several years finding her footing, but learning many different career-areas to use her vast people and training skills. San Francisco was *again* the perfect place to continue to work on herself, knowing after her approach to relationships - rescuing Jeffrey - still needed changing. She *again* took many classes, seminars, studied and read a lot of books on New Age-metaphysics and Spirituality. Beth wanted a better, happier life and then found that the human resources area ensconced most of what she knew so well, and could be a good benefit to people and companies.

One job on top of another, she built herself up in knowledge, certifications and experience, as well from a small apartment in the 'Little Saigon' area. It was in the shadow of the big Federal Building - not a good place to be after "9/11" - to an amazing, apartment on a high hill in Pacific Heights, with great views. Ironically, the Dot-Com Bubble had made all the apartment rents collapse, and SF - as she called it - was a rent-controlled city, so while the rent was still high, it wouldn't be going up very fast.

Once settled, and doing well financially, Beth excitedly invited Connie and Michael to come for a visit. Connie had been out there once to visit Matt in Oakland, while he was in the Navy, but she'd not spent much time in SF. Michael had at last found her almost-dream job, working in a group-home for the county, managing mentally-challenged adult residents. Bar-management had proven to be too-stressful for her pain-ridden physical body. She had gone way-beyond pain-meds, and was now into an advanced-form of bio-feedback, that she did with her visualization-techniques three-times a day. She wouldn't be able to do any real strenuous work or quick movements, but she was fully functional within those restrictions. It was her passion for compassion that made her so good at helping others, or her *justified-rescuing* - her job to do it.

Beth took to the SF hills like she was a native, loving the exercise, as well observing all the old Victorians, and other classical-styles the city was so rich with. Living on a high hill with public transportation was wonderful, except that Connie and Michael had to walk up or down the hills to get to it. Renting a car was only good for going out of town, because parking was difficult and very expensive. Beth told them to buy Muni-passes for the Cable Car, Streetcars and the buses that would take them around the city. The California Street Cable Car started right at the bottom of her street, though Connie and Michael preferred the two-block walk-around rather than going straight down the hill. They were off to Sunday Brunch at the 'Top of The Mark,' and stopping at the glorious Fairmont later coming back.

Rather oblivious to their problem of physical movement, Beth thought it'd be fun to walk the couple of blocks down the hill to China Town. The two of them almost killed her, yelling didn't she understand - as to Connie's knee and ankle issues and Michael could barely-walk *flat!* On another bus ride, Beth told them that it was like 'free' entertainment watching the 'characters' that rode the bus, they laughed, as neither ever took public transportation. Not believing it could truly be all that bizarre, proof came when two men in 'skin-tight,' full-body-snake-costumes stepped aboard.

Michael, sitting next to Connie across from Beth, began to bury her face in Connie's hair, as the two men stood 'frontal-pose' of them. Connie's eyes were about to pop-out of her head, and Michael could not control her muffled laughter. Beth shook her head, and pulled in her lips, containing her snickers. The men's matching costumes - green-yellow, and blue-yellow, had matching makeup with adorned swim-cap head-gear. It wasn't even close to Halloween, which Beth told them was better than Mardi Gras, so no explanation.

They rented a car to go over the Golden Gate Bridge to Richmond, for the new 'Rosie the Riveter' Memorial Museum, and then onto Napa and Sonoma for wine-tasting. Trips to the Golden Gate park and the ocean were also covered, with Connie chasing down restaurants for all of their eating out, though Beth felt she knew some, she'd been to since living there. Of course, Fisherman's Wharf and Ghirardelli Square, as they were non-stop everyday, even going out to Alcatraz Island.

There was nothing like the three of them being together, laughing themselves silly, and Beth glad she had the room for them, as the weather was perfect. Connie returned twice more, once for Halloween, and traveling down the coast to Monterrey, but mainly eating at good restaurants planned in advance with on-line, super-discount coupons for the gourmet places.

Michael gave a Beth an update on April, as sadly, but truly losing her mental-capacity in her actions and deeds. Deidra got her husband to get his vasectomy reversed, and they had a daughter, which she would not let April see, when she found out through a friend. One night after Deidra left work, April went to the exclusive shop, saying she'd been there the day before, and left her sunglasses, then she'd been called to come pick them up. She went to Deidra's station, and stole the photo of her granddaughter. Deidra was furious, threatening police action. As April's 'collection' turned into full-fledged-hoarding, also *collecting* credit cards. "They sent them to me, why not use them?" She bought multiples of things from the television 'sale' channels. She did elder-care, with no training or certification, and was fired several times for stealing.

Once Mike divorced Cathy, he'd began work on his dream home at the farm, and several women meandered through his life, but not-sticking for more than a year or so. He began to drive alone to south Texas in February, to get away from the winters in northern Illinois. Jason kept up tabs of his parents, support of Mike at the farm, and Barb living next door to him, while Jackie and his family lived outside Detroit.

Mike visited several different places, but once he found South Padre Island, northeast of Brownsville - he'd found his 'happy place' to be. In 2004, Jason talked Michael into joining him and Mike, as her brother Web and wife Cindy were coming to Padre Island also. They continued to be good friends, through all the relationships changing over the years. Everyone mellowed with age, though the deep connections were not forgotten.

Connie, on the other hand, started making trips to Florida to visit various friends, to escape from the 'melting-mud,' as she called the long, April month in the UP. She couldn't snowmobile, and the numerous feet of snow-melting everywhere aggravated her. The bar was going gang-busters, raking-in-the-dough, so Matt managed the bar and Greg the dogs. His age gaining on him, Greg no longer had much interest in the hassle of travel, and his outlook on life often pessimistic. Beth called frequently, catching Greg home rather than Connie, and his usual response to how things were going: "Same shit, different day. I'll give her the message."

Obviously, Greg had lost many of his friends in the Chicago area, and the 'local-yokels,' as he called them in the UP, didn't hold his interest for discussions. Beth had remarked to Connie about it, when she caught up with her, but she only commented that he was old, and not really interested in doing anything but watch TV. "It was the problem of marrying someone so much older, if they weren't interested in keeping busy." Sounded as if she'd become resigned to the situation, as she had all the intentions of doing what she wanted, with or without him. It was sad, but time does take it's toll.

Beth made regular trips back to San Antonio to see Jeremy, and at last - like his mother - he graduated the university in May, 2003 with honors. His opportunities for advancement were now totally unlimited, for his brilliant-mind and unlimited-talent in the IT field. He said IBM, that had installed a new system at the company he worked for, had already offered him a job. But Beth told him he'd only be a number to them, and he needed to find a challenging, boutique-growing company for those rare, communicative-skills he had that most ITs lacked.

Jeremy next offer included travel, dealing with Fortune 500 manufacturing companies, installing programs went from two-hundred to six-hundred million dollars. Beth suggested he might want to think about moving to Dallas, as it had many more flights than San Antonio - he'd outgrown the city. With his left-brain-right-brain skills, Jeremy was still pursuing his acting, and now added improvisation with a couple of friends. Beth could not be more proud of him, as truly following more like her, than his father. Unfortunately, that also meant he'd become a rescuer of 'broken-winged' damsels.

While in San Antonio, Beth reconnected with a old mutual friend of Jim and her, who caught her up on his doings. Jim had finally gotten an overseas job fitting his engineering and mental background - rebuilding Serbia-Kosovo and the former Yugoslavia. Beth learned how truly prejudice Jim was, while living in Japan, as he'd watched his comments prior. He also got involved with a rather young, East Texas girl, and had a son.

While Beth was happy he fulfilled his dream, the later years with Jeremy had become difficult for Jim, as he realized Jeremy was much smarter than he was. Jeremy's easy ability to 'consume all' regarding new computer technology was mind-boggling, it pricked Jim's insecurities. But the kicker came, when she concluded by saying, that 'Mr. Clean-freak' had picked-up one of those 'blood-viruses' in some cut he got, which killed him in less than a week. Always getting a tetanus, when not needed to make sure of any wound, Beth thought how sad and ironic.

Beth found out after Jim left Japan, from his only good friend, he really did want to choke her, as he so resented how she always spoke with such confidence. Jeremy had also, surprisingly, run into Jim when over at a friend's house, when he showed up to pick of the friend's mother for a date. Beth was glad she never found out what he was capable of, and felt sorry for the naive, East Texas girl now raising a son alone, as never married, so no legal-access to any money he may have made those years he worked. Mainly, it closed an interesting chapter of Beth's life, and once again her domino-theory of how *'one-unexpected-thing'* can lead to a major change in one's life. Jim convinced *her* to work overseas, and she never doubted that Japan's hallmark-affect on her life and all those experiences there, would continue to influence her.

With her staunch belief in 'right and wrong,' Beth began to have a problem at the huge corporate entity, where as Regional Human Resources Manager, she had over a thousand employees covering from San Jose to Sacramento. She did extensive training for the Supervisors, and weekly classes for the new employees, but it was the managers who just didn't seem to believe that sexual harassment and discrimination laws regarded them. When the company bought-out another competitor, whose owner's son's sexist reputation proceeded him, work conditions became intolerable. Connie couldn't believe that Beth let principles end a great job, but all her life Connie skimmed-the-system in various ways, and saw nothing wrong with that.

Michael, Connie and Beth were kind-of rolling along, keeping up with each others' lives when Mike surprised them all, with his maybe-minute quasi-fame came along. Immensely enjoying his retirement, buying old equipment and rebuilding it for the sake of the machinery, he hit bingo. Mike rebuilt an old, war-worn Cat D-9 bulldozer back into full working order, and advertised it in the collector-trade magazine. Clint Eastwood was filming the two World War II movies - *'Flags of Our Fathers'* and *'Letters from Iwo Jima,'* with his need for authenticity, his people tracked-down Mike and purchased the old D-9 work-horse, to become a supporting player in both movies. Of course, Mike became a local hero - not for the first time - went to see both films, then bought copies of the DVDs when they came out.

Beth took several independent contracts, did some volunteer work and as usual, when she had time, did her poetry and writing her blog about letting go of one's past. Her two best and biggest experiences were the classes she took in Memoir Writing at SF State - Downtown Campus, and the Intuitive Classes that partnered-her-up with Cheryl, an artist from Long Beach that recently moved to SF. They took the BART to their East Bay pick-up ride over to the classes. It was a new friendship of epic portion for Beth's cultural expansion. One of the things that she loved so much was all of the museums that SF had to offer, now she had someone to enjoy them with, as well as numerous gallery shows and openings. They also explored 'dowsing' and again traveled together over to the East Bay, meeting a most fascinating group of women and men, through an amazing older woman named Shirley.

While Beth rarely had any straight-male interests, but had many gay, men-friends that she thoroughly enjoyed. Her life took an interesting turn with a constant selection of new people, as her spiritual blog started her sharing many of the things she'd learned in all of her classes and studies. As she got into 'Life Coaching,' Beth began doing presentations, workshops and taking private clients.

Then corporate called her again, as she got involved with an executive-limousine-travel dealing with the biggie-clients in Silicon Valley. There were many benefits of concerts, limo-parties and big-name clients, speaking engagements and various events for every holiday. There was a busyness, yet also a shallowness that it seemed only her writing could curb. She was getting restless, and yet not sure what she did want, or why she wasn't quite happy.

Connie had just left for another one of her Spring trips to visit Mary in Florida in 2007. Barely settled in, when she got the call that Greg had a major-stroke and was in the hospital. It took her another whole day to return, as the flights in and out of the UP were slim at best. It seemed faster to fly into Green Bay, and have Matt come down to get her. Greg struggled on, and in a week or so, improved enough to go into rehab in a facility one town-over.

He didn't have a lot of enthusiasm to recover, then he realized it was the same facility that Connie had her mother in, though she was at the 'Assisted Living' section. Greg got so upset he had another stroke. He could not make sense of the *worth* of living his life, if that was all it was going to be. He didn't want to live-unconsciously, being a part of the dreaded-treadmill of life, never having to think beyond four walls, or letting go of the physical conditions placed upon his existence. He hovered over the edge-of-life, waiting for a better moment to live, and it just didn't come. He died, when he didn't need to, but chose to. Connie was both devastated and relieved.

No need for people to put-up-with all of the bad weather, Connie wanted to make it a full memorial over Fourth of July holiday, as she was doing a cremation. Beth felt she needed some time off herself, so decided to spend some with Jason, Barb and Mike before driving up to the memorial with Michael and her daughters.

There was something nice about being chauffeured up, not having to worry with traffic and talking non-stop. It'd been a long time since Michael and Beth enjoyed endless talk about movies, books and TV shows. Connie packed the dozen or so people in on all levels of the house, with almost a pajama-party atmosphere. At the community park on the lake, Connie asked Greg be given a full military tribute he'd earned for his years of service, with Veteran Guards honoring him and giving the symbolic flag to her.

She asked Beth to give the eulogy, and she wrote with remembrance of those early days together of flowers, cards, trips to the circus and more. Connie sobbed, realizing how much she loved Greg, though the later years were sometimes difficult. they'd had over twenty years together. His ashes were poured into the lake he'd come to love, and they went out on her pontoon boat later for the sunset.

Unfortunately, Michael's girls didn't use the GPS on the drive back to Chicago, and got horribly lost, returning quite late to Chicago. Beth had to fly out first thing in the morning back to SF, so missed the special, fresh-salmon dinner Barb fixed for them. A disappointing end to a wonderful visit, and good-bye to Greg, with another wake-up call that they were all definitely getting older.

Returning to work, Beth had one confrontation after another from several of the managers, the only female among the twelve management-men. None of them had any respect for what she did, and again their exception for having to follow the laws. The absurdity sometimes blew her mind, as one manager who was Mormon, constantly argued with a supervisor who was into Scientology - all she could think was WTF?!?!? The CEO called her into his office regarding the complaints of three managers, that she had to stop harassing them regarding their behavior.

"My job for you, as HR Manager, is to keep you from getting sued. They are violating the laws, and if they don't stop, you will be sued. So, that's your choice if you want them to change or me to leave." Much younger than her, he truly didn't take her seriously, as he also did not take the laws that she taught the employees so well about, needing to be enforced.

He laughed, "Well, there's three of them and one of you - the majority rules, right?"

"Fine," Beth said as she stood up, "I'll be out of here by five o'clock, and leave an info-sheet as to what is in process." She was suddenly feeling a tremendous release in her words.

He laughed again, "Don't be ridiculous, we can all get along."

"Either you want me to do my job, or you don't - which is it?" She was giving him and her an out, but making him choose.

He couldn't believe she was putting him in such a position, and got defensive, "I need my managers." She was out of his office without another word. By noon he heard she'd been giving info to several people, talking to accounting about time and money coming to her, as well clearing off her desk. He walked in her office and asked, "Are you really doing this?"

Beth turned to look at him, "Your choice - you want to allow them to be in violation of the laws of harassment and discrimination." She turned back to writing-down notes regarding several employees.

A few minutes after five, she was heading out of the building, when he came running after to stop her and say, "You were the best employee I've ever had, I'm really sorry you're leaving." He then gave her a big hug. Beth was totally flabbergasted, as she pulled herself together, carrying her personal items and went on to meet a few friends for a celebratory-drink. It had all been so quick, yet the best way to close the door.

For the next year, she stayed busy with contracts and even did some work for the county in Work Force Development Training. Then, from self-publishing her *Move Past Your Past* book, her Life Coaching, workshops and presentations increased. So, no real money concern until the ugly, housing-mortgage-scam began growing, in late 2008, then spread beyond California and across the country, in 2009 and 10 devastated all.

Connie talked to Beth about qualifying for Jim's Social Security, as they'd been married for more than ten years, so Beth checked. Since she missed ten years of 'prime-income years' regarding Japan, for adding to her own Social Security, she would get more money using Jim's. It was a simple process of proving their marriage and his death, and her financial needs would be growing quickly, as the recession fully took over the country.

No one knew better than Beth, that proving 'ageism' was almost impossible, when so many qualified people were out of work. Sitting across the desk from the HR Assistant for her first-level interview, the woman was younger than Jeremy, and had no clue regarding Beth's heavy resume.

She kept flipping back and forth the two pages, plus her addendum sheet of her certified training programs she did. Without question, Beth was over-qualified for the position she applied for, and without coming off as pleading, she tried to assure the woman, she did not want her job, just a job. She'd gone over a year with only part-time from the temp-agency. "You know, of course, we've got applicants at half your age, and for half your prior money."

Beth was totally shocked at the illegal-statement the ignorant, young woman just said. "So, I'll be a real bargain for you, getting all of my experience without having to pay for it." Trying to stay positive, but her smile was very forced, as was her positive, confident attitude. It's so easy to define one's self by everything she was not - like definitely not young. Or, see the faults and imperfections far more easily than the brilliance and experience. There was no need to focus on what she was not, or the sum of what she hadn't achieved - less than great computer competence, nor the sum of her failures in 'needing to do the right thing.'

Her nephew Jason called, greatly concerned, offering Beth to return to Chicago, as he had room for her in his duplex, and was sure he could find her employment. He'd been connected for sometime in management regarding warehousing and logistics, with lots of large manufacturing facilities. Beth steadily marched through her stocks and 401k. Her rent alone, exceeded the Social Security she received, and her credit card was used to buy food. She'd always been frugal, when she had good money coming in. Her artist friend, Cheryl also lost her website job, then her sister died, leaving Cheryl the family home near the desert, as her two sisters had no interest in it. Her leaving SF would leave a huge gap in Beth's life. The reality of vacating her beloved SF no longer could be avoided, but she did not want to go back to Chicago, though she loved Jason.

My Friend

I come to you seeking truth,
and with it I receive knowledge.
You tell me if there is no honesty between people,
there is no worthwhile relationship.

I come to you seeking approval,
and with it you give me love.
Not as a counselor, but as a friend,
sharing more than words; an acceptance of who I am.

I come to you seeking criticism,
and without it you give me wisdom.
You show me no boundaries
and tell me there-in lies no limits.

I come to you seeking hope,
and you tell me there is only belief in myself.
You say not to depend on anyone or expect anything,
and I will then not be disappointed.

I come to you when I question
the words and deeds of others.
You show me the gift of forgiveness and
the uselessness of being vindictive.

I come to you to find the answers,
and with you I find myself.
I know I can never be as honest as you, but then,
to be myself is more than enough you say.

CHAPTER 42

Last Reunions and Goodbyes

Sunday afternoon, Beth was cleaning closets to clear out her mind, questioning where she could be happy moving to, but importantly afford living, when her phone rang. Accumulated frustration of it all peaked, as she answered Connie, calling from the UP. Before she could say much, Beth dumped it all out on her - no job in sight once she finished her current Census work, and not much of a retirement income left to live on.

Quietly listening, Connie then calmly stated, "It's two hours later here, the middle of July, with seventy-five degrees, breezy and no humidity. And, it certainly is affordable to your restricted income." More than a whirlwind as they talked, and went over the pros with few cons to consider, the moving-seed planted, to be mulled over the next few days. It amazed Beth how comfortable it felt in her gut. By the time Connie visited the newly refurbished apartments - fifteen miles from her home - and sent Beth the photos of the renovated historic building, Beth was hooked.

The application was on its way to her, as she gave notice to her shocked building manager. The clock now ticking, as to packing up, shipping it all out to Connie's house and moving-on once again. Interesting, as Beth began to notice things that aggravated her about the city, that had not jumped out before, like the increase of rude traffic at crosswalks and noise.

Reinventing herself once again at her age, most friends were surprised, but Jeremy now in Dallas was shocked, and worried of the dramatic change. He regularly referred to her as his 'hippie-super liberal' mother, who considered him to be conservative. Beth was also a source of entertainment for Jeremy's stories to his friends, as she was always up-to something - 'never boring is her motto' he often said. "I know Jeremy, this is rather sudden, but trust me, this feels right to my intuition, and I know it is something that I'm supposed to do. It's not just about the money, and you know, I will not have my son supporting me, or *me* living with you."

"But, Mom, those people up there, they are so conservative, and believe so totally different than you do . . . You even said your 'wild and crazy' friend has become a died-in-wool conservative. And, what about your movies, you go almost every week, and the symphony, opera, all the museums, gallery openings with your artist friends . . . and walking everywhere to do things, your friends . . . " She could hear the earnestness in his voice, his dire concerns for her mental health, and she truly loved him for it.

"I know there will be some challenges, and maybe that is what all of this is about - I've got some new lessons to learn. Please don't worry so much about it. I'm sure I will find some like-minded people, and I'll survive without my movies or museums. I've adapted before - you know I did it in Japan against all odds, and was quite successful. I think I'm ready to get away from all of the city life, and really get 'back to nature' for completely releasing my stress. Trust me, I can do this . . . and if I truly fail, you know I'm the best at coming up with a 'Plan B.' I've done it before, remember I survived my business-disaster in Hawaii, so I can overcome just about anything." At least he knew better than to say she was 'too old' for another change. He then surrendered to her, as he knew it was always a losing-battle of the wits. He may be a computer super-geek, but she could trump just about anyone with her words.

A few days later, she got Jeremy's tacit-acceptance as he put a thousand dollars into her checking account. This aided greatly her expense of the continuous - over thirty boxes of her 'life-stuff' she shipped out daily from her Mail Boxes, Etc. two blocks down. After many trips down to the "Out of the Closet" donation store, a trip out to the SCRAP art-recycle-center and finally the Salvation Army clear-out, what she had not been able to sell.

Beth finished cleaning the apartment. Totally exhausted with the physically-busy month, she stretched out on Connie's air mattress she'd brought to San Francisco on that first visit so many years past. Bags for the airport were packed, along with the stuff she was giving to Cheryl, who was taking her to the airport. Just finishing her sandwich when her phone rang, Beth saw it was Connie, *"Probably making sure that I'm all ready to fly out in the morning,"* she then said into the phone, "Hello My Sweet! Yes, I'm all ready to go."

"Well, is there any way you can put this off? I got a message from the site-manager at the building, and it's going to be at least three or more weeks before they can let anyone move in - contractor delays on some State inspector stuff." Her voice was a little pensive, worried about what she would do with Beth for that time period.

"Connie, where would I go even if I could change the flight?" Beth was surprised at the question. "I know it's an inconvenience, but I guess I'll have to stay with you. Can you put up with me for that long?" Now a mutual concern, since they'd been living so far apart for so many years, with only four to five day visits when together. Such a long period of time together for the independent women might damage their friendship.

"Well, . . . yea, . . . sure. It's just that I've scheduled to be out of town, and I don't want to leave you by yourself . . . You know, without a car and all."

"Hey, I've been living by myself, and entertaining myself for a very long time, *thank you*. Remember, I'm really adaptable when I have to be and I'll manage to keep busy helping you however I can. I mean if you can put up with me, I can certainly try not to invade your life, too much. It is a big house . . . and big yard." Beth could see this would be one of her first new challenges.

There were hesitations on both ends of the line, realizing what a huge commitment they were both entering into with each other. Neither was the same woman they had been thirty years before, when their lives had been so daily-entwined.

"OK," Connie responded cautiously, trying to get a sense of irony into it. "I guess if we don't kill each other, it will work out." Beth laughed heartily in acknowledgement, affirming her gut was still with her on all of this.

"OK, I'll call you from Minneapolis to let you know I made it, and no delays are expected on the hopper-flight." She took a deep breath and drew up some resolve, "I love you, and I really am excited about all of this. I'm ready for the change." Now, it was Connie on the other end giving out a rather loud laugh. What were they both doing?

With the long wait between flights, Beth closed her eyes to visualize clearing herself from top to bottom, so she would keep the positive energy flowing into and through her. For the last couple of years her positive regiment really helped to change her around, and totally use her Metaphysical beliefs into a clearer accepting. Just believing, knowing she was protected and guided, made staying positive with it life-stuff so much easier.

Then, Beth promised to herself, *no* preconceived-expectations, that she chose to make this drastic change to her life, and that she would continually remind herself to let it all unfold. She took another deep breath, and the relaxed feeling told her once again, it was the right move she was making. She felt there were more big things coming, that would stem from this. There was no asking why or when, let it unfold - be positive, her intuition said.

Her hopper-flight landed at Rhinelander's small airport, and she spotted Connie there at the single-baggage carousel immediately. She let her premature, silvering-hair do her frosting, and it looked great with her dark eyes. They were both about the same build, having added a few extra pounds over the years. With a big hug and kiss planted on the resistant Connie, Beth excitedly asked, "So, how soon until I can call myself a "Yooper?" Connie laughed and shook her head, still often amazed at her cheerleader-enthusiasm.

"Once you've lived through one of our winters and still want to live here, it's that simple. So, we'll see how you do with it. You said it's almost thirty years since you even lived in a full, four seasons. You look good, all that exercise with packing must of helped. How many bags do you have?" Connie picked up the small, tote-bag heading for her white, luxury Jeep - the dichotomy was her.

She really wondered how this was all going to turn out, as it not an easy life she had chosen for herself to escape Chicago. Beth's last visit had been three years prior for Greg's Memorial. Settled in the car, Connie turned toward her, serious in what she was about to say. "OK, you've heard me bitch and complain about the limited food selection and the people, but I'm telling you that you need to watch what you say, if you want to be accepted at all."

Beth ran her hand through her hair, and rolled her shoulders back stretching to get comfortable. Connie pulled out of the parking lot and turned easily onto the highway. "Let me tell you about this asshole who recently moved up here from the Chicago-area to open a bar, . . ." Most outside people managed to fit in as Connie did, by keeping a low profile, and not bragging about any past success, or hiding-well any past secrets. She then added that no one knew about any of their past escapades they had done. At this, Connie looked over at her, and Beth slid her thumb and forefinger over her lips to show they were sealed.

"So, you need to limit how much you talk about yourself - you know Japan and all of your education and stuff - until you get to know someone, or they ask for more details. Just being from California, and especially San Francisco will raise some eyebrows and they'll expect some liberal-stuff from you. Now, my friends know who you are, as I've told them you were moving here and they remember my trips out to see you, along with the food we ate." She laughed at this comment, as the trips had given her a certain bragging-right. "I'm going to miss that. Anyway, I've told you before that everyone is related to everyone, so you need to be aware *not to talk* about somebody, as they'll take offense regarding a relative, even if they know the person is a jerk or whatever."

Beth glanced out the window at the common, open small town scenery. "And, I've also got my responses, as to them inviting me to things I'm not interested in, so I don't hurt or offend anyone. I know they probably don't understand my whole metaphysical-belief-thing. I know you don't really either, but you don't care about how I believe or think anyway, as long as I don't tell you how to either. I guess that's how we've continued to get along over the years as we've changed." Very quiet for a minute or so, Beth decided to finish it off with one of Connie's favorite come-backs. "All-righty then, I guess we've gotten that all covered." They both laughed, more relieved as to how it was all going to come out for them.

"You know I really appreciate all you've done for me with this, and I sure hope that you didn't try to pick-up or move any of those heavier boxes by yourself. Oh, and the last four should be coming this week." She may not always be able to handle Connie's chiding, or especially the sarcastic teasing, but Beth did have quick humorous retorts she could unleash. To Connie they were actually appreciated, and not taken with offense. It might take a bit, but they would get back into each other's syncopation, and that comfortable honesty they'd always had. It wasn't quite a mutual sigh of relief, but it was going to be OK. *"Unfolding,"* Beth said under her breath, *"just let it all unfold and accept it all as it is - new lessons learned without expectations."*

Back at the house, Connie was behind the kitchen counter sipping her glass of white wine, with dinner in the oven and another wine glass waiting. Beth came down the hall from her bedroom, after changing her clothes. She was adjusting the straps and tucking her boobs to make sure they were straight and balanced. "Keep those girls straight and looking up," Connie joked.

"Yea, so many women don't know how stodgy and old they look with saggy, hanging boobs. It easily takes ten-years off when they are up and perky." They both laughed.

Connie, still slightly shaking her head, then directly asked, "How difficult is all this for you to handle?" She had a real concern for Beth, now that she was there.

"I've told you before how much I loved it here, I'll adapt and adjust to it all."

"No, I don't mean *just here*. I mean difficult not having money, when you've been used to having so much for so long. And, difficult not getting a job or work when you've got so much experience and education . . . how are you doing with *all that*?" Connie swallowed a sip of wine.

"Do you have some red wine?" She wasn't ready to answer the heavy questions without a little imbibing. She sat on a bar stool, it becoming her side of the counter.

Connie walked over to the wine rack and pulled out two bottles. "That's all the red I have." Beth read both labels, chose one and put the other back, as Connie pulled out the corkscrew. "It doesn't exactly need to breathe, but it's not bad I understand." It was almost like an homage to their years working in the French restaurant together. Beth almost fell off the stool with her laughing, and Connie cracked up at her own excellent foil.

Connie, obsessed with her TiVo recording system, only watched her programmed shows. Beth watched a lot of PBS, but of no interest to Connie. "I've got my 'right-winged, conservative-stuff' as you call it coming on, so you can go to your room and read, you won't hurt my feelings one bit." It *was* her giant-screen TV and house, so Beth did just that. What disturbed Beth most was when Connie, purposefully used the pejorative of 'nigger,' and Beth jumped on her asking, what about us going to see to your love - Lou Rawls. That's different, she'd said.

Beth had only been at Connie's a few days, but already had helped clean out the basement, and cleared out residuals of the past few years from the lower-level family room. She questioned the large, wooden shelves with the stacks of at least fifty good-sized boxes, depicting expensive ornamental-candles. "Those are my hostess gifts from all my candle parties over the past few years. I'm going to use them for wedding gifts, or special birthday gifts for people."

Beth looked at her and tried to joke, "You sure you're not 'collecting,' or actually becoming a hoarder like April? You could sell these with a humongous garage sale for the animal shelter, to almost pay-off its mortgage that you're so concerned about!" She chuckled.

Surprisingly, Connie shocked her, "They're MINE, and I'll decide what happens to them." She realized she had over-reacted, "Well, I like them, and maybe I'll use them."

With the lower-level glass patio-doors wide open, the woodsy smell freshened everything. "Sure is wonderful out here." Beth walked outside to deep breathe and let herself stare-off across the deep lawn down to the large lake, with the sun shimmering-off it. She took another deep breath, so appreciating the glorious nature, as the last bit of stress released itself from her shoulders and back. They would work through these things, she was sure.

Connie followed her out, "I would appreciate you packing-up of the last of some of Greg's things for his kids back East. I've been putting-off that project." They then sat and talked outside, still catching-up on more details of the past few years, not covered in phone calls. Living alone, Connie then expressed that she was happy with the company, and glad that they had the extra time together before Beth's move to the new apartment. As her trip down to Wisconsin had been cancelled due to an illness, she said they could maybe plan some site-seeing for Beth to get more familiar with places she'd not taken her to before. Considering that she no longer enjoyed the driving, because of problems with her back and legs, Beth took it as a kind gesture.

The weeks flew by, and Beth was soon finishing the touches on her new apartment in the old refurbished building, when there was a knock on the door. She swung it open to see Michael standing there, and she yelled out, "Oh, my God! What are you doing here?" Michael laughed and gave Beth a big hug and kiss, then introduced her to her friend Susan, who'd driven up with her. Beth remembered Michael mentioning her, but they'd never met and Michael really couldn't drive such a long trip by herself any more.

Connie stepped into view, "Surprise! I thought you might enjoy some time together, so I had them come up to visit, so we can all go site-seeing for the leaves, it's such a beautiful day." They had three days together, enjoying the incredible fall trees and eating themselves silly, where Connie knew to be the best places. The talk was non-stop, as Beth asked Michael about what new movies she'd seen, while she and Susan commented, as they usually went together.

Michael still loved her job with the county, helping her residents at the group home and all of their activities or jobs that they had. Connie also took them over to see the new animal shelter, as they'd gotten the new place built, then immediately filled with cats and dogs for adoption. She was so proud of it all, with her involvement in getting it done. Too quickly, they left for the six-hour drive back. It was a respite for them to have refilled their well of friendship.

Beth wanted a job, and without a car yet, she'd have to keep it all close by. She heard about the city looking for volunteers for a festival coming up, and they were meeting in the lobby of her building, since several residents were involved. It was a double accomplishment for Beth as she met Pat, who worked with the sponsor group and Dorothea, who was City Manager. City Hall, with the Fire and Police departments, were directly across from her apartment building. It took Beth a while to convince Dorothea, but soon she was Special Assistant to the City Manager - granted, eight dollars an hour and only twenty hours a week, but great fun for both.

Getting to know Pat was truly finding a 'like-minded' friend, while she'd been born and raised till grade school in the area, then she and her mother moved to Chicago after her father died. Pat had worked almost thirty years in the corporate world, so she totally understood what Beth'd put up with there, also.

Luckily, an easy winter for Beth, though more than once she managed to slip on the ice walking down to the community center for the aerobics class. Connie's schedule and the fifteen-mile drive kept them apart more than Beth expected, so she learned she was going to have to create her own friend-community of support. She made a few more friends in the building, of particular note, Lois down the hall, who was from Rockford, Illinois, so commonality with her of sorts. Most importantly though, working at City Hall gave Beth access to meeting many of the town's people. As Connie said, they looked at her for being an oddity, not just California, but 'crazy San Francisco.' To many, as Beth may be helping out collecting the payments on water, electric and cable, she added she was originally from Chicago, which made her a little more palatable to them.

Thanksgiving was Beth's first full-family visit, as this year Matt and Kathy, his long-time fiancee, were hosting. Sharon was coming with her younger son Eric, who was in from college in Green Bay. Connie picked Beth up Wednesday to help prepare her share for the dinner, as well bring what Beth wanted to drink - she found a bottle of Pinot Noir, which surprised her, as their wine selections were limited. "Kathy's son Eddie is coming up from Chicago, and he's gay, so you'll probably like him, since you had so many as friends. Though I heard, he's bringing some female-friend who wanted to get away."

Beth chuckled, Connie was right, she and Eddie bonded, as he had been told about her. The friend was very uncomfortable, and didn't bring her own wine, so hit Beth's to chug-a-lugg it into a water glass. Connie then jumped on her for doing so. Beth got a smaller wine glass to pour some into, "It's not that kind of wine, . . . it's not sweet and you sip it." At dinner, she asked for catsup, then proceeded to pour it all over the turkey, dressing and potatoes.

Connie, three-sheets-to-the-wind, let out a roar, "What the fuck are you doing?" Kathy and Sharon both tried to calm her, as Eddie got really upset at Connie being so tacky.

"*Connie*," Beth sternly said, "It's her food, and you've had enough to drink." The others looked at Beth, shocked she'd say something, as Connie put her glass back down.

"I'm sorry," she looked at Eddie, "it's your food," but stuck her tongue out in disgust.

Connie *again* invited Beth for Christmas, joining the family celebration at her house. Beth came to stay overnight, *again* to help with the cooking and cleaning-up of everything. Good to belong, whatever the situation. Beth's budget limited, she wrote poems and little things for everyone, but they were all nice giving her gifts and complimented her on dinner. They were also grateful that Beth kept Connie's drinking more controlled, as well her mouth.

* * * * * *

Interestingly, April came after Christmas to visit Michael, trying to get Michael to let her move in with her. But this time, she resolved in saying 'no.' It seemed, April was being evicted, as she'd filled her apartment with all of her hoarding. Apparently, a fire hazard, so not safe to live there, as there no space to move around at all. Even her balcony was filled to the brim. April came loaded-down with 'gifts' for Michael. Leather jackets, jeans and other stuff she continually purchased on one credit card after another, never paying-off any of them. At the same time, she never gave Michael a cent for gas, though she had her running all over for her to buy more stuff. Nor did she contribute money for groceries or meals eaten out. Since Michael had a regular job, not great money, but April still expected her to pay.

Once Michael confirmed again, she could not move in with her, April said she'd probably load all of her loot into a U-Haul and drive out to Oregon. Her daughter Teresa lived there with her husband. Since Teresa and her husband were both very, busy environmental attorneys, they did not want her, but it didn't matter to April. This all recapitulated once again, why no one wanted anything to do her. As Michael held firm on not letting her stay with her. As she discussed it all with Connie and Beth, they couldn't begin to agree more on April's serious-craziness. Also, not in the best of health, with her diabetes and recurring heart problems. Though she used them for sympathy, April didn't follow medical restrictions.

It'd not been an easy time for Michael, not that April took any of that into consideration. Travis, her son, was in the hospital for his alcoholism, without any good prospects. By the end of the first week of the New Year, 2011, Travis died, but Michael really didn't want to talk about it at all. Just as she didn't want to talk about Travis' young, teenage-daughter having a child, which made Michael a great-grandmother. Whenever Michael could, she'd send her granddaughter money for the child, as Travis had done very little to support any of his half-dozen children.

When April returned to San Antonio, she recruited a few acquaintances, playing on her health issues. They helped load up the large, moving-van with her hoarded-collection from several storage locations. Still it wouldn't all fit in the largest van. Sometime in March, April headed west to Oregon, letting Teresa know she was coming. Teresa informed her again, they themselves, were moving to northern California for a new job, so not come. April didn't believe them, and headed out across country. When she arrived, they were telling the truth, in the full-process of having their moving-van loaded. The stress of the trip, and her emotional anger-frustration of not getting what she wanted, yet felt she deserved, April had a massive heart attack.

Teresa put her in the hospital, then left, as their jobs were waiting. She returned once, but kept contact with the hospital, until April died after several more heart attacks in the next few weeks. When Michael shared the information, Connie and Beth could only shake their heads, as to what had happened to make April go so nuts. Michael had been her only recent connection, and they hoped April was finally at peace with the world. She had known through her astrology and metaphysics how to live consciously in life's fleeting moments, and how to breathe to stop being so frantic. Yet, she had lost her way to living honestly, when she lost her passion about living intuitively. How and why she got so lost, they'd never totally understand, as she wouldn't talk about it.

* * * * * *

Beth saved up money for a down-payment on a new car. Her nephew Jackie, had gotten back in contact with her and suggested a 'family & friends' discount on a Ford, so Connie helped her find one on-line. The closest dealer was over an hour away, but they secured the Fiesta for her. Jeremy promised to give her a thousand dollars, and Beth got a car loan from the credit union she joined. All money in place by April first, Connie drove Beth to the dealer, though another big, snow storm was on its way toward them. Although Connie had a bad cold, they went on to get Beth's little 2011 Magenta-colored Fiesta purchased. Beth'd not had a car since she lived in Hawaii, but through the snow storm she mustered on to safely arrive in her apartment parking lot. Now, she had wheels and her whole life changed for the better! Excited, she could take her turn driving, where as Lois and Pat had been happily taking her places.

Beth planned her first big trip down to Mike's farm for Memorial Day weekend. Barb was coming out ahead of time, and Jason bringing Michael in with him. So good to all be comfortable together, to laugh, drink and eat good food. It was Beth's first time to see Mike's house, as they reminisced about all the good times in the old trailer, that had housed them for so long. Barb and Mike were now travel-buddies, though she always affirmed there was no sex.

They still snipped and barked at each other, when they'd had too much to drink, until Jason came in between. Beth also noticed that Michael's stability was getting worse, and the residual from her cancer-toxicity caused her muscle deterioration to be more extensive. She had another year before she'd be on Medicare, so she was lucky to have her job with the county, and still be able to do it. Barb took Beth into town, and it was fun to see all the places she'd remembered from so long before. So many special times and special memories, that they'd all hold dear.

With Jeremy traveling so much, he had lots of American 'frequent-flyer' points, and brought Beth to Dallas twice a year - to see him and friends perform their Improv at the Renaissance Faire. Then again at Thanksgiving or Christmas. Even with him getting the tickets, not an easy trip, as one flight out, seven in the morning to Chicago. And, one flight in, six-thirty in the evening back to Marquette around nine. Luckily, there were plenty of flights between Chicago and Dallas. Marquette was the largest UP city, thirty thousand, one and half hours from where Beth lived. Much of the time, there was fog in the morning, so not an easy drive, and then a late night-drive home.

The Upper Peninsula of Michigan had a whopping three-hundred thousand people in an area three-times the size of New Jersey.

But it also had the oldest, largest virgin-hardwood growth, and more waterfalls than any other state. It was beautiful and Beth loved exploring it with Pat or Lois, whenever she had the chance to do so. And, Autumn was the most incredible she'd ever experienced. God's paintbrush, worked overtime!

Though sometimes getting together with Connie, seemed more convoluted. If Beth planned it and worked it around Connie's schedule, no problem. But trying to get her to set-up regular outings with Beth was almost impossible. At the same time, Connie did relate back things she was always doing with others. Beth wanted to understand why she wasn't included more often. Connie did enjoy having her candle-home party sales, and asked Beth to come over to help set it up. Since having a car, it was fun meeting some of her other friends. Beth did get Connie to go with her to Door County, when Pat got sick and couldn't go. Connie hadn't been there in years, before with Cam. If Beth could get them together, they had a great time, but doing so was often like pulling teeth.

Connie did what she jokingly called, "Mommy and Me" days with Matt, snowmobiling, as well as off-road driving in her four-wheel-drive 'dunes-buggy' vehicle. Though Beth always loved snow-mobiling, Connie made it very clear, it was too expensive for her to be involved with. But, when she had an accident from drinking too much, which she denied, she called Beth to come take her home.

Still, to Beth any chance of spending time together was better than none. They did make a trip down to Green Bay, when Beth had to have some special dental surgery, and Jeremy got them a room at one of the Hilton affiliates. As Connie's ignoring accumulated, Beth began spending more of her time and holidays with Pat and her cousin LaDena. They *really wanted to time with her.* Then when Connie called at the last minute for Beth to join them, she was busy, and Connie was shocked.

Michael surprised Beth when she called saying she was trying to get a substitute to take her place at work, so she and Susan could come back up in the fall. Yet the restrictions the county put on the replacement people, required arrangements to be made way in advance. Michael still didn't do planning-ahead very well, so wasn't able to return, to Beth's great disappointment.

Beth was really excited for Jeremy, when he began working in Europe in late 2011 until end of June in 2012, with returns to the U.S. every three to four weeks. She kept giving him suggestions for exploring on those weekends he had in Switzerland, as the trains connected to so many countries, and he took advantage to travel often. She missed her own international travel, and truly hoped one day to be doing it again.

Jason surprised Beth, planning on a trip up to see her, and bringing Mike along. He was having so many problems with his knees he sat in Jason's truck, while she showed him all of her favorite spots for photographing. The time would be coming soon when Mike would need to have the knees replaced, though he didn't want to deal with it. At least, Connie was able to join them for dinner one night at her favorite restaurant, where she knew the owner from her early days there with Greg.

Christmastime, Connie called Michael. She mentioned she'd probably retire with her next birthday in April, as she would be sixty-five and get her Medicare. She was seriously thinking of moving to the UP to join them both, as soon she would have to use a walker, and from there into a wheelchair. Connie jumped on it, "I've still got my mother's mobile home, which I'm renting out, and it's all set up for accessible, so I could get you into it. Then I could pick you up, we'd go zipping you all over town in your wheelchair!" She laughed at it, "How funny we'd be compared to the early days, when bar-hopping and chasing men." Connie didn't notice Michael wasn't laughing.

When she mentioned it Beth, she said, "My God, Connie, what's wrong with you? You know Michael doesn't want to think about using a walker, much less a wheelchair. She doesn't want to look like a little old lady, she's not like your mother, happy to be pushed around. She wants to be up here, because she *doesn't* know anyone."

Connie got defensive, "What are you talking about, she knows this all is inevitable! There's nothing they can do to slow it down, she's known it for years now." Connie didn't get it. Some things and how people reacted, Connie could be so oblivious. Beth had always felt she could have been more inclusive with Greg as he aged, but she saw no need to urge him to join her.

The New Year of 2012 came and went without fanfare. Whether it was the anniversary of Travis' death or just time, the call came from Jenny, Michael's daughter, she had died from a massive heart attack. It happened right at work, she grabbed her chest, sat down on a chair and died instantly, with several patients around her. Beth couldn't understand a word Connie was saying, when she called crying and screaming into the phone. She finally got her to calm down long enough to understand, it was Michael she was talking about. It took her daughters a few days to get organized, but the Memorial would be right after Connie's birthday. With a heavy heart, Beth called Jason who was devastated. She then asked him to call Mike as soon as he could, so he'd hear it from him, rather than her brother Web calling to tell him.

Jenny called back a few days later and asked Connie if she and Beth could stay at Michael's place and clean it out somewhat - mainly the clothes and personal items. They just couldn't deal with it. Beth had never been inside, yet she recognized many of the photographs on her walls. They totally filled, top to bottom, and other items she had collected for so many years. Almost spooky, as her presence revealed everywhere, as if any moment she'd come through the door, so happy to see them.

Connie said to Beth, "Go through the clothes to see if any of them fit you, I know they're too small for me. And, I'll take what's left to the bar, to put them out for people to take what fits." Then, all too eerie, as Beth understood her daughters had enough to deal with, so she was gingerly pushing through the hangers.

Connie started digging through the pantry, throwing stuff away into the large, trash-container when she began screaming, sat down at the table and cried. Beth came running into the dinning room, and saw Connie holding a package in her hand of diet pills. The label very clearly stated they could cause heart attacks, this was a notorious brand recently banned. "How could she do this? She knows this stuff is shit, and so dangerous." Most of the packet was gone, and looking at the ones remaining in the cellophane, Michael had probably taken two or three of the packets. Beth read the directions, figuring she'd been on them right as the New Year started.

Beth got a cold chill down her spine, "Connie, I think she knew quite well what these pills would do. You remember how she used to say, 'I want to go out in a flash, no long-lingering.' Well, these would do it with her health issues. There was no way, she was going to go into a wheelchair, and especially not have you pushing her around town in front of everybody. I told you, she wanted to come up to the UP, where nobody would know her or feel sorry for her." Beth held the pills in her hand, "This is what she wanted, this is how she wanted to die." Connie would not accept it, she couldn't see the degradation Michael would feel being helpless in a wheelchair. *She* was the one who helped people, and not them helping her. She'd rather have a quick death than a slow, withering-away being taken care by others.

"When you can Connie, you need to write something down and I'll read it for you. I wrote most of mine on the way down, as I'd been thinking of it for a few days." They'd gone out for Italian beef for Connie's birthday for lunch, as she was going out with her sister and some friends that night to celebrate, though she was in no mood. Beth would be meeting Jason for dinner, and she knew he'd need more comforting than she would. Beth had become more accepting of death in the last few years, as more of a release for peace. She would cry in her own time, and her words were where her love was expressed. Connie found the calendar marked for having Marie and Cindy for dinner on Marie's birthday, the end of the month. Beth made no comment, just shook her head, thinking how Michael liked to take care those she thought worse-off than her.

Though hung-over from getting so shit-faced for her birthday, Connie insisted she wanted to go see Little Mary from the Cafe' days, as she lived not too far away. Yet, she refused to call to get the directions clarified, and drove around getting them there almost an hour late. Beth kept thinking there was something more to it, when they'd only been there about thirty minutes, and Connie began angling to go. Beth hadn't seen Mary in years, and really wanted to stay. She'd put out snacks, which Connie ate, but kept saying they had to go. Once in the car, she asked, "What was that all about, you were almost rude?" Connie ignored her, and just drove, now knowing where she was without any confusion. Beth felt a volcano brewing inside Connie, as she'd not handled the whole quasi-suicide-thing she proposed. Beth could only think of one of the basics of Metaphysics and Spirituality - "No one dies before their time."

Her daughters put up some wonderful photos, and Beth slowly studied them one by one. Out of the corner of her eye, she saw Cindy and Marie come in, with Jenny helping Marie get her coat off. All

Beth thought only of the letter the attorney sent her years ago to never speak to Marie directly, but only through him. He was now dead. With the irony, she almost chuckled, thinking she'd follow the order, and not talk to either one of them. To do so would be hypocritical of her.

Beth mentioned to Jenny when she first came in she would be reading both Connie and her remarks. Beth not sure if Connie said something to Jenny regarding the diet pills, so she did. She clearly commented, "Mom was very vain, there's no way she would have ever been seen in a wheelchair." Beth had been right in her prognosis of Michael's choice to exit in her own time. Connie, even more upset, and almost angry as to Michael choosing to leave them - *her*.

Quite a few people came and went, including all of the patients brought in who Michael worked with, before the start of the Memorial. As Beth listened to the Minister, she thought it was a good thing Michael had been cremated, as she would have sat up in a casket and yelled, *"Where the hell did you get this guy? Are you serious in him for me, and my beliefs?"* He also managed to drone on way, too long. Jason had been sitting with Beth, but when she got up to read, Connie really began to lose it, though crying some before.

Jason moved over and put his arm around her, and it did help. Connie's comments Beth read were light and fun regarding 'chasing men and living down the hall from each other.' Beth then told the story of how the four of them had been brought together, what they'd been through and how even forty years later they were still friends. She spoke for about five minutes, mostly calm and clear, though she choked once or twice. she acknowledged Michael contributed greatly to Beth's changing, especially in the early years regarding Bruce, and she'd always carried her within her heart.

Beth and Connie were surprised Jason was not included in the dinner following the memorial. But Michael had very much separated her relationships, not sharing her closeness of one with another - almost compartmentalizing them. The girls had no idea of the closeness of Jason and Michael at all. In the morning, Beth helped Connie bag-up the huge amount of clothes, with at least fifty pairs of jeans - many with the waists clipped to accommodate her 'muffin top. And, at least a dozen black-hoody sweatshirts. Michael was consistent in her look, always James Dean, if there was a collar to turn up. Beth found a few things she to wear, but couldn't believe the redundancy in her wardrobe, as Beth liked color rather than Michael's repeat of black or denim. The Jeep was filled to the brim, and there would be a few memories to keep.

Connie talked very little on the drive back, again putting on her Sirius-radio to the Motown, Blues, or Jazz channels, as Beth kept busy writing, knowing Connie was not in a talking mode. As they got closer to home, she felt Connie pulling away even more, and Beth hoped she wasn't going into a depression.

She'd been on multiple anti-depressants for a few years even before Greg died. She didn't have much more in her life than her Animal Shelter. Connie rarely got involved with the bar any more, except to count the money. When Eric, her younger grandson finished college, he went to Portland joining his brother to work in sound-engineering. Maybe there'd be more snow, and she could go snowmobiling with Matt. She needed something to distract her from it all. Eventually, Connie shared she didn't want to know Michael may have wanted to kill herself. She truly felt it was 'greedy' of Michael to deprive her friends of her company.

* * * * * *

Beth started teaching Memoir Writing at the Community Center, and then moved it to the Library. The group was small, as compared to those she'd done in San Francisco, and usually consistent with the snowbirds returning. One student she worked with editing, she helped get his book published, over the couple of years together. She worked on her own idea for a novel from a poem she'd written some time back, but Connie wasn't happy she was in the story.

The monthly writers group gave Beth another outlet for her creativity, though they rarely understood her poetry. Beth came and stayed with Connie when she had hand surgery, then didn't hear from her for a while. Out-of-the-clear-blue, she called to invite Beth to dinner. Connie opened up about Greg, how he loved her so, though, she'd felt controlled sometimes. After several drinks, she talked about Michael and how much she missed talking to her. Beth agreed.

Beth continually worked at having a variety of things going on in her life, so it was never boring. She planned a trip to Mackinac Island with Pat just before Memorial Day, when the prices went up,

They had a fantastic time, even with Pat's slight mobility issues. They traveled well together, and Beth enjoyed her company as she loved to talk and they never ran out of topics. Also, Pat never missed church since moving to the UP, and Beth enjoyed attending with her when they traveled. Dorothea always had new projects for Beth to take on at City Hall, and she loved working the elections. The whole situation of small-town politics fascinated Beth, and she took pride she'd helped refurbish the recycling program for the city.

Beth was supposed to meet Jeremy in Chicago that July, as he was once again taking the Second City Improv-Training, and she'd get to see him perform there. He'd been having some problems with his intestines, then they discovered an obstruction in his bowel, and he needed emergency surgery just before the date. He told her to go ahead, as he preferred her there, than worrying over him in Dallas. Jeremy ate a lot of fast food, and Beth was sure it was also from all of the GMOs, she'd been reading a lot about, and how damaging they were to the intestines.

It turned out to be an amazing trip for Beth, as she hadn't spent much time in Chicago since she'd worked on North Michigan Avenue for the advertising agency, before she got married. There were so many incredible things to explore that hadn't been there before, and she even took the architectural tour on the river. Navy Pier was wonderful, and had a very large exhibition on Nicolai Tesla, whom Jeremy really enjoyed reading about, so she picked up lot of info to give him. She went on the giant, ferris wheel, with the glorious view over Lake Michigan. Jason came in to have dinner with her, though the rainy weather was terrible. She checked on Jeremy several times a day, and the time flew by escaping into another world.

In the fall, Jeremy came over from Minneapolis to visit for a weekend. He flew to Chicago, then come up from there, seeing how Beth had to deal with the difficult connections. He could have almost drove over faster than flying. Beth was getting good at being the tour guide, and she did love showing off the amazing nature they were surrounded by everywhere. What Jeremy also picked-up on, was the lack of cell-phone service for long stretches, and the emptiness of the excellent roads. He talked to her about the situation in the winter, as she'd been lucky about having milder weather the past two years.

Then, because she didn't want him to miss his flight back to work, Beth thought they should stay at a motel in Marquette, on the road that lead to the airport, in case there was fog. The long drive from her apartment could have delayed them with it. Beth then came for Thanksgiving, and was happy that he'd separated from the long-term girlfriend, as she really didn't liked her at all. Jeremy's, best friend of twenty years and improv partner, Brian stayed at the big house to take care of it while Jeremy worked out of town. He loved to cook, so they had a great holiday dinner, and many laughs together telling stories.

Only back a few weeks, Beth got a call from a sobbing Jeremy. She calmed him down, to understand that Brian had a massive, heart attack and died. This was too scary, as he was only a few years older than Jeremy. Apparently, Brian went to bed early, thinking he had the flu, but the autopsy showed a congenital heart problem that was never diagnosed. It was almost an instant death, though no consolation.

Nothing like losing a best friend, close in age, to make you realize time *is too short*. With this trauma, everything changed in Jeremy's life - he got out of the big house, contacted a woman he had feelings for years before and they were soon involved. He'd always wanted children, and she had a young daughter, but wanted more. The chemistry they had before blossomed, as 2013 rolled onto the calendar.

From a retreat Beth attended the past summer, she'd been ask to speak at one herself. She got to promote and sell several of her *Move Past* books, along with doing some private sessions as a Life Coach. Once again, she was reminded that her talents in helping people were needed and wanted. She then did several workshops with a holistic group in Green Bay, so knew she really needed to get back into a city with more people, as well those open to her talents in helping them.

In the Spring, Jeremy talked to her about considering moving to Dallas, as concerned about a car accident, and no access to help her. He said he'd send her some info about the community colleges there, they may be interested in her teaching her memoir writing. Not responding positively, quickly enough, he added, "Steph and I are talking about getting married, and want to expand the family as soon as we can. I thought you wanted to be a grandmother?" He said the magic-word, and she jumped-on-the-bandwagon, which she'd already been considering, but nothing got her quicker than the prospect of being a grandmother. At Easter dinner at Pat's house, Beth dropped the bombshell, saying she'd look for an apartment and job when she went for her annual trek to see Jeremy. She would go for the *Renaissance-Faire* over Memorial weekend, with the idea of moving down there by the '4th of July.'

Pat's cousin LaDena immediately volunteered herself and her friend Ron, "We'll drive the moving-van if you want, since we've never been to Texas!" LaDena was one of the first Peace Corp volunteers, and spent many years working with Ethiopia, including the escape of the fifteen thousand from Idi Amin to Israel. Not too shocked and happy, Beth could see the synchronicity in it all working out. She began tracking the community colleges, and sending emails, with a very strong, positive return from the one college just north of the city. Beth let Dorothea know she might stay a few days longer, but would talk to her from Dallas.

Beth next called Connie to let her know of her plans, and she questioned, "I didn't know you weren't happy here?" She was a bit stunned that Connie hadn't seen how her not extending-herself out more to Beth, totally left her to fend for herself. Which she did do rather well, but more closeness to and with Connie had been expected, as well wanted. Still, it was for the best.

"Well, you have to admit, we never did very much together on a regular basis. I was the one usually doing the inviting, unless a candle party or some fund-raiser." Beth did not mean for it to come off as so direct or rude, but all true. "Your grandkids are grown, Connie, I'm going to have mine late in life, but at least I'm getting them. I do want to be there to enjoy."

The time flew by, as packing once again began, but this would be the first move where she also took her furniture. After the fun of Faire, Beth was set with a new job at the college and a very, nice two-bedroom apartment in a retirement community, with the rent only about one hundred-fifty more than what she was paying there, so it should work. Beth planned out the trip, with them staying three-nights over the twelve-hundred miles, and Jeremy found Hilton-affiliates with his points. Beth asked him for a first-class airline ticket one-way from wherever LaDena and Ron wanted, back to Marquette. Jeremy was more than happy to comply, as otherwise he had to take off work to drive the moving-van down. LaDena and Ron planned on going camping and hiking out west around Grand Canyon, so would end up in Las Vegas to return home.

Connie came over as the packing was finished, and joined Beth at the same restaurant they ate at after she'd arrived. Not a sad-leaving, though Beth was not sure if she had fulfilled her purpose for the move. They certainly had more time together than they would have, so maybe the expectation was fulfilled. It popped in her head Michael had always said 'her expectations were too high, and why she'd get disappointed.'

After Greg passed, Connie continued to make her spring trips to Florida, but for a rental house for the month, so taking the dogs with her in the car. Sharon would go with her for the drive down, then fly back, then reverse at month's end. Connie would schedule out a week or so for Matt and Cathy, and several others to join her, but she never invited Beth, though she knew Jeremy would have covered her air fare. Beth asked her once, but the answer was so superfluous, as if Connie became oblivious of her even being there for consideration. Thinking of this, Beth suggested, "Maybe you can stop and stay overnight, on your way to Florida to see me."

Connie looked at her matter of factly, "Oh, . . . no, it's off our main route I take going down. I'm just trying to get there as fast as we can, we just snooze and change drivers." As usual, Beth was the one giving the hugs and kisses, as Connie never really did. Mutual 'I love you' ended the meeting, Connie's teary eyes surprised Beth somewhat.

With only a few glitches weather-wise, directionally speaking, the drive, hotels and all went well. LaDena had some friends in Dallas, and they were soon off on their own travels. That weekend, Beth picked up the Sunday paper to see there was a poetry conference the following weekend, and perfect for where she felt her life was leading. She joined the Poetry Society of Texas group and the local chapter, then ended up winning a first place in one of their one hundred annual contests in the fall. Beth had never been so excited to be acknowledged and win twenty-five dollars before. She'd found some of the 'like-minded' people she'd looked for.

The next big leap was her Memoir Writing classes, and her department coordinator - DeBorah, was a delight to work with, as she ran the '50+' group - classes for people over fifty. Using her own designed procedure for the teaching in small groups, her niche had been found and she totally blossomed so much more than in the UP, or even San Francisco. She wrote a wedding poem for Jeremy and Steph, then a gay couple they knew were getting married, so she wrote another one for them. The poetry fed her deeply, her inner-soul, and then she started a new blog called "EveryDay Empowerment," which she felt her life was turning into. But the best day was, when she saw the ultrasound-images of their new baby, as she was spending time with Steph's daughter Sera, from her first marriage. Later, Pat came down with several ladies for a quilting conference. Beth greatly enjoyed her staying with her, as they went to several places, but rainy weather interfered with some longer trips outside Dallas. They talked weekly, as their friendship grew deeper, while Beth only talked occasionally with Connie.

The grand boy, Magnus, made his entry in mid-June of 2014, and Beth's life would never be the same again. How perfect and wonderful, as she had both a granddaughter and a grandson. Life was good, and quite busy with part-time jobs, teaching her Memoir Writing classes and her own writing of her blogs and poems. Beth also helped her students with editing their writing to self-publish. The only thing missing was a man in her life, yet there was no real-urge or gaping-hole. She did miss seeing the spectacular, autumn season in the UP, and both winters following her leaving had tons of snow dropping on them, with unlimited days below zero. She had been blessed to leave when she did. Yes, Dallas did get a day or two of ice, and the rare snowfall, but most days no heavy coat at all was needed.

Beth called Connie mid-January, 2015 for her birthday, though she'd sent a card and poem, to see how she was celebrating it. Connie mentioned Eddie and his partner, Dustin were getting married in Vegas on Valentine's day weekend. So she, Matt and Kathy, Eddie's mother, would be going along with two more couples. Beth got excited, as she always enjoyed Eddie, and wanted to know if she could join them all. "Yes, I'm sure he'd love it, as he always enjoyed you so much. You can even share my room, and I'll have somebody to hang out with."

"Great, send me the time your flight gets in, and I'll try to match it. I'll get Jeremy to book me, as soon as I get the info from you. We'll have lots of fun." By the time they all got together, Beth was fighting-off some bad bronchitis, but constantly taking her zinc lozenges to keep it from getting worse. Connie wanted to go to a

Motown music review that night, which was fine with Beth, doing dinner before at an Italian restaurant. It had been more than twenty years since Beth had been to Vegas, with so many new places to see and walk around. The day of the wedding, they were all invited over to Eddie's grandmother's apartment, who was a real hoot, that Beth and Connie enjoyed laughing and sharing stories with.

An arranged shuttle got them to the ceremony at the Little White Chapel. They'd never seen such an assembly-line of various couples - more than usual, since being Valentine's Day. Beth reassured Kathy that she looked wonderful, as the 'Mother of the Groom' - Eddie. They managed to have it as nice as they could, though a totally controlled production. They all headed over to the restaurant, while the boys got some scheduled-photos by the fountains.

And, Connie even *asked* Beth to make sure she didn't drink too much. Dustin was very nice, talking to Beth several times, while Eddie let her know how happy he was that she came. After brunch the next day, Beth presented her framed-poem for the two of them. Eddie cried, as he asked her to read it for everyone. It cracked Beth up, that one of the other couples that didn't know her, asked who wrote the poem. Connie and Kathy proudly piped up, "She's even won awards, she's really good, and Eddie knew her when she lived in the UP." The acknowledgement surprised and delighted her.

Eddie was so thrilled, giving Beth another hug and kiss, telling Dustin, "I know right where we can hang it, so everyone will see it." The warm accolade thrilled Beth.

Back in the room, Connie was now feeling like she was coming down with something. "Oh, Connie, I'm so sorry, I hope I didn't give this to you, it's been going on for some time."

"No, I was sick a few weeks ago, and I don't think I got rid of it totally." A few hours later, they all piled into the shuttle to go back to the airport. Other than Kathy having a problem with Matt gambling and drinking too much, it was a good, fun weekend with some great laughs and talks.

Nothing like the wildness it would have been in the old days, but those were behind them. Connie called a few weeks later, saying she'd really been sick, and the doctor wanted her to go for a chest x-ray because the coughing had been so heavy and still going on. "I better be rid of this thing soon, we leave in another week to drive to

Florida. Beth's finally cleared, and she was doing well as it got warmer in Dallas. A week later Connie called, "Did you get a chest x-ray for your bronchitis?" There was a shallowness in Connie's voice.

Beth said, "No, mine was waning as we left Vegas. I'm doing fine now, what's up?"

"Well, I'm leaving for Florida with Sharon anyway, but I've got a spot on my lung. My doctor said she'd send an order for a Cat-scan or something, when I get there." She tried not to show concern, as just an annoyance. A week later, Connie called back, now sounding really pissed. "Well, I've got cancer, but they said no problem, it's small and can be fixed easy. I'm going to have a treatment here and then head back for Chicago. They've got the best doctors, they've kept Cheryl's asshole-husband alive for twenty years. I'm really upset, as we have to cancel all the plans for everyone coming to visit. I'll get some of my payment back on this house, then drive back when Matt gets here after the treatment." There was a real-heaviness in her resign.

Beth could only say, "You'll be in my prayers, and hope it all goes as they say." Then a week or so later, Beth began having problems catching her breath, noticing it when she did her water aerobics and walking across the campus parking lot to class. Once Beth'd sat down, it cleared, but she decided to see her primary doctor the next day. She gave her an EKG, but though nothing showed, so told her to get to the Emergency Room for more tests. Beth went right there thinking about Connie.

It took several tests, but finally the excellent ER doctor discovered some minute, blood clots on one lung-lining. They whizzed Beth into a hospital room, immediately put her on blood thinners. Then an excellent hematologist showed up at her side, with a thousand questions and more tests. She stayed for two and a half days, but the frustrated hematologist could not find any cause, but said they'd monitor her as it cleared. Jeremy came to pick her up, and did his usual, comedic-routine, yet she knew his vitally concern. She'd always been good about staying healthy with her diet and exercise. Beth called Connie, reassuring her all was well on her end.

Once settled into her sister Cheryl's house, the phone calls between them were every few days, with details as to Connie's treatment program, ". . . now there's a crack in my back which has the cancer also, but it doesn't need chemo, just radiation. They said it's manageable." Beth noted the cancer went from 'easily fixed' to 'manageable.' She got bad-vibes and called Jason. "If she thinks she's going to be there through Memorial Day, I'm going to ask her if I can come visit - can I stay with you? Maybe Mike wants to come in, and we can all have dinner or cook out, if she's up to it." Jason, as usual, was more than accommodating.

Beth headed to O'Hare for Memorial weekend, as Connie started more treatments of alternating chemo and radiation. She wasn't doing too bad, but took a lot of pain pills, and preferred dinner-out than doing barbecue. Mike drove in from the farm, and Connie didn't look too bad, as she still had her hair, though she'd gotten a wig for the future, as the treatments would continue another month or so. The dinner was great, but she started to wane, and felt she needed to get back to Cheryl's. At the end of June, the doctors said the treatments would need time to do their job, so she could go back to the UP if she wanted. Connie really missed her dogs, and sleeping in her own bed, so Matt was flying in to drive her home.

Beth talked to her every week over the next couple of months, trying to remind her to stay positive, but Connie wasn't accepting of just using that, and not feeling good at all. The call came in late August that the cancer advanced into her lymph nodes, so not much more they could do. Beth didn't understand, how it went from curable to death, so quickly. "There going to move me from the hospital to the nursing home - the one where my mother and Greg were. They were real good to them there." Her voice was breathy, and low, rather raspy.

"Can I come up and visit you Connie? Would it be alright?" She felt her voice catch.

"Yea, thank you, I think I'd like that." She'd have something to look forward to.

Pat could not have been more supportive and accommodating, from picking Beth up in Marquette that late Friday night, after the delayed flight, to lending her SUV for the thirty-five mile trek, one-way from her house to the nursing home. Connie could only handle three hours a day of company. That first day, it was Kathy, Sharon and her friend Marge, that Beth had met a few times before at Connie's. Lunch had been ordered from the restaurant in town, and they'd all visit and eat with a thermos of margaritas - a real reunion.

Beth got there early, and asked directions to Connie's room, when she turned to walk in the room, she stopped at the door, thinking she had the wrong one. Sitting in the recliner, facing the television, was a slumped, old man with fuzzy, gray-wisps on his head.

Beth backed out quickly to the hall, away from the door which did have Connie's name on it. Beth's breath sucked-out of her. She turned to the wall, trying to get it back, realizing that *was* Connie. She practiced her old mantras: "I can do this." "Please, God, help me to do this." "I can do this."

Beth took a full minute to get herself under emotional control. She could not remember being in such a position before with anyone, much less someone she loved so much. She swallowed several times, and tried to take as deep a breath as she could. With a plastered smile on her face, that she hoped didn't look too phony, she walked in the room. "Hey, Kiddo! Guess who's coming for lunch?" Beth's jaw was tight, trying not to let it slip, and choke her up into crying. She kissed Connie, and hugged as much of her shoulders as she could.

Talking slow and very gravelly, Connie asked, "Get a nurse to help move me, . . . so when the others come in, . . . we can all sit together." Beth followed her instructions, and watched her as much as she could without Connie noticing her wince. She would have to find somewhere to look, that wouldn't affect her too much, but she could not find any safe spot. Connie asked how the flight was, and Beth responded as cheerily as possible.

"Oh, you know, a hassle out of Chicago with delays, so Pat had a bit of wait, and the long drive back. She's loaned me her SUV to drive over, . . . and wanted you to know they're all praying for you at her church." Connie asked how her grandson, Magnus was, and Beth whipped out the latest photos to show her and the others came in as they finished talking. Beth was always glad to especially see Sharon and also Kathy, as well Marge, as they'd all been helping out as much as possible. Connie ate as much as she could, enjoyed the margaritas, which she shouldn't have too much with her meds, but it didn't make much difference any more. Within the hour, they gathered themselves up to leave, so Beth would have more time to spend with Connie.

Knowing Connie couldn't talk much, Beth jumped right in to keep the conversation going. "So, you remember me telling you about my Memoir Writing classes at the college when we were in Vegas, well my first session starts for the new semester soon, and I'm doing two days a week now, with so many more people. I've got some great newbies, as well as my wonderful returnees, so, . . . you want to hear more of their stories?" Beth figured it would be the best thing to take both their minds off it all, and she'd already caught Connie up on Mike and Jason, as not really any other mutual friends left to discuss. Beth'd been rolling along, with Connie nodding occasionally, and she thought she may have dozed off, but she kept talking.

Connie's head popped back slightly, and her eyes came open, "Oh, Shit! I dozed-off from these drugs," really upset, she added, "Don't let me do that! Kick me in the foot or hit my arm, if I start dozing off again. I don't want to waste any of our time together, they'll be kicking you out soon." Beth tried to chuckled, but the truth of the situation was quite painful, this weekend really would be the last time they were together.

Beth took a deep breathe, and continued on. "Well I'll go back a little bit, so you get the end of her story so far, and then I'll start with the next one, I know you'll enjoy it." Beth clinched her teeth and pulled her jaw in to continue, saying again to herself that she could do this. *She had to do this!* Not too much longer, before the nurse came in with more pills, and told Beth her time was up for today. She took another deep breath, kissed and hugged Connie's shoulder. "All-Righty, then." as Connie had often said, "I'll see you tomorrow, same time, same station and we'll continue 'Beth's exciting tales.' If we're not the ones creating the excitement any more, at least, other people are, that I can share with you." She had her teeth clinched again, to hold it in.

Connie looked up and smiled as much as she could, "Thank you, . . . I love you."

Beth quickly nodded, "Me, too," turned and exited before she lost it all. She barely got more than a few yards, when she had to put her hand on the wall to balance herself, take some more deep breaths, and get to the end of the hallway past the nurse's station. They all watched, saying goodbye, as Beth called back to them. "I'll be back tomorrow morning." She didn't even make it to the SUV, before the sobs ran almost violently out of her.

"Hell-of-a-way to build back up their closeness, but something's better than nothing." She sat in the car for almost five

minutes before she had enough control to drive the thirty-five miles back to Pat's. Distractions came to her, as she passed the various landmarks that had become so familiar the three years she'd lived in the UP, and of course, how little it had changed from the two years being gone.

Pat was a most-valuable friend, being her usual positive and cheery self, not only how they were so much alike in always being supportive of others, but their Spiritual beliefs. There was nothing they couldn't talk about, or agree to disagree, with the rare-topics that they differed on. Prior to coming, Beth contacted, Dorothea, her boss - the City Manager about visiting, and called to see if she and her husband Chuck were available, so Beth and Pat headed over to them.

Dorothea recently went through her own bout with breast cancer, which she caught early, and only had to have radiation. It was good to have some laughs, as Dorothea told her all the local politics and *crapola*,' once again reiterating how she looked forward to retiring next year. Once back to Pat's and some dinner, they watched a DVD. Beth mentioned about really needing some sleep, as all the emotional stuff totally drained her. Pat, reminded her what time they had to get up, as Beth would be dropping her off at church, before going to visit with Connie.

As Beth drove into the parking lot of the nursing home on Sunday morning, she again sat for several minutes to deep breathe and pull her emotions in tightly. When she felt she could handle it all, she walked inside. Connie dozed with the television on. "Good Morning, Sunshine! How are you today?" A slight smile came across Connie's face, as happy to see Beth returned. "Have you had any visitors since I left yesterday?" she asked, as she kept smiling.

Connie adjusted herself in the recliner, and took a sip of water for her rusty-throat. "Yes, Matt came, before going to open the bar, but . . . I made him leave . . . he wouldn't stop crying. I mean, why does he have to come here and sob? And, all he says is, 'What am I going to do?' over and over again."

Beth kept her eyes steady on Connie, trying not to show any judgment or comment pulling her lips in. With her non-remark, Connie continued. "You're right. You've always been right about me spoiling him. I did too much for him . . . he's weak. I don't know if he is going to make it." She was quiet again, so Beth thought of something positive to say.

"Don't worry, you've got a great bar staff. They'll keep him going. And, he's got Kathy, who can support him, too." Not really the time to punish herself for how she raised Matt.

Even before her son Jeff was killed, Connie always spoiled Matt. She looked at Beth, knowing she was just placating the inevitable. She had to admit, if only to herself, that Matt's 'trifecta addictions' - as Connie referred to them - of alcohol, drugs and gambling - were not a good combination for running a very successful business. "I bet you don't worry about Jeremy doing his job, . . . he's so successful, and you raised him to be very independent. He's a got a great wife and family. I bet you're really proud of him." Connie sighed at a life filled with regret.

Beth took a deep breath, wanting to acknowledge, but not brag or gloat. "Yes, he's very successful, and he's the one who *does* for me. I mean, I wouldn't be able to do this," she swept her hand around, "if he didn't get the airline tickets for me. And, my grandchildren - that I waited a long time for - are such a joy to me. I love to babysit." Perhaps Connie was trying to clear her own conscience, and Beth was the best one to confess to who'd truly understand.

Connie then thought of all the effort Beth was going through to be with her. "I want you to be sure and thank Pat for all she's doing, too, so you can be here with me. Also, . . . I don't want you to bother coming back for the Memorial . . ." She looked straight at Beth.

"What do you mean?" Beth was shocked at both the statement and the acknowledgement of her near death. "You know I write the best eulogies!" She was trying now to soften the blow.

"I know," she chuckled, "You'd have them laughing and crying at the same time. I don't want you to have to deal with Cheryl, or anyone else. *This is our time* . . ." She started to tear up.

Beth quickly broke in, "Well, then, let's get started. . ." She took a deep breath to begin again, "OK, I think I last left you with my Swedish student, why don't we move into a really-great story about a World War II, fantastic hero . . ." Connie nodded, trying to smile. Beth had been rambling on for some time when the phone rang stopping her. It was her sister Cheryl.

"No, I can't talk now . . ." Cheryl continued. "I don't want to talk to you, Beth is here, . . ." Cheryl still continued. "Beth is telling me interesting stories, and you're always boring, I'm hanging up now," and she did, laughing. "OK, . . . we're in Italy, now right?" They both laughed, and it really felt good. Beth later helped Connie with her lunch, as she continued on with the incredible war story.

Too soon after, the nurse came back to say Beth's time was up for the day. Connie asked with hope, "Same time tomorrow, . . . more stories?" Beth nodded 'yes' as she got up to hug and kiss her again. This time, Connie was the first to say, "I love you, . . . and thank you and, . . I'll be waiting right here . . . for you tomorrow." It was all Beth could do to get out of the door before the tears poured out.

Once again, it took more than five minutes before she could leave the parking lot to drive back. She was meeting Ron and Pat for lunch, he'd picked her up after church, so they could all visit. LaDena was in Chicago with her Ethiopian group, but it was good to see Ron.

It had been a couple of years since they'd helped Beth move to Dallas. Refilling her emotional-well with happiness, was a lifesaver, laughing at the funny things the couple did. Beth told Pat later, she hoped she'd be able to make it through the third day, and saying goodbye to Connie. The Labor Day holiday, happily was another beautiful-weather day, and buoyed Beth's emotions in fulfilling her forty-year friendship with Connie. With a deep breath, and big smile on her face she entered the little room, "It's a beautiful day in neighborhood!" she sang 'a la Mr. Rogers,' as Connie turned and laughed at the children's memory, very happy to see Beth.

Her voice still hoarse from the drugs and all, "I've been thinking, . . . while I still can, " they both laughed, and Beth sighed, it was going to be OK. "I don't give-a-shit any more, what anybody up here, or anywhere else thinks about me any more. I want you to get that damn book out and published, I want to be 'infamous!' I want to be remembered for the crazy, I really was." She laughed again, "I mean, you know, we owe it to Bobby Ryan, to let everyone know how great he was!" They were both laughing, until Connie started coughing, which stopped them both. "I mean it, . . . promise me you'll do that." Before the welled-up tears could be released on both sides, Beth got them back on track.

"Yes, I promise I will, . . . and let's get back to my students' memoirs. I've still got a few more interesting ones to tell you." Again, Beth later helped Connie with her lunch, so the nurse didn't have to, and the time, *again*, sped by until she returned to say Beth's time was up. She was slow to get up from her chair, not having planned how she'd say goodbye, and Connie stopped her by speaking first.

She looked Beth straight in the eye, as they were both tearing-up, "I'll call you to say goodbye, I love you, . . . and thank you for all this. . ." It was as far as she could get.

Beth hugged and kissed her, whispering, "I love you so much." This time, already crying as she left the room. She stopped several times in the hall, before she got to the door and outside. The drive to Pat's barely realized, and thank goodness the holiday had so little traffic. Pat was invited to a big party at a mutual friend's, on the Paint River, which came through town and gave it the falls of its name. Again, the community and friendship helped Beth recover, particularly the wonderful boat ride up and down the river, generously offered to her by the host.

The five o'clock morning drive to the Marquette airport for Beth's seven-thirty flight to Chicago, was almost silent for them both. "You know Pat, there is no way I could have done this without you, and I do truly appreciate your time, patience and love on this." They stopped for Beth to fill the gas tank for Pat as promised, stretch and talk. At the airport, it'd be too emotional, so Beth wanted her to just drop her at the door, and not come inside at all. "Please stop and have a nice breakfast before you make that long drive back." Pat believed as Beth did, even with all Pat's physical ailments, you keep putting one foot in front of another, until you weren't around to do so. Life was all about lessons learned, whatever was thrown at you by the Universe.

"Yes, I think I'll need it, and please do call me when you get home in Dallas." Beth did call from Dallas, as exhausted as she was. It was soon back to teaching her Memoir Writing and part-time job at the phone center. Though frequently distracted by memories of how pitiful Connie looked, she hoped she wasn't in any pain. At the strangest times, some silly, simple habit of Connie's would blast her back into Beth's head. In the restroom, she noticed the toilet paper come over the front, and cracked up snickering. How many times, Connie would announce how she *'had to'* change the toilet paper in some public facility, so that it went behind, rather than over the top. "Don't these idiots know, the toilet paper *'has to'* drop behind, so it doesn't get stuck." Connie took-it-on as her 'duty' to *convert* all toilet paper. Beth shook her head, as tears welled into her eyes. These silly, little things would haunt her as memories.

Beth accepted the Divine Right Order of Life in the Universe, as acknowledged and asked for in her daily affirmations. There was a mystery of being-beyond, thus wisdom in focusing on things you can change and trust. As well, the things one needed to accept, when not being able to understand life, or in the unseen realm. Some believed holding onto things made them stronger, she learned it was the letting go - let life flow, in the most positive way creates an inner strength.

Epilogue

Beth knew we all have our broken pieces, big or small, because no one was raised in Disneyland, and it certainly wasn't a Disney World. And, she'd come to believe we're all here for lessons to be learned, however much we can and choose to learn for changing and growing for happier lives. When lessons are done, or we no longer choose to work on them, then so is our time - purpose. Yes, as the ladies learned, change took work and first tries rarely work. Also learned, no one can truly fix us, but ourselves. No one, no matter how at the time we think they can fix, or forever make us happy. No one is perfect, yet we have to learn to love ourselves - warts and all! And, the biggie - forgiveness - of ourselves and others - is the foundation of loving ourselves, we all made mistakes - as did our parents.

    No person or thing from the outside can be more than a bandaid, as the only one who can fill up that hole inside is us, loving and forgiving ourselves. Most of us are doing the best we can or are capable of doing - if you don't learn that, then your life will be a pure facade from head to toe. Friends can help to support us, but even they need to be changed as we do. Life will become a cliche if you don't change, and then it doesn't have much purpose left. It's important to stop feeling we need to be more, do more or achieve more in order to be happy. We each need to find our own ways of working out how to live with life, and need to start having the confidence to let our intuitions lead the way.

    Beth took time to reexamine her own life - she certainly wasn't perfect, and not looking to be so, but her life was good - good for her and that's what counted. She took care of herself, her health by doing her water aerobics four or five days a week, while watching her diet, except when she went out - indulging in more carbs than usual. But more than anything, Beth's enjoyment came from within - loving her life, knowing she was loved, especially by God/Source. Her grandchildren now, were such a joy - so pretty, so bright and talented Seraphina, along with so very curious, clever and happy Magnus - babysitting or visiting, they made her very happy.

Beth wished she'd been able to get April to understand - accept, the true power of forgiveness. Perhaps if she'd done so with her father, her daughters would have learned to do it with her, regarding Alex mistreating them. Maybe then, it could have all been much happier for her, with her girls in her life. Beth thought, April had what was called today, *Entitlement* issues, in a psychosis form, expecting everyone to cater to her every whim. Truly, sad how she ended, looking to the outside - the material things to make her happy.

Beth found her niche with the Memoir Writing. Her joy in her students' accomplishments of expressing themselves, and letting go of whatever they'd been holding onto from their pasts. She thanked them, as she told how she shared their stories with her dying friend and how happy it made her to hear them. They were amazed. She also told them she'd be doing hers now.

Life was good, and she was grateful for it without all the entrapments of material things, or a need for a surplus of money. Even when she made good money, she only collected those mementoes from her travels. She didn't like clutter, so the closest to hoarding was maybe, 'buy one-get one free' sale. The occasional glass of wine was her drinking these days, and her drug of choice was ibuprofen, if over-doing the exercise. She learned from her mistakes, and her mantra now to live a very long, very healthy and happy life to see her grandchildren grow to adulthood.

Cheryl, Connie's sister, sent an email the week after Beth left, Connie was sent back to the hospital. Two weeks later, another came announcing Connie begged to go back home for a last visit with her dogs. Friday afternoon Beth's phone rang, and showed the call from Connie. Beth couldn't believe it, but instantly answered, "Hi Kiddo, how-ya doing?"

"It's Cheryl, Beth, I'm going to give you over to Connie, she wants to say a last goodbye." Beth's breath was immediately sucked out of her, as tears started seeping out.

A very graveled-voice slowly came on the line, "Beth, . . . love you . . ." she started choking, then mumbled about the "rocking-chairs . . ."

Beth knew and helped her, "Yes, I know, . . . us watching the sunset in the rocking-chairs, at the rest-home for 'Wayward-Waitresses,' we're not going to make . . . and no more Scrabble games either." Connie was trying to laugh through her obvious tears.

"Good-bye, . . . and I'll see you soon," there was open sobbing now.

But Beth had to answer, "Not too, soon. I've got my grandkids to live for now . . . Always, love you, Connie. . . Bye." They were both crying into the phone, as Beth heard the disconnect on Connie's end. Cheryl sent an email Sunday afternoon Connie had returned to the hospital and passed there.

Beth took to her writing, her 'great release' of her emotions. In both her *EveryDay Empowerment* blog, then several poems regarding both Michael and Connie's death. The words helped some, as the little snatches of memories would bring a shake of a head and a snicker, then tears. The 'last one standing,' as they say, of a forty-year run, not that a prize or grand bottle of booze designated. All Beth had were her memories of her friends, she could put those into words, of who they were and how they changed each others' lives over the years. She let go of any ideas of how things 'should have been,' to not judge any of them, or herself the way they chose to live and to die. They were 'friends' - 'warts and all.'

An Old Soul

You feel this presence, ancient - older than time itself.
An enigma, vastly beyond the sphere of our Universe.
Feel the strength of breath in the convictions held.
We are but a mirror reflection of our inner core.

You were carved from tuned schematics
in a place where time did not exist.
Created to be loyalty's best paradigm,
to live in a place of an honored heart.

Most beings keep their best parts hidden,
to not show vulnerability or softness.
Yet, it is this empowerment energy
that proclaims itself through-out the cosmos.

It is a heart-strength taught by the Creator.
Like all life-forces, you too, seek to learn what is hidden.
You want to know what cannot be seen, or spoken of.
You understand the priceless power it gives you.

Within the human genome is the surprise element of Magic.
That secret ingredient withheld by the galactic alchemists.
Man searches for immortality, like lightening -
what would he do with it, if by chance caught?

Forever is a long time in anyone's light years.
And, the heart does not yearn for timelessness.
Choices already live within your mirror reflection -
bloom your true essence where angels live to tread.

Love is far from the perceived sweetness or flowers.
It is instead a mighty force that can return
even the most fractured, broken pieces
into a state of wholeness, no matter what it takes.

Author's Bio

Originally from Chicago, Alice Parker has degrees in psychology, marketing, and English ESL-bilingual–bi-cultural studies in graduate school. A Dale Carnegie Trainer for 3 years, leading classes, she's traveled to 36 countries and 40 states – lived in 6, and wrote for an international business-travel magazine, and others.

A corporate business trainer in Japan for 7 years, then 8 years in San Francisco as HR Mgmt. to 1000 employees. As a Life Coach, she used her published Self-Help book, *Move Past Your Past - A Process for Freeing Your Life,* to do numerous workshops. She's passionate about her poems and empowering published memoir *Choices, Changes & Friends - 1970s After Divorce.* Four friends got their divorces together in the crazy 1970s, with satirical humor they dealt with it all and grew into independent women.

In the Dallas area since 2013, member of Poetry Society of Texas, winning 1st in State several times, and past President of the local Mockingbird Chapter, 3 years. Alice is also a proud member of the weekly, international poetry group, Corroboree.

For over 10 years she has taught memoir writing classes, and did editing to help her students publish. Her most recently published book is on Australia, *A Trip To Oz - A Memoir of Self-discovery thru Australian Adventures.* And, ready to publish is her novel on Croatia *Change of View - A Romantic Adventure.* She's has also finished 2 biographical books regarding the American Occupation of Japan: *Occupied Hearts - Love the Long Way Around* and *Japan as the Occupier and Occupied.*

www.ingramcontent.com/pod-product-compliance
Lightning Source LLC
Chambersburg PA
CBHW021436070526
44577CB00002B/190